ARCHAEOLOGIES OF THE FUTURE

The Desire Called Utopia
and Other Science Fictions

FREDRIC JAMESON

VERSO

London • New York

First published by Verso 2005
© Fredric Jameson 2005
This edition published by Verso 2007
© Fredric Jameson 2007
All rights reserved

3 5 7 9 10 8 6 4 2

Verso
UK: 6 Meard Street, London W1F 0EG
USA: 180 Varick Street, New York, NY 10014–4606
www.versobooks.com

Verso is the imprint of New Left Books

ISBN 978-1-84467-538-8

British Library Cataloguing in Publication Data
A catalogue record for this book is available from the British Library

Library of Congress Cataloging-in-Publication Data
A catalog record for this book is available from the Library of Congress

Printed in the USA by Quebecor World, Fairfield

For my comrades in the party of Utopia:
Peter, Kim, Darko, Susan

*If the hoar frost grip thy tent
Thou wilt give thanks when night is spent.*

Contents

PART TWO AS FAR AS THOUGHT CAN REACH

ESSAYS

PART ONE
THE DESIRE CALLED UTOPIA

Introduction:
Utopia Now

Utopia has always been a political issue, an unusual destiny for a literary form: yet just as the literary value of the form is subject to permanent doubt, so also its political status is structurally ambiguous. The fluctuations of its historical context do nothing to resolve this variability, which is also not a matter of taste or individual judgment.

During the Cold War (and in Eastern Europe immediately after its end), Utopia had become a synonym for Stalinism and had come to designate a program which neglected human frailty and original sin, and betrayed a will to uniformity and the ideal purity of a perfect system that always had to be imposed by force on its imperfect and reluctant subjects. (In a further development, Boris Groys has identified this domination of political form over matter with the imperatives of aesthetic modernism.)[1]

Such counterrevolutionary analyses – no longer of much interest to the Right since the collapse of the socialist countries – were then adopted by an anti-authoritarian Left whose micropolitics embraced Difference as a slogan and came to recognize its anti-state positions in the traditional anarchist critiques of Marxism as Utopian in exactly this centralizing and authoritarian sense.

Paradoxically, the older Marxist traditions, drawing uncritical lessons from Marx and Engels' historical analyses of Utopian socialism in *The Communist Manifesto*,[2] and also following Bolshevik usage,[3] denounced its Utopian competition as lacking any conception of agency or political strategy, and characterized Utopianism as an idealism deeply and structurally averse to the political as such. The relationship between Utopia and the political, as well as questions about the practical-political value of Utopian thinking and the

---

1 Boris Groys, *The Total Art of Stalinism* (Princeton, 1992 [1988]).

2 See Karl Marx and Friedrich Engels, *The Communist Manifesto*, Section III, "Socialist and Communist Literature"; and see also Friedrich Engels, "Socialism Utopian and Scientific". Yet Lenin and Marx both wrote Utopias: the latter in the *Civil War in France* [1871], the former in *State and Revolution* [1917].

3 The so-called "theory of limits" or "theory of nearer aims" ("teoriya blizhnego pritsela"): see Darko Suvin, *Metamorphoses of Science Fiction* (New Haven, 1979), pp. 264–265.

identification between socialism and Utopia, very much continue to be unresolved topics today, when Utopia seems to have recovered its vitality as a political slogan and a politically energizing perspective.

Indeed, a whole new generation of the post-globalization Left – one which subsumes remnants of the old Left and the New Left, along with those of a radical wing of social democracy, and of First World cultural minorities and Third World proletarianized peasants and landless or structurally unemployable masses – has more and more frequently been willing to adopt this slogan, in a situation in which the discrediting of communist and socialist parties alike, and the skepticism about traditional conceptions of revolution, have cleared the discursive field. The consolidation of the emergent world market – for this is really what is at stake in so-called globalization – can eventually be expected to allow new forms of political agency to develop. In the meantime, to adapt Mrs Thatcher's famous dictum, there is no alternative to Utopia, and late capitalism seems to have no natural enemies (the religious fundamentalisms which resist American or Western imperialisms having by no means endorsed anti-capitalist positions). Yet it is not only the invincible universality of capitalism which is at issue: tirelessly undoing all the social gains made since the inception of the socialist and communist movements, repealing all the welfare measures, the safety net, the right to unionization, industrial and ecological regulatory laws, offering to privatize pensions and indeed to dismantle whatever stands in the way of the free market all over the world. What is crippling is not the presence of an enemy but rather the universal belief, not only that this tendency is irreversible, but that the historic alternatives to capitalism have been proven unviable and impossible, and that no other socio-economic system is conceivable, let alone practically available. The Utopians not only offer to conceive of such alternate systems; Utopian form is itself a representational meditation on radical difference, radical otherness, and on the systemic nature of the social totality, to the point where one cannot imagine any fundamental change in our social existence which has not first thrown off Utopian visions like so many sparks from a comet.

The fundamental dynamic of any Utopian politics (or of any political Utopianism) will therefore always lie in the dialectic of Identity and Difference,[4] to the degree to which such a politics aims at imagining, and sometimes even at realizing, a system radically different from this one. We may in this follow Olaf Stapledon's space-and-time travelers, who gradually become aware that their receptivity to alien and exotic cultures is governed by anthropomorphic principles:

At first, when our imaginative power was strictly limited by experience of our own worlds, we could make contact only with worlds closely akin to our own.

4 See G.W.F. Hegel, *Encyclopedia Logic*, Book Two, "Essence" (Oxford, 1975 [1817]).

Moreover, in this novitiate stage of our work we invariably came upon these worlds when they were passing through the same spiritual crisis as that which underlies the plight of *Homo sapiens* today. It appeared that, for us to enter any world at all, there had to be a deep-lying likeness or identity in ourselves and our hosts.[5]

Stapledon is not strictly speaking a Utopian, as we will see later on; but no Utopian writer has been quite so forthright in confronting the great empiricist maxim, nothing in the mind that was not first in the senses. If true, this principle spells the end, not only of Utopia as a form, but of Science Fiction in general, affirming as it does that even our wildest imaginings are all collages of experience, constructs made up of bits and pieces of the here and now: "When Homer formed the idea of *Chimera*, he only joined into one animal, parts which belonged to different animals; the head of a lion, the body of a goat, and the tail of a serpent."[6] On the social level, this means that our imaginations are hostages to our own mode of production (and perhaps to whatever remnants of past ones it has preserved). It suggests that at best Utopia can serve the negative purpose of making us more aware of our mental and ideological imprisonment (something I have myself occasionally asserted[7]); and that therefore the best Utopias are those that fail the most comprehensively.

It is a proposition which has the merit of shifting the discussion of Utopia from content to representation as such. These texts are so often taken to be the expressions of political opinion or ideology that there is something to be said for redressing the balance in a resolutely formalist way (readers of Hegel or Hjelmslev will know that form is in any case always the form of a specific content). It is not only the social and historical raw materials of the Utopian construct which are of interest from this perspective; but also the representational relations established between them – such as closure, narrative and exclusion or inversion. Here as elsewhere in narrative analysis what is most revealing is not what is said, but what cannot be said, what does not register on the narrative apparatus.

It is important to complete this Utopian formalism with what I hesitate to call a psychology of Utopian production: a study of Utopian fantasy mechanisms, rather, and one which eschews individual biography in favor of historical and collective wish-fulfillment. Such an approach to Utopian fantasy

---

5 Olaf Stapledon, *The Last and First Men/Star Maker* (New York, 1968 [1930, 1937]), p. 299. The English novelist Olaf Stapledon (1886–1950), whose two most important works, just cited, will be discussed in Chapter 9 below, derives from what may be called the European art tradition of H.G. Wells' "scientific romances" or speculative fiction, rather than from the commercial pulps in which American SF emerged.

6 Alexander Gerard, *Essay on Genius*, quoted in M.H. Abrams, *The Mirror and the Lamp* (Oxford, 1953 [1774]), p. 161.

7 See Part Two, Essay 4.

production will necessarily illuminate its historical conditions of possibility: for it is certainly of the greatest interest for us today to understand why Utopias have flourished in one period and dried up in another. This is clearly a question that needs to be enlarged to include Science Fiction as well, if one follows Darko Suvin,[8] as I do, in believing Utopia to be a socio-economic sub-genre of that broader literary form. Suvin's principle of "cognitive estrangement" – an aesthetic which, building on the Russian Formalist notion of "making strange" as well as the Brechtian *Verfremdungseffekt*, characterizes SF in terms of an essentially epistemological function (thereby excluding the more oneiric flights of generic fantasy) – thus posits one specific subset of this generic category specifically devoted to the imagination of alternative social and economic forms. In what follows, however, our discussion will be complicated by the existence, alongside the Utopian genre or text as such, of a Utopian impulse which infuses much else, in daily life as well as in its texts (see Chapter 1, below). This distinction will also complicate the very selective discussion of SF here, since alongside SF texts which deploy overtly Utopian themes (as in Le Guin's *Lathe of Heaven*) we will also reference works which, as in Chapter 9, betray the workings of the Utopian impulse. In any case, "The Desire Called Utopia", unlike the essays collected in Part Two, will deal mainly with those aspects of SF relevant to the more properly Utopian dialectic of Identity and Difference.[9]

All these formal and representational questions lead back to the political one with which we began: but now the latter has been sharpened into the formal dilemma of how works that posit the end of history can offer any usable historical impulses, how works which aim to resolve all political differences can continue to be in any sense political, how texts designed to overcome the needs of the body can remain materialistic, and how visions of the "epoch of rest" (Morris) can energize and compel us to action.

There are good reasons for thinking that all these questions are undecidable: which is not necessarily a bad thing provided we continue to try to decide

---

8 Suvin, *Metamorphoses of Science Fiction*, p. 61.

9 The conventional high-cultural repudiation of SF – its stigmatization of the purely formulaic (which reflects the original sin of the form in its origins in the pulps), complaints about the absence of complex and psychologically "interesting" characters (a position which does not seem to have kept pace with the postcontemporary crisis of the "centred subject"), a yearning for original literary styles which ignores the sylistic variety of modern SF (as Philip K. Dick's defamiliarization of spoken American) – is probably not a matter of personal taste, nor is it to be addressed by way of purely aesthetic arguments, such as the attempt to assimilate selected SF works to the canon as such. We must here identify a kind of generic revulsion, in which this form and narrative discourse is the object of psychic resistance as a whole and the target of a kind of literary "reality principle". For such readers, in other words, the Bourdieu-style rationalizations which rescue high literary forms from the guilty associations of unproductiveness and sheer diversion and which endow them with socially acknowledged justification, are here absent. It is true that this is also a reply which the readers of fantasy could very well address to the readers of SF itself (see below, Chapter 5).

them. Indeed, in the case of the Utopian texts, the most reliable political test lies not in any judgment on the individual work in question so much as in its capacity to generate new ones, Utopian visions that include those of the past, and modify or correct them.

Yet this undecidability is in reality a deep-structural rather than a political one; and it explains why so many commentators on Utopia (such as Marx and Engels themselves, with all their admiration for Fourier[10]) should have emitted contradictory assessments on the matter. Another Utopian visionary – Herbert Marcuse, surely the most influential Utopian of the 1960s – offers an explanation for this ambivalence in an earlier argument whose official subject is culture rather than Utopia as such.[11] The problem is however the same: can culture be political, which is to say critical and even subversive, or is it necessarily reappropriated and coopted by the social system of which it is a part? Marcuse argues that it is the very separation of art and culture from the social – a separation that inaugurates culture as a realm in its own right and defines it as such – which is the source of art's incorrigible ambiguity. For that very distance of culture from its social context which allows it to function as a critique and indictment of the latter also dooms its interventions to ineffectuality and relegates art and culture to a frivolous, trivialized space in which such intersections are neutralized in advance. This dialectic accounts even more persuasively for the ambivalencies of the Utopian text as well: for the more surely a given Utopia asserts its radical difference from what currently is, to that very degree it becomes, not merely unrealizable but, what is worse, unimaginable.[12]

---

10 Marx and Engels, *Selected Correspondence* (Moscow, 1975): for example, October 9, 1866 (to Kugelmann) attacking Proudhon as a petty-bourgeois Utopian, "whereas in the Utopias of a Fourier, an Owen, etc., there is the anticipation and imaginative expression of a new world" (p. 172). And see also Engels: "German theoretical Socialism will never forget that it stands on the shoulders of Saint-Simon, Fourier and Owen, three men who despite their fantasies and utopianism are to be reckoned among the most significant minds of all times, for they anticipated with genius countless matters whose accuracy we now demonstrate scientifically" (quoted in Frank and Fritzie Manuel, *Utopian Thought in the Western World* [Cambridge, MA, 1979], p. 702). Benjamin was also a great admirer of Fourier: "Il attendait la libération totale de l'avènement du jeu universalisé au sens de Fourier pour lequel il avait une admiration sans borne. Je ne sache pas d'homme qui, de nos jours, ait vécu aussi intimement dans le Paris saint-simonien et fouriériste." Pierre Klossowski, "Lettre sur Walter Benjamin", *Tableaux vivants* (Paris: Gallimard, 2001), p. 87. And Barthes was another such passionate reader (see Chapter 1, note 5).

11 See "On the Affirmative Character of Culture", in *Negations* (Boston, 1968).

12 From another standpoint, this discussion of the ambiguous reality of culture (that is to say, in our context, of Utopia itself) is an ontological one. The presumption is that Utopia, whose business is the future, or not-being, exists only in the present, where it leads the relatively feeble life of desire and fantasy. But this is to reckon without the amphibiousness of being and its temporality: in respect of which Utopia is philosophically analogous to the trace, only from the other end of time. The aporia of the trace is to belong to past and present all at once, and thus to constitute a mixture of being and not-being quite different from the traditional category of

This does not exactly leave us back at our beginning, in which rival ideological stereotypes sought to pass this or that absolute political judgment on Utopia. For even if we can no longer adhere with an unmixed conscience to this unreliable form, we may now have recourse to that ingenious political slogan Sartre invented to find his way between a flawed communism and an even more unacceptable anti-communism. Perhaps something similar can be proposed to fellow-travelers of Utopia itself: indeed, for those only too wary of the motives of its critics, yet no less conscious of Utopia's structural ambiguities, those mindful of the very real political function of the idea and the program of Utopia in our time, the slogan of anti-anti-Utopianism might well offer the best working strategy.

·

Becoming and thereby mildly scandalous for analytical Reason. Utopia, which combines the not-yet-being of the future with a textual existence in the present is no less worthy of the archaeological paradoxes we are willing to grant to the trace. For a philosophical discussion of the latter see Paul Ricoeur, *Time and Narrative*, Volume III (Chicago, 1988), pp. 119–120.

I
Varieties of the Utopian

It has often been observed that we need to distinguish between the Utopian form and the Utopian wish: between the written text or genre and something like a Utopian impulse detectable in daily life and its practices by a specialized hermeneutic or interpretive method. Why not add political practice to this list, inasmuch as whole social movements have tried to realize a Utopian vision, communities have been founded and revolutions waged in its name, and since, as we have just seen, the term itself is once again current in present-day discursive struggles? At any rate, the futility of definitions can be measured by the way in which they exclude whole areas of the preliminary inventory.[1]

In this case, however, the inventory has a convenient and indispensable starting point: it is, of course, the inaugural text of Thomas More (1517), almost exactly contemporaneous with most of the innovations that have seemed to define modernity (conquest of the New World, Machiavelli and modern politics, Ariosto and modern literature, Luther and modern consciousness, printing and the modern public sphere). Two related genres have had similar miraculous births: the historical novel, with *Waverly* in 1814, and Science Fiction (whether one dates that from Mary Shelley's *Frankenstein* in the same years [1818] or Wells' *The Time Machine* in 1895).

Such generic starting points are always somehow included and *aufgehoben* in later developments, and not least in the well-known shift in Utopias from space

---

1 But see, for an authoritative statement, Lyman Tower Sargent, "The Three Faces of Utopianism", *Minnesota Review*, Vol. 7.3 (1967), pp. 222–230 and "The Three Faces of Utopianism Revisited", *Utopian Studies* 5.1 (1994), pp. 1–37. As Utopian studies are a relatively recent disciplinary field, bibliographies of theoretical interventions in it are still relatively rare: but see those in Tom Moylan, *Demand the Impossible* (New York, 1986) and in Barbara Goodwin and Keith Taylor, *The Politics of Utopia* (London, 1982). The journal *Utopian Studies* can be consulted for recent developments in this area. Theoretical contributions to the study of Science Fiction are another matter: see Veronica Hollinger's splendid overview, "Contemporary Trends in Science Fiction Criticism, 1980–1999" (*Science Fiction Studies*, No. 78 [July 1999], pp. 232–262), and for a more Francophone perspective, the bibliography in Richard Saint-Gelais, *L'Empire du pseudo* (Quebec City, 1999). For both, of course, we are fortunate to be able to draw on the superb *Encyclopedia of Science Fiction* of John Clute and Peter Nicholls (New York, 1995); and for Utopias, on the *Dictionary of Literary Utopias* of Vita Fortunati and Raymond Trousson (Paris, 2000).

to time, from the accounts of exotic travelers to the experiences of visitors to the future. But what uniquely characterizes this genre is its explicit inter-textuality: few other literary forms have so brazenly affirmed themselves as argument and counterargument. Few others have so openly required cross-reference and debate within each new variant: who can read Morris without Bellamy? or indeed Bellamy without Morris? So it is that the individual text carries with it a whole tradition, reconstructed and modified with each new addition, and threatening to become a mere cipher within an immense hyper-organism, like Stapledon's minded swarm of sentient beings.

Yet the lifework of Ernst Bloch is there to remind us that Utopia is a good deal more than the sum of its individual texts. Bloch posits a Utopian impulse governing everything future-oriented in life and culture; and encompassing everything from games to patent medicines, from myths to mass entertain-ment, from iconography to technology, from architecture to eros, from tourism to jokes and the unconscious. Wayne Hudson expertly summarizes his magnum opus as follows:

> In *The Principle of Hope* Bloch provides an unprecedented survey of human wish
> pictures and day dreams of a better life. The book begins with little day dreams
> (part I), followed by an exposition of Bloch's theory of anticipatory conscious-
> ness (part II). In part III Bloch applies his utopian hermeneutics to the wish
> pictures found in the mirror of ordinary life: to the utopian aura which sur-
> rounds a new dress, advertisements, beautiful masks, illustrated magazines, the
> costumes of the Ku Klux Klan, the festive excess of the annual market and
> the circus, fairy tales and kolportage, the mythology and literature of travel,
> antique furniture, ruins and museums, and the utopian imagination present in
> dance, pantomime, the cinema and the theatre. In part IV Bloch turns to the
> problem of the construction of a world adequate to hope and to various
> 'outlines of a better world'. He provides a 400 page analysis of medical, social,
> technical, architectural and geographical utopias, followed by an analysis of
> wish landscapes in painting, opera and poetry; utopian perspectives in the
> philosophies of Plato, Leibniz, Spinoza and Kant, and the utopianism implicit
> in movements agitating for peace and leisure. Finally, in part V Bloch turns to
> wish pictures of the fulfilled moment which reveal 'identity' to be the funda-
> mental supposition of anticipatory consciousness. Once again, the sweep is
> breathtaking as Bloch ranges over happy and dangerous experiences in ordinary
> life; the problem of the antinomy between the individual and the community;
> the works of the young Goethe, *Don Giovanni*, *Faust*, *Don Quixote*, the plays of
> Shakespeare; morality and intensity in music; hope pictures against death, and
> man's increasing self-injection into the content of religious mystery.[2]

---

2 Wayne Hudson, *The Marxist Philosophy of Ernst Bloch* (New York, 1982), p. 107. We must also note Ruth Levitas' critiques of the notion of a Utopian "impulse" in her *Concept of Utopia* (Syracuse, 1990), pp. 181–183. This book, central to the constitution of Utopian studies as a

We will return to Bloch shortly; but it should already be clear that his work raises a hermeneutic problem. Bloch's interpretive principle is most effective when it reveals the operation of the Utopian impulse in unsuspected places, where it is concealed or repressed. But what becomes, in that case, of deliberate and fully self-conscious Utopian programs as such? Are they also to be taken as unconscious expressions of something even deeper and more primordial? And what becomes of the interpretive process itself and Bloch's own philosophy of the future, which presumably no longer needs such decoding or reinterpretation? Yet the Utopian exegete is not often herself the designer of Utopias, and no Utopian program bears Bloch's own name.[3] There is here at work the same hermeneutic paradox Freud confronted when, searching for precursors of his dream analysis, he finally identified one obscure aboriginal tribe for whom all dreams had sexual meanings – except for overtly sexual dreams as such, which meant something else.

We would therefore do better to posit two distinct lines of descendency from More's inaugural text: the one intent on the realization of the Utopian program, the other an obscure yet omnipresent Utopian impulse finding its way to the surface in a variety of covert expressions and practices. The first of these lines will be systemic, and will include revolutionary political practice, when it aims at founding a whole new society, alongside written exercises in the literary genre. Systemic will also be those self-conscious Utopian secessions from the social order which are the so-called intentional communities; but also the attempts to project new spatial totalities, in the aesthetic of the city itself.

The other line of descent is more obscure and more various, as befits a protean investment in a host of suspicious and equivocal matters: liberal reforms and commercial pipedreams, the deceptive yet tempting swindles of the here and now, where Utopia serves as the mere lure and bait for ideology (hope being after all also the principle of the cruelest confidence games and of hucksterism as a fine art). Still, perhaps a few of the more obvious forms can be identified: political and social theory, for example, even when especially when – it aims at realism and at the eschewal of everything Utopian; piecemeal social democratic and "liberal" reforms as well, when they are

---

field in its own right, argues for a structural pluralism in which, according to the social constructions of desire in specific historical periods, the three components of form, content and function are combined in distinct and historically unique ways: "The main functions identified are compensation, criticism and change. Compensation is a feature of abstract, 'bad' Utopia for Bloch, of all utopia for Marx and Engels and of ideology for Mannheim. Criticism is the main element in Goodwin's definition. Change is crucial for Mannheim, Bauman and Bloch. Utopia may also function as the expression of education of desire, as for Bloch, Morton and Thompson, or to produce estrangement, as for Moylan and Suvin. If we define utopia in terms of [only] one of these functions we can neither describe nor explain the variation." (p. 180)

3   Tom Moylan pertinently reminds me that Bloch already had a concrete Utopia; it was called the Soviet Union.

merely allegorical of a wholesale transformation of the social totality. And as we have identified the city itself as a fundamental form of the Utopian image (along with the shape of the village as it reflects the cosmos),[4] perhaps we should make a place for the individual building as a space of Utopian investment, that monumental part which cannot be the whole and yet attempts to express it. Such examples suggest that it may be well to think of the Utopian impulse and its hermeneutic in terms of allegory: in that case, we will wish in a moment to reorganize Bloch's work into three distinct levels of Utopian content: the body, time and collectivity.

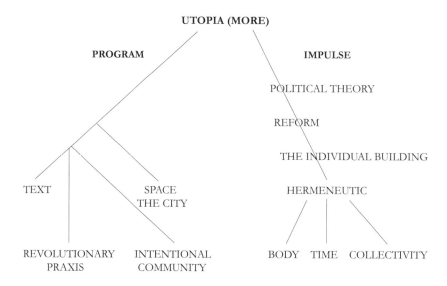

Yet the distinction between the two lines threatens to revive the old and much-contested philosophical aim of discriminating between the authentic and the inauthentic, even where it aims in fact to reveal the deeper authenticity of the inauthentic as such. Does it not tend to revive that ancient Platonic idealism of the true and false desire, the true and false pleasure, genuine satisfaction or happiness and the illusory kind? and this at a time when we are more inclined to believe in illusion than in truth in the first place?[5] As I tend to sympathize with this last, more postmodern, position, and also wish to avoid a rhetoric which opposes the reflexive or self-conscious to its unreflexive opposite number, I prefer to stage the distinction in more spatial terms. In that case, the properly Utopian program or realization will involve a commitment to closure (and thereby to totality): was it not Roland Barthes who

4 See Claude Lévi-Strauss, "Do Dual Organizations Exist?" in *Structural Anthropology* I (Chicago, 1983 [1958]); and also Pierre Bourdieu, *Outline of a Theory of Practice* (Cambridge, 1977 [1972]).

5 See Gilles Deleuze, *Cinéma* II (Paris, 1985 [1952]), Chapter VI, on "le faux"; and also Jean-Paul Sartre, *Saint Genêt* (New York, 1983), on "le toc", pp. 358ff.

observed, of Sade's Utopianism, that "here as elsewhere it is closure which enables the existence of system, which is to say, of the imagination"?[6]

But this is a premise that is not without all kinds of momentous consequences. In More, to be sure, closure is achieved by that great trench the founder causes to be dug between the island and the mainland and which alone allows it to become Utopia in the first place: a radical secession further underscored by the Machiavellian ruthlessness of Utopian foreign policy which – bribery, assassination, mercenaries and other forms of *Realpolitik* – rebukes all Christian notions of universal brotherhood and natural law and decrees the foundational difference between them and us, foe and friend, in a peremptory manner worthy of Carl Schmitt and characteristic in one way or another of all subsequent Utopias intent on survival within a world not yet converted to Bellamy's world state: as witness the sad fate of Huxley's *Island* or the precautions that are required by situations as different as Skinner's Walden communities or Kim Stanley Robinson's Mars.[7]

Totality is then precisely this combination of closure and system, in the name of autonomy and self-sufficiency and which is ultimately the source of that otherness or radical, even alien, difference already mentioned above and to which we will return at some length. Yet it is precisely this category of totality that presides over the forms of Utopian realization: the Utopian city, the Utopian revolution, the Utopian commune or village, and of course the Utopian text itself, in all its radical and unacceptable difference from the more lawful and aesthetically satisfying literary genres.

Just as clearly, then, it will be this very impress of the form and category of totality which is virtually by definition lacking in the multiple forms invested by Bloch's Utopian impulse. Here we have rather to do with an allegorical process in which various Utopian figures seep into the daily life of things and people and afford an incremental, and often unconscious, bonus of pleasure unrelated to their functional value or official satisfactions. The hermeneutic procedure is therefore a two step method, in which, in a first moment, fragments of experience betray the presence of symbolic figures – beauty,

---

6   Roland Barthes, *Sade, Fourier, Loyola* (Paris, 1971), p. 23.

7   And we might have added the historical tragedy of Winstanley and St George's Hill (along with the fate of Goetz's Utopian commune in Sartre, *Le Diable et le bon dieu*: it is true that this last is imposed rather than intentional, which was presumably the other point the philosopher of freedom and praxis wanted to make). As is well known, Huxley's late work, *Island* (1962), represents his attempt to rectify the satiric *Brave New World* of 1932 with the construction of a "serious" (although narrative) contribution to the Utopian genre. B.F. Skinner (1904–1990), one of the more idiosyncratic American theorists of behaviorism and the inventor of the so-called Skinner box, wrote a major Utopia in *Walden Two* (1948), in which (in my opinion) "negative conditioning" plays little part: see the brief discussion in Chapter 4 below. Kim Stanley Robinson (1952–) is the author of not one, but two Utopian cycles, the so-called Orange County trilogy (1984–1990) and the Mars trilogy (1992–1996), with a third one, centering on ecological disaster and its Utopian possibilities, on the way. On the Mars trilogy, see Part Two, Essay 12, below).

wholeness, energy, perfection – which are only themselves subsequently to be identified as the forms whereby an essentially Utopian desire can be transmitted. It will be noted that in this Bloch often appeals to classical aesthetic categories (which are themselves ultimately theological ones as well), and to that degree his hermeneutic may also be grasped as some final form of German idealist aesthetics as it exhausts itself in the late twentieth century and in modernism. Bloch had far richer and more varied tastes than Lukács, and attempted to accommodate popular and archaic culture, modernist as well as realist and neoclassical texts, into his Utopian aesthetics: but the latter is perfectly capable of assimilating postmodern and non-European, mass-cultural tastes, and this is why I have proposed to reorganize his immense compendium in a new and tripartite way (body, time and collectivity) which corresponds more closely to the levels of contemporary allegory.

Materialism is already omnipresent in an attention to the body which seeks to correct any idealism or spiritualism lingering in this system. Utopian corporeality is however also a haunting, which invests even the most subordinate and shamefaced products of everyday life, such as aspirins, laxatives and deodorants, organ transplants and plastic surgery, all harboring muted promises of a transfigured body. Bloch's reading of these Utopian supplements – the doses of utopian excess carefully measured out in all our commodities and sewn like a red thread through our practices of consumption, whether sober and utilitarian or frenzied-addictive – now rejoins Northrop Frye's Blakean myths of eternal bodies projected against the sky. Meanwhile the overtones of immortality that accompany these images seem to move us urgently onwards towards the temporal level, becoming truly Utopian only in those communities of the preternaturally long-lived,[8] as in Shaw's *Back to Methusaleh*, or the immortal, as in Boorman's film *Zardoz* (1974), significantly offering fodder for the anti-Utopians in the accompanying deterioration of the Utopian vision: the suicidal tedium of Shaw's long-lived elders, the sexless ennui of the inhabitants of *Zardoz*'s Vortex. Meanwhile, liberal politics incorporates portions of this particular impulse in political platforms offering enhanced medical research and universal health coverage, although the appeal to eternal youth finds a more appropriate place on the secret agenda of the Right and the wealthy and privileged, in fantasies about the traffic in organs and the technological possibilities of rejuvenation therapy. Corporeal transcendence then also finds rich possibilities in the realm of space, from the streets of daily life and the rooms of dwelling and work place, to the greater locus of the city as in ancient times it reflected the physical cosmos itself.

But the temporal life of the body already resituates the Utopian impulse in what is Bloch's central concern as a philosopher, namely the blindness of all traditional philosophy to the future and its unique dimensions, and the

8 See Part Two, Essay 7, "Longevity as Class Struggle".

denunciation of philosophies and ideologies, like Platonic anamnesis, stubbornly fixated on the past, on childhood and origins.⁹ It is a polemical commitment he shares with existential philosophers in particular, and perhaps more with Sartre, for whom the future is praxis and the project, than with Heidegger, for whom the future is the promise of mortality and authentic death; and it separates him decisively from Marcuse, whose Utopian system drew significantly, not merely on Plato, but fully as much on Proust (and Freud), to make a fundamental point about the memory of happiness and the traces of Utopian gratification that survive on into a fallen present and provide it with a "standing reserve" of personal and political energy.¹⁰

But it is worth pointing out that at some point discussions of temporality always bifurcate into the two paths of existential experience (in which questions of memory seem to predominate) and of historical time, with its urgent interrogations of the future. I will argue that it is precisely in Utopia that these two dimensions are seamlessly reunited and that existential time is taken up into a historical time which is paradoxically also the end of time, the end of history. But it is not necessary to think of this conflation of individual and collective time in terms of any eclipse of subjectivity, although the loss of (bourgeois) individuality is certainly one of the great anti-Utopian themes. But ethical depersonalization has been an ideal in any number of religions and in much of philosophy as well; while the transcendence of individual life has found rather different representations in Science Fiction, where it often functions as a readjustment of individual biology to the incomparably longer temporal rhythms of history itself. Thus, the extended life spans of Kim Stanley Robinson's Mars colonists allow them to coincide more tangibly with long-term historical evolutions, while the device of reincarnation, in his alternate history *Years of Rice and Salt*, affords the possibility of reentering the stream of history and development over and over again.¹¹ Yet a third way in which individual and collective time come to be identified with each other is in the very experience of everyday life, according to Roland Barthes the quintessential sign of utopian representation: "la marque de l'Utopie, c'est le quotidien".¹² Where biographical time and the dynamics of history diverge, this day-by-day life in successive instants allows the existential to fold back into the space of the collective, at least in Utopia, where death is measured off in generations rather than in biological individuals.

9 See Ernst Bloch's attack on anamnesis in *The Principle of Hope* (Cambridge, MA, 1986 [1959]), p. 18.

10 Herbert Marcuse, *Eros and Civilization* (New York, 1962), p. 18 and Chapter 11.

11 *Years of Rice and Salt* (2002) offers the chronicle of a world from which Europe and Christianity have been eliminated by the Black Death in the fourteenth century AD, a world in which a "native American" high civilization flourishes in the Western hemisphere and China and Islam have become the major subjects of a history that concludes with equivalents of "our" First World War, "our" revolutionary 1960s, and (hopefully) a different kind of future from our own.

12 Barthes, *Sade, Fourier, Loyola*, p. 23.

Stapledon's traveler, meanwhile, lives time in an indeterminable Einsteinian relativity, but also combines with a host of other individuals and their temporalities in a collective experience for which we have no ready-made linguistic or figurative categories. It is an account worth quoting in its own right, and marks the way in which a temporal investment of the Utopian impulse moves towards that final form which is the figure of the collectivity as such:

> It must not be supposed that this strange mental community blotted out the personalities of the individual explorers. Human speech has no accurate terms to describe our peculiar relationship. It would be as untrue to say that we had lost our individuality, or were dissolved in a communal individuality, as to say that we were all the while distinct individuals. Though the pronoun "I" now applied to us all collectively, the pronoun "we" also applied to us. In one respect, namely unity of consciousness, we were indeed a single experiencing individual; yet at the same time we were in a very important and delightful manner distinct from one another. Though there was only a single, communal "I," there was also, so to speak, a manifold and variegated "us," an observed company of very diverse personalities, each of whom expressed creatively his own unique contribution to the whole enterprise of cosmical exploration, while all were bound together in a tissue of subtle personal relationships.[13]

At this point the expression of the Utopian impulse has come as close to the surface of reality as it can without turning into a conscious Utopian project and passing over into that other line of development we have called the Utopian program and Utopian realization. The earlier stages of Utopian investment were still locked into the limits of individual experience, which is not to say that the category of collectivity is unbounded either – we have already hinted at its structural requirement of closure, to which we will return later on.

For the moment, however, it suffices to observe that, short of any conscious Utopian politics, the collective knows a variety of negative expressions whose dangers are very different from those of individual egotism and privilege. Narcissism characterizes both, no doubt: but it is collective narcissism that is most readily identified in the various xenophobic or racist group practices, all of which have their Utopian impulsion, as I've notoriously tried to explain elsewhere.[14] Bloch's hermeneutic is not designed to excuse these deformed Utopian impulses, but rather entertains a political wager that their energies can be appropriated by the process of unmasking, and released by consciousness in a manner analogous to the Freudian cure (or the Lacanian

---

13 Olaf Stapledon, *The Last and First Men/Star Maker* (New York, 1968), p. 343.
14 See the Conclusion to my *The Political Unconscious* (Ithaca, 1981), and also my review article "On 'Cultural Studies'", in *Social Text*, No. 34 (1993), pp. 17–52.

restructuring of desire). This may well be a dangerous and misguided hope; but we leave it behind us when we pass back over into the process of conscious Utopian construction again.

The levels of Utopian allegory, of the investments of the Utopian impulse, can therefore be represented thus:

THE COLLECTIVE (anagogical)

TEMPORALITY (moral)

THE BODY (allegorical)

UTOPIAN INVESTMENT (the text)

2

The Utopian Enclave

To see traces of the Utopian impulse everywhere, as Bloch did, is to naturalize it and to imply that it is somehow rooted in human nature.[1] Attempts to realize Utopia, however, have been historically more intermittent, and we need to limit them even further by now insisting on everything peculiar and eccentric about the fantasy production that gives rise to them. Daydreams, in which whole cities are laid out in the mind, in which constitutions are enthusiastically composed and legal systems endlessly drafted and emended, in which the seating arrangements for festivals and banquets are meditated in detail, and even garbage disposal is as attentively organized as administrative hierarchy, and family and child-care problems are resolved with ingenious new proposals – such fantasies seem distinct enough from erotic daydreams and to warrant special attention in their own right.[2]

The Utopians, whether political, textual or hermeneutic, have always been maniacs and oddballs: a deformation readily enough explained by the fallen societies in which they had to fulfill their vocation. Indeed, I want us to understand Utopianism, not as some unlocking of the political, returning to its rightful centrality as in the Greek city-states; but rather as a whole distinct process in its own right. On a first approach, I want even those dealings with the political which it seems to presuppose to retain an awkward and suspect character. We must accustom ourselves to think, in our societies in which the political has so successfully been disjoined from the private, of the political as a kind of vice. Why else should those prototypical political thinkers *par excellence*, Machiavelli and Carl Schmitt, be forever surrounded with an aroma of scandal? But what they dared to enunciate publicly, in a heroism indissociable from cynicism, our Utopians grasp more furtively, in forms more redolent of perversion than of paranoia, and with that passionate sense of mission or calling from which *jouissance* is never absent.

---

1 As befits a defender of natural law: see Bloch, *Natural Law and Human Dignity* (Cambridge, MA, 1961).

2 I hope it is clear that psychological explanations, particularly those in terms of "sublimation", are incompatible with the kind of productions described here.

It is however not a psychological account we now seek, but rather a more historical one, which theorizes the conditions of possibility of these peculiar fantasies. Utopias seem to be by-products of Western modernity, not even emerging in every stage of the latter. We need to get some idea of the specific situations and circumstances under which their composition is possible, situations which encourage this peculiar vocation or talent at the same time that they offer suitable materials for its exercise.

The Utopian calling, indeed, seems to have some kinship with that of the inventor in modern times, and to bring to bear some necessary combination of the identification of a problem to be solved and the inventive ingenuity with which a series of solutions are proposed and tested. There is here some affinity with children's games; but also with the outsider's gift for seeing over-familiar realities in a fresh and unaccustomed way, along with the radical simplifications of the maker of models. But there is also the delight in construction to be taken into account, something wonderfully conveyed by Margaret Cavendish's "spirits":

> "for every human creature can create an immaterial world fully inhabited by immaterial creatures, and populous of immaterial subjects, such as we are, and all this within the compass of a head or scull; nay, not only so, but he may create a world of what fashion and government he will, and give the creature thereof such motions, figures, forms, colours, perceptions, etc. as he pleases, and make whirlpools, lights, pressures and reactions, etc. as he thinks best; nay, he may make a world full of veins, muscles, and nerves, and all these to move by one jolt or stroke: also he may alter that world as often as he pleases, or change it from a natural world of ideas, a world of atoms, a world of lights, or whatsoever his fancy leads him to. And since it is in your power" (the spirits conclude) "to create such a world, what need you to venture life, reputation and tranquility, to conquer a gross material world?"[3]

But such creation must be motivated: it must respond to specific dilemmas and offer to solve fundamental social problems to which the Utopian believes himself to hold the key. The Utopian vocation can be identified by this certainty, and by the persistent and obsessive search for a simple, a single-shot solution to all our ills. And this must be a solution so obvious and self-explanatory that every reasonable person will grasp it: just as the inventor is certain his better mousetrap will compel universal conviction.

---

3 Margaret Cavendish, *The Description of a New World Called the Blazing World* (New York, 1992 [1666]), pp. 185–186. Cavendish (1623–1673) is truly the descendant of Bacon in this Utopia which, however fantastic, is based on a constructional play with "scientific" elements drawn from all the current theories of her own time, including those of Descartes and Hobbes, whom she claimed to have known personally. Constructivism celebrates its coronation in her ambition "not only to be Empress, but Authoress of a whole world" (p. 224).

Yet it is the social situation which must admit of such a solution, or at least of its possibility: this is one aspect of the objective preconditions for a Utopia. The view that opens out onto history from a particular social situation must encourage such oversimplifications; the miseries and injustices thus visible must seem to shape and organize themselves around one specific ill or wrong. For the Utopian remedy must at first be a fundamentally negative one, and stand as a clarion call to remove and to extirpate this specific root of all evil from which all the others spring.

This is why it is a mistake to approach Utopias with positive expectations, as though they offered visions of happy worlds, spaces of fulfillment and cooperation, representations which correspond generically to the idyll or the pastoral rather than the utopia.[4] Indeed, the attempt to establish positive criteria of the desirable society characterizes liberal political theory from Locke to Rawls, rather than the diagnostic interventions of the Utopians, which, like those of the great revolutionaries, always aim at the alleviation and elimination of the sources of exploitation and suffering, rather than at the composition of blueprints for bourgeois comfort. The confusion arises from the formal properties of these texts, which also seem to offer blueprints: these are however maps and plans to be read negatively, as what is to be accomplished after the demolitions and the removals, and in the absence of all those lesser evils the liberals believed to be inherent in human nature.

With this fundamental qualification in mind, we can then take an inventory of the most influential Utopian formulations, beginning with More's canonical solution in the abolition of money and property. This first basic step does not disappear in later Utopias, but is often improved by additional concerns, which prompt new motifs and new embellishments. So it is that Campanella emphasizes the order to be realized by a generalization of the space of the monastery. For Winstanley it is rather the abolition of wage labor in the new space of the commons which heralds the beginning of the end of social misery, while all of Rousseau's ideas about freedom turn on the bitter experience of dependency. Fourier and desire; Saint-Simon and administration; Bellamy and the industrial army; Morris and that non-alienated labor he called art – all were able to offer Utopian programs that could be grasped with a single slogan and seem relatively easy to put into effect.

With Chernyshevsky it is marriage and "the woman question" which become central, while in the contemporary period it is not only subjectivity that complicates Utopian production. *Ecotopia* answers standard capitalist objections by offering an ecological which is also an entrepreneurial Utopia, while Le Guin's Tao is an equally ecological remedy for a fundamentally aggressive

---

4 The argument is developed further in Chapter 11. Yet it is worth wondering whether the protean analyses of the pastoral impulse in Empson's classic *Versions* do not bring it fairly close to the Utopian impulse as such (William Empson, *Some Versions of Pastoral* [London, 1935]).

and destructive modernity. In Skinner pedagogy primes all else (whatever he may call it), while in Marge Piercy's *Woman on the Edge of Time* the now familiar contemporary triad of race, class and gender replaces More's old triad of greed, pride and hierarchy (see Chapter 3 below) and offers a succinct and interrelated target.[5]

Yet despite what has been said about the eccentricities of the Utopian analyst, these themes and social diagnoses are neither random nor willfully invented out of obsession or personal whim. Or rather, it is precisely the Utopian's obsession which serves as a registering apparatus for a given social reality, whose identification then hopefully meets with collective recognition. But nothing guarantees that a given Utopian preoccupation will strike the mark, that it will detect any really existing social elements, let alone fashion them into a model that will explain their situation to other people. There is therefore, alongside seemingly random biographical chapters, a history of the Utopian raw material to be projected:[6] one that is bound up with representation insofar as it is not only the real contradictions of capitalist modernity that evolve in convulsive moments (like the stages of growth of the eponymous monster of Ridley Scott's film *Alien* [1979]), but also the visibility of such contradictions from stage to historical stage, or in other words the capacity of each one to be named, to be thematized and to be represented, not only in epistemological ways, in terms of social or economic analyses, but also in dramatic or aesthetic forms which, along with the political platforms and slogans so closely related to them, are able to grip the imagination and speak to larger social groups. And as with the Alien itself, it is conceivable that each moment of representation will seem radically different from its predecessors: thus, the dilemmas of industrialization no longer seem to have much in common with the misery caused by enclosure – save as a source of immense collective suffering.

Yet in order for representability to be achieved, the social or historical moment must somehow offer itself as a situation, allow itself to be read in

---

5 We sometimes forget that Chernyshevsky's *What's To Be Done?* (1863), which gave its name to Lenin's equally famous pamphlet, was as influential world-wide as Bellamy's *Looking Backward* of 1888. *Ecotopia* (1975), by Ernest Callenbach (1929–), is the most important Utopia to have emerged from the North American 1960s: it depicts a state which includes the present Oregon, Washington and Northern California, which, having seceded from the United States, is isolated for decades by an economic and informational blockade. As for Ursula Le Guin (1929–), it will frequently be a question of her works in what follows, particularly in Chapters 5, 6 and 10 below, and also in Part Two, Essay 3. She is one of the most important contemporary American writers (and not only of SF and fantasy): her novel *The Left Hand of Darkness* (1969) made a fundamental contribution to feminism and gender studies, just as her electrifying political intervention, *The Dispossessed* (1974), did to the political debates of the 1970s.

6 But this book is not that history: the play of raw material will be chiefly rehearsed in Chapter 3, on More's *Utopia*; while the emphasis elsewhere will be a more formalist one, inquiring into the representational constraints which deform a text they enable in the first place.

terms of effects and causes, or problems and solutions, questions and answers. It must have reached a level of shaped complexity that seems to foreground some fundamental ill, and that tempts the social theorist into producing an overview organized around a specific theme. The social totality is always unrepresentable, even for the most numerically limited groups of people; but it can sometimes be mapped and allow a small-scale model to be constructed on which the fundamental tendencies and the lines of flight can more clearly be read. At other times, this representational process is impossible, and people face history and the social totality as a bewildering chaos, whose forces are indiscernible.

For good or ill, this second type of Utopian precondition – the material – would seem to distinguish itself from the first – the vocation – as object to subject, as social reality to individual perception. Yet the traditional opposition is little more than a convenience, and we are more interested in the mysterious interaction of both in Utopian texts in which they in fact become inextricable. To separate them inevitably involves a figural process, even in objective disciplines like sociology. So if in a first moment I have characterized the Utopian's relationship to her social situation as one of raw material, we may now ask what kinds of building blocks the historical moment provides. Laws, labor, marriage, industrial and institutional organization, trade and exchange, even subjective raw materials such as characterological formations, habits of practice, talents, gender attitudes: all become, at one point or another in the story of utopias, grist for the Utopian mill and substances out of which the Utopian construction can be fashioned.

But we have also evoked a kind of Utopian workshop like the inventor's, a garage space in which all kinds of machinery can be tinkered with and rebuilt. Let's now for a moment follow this spatial figuration, which has been most complexly elaborated in Niklas Luhmann's so-called systems theory, with its concept of "differentiation" as the fundamental dynamic. Thus, a Luhmann-inspired metaphysic would posit something like an undifferentiated substance which begins internally to differentiate itself into so many related but distinct, semi-autonomous "systems".[7] We may think of these systems in any form we like: Kant's witty identification of the faculties of the university with the older tradition of the mental faculties offers a good random starting point, for it projects a comparison between the increasing differentiation of the various bodies of the specialized academic disciplines with the separation from each other of "parts" of the psyche, such as cognition or the will. That these are ongoing and increasingly complex differentiations is a matter of empirical history: the traditional disciplines begin to hive off new ones, such as sociology or psychology, or in our time molecular biology, while modern literature testifies to the emergence of all kinds of new psychic functions which were

---

7   See, for example, Niklas Luhmann, *The Differentiation of Society* (New York, 1982).

not registered in the traditional literary genres. But now the juxtaposition of these two evolving fields (the academic disciplines, the psyche) remind us of the multiplicity of other such fields contained within the social totality (or "system"): social classes, for example, which then differentiate into a host of strata, professional specializations and the like; or productive activities, which multiply as industry itself becomes refined into ever more varied technological and scientific processes, while the products thus produced (and the demand for them) are multiplied virtually without limit. Meanwhile the political system itself hives off the jurists, who become a separate profession governed by a distinct field of knowledge in its own right, from its administrators and bureaucrats, elective officials, state, municipal and federal employees, along with the multiplications of the welfare state, the appearance of social workers, and the various branches of public medicine as well as scientific research; and so on and so forth. Luhmann defines modernity by way of the onset of this process; postmodernity could then be seen as a dialectical saturation in which the hitherto semi-autonomous sub-systems of these various social levels threaten to become autonomous *tout court*, and generate a very different ideological picture of complexity as dispersed multiplicity and infinite fission than the progressive one afforded by the preceding stage of modernity.

What does this interesting picture of social differentiation have to offer a theory of Utopian production? I believe that we can begin from the proposition that Utopian space is an imaginary enclave within real social space, in other words, that the very possibility of Utopian space is itself a result of spatial and social differentiation. But it is an aberrant by-product, and its possibility is dependent on the momentary formation of a kind of eddy or self-contained backwater within the general differentiation process and its seemingly irreversible forward momentum.

This pocket of stasis within the ferment and rushing forces of social change may be thought of as a kind of enclave within which Utopian fantasy can operate.[8] This is a figure which then usefully allows us to combine two hitherto contradictory features of the relation of Utopia to social reality: on the one hand, its very existence or emergence certainly registers the agitation of the various "transitional periods" within which most Utopias were composed (the term "transitional" itself conveying this sense of momentum); while, on the other, it suggests the distance of the Utopias from practical politics, on the basis of a zone of the social totality which seems eternal and unchangeable, even within this social ferment we have attributed to the age itself. The court, for example, offers a figure of a closed space beyond the social, a space from

---

8 I toy elsewhere with figures from Lacan ("extimacy") and Derrida ("encryptment"). See my essay "The Politics of Utopia", *New Left Review*, No. 25 (January/February 2004), p. 43; the essay is something of an early and tentative sketch of positions more fully developed in the present book, which constitutes the concluding volume of *The Poetics of Social Forms*.

which power distantly emanates but which cannot itself be thought of as modifiable except in those rare moments in which revolutionary politics shakes the whole edifice. For the earlier Utopias, then, the figure of the court as an ahistorical enclave within a bustling movement of secularization and national and commercial development offers a kind of mental space in which the whole system can be imagined as radically different. But clearly, this enclave space is but a pause in the all-encompassing forward momentum of differentiation which will sweep it away altogether a few decades later (or at the very least reorganize it and plunge it into secular society and social space as such). The Utopians, however, reflect this still non-revolutionary blindness as to possible modifications in the power system; and this blindness is their strength insofar as it allows their imagination to overleap the moment of revolution itself and posit a radically different "post-revolutionary" society.

Meanwhile, to identify another such enclave, the eighteenth-century hobby of the drafting of new constitutions – something vividly to be observed in the instructive context of Jean-Jacques Rousseau's more general (and differentiated) fantasy production – illustrates in another way the sense of the differentiation of administrative and bureaucratic power from social life in general, and the possibilities this differentiated enclave opens up for Utopian reconstruction, until in the nineteenth century it suddenly expands into society itself and is no longer available for Utopian speculation, having become diffused and indeed virtually coterminous with the new industrial society itself. Saint-Simon's is perhaps the last Utopian vision of bureaucratic reorganization until we reach the constitutional activities of Kim Stanley Robinson's Mars, which reflect the emergence of new transnational bureaucracies – in some galactic United Nations and multiplanetary corporate systems.

Such enclaves are something like a foreign body within the social: in them, the differentiation process has momentarily been arrested, so that they remain as it were momentarily beyond the reach of the social and testify to its political powerlessness, at the same time that they offer a space in which new wish images of the social can be elaborated and experimented on.

So it is that despite the commercial bustle of More's London the money form is still relatively isolated and sporadic in the agricultural world that surrounds it (enclosure will be the essential step that opens this older world up to wage labor). We may thus posit the money form as leading a kind of enclave existence within More's historical moment, thereby proposing a cognate figure to the one Marx famously uses about the international role of money in an earlier period: "trading nations, properly so called, exist only in the interstices of the ancient world, like the gods of Epicurus in the *intermundia*, or the Jews in the pores of Polish society".[9] Here too, in this still largely medieval moment of "early modernity", money and commerce will have remained episodic,

9 Karl Marx, *Capital*, Volume I (London, 1976 [1867]), p. 172.

embodied in the decorative ostentation of gold on the one hand or the excitement of the great fairs on the other: but this enclave status of money is precisely what allows More to fantasize its removal from social life in his new Utopian vision. It is an absence which will become unthinkable when the use of money is generalized to all sections of the "modern" economies, at which point Utopian speculation will take the form of various substitutions – stamp script, labor certificates, a return to silver, and so forth, none of which offer very convincing Utopian possibilities. Yet the paradox which More's fantasy allows us to glimpse is the way in which this monetary enclave, and this strange foreign body as which money and gold momentarily present themselves, can at one and the same time be fantasized as the very root of all evil and the source of all social ills and as something that can be utterly eliminated from the new Utopian social formation. The enclave radiates baleful power, but at the same time it is a power that can be eclipsed without a trace precisely because it is confined to a limited space.

In More's near-contemporary Campanella the enclave status plays a somewhat different role: it is because the monastery is an enclave within a more generally differentiated and complicated society that it can be generalized outwards and serve as a Utopian model for a social simplification and discipline. The irony of the success of this counterreformation Utopia among Protestants is to be explained by Weber's observation: the Protestant elimination of the monasteries turned the whole world into one immense monastery in which, as Sebastian Franck put it, "every Christian had to be a monk all his life".[10]

A similar inversion takes place in Bacon, where the enclave emergence of secular science and its episodic transnational networks, foreshadowing the founding of the Royal Society, determine the fantasy of a whole world organized along the new research principles.

Both these models, which deploy ideologies of the old and the new forms of the intellectual, remain attractive to intellectuals in various modern versions, it being understood that the intellectual is quintessentially the dweller in just such enclave spaces. This is something Kim Stanley Robinson's Martians come to realize, as their own social environment becomes gradually enlarged and differentiated:

"When we first arrived, and for twenty years after that, Mars was like Antartica but even purer. We were outside the world, we didn't even own things – some clothes, a lectern, and that was it! ... This arrangement resembles the prehistoric way to live, and it therefore feels right to us, because our brains recognize it from three millions of years practicing it. In essence our brains grew to their current configuration in response to the realities of that life. So as a result

---

10 Max Weber, *The Protestant Ethic and the Spirit of Capitalism* (New York, 1958 [1902]), p. 121.

people grow *powerfully attached* to that kind of life, when they get the chance to live it. It allows you to concentrate your attention on the real work, which means everything that is done to stay alive, or make things, or satisfy one's curiosity, or play. That is utopia, John, especially for primitives and scientists, which is to say everybody. So a scientific research station is actually a little model of prehistoric utopia, carved out of the transnational money economy by clever primates who want to live well."[11]

The absence of money – More's fundamental principle – is the precondition for this enclave utopia, but no longer its thematic focus; while the instinctual – we might even say socio-biological – defense of utopia as a pre-monetary life recalls Freud's remark on the absence of money from the unconscious (or even Habermas' account of money as the "noise" in an essentially communicational system).[12]

The anthropological note also reminds us of the next development in Utopian form which is enabled by geographical exploration and the resultant travel narratives, which combine with philosophical materialism to produce a new and geographical experience of the enclave, in which new information about tribal societies and their well-nigh Utopian dignity are conjoined with Montesquieu's climatological determinism. The exotic travel narrative, along with Rousseau's near-Utopian fantasies about closed spaces such as Poland or Corsica,[13] develops on into various influential post-Utopian ideologies: most directly into the primitivism revived by Lévi-Strauss and renewed study of

11 Kim Stanley Robinson, *Red Mars* (New York, 1993), pp. 309–310; quoted from Damien Broderick's fine book *Reading by Starlight* (London, 1995, pp. 107–108), which intersects in many ways with my concerns here and which has clarified my decision to limit my engagement with SF to its Utopian functions. Broderick's work indeed reproduces, at a very high level of energy and intelligence, the standard aim of traditional aesthetics, namely to identify the specificity of the aesthetic as such: in other words, for standard literature, to differentiate fiction from other discourses; or, in the case of SF, to differentiate its narrative sentences and their content, not only from realism, but also from the literary fantastic or "maravilloso" as well as from fantasy, horror and other paraliterary forms. In my opinion, this is not in the long run a very interesting or productive line of inquiry, although it can certainly throw off many useful or striking insights in the process. Indeed, the sterility of the approach documents the structural limits of aesthetic philosophy as such and confirms its obsolescence. (I am inclined to make an exception for the study of the specificity of poetic language.) Yet, as far as I can judge, all general approaches to SF as a mode find themselves fatally diverted into these channels, from which only the historical conjuncture or the Utopian impulse seem capable of rescuing them. But see, for a Marxian approach to the whole SF tradition, Carl Freedman, *Critical Theory and Science Fiction* (Hanover, NH, 2000).

12 See Habermas' concept of money as "norm-free" within the system: *The Theory of Communicative Action* (Boston, MA, 1984 [1981]), Volume II, pp. 171–172, 264–265 and 343–346. For Freud's idea that the unconscious has no concept of money at all, see Norman O. Brown, *Life Against Death* (Middletown, CT, 1970).

13 Jean-Jacques Rousseau, *Oeuvres*, Volume III (Paris, 1964): "Project de constitution pour la Corse" (1765), and "Considérations sur le gouvernement de la Pologne" (1770–1771).

primitive communism or tribal society;[14] as well as more indirectly into the closures of nationalism on the one hand, which very much vehiculates a geographical secession specified as a racial uniqueness; and into ecology on the other, reemerging from the closure of the planet itself.

Yet with the bourgeois era and Fourier something new begins to appear: that realm of subjectivity which Rousseau had still kept separate from his political fantasies about Plutarchian virtue – a veritable new construction of the subject or psyche which the later discipline of psychology will attempt to colonize and on which Freudian psychoanalysis will establish its beachhead. It is characteristic of this production of the new individualism and its subjectivities that the latter should now be felt to be incommensurable with the dry and more seemingly objective issues of social construction and Utopian statecraft. Fourier's dazzling set of Utopian permutations are the last bravura solutions to this dawning incompatibility, as objectivity and subjectivity are reconciled in a host of objective tasks that correspond to the new multiplicity of subjective passions, and are organized by feminist and anti-capitalist values.

After Fourier's grand synthesis (which has been compared to the complexities of the Hegelian dialectic),[15] this new psychic enclave which is bourgeois or modern subjectivity will essentially be dealt with in that separate codicil called cultural revolution. Chernyshevsky is the great forerunner of this parallel revolution, and at once raises all the feminist and gender issues that will dominate contemporary utopias, while deriving his cooperative economic revolution from cottage industries specifically identified as women's work, namely Vera Petrovna's textile workshops.

For the most part, however, the emergence of a new industrial order will reconfirm that fundamental modern differentiation between the subjective and the objective, and Bellamy's paradigmatic success is due to the Utopian form with which he greets and "solves" the problem of industry and technology,[16] while Morris' counterstatement, in the distant wake of the Luddites,[17] remains

---

14 Characteristic are Marshall Sahlins, *Stone Age Economics* (Chicago, 1972) and Colin Turnbull, *The Forest People* (New York, 1961).

15 "Fourier ... uses the dialectic method in the same masterly way as his contemporary, Hegel" (Friedrich Engels, *Anti-Dühring* [Moscow, 1977 (1878)], p. 315); see also my essay on Fourier, Essay 1 of Part Two of the present volume.

16 Edward Bellamy, *Looking Backward* (New York, 1986 [1888]), p. 69:

"The national organization of labor under one direction was the complete solution of what was, in your day and under your system, justly regarded as the insoluable labor problem. When the nation became the sole employer, all the citizens, by virtue of their citizenship, became employees, to be distributed according to the needs of industry."

"That is," I suggested, "you have simply applied the principle of universal military service, as it was understood in our day, to the labor question."

17 See Kirkpatrick Sale's enlightening *Rebels against the Future* (Reading, MA, 1995); and for a more general critique of the notion of peasant "spontaneity" and allegedly spontaneous and unorganized uprisings, Ranajit Guha, *Elementary Aspects of Peasant Insurgency in Colonial India* (Oxford, 1983).

reactive in its attempt to rescue non-alienated labor from the dreariness of factory work (a labor which however reflects and expresses in a different register the new autonomy of art also generated by the differentiations of the modern).

Other potentially Utopian enclaves appear at this point: space and urbanism, for example, in which the Utopia of the garden city appears,[18] and in the next generation that of the Bauhaus and a very different kind of revolutionary modern architecture. Unlike Morris, these efforts show the renewed influence on the concept of Utopian secession: the various anarchist cooperatives, for example, and the rural communes that follow them much later in the 1960s, are all predicated on an idea of utopian closure which Skinner's already suburban Utopia perhaps does not programmatically enough express. Industrialization greatly increases the wealth of nations (Marx's so-called General Intellect spreading through the whole social order),[19] but is not felt in the modern period to have so completely colonized social space as to close all the loopholes and make an enclave-type withdrawal impossible. Indeed, it is precisely the closing of those loopholes (and the advent of the perspective of a concrete World Market) which is now called postmodernity (or global-ization) and spells an end to this type of Utopian fantasy.

At the same time, a kind of dedifferentiation already begins to reappear in the modern era which is registered in the conflation, from Bellamy onwards, of Utopia and socialism. We have indicated, indeed, that More's initial utopian gesture – the abolition of money and property – runs through the Utopian tradition like a red thread, now aggressively affirmed on the surface, now tacitly presupposed in milder forms or disguises. (Indeed, a closer look at More's text itself is obviously on our agenda and will be undertaken in the next chapter.)

But the confluence of socialism and the Utopian form obviously presents some problems for the latter's autonomy, seeming to relegate the latter to the secondary status of illustration or propaganda. Communist utopias form a special subset of this group, since they reflect the closure and international secession of that enclave called "socialism in one country"; they are, moreover, post-revolutionary: either seeming to express a Utopian imperialism of further worlds to conquer, both geographically and, scientifically (as in Bogdanov or Efremov), or to revert, in the pastorals of socialist realism, to what we have called mere expressions of the Utopian impulse.[20] There are also Utopias

---

18 Ebenezer Howard, *Garden Cities of Tomorrow* (Cambridge, 1965 [1902]).

19 Marx's notion of the "General Intellect" (so named in English in his text) is to be found in the *Grundrisse* (London, 1973 [1857–1861]), p. 706; it was an energizing conception of Italy's Autonomia period (see the essay by Maurizio Lazzerato in Michael Hardt and Paolo Virno, eds, *Radical Thought in Italy* [Minnesota, 1996]) and is central to the hotly debated current notion of "immaterial labor" in the cybernetic age.

20 *Red Star* (1908), by the remarkable Alexander Bogdanov (1873–1928), is of course pre-revolutionary in the technical sense; while the *Andromeda* (1958) of I.A. Efremov (1907–1972), the inaugural salvo of a return to Soviet Utopian SF after Stalin's death, opens the way for major

which express the profound disillusionment with the stalling or the denaturing of Lenin's original Utopia – that ambiguous work *We* has indeed been shown to be both Utopia and dystopia all at once.[21]

But the history of the communist adventure is not co-terminous with the history of socialism as such; and it is hard to see how the problems of a modernizing industrial society could be resolved without the Utopian solutions afforded by socialism. The third stage of capitalism, however, which issued in the radically different technology of cybernetics and computers, now seemed to render the dilemmas of heavy industry and modern factory production obsolete, and to enable a return to non-socialist utopias, such as those of Nozick's anarchism or those implicit in that romance of finance capital to be found in cyberpunk. Cyberspace is indeed an enclave of a new sort, a subjectivity which is objective and which, like Luhmann's systems theory, but also like the structuralism and poststructuralism which preceded it, once more does away with the "centered subject" and proliferates in new, post-individualistic ways. Those ways, however, cannot but be collective (albeit in unrecognizable new forms as well), and we will try, in a final chapter, to reidentify the vital political function Utopia still has to play today.

---

contributions to the tradition by the Strugatsky Brothers (Arkady, 1925–1991, and Boris, 1933–), on whom see below, Chapter 6. It should be noted, however, that a long-standing Russian tradition of Verne-like SF continued to be published throughout the Soviet period under the rubric of children's literature. For the strange case of Platonov's *Chevengur* (1928–1929), see my *Seeds of Time* (New York, 1994), pp. 73–128; and, for the contemporary Russian scene, by all means read Viktor Pelevin, *Homo Zapiens* (New York, 1999; and see Chapter 6, note 8, below).
21 The structural ambiguity of Zamyatin's *We* has been stressed by two of the fundamental works of Utopian literary theory (as well as by Gary Saul Morson: see Chapter 11). In *Metamorphoses of Science Fiction* (New Haven, 1979), Darko Suvin argues against the classification of *We* as anti-Utopian, seeing it rather as an intersection between two tendencies within the Utopian tradition: "The defeat in the novel *We* is not the defeat of the novel itself, but an exasperated shocking of the reader into thought and action. It is a document of an acute clash between the 'cold' and the 'warm' utopia: a judgement on Campanella or Bacon as given by Rabelais or Shelley" (p. 259). Phillip E. Wegner's *Imaginary Communities* (California, 2002) elaborately maps out this position by a demonstration of the "play of possible worlds" within Zamyatin's polyphonic text.

3

Morus: The Generic Window

I

Can we invent a way of reading More's *Utopia* (1516) so as to recover something of the shock and freshness of its elegant new Latin for the first European readers? Not the components, however, nor even their individual modes, but rather the unaccustomed combination of hitherto unrelated connotations, make up this generic hapax legomenon; and a type of syntax which might ordinarily say "humanism" finds itself oddly transformed as part of a complex message which is itself a kind of semantic "one of a kind".

Even from the outset, however, we have a decision to make which will confront us with two distinct interpretations, inasmuch as Book Two, the properly Utopian part of the text, is known to have been written first. Are we then to reincorporate this philological knowledge, and to treat Book One as a kind of afterthought or cautious and politically prudent (but also daring) recontextualization of the account of the island itself, one which carefully distances Hythloday's enthusiasms and hedges all the bets? Or should we let the present order continue to dictate a processual dynamism in which the Utopian vision emerges dialectically from the very contradictions of both Part One and the historical present? This second alternative reading, and the interpretive decision it calls for (to take More's vision seriously), is reduced and caricatured by the revisionist and anti-Utopian position (which always seems to reemerge in periods of political stagnation) according to which "Utopia" is really a *jeu d'esprit* after all, and the idiotic names (Hythloday = Nonsenso, etc.)[1] are meant to be taken satirically. The best method is always to turn such a problem into a solution in its own right, and to make of this objective and incompatible alternation an interpretive phenomenon at some higher (meta) level.[2] Here reading and interpretation confront the fundamental ethical binary

---

1 See Paul Turner's translation of Thomas More, *Utopia* (London, 1965 [1516]), p. 8. This view of Utopia as a *jeu d'esprit* (More was a great joker, Erasmus tells us) is classically expressed by C.S. Lewis in *English Literature in the Sixteenth Century* (Oxford, 1954), pp. 167–171.

2 This is, I believe, what Adorno meant by "second reflexion" in *Aesthetic Theory* (Minnesota, 1997), translated by R. Hullot-Kentor, pp. 26–27; or, as far as that goes, what I call metacommentary in the essay of that name in my *The Ideologies of Theory* (Minnesota, 1988 [1970]).

with a vengeance; and are at once asked to take a position on that ideological question *par excellence* which is also the fundamental political one, namely whether Utopias are positive or negative, good or evil.

Yet this is not to be asked first but rather last of all: and the initial interpretive signals, those that revolve the hermeneutic wheel at some outside level of reading and decipherment, will be the generic ones. Genre presumably governs the interpretation of the narrative or representational details within its frame; and in More's text it again offers a relatively stark and global alternative between two possibilities. But they are not, I think, those proposed above between Utopia taken seriously as a social and political project and Utopian thought ridiculed as a pipe dream. Nor does that opposition correspond to Robert C. Elliott's great dialectical proposition that, as a genre, Utopia is the opposite and the structural inversion of satire as such.[3] For what Elliott meant by satire was not anti-political rejection of the unrealistic and fanciful Utopian programs such as the abolition of money and private property, but rather the passionate and prophetic onslaught on current conditions and on the wickedness and stupidity of human beings in the fallen world of the here and now. Put this way, we can see that Elliott's generic alternation rather corresponds basically to the opposition between the two books of *Utopia* itself:[4] and it follows that the generic interpretation of the text as a whole will very much depend on which part we take to be prior and to offer the fundamental hermeneutic key. Thus, if we posit the priority of Book One, we will want to foreground satire and its generic structure; if Book Two (and insofar as Utopia as a genre does not yet exist), it will be travel narrative that sets the generic agenda.

II

Whatever else it does, travel narrative marks Utopia as irredeemably other, and thus formally, or virtually by definition, impossible of realization: it thus reinforces Utopia's constitutive secessionism, a withdrawal or "delinking" from the empirical and historical world which, from More to Ernest Callenbach's *Ecotopia*, problematizes its value as a global (if not universal) model and uncomfortably refocuses the readerly gaze on that very issue of its practical political inauguration which the form promised to avoid in the first place. (These contradictions are clearly modified when Utopia is set in a temporal future rather than at a geographical distance, but after all today space is once again on the postmodern agenda.) Yet Utopian politics takes place within this gap between

---

3 Robert C. Elliott, *The Shape of Utopia* (Chicago, 1970), Chapter 1.
4 The definitive study of the relationship between Books One and Two (the latter having according to all evidence been composed *before* the former) is J.H. Hexter's *More's Utopia: The Biography of an Idea* (Princeton, 1952).

Utopus' newly created island and its non-Utopian neighbors: and this gap is the point at which More's Utopianism begins to seem indistinguishable from Machiavelli's practice (whose codification, as noted above, is virtually contemporaneous with More's text).

As with the imaginary construction of the chimera, however, even a no-place must be put together out of already existing representations. Indeed the act of combination and the raw materials thereby combined themselves constitute the ideological message. We cannot try to read Book Two as a generic travel narrative without making an effort to see the place and to sense that exoticism it uniquely offers. I think myself of the figures in Dante or Giotto: realistic statuary, but without any of the technical detail and complex and perspectival verisimilitude of the Renaissance – hooded forms, whose robes and folds mark a conceptual relationship to the classical world, while their monkish overtones retain connotations of the medieval and Catholicism. Yet the Utopians will have to learn about both these family likenesses from their visitor Hythloday, who brings with him both the Greek classics and the Christian gospels. They confirm the family likeness by recognizing Christianity as their ethos, and also by way of the revelation that in fact they are descendants of Greeks shipwrecked, many generations earlier. Yet if this island has nothing of the empirical exoticism of Cortez's Mexico, or of that China and Japan to which Columbus tried again and again to sail, it is nonetheless situated in the Pacific, between Ceylon and America, and deserves at least some quotient of a properly New World association. In fact, as Arthur Morgan has pointed out in some detail, the association suggests a distant identification with the Inca empire, whose "communistic" social system has not ceased to fascinate the West down to our own time (as in Godelier's reclassification of it under the category of Marx's Asiatic mode of production).[5]

Nor must we omit a final cultural association here: for despite his subsequent ferocious denunciations of Luther, there cannot but breathe through the text of Erasmus' friend something of the spirit of what will only later be called Protestantism, a milder fellow-traveling sympathy with reform easily ·chastened by very real political dangers and (at least in More's case) open to other incursions of the unconscious, particularly of a sexual nature (he seems to have ceased all sexual relations at a relatively early age, and to have worn a hair shirt the rest of his life). But this flavor of Protestantism, although registered in some practical details (the priests marry, for example), is rather to be understood in the cultural sense, as a return to that spirit of primitive Christianity which is also a discovery and a new intellectual enthusiasm (very much like that humanism with which it is at first intimately related).

Greece, the medieval, the Incas, Protestantism: these are the four crucial elements of More's Utopian text, the four raw materials of its representation.

---

5   Arthur Morgan, *Nowhere Was Somewhere* (Chapel Hill, NC, 1946). And see note 19 below.

Utopia is a synthesis of these four codes or representational languages, these four ideologemes, but only on condition it be understood that they do not fold back into it without a trace, but retain the dissonances between their distinct identities and origins, revealing the constant effort of a process that seeks to combine them without effacing all traces of what it wishes to unify in the first place. For these four reference points include superstructure and base, that is to say, contemporaneous or even modern intellectual movements and passions along with social institutions barely surviving from the past. Their combination is a whole political program and in effect implicitly identifies those still-existing social spaces in which the new ideological values might be incarnated.

Thus Greece clearly means humanism and the conceptual enthusiasm aroused by the rediscovery of the linguistic possibilities of the classical languages; it stands for a unique perspective in which language and thought are once again for one long moment inseparable, in which the philosophical richness of the ancient texts is grasped as being at one with the stylistic and syntactical richness of the culture languages of antiquity. Norbert Elias has observed that this extraordinary revival is comparable to nothing quite so much as to the rediscovery of Marxism and the great dialectical texts and traditions in the 1960s:[6] an excitement that identifies a forgotten or repressed moment of the past as the new and subversive, and learns the dialectical grammar of a Hegel or an Adorno, a Marx or a Lukács, like a foreign language that has resources unavailable in our own. The style of classical Greek is thus at one with the discovery of an alternate conceptual universe (even the very modern notion of a language revolution is faintly present in More, in the theme of the old and the new languages spoken by the Utopian population);[7] and this glimpse of the fleeting unity between thinking and syntax will rapidly generate the first new image of the role of the intellectual since the Augustinian vision of the priesthood and the emergence of the various orders. Indeed, these new humanistic intellectuals will, Max Weber tells us, lay their own claim to political power and entertain a brief but intense ambition to become a new ruling class comparable to that of the Chinese mandarins, equally text-oriented and prepared to assume the functions of a heroic bureaucracy.[8] Ironically, More himself prematurely fills just such a role, and his tragic end offers at least one figure for the general collapse of humanist intellectuals' political project (who are replaced by the more familiar and more successful

---

6 See Norbert Elias, "Thomas Morus' Staatskritik", in *Utopieforschung*, ed. Wilhelm Vosskamp (Frankfurt, 1985), Volume III, p. 114.

7 See, on Utopia's two languages, Emile Pons, "Les langues imaginaires dans le voyage utopique", *Revue de littérature comparée*, XIII (1931).

8 See *From Max Weber: Essays in Sociology*, ed. H. Gerth and C. Wright Mills (Oxford, 1946) "Politics as a Vocation", p. 93. The humanist failure is narrated in a somewhat different way by Lucien Goldmann in *The Hidden God* (*Le Dieu caché*) (Paris, 1959).

grande bourgeoisie). Paradoxically, although *Utopia* can in that sense be read as a kind of manifesto for just such humanist intellectuals, the society it represents does not contain any, for its realization is meant to spell the end of all such (Utopian) political projects.

This, then, is the point at which a humanist ideology gives way to a Protestant one, and in which the description of the political and economic features of the Utopian system (if one may call them that) give way to an account of its relationship to religion (pluralist and deist, but excluding atheism) and of its priests and lay orders. In effect, Protestantism adds a third language (Hebrew) to the twin arsenal of humanism; and it is crucial to grasp the way in which both these revivals (of the classics and of primitive Christianity) are felt to be avant-garde causes. Together they constitute the Novum of the day: that is to say, a conceptual and an ideological revolution whose innovation constitutively includes passion and excitement within it ("les grands âges sont révolus," as Gargantua puts it).

These are the superstructural impulses of *Utopia*. Its other two dimensions then correspond to an imagination of institutions, and in particular of institutions capable of embodying the spirit of the two intellectual movements (Plato's *Republic*, early Christian communism) and indeed of housing it in a space of possibility. In addition, the second set of options has the advantage of offering an already existent and fully realized world empire on the one hand, and an enclave structure on the other, which can persist locally within a social space of a wholly different type.

I am tempted to see the Inca model as a way of incorporating the economic into More's vision; but also as a strategy for effacing the political problem of the persistence of the ruler and the power center within an allegedly egalitarian republic (it will be remembered that some of the most powerful readings in Louis Marin's classic *Utopiques* turned precisely on the cartographic slippage between markets and administrative centers).[9]

As for what I have called the medieval element, however, it is to be understood as a uniquely European social institution, namely the monastery as such. More's youthful experiences in a monastery document his admiration for this institution, about which Weber said that in the early Middle Ages its various forms constituted enclaves within which rationality developed, in isolation from the surrounding agricultural society (think, for example, of the rationalization of time for purposes of orderly work and prayer alike, and also that of space in the way in which the buildings were constructed and the plantations laid out).[10] It may well have been Henry VIII's closing of the monasteries and his plundering of their collective treasures that generated More's ultimate refusal far more than abstract questions of belief or of papal authority. At any rate,

9   Louis Marin, *Utopiques* (Paris, 1973), Chapter 6.

10   See Max Weber, *The Protestant Ethic and the Spirit of Capitalism* (New York, 1958 [1904–5]), p. 118.

the kinship of the Utopian structure with the monastery has often been noted, and the great Utopian experiments of the Jesuits in eighteenth-century Paraguay come as a belated confirmation of this common spirit (when they were not indeed themselves inspired by the example of the textual predecessor). In this sense, the surviving institution of the monastery may be said to play something of the role in More's imagination of Utopia that the institution of the traditional common lands – the *mir* in Russia, the *ejido* in Mexico – played in nineteenth-century socialist thinking (not least in that of Marx himself, as in the famous letter to Vera Zasulich).[11] Nor is it without significance that both these social realities – the Inca empire and the monastic compound – are in the process of wholesale dissolution in More's own time: the former by way of the Spanish conquest, the latter by way of Henry VIII's reforms. We can see, in the impact of globalization in our own period, that historical processes in which older institutions and cultures are tangibly being destroyed before our own eyes tend to arouse very special kinds of political passions and indignations, which it does not seem to me far-fetched to attribute to More himself (particularly in the light of his denunciation of enclosure in Book One).

It is also important to register an extraordinary interpretive moment in Christopher Kendrick's pathbreaking essay on *Utopia* in which what are essentially the same four dimensions or cardinal points in the text (he does not thematize them as such), are reread as reenactments of four distinct types of what Marx called precapitalist modes of production. The lengthy passage is important enough to be quoted in full: .

> What are the ultimate elements of Utopian society? It represents an imaginary combination of modes of production, including major aspects of at least four distinct modes. First, its economic arrangements are partly modeled upon those of tribal communism: consider, for example, the utopian practice of sending retinues to the country to manage two-year farming stints, with the "communalization" of agrarian and urban labor that this entails; and consider the relative arbitrariness of the household or family that obtains in the Utopia, and the consequent predominance of a quasitribal group structure. The encounter with tribal communism in the New World doubtless provoked

11 March 8, 1881: "Thus the analysis given in *Capital* does not provide any arguments for or against the viability of the village community, but the special research into this subject which I conducted, and for which I obtained the material from original sources, has convinced me that this community is the fulcrum of Russia's social revival, but in order that it might function in this way one would first have to eliminate the destructive influences which assail it from every quarter and then to ensure the conditions normal for spontaneous development." Marx and Engels, *Selected Correspondence* (Moscow, 1975), p. 320. There has been a political revitalization of the theme of enclosure and the commons since globalization: see Midnight Notes Collective, "The New Enclosures", in *Midnight Oil* (Brooklyn, 1992); and Naomi Klein, "Reclaiming the Commons", *New Left Review*, No. 9 (May/June 2001).

Utopian communism, yet More's island – mirror for England that it is – hardly takes the print of New World tribalism in any sort of serious way; the more important subtext, which might be considered to be activated by the New World experience, is that of Germanic communal society (and this is especially obvious not so much in the economic as the political sphere, i.e. in the resemblance of the utopian system of political representation to the immemorial English municipal system). Yet, utopian communism can hardly be accounted for as a modernized version of the tribal system, it must also be drawn from the representation of "accomplished" communism, a mode which may be assumed to exist in More's time insofar as its social relations inhere in the feudal mode of production. The accomplished nature of utopian communism pronounces itself in such features as the insistence upon the social rights adhering to work, the militant rejection of any form of private possession, the assumption of an existing abundance of goods as the system's premise, and so forth. Third, *Utopia* "regresses" to the classical mode of production for its emphasis upon urban crafts, for the sweet reason of the hedonistic utopian philosophy, and – perhaps most obviously – for its slavery. Fourth, the description builds mainly upon feudalism in its representation of the household as the central social institution, and of religion as the naturally dominant force of social cohesion.[12]

Kendrick thus identifies a kind of substructure within the Utopian text in which all the precapitalist modes of production live on in a residual way (as for capitalism, Louis Marin has famously detected its absent, impending emergence in the holes in the Utopian map, most notably the missing space of the market).[13] The argument is that late feudalism constitutes a chaotic transitional period in which traces of all these modes survive, and thus in which what is positive (or "Utopian" in the customary sense of the word) in each of them can be separated off by the political Imaginary and combined to produce a synthesis of desirable social features. In the preparatory 1857 notebooks for *Capital*,[14] indeed Marx identified what seemed to be five distinct precapitalist modes: primitive communism or tribal society; the Asiatic mode (later vulgarized by Wittfogel as "oriental despotism"); the ancient mode, which is to say the *polis* and the slavery on which it is based; the Germanic mode (yeomen farmers who meet periodically in an assembly or *Ding*); and feudalism. In fact, it would seem that Marx theorized the Asiatic mode as an organic development out of primitive communism, on the basis of the continuity in

12   Christopher Kendrick, "More's *Utopia* and Uneven Development", in *boundary two*, XIII, 2/3 (Winter/Spring 1985), p. 245. (This text is not included in his important recent book, *Utopia, Carnival and Commonwealth in Renaissance England* [Toronto, 2004]).

13   See note 9 above.

14   Marx, *Grundrisse* (London, 1973). The section of these notebooks that Marx himself entitled "Forms which Precede Capitalist Production" is to be found on pp. 471–514.

agriculture production as such.[15] In any case, any future theory of the periodic reemergence of the Utopian text (and not only this inaugural one of Thomas More) needs to take into account the Marin/Kendrick proposition that such apparently substantive visions arise from the "kaleidoscopic" vision of a class "without a project or nation",[16] that is to say, without an articulated analysis of the situation (Marin) and without the lineaments of a political strategy (this might well characterize our own post-Cold War and post-neoliberal positions). At any rate, what is productive about the Utopian text can on this view best be grasped if we take it to be a registering apparatus for detecting the feeblest positive signals from the past and the future and for bricolating and combining them and thereby producing what looks like a representational picture. I would only want to add that these elements and impulses need to be translated into cultural or ideological representations in order to be effectively mediated into the present situation.

Thus I would want to reinterrogate my own picture of the fourfold ideological mediations in More for their relevance to later Utopias and to Utopian thought in general. Is it enough to identify two groups of subjective and objective components, where the first includes the example of conceptual and linguistic speculation and excitement alongside a vision of subjective purification and action on the self; and the second includes global and local institutions, an economic structure and a self-contained machine for organizing and living the everyday?

Let us then map out these four poles as follows, according to the Greimas semiotic square.[17] We will first grasp the twin impulses of humanism and Protestantism as related yet contradictory poles, on the one hand the rediscovery of Greek and on the other the acquisition of Hebrew. Both of these positions and passions are thus text-based, and indeed mark out the historical possibilities of intellectuals in this early Renaissance era. Their Utopian reconciliation or resolution is certainly that of humanism itself – after all,

---

15 Engels published his own version of the pre-capitalist modes of production in 1884 after Marx's death, under the title. *Origins of the Family, Private Property and the State*, significantly omitting the Asiatic mode from his enumeration. Obviously, the existence of a properly Marxian theory of the latter could not have been known until the first publication of the *Grundrisse* in 1939: since then, debate on the subject has been extensive, not to say interminable.

16 Kendrick, pp. 245–246; and see below. And on the relationship between Utopia and the construction of the nation, now see Phillip Wegner, *Imaginary Communities* (California, 2002).

17 This encapsulates the principal thesis of Marin's *Utopiques*, namely that (following the terminology of the Greimas semiotic rectangle) the Utopian text is not a synthesis of opposites or what Greimas calls a complex term; rather it is a synthesis of their negations or in other words a neutral term. (I will provide a reading of such neutralization in Chapter 11.) At any rate, the Utopian text is accordingly not to be seen as a vision or a full representation, but rather as a semiotic operation, a process of interaction between contradictions and contraries which generates the illusion of a model of society. I have discussed Marin's book in an earlier essay, "Of Islands and Trenches", in *The Ideologies of Theory* (Minnesota, 1988), Volume II, pp. 75–101.

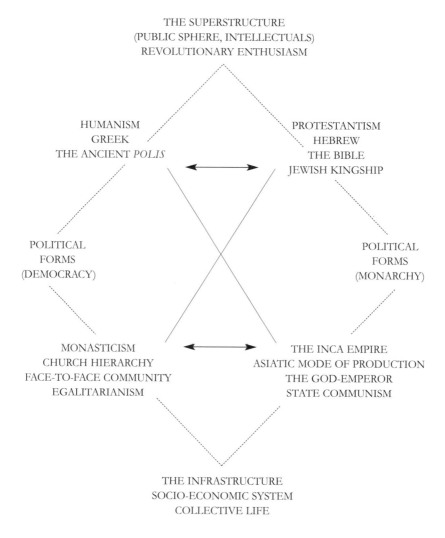

THE SUPERSTRUCTURE
(PUBLIC SPHERE, INTELLECTUALS)
REVOLUTIONARY ENTHUSIASM

HUMANISM
GREEK
THE ANCIENT *POLIS*

PROTESTANTISM
HEBREW
THE BIBLE
JEWISH KINGSHIP

POLITICAL
FORMS
(DEMOCRACY)

POLITICAL
FORMS
(MONARCHY)

MONASTICISM
CHURCH HIERARCHY
FACE-TO-FACE COMMUNITY
EGALITARIANISM

THE INCA EMPIRE
ASIATIC MODE OF PRODUCTION
THE GOD-EMPEROR
STATE COMMUNISM

THE INFRASTRUCTURE
SOCIO-ECONOMIC SYSTEM
COLLECTIVE LIFE

More's friend Erasmus encompassed both languages, both cultures and texts, his mediation seeming to offer some Utopian possibility in its own right, until history and the ferocious factionalisms and religious wars of the age demonstrated the fragility of this achievement (and determined a singular prudence in the conduct of the scholar himself). But I believe that the Weberian account gives us a more striking version of these contradictions and the syntheses in which they were unable to be resolved and *aufgehoben*. For this whole dimension of our semiotic square is that of superstructures: of the intellectual missions and vocations of the emergent secular intellectual: but it might be even better described in terms of a nascent public sphere. It is that public sphere that is in reality and in history unable to come into being: that situation of mandarin governmental power and authority that the humanist intellectuals are unable to achieve (owing not least to the very virus of Protestantism which the contradiction underscores).[18]

Yet there is another Utopian element we must not omit in articulating this first level: for both elements are driven by an intellectual passion – that of reappropriating the original text, whether in Greek or in Hebrew – an element characterized by that highly suspicious word *enthusiasm*: this is the intellectual vocation at its most feverish and committed, at the very height of its potential excitement, in a mission that more than any other seems to concentrate what defines the intellectual as such, namely the relationship to writing. Not the Socratic commitment to ideas, but rather this one of the text and its translation – Dürer's image of Saint Jerome toiling over his version of the sacred pages – marks out the space and function of the modern intellectual. Is this to say that Utopia is defined (and limited) by its social determination as the expression of intellectuals as a caste? Not necessarily; but this one certainly is, and it is no accident that More's career – uniquely, in the early modern – runs the gamut of possibilities of intellectuals as such, from humanist and counselor to princes all the way to dissident and martyr.

This choice of terms (and I have observed elsewhere that it is the initial positioning of the terms that constitutes the interpretive act as such) then assigns the remaining pair to that dimension in which they are mere cancellations of the first two (contradictory) terms. I posit the Inca empire as the negation in exoticism of everything the classical world stands for in the Western tradition: discovering the New World is indeed a rather fundamental cancellation of the classical tradition, inscribing a very different kind of empire and a very different kind of political formation in the place of everything codified in Greece and Rome. Indeed, that it should be assigned, by Maurice Godelier,[19] to Marx's early category of the Asiatic mode of production suggests that, repositioned in the context of the Western classical references, the Incas could only be fantasized in terms of Asia, the great other of both Greece – the Persian empire – and Rome – the Carthaginians (as in Flaubert's *Salammbô*).

As for monasteries and Protestantism, it is only too clear how the latter cancels the former – the liquidation is a physical one and underwrites the separation from the church of both Luther himself and Henry VIII. I want to understand the process in a more general way, not as the opposition between two religious principles, but rather as that obtaining between a kind of individualist inner-directedness and the communal forms taken by the orders. For it is this last essentially social element that will bind together the pair of lower forms: both

---

18 See note 8 above.
19 Maurice Godelier, *Horizon, trajets marxistes en anthropologie* (Paris, 1973), pp. 83–92 and 343–355. Godelier is among the most eminent anthropologists to defend the value of Marx's concept of the "Asiatic mode", which he has rescued from Orientalism by application to the Inca empire.

are socio-economic representations, and their juxtaposition along this particular semiotic axis underscores the uniqueness of both as modes of social organization and forms of economic production and distribution, rather than as forms of power. Thus, in this semiotic context (that of the lower level of the square), the Inca empire becomes visible as a kind of state-organized communism (rather than as a structure of imperial power crowned by a god-king); while not the hierarchical organization of the order and the Church itself is foregrounded in the other term so much as the egalitarian nature of the monastic community. This level then expresses what in the previous chapter I called a socio-economic system, rather than the thematics of a form of government.

It is thus this last – or the political in its most specialized form – which is inscribed in the two lateral axes of the square, the twin negations of each of the two positive terms. For here the combination of the terms *Protestant* and *Inca empire* draws the first of these into the realm of the content of Hebrew scripture, namely the history of the Jewish kings; while now the vision we have of the Incas rotates until its properly political dimension, that unique form of imperial power minimized in the lower or neutral axis, comes preeminently into the light.

Meanwhile a comparable semic reorganization takes place on the other side of the square: as C.S. Peirce puts it in another context:

> a conception is framed according to a certain precept, [then] having so obtained it, we proceed to notice features of it which, though necessarily involved in the precept, did not need to be taken into account to construct the conception. These features we perceive take radically different shapes; and these shapes, we find, must be particularized, or decided between, before we can gain a more perfect grasp of the original conception.[20]

So now, a humanism considered primarily as an intellectual passion, and a project of the public sphere, becomes reoriented around its political content, namely the structure of the ancient *polis* (including, or not, its evolution into the unique political organization of the Roman empire); and by the same token, the monastic order now begins to exhibit its essentially spatial nature as a small face-to-face political community, a kind of medieval version of the *polis*.

We thus observe the emergence of a medial band which cuts across the square, and in effect separates the superstructure (humanism in its two linguistic forms, Greek and Hebrew) from something like an infrastructure in the twin forms of socio-economic communism. This medial band is the place of the political in our earlier sense, and its position here dramatizes its isolation from a daily life in which superstructure and infrastructure commingle. For unique historical reasons, in other words, the political dimension of More's

---

20 C.S. Peirce, *Collected Papers* (Harvard, 1931), Volume I, p. 262.

Utopia has been disjoined from society, very much after the fashion of the royal court itself, and has thus, as a kind of enclave, been opened up for the play and reconstruction of the Utopian imagination, which indeed combines small political groups with monarchies of utterly different dimensions, in a federalism which exemplifies Polybius' mixed forms of government in a very different way from the standard recipes of the tradition.[21] The heterogeneous elements of More's peculiar text, all the while combining to produce the prototypical Utopian image we inherit from him, at one and the same time betray the peculiar and infrequent constellation of historical elements that make the emergence of that text possible in the first place.

III

But now we need to turn to *Utopia*, not as travel narrative, but as satire: which is to say that we must now reorganize the text around Book One. For however the text emits its various signals of otherness and difference, the obvious has often been remarked, namely that the fifty-four cities of Utopia replicate the fifty-four boroughs of London, so that More's imaginary island is simply a literal inversion of the actually existing kingdom of Henry VIII. The alleged Utopian vision is therefore little more than a point-by-point commentary on English affairs and the English situation, and its structure falls apart into so many opinions and punctual thoughts for improving laws, customs and conditions, at which point Book Two begins to resemble the later Book One in form and effect. This is certainly the case, and there can have been few "satiric" texts quite so savage (and Science-Fictional) as the famous one:

> Your sheep ... which are usually so tame and so cheaply fed, begin now, according to report, to be so greedy and wild that they devour human beings themselves and devastate and depopulate fields, houses and towns.[22]

It is a grim inversion of LaBruyère on the peasants;[23] and a swift and figurative operation in which the sinful passions of the human beings begin to infect placid animals, while the former have become themselves implicitly bestialized.

---

21 Polybius, *Rise of the Roman Empire* (Penguin, 1979), pp. 303–318. This traditional classification scheme has been revised and applied, with extraordinary originality and suggestiveness, to present-day globalization by Michael Hardt and Antonio Negri in *Empire* (Cambridge, 2000), pp. 162–164 and pp. 314–316. See also Antonio Negri, *Insurgencies* (Minnesota, 1999), pp. 67–69 and 107–110.
22 Thomas More, *Works* (New Haven, 1963–1997), Volume IV, p. 65–67.
23 Auerbach quotes the famous passage from the *Caractères* in *Mimesis* (Princeton 1953 [1946]), p. 366: "One sees certain ferocious animals, male and female, scattered over the countryside, black, livid, and burned by the sun, bound to the soil which they dig and turn over with unconquerable stubbornness; they have a sort of articulate voice, and when they stand up they exhibit a human face, and in fact they are men [et en effet ils sont des hommes]."

Yet the interest of the two books and their radical distinction in mode lies primarily in the problem of the transformation of the one into the other, and according to our present scheme (the alternative reading according to which we deduce Book Two from Book One) poses the question of how the fantastic and Utopian representation has been somehow derived or generated from the incisive and "realistic" debate on current conditions. Here again I think Kendrick is on the right track when he asserts that England "provides [Utopia] with the raw material from which [the text] is spun":

> The content of the political unconscious is largely composed of a group of received social representations … The political unconscious may be imagined … as working something like a kaleidoscope: compulsively breaking down, scrambling, and reassembling its collection of "social images" from the past of ideology, in response to the recurrent dilemmas, conflicts, traumas appertaining as a matter of course to the daily life imposed by all hitherto existing modes [of production].[24]

It is worth pausing at this point to underscore the production process of the Utopian text: that process has a conceptual level (as Lévi-Strauss taught us long ago for the case of tribal stories or myths), in which it not only thinks through figures but also solves contradictions. *Utopia* thus has a specifically aesthetic level, about which most of the literary critics have been singularly unhelpful, and eager to agree with the stereotypical boredom of the form; but what if there were also a level in which the text proves not only to be what Plekhanov called the "social equivalent", the correlative namely of ideology and of a class standpoint, but also a kind of gestural equivalent? Here the Utopian text and its mechanisms would correspond to something like an activity in daily life, and would constitute a rehearsal of the latter on the purely symbolic level, offering a kind of supplementary pleasure derived from the latter's imitation. I would want at least provisionally to distinguish this pleasure from what obtains on the representational level, where I want to suggest that it is to be theorized in terms of miniaturization. The activity satisfactions of Utopia are to be sure closely related to that aesthetic or representational process; but we gain something in the way of insight by trying to classify the operations involved, which it is far too general to subsume under the old aesthetic catchall of play (Marin's work targets a very specific kind of spatial play, geometrical and cartographic, which is theoretically and diagnostically distinct from the old anthropological category).

I have already observed above that we need to grasp the Utopian operation in terms of home mechanics, inventions and hobbies, returning it to that dimension of puttering and active *bricolage* from which Lévi-Strauss' source in

---

24 Kendrick, "More's *Utopia* and Uneven Development", pp. 243–244.

Dickens immediately distanced it (Mr Weller is a naïf artist, building a garden like the inspired planners of the Watts Towers or the Chandighar Rock Garden).[25] For it is precisely this dimension of a hobby-like activity, which anyone can do in their own spare time, at home, in your garage or workshop, that organizes the readership of the Utopian text, a better mousetrap which you also can emulate, thinking of new twists on existing laws and customs and coming up with ingenious models of your own. (More was a most unlikely candidate for the launching of this peculiar new form, into which generations of crackpots have enthusiastically plunged.) Utopia is thus by definition an amateur activity in which personal opinions take the place of mechanical contraptions and the mind takes its satisfaction in the sheer operations of putting together new models of this or that perfect society.[26] Perhaps the printing press and the enlargement of literacy in the early Tudor period encouraged such activities among More's contemporaries (just as the later industrial age will do in the late nineteenth-century US, one of the most fertile moments for the propagation of Utopias of all kinds).

I would not want this to serve as a sketch for some more immediate definition of Utopia as a genre, however, for I suspect that it is rather an ad hoc combination of various genres at any given time; while Elliott's notion of "satire" seems best taken as the designation of a mode.[27] In fact, just as the travel narrative presided over our discussion of Book Two, without ever coinciding absolutely with the genre in question, so also here, in the political commentary and motivation of Book One, a number of traditional genres propose themselves (either positively or negatively) which may help to specify the problem of the Utopian genre more sharply even if they do not "define" it. It seems to me that it is helpful to juxtapose the Utopian process of production with two other discursive operations which have received a certain analytical attention in contemporary or post-semiotic times: these are, on the one hand the writing of constitutions (an activity which will reach its paroxysm in the eighteenth century, but which is not extinct even today, in the two periods of decolonization and of the post-communist states), and on the other the political manifesto, in terms of which Althusser attempted to reread Machiavelli's *Prince*. Alongside these discursive modes, two others may be adduced, namely the Mirror for Princes, of all these genres the closest to More's own time, and all the more relevant for Hythloday's passionate refusal to assume that vocation of courtier and counselor to the king that the real-life More himself was about to embrace; and that of great prophecy, a discourse which equally combines Elliott's two modes of satiric denunciation of a fallen present and the evocation of a society transfigured, and whose strange lack of fit with *Utopia* itself ought to suggest a useful differentiation between the prophetic and the Utopian.

25 Claude Lévi-Strauss, *La Pensée sauvage* (Paris, 1962), p. 26.
26 But see, on Utopian opinion, Chapter 4.
27 See note 3, and also Robert C. Elliott, *The Power of Satire* (Princeton, 1960).

The genre of the written constitution would seem best initially approached by way of a distinction with that other discursive form which is the individual law, and which is presumably constructed as an interdiction on specific anti-social acts (if not a way of clarifying exchanges and agreements).[28] In that case, it would seem as though the constitution as such were devised to forestall certain kinds of political and historical events and catastrophes: most notably revolutions, but also more limited types of power seizure and power imbalance. Constitutions are thus structured, not to define and judge individual acts, but rather to prevent historical events of specific types. The question is thereby raised, for the Utopian text, whether this kind of management of history is at all comparable with the form of a text of which it has so often been asserted that it is designed to preclude history altogether. Must Utopia then not implicitly or explicitly define history itself by way of a splitting or a reduction in which it is bad history – political history – which is channeled into that category and neutralized (what Marx calls "pre-history", for example), while what remains – something like Utopian everyday life, perhaps – then emerges as truly utopian? More's text assuredly gives us something like a constitution of Utopian society, including any number of laws and customs; but it is an imaginary constitution and a thought experiment which is designed to forestall, not historical events as such, but rather private property as such.

Meanwhile, it is clear enough that Utopus' foundational gesture is not meant to be a call to practical political action or to emulation; and that whatever its undoubted impact, More's text is fundamentally different from Machiavelli's in its effects and consequences (it was not even translated into English until 1551). To be sure, we must at least try to separate the historical and structural uniqueness of Machiavelli's own discursive position from that implied in other manifestos; so it is not clear whether Althusser only and exclusively has Machiavelli in mind when he defines a manifesto as a focus simultaneously on the nature or knowledge of the political in general and on a specific and concrete political problem in particular such that this focus includes the identification of agency and the question of political practice as such.[29] At any rate this shifts the problem of the Utopian text in a new direction, displacing the old anti-Utopian objection that the practical question of implementation is never raised in the standard Utopias (or is at least given over to some pious liberal hope for reasoning and persuasion, for a peaceful common-sense transition), and foregrounding on the contrary the question of whether Utopia has any formulable relationship to the political in the first place. It is a question which then yet again replaces that of the nature of the political on the agenda:

28 And see on constitutions, Kenneth Burke, *A Grammar of Motives* (Berkeley, 1969), Part Three, Chapter 1, pp. 323–401; and on laws or the "casus", André Jolles, *Einfache Formen* (Tübingen, 1982).
29 Louis Althusser, *Écrits philosophiques et politiques*, Volume II (Paris, 1995), p. 59.

thus, if one follows Carl Schmitt's formula, that the political is first and foremost the decision about friend and foe,[30] it is clear enough that this is a central and constitutive issue both in Machiavelli and in Marx and Engels, but less certain how it could be raised on the occasion of More's vision of Utopia or even of his positions in Book One.

There at any rate politics and the political are framed by the absolutist court as such, a context which sunders means from ends far more decisively than in the two classic manifestos (in which the means – nation or proletariat – are at one with the ends). Utopus must somehow abolish himself and his monarchy in order to allow Utopia to come into existence; nor is the prophetic voice and the individual prophet more clearly in evidence in the new collective scheme. The two final generic references are thus somehow shortcircuited by the gap they imply between the individual leader and the collective state of things.

Thus in some sense the Utopian form (genre or not) comes into being to complement these various imperfect genres and to fulfill or to forestall each of them in unexpected ways. It is a paradox that a form so absolutely dependent on historical circumstance (it flourishes only in specific conditions and on certain rare historical occasions) should give the appearance of being supremely ahistorical; that a form which inevitably arouses political passions should seem to avoid or to abolish the political altogether; and that a text so uniquely dependent on the caprice and opinion of individual social dreamers should find itself disarmed in the face of individual agency and inaugural action. Yet perhaps the generic question has some further lessons

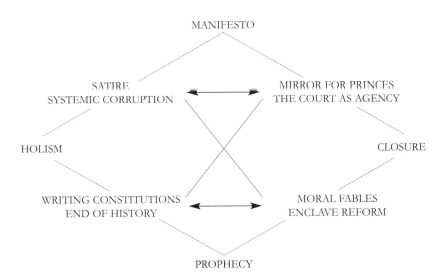

30 Carl Schmitt, *The Concept of the Political* (Rutgers, 1976 [1933]).

for us; in any case we have not yet fully combined the problems of representation with those of ideological analysis in understanding how Utopia can be grasped as having necessarily to emerge from the more purely political discussions of Book One.

For the first of these lines of inquiry, it will be formally crucial to interrogate the interpolated narratives, those involving yet a different genre, namely the moral fables about non-existent states, the Polylerites, the Achorii, and the Macarenses: for these interpolated episodes should tell us two antithetical things, namely why More needed to have recourse to non-existent or imagined places, and then why none of them could have fulfilled the function that the fourth and final, but very different non-existent state of Book Two, namely Utopia itself, was called upon to fill. Why, in other words, does the image or full figure of Utopia necessarily emerge from previous but local and analogous figures? The latter are, to be sure, imagined as enclaves within our existent world; whereas, despite the positioning and the supplementary explanations, Utopia is somehow felt to replace our world altogether.

Our three enclave states (or examples), whose nonsense names seem to take the measure of the reforms,[31] demonstrate (in reverse order): how to limit the king's finances (the Macaranses, translated by Turner as Happiland); how to discourage foreign conquests (the Achorii, or Nolandia); and most extensively, how to turn the severe English penal system to the advantage of the citizenry (the Polylerites, or Tallstoria). The two initially mentioned imply common-sense rules and limits for monarchs: they are thus both situation-specific in their reference, and not unrealizable. Nor, when we come to the longest example, the Polylerites, are the more moderate punishments and the forced labor of the convicts unrealizable either, although they obviously collide with widespread prejudice and popular doxa, as the heated discussion shows.

But, as Marin has demonstrated,[32] this longest extrapolation is internally contradictory in two distinct ways, and this constitutes the formal interest of the episode. The first problem has to do with the very existence of theft itself: if this country is so happy and peaceful, why does it generate the poverty and misery which impel people to steal? If on the other hand, there is very little theft, in comparison to the societies we are familiar with, in what way can its penal system be exemplary for us? How, in short, to demonstrate that it is the penal system which is responsible for reducing crime rather than the other way round? We, who have read Book Two, know the answer to these questions, which turns on the continuing presence of private property and therefore the continuing existence of goods and money to steal.

This suggests that in effect More's extrapolation, by its very internal contradiction, is still bound up with the real empirical world, and that it can only solve

31 See note 1.
32 Marin, *Utopiques*, Chapter 7 (and also see Wegner, *Imaginary Communities*, pp. 40–45).

that representational contradiction by generating and producing a purer one (Utopia proper) from which the links to historical reality have been more absolutely sundered. (Or, if you prefer to read the text according to its compositional chronology, More has here, in the later Book One, excavated the representational precondition for the earlier model of Book Two.) We can say all this in a rather different way by pointing to a principle of totality at work in such representations, one based on the overdetermination of the historically real itself. One cannot – such is the lesson of these extrapolations – change individual features of current reality. A reform which singles out this or that vice, this or that flaw or error in the system, with a view towards modifying that feature alone, quickly discovers that any given feature entertains a multitude of unexpected yet constitutive links with all the other features in the system. In the area of representation, the symptom of this discovery is to be found in what we have called a representational contradiction. Thus, in order adequately to represent such changes, the modification of reality must be absolute and totalizing: and this impulse of the Utopian text is at one with a revolutionary and systemic concept of change rather than a reformist one.

In Utopia, however, the mark of this absolute totalization is the geopolitical secession of the Utopian space itself from the world of empirical or historical reality: the great trench which King Utopus causes to be dug in order to "delink" from the world, and to change his promontory into an island – surely an extraordinary anticipation of the great public works projects of modern or socialist times (and perhaps also the well-known hydraulic society projects that anticipated them),[33] including the marshalling of the army and the suggestion of forced or slave labor. This brings us to the second contradiction, or at least the second representational symptom betrayed by the Polylerite extrapolation. For in that example there is no trench: the Polylerites are separated from the Persian empire by a mountain range, and they pay tribute to the Persian monarch for protection – a dependency quite different from the Machiavellian foreign-policy system of the Utopians themselves, and one which puts a different kind of burden on what remains a money economy. This geopolitical dependency seems to me to constitute an autoreferential allegory about the structure of the representation itself, which still depends on external references and empirical contents. If you like, it is still protohistorical and not yet sufficiently aesthetic, in the sense of its autonomy from reality contexts – something which will be achieved only with Book Two and the representation of Utopia itself, and which may well shed new light both on the aesthetics of the Utopian text itself and on the Utopian character of aesthetics (as Marcuse developed it in his great essay on the "affirmative character of culture").[34] Utopia is thus in that sense a representation which

---

33 The classic (anti-Marxist) text is Karl Wittfogel, *Oriental Despotism* (New Haven, 1957).
34 See the brief discussion of this essay in the Introduction.

has become a closure, as far as possible (and it is of course impossible) autonomous and self-referential: at some outside limit, purely formal and without content, or rather, whose content has been sublimated by itself becoming self-referential.

This is, however, so far merely a formal account of the text, which seems interminably to postpone the essential, namely any discussion of the wish at the heart of More's invention. It will no doubt be even more frustrating to learn, as we will in the next chapter, that wish-fulfillments are themselves internally contradictory, and therefore scarcely to be taken at face value. They are, moreover, necessarily clothed in ideology and as inseparable from the latter and its historical determinants as the body from the soul (an issue to be confronted only much later on, in Chapter 10).

None of which means that nothing of significance can now be said about the wish-fulfillment that drives *Utopia* and that lends it its transhistorical freshness. Yet it does so by way of a unique structure, which can be identified as a slippage around three ideological themes, which it amplifies and neutralizes all at once. The first of these themes is clearly that of money itself, and the evils of gold, a commonplace that absorbs a tradition of prophecy and invective whose beginnings are lost in the mists of time along with those of money itself. Marx effectively demolished the presuppositions of these denunciations of money in his attacks on Proudhon and in the *Grundrisse*.[35] That in More they lead to a form of "communism", that is to say, to the abolition of private property, is less significant than the triangular movement whereby the theme of money is ideologically neutralized.

For the conceptual vice of the critique of money and gold is that it is neither political nor economic but rather ethical in its ultimate sources and consequences. But in More the place of the ethical is occupied by a different theme or ideologeme, namely pride as a psychological and indeed "theological" phenomenon. This displaces the evils of money and its accompanying sins (most notably greed) with a rather different set of social phenomena, namely vainglory, ostentation, social position, hierarchy and the like; and the latter lead us on to the third term in More's ideological triangle, namely the emphasis on equality and egalitarianism. Yet the latter is not simply a correction or cancellation of the effects of pride; it is a move from one dimension to another, from the realm of the self and the soul to that of social existence, both of these being in their turn distinct from the realm in which money and gold hold sway. As Luhmann has shown, these various realms of the psychic and the social and the economic are not yet in traditional societies (or even in societies like More's which are emerging from the traditional and the feudal) fully differentiated. The rotating movement from one to another is in part a

---

35 See Karl Marx, *The Poverty of Philosophy* (New York, 1963 [1847]), especially pp. 69–79; and also the *Grundrisse*, chapter II (the chapter on money).

reflection of that lack of differentiation: no single realm can define its elements completely in its own terms, but must borrow from the other ones at the same time that it differentiates itself from them. This makes for a welcome multiplicity of consequences and effects for More's representations themselves, which can be interpreted in the light of their social implications, but also for their consequences in terms of the individual subject, and not least for the practical policies they seem to entail particularly in the principle of the abolition of private property. The ambiguity of the tripartite framework is such that we can overlook the ethical origins of this principle and take it for a whole political program and a way of realizing Utopia as such. The rotation of these three ideologemes is itself the source of Utopia's seeming autonomy on the representational level, and rescues the text from the status of a mere tract on any one of the themes (a pamphlet against money, for example, or a theological treatise on pride, a revolutionary broadbill denouncing social hierarchy).

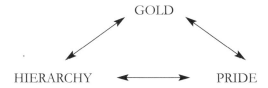

This rotational operation forestalls the thematization or reification of any single factor into an ideological system or vision of human nature (a problem to be discussed in Chapters 10 and 11). This is, I believe, what Louis Marin termed "neutralization" in his fundamental work on Utopias, and it will require and receive an explanation, at the appropriate time, of how neutralization can be grasped as production, rather than as simple cancellation or effacement. Most immediately, however, it demands subsumption into the structure of wish-fulfillment itself.

4

Utopian Science versus Utopian Ideology

Yet few texts would seem to reveal the structure of the Utopian wish-fulfill-ment quite so transparently as More, in which Book One offers a frightening picture of English society and its contradictions, to which Book Two responds with a series of ingenious yet plausible solutions. The opposition is, however, more complicated than this description would suggest, for it seems shadowed by another tension between collective evaluation and individual proposal, between a relatively objective inventory of injustices, vices and suffering, and a play of Latin wit and invention that can scarcely be attributed to anyone but the increasingly well-known public figure who is its author. Still, this individ-ual figure also stands for a collective reality, namely humanism as a social and intellectual movement, so that any attempt to subsume this particular tension under the familiar distinction between the objective and the subjective collapses.

Is the opposition between the social analysis of Book One and the aes-thetic solutions of Book Two any more productive? Perhaps: but it is first necessary to emphasize what is at stake in these terminological and concep-tual issues. On the one hand, we confront a truly ferocious indictment of contemporary society, violent and oppressive, riddled with corruption and injustice, hierarchical as well in its reproduction of class privilege and inequal-ity. Yet this "savage indignation", which is not only to be attributed to More, but also to Rousseau and Fourier, to Owen and Chernyshevsky, is evidently trivialized by our simultaneous insistence on the eccentricities of the Utopian inventors, and their delight in the cloud-cuckoo-lands in which they indulge themselves. How to reconcile these seemingly incompatible perspectives, or if that is not possible, how to decide between them? Are we simply to go care-fully through the list, and decide that More was clearly a serious character, whereas Fourier can equally obviously be seen to be a charlatan and a crackpot, at best an ineffectual dreamer, mainly known for the notorious "oceans of lemonade"?

Enough has been said, however, to suggest that it is not only political passion that is involved here, and that the Utopians were not exclusively driven by indignation at social injustice or compassion for the poor and the oppressed.

They were also intellectuals, with a supplementary taste for systems (as Barthes argued[1]), for maps (see Marin[2]) and for schemes of all kinds (see the Manuels[3]); know-it-alls willing tirelessly to explain to anyone who would listen the solutions to all those problems; tinkerers, blackening reams of paper writing and rewriting their projects and their propaganda pamphlets, drawing up endless seating charts and plans and urban reconstructions: in short, obsessives and maniacs, even where they seemed to be no more than public figures with a literary hobby (like More) or men-about-town with a wide curiosity (like the young Saint-Simon), or indeed Science Fiction writers with a sideline. Yet for many of them being a Utopian approached full-time professional status on the model of the professional revolutionary, while others, like Rousseau, refusing all professional status on principle, passed their Utopian activities off as yet another form of idle day dreaming.

I think that it is impossible to reconcile our two initial antithetical characterizations any more than it is possible to choose one or the other without distortion: More was just as notoriously a joker (we have it on Erasmus' testimony) and Fourier's social passion and commitment cannot be doubted by anyone who studies his works.[4] I fear that the only way of dealing with this contradiction is to think both perspectives together simultaneously.

They correspond, indeed, to a tension Adorno has identified as a very fundamental one indeed in aesthetic theory:[5] and this is the tension between expression and construction. Even the driest artistic production – a collage of sounds by Cage, for example, or the dissonance of various geometric shapes in Malevich – retains an echo of expressiveness, or better still, necessarily acquires one, for those human viewers or listeners we still are; while the most minimal expressionist shriek is still necessarily a construction. What does happen is that the avant-garde aestheticians themselves emphasize one of these features over another in their programs and manifestos. Yet satire itself,[6]

---

1 Barthes, *Sade, Fourier, Loyola* (Paris, 1971).

2 Louis Marin, *Utopiques* (Paris, 1973)

3 Frank and Fritzie Manuel, *Utopian Thought in the Western World* (Cambridge, MA, 1979); see in particular their account of the proliferation of religious-revolutionary "sects" during the English Revolution: "Edwards was only the most noteworthy of the specialists who, in cataloguing a wide variety of abominable heresies theological and social, succeeded in conveying the impression that they were all of one ilk. Ephraim Pagitt's *Heresiography* (1645), more restricted in its field of inquiry, treated of some twenty sorts of Anabaptists alone: Muncerians, Apostolikes, Separatists, Catharists, Silentes, Enthusiasts, etc." (pp. 334–335). One is reminded of the paradigmatic account in Flaubert's *Éducation sentimentale* of the political sects during the revolution of 1848.

4 Or who reads Jonathan Beecher's admirable biography, *Charles Fourier: The Visionary and his World* (California, 1986).

5 T.W. Adorno, *Philosophie der neuen Musik* (Frankfurt, 1958 [1948]), pp. 41ff; and *Aesthetic Theory* (Minneapolis, 1997 [1970]), pp. 44–45, 56–58, 244–245.

6 So presciently linked to Utopia by Robert C. Elliott in his diptych *The Power of Satire* (Princeton, 1960) and *The Shape of Utopia* (Chicago, 1970).

no matter how authentic it claims to be as a passionate and spontaneous reaction to intolerable injustice, must also find its rhetorical figures ("sheep devouring men") and document its reactions with representations that move the reader. Yet is this to say any more than that the Utopians, besides being intellectuals, are also artists and rhetoricians?

We may perhaps make a new beginning on such oppositions by recalling Coleridge's distinction between Imagination and Fancy (derived, in the long run, I think, from Kant's foundational opposition between the Sublime and the Beautiful).[7] This takes us on to the point where the aesthetic is no longer a secondary hobby but rather goes around behind creation to identify the very sources of reality as such. On some metaphysical level, Imagination is a theoretical concept, designating the primal creative force of God: which an aesthetic context reduces to the shaping power appreciated in the architecture of monumental literary plots (the so-called primary and secondary imaginations). Fancy then on that level stages Coleridge's indictment of eighteenth-century allegory and of the local rhetorical decoration of the art of that period with which the Romantics sought so decisively to break. Architectural parallels are even more telling: and as recently as yesterday Robert Venturi's concept of the "decorated shed"[8] revived something of the older tensions between the vocation of architecture to sculpt and form the void and that secondary ornamentation of the building which Adolf Loos denounced as crime and degeneracy.[9]

The origination of such oppositions in a distinction between two period styles – modern versus postmodern, or Romantic versus eighteenth century – suggests that we may in fact here have to do with two very different types of wishes (or desires, to use the postcontemporary word). Yet it may be worth

7   As is well known, Coleridge only touched on this, his most famous theoretical contribution, in one central place in his work: chapters XII and XIII of *Biographia Literaria*. It is therefore worth quoting this relatively brief exposition in full: "The imagination then I consider as either primary, or secondary. The primary Imagination I hold to be the living power and prime agent of all human perception, and as a repetition in the finite mind of the eternal act of creation in the infinite I AM. The secondary Imagination I consider as an echo of the former, coexisting with the conscious will, yet still as identical with the primary in the *kind* of its agency, and differing only in *degree*, and in the *mode* of its operation. It dissolves, diffuses, dissipates, in order to re-create; or where this process is rendered impossible, yet still at all events it struggles to idealize and to unify. It is essentially *vital*, even as all objects (*as* objects) are essentially fixed and dead.

"Fancy, on the contrary, has no other counters to play with, but fixities and definites. The fancy is indeed no other than a mode of memory emancipated from the order of time and space; while it is blended with, and modified by that empirical phenomenon of the will, which we express by the word Choice. But equally with the ordinary memory the Fancy must receive all its materials ready made from the law of association." *Biographia Literaria* (London, 1949 [1817]), pp. 145–146.

8   The term opposes "decoration", or the façade of the building, to the void of the shed behind it: see Robert Venturi, Denise Scott-Brown and Steven Izenour, *Learning from Las Vegas* (Cambridge, MA, 1972).

9   See Adolf Loos' astonishing *Ornament and Crime* (Riverside, CA, 1998 [1908]).

a detour through Freud's own discussion of wish-fulfillments and art to observe the theorization of a relationship between these two drives or impulses within a single work. Freud does not, indeed, draw the line where one might expect it to fall, between the conscious and the unconscious, or between daydreams and the authentic nighttime variety. He positions it squarely within the daydream in his major pronouncement on aesthetics, the essay "Creative Writers and Day-Dreaming",[10] a text sometimes felt to be as vulgarly orthodox within the psychoanalytic canon as Zhdanov in Marxism.

Yet the same opposition can be identified within the nighttime dream, where it serves to distinguish between the wish the dream comes into being to fulfill and the more purely formal afterwork of so-called secondary elaboration or revision (or "overdetermination", a term borrowed by the Althusserians for the altogether different matter of historical causality).[11] *The Interpretation of Dreams* thus seems to confirm the priorities of German (or Coleridgean) idealism: the wish, or the Imagination (or even the Sublime) is the noble term, Fancy or secondary elaboration a mere decorative afterthought. (Perhaps the relevance of the distinction can be dramatized by a conundrum: to which terms of Coleridge's opposition do More's two books correspond?)

But the essay on daydreaming, that is to say, on literary production as such, complicates this simple scheme, which we are tempted to assimilate to the opposition between the objective – the world itself, the space of the great cathedrals – and the subjectivity of mere embellishment or wallpaper, of individual fantasy association. For here the shaping wish-fulfillment of the literary work is firmly resituated in the subjectivity and the private history of the writer or artist himself. (Indeed, the very source of such wishes in the archaic memory of gratification powerfully supports and documents the Marcusean Utopia of anamnesis: "whoever understands the human mind knows that hardly anything is harder for a man than to give up a pleasure which he has once experienced".[12])

It is this private and indeed childish formation of the central wish to be "fulfilled" which marks the daydream with its three fundamentally ungeneralizable characteristics: first, it turns on the conviction of providentiality – that "true heroic feeling, which one of our best writers has expressed in an inimitable phrase: 'Nothing can happen to *me*!'"[13] And this feeling of ontological security and even omnipotence is the other face of the daydream's narrative organization around the self as such: "through this revealing characteristic of invulnerability we can immediately recognize His Majesty the Ego, the hero alike of every day-dream and every story".[14]

10 Sigmund Freud, *The Standard Edition of the Complete Psychological Works of Sigmund Freud*, (London, 1954), Volume IX, pp. 143–153.
11 Ibid., Volume V, p. 488.
12 Ibid., Volume IX, p. 145.
13 Ibid., p. 150.
14 Ibid.

Finally, the centered narrative subject inevitably posits the ancient ethical binary most famously denounced by Nietzsche: "the other characters in the story are sharply divided into good and bad, in defiance of the variety of human characters that are to be observed in real life. The 'good' ones are the helpers, while the 'bad' ones are the enemies and rivals, of the ego which has become the hero of the story."[15] Yet this incorrigibly egocentric organization of the daydreaming wish-fulfillment now dramatically restructures the opposition we have been rehearsing here: the primal architectonic of the Imagination, plot formation – the structure of the "phantasm" – has here now abruptly been discredited and degraded into a sheerly private hobby whose objective relevance has suddenly become something of a mystery. Indeed, it is when at the very end, he comes to the "innermost secret" of the artist – his "ars poetica" and the instinct for representation which makes him an artist in the first place – it is here that Freud lets fall a curious insight:

> You will remember how I have said that the day-dreamer carefully conceals his phantasies from other people because he feels he has reasons for being ashamed of them. I should now add that even if he were to communicate them to us he could give us no pleasure by his disclosures. Such phantasies, when we learn them, repel us or at least leave us cold … The essential *ars poetica* lies in the technique of overcoming the feeling of repulsion in us which is undoubtedly connected with the barriers that rise between each single ego and the others.[16]

It is an extraordinary moment: and anyone who compares the fascination we often feel for our own dreams with the boredom that suddenly overcomes us in listening to the account of another's will know what Freud means (nor is it an uninteresting professional revelation to find a psychoanalyst making).

And yet the work of art, for Freud, remains a wish-fulfillment, however much the writer "softens the character of his egoistic day-dreams by altering and disguising it". We must therefore distinguish between two forms presented by the wish-fulfillment: a repellent purely personal or individual "egoistic" type, and a disguised version which has somehow been universalized and made interesting, indeed often gripping and insistent, for other people. The border

---

15 Ibid.
16 Ibid., pp. 152–153. As this discussion, more purely formalistic, seems to leave little place for any identification of the Utopian (or artistic) readership with the original wish or desire, it is perhaps worth adding a remark of Freud's elsewhere, about the artist's successful projection of his own wish-fulfillment: "he can only achieve this because other men feel the same dissatisfaction as he does with the renunciation demanded by reality, and because that dissatisfaction, which results from the replacement of the pleasure principle by the reality principle, is itself a part of reality". "Formulations on the Two Principles of Mental Functioning", *Standard Edition*, Volume XII, p. 224.

between these two kinds of symbolic acting out of the wish is drawn by uncon-scious resistance, and if on the one side it is maintained by that feeling of repulsion Freud indicates, on our own it is patrolled by embarrassment. One thinks indeed of that marvelous scene from Jean Renoir's film *La Règle du jeu* (1939) which Lacan singles out precisely in the present context:[17] the nascent embarrassment of Dalio as he exhibits his heart's desire, the greatest acquisi-tion of his collection of automata, an immense mechanical orchestra, which, in full animation, leaves its owner to blush and prance awkwardly in imitation alongside it.

Freud thus leaves us with a perspective in which the dimensions within the daydreaming wish-fulfillment are themselves restructured and reorganized around two distinct pairs of oppositions: for now, alongside the tension between the objective and subjective, we find ourselves obliged, in the openly aesthetic context, to accommodate an opposition between the particular and the universal which is also intimately related to that between the writer and his public, or in other words, between the individual and the collective. Freud's dramatic "solution" will consist in reenlisting fantasy and the decorative on the side of the universal and the collective itself:

> The writer softens the character of his egoistic daydreams by altering and disguising it, and he bribes us by the purely formal – that is, aesthetic – yield of pleasure which he offers us in the presentation of his phantasies. We give the name of an *incentive bonus*, or a *fore-pleasure*, to a yield of pleasure such as this, which is offered to us so as to make possible the release of still greater pleasure arising from deeper psychical sources.[18]

Here then, the faculty which produces aesthetic or artistic decoration has suddenly become more public and more collective in its function than the "august shaping power" of Imagination or primal wish-fulfillment, which sinks to a rather shameful and private activity that needs to be disguised at all costs.

With this reversal, we seem farther than ever from any structural clarifica-tion of what we have speculated to be some collective wish-fulfilling mechanism at the heart of Utopian fantasy and Utopian textual production. At this point, perhaps, the Freudian or psychoanalytic complication of our initial problematic needs itself to be recomplicated by an epistemological dimension which restores something of the dignity of social knowledge to the suggestion of playful and arbitrary construction apparently inherent in any conception of fantasy.

The new wrinkle can be traced at least as far back as Plato, who very cen-trally and insistently distinguished between sheer opinion and philosophical

17 Jacques Lacan, 1958–1959 Seminar, *Le Désir et son interprétation*, 10 December 1958.
18 Freud, *Standard Edition*, Volume IX, p. 153.

knowledge, or in other words *doxa* and *episteme*:[19] the first the personal and highly unreliable province of sheer opinion or belief, the second the realm of the Ideas and of some impersonal "knowledge" that compels immediate conviction, on the order, for example, of the mathematical certainties discovered by Pythagoras. Characteristically, Plato's reasoning here is brought to bear on that object preeminently ambiguous in this respect, namely that opinion which turns out to coincide with true knowledge without for all that becoming any more reliable or shedding its doubtful epistemological status.

Yet it still remains unclear and paradoxical how any Utopian fantasies could be sorted out according to the Platonic standards of true knowledge and mere personal opinion or belief. Perhaps the example of a historical interpretation we owe to Plato's modern follower, the historian of science Alexandre Koyré, will be more suggestive in this respect: for one of Koyré's most notorious reinterpretations of the emergence of modern science involved the proposition that Galileo's fundamental principle – the mathematicalization of nature – was based not on scientific knowledge, but was rather motivated by what we may call a philosophical opinion or Platonist ideology, the Pythagorean conception of number.[20]

Indeed, the term *ideology* now suggests a further turn of the screw in which a now traditional Marxian opposition between ideology and science comes to enrich and complete the Platonic one from which it is itself derived. It is not necessary to revive the much-misused distinction between bourgeois ideology and Marxist science (in *The German Ideology* Marx and Engels observe, "We know only a single science, the science of history")[21] to grasp the usefulness of a differentiation of *Ideologie* from *Wissenschaft* (a word far less suffused with positivist overtones than its French or English translation). It is a renewed usefulness which derives from the fact that now private opinion or sheer personal belief, under its new incarnation as ideology, has recovered a collective dimension, being henceforth associated with a specific group or class. There are no personal ideologies, except by a metaphorical transfer in which the function of purely private associations and symbolic images in the psychic economy of a given individual is compared to the dynamics of the social economy generally.

Meanwhile, this new version of Platonic doctrine is then returned to the shadow of Freudianism by an Althusserian rewriting of the distinction of science and ideology in what are now Lacanian terms.[22] Althusser seeks indeed

19 Plato, *Complete Works* (Indianapolis, 1997): see in particular, the *Meno*, p. 97; *Letter VII*, pp. 1659–1660; and the *Theaetetus*, pp. 189–190.
20 Alexandre Koyré, *Études Galiléennes* (Paris, 1939). It is worth adding that this canonical reinterpretation of Koyré (which implies that Galileo's theories were anti-experimental "thought experiments") has been at the center of an important debate in contemporary "science studies": see Dušan I. Bjelic, *Galileo's Pendulum* (Albany, New York, 2003), pp. 10–11 and p. 164, note 34.
21 Marx and Engels, *The German Ideology* (Moscow, 1964 [1845–46]), p. 34.
22 Louis Althusser, *Lenin and Philosophy* (New York, 1971).

to dispel the orthodox misconception that we emerge from the errors of ideology, once and for all, into the scientific truth of Marxism. For him, on the contrary, Marxism can be both science and ideology all at once; the various distinctive Marxist ideologies are then radically to be dissociated from that Marxian science or truth to be found in Marx's own text which famously consists of a writing "without a subject",[23] something that explains why Marx felt it necessary on one occasion to declare that he himself was "not a Marxist". The famous Althusserian definition of ideology as "the Imaginary relationship of the subject to its Real conditions of existence"[24] is intended to remove the stigma of sheer error from ideology by assigning wholly distinct functions and statuses to these two social and psychic instances.

With this move, our coordination of the dynamics of wish-fulfillment with the Platonic–Marxian epistemological analysis of doxa and ideology is complete. But it remains to be seen what its consequences are for the texts in question here. Utopian science versus Utopian ideology? If the conceptual frameworks outlined above have any relevance, we ought to be able at the very least to register Utopian opinion or doxa by our own readerly reactions, by the barely perceptible movements of irritation or annoyance that are aroused by this or that detail of the Utopian scheme, by momentary withdrawals of credibility and trust, by punctual exasperation that can only too easily be turned against the writer in the form of contempt or amusement. Paradoxically, these are not the reactions one brings to the principal proposals and as it were the very scaffolding of the Utopian plan itself; and this, despite the anti-Utopian arguments of the commentators who want us to take More's parodic names literally, as the sign of his satirical disavowal of the whole enterprise.

It is rather in the detail, the implementation and decoration or embellishment, of the scheme that we are sometimes drawn up short. Thus, for example, More's account of the Utopian churches may startle us, owing to the seemingly gratuitous character of the choice of feature and the explanation given it:

> The temples are all rather dark. This feature is due not to an ignorance of architecture but to the deliberate intention of the priests. They think that excessive light makes the thoughts wander, whereas scantier and uncertain light concentrates the mind and conduces to devotion.[25]

23 Ibid., p. 171.
24 Ibid., p. 162. Althusser seems here to have omitted the third term in the Lacanian triad, namely the Symbolic Order, opposed both to the Imaginary (or mirror stage) and to the Real itself, which Lacan famously defined as "what resists symbolization absolutely". Nonetheless, I believe that Althusser can be read as presupposing two distinct attempts to come to terms with the Real: the ideological one, in which the Imaginary function includes the self; and that of "science", from which the self is omitted, and which attempts to map the Real in "symbolic" or in other words in purely syntactic terms (like a mathematical formula).
25 Thomas More, *Works* (New Haven, 1963–1997), Vol. IV, p. 142.

The reader at once tends to transfer this opinion to More himself, particularly since in the context, the point being made has to do with the pluralism of practices and the freedom of belief (but not of non-belief, it should be added). Some commentators have interpreted this detail as a taste for Romanesque churches over Gothic ones, thus adducing a further sign and symptom of the medieval cast of More's imagination: if so, our reaction can only be thereby strengthened.

This minor blemish thus rejoins the more famous moments in which not Utopian custom but More's own prejudices seem to speak through the text: the engagements, for example, in which the marital pair-to-be are called on to exhibit themselves to each other naked (caveat emptor!); or, on a somewhat different level, the Utopian practice of using gold exclusively for chamber pots. The darkened churches seem to express a preference; the marriage pre-cautions seem wryly to betray an experience or a personal disappointment; the chamber pots, however, and whatever their classical sources, give off something of the exhilaration of a find, of a bright idea, that flash of quick wit for which, we are told, More was known.

It is therefore important to grasp the various forms in which what we have begun to call Utopian opinion takes: only the variety of such seemingly inappropriate and generically illicit interjections can lead us to what they have in common and direct us to their source. Thus, although the notion of human programming (and its pedagogical method) is something like a personal invention of B.F. Skinner and his intellectual private property, this particular overarching structural principle is not felt to be sheer or gratuitous opinion in that neglected and underestimated modern Utopia called *Walden Two*. Indeed, one might well argue that programming is the very essence of childhood pedagogy and formation; and that the theme of reprogramming (or deprogramming) is a neglected feature of Utopias that repress the problems of their transition or emergence, just as it is an essential feature of any Cultural Revolution, which must substitute new habits for those of the past and the old order. The reflexive paradoxes of reprogramming – the educators must themselves be educated or reeducated – are common to revolutions and Utopias alike.

Yet the standard guided tour of Utopia which Skinner, like all his forebears and successors, is obliged to offer us includes many everyday features and details that have nothing to do with programming. Thus he draws our attention to the following during a visit to the cafeteria:

> In spite of Castle's obvious impatience with the details of a domestic technology, Frazier talked at length about the trays. One of their innumerable advantages was the transparency, which saved two operations in the kitchen because the tray could be seen to be clean on both sides at once … "The main advantage of the tray," [Frazier] went on, "is the enormous saving in labor.

You will see what I mean when we visit the dishwashery. Commercial restaurants would give anything to follow our lead, but it requires a bit of cultural engineering that's out of their reach."[26]

This is an issue that must have caught Skinner's attention, one feels, during luncheon lines and stray moments of attention to the dining-room staff, and which generates what, following Barthes, we may term the "narcissistic punctum". He must have been very proud indeed of the inventiveness and the intellectual resourcefulness and freedom from traditional constraints which enabled him to cook up this particular solution, which he thought well enough of to insert into the Utopian text itself, less as an illustration of programming (the "cultural engineering" in question) than of his pleasure in his own ingenuity. Did not Thomas More himself observe: "After all, it's a natural instinct to be charmed by one's own productions. That's why raven chicks are such a delight to their parents, and mother apes find their babies exquisitely beautiful."[27]

Nor can Skinner have been said to have ignored the predictable reactions of his public: which here, following the example of the repulsion of Freud's readership with open and obvious personal wish-fulfillments, can be anticipated to feel some annoyance with this self-indulgent intrusion of Skinner-Frazier's pride into more serious matters. Indeed, he inscribes it back into the text, attributing the reaction to another character – Castle – against whom he is thus entitled to debate the matter further and to assert the full Utopian appropriateness of just such details.

Nor are his arguments necessarily fallacious: "Through some principle of behavior which I did not fully understand," the narrator tells us, "it appeared that the ingestion of food had something to do with the development of aesthetic preference or tolerances."[28] But over and beyond the merely aesthetic, it is certain that the issue of the kitchen and the dining room is a central feature of the Utopian text from More to Bellamy and down to our own time. This

---

26 B.F. Skinner, *Walden Two* (New York, 1948), pp. 48–49. To avoid the accusation of arbitrariness, I will also adduce the example of the founding father of SF. I am indebted to Dan Smith (in a forthcoming book on material culture in literature) for the strange case of H.G. Wells' chairs, as they rather gratuitously furnish the apartment of the protagonist of the first modern SF novel, *The Time Machine* (1895): "Our chairs," the narrator tells us, "being his patents, embraced and caressed us rather than submitted to be sat on." Smith reads this detail, plausibly enough, as a judgment on William Morris and his nostalgic Utopia, who not only patented his own cushioned chair, but is also allegedly present in fictive form among the small group of friends to whom the Time Traveller relates his adventures. Wells' exercise of Fancy here is thus of a piece with a whole secondary production of modernity as a material Utopia, despite the unhappy outcome for the human race of this first Scientific Romance, and despite his own ambivalent feelings about Utopia as such.

27 I have cheated by using Paul Turner's translation, p. 42 (see note 1 of Chapter 3 above); compare *Works*, IV, p. 57.

28 Skinner, *Walden Two*, p. 46.

bears on gender and on the "woman question" and the equality of the sexes in Utopia; and the communal kitchen and dining area is allegorical of that Utopian equality as well as instrumental in bringing it about – a matter of Utopian science rather than Utopian ideology, one would think, even though Skinner's tray shows how easy it is to slip from the first into the second, of which it surely remains an irredeemable example, even though, on some other level, it may constitute a forlorn and pitiful symbol or symptom of gender itself.

But perhaps it is impossible to write the Utopian text in the first place without its infusion by such ideological or wish-fulfilling impulses. Thus, a contemporary Utopia of far greater quality and ongoing relevance than that of Skinner – Ernest Callenbach's *Ecotopia* (from 1968, exactly twenty years after Skinner's) – also incorporates episodes and details that startle and alienate the reader more than they enlarge a truly political and Utopian imagination.

It may not be necessary to dwell on the narrator's sexual escapade in the hospital, which rather improbably proves to be "standard operating procedure", but it is interesting that these wish-fulfilling bright or ingenious ideas mostly turn out to be sexual in origin. This is also the case, but on a higher anthropological and philosophical level, with that invention of Callenbach's which has always seemed to pose the greatest problem even for his most sympathetic readers, namely the all-male institution of the War Games, in which periodically the men revert to the most primitive weapons – clubs, bows and arrows – and let off steam assaulting each other physically in two opposing groups, sometimes with real casualties. The assumption of an essentialist and innate aggressivity of the male of the species is here presupposed, and then ingeniously dealt with. The ritual combat has no content, no political purpose, unlike More's Utopian foreign policy (which in any case marshals mercenaries). It is clearly enough intended to address the question – also central in Ursula Le Guin, as for example in *Always Coming Home* (1985) – of the relationship between Utopian society and the aggressive instincts or impulses (if such things can be posited as existing in the first place); and this particular theme can be expected to spill over into other kinds of anti-Utopian themes, such as the boredom of Utopian peace, for example, or the question of policing anti-social physical violence. But the solution in reality produces the problem it was to have resolved; and conjures up some eternal human aggressive impulse as a given. Women run this society politically, but it is not clear to me why they would not feel excluded from an institution which in any case replaces the collective sports well known from both Communist and Fascist traditions.

But if contact sports and aggressivity replicate the masculine side of the stereotypical gender dualism, Skinner's remark about "aesthetic preferences" fills in the feminine pole and reminds us that, for the American male, indeed, aesthetics – the "science of beauty" – is, like the kitchen itself, conventionally assigned to woman's domain. Even the episode of Mrs Colson,[29] ostensibly designed to show how insignificant Frazier's status is within his own Utopia (she does not even know who he is), in reality secures the ongoing persistence of traditional "housewifery" in this highly reflexive blueprint for radical social transformation. Bellamy and Morris are even more suspect in this regard, while More's chicks and baby monkeys also unwittingly display an unconscious pre-occupation with "social reproduction" and a gendering of Utopian fancy.

I will later have occasion to suggest that what is repressed may not be the problem of gender inequality so much as the question of the institution of the family itself: but at this stage these topics are inextricably identified with each other, and it does not seem farfetched to interpret at least some of these gratuitous Utopian fancies as placeholders and symptoms of a more funda-mental repression, of the coming up short of the Utopian imagination against taboos that prevent any wholesale redesigning of the social order as such. Are such taboos to be identified as the baleful effect and influence, the counter-force, of some anti-Utopian drive, which like anti-matter or negative energy is called into being by the very activation of the Utopian imagination itself? I am unwilling to recognize anti-Utopian prejudice as a positive force, some-thing which would resuscitate Manichaeanism and the conception of evil as a reality in its own right. Indeed, in a later chapter I want to argue that the fear of Utopia takes privative forms, which have their own ideological determina-tion and meaning. That there is such a thing as a reality principle at work within the wish-fulfillment, however – this I will show in the next chapter but one.

Still, we must acknowledge that the flowering of Utopian fancies across this landscape, like the wisps of underground gases escaping their multiple pores and punctures across the length and breadth of the Utopian moor, are to be analyzed as so many emanations of that rather different element which is the Utopian impulse itself, of which we have affirmed from the outset that it is to be distinguished from the primal architecture of the Utopian Imagination as such, or of Utopian "science".[30] In these minute nooks and niches, indeed, we can observe the work of no less an energy – call it wit, invention, decoration or ornament – than that august power of plot-formation which Aristotle made central to what was after all limited by theater as a form and a medium. Here also, we find Utopian satisfactions which are no less worthy of aesthetic admi-ration than those "details" of her dress Marcel discovered with astonishment during his walks in the Bois de Boulogne with Mme. Swann:

> And I realized that it was for herself that she obeyed these canons in accor-dance with which she dressed, as though yielding to a superior wisdom of which she herself was the high priestess: for if it should happen that, feeling

29 Ibid., pp. 218–221.
30 I am indebted to Jonathan Flatley for this observation.

too warm, she threw open or even took off altogether and gave me to carry the jacket which she had intended to keep buttoned up, I would discover in the blouse beneath it a thousand details of execution which had had every chance of remaining unobserved, like those parts of an orchestral score to which the composer has devoted infinite labour although they may never reach the ears of the public: or, in the sleeves of the jacket that lay folded across my arm I would see, and would lengthily gaze at, for my own pleasure or from affection for its wearer, some exquisite detail, a deliciously tinted strap, a lining of mauve satinette which, ordinarily concealed from every eye, was yet just as delicately fashioned as the outer parts, like those Gothic carvings on a cathedral, hidden on the inside of a balustrade eighty feet from the ground, as perfect as the bas-reliefs over the main porch, and yet never seen by any living man until, happening to pass that way upon his travels, an artist obtains leave to climb up there among them, to stroll in the open air, overlooking the whole town, between the soaring towers.[31]

As grotesque as gargoyles, no doubt, the Utopian version of such details: and gender, along with the Freudian unconscious, expresses itself through them as a kind of distorted mask which is Utopia's disguise and protection of itself – the private awkwardness concealing the public desperation, embarrassment once again marking the place of the desire of the other: only in Fourier do we come upon a joyous tapestry of a myriad public eroticisms, as barefaced as a host of cupids whose clusters design the overall shape of the Phalanstery itself.

No doubt, as with any dualism – beauty and the sublime, plot and character, center and margin, subject and other, studium and punctum, over-determination and wish-fulfillment, strategy and tactics, metaphor and metonymy, sun and moon, good and evil – the interrelated pair Imagination and Fancy is incorrigibly susceptible to reinterpretation in gender terms (just as the latter can then be reinterpreted in terms of power, or indeed any of the other dualisms competing for some illusory "ultimate determining instance"). What is more significant is that it is always the subordinate term which seems more clearly defined than the dominant one – it was always easier to propose a reading of Coleridge's Fancy than to say what he meant by the Imagination – but also that, as with all dualisms, the terms keep swapping places ceaselessly, in an alternation in which the tenor becomes the vehicle, and what counted as Imagination and overarching form unexpectedly turns into a play of wit and ingenious artifice, while the formerly decorative principle unexpectedly assumes an architectonic function. We have already observed the way in which Skinner's tray marks the place of gender and the Utopian transformation of

31 Marcel Proust, *Remembrance of Things Past*, trans. C.K. Scott-Montcrieff (London, 1982 [1913]), Volume I, pp. 686–687 (French reference, Pléiade vol. I, pp. 626–627 [Paris, 1987]).

kitchen and dining space, of women's work, and even of the aesthetic – all features which will become central organizing principles in the feminist Utopias which follow *Walden Two* in the next generation. (Meanwhile, with a little ingenuity, the transparency of the tray itself can come to figure an access to the social totality, the cognitive mapping of production, that deconceal-ment of social and structural relationships which was one of the fundamental casualties of Taylorist labor and of the centralized authority of Fordist capi-talism.) Callenbach's war games also can easily come to figure the collective rituals whereby a society reaffirms itself and substitutes for the immediacy of individual conflict the mediated and institutional kind.

However, a more fundamental transformation may well be at stake here than any merely cyclical rearrangement of the tropes: this is the structural shift in Utopian problem-solving determined by the emergence of industrial capital-ism itself, which effaces beyond any recall but the nostalgic kind that simpler pastoral or village existence on which earlier Utopias were able to draw for their account of utopian daily life, and in which Fancy found its fundamental material and its terrain of operation. Now the task of Fancy will slowly become an extraordinarily complex one; while the operation of Imagination will be dra-matically simplified, since a single system or mode of production has now supplanted all the others, leaving Utopia with the relatively straightforward program of abolishing it. In More or even Plato, this could be achieved simply by banishing money, a solution which today raises more problems than it solves.

But when the commercial and industrial process is itself recognized to be a system in its own right – a dawning recognition whose maturation runs from Adam Smith to Marx – at that point the overarching structure of capitalism has taken the place of any of the grand constructions to which Imagination might lay claim; while its one great alternative – socialism – has also emigrated from the world of Utopian fantasy to that of practical politics. Thus in either case the capitalist or the socialist frameworks become posited in advance and presupposed by the Utopian Imagination; and the center of gravity of Utopian construction passes to Fancy, which begins tireless to elaborate schemes by which capitalism is ameliorated or neutralized, or socialism is constructed in the mind. At this point, the dominant theme of money proliferates into a mul-tiplicity of funny-money schemes and crackpot currency proposals, which become the central determining mechanisms for this or that new Utopian fantasy (political forms of collective organization taking on much the same function in socialist Utopias). But clearly enough, at this point the very spirit of Utopian invention has been modified, its difficulties increased from the point of view of Fancy, while the function of Imagination slowly atrophies for want of use; it is this process which we have called the waning of the Utopian impulse, the enfeeblement of Utopian desire, and which saps our political options and tends to leave us all in the helpless position of passive accomplices and impotent handwringers.

Where the Utopian Imagination does flourish, it does so in the former space of Utopian Fancy, namely in the attempt to imagine a daily life utterly different from this one, without competition or Care, without alienated labor or the envy and jealousy of others and their privileges. It is an attempt which then slips effortlessly into metaphysics, such as the calm of the Heideggerian return to Being. Fancy, meanwhile, wracking its brain for new systemic schemes, like the scribbling cherub in Dürer's *Melancolia* – the two central figures of Melancholy and her small partner might indeed stand as allegorical figures for Imagination and Fancy as such – produces ingenious but social-democratic inventions such as the Tobin Tax, or else extraordinary systemic proposals like Barbara Goodwin's lottery society;[32] but somehow fails to rise to the height of energizing visions of the older Utopian texts. Yet the opposition between the two, and their formal cooperation in tension and complementary, remains a political reality even in the present day, and I will suggest in a final chapter that they correspond to something like the current antagonism between the rival left ideologies of Marxism and anarchism – the totalizing Imagination of the former grasped as the defense of organization, the state and the party, while the commitment of the anarchists to the freedoms of the everyday and a life beyond centralization, power and dependency necessarily draw on the best traditions of Utopian Fancy, very much including Fourier's extraordinary libidinal "details".

This shifting structure of the wish-fulfillment, however, has tended to distract us from the content of the Utopian wish as such, as well as from the nature of the process by which wishes are fulfilled. Meanwhile the emphasis on Utopia as a kind of fantasy or wish-fulfilling production raises an unexpected terminological confusion compounded by the term fancy itself. This is the assimilation of the Utopian genre to what is today commercially termed "fantasy", alongside its generic and marketing opposite number in Science Fiction. We must now lay this misunderstanding to rest, before returning to different but no less significant problems posed by the fulfilling of a wish as such.

---

32 Barbara Goodwin, *Justice by Lottery* (Chicago, 2001).

5

The Great Schism

If indeed Utopia is a "socio-economic subset of Science Fiction",[1] the new and unexpected terminological conflict pits it against what is today generically identified as "fantasy", which has indeed a far older historical lineage than Science Fiction itself (conventionally assigned an inaugural date of 1895 – Wells' *Time Machine* – if not 1818 – Mary Shelley's *Frankenstein*). Whether legitimately or not, the scientific pretensions of SF lend the Utopian genre an epistemological gravity that any kinship with generic fantasy is bound to undermine and seriously to unravel: associations with Plato or Marx are more dignified credentials for the Utopian text than fantastic trips to the moon in Lucian or Cyrano. It would seem, therefore, that we need to pause for a brief detour through this new generic debate, first addressing the structural differences to be established between SF and fantasy, before touching on the relevance of the latter for Utopianism and Utopian construction.

In recent years, to be sure, the competition between SF and fantasy – which has evolved largely to the benefit of the latter, especially among younger readers of innumerable multi-volume series – has seemed to take on overtones of that bitter opposition between high and mass culture crucial to the self-definition of high modernism but far less significant in its postmodern avatar. Not only do the sales of fantasy lists far outweigh those of a diminished "serious" SF, but the latter now has a specialized following that can scarcely be compared to the readership developed by Tolkien (posthumously) or Harry Potter (very actual indeed). The increasing number of films drawn from the work of Philip K. Dick have not particularly encouraged a reevaluation of this major American literary figure (particularly since even the greatest of these adaptations, Ridley Scott's *Blade Runner* [1982], offers an elegant futuristic melancholy very much at odds with its literary source, *Do Androids Dream of Electric Sheep?* [1966]). But even a mass public would not seem to warrant extended comparisons between the current fantasy bestsellers and the Utopian craze inspired by Bellamy's *Looking Backward*; as for

1 See Introduction, note 8.

Morris, along with Le Guin one of the few practitioners of both Utopia and fantasy alike, his Utopian achievement is not particularly enhanced by a commitment to medieval fantasy or romance which tends to refocus *News from Nowhere* as idyll or pastoral.

Fantasy has indeed, as a genre, stronger affinities with medieval content than with such Renaissance forms; and this will indeed be one of the topics to be explored in what follows, particularly in the light of the medieval currents that continue to inform More's *Utopia*. But I will also want to address two other structural characteristics of fantasy which contrast sharply with SF and can also serve as *differentiae specificae* for this genre, namely the organization of fantasy around the ethical binary of good and evil, and the fundamental role it assigns to magic.

We will return to magic in a moment. As for ethics, however, it would not seem particularly necessary, after Nietzsche, to argue its regressiveness; but perhaps Nietzsche's point is only reinforced by the perpetual necessity of doing so.[2] He himself sought to strike at the heart of Christianity by demonstrating the aggressivity inherent in the latter's imperative of charity: not only does doing good to others secure their gratitude and thus my power over them, but in Nietzsche's larger historical vision neighborly love disarms the strong and inaugurates the new religion of the weak. More recently, Sartre analyzed the function of the ethical binary itself as a way of securing the centrality of the self and its ideologies and literally marginalizing the other, who becomes the locus of evil; Foucault elaborated this view into an investigation of the policing operations inherent in the opposition of good and evil, and the institutionalization of the norm over the abnormal and the exception. But perhaps the remarks of Freud quoted in the preceding chapter are enough to underscore the essentially infantile spirit of an opposition between heroes and villains which reconfirms the narcissistic perspective of the self on other people and other realities.

Medieval material, as well as a Christian (or even Anglican) nostalgia particularly pronounced in Tolkien and his fellow-travelers as well as in the Harry Potter series, must first be radically distinguished from the historicisms at work in the SF tradition, which turn on a formal framework determined by concepts of the mode of production rather than those of religion: a work like Keith Roberts' remarkable *Pavane* (1968), in which the triumph of the Spanish Armada secures England for an essentially medieval Catholic domination well up into chronologically modern times, cannot be said to express any nostalgia for this alternate history any more than the cognate *Hard to Be a God* (1964)

---

2 Terry Eagleton objects to this position (see *After Theory* [New York, 2003] pp. 142–143); but rather than engaging in debates about "human nature", I would prefer to point to the disastrous results of ethical politics, such as those of the Second International (or even the American New Left in the 1960s). See also, on ethics, the positions of Fourier (Part Two, Essay 1, below).

of the Strugatsky Brothers (and indeed most such "alternate histories", from the steam punk of books like Gibson and Sterling's *The Difference Engine* [1990] to Aldiss' *Helliconia* trilogy [1982], Brunner's *Crucible of Time* [1983], or Kim Stanley Robinson's *Years of Rice and Salt* [2002], still owe allegiance to Enlightenment values).[3]

Nonetheless what I would characterize as a mode-of-production aesthetic shares with the historicism of fantasy a well-nigh visceral sense of the chemical deficiencies of our own present, for which both offer imaginary compensations, albeit of very different types. The various SF historicisms – galactic Roman empires, Orientalist fantasmagorias, samurai worlds, medieval-corporate Foundations – stand on an equal footing with images of this or that fantastic future; and, whatever their more fantastic details, such as the spice worms of Frank Herbert's *Dune* (1965), reinforce components of an essentially historical situation, rather than serving as vehicles for the fantasies of power. Herbert's remarkable ecological construction, indeed, offers a revealing textual contrast to related fantasy worlds of the "sword-and-sorcery" type. Even the tell-tale figure of the redeemer–savior, common to much other 1960s SF such as Heinlein's *Stranger in a Strange Land* (1961),[4] stands as a symptom of that historical era and as the expression of a sense of impending well-nigh Utopian change, rather than as a figure from the stock formulaic cast of fantasy characters, where, as with Georges Dumézil's Indo-European separation of functions, the warrior-hero tends to be radically dissociated from the magician-priest (whom we will examine in a moment). Meanwhile postmodern SF, and in particular Bruce Sterling's cyberpunk, shows a seemingly insatiable appetite for historicist visions of other modes of production, a phenomenon no doubt related to that postmodern genre I have elsewhere

3 The work of the Strugatsky Brothers, the major writers of the recent Soviet SF tradition, will be examined in Chapter 6, below: *Hard to Be a God* teaches the historical lesson on non-intervention from a Marxist perspective, in which the altruistic attempt to intervene in the evolution of the modes of production and to humanize a feudal system of great brutality catapults the latter beyond capitalism into fascism. William Gibson (1948–) and Bruce Sterling (1954–) are generally acknowledged to be the founders of so-called cyberpunk: see Part Two, Essay 11 below. Brian Aldiss (1925–) is one of the most considerable figures in the British SF tradition (his first novel, *Starship* [1958] is discussed in Part Two, Essay 2, below); The Helliconia trilogy stages an immensely ambitious history of another planet and the evolution of its civilization across a more than two-thousand-year-long Great Year. He is also the author of an important history of SF (*The Billion Year Spree*, New York, 1973: rewritten in 1986 as *The Trillion Year Spree*). The British novelist John Brunner (1934–1995) left a large and mixed body of SF work, including a tetralogy of four massive and influential dystopian novels: *Stand on Zanzibar* (1968), *The Jagged Edge* (1969), *The Sheep Look Up* (1972) and *The Shockwave Rider* (1975). On Robinson's novel, see Chapter 1, note 11, above.

4 When asked who was the greatest French poet, André Gide famously replied, "Victor Hugo, alas"; an answer to the question about the greatest American SF writer would have to identify Robert A. Heinlein (1907–1988) in much the same way. But see H. Bruce Franklin's excellent *Robert A. Heinlein: America as Science Fiction* (New York, 1980); and see also on Heinlein Part Two, Essays 2 and 7, below.

called nostalgia film.[5] But this SF avidly searches out the entrepreneurial features of past and future, and, whether neo-conservative or not, is certainly not technically reactionary in the spirit of fantasy.

The latter indeed breathes a purer and more conventional medieval atmosphere, and dreams this non-historical vision along certain sharply articulated lines, from religion to village life, from superstition and legends all the way to the great struggles between the nobility and the peasantry. It is more appropriate to identify these strata as castes rather than as classes (in the modern industrial-capitalist sense), inasmuch as they are characterized by a sense of physical and mental difference analogous to (but not identical with) the modern racialisms. Indeed, one of the signal features that differentiate caste from modern notions of race and class lies in the distinctive culture attributed to each of these structural populations of feudalism. That the hegemonic caste should generate its own aesthetic is scarcely surprising, although the death-oriented haughtiness of the medieval aristocracy, with its samurai cult of honor and masculinity, is obviously very different from the spirit of a later bourgeois dominant culture. But it is in the culture of the peasantry that we find the most original features of medieval life, particularly when compared with the exhaustion and alienated lives of modern factory workers, to whom socialism (and later on, mass culture) must first bring culture from the outside. Peasant culture, however, constitutes a fundamental negation and repudiation of its aristocratic masters, with its Brechtian slyness and "cowardice", its mutism and attachment to the Taoist rhythms of nature, its secret homage to the primordial trickster figure.[6] The opposition between these two caste aesthetics indeed cuts right across religion itself, where the wealth of the church and its princes and sumptuous rituals, its tortured god and its obsession with sin and judgment, stand in sharp contrast to the survival of the older nature cults among the peasantry, along with the joyous poverty of the Franciscan order, and the plebeian revelry of the festivals and the great pilgrimages. Each of these cultures then projects its own unique forms and genres, and the *chanson de geste* expresses the ethos of the feudal barons as dramatically as the fairy tale expresses the hopes and beliefs of the peasants. Medieval culture-material then offers a mixture of these aesthetic voices and practices: the omnipresence of the binary opposition between good and evil and the sense of radical otherness already informing the first crusades and the hatred of Islam coexisting with the plebeian Christianity of the villages and their egalitarianism.

In modern fantasy, however, these incompatible cultural styles are combined in an unexpected way: thus in Tolkien a village nostalgia is deployed in order to authorize a baleful, more properly aristocratic vision of the epic

---

5 See, for example, my *Postmodernism, or, the Cultural Logic of Late Capitalism* (London/Durham, NC, 1991), pp. 287, 369.

6 See my *Brecht and Method* (London, 1998), pp. 136–140.

battle of Good and Evil quite inconsistent with the aesthetic of the peasant fairy tale. Meanwhile the antagonistic religious ideologies of the Middle Ages are here harmoniously combined into a contemporary anti-Enlightenment spiritualism which speaks across the spectrum to those dissatisfied with modernity, from know-nothing American fundamentalisms all the way to the higher-toned Anglican reactionaries. It is also worth mentioning the ahistorical nature of these ethical preoccupations, inasmuch as it would seem to be the absence of any sense of history that most sharply differentiates fantasy from Science Fiction and must also be factored into any systematic comparison with Utopian form. Still, a displacement from politics to ethics and an essentially non-historical perspective on social life are surely not sufficient to distinguish the inner logic of modern fantasy as a genre or mode from any number of other contemporary literary forms (very much including those of high literature or high culture). Nor is the peculiar religious framework itself formally distinctive until we enlarge our conception of religious ideology to include what official religion has always denounced and rejected, namely the practice of magic as such, whose figural meaning we now need to address.

As for medieval religion itself, however, it is important to understand the unique conceptual resources of medieval theology, which lie not so much in any particular piety as in its structure as a remarkably sophisticated form of what Lévi-Strauss called *pensée sauvage*, in its primitive forms a kind of purely perceptual knowledge developed in the absence of abstract or properly philosophical concepts and conceptualities. Medieval theology, like tribal thought, is figural rather than conceptual; but unlike myth it is an extraordinarily elaborated and articulated system of thought, developed after the emergence of classical philosophy as such and in full awareness of the latter's conceptual and linguistic subtleties and of the richness of its problematics. Theology thus constitutes a repository of figuration and figural speculation whose dynamics were not recovered until modern times, with psychoanalysis and *Ideologiekritik*. But it is important not to confuse this remarkable language experiment with religion as such, and better to focus on its fundamental mechanisms, rather than on any alleged subjective content such as faith or belief.

Those mechanisms are summed up by the word *allegory*, which, as enigmatic as it may be, must always offer the central challenge of any attempt to go to the heart of the medieval. But allegory is already implicit in the very conception of *pensée sauvage*, which even in the thinking of Lévi-Strauss' Indians posits the intellectual prestidigitation of individual items promoted to their own generic idea or universal, such that they become classes of themselves. Allegory foregrounds this strange process by way of a unique autoreferentiality or self-designation in which a text's language necessarily acts its content out, and uses itself to articulate the inexpressible. Let Adrian Leverkühn's musical setting from *Paradiso* illustrate this complex process in a succinct and graphic way:

Thus in the piece which especially took me, and Kretschmar too had called very good, where the poet in the light of the planet Venus sees the smaller lights – they are the spirits of the blessed – some more quickly, the others more slowly, "according to the kind of their regard of God" drawing their circles, and compares this to the sparks that one distinguishes in the flame, the *voices* that one distinguishes in the song "when the one twines round the other". I was surprised and enchanted at the reproduction of the sparks in the fire, of the entwining voices.[7]

> E come in fiamma favilla si vede,
> e come in voce voce si discerne,
> quand' una è ferma e altra va e riede,
> vid' io in essa luce alter lucerne
> muoversi in giro più e men correnti,
> al modo, credo, di lor viste interne.
> Di fredda nube non disceser venti,
> o visibili o no, tanto festini,
> che non paressero impediti e lenti
> a chi avesse quei lumi divini
> veduti a noi venir, lasciando il giro
> pria cominciato in li alti Serafini;
> e dentro a quei che più innanzi appariro
> sonava *"Osanna"* sì, che unque poi
> di rïudir non fui sanza disiro.
>
> *Paradiso*, VIII

And as we see a spark within a flame, and as a voice within a voice is distinguished when one holds the note and another comes and goes, I saw within that light other lamps moving in a circle more and less swift according to the measure, I believe, of their internal sight. From a cold cloud winds, whether visible or not, never descended so swiftly that they would not seem impeded and slow to one who had seen those divine lights come to us, leaving the circling first begun among the high Seraphim; and within those that appeared most in front *Hosanna* sounded in such wise that never since have I been without the desire to hear it again.[8]

Here already a kind of Utopian body is projected as the senses swap places, lights doing double duty for sounds and then vice versa: this is the very element of allegory, whose *pensée sauvage*, divested of abstractions, must use

---

7 Thomas Mann, *Dr Faustus* (New York, 1948 [1947]), p. 162.

8 Dante Alighieri, *Paradiso* (Princeton, 1975: Singleton translation), Canto VIII, verses 16–30, pp. 82–85.

each singular perception to express the other, then appropriating the other in order to return on itself to shore up its own existence as representation. So it is that Adrian's music needs not add some third dimension to Dante's allegorical scheme but merely insert itself in the ceaseless exchange from tenor to vehicle.

And although I have minimized the theological content of this form, it can certainly be argued that it is the supreme non-representability of the godhead that furnishes the mystical text with its fundamental vocation and motivates allegory as an extreme structure of language itself.

It is precisely this allegorical dimension which is lacking in modern fantasy, whose medieval Imaginary seems to be primarily organized around the omnipresence of magic, itself enlisted in the pursuit of power by the great magicians in their reenactment of that cosmic struggle between Good and Evil which, as we have seen, expresses the aristocratic ideologies of the medieval aesthetic. Magic is indeed the more problematic component of generic "sword and sorcery", since the armed struggle as such is easily understood as a regression to the pre-technological era and an attempt to recreate the immediacy of a face-to-face conflict between individuals.

Magic on the other hand reawakens all the unsolved generic problems inherent in distinguishing fantasy from SF, and in particular in determining why any number of fantastic SF technologies, such as teleportation or time travel, superhuman computers, telepathy, or alien life forms, should be regarded any differently from magicians or dragons. Darko Suvin's influential conception of SF as "cognitive estrangement",[9] which emphasizes the commitment of the SF text to scientific reason, would seem to continue a long tradition of critical emphasis on verisimilitude from Aristotle on (who famously explained that history only describes what did happen, while "poetry" – in the larger sense – describes happenings probable or believable).[10] The role of cognition in SF thus initially deploys the certainties and speculations of a rational and secular scientific age: Suvin's innovative use of this concept presupposes that knowledge today – Marx's General Intellect[11] – includes the social, and that therefore the reception of SF ultimately includes the Utopian.

It is perhaps in the borderline phenomena that the distinction meets its crucial test: Jules Verne seems to face backwards and to sum up that whole tradition of fantastic machinery that passes through Cyrano on its way back to Lucian. Meanwhile in fantasy itself the dragon can be seen as the equivalent of the spaceship or of teleportation in SF. Yet as a living being the dragon is also able

9 Darko Suvin, *Metamorphoses of Science Fiction* (New Haven, 1979), Chapter 1. We should not invoke Suvin's authority here without noting his negative judgments on fantasy as such: see "Considering the Sense of 'Fantasy' or 'Fantastic Fiction'", *Extrapolation* 44.3 (2000), pp. 209–247.

10 Aristotle, *Poetics*, 1451.

11 See Chapter 2, note 19 of this volume above.

to incarnate sheer otherness, so that its symbolic capacities well exceed those of inanimate machinery. Indeed, in Delany and Anne McCaffrey the ecstasy of dragons in flight rehearses intensities at the very limit of the human; in Le Guin the dragon's preternatural wisdom and knowledge, and its symbiotic relationship with humans, equally make it into a vehicle for transcending ordinary human possibilities.[12] In Science Fiction, however, the relationship to the spaceship as artificial intelligence (as most famously in *2001*) or to other kinds of bio-technology, such as the intelligent house,[13] is a relatively lateral development which only becomes central to the genre with the thematics of robots (Asimov), androids (Philip K. Dick), and later cyborgs (Donna Haraway). But these are machines that have already become Others, and have been promoted into something like a new and distinct, alternate, species to the human.

Nonetheless fantasy remains generically wedded to nature and to the organism; and in that effacing of boundaries at work in current ideas of the posthuman, the tug of war between organism and machine increasingly inclines to the preponderance of the latter, in genetic engineering and in the promotion of biology over physics as the prototypical science. The reincorporation of organic material in the imagery of the cyborg or of intelligent computers, however, tends to transform the organic into a machine far more than it organicizes machinery. Thus, postmodern or cybernetic technology becomes if anything even more "unnatural" than the older heavy-industrial kind. This is the historical context in which fantasy and its ethical dynamics and magical powers can today be seen as a compensation for that continuing technological bias of Science Fiction which, although no longer mechanical in the spirit of its "golden age", nonetheless testifies to the omnipresence of a built environment, and indeed to the virtual abolition of a nature so oddly paired in modern fantasy with religion.

Nature thus seems to function here primarily as the sign of an imaginary regression to the past and to older pre-rational forms of thought. But we probably do not want to be caught in that "dialectic of Enlightenment" which Hegel already denounced as a vicious circle in *Phenomenology of Spirit*,[14] in which

---

12 Samuel R. Delany (1942–), one of the foremost practitioners (alongside his SF novels) of a very sophisticated fantasy indeed in his *Neveryon* series, and a considerable theorist of SF from a linguistic or "structuralist" point of view, is a central figure in what I will call a new "aesthetic" or perceptual stage of SF (see Chapter 7, below). Anne McCaffrey (1926–) is best known for her very successful dragon or Pern series, which is generally considered to be fantasy rather than SF. And on dragons more generally, see Susan Willis, "Le Guin's Dragons: Gender and Utopian Transformation", (lecture at the Summer Institute of Theory, University of Southern Maine, August 2002).

13 See China Miéville, "The Conspiracy of Architecture," in *Historical Materialism*, No. 2, Summer 1998; and also see the interesting special issue of the same journal on "radical fantasy" (Volume X, Issue 4 [2004]), in which an early draft of the present chapter appeared.

14 G.W.F. Hegel, *The Phenomenology of Spirit* (Oxford, 1977 [1807]), Chapter VI, subsection B-II, "Enlightenment".

Enlightenment rationality and religious irrationalism confront each other as mutually exclusive thought-modes one of which is historically called upon to disappear. The denunciation of religion (or medieval fantasy) as sheer mystification and obfuscation to be eliminated has as its dialectical consequence the limits of Enlightenment radicalism and its shallow affinities with rationalism and liberalism. Hegel, whose sympathies with the French Revolution were already profound and considerable, was also capable of proposing a historically original post-Enlightenment "solution" to the problem of religion and so-called irrationalism. The mistake of the Revolution, he argues, was to have insisted on the elimination of its cultural antithesis; and the result of this insistence was the Terror. Hegel's dialectic on the other hand suggests (it is a whole political program) that we need to go all the way through religion and come out the other side: absorbing all its positive features – it is after all in this period culture and desire, the very content of the premodern superstructure as such – in order to combine them with an Enlightenment impulse no longer menaced by reduction to instrumental reason and the narrower forms of bourgeois positivism. We might well want to look at the traditional (and irreconcilable) antithesis between SF and fantasy from the perspective of Hegel's lesson here.

But it is in fact in Feuerbach that we find an even more practical solution for our generic problems. For Feuerbach in many ways taught us how to set the Hegelian position in motion, how to make it over into a practical program for analysis and politics alike. Feuerbach, indeed, completes the Enlightenment view of religion as superstition (and an ideological bulwark of tyranny) by asking the complementary question about the source of religion's attraction and power. The conventional wisdom (famously replicated by Marx) which posits it as a "haven in a heartless world" still carries with it the implication of sheer deception and manipulation.

Feuerbach on the other hand had the ingenious idea of grasping religion as a projection: it is, he argued, a distorted vision of human productive powers, which has been exteriorized and reified into a force in its own right.[15] Divine power, of which the various theologies are so many abstractions and elaborations, is in fact unalienated human creativity which has then been re-alienated into an image or a figural form. In it labor and productivity, including human intelligence and imagination, the "general intellect" of humanity, have been hypostatized and subsequently appropriated and exploited like any other human product. We do not read Marx's great footnote – the *Theses on Feuerbach* – fully and correctly unless we appreciate the nature of this revolutionary

---

15 "In the religious systole man propels his own nature from himself, he throws himself outward; in the religious diastole he receives the rejected nature into his heart again" (Ludwig Feuerbach, *The Essence of Christianity* [Amherst, NY, 1989 (1841)], p. 31). This philosophically original doctrine of projection can then be seen as a precursor of Bloch's hermeneutic as well: "The deity is an idea the truth and reality of which is only happiness" (*The Essence of Religion* [Amherst, NY, 2004 (1851)].

analysis, which has immense implications for all cultural and superstructural analysis and not only that of religion.

In our present context, indeed, it has immediate consequences for our reception of that fundamental motif of fantasy which is magic as such. If SF is the exploration of all the constraints thrown up by history itself – the web of counterfinalities and anti-dialectics which human production has itself produced – then fantasy is the other side of the coin and a celebration of human creative power and freedom which becomes idealistic only by virtue of the omission of precisely those material and historical constraints. Magic, then, may be read, not as some facile plot device (which it no doubt becomes in the great bulk of mediocre fantasy production), but rather as a figure for the enlargement of human powers and their passage to the limit, their actualization of everything latent and virtual in the stunted human organism of the present. Let Le Guin's extraordinary evocation of one specialized magical talent stand for this motif as a whole:

> The first sign of Otter's gift, when he was two or three years old, was his ability to go straight to anything lost, a dropped nail, a mislaid tool, as soon as he understood the word for it. And as a boy one of his dearest pleasures had been to go alone out into the countryside and wander along the lanes or over the hills, feeling through the soles of his bare feet and throughout his body the veins of water underground, the lodes of knots of ore, the lay and the interfolding of the kinds of rock and earth. It was as if he walked in a great building, seeing its passages and rooms, the descents to airy caverns, the glimmer of branched silver in the walls; and as he went on, it was as if his body became the body of earth, and he knew its arteries and organs and muscles as his own. This power had been a delight to him as a boy. He had never sought any use for it. It had been his secret.[16]

In such a passage the very nature of magic itself becomes a whole literary program of representation; and this is why the most consequent fantasy never simply deploys magic in the service of other narrative ends, but proposes a meditation on magic as such – on its capacities and its existential properties, on a kind of figural mapping of the active and productive subjectivity in its non-alienated state. By the same token, the approach to this power and its representation will generally not take the form of its plenitude or mature achievement (the aged wizards who compel awe and fear), but rather that of the *Bildungsroman*, in which (like the hero of *The Wizard of Earthsea*) the novice gradually comes to witness and guide the awakening of this peculiar talent.

But we may now, recalling Le Guin, go even further than this: for her fantasy novels put us on track of both our two still outstanding problems: the question

16 Ursula Le Guin, *Tales from Earthsea* (New York, 2001), pp. 13–14.

of history and the role of the ethical binary of good and evil. The Earthsea series in fact begins with the awakening of evil (in Ged's first misguided consultation of the spells, and developing through to its confrontation with the shadow, or evil, self at the end of that first volume) and ends with the attempt to resolve what has become a world-wide historical crisis, in the gradual disappearance of magical powers everywhere in Earthsea. Le Guin thus begins in ethics and ends up in history; and in a materialist history at that. For in its purely thematic form, the vision of an immense historical degradation and the end of the old world, the old society and the old ways, is everywhere apparent in fantasy (and in myth itself). Tolkien affords us the prototypical expression of this reactionary nostalgia for Christianity and the medieval world, and Le Guin starts out, like so many others, as his disciple. But her village paradigm, a nostalgic celebration of the societies of an older Native American mode of production, switches train tracks from the Church of England to the politics of imperialism.

Meanwhile, even her deployment of the paradigm of the struggle between Good and Evil becomes socialized and historicized by way of feminism. The patriarchal, in *Always Coming Home* (1985), is identified with the imperialistic (and see the great war novel *The Word for World Is Forest* [1972], unjustly neglected since the end of the Vietnam War). By the same process, the representational evolution of *The Wizard of Earthsea* pentalogy, from the evil "shadow" of the first volume to the truly chilling appearance of Jasper in *Tehanu* (1990) – a character in whom *ressentiment* and misogyny, class superiority and the dehumanizing will to vengeance, are memorably compounded – affords a vivid picture of submission to the other's magic as a paralyzing force, and truly resituates us in the concrete social world of alienation and class struggle, of subalternity and oppression. Le Guin thereby triumphantly demonstrates that fantasy can also have critical and even demystificatory power.

But we must also take into account the way in which history and historical change inscribe themselves in even the most ahistorical forms. Postmodernity, which names wholesale modifications in the life world, can also be expected to mark that merely imaginary reality which is the shape and function of magic in fantasy texts: perhaps, indeed, it is this deeper rhythm of history which Le Guin's own work, ostensibly registering the secularization and the literal *Entzauberung* of an older world by modernity, in fact detects and expresses.

But the more immediate shifts are to be identified in the paradigm shift in modern science itself from physics to the life sciences: a shift calculated to make problems for conventional SF representation and narrative. Indeed, it seems likely that today the complexities of biology and the genetic, indeed bio-power itself, offer a content and a raw material far more recalcitrant to plot formation than even Einsteinian cosmology and the undecideability of atomic sub-particles. Greg Bear's influential *Blood Music* (1983) can serve as a useful chronological marker for this watershed, while I am probably not alone in finding the latest hard SF based on informational processes (even by so estimable a writer as Greg Egan) relatively unreadable.

The seemingly irrecuperable ascendancy of fantasy has in that case no little to do with the literary advantages offered by its new content in ecology and a now far more extensive exploration of the possibilities inherent in the human body; while so-called cyberpunk, for all its energies and qualities, can historically be interpreted as SF's doomed attempt at a counteroffensive, and a final effort to reconquer a readership alienated by the difficulties of contemporary science, increasingly hostile ideologically to the radicalism of more social SF (now generationally distanced by the youth culture), and frustrated by the diminishing production of new yet formulaic easy reading in the SF area.

Yet it would not be altogether correct to stage the opposition between SF and fantasy as a replay and variant of the more familiar modern antagonism between high and low or mass culture – or at least it is a position one can take only after registering the postmodern attenuation of these boundary lines, the *rapprochement* between high and low culture in the last decades, and the blurring of distinctive generic characteristics which characterizes postmodernity here as elsewhere. Not only are some of the best recent works and writers difficult to classify, but the disputes about what cannot be admitted into the SF canon have come to seem increasingly unproductive, even though the genre itself depends on them and is constituted by generic recognition (or its accompanying opposite number, generic undecidability). The work of Gene Wolfe (1931–), richly developing in the spaces between fantasy and SF, can perhaps serve as a central exhibit in these debates: for myself, I acknowledge its quality but feel a deep reluctance to abandon these generic distinctions. Perhaps the qualitative judgments that are so easy to make in SF are unavailable in so amorphous a world of discourse as fantasy.

This does not mean that distinctive contemporary fantasy texts cannot emit signals and vibrations which are comparable to those of the best SF and yet as different from it generically as they are from more traditional fantasy as such. The rising flood designed to submerge the Eastern seaboard in Michael' Swanwick's remarkable *Stations of the Tide* (1991) is as "historical" an event as the waning of magic in Le Guin; but its deeper historical originality lies in the transposition of this entire simulated "Eastern seaboard" to an alien planet in the first place. As in Le Guin, Swanwick's novel constitutes a reflection on magic as such, on its powers and its nature; yet it opens a unique place for itself in a narrative play on the two distinct senses of this word, only one of which exists in the generic discourse of fantasy. That "literary" meaning, to be sure, designates the powers possessed by "real" magicians (where real designates the conventions of the genre). But in the real world (using the other sense of reality) a real magician is one who exercises a profession and performs specialty acts in venues ranging from children's birthday parties to circuses and television spectacles. Swanwick's magician Gregorian – who had the makings of a villain as sinister and chilling as Le Guin's Jasper – effortlessly modulates between the two roles, as in the following performance:

> "The rainbird is a typical shapeshifter. When the living change comes over the Tidewater, when Ocean rises to drown half the continent, it adapts by transforming into a more appropriate configuration." Suddenly he plunged both hands deep into the bowl of water. The bird struggled wildly and disappeared …
>
> When the water cleared, a multicolored fish was swimming in great agitation in the water …[17]

Yet this seeming demonstration of the peculiar ontology of this planet with its dimorphic life forms turns out to have been sheer illusionism of the proverbial rabbit-and-hat variety, as Swanwick's next chapter reveals. The magical powers of Gregorian thereby become as ambiguous as those of Bergman's *The Magician* (1958) and no less troubling. But what in Bergman is a metaphysical hesitation about the supernatural itself (in something of a textbook illustration for Todorov's rather pedestrian theory of the fantastic) here becomes a narrative shell game and a postmodern play with generic frameworks that fade in and out of each other.[18] This movement produces an intricate alternation between Coleridge's familiar suspension of disbelief and some less familiar suspension of belief, in which the prosaic reality of the faker and illusionist fades in and out of the fantasy conventions and somehow covers them as well, in a virtuosity itself quite different from the way in which Dick motivates and secures his visions by drugs and/or schizophrenics.

This truly postmodern inventiveness is then confirmed by another feature of Swanwick's work which seems to have its SF affinities (in Van Vogt as well as in Dick), but which is also historically and generically very different from the openings onto other worlds they so often posit:

> The Bureaucrat was the last to leave. He stepped out into the hall of mirrors: walls and overhead trim echoing clean white infinity down a dwindling line of gilt-framed mirrors before curving to a vanishing point where patterned carpeting and textured ceiling became one. Thousands of people used the hall at any given instant, of course, popping in and out of the mirrors continually, but the Traffic Architecture Council saw no need for them to be made visible. The bureaucrat disagreed. Humans ought not go unmarked, he felt; at the very least the air should shimmer with their passage.
>
> All but weightless, he ran down the hall, scanning the images offered by the mirrors: A room like a black iron birdcage that hummed and sparked with

---

17 Michael Swanwick (1950–), *The Stations of the Tide* (New York, 1991, p. 17).
18 See Part Two, Essay 2, for an earlier conceptualization of such "generic discontinuities", which have here developed out into a play of simulacra.

electricity. A forest glade where wild machines crouched over the carcass of a stag, tearing at the entrails. An empty plain dotted with broken statues swathed in white cloth, so that the features were smothered and softened – that was the one he wanted. The traffic director put it in front of him. He stepped through and into the antechamber of Technology Transfer. From there it was only a step into his office.[19]

Still, Dick's "motivations of the device"[20] alerted us to experiential analogies in the "real world" with their drugs and schizophrenic episodes; but here the analogies – walking down a bustling hallway (or an empty one) – seem rather secondary. Van Vogt's door, meanwhile, functioned as portals onto the mysteries of being of other worlds entirely:[21] something like tourism before the Second World War. That otherness is now the historical difference between Van Vogt and Swanwick, whose narrative merely offers a sampling of various landscapes, with one new wrinkle, namely that it is also a sampling of various temporalities. The old one is indeed put on hold after you enter another dimension of space, and you can live through entire conversations in time before picking up your older chronology again where you left off when you passed through that particular doorway.

That would already set Swanwick's narrative a notch above the mimesis of a purely filmic experience which is now the standard analogon or experiential equivalent for so much contemporary writing (and not only that of fantasy). We may well feel ethical qualms about the phenomenological basis of representations drawn not from our most authentic corporeal experiences but merely from their cinematographic expansion, by way of the image, into areas we have never ourselves physically frequented (even though that expansion is itself predicated on the memory of lived equivalences): but something surely changes when the mimesis of filmic experience becomes reflexive and thematized, itself the deeper subject of the text.

In any case, here the text unexpectedly designates itself by way of the representation, not merely of cinema, but of cinema's "special effects", and indeed of effects inconceivable for the cinema of Van Vogt's time. This is therefore neither modernist reflexivity nor the visionary metaphysics and spirituality vulgarly associated with fantasy, but either something entirely different: namely the mimesis of technology, and of a very specific historical moment of technology at that. (We are told, indeed, that the current development of special-effects technology can be dated from George Lucas' establishment of a *Star Wars* laboratory in 1977.) Swanwick's unique narrative is thus postmodern, not only in the way in which it represents the reality of the image, but also by

---

19 Swanwick, *Stations of the Tide*, p. 126
20 A Russian Formalist term and concept: see Viktor Shklovsky's *Theory of Prose* (1925).
21 See Part Two, Essay 6.

carrying within itself the very cybernetic technology which is the marker, if not the cause, of postmodernity in the first place. It thereby becomes more realistic, as a social document, than much of what purports to pass for a postmodern social realism; and, over against cyberpunk in SF, documents a claim of contemporary fantasy for its own unique mimetic possibilities.

In any case, the charm of the world of magic makes a more permanent claim of its own, as it persists in medieval romance, of which the Arthurian cycle is the fundamental expression. And like all the genres of modes of production different from our own – myth, tragedy, epic, Chinese lyric – it also offers that unique "Luft aus anderen Planeten", that air from other planets (which Stefan George evoked and which Schoenberg set to music), that signals some momentary release from the force of gravity of this one. So also our own genres – modernism in one way, SF in another – struggle desperately to escape our force field and the force of gravity of our historical moment. But romance – all the way from Chrétien to its most modern echoes in Wagner's *Parsifal* (1882) or the *Lancelot* (1974) of Robert Bresson – retains the fascination of a magical transformation of human relations – conflict, violence, desire, sovereignty, bonding, love and vocation – all uniquely reconfigured under the central narrative category of the adventure. Yet the invocation of magic by modern fantasy cannot recapture this fascination, but is condemned by its form to retrace the history of magic's decay and fall, its disappearance from the disenchanted world of prose, the "entzauberte Welt", of capitalism and modern times. It is only at this point, when the world of magic becomes little more than nostalgia, that the Utopian wish can reappear in all its vulnerability and fragility. In Morris and Le Guin both there visibly reappears that mysterious bridge that leads from the historical disintegration of fantasy to the reinvention of the Novum, from a fallen world in which the magical powers of fantasy have become unrepresentable to a new space in which Utopia can itself be fantasized.

6

How to Fulfill a Wish

Neither generic differentiation, however (the constitutive difference between Science Fiction and fantasy), nor structural description (Imagination and Fancy, the wish and its secondary elaboration), seem to have brought us any closer to the nature and source of the Utopian wish itself (whose vacuous evocation as the image of a perfect society or even the blueprint of a better one are best set aside from the outset without further comment). Nor does the identification of Utopian ideology seem to have helped us much in determining Utopian science. Is there indeed any formalist method for describing the august function of Coleridgean Imagination in Utopian textuality which does not find itself passing through content, and falling back on the various above-mentioned Utopian schemes organized around the abolition of money, desire, non-alienated labor, the liberation of women, etc.? Not only were all these themes the result of a negation of the existing order, rather than the construction of a new one; they do not seem to entertain any privileged relationship to the structure of the Utopian text and might just as easily have been outlined in a political pamphlet or a treatise on political theory. In that form, in other words, they are not yet wish-fulfillments; and it therefore seems necessary to return to the problem of the properly Utopian wish-fulfillment in order to identify a process distinct from Utopian ideology or the gratifications of the narcissistic punctum.

Here, indeed, the reflexive turn of our analysis of magic in the preceding chapter may serve as a precedent, for it does not seem irrelevant to inquire how the Utopias themselves, or their SF analogues, stage wishing as such, and what counts in them in particular as the fulfillment of just such wishes. Two works of great quality come to mind as representations of the very process of forming and satisfying the Utopian wish: Ursula Le Guin's *Lathe of Heaven* (1971) and, on the other side of the Iron Curtain, the Strugatsky Brothers' virtually contemporaneous *Roadside Picnic* (1972).[1]

---

1 Ursula Le Guin, *The Lathe of Heaven* (New York, 1971); Arkady and Boris Strugatsky, *Roadside Picnic* (New York, 1977); page references to both editions will henceforth be given in the text.

The Strugatskys give us Utopia as it were backwards, or from the other side of the mirror. It is simply the Zone, an enigmatic and dangerous space of otherness that makes its appearance in their novels under various guises (see for example the Forest, in *The Snail on the Slope* [1968]). The Zone is a magical, incomprehensible area of radically other space – a space beyond the law, an ontological Chernobyl – which contains unusual objects: enigmatic objects like the "empties" ("two copper disks the size of a saucer, about a quarter inch thick, with a space of a foot and a half between them" [8]); deadly objects like the burning fluff, the "shimmering, a trembling, sort of like hot air at noon over a tin roof" [22], and the silvery cobwebs that poison Kirill in the opening section; along with objects of inestimable value and use – the reward for all this and the true treasures of the Zone, like permanently charged batteries – and which are of especial interest to the military-industrial complex.

These are the objects of our Utopias seen through the distorting mirror of alien eyes: what is the use of a transparent lunch tray, indeed what is a cafeteria tray in the first place? What is a chamber pot, let alone a gold one, or a low-power electric vehicle for moving in the woods? What are the machines of Bellamy's new factories? No alien could figure it out; and we have similar problems with their Zone, which we can only conceptualize as a malevolent space in which, from time to time, we discover objects you can make a fortune with. We thus continue to wield our earthbound binary categories of good and evil (good for us, evil for us), albeit now utterly dissociated from each other, and coexisting like two distinct and incommensurable dimensions, thereby ignoring the warnings of a Stanislaw Lem that the radically alien cannot be grasped by any human categories.[2]

Aliens are neither benevolent nor malevolent, despite the dialectic rehearsed in books like Arthur C. Clarke's *Childhood's End* (1950) or James Blish's *Case of Conscience* (1959). Specks or blips on the margins of the alien's field of vision, we are invisible to them, or at best indifferent, a situation that does not exclude grim accidents. *Roadside Picnic*, indeed, tells the story of one such extraterrestrial accident.

Yet the extraordinary density of the Strugatskys' little novel is to be explained by the variety of humans and human groups who bring their limited thought processes, and their varying interests, to bear on this space which has appeared as though by cosmic miracle: among them, scientists trying to understand, the media trying to sensationalize, businessmen estimating possible returns, and military men weighing the chances for new "weapons of mass destruction"; the mafia, finally, organizing contraband and smuggling, doing a brisk traffic in forbidden items on the Canadian border, famously the locale of the earlier classic smuggling operations of Prohibition itself. But the Zone has also brought into being a new profession, and a new form of human

2 See Chapter 8.

prowess and intrepidity – that of the stalker, who risks his life, health and freedom in illegal forays into the Zone.[3]

One of these marginals and subversives is the protagonist, whose reward for his efforts has been a genetically deformed or mutant daughter. We are to understand that his motives are not financial, but that he desperately seeks a wonder-working cure for her condition in the very place of miracles: and, barring a specific cure, he seeks a legendary object which now flings our text generically over into the fairy tale (whose borders the Strugatskys in any case frequently transgressed in other works).[4]

But it is precisely the nature of such generic borders which the reflexive wish-fulfillment seeks to explore, sometimes by way of an illicit commingling that dramatizes their incompatibility. So it is that in early Le Guin a Tolkien-inspired countryside of magicians and dragons oddly coexists with spaceships and SF explorers from other planets. Le Guin has herself characterized such works as youthful errors; yet the generic category mistake very sharply fore-grounds the strengths of each and can stand as a reflexive meditation on the two distinct systems. So the creative power of magic (which we have examined in the previous chapter) and the sheerest ecstasy of dragon flight contrast sharply with the resistance of matter in the SF mode and its systematic exploration of otherness and alien culture. Yet there is an allegorical thread that links the two modes in Le Guin's galactic UN (the Ekumen), whose peaceful coexistence is secured by a simultaneous faster-than-light communications device – the ansible – discovery of which by Shevek is only retroactively narrated in the later *Dispossessed* (1974).

In Le Guin, then, we confront something like a binary alternation between the reality principle of SF and the pleasure principle of fantasy. Perhaps in that sense Utopia does constitute a working synthesis of these two incommensurables: the supreme creativity or shaping impulse of fantasy marshalling the most recalcitrant raw material of all, in the state and the social order. So it is that as Science Fiction approaches the condition of Utopia (as in the two novels currently under consideration here), a peculiar fairy-tale topology begins to rise towards the surface like a network of veins.

At any rate, the ultimate lost object of desire of the Strugatskys' Zone turns out to be, not some brilliant technological equipment utilizing utterly incomprehensible, physical processes, but rather a magical object of a unique kind: "a mythical artifact located in the Zone in the shape and form of a gold ball that grants human wishes" (93). It is this Golden Ball for which the stalker

---

3 It is worth noting that Andrei Tarkovsky's film *Stalker* (1979) is now only distantly related to the Strugatskys' original. The story goes that the film stock on which a relatively faithful first version was shot proved to be defective, and that financial shortages unfortunately determined the cheaper allegorical solutions of the final product.

4 In particular, such works as the 1965 novel translated as *Monday Begins on Saturday* (New York, 1977).

protagonist of *Roadside Picnic* searches: and the reader has the feeling that the success of the quest is somehow dependent on the quality of the wish itself. Can it be merely personal and egoistic? Which is to say, in our society, the wish for lots of money (to which health and youth are by definition added)? But the money, and even the scientific miracles, were already somehow premised in the other more utilitarian objects. If this wish is then abstracted into a more general one – happiness, let us say, or *jouissance* – it somehow meets the absent presence and implied ontological· competition with that other, alien, realization of *jouissance* around which the entire novel incomprehensibly turns.

For is not the hypothetical "picnic" itself just such an alien and transfigured form of *jouissance*, the carnival holiday of beings utterly unimaginable to us except by their inconceivable superiority? The scientific hypothesis, indeed, which best explains the Zone and the Visitation from which it presumably comes is the one that gives the novel its title:

> Imagine a picnic … Picture a forest, a country road, a meadow. A car drives off the country road into the meadow, a group of young people get out of the car carrying bottles, baskets of food, transistor radios … In the morning they leave … And what do [the animal witnesses of the region] see? Gas and oil spilled on the grass. Old spark plugs and filters. apple cores, candy wrappers, charred remains of the campfire … a roadside picnic in the cosmos. (107)

But these remains, which testify to the absolute indifference of the aliens to human existence – for we ourselves are precisely those "animal witnesses" – are also the traces and the marks of superhuman pleasure, which individual humans can scarcely imagine.

So it is that Redrick's wish is not for himself but for the cure of his mutant daughter; but in the process of approaching this goal – and the novel breaks off with the discovery of the Golden Ball itself – another sacrifice is demanded: as it were the substitution for his own debt payment (genetic damage in return for valuable discoveries in the Zone) of the payment of another life. For this purpose Redrick borrows the life of an innocent party, son of the crippled competitor with whom he has agreed to share the profits of this particular expedition. Arthur is obliged to precede the stalker, much as you might use an unwitting victim to navigate a minefield, and with much the same consequences. Yet the young man also has a wish, one singularly free of self-interest and even more altruistic than Redrick's paternal one. Indeed, his wish inscribes the very Utopian impulse itself, a universal philanthropy, the purest longing for the good of mankind: "Happiness for everybody … Free! … As much as you want! … Everybody come here! … There's enough for everybody! Nobody will leave unsatisfied! … Free! … Happiness! … Free" (151). The death of the boy which opens the path to wish-fulfillment for Redrick himself is thus a kind of murder (as well as a revenge on the father and also the substitution of the sacrifice of one paternal bond for another), but it is also a shortcircuiting by the SF text of the Utopian impulse, which this mode of narrative can seemingly not tolerate. The SF framework electrocutes the Utopian dreamer just as surely as the poisonous cobwebs of the Zone fatally infect humans who come into contact with them. The bitter outcome (whatever the fate of the deformed child) is the inevitable reconfirmation of SF's reality principle.

At the same time the issue of the quality of the wish – its relative interest or disinterestedness – far from introducing moral or ethical questions into the discussion, returns us abruptly to Freud's insights into the universal and the particular. He identified the particularity of the wish as the insatiably egoistic fantasy which repels us not because it is egoistic but because it is not mine: a formulation which discloses an unpleasant swarm of competing and irreconcilable desires behind the social order and its cultural appearance. As for universality, it is less a social possibility than the very disguise which makes that cultural appearance possible: something like a non-figurative system of ornamentation and elaborate decoration which simulates impersonality and offers an abstraction in which everyone can acquiesce: a more perfect society, "that no one shall go hungry any longer", "happiness for everybody, as much as you want". In that case, is not the Utopian order to be read as a Machiavellian structure of practical social organization concealed behind the sham universality of the various Utopian regimes? And have we really come to the innermost secret of Utopian form when it thus dissolves into the private fantasme on the one hand and the practical–political on the other?

Such questions prepare us for the far more elaborate exploration of wishfulfillment in *The Lathe of Heaven*. Le Guin's only contemporary novel, so to speak, it also stages the apotheosis of her adopted city of Portland, Oregon, and brilliantly illustrates the formal relationship in which SF stands with respect to the historical novel as such. For if the great historical novels replay key moments of the past of their settings, finally endowing them with a rich set of invented traditions and a whole ontological resonance (as witness what Faulkner's chronicles do for Mississippi), the SF novel on the contrary, and in particular this one, enriches the cityscape with a whole variety of imaginary futures, from the backwater provincial Portland of the Plague Years to the glittering mega-Portland capital of the United Nations. The future historical perspective is thus a kind of supplementary or lateral bonus of the Utopian dimension of a novel, full of extraordinary estrangements, as when Le Guin's hero George Orr, whose "effective dreams" produce these cataclysmic yet immediate transformations, finds it hard to understand how an underwater tunnel functions:

> The Willamette was a useful element of the environment, like a very large, docile animal harnessed with straps, chains, shafts, saddles, bits, girths, hobbles … Above the heads of those now riding the GPRT train in the Broadway

Tunnel were tons of rock and gravel, tons of water running, the piles of wharves and the keels of ocean-going ships, the huge concrete supports of elevated freeway bridges and approaches, a convoy of steamer trucks laden with frozen battery-produced chickens, one jet plane at 34,000 feet, the stars at 4.3 light years. (40–41)

Shades of the racehorse that is the symbol of power in one of George's earlier dreams: but this harnessing and overbuilding of Nature also serves to reveal and to defamiliarize the natural as well, and in particular water not thus harnessed and instrumentalized:

[Heather] went to the door and stood half inside, half outside, for a while, listening to the creek shouting and hollering eternal praise! eternal praise! It was incredible that it had kept up that tremendous noise for hundreds of years before she was even born, and would go on doing it until the mountains moved. (108)

But she is wrong about this, as the very fate of water ebbs and flows with George's dreams; and it would be worth tracing the fate of water throughout our Utopian tradition, from the half-moon bay in the original[5] to the question of plumbing and sewage in more modern texts. Still, this passage from *The Lathe of Heaven*, in which the running stream stands for nature itself, gives us at least one standard by which to judge the Utopian text and what it enables just as much as what it represses.

Yet this "realistic" Portland novel is also a fairy tale, indeed a rather grisly embodiment and elaboration of one of the archetypal fairy tales of wish-fulfillment as such: namely that of the fisherman to whom the immortal fish promises three wishes, with the results we know ("I wish I had some sausages"; "I wish those sausages were stuck on your nose!"; with the third and last wish inevitably following).[6] The premise is one of totality: that the world is one immense and self-sufficient system   change anything in it, no matter how small, and the rest will necessarily be altered in unexpected ways. It is a vision that works diachronically as well as here synchronically: remember the unhappy butterfly, in Bradbury's "Sound of Thunder" (1952), which, crushed during a time-travel visit to the Paleolithic past, changes the present beyond recognition when its hapless traveler returns.[7]

So George's "effective dreams" are always realized on the order of the legendary treachery of oracles ("when Croesus crosses the river Halys, a

5 Marin is particularly good on this peculiar geographical detail: see Louis Marin, *Utopiques* (Paris, 1973), pp. 153–155.

6 Günter Grass has used this fairy tale as the framework for an extraordinary history of the human race, in *Der Butt* (*The Flounder*), 1977.

7 Ray Bradbury (1920–), the author of *The Martian Chronicles* and *Farenheit 451*, is another crossover writer in whose works the boundaries between fantasy and SF often seem blurred.

mighty empire will fall!" – namely, his own). There is a laterality of attention: what his unconscious centers as the explicit object of its concentration turns out to be a mere detail of a picture ordered in a quite different way. His minder thinks of this as of "the overliteralness of primary-process thinking" (61), which it may also be, in that case reflecting the way in which the literal signifiers can be shifted around, remaining serenely equal to themselves all the while that their fundamental meanings and consequences vary wildly. From another perspective, to be sure, we here witness the unexpected aftereffects of that alternation between Fancy and Imagination discussed in an earlier chapter: what was to have embodied the work of Imagination is suddenly displaced and trivialized by the catastrophic centrality of an element of mere Fancy, a hitherto insignificant detail of the context Imagination turned out to presuppose. Here is an example: the world is no longer to be overpopulated. But this welcome development must now be rationalized in retrospect by the deaths of six billion people in the Plague Years (a hitherto non-existent event which rapidly finds its place in our chronological memory of the recent past, like Proust's furniture racing to reach their correct stations in bedroom space before he is completely awake). Is the episode not itself a kind of anti-Utopian fable (the inevitable suffering entailed by all Utopian experiments)?

But that depends on how we read the Utopianism of George's dream director, the sleep specialist William Haber. He certainly has big plans, but one feels that this fable comes down rather hard on him, all things considered, and that his undoubted "will to power" – Nietzsche after all showed that it was active in the smallest as well as in the greatest things – is sometimes denounced mainly as a foil to Le Guin's Taoist agenda:

> The quality of the will to power is, precisely, growth. Achievement is its cancellation. To be, the will to power must increase with each fulfillment, making the fulfillment only a step to a further one. The vaster the power gained, the vaster the appetite for more. As there was no visible limit to the power Haber wielded through Orr's dreams, so there was no end to his determination to improve the world. (128)

Haber's "comeuppance" at the end is the rather predictable moral lesson that serves him right; while Orr's personality is the opposite of his in every way:

> The infinite possibility, the unlimited and unqualified wholeness of being of the uncommitted, the non-acting, the uncarved: the being who, being nothing but himself, is everything. (95)

So Heather sees George's seeming passivity as a remarkable and unusual kind of strength; and even unknowns and passersby seem to draw comfort from it:

So great a joy filled Orr that, among the forty-two persons who had been jamming into the car as he thought these things, the seven or eight pressed closest to him felt a slight but definite flow of benevolence or relief. The woman who had failed to get his strap handle away from him felt a blessed surcease of the sharp pain in her corn … (42)

One may well subscribe to Le Guin's Taoism as it is expressed in such passages without feeling altogether comfortable about the way she uses Haber to score the point. The pop-psychological diagnosis for example: "The doctor was not … really sure that anyone else existed, and wanted to prove they did by helping them" (32). For the point has to be made (and is, over and over again) that Haber wants to improve things and to help people; "to a better world!" (73) is not, for him, an idle toast, whatever unconscious Nietzschean motives stir beneath the surface. His ethos is meant to be contrasted with Heather's:

A person who believes, as she did, that things fit: that there is a whole of which one is a part, and that in being a part one is whole: such a person has no desire whatever, at any time, to play God. (106)

Hers is an ethos of being rather than of praxis:

Things don't have purposes, as if the universe were a machine, where every part has a useful function. What's the function of a galaxy? … What matters is that we are a part. Like a thread in a cloth or a grass-blade in a field. It *is* and we *are*. What we do is like wind blowing on the grass. (82)

But, as with Orr, Le Guin has gone to a good deal of trouble to motivate Haber's character: he is someone who likes to do good and to change things: "I frequently daydream heroics. I am the hero. I'm saving a girl, or a fellow astronaut, or a besieged city, or a whole damn planet. Messiah dreams, do-gooder dreams, Haber saves the world!" (36) The contradiction at the heart of the lesson is the one that inhabits any ethic of becoming what you are already. The problem is that Haber himself, along with his do-gooding personality and complete with his own inner will-to-power, is also already part of the fabric of being. The will to power is not something outside of being, that we could omit in order to exist in some more peaceful state. It is Being itself; as witness the way in which Heidegger is able to transform Nietzsche's version of the impulse (as we traditionally understand it, and as Le Guin understands it) into Aristotelian *energeia*, that is, into the very force of life and activity itself. When it is a question of the totality of being, indeed, how can one presume to pick and choose, to accept Orr's impulses and repudiate Haber's?

The same argument could be used for Orr himself, who, whatever his relationship to being, is also forced into action – very specifically against Haber and against the latter's millenarian schemes which he must somehow arrest and neutralize. For action and changing things are themselves a necessary part of being and implicate the dreamer fully as much as his director. Indeed, the most interesting confusion lies in the matter of Utopian agency itself: is Orr the Utopian, whose dreams change everything without his wanting them to; or is not the true Utopian Haber, who simply wants them to? In that case, Haber would stand as the representative of Fancy, in contrast to Orr's embodiment of the power of Imagination itself. And what is the nature of the strange Utopian power – the exceptionality of the *iahklu'* – that it falls to Orr for a moment to bear? We are apparently not to judge this power as evil or catastrophic (although its results seem almost exclusively to deserve that description): and not the least beauty of the novel lies in the mystery of this strange rhythm at the heart of being itself, shrouded in some of that same mist that surrounds the aliens, whose own improbable unreality is their very representation.

It does not seem particularly promising to argue against the premises and the meaning of a novel; and in fact I do so only in order to bring out its representational problems and contradictions, which emerge starkly if we take *The Lathe of Heaven* to be an anti-Utopian work. If on the contrary we reduce the stakes somewhat, and make of Haber not a Utopian revolutionary, who wishes to change everything and to transform the very totality of being, and read him rather as a New Dealer and a liberal or social democrat, eager for reform rather than revolution, and intent on changing now this, now that, as he encounters the various ills of society one by one on his path; then from an anti-Utopian work the novel swings around into a rather different tradition of inspiration, and *iahklu'* becomes the very code word for revolution itself as the dream of a total process. But this interpretive choice should not be allowed to weaken the fundamental ambiguity here: Le Guin is a Utopian writer with mixed feelings, and offers the constitutive undecidability of a representation which affirms and foregrounds Utopia in the very same act by which it calls it fundamentally into question. This is scarcely surprising insofar as the Taoism which is used as a critical and negative instrument against the Haberian Utopia is itself Utopian in its serenity. .

The author herself has characterized *The Lathe of Heaven* as her tribute to Philip K. Dick; it is certainly the closest she comes to a pastiche of the great flows of schizophrenic metamorphosis that are for many the most unique moments in his work (Lem also undertook several pastiches of these sequences, most notably in *The Futurological Congress* [1970]). But her possibility of doing this is intimately related to the very nature of her philosophical premise here, namely that reality is a seamless web in which no thread can be tugged without a simultaneous alteration of the whole. It is in fact our old friend the synchronic totality, and the passage from one of these totalities to another is the navigation of a delirious and uncharted zone whose being shudders with incomprehensible waves and pulses:

He could not go on talking. His mouth had gone dry. He felt it: the shift, the arrival, the change. The woman felt it too. She looked frightened. Holding the heavy brass necklace up close to her throat like a talisman, she was staring in dismay, shock, terror, out the window at the view … She was there at the center, like [Haber]. And like him had turned to look out the window at the vanishing towers fade like a dream, leave not a wrack behind, the insubstantial miles of suburb dissolving like smoke in the wind, the city of Portland, which had had a population of a million people before the Plague Years but had only about a hundred thousand these days of the Recovery … (63–64)

Perhaps, indeed, Le Guin's very emphasis on the change itself is to be contrasted with the insidious way, in Dick, that reality gets modified without our immediate awareness: the nightmare stirring at the very corner of our field of vision in an otherwise normal world. Compare, in this sense, two of the climactic scenes in these works. On the one hand, the desperate anxieties of the rendezvous given or taken in a world in full temporal and geographical flux:

Orr had made a date, last week, to meet Heather LeLache at Dave's for lunch on Thursday, but as soon as he started out from his office he knew it wouldn't work … He could not find Dave's of course. He couldn't even find Ankeny Street. He remembered it so vividly from so many other existences that he refused to accept, until he got there, the assurances of his present memory, which simply lacked any Ankeny Street at all. Where it should have been, the Research and Development Coordination Building shot cloudward from among its lawns and rhododendrons … He could not recall the name of Heather's firm exactly; was it Forman, Esserbeck, and Rutti, or was it Forman, Esserbeck, Goodhue and Rutti? He found a telephone booth and looked for the firm. Nothing of the kind was listed, but there was a P. Esserbeck, attorney. He called there and inquired, but no Miss LeLache worked there. (123, 125)

On the other, Joe Chip's epic flight to DesMoines, Iowa, through a world rapidly deteriorating into the past:

Can I get to Des Moines in a 1939 LaSalle automobile? He asked himself …. Wait a minute, he thought. Air transportation existed in 1939. If I could get to the New York Airport – possibly in this car – I could charter a flight. Rent a Ford trimotor plane complete with pilot … An hour later he arrived at the airfield, parked and surveyed the hangars, the windsock, the old biplanes with their huge wooden props … Ten minutes later the Curtiss-Wright biplane had been gassed, the prop manually spun, and with Joe Chip and Jesperson aboard, it began weaving an erratic, sloppy path down the runway, bouncing into the air and then collapsing back down again … At three in the afternoon the following day they reached the airfield at Des Moines.[8]

But Joe Chips' temporal regression is the result not of an aberrant wish-fulfillment, but rather of the malignancy of being itself which will later on in *Ubik* be personified by one of Dick's incomparable villains.

What is closer in register is the result, and the sheer ravages of decay and disintegration in the two works. Dick is notoriously the epic poet of entropy and of the transformation of the world into kipple, the layers of dust, the rotting of all that's solid, a destruction of form itself that is worse than death:

> The carpet of the office beneath his feet rotted, became mushy, and then sprouted, grew, alive, into green fibers; he saw that it was becoming grass. And then the walls and the ceiling caved in, collapsed into fine dust; the particles rained noiselessly down like ashes.[9]

(And if we momentarily withhold the last sentence of the paragraph, it is in order parenthetically to add what is less often noticed, that, like Platonov's baste shoes that sprout and come alive like plants,[10] this entropy can also have a far side in resurrection itself: "And the blue, cool sky appeared, untouched, above.")

But in Le Guin the breakdown is motivated:

> The buildings of downtown Portland, the Capital of the World, the high, new, handsome cubes of stone and glass interspersed with measured doses of green, the fortresses of Government – Research and Development, Communications, Industry, Economic Planning, Environmental Control – were melting. They were getting soggy and shaky, like jello left out in the sun. The corners had already run down the sides, leaving great creamy smears. (164–165)

This particular nightmare expresses the emptiness of Haber's being (he is the last "effective dreamer") more than it does any malevolence of the type that drives Dick's preternatural figures (like Palmer Eldritch or Jory). There is certainly aggressivity in Le Guin, but it is identified with the militarists and the misogynists (like the Condors) who far from depriving the world of its ontological reality simply wreck and destroy it.

There is, finally, the question of small business and of Dick's nostalgic fascination with it. But this is also the question of the ending of *The Lathe of*

---

8 Philip K. Dick, *Ubik* (New York, 1969), pp. 138–144. It would be instructive to compare these two nightmarish Western transformation scenes with their postmodern Russian counterparts in Viktor Pelevin's extraordinary *Homo Zapiens* (1999), where the descent into the image cuts far deeper into the sources of commodification and spectacle society.

9 *Ubik*, p. 102.

10 See the chapter on Platonov's *Chevengur* in my *Seeds of Time* (New York, 1994).

Heaven. How indeed to conclude this interminable series of wishes, which is also, for George Orr, the problem of divesting himself from his frightening and mysterious powers? Le Guin achieves this by a series of generic discontinuities that shift the register of the novel, first into the more conventional SF of aliens and galactic warfare, and then onto the level of outright fantasy, in which the benevolent aliens, floating like giant turtles, remove the *iakhlu'* and themselves settle peacefully in a now stabilized Portland like any other wave of American immigrants. Orr's visit to the alien's antique shop, built underneath the old freeway, offers a *deus ex machina* that owes everything to Dick's lifelong obsession with small record stores and with the related traffic in American memorabilia in which Dick's own nostalgia for the American 1950s is so wondrously captured and expressed. At this point, then, the aliens (who seem to share but a single consciousness) probably owe more to Dick's helpful and sympathetic automata, like the Lincoln and the Stanton in *We Can Build You* (1962), than to the more frightening apparitions in the latter's work.

But their previous avatar – the alien seizure of the moon as a response to Orr's effective dream of "peace on earth" – is not only a replay of Wells' paradigmatic *War of the Worlds*; it also dramatizes a fundamental theme of Sartre's theory of collectivities: namely that a group is unified only from the outside, by a common threat or enemy. So it is that George's effective wish for peace on earth has as its logical but unintended result the unification of the human race by an attack from beyond it. And this unexpected consequence has an unexpected consequence of its own, namely to open up Le Guin's narrative to the possibility of a beyond in which its unexplained premise (the "effectiveness" of Orr's dreaming) can itself be grounded, if not explained: a beyond of the historical realism of the Portland text.

Is it any longer possible for the wish-fulfilling text to project its wishes in the form of some naïvely satisfied and satisfying realization? Wish-fulfillments are after all by definition never real fulfillments of desire; and must presumably always be marked by the hollowness of absence or failure at the heart of their most dearly fantasized visions (a point Ernst Bloch never tired of making). Even the process of wish-fulfillment includes a kind of reality principle of its own, intent on not making things too easy for itself, accumulating the objections and the reality problems that stand in its way so as the more triumphantly and "realistically" to overcome them. I have always found Proust's fantasized love letter paradigmatic, not only of the daydream, but of the reality principle it must include in order to be operative and which ends up unraveling the whole process:

> Every night I indulged myself in imagining this letter, I went through the
> motions of reading it, I recited its every sentence to myself. Suddenly I broke
> off, terrified. I had just understood that were I ever to receive a letter from
> Gilberte, it could in any case never be this one, for I had just composed the

latter myself. And from that point on I forced myself to avoid thinking those words I would have liked to have her send me, for fear that by enunciating them I would exclude those very words – the dearest, the most longed for – from the field of possible realizations. Even if, by some improbable coincidence, it should have been this very same letter invented by me that Gilberte on her side would have sent me, in recognizing in it my own work, I should never have had the impression of receiving something that did not come from myself, something real and new, a joy external to my own mind, independent of my will, and truly given by love.[11]

A collective wish-fulfillment, then – the Utopian text – would have to bear the marks of this inner reality principle as well, by which alone it manages to represent its successful achievement. Can we speak here, as Freud might have of dreams, of a compromise between the wish and what contradicts it? That would certainly trivialize the process, and reduce the political content and import of Utopian fantasy to an easily deluded satisfaction. We need a nobler word than *frustration* to evoke the dimension of Utopian desire which remains unsatisfied, and which cannot be felt to have been fulfilled without falling into the world and becoming another degraded act of consumption. Bloch's allegory of the Egyptian Helen might be suggestive in such a conceptual quest (the real Helen having lived through the Trojan War in Egypt, while a simulacrum inhabited Troy): at any rate, what is wanted is a concept which will not transfer the theory of the split subject to the collectivity (see the concluding chapter, below); nor will it encourage an apolitical mysticism of the infinite or the unattainable. The desire called Utopia must be concrete and ongoing, without being defeatist or incapacitating; it might therefore be better to follow an aesthetic paradigm and to assert that not only the production of the unresolvable contradiction is the fundamental process, but that we must imagine some form of gratification inherent in this very confrontation with pessimism and the impossible. At the very least, however, the other path – whereby, as in Le Guin, the Utopian text reflexively charts the impossibility of that achievement and the ways in which the wish outtrumps itself – may also be taken to be a mode whereby the Utopian wish is authentically registered and set down.

11 Marcel Proust, *À la recherche du temps perdu* (Paris, 1987 [1913]), Volume I (*Du côté de chez Swann*), p. 402: "Tous les soirs je me plaisais à imaginer cette lettre, je croyais la lire, je m'en récitais chaque phrase. Tout d'un coup je m'arrêtais effraýe. Je comprenais que si je devais recevoir une lettre de Gilberte, ce ne pourrait pas en tous cas être celle-là puisque c'était moi que venais de la composer. Et dès lors, je m'efforçais de détourner ma pensée des mots que j'aurais aimé qu'elle m'écrivît, par peur en les énonçant, d'exclure justement ceux-là – les plus chers, les plus désirés – du champ des réalisations possibles. Même si par une invraisemblable coincidence, c'eût été justement la lettre que j'avais inventée que de son côté m'eût addressée Gilberte, y reconnaissant mon oeuvre je n'eusse pas eu l'impression de recevoir quelque chose qui ne vînt pas de moi, quelque chose de réel, de nouveau, un bonheur extérieur à mon esprit, indépendant de ma volonté, vraiment donné par l'amour."

7

The Barrier of Time

Say that the present state of the world is the cause of that total state which follows next on it. Here, again, is ... self-contradiction. For how can one state a become a different state b? It must either do this without a reason, and that seems absurd; or else the reason, being additional, forthwith constitutes a new a, and so on for ever. We have the differences of cause and effect, with their relation of time, and we have no way in which it is possible to hold these together. Thus we are drawn to the view that causation is but partial, and that we have but changes of mere elements within a complex whole.

F.H. Bradley[1]

Our perversely formalist approach to Utopia as a genre has thus displaced the inquiry away from content; and it has led us to substitute the question, What difficulties must be overcome in imagining or representing Utopia? for the seemingly more urgent investigation of the nature of Utopian desire and the substance of its hope. We have found indeed that the answer to this second kind of question about the content of the Utopian wish will be a generic or an intertextual one. The content of Utopian form will emerge from that other form or genre which is the fairy tale: if not a purer form of collective desire, then at least a more plebeian one, emerging from the life world of the peasantry, of growth and nature, cultivation and the seasons, the earth and the generations; a figuration that lives on in the industrial or post-industrial era only in the mocking remnant of "birth, copulation and death". It will then scarcely be a matter of astonishment that the Utopian form carries within it this memory of the land and the village, this half-forgotten trace of the experience of peasant solidarity and collectivity.

Even this hypothesis, however, suggests that our next formal problem will be an essentially temporal one, and will have to confront the way in which the secession of the Utopian imagination from everyday empirical Being takes the form of a temporal emergence and a historical transition, and in which the

---

1 *Appearance and Reality* (Oxford, 1930), p. 194.

break that simultaneously secures the radical difference of the new Utopian society makes it impossible to imagine.

This dilemma is best initially confronted in the aporia of the founder himself. Utopus, to be sure, is one of those legendary figures now lost in the mists of time, who seems to have programmed himself out of existence, substituting the more democratic institution of the elective prince (More's Latin word *princeps* is deliberately ambiguous in this context).[2] This actantial form of transition in the person of the vanishing mediator himself is mostly replaced by the no less mysterious temporality of the revolutionary event – peaceful in Bellamy, violent in Morris; while Le Guin's great Utopian and revolutionary founder, Odo, is disambiguated by the fact that, like Moses, or indeed like Marx himself, she dies before resettlement to the promised land and thus can not be suspected of any personal complicity in its later organization and institutionalization. Of modern Utopias only Skinner's is frank enough to pose the personal question in the deliberately unattractive figure of Frazier, a God or creator who is utterly powerless in his new world and lives within it incognito, treated as a harmless crackpot by the new Utopian citizenry).[3]

As for the antinomy at work here, we find its strongest formulation in Rousseau, who, formed on Plutarch, necessarily returns to the latter's portraits of Lycurgus and Solon for his representation of the dilemma posed by such mythic founders. He thus stages a mystery of personification which has survived on into current ideological stereotypes of totalitarianism, in which a fear of the emergence of the Dictator accompanies any such image of a new beginning or an absolute break. Indeed, much of the force of the anti-Utopia as a genre derives from this essentially narrative fear, in which the name of Big Brother or Zamyatin's Benefactor can only itself be figured as an absence or an actantial fiction which has real and baleful results.

Unsurprisingly, Rousseau, with his ideological revulsion for any sort of dependency, offers the clearest and most striking philosophical expression of this antinomy: the mythic founder must be without all human frailties, in order to be able to stand outside a corrupt society and to reform it; but he must also acquire no political or personal prestige from this feat which might otherwise threaten the abuses of the father figure (Stalin) or the charismatic fascist leaders. The dilemma is grist for Rousseau's mill and results in one of those paradoxical formulations which slash through his theoretical texts: "We therefore find combined in the work of legislation two things which seem incompatible: an enterprise far above human powers, and, in order to execute it, an authority which is reduced to nothing."[4] The Legislator must thus be at one and the same

2 See the note on this word in More, *Works* (New Haven, 1963–1997), Volume IV, p. 399.

3 See the episode of Mrs Colson, in B.F. Skinner, *Walden Two* (New York, 1948), pp. 218–221.

4 Jean-Jacques Rousseau, *Oeuvres*, III (Paris, 1964), p. 383: "Ainsi l'on trouve à la fois dans l'ouvrage de la législation deux choses qui semblent incompatibles: une entreprise au-dessus de la force humaine, et pour l'exécuter, une autorité qui n'est rien."

time a God and a non-citizen without any power over the laws thus promulgated: accordingly, Lycurgus commits suicide.

Yet equally characteristically, Rousseau reformulates this dilemma in terms of time and those temporal paradoxes we have here been assimilating to the structural antinomies of narrative itself: indeed, he restages it very much in the form in which modern cultural revolution will reformulate this seemingly unresolvable antinomy:

> In order for an emergent people to develop a taste for the healthy maxims of politics and to follow the fundamental rules of reason as it applies to the State, it would be necessary for the effect to become the cause, for the collective spirit meant to be the result of the institution to have presided over the institution itself, and for men already, before the giving of the laws, to be what the laws were supposed to make them.[5]

Yet in recent times, this conundrum will be attributed to the very paradox of time itself and of what is in history called "transition" and in narratology simply the event itself. The antinomies of cause and effect are today exasperated by the emergence of the notion of system.

Indeed, Bradley's elegant formulation warns us of the self-defeating price to be paid for any truly thoroughgoing exercise of systemic thinking in history; and this, whether we have to do with a relatively contemporary (structural) conception of the synchronic (or of totality, or the mode of production, or the Foucauldian episteme), or simply (as in Bradley) of some state a/state b progression, or indeed with some more general sense of the present as an immense and interrelated web from which not even a dead butterfly can fall at the peril of the whole. The theory of history has certainly moved in this direction: and it is as though the ever greater accumulation of facts about a given period (very much including our own) determines a gravitational shift from diachronic thinking (so-called linear history) to synchronic or systemic modeling. It is a shift that can be measured (following Bradley's hint) by the increasing frequency of attacks on causality (Hume being pressed into post-contemporary service) and even by the hegemonic emergence of various anti-causal doxa.[6] But I think that the attack on "causality" as such is misplaced; Kant has taught us (along with many others) that in that sense cause and causality are mental categories,

---

5 Ibid., p. 383: "Pour qu'un peuple naissant pût goûter les saines maximes de la politique et suivre les règles fondamentales de la raison d'État, il faudrait que l'effet pût devenir la cause, que l'esprit social qui doit être l'ouvrage de l'institution présidât à l'institution même, et que les hommes fussent avant les loix ce qu'ils doivent devenir par elles."

6 See the comprehensive discussion of these historiographico–philosophical debates in Paul Ricoeur, *Time and Narrative*, vol. I (Chicago, 1984), Part Two; and on the relationship between the emergence of new disciplines and the becoming-synchronic of history, Fernand Braudel, *On History* (Chicago, 1980).

about which it makes no sense to assert that they are either true or false. It would be more plausible and useful to think of causality as an essentially narrative category: in which case its current bad press is more easily explained, and can be argued in terms of that multiplicity of "factors" or of historical events and perspectives already alluded to. In other words, as the number of things that historical inquiry is willing to accept as determinants increases – gender relations, writing systems, weaponry – each becomes a candidate for a new version of that "ultimately determining instance" or cause which in its turn dictates a new historical narrative, a fresh way of telling the story of the historical change in question.

For if explanation is the interpretation that makes us grasp necessity as such,[7] then we can understand better how the practice of historical causality has slowly evolved from a diachronic to a synchronic perspective. Diachronic causality, the single string of causes, the billiard-ball theory of change, tends to isolate a causal line which might have been different, a single-shot effectivity (even an ultimately determining instance) which can very easily be replaced by an alternate hypothesis. But if, instead of this diachronic strand, we begin to posit causality as an immense synchronic interrelationship, as a web of overdetermination, a Spinozan substance made up of innumerable simultaneously coexisting cells or veins, then it is harder to object some causal alternative: all causes are already there, in what Hegel called the "ground":

> existence is the indefinite multitude of existents as reflected-into-themselves, which at the same time equally throw light upon one another – which, in short, are co-relative, and form a world of reciprocal dependence and of infinite inter-connection between grounds and consequents. The grounds are themselves existences: and the existents in like manner are in many directions grounds as well as consequents.[8]

A proliferation of narratives thus emerges which raises the terrifying specter of postmodern relativism and which is scarcely reduced by assigning each one its specific sub-field and then attempting to reconstruct some new and more "complex" or "differentiated" discipline as a whole (indeed, the current Luhmannian slogans of complexity and differentiation, or the Althusserian concept of overdetermination, are little more than symptoms of this dilemma, rather than solutions to it). From a limited series of conventional and reassuringly simple narrative options (the so-called master narratives), history becomes a bewildering torrent of sheer Becoming, a stream into which, as Cratylus put it long ago, one cannot even step once.

---

7 Hegel, *Encyclopedia Logic* (Oxford, 1975 [1817]), p. 174: "The aim of philosophy is ... to ascertain the necessity of things."
8 Ibid., p. 179.

It then proves reassuring to abandon these diachronic dilemmas altogether, and to turn towards a perspective and a way of looking at things in which they do not even arise. Such is the realm of the synchronic, and we may well ask ourselves what replaces narrative here and what representational forms are available to articulate this new systemic view of the multiple coexistence of factors or facts, what mode of *Darstellung* could possibly accommodate this historiographic material. Only to do so properly would involve a review of everything from the so-called plotless or poetic, "modernist" novel (*Ulysses* is the quickest shorthand reference) to experiments in historiography from Braudel's *Mediterranean* to Benjamin's *Arcades*, with more than a brief glance at Althusser's conception of structural causality. For the moment it is appropriate to add the warning of the theoreticians of the synchronic that this is not a temporal matter either, and that synchronic history of this kind has nothing to do with a present, eternal or otherwise, and is not to be grasped in terms of lived or existential time.

We stress this (quite proper) proviso in order to point out the obvious, namely that few enough people observe it, and that a slippage from synchronic *Darstellung* into the paradoxes of human temporality is so frequent as to be pronounced inevitable. Thus the systemic or synchronic perspective on events not only makes for representational dilemmas (the latter can always be productive and interesting ones), it also generates low-level or everyday ideological questions about change itself. The more successful the historiographic construction – the conviction that everything is of a piece, that the relations between existences and facts are much stronger than their possible relationship to what is no longer and what is not yet, that actuality is a seamless web and the past (or tradition) a mere intellectual construct in the present – the stronger this case is made intellectually, the more inevitable is our entry into a Parmenidean realm in which some eternal system reigns around us like a noon beyond time only faintly perfumed with the odor of heated plants and informed by the echo of cicadas and the distant and incomprehensible memory of death. Proust and Bergson, Plato and Parmenides: is it idealism as such that generates this ideological illusion, or on the contrary the historiographic arguments that are themselves the source of the idealistic mirage? Or do both spring from some modification in the social order? To offer an answer to these questions is then to propose a specific narrative option (indeed, we have already implicitly suggested one, in evoking the accumulation of information in the contemporary world) which flies in the face of the synchronic hypothesis itself.

So it is that the synchronic historian works against himself: winner loses, as Sartre liked to put it: the more airtight the synchronic system laid in place all around us, the more surely history itself evaporates in the process, and along with it any possibility of political agency or collective anti-systemic praxis. The local changes it is possible to make now obey the law of

Bradbury's crushed butterfly and are laden with unintended consequences. Indeed, the surest arguments against Utopia – as just such a sealed and imputable system beyond the reach of our own concrete synchrony, as a kind of alternate universe to our own, with which it is impossible to communicate – are to be found here, in the doctrine that all such unintended consequences tend towards violence, and that the punctual Utopian intervention, by destroying a customary and conventional order of some kind, leads to tyranny (or totalitarianism, as it used to be called). I will return to these issues later; I raise them now, however, in order to grasp the inextricable relationship between the question of synchrony and that of the construction of Utopian representations.

It thus becomes logical to interrogate the representation of temporality in SF, and in particular of synchrony and of systematizing periodicity, as one step towards the problem of the representation of Utopia as such. We then find that this proves to be less a set of questions turning on the content of a given system – these make up what can be called a kind of anthropological SF[9] – than a more purely formal puzzlement about the possibilities of figuration of a radical historical break which it may be premature even to term a transition. Better, for the moment, to have recourse to the traditional Russian term, the "time of troubles", in which the centers of civilization are destroyed, the cities are deserted and the countryside is ravaged by armed marauders, custom and law are swept away, a social chaos ensuing from which a new social order emerges only slowly and from new and unpredictable, hitherto marginal areas. This kind of historical caesura is a very different concept from that of the Western Middle Ages (after all, a period in its own right, with its own cultural and social stability), and it tends to encourage a cyclical view of history.

Indeed all of these features have found classical representation in one of the central texts of SF's "golden age", the 1941 novella *Nightfall*, by Isaac Asimov (1920–1992). Here it is the planet Lagash whose population descends into barbarism and madness every two and a half thousand years, setting its cities afire and sinking into a new Stone Age, from which it laboriously reinvents civilization and science, technology and enlightenment, only in time to face the next cyclical catastrophe. The trigger is a rare total eclipse, whose cataclysmic effect can be grasped only when we understand that this planet is governed by six suns, one or several of which are always present even dimly during the everyday "nighttime" of the previous period.

To be sure, we need not examine the scientific premise any too closely, since it is rather the mimesis of a scientific premise which is the crucial feature (and which, according to Aristotle, must be plausible rather than necessarily true). Yet science – at least of some *Popular Mechanics* and Sunday supplement variety

9 I list a few of these novels in Chapter 5 as examples of the Enlightenment view of history (see page 59, above).

– has always been thought to characterize the golden age of SF, at least in the US, where the pulps constitute a different kind of beginning for the genre than either its classical prototypes (in Lucian and Cyrano) or its European art-novel progenitors, such as Wells, Čapek and Stapledon.

Indeed, the veteran writer to whom we owe "Nightfall", and whose remarkable and productive career spanned SF's first half-century, once periodized the generic history of that half century as follows: adventure, then a scientific moment, followed by a sociological one.[10] We will interpret the scientific moment in a relatively formal way, although its content need not be underestimated. There is, for example, the well-known episode of Cleve Cartmill's 1944 short story about the atomic bomb, which earned his editor (John Campbell) an investigation by the FBI. Then, too, there is the undoubted influence of imaginary SF projects on real space and scientific research (an influence parallel to that of early twentieth-century SF illustrations on the modernist architects of the day).[11]

Still, it seems to me that literary analysis is best served by a conception of such scientific content as constituting a formal device: here, in other words, a specific scientific effect or mathematical paradox (or, if you prefer, the plausible mimesis of those things) serves as a frame, or better still a pseudo-causal hypothesis to be matched up with a story type of a wholly different order. These two dimensions are somehow to fit together in such a way as to produce a reversible narrative object, a kind of narrative Gestalt which can be seen from two distinct perspectives, the scientific and the non-scientific, each one alternatively serving as the "example" of the other taken as theme (or as the vehicle of the other's tenor, to use an older technical language). In this case, the non-scientific content is relatively more social in character: this is consistent with what is known about the life of Asimov, who is said to have participated in the 1930s in groups which made a systematic study of Marx and Marxism, and whose concept of "psychohistory", in play here and in the *Foundation* series, was suggested by that of the "mode of production".

But we also need to specify the nature of Asimov's third moment in SF history: for the term "social" I have used about the content of "Nightfall" is not altogether the same as what Asimov calls sociological, which I take to designate social satire. It is a long and honorable tradition to date this new period from the publication of Pohl and Kornbluth's *Space Merchants* in 1953. This novel, which was characteristic of American public preoccupations of that period (the titles of some of its mainstream bestsellers – *The Hucksters*; *Organization Man* – are significant markers), dealt with the merchandizing,

10 Isaac Asimov, *Soviet Science Fiction*, (New York, 1962), "Introduction", pp. 10–12.
11 A point Reyner Banham never tired of making, and which came into its own in Archigram. See also Rem Koolhaas on Hugh Ferriss (and on much else) in *Delirious New York* (New York, 1978).

in outer space, of products to which a public had been systematically addicted (shades of P.K. Dick's Can-D and Chew-Z[12] or, indeed, of Coca-Cola or tobacco!). To be sure, "Nightfall" is a typical pulp product, with clichéd dialogue and a dose of stereotypical social satire, with its cartoon Gotham-style investigative reporter, its hidebound academics, its "general public" and its religious fanatics. The notion of a historical system, such as the "high civilization" broken off by the catastrophe, will find its fuller development only in later SF.

In "Nightfall" the scientific paradox is no doubt constituted by the conception of an eclipse of all six suns, caused by the shadow of a hidden twin planet whose existence had until then only been hypothesized. Meanwhile the astronomical ignorance on which these shattering effects are predicated is itself ingeniously explained: one of Lagash's astrologists hypothesizes the movements of a planet within a solar system organized around a single sun, and the greater ease of theoretical research: "astronomers on such a world would start off with gravity probably before they even invent the telescope";[13] and it is clear that with the regularity of the exchange of day and night such scientists would learn something else the inhabitants of Lagash do not suspect.

I think it might be better to take an immediate lesson from our own immediate theme of the synchronic system versus the diachronic narrative, and to rewrite Asimov's periodizing narrative of SF history in terms of so many possible dominants which form different functional constellations in any given period. So here in Asimov, and under the scientific "dominant", the sociological one, the realm of social satire, takes a subordinate place from which it will emerge triumphantly in the next period.

Forty years after Asimov's 1962 preface, indeed, we are in a position to posit several more stages in the development of SF, particularly inasmuch as the "sociological" stage in which he obviously includes his own later work has come in hindsight to seem parochial and a limited form of American culture critique contained by Cold War fears and strategies. Yet the age of Dick and Le Guin does not seem adequately characterized by a move from sociology to psychology either, or by the emergence of those complicated and interesting characters whose alleged absence from SF has so often been deplored by modernist readers of canonical high literature. Psychology is not merely disqualified by its humanist overtones (psychological tricks and paradoxes probably belong back in Asimov's second or "science-and-technology" stage); it also finds itself displaced by psychoanalysis and relegated to the status of a pseudo-science if not to that of applied science and of testing and marketing techniques. "Subjectivity" is a more capacious and less dogmatic category under which to range what we find at work in Dick's hallucinations as well as

---

12 In Philip K. Dick, *The Three Stigmata of Palmer Eldrich* (New York, 1965).
13 Isaac Asimov, "Nightfall", in *Famous Science-Fiction Stories*, ed. R.J. Healy and J.F. McComas (New York, 1957) p. 404.

in Lem's cognitive paradoxes or Le Guin's anthropological worlds: this would add a fourth moment to Asimov's three.

Yet I would also be tempted to take into account the rhetoric and propaganda for a "New Wave" in Science Fiction (particularly in Britain, with Moorcock and his colleagues, but also with Samuel Delany in the US) as the global dawn of a hallucinogenic age, and to infer from all these widely varied symptoms the coming into being at this point of something like a fifth or aesthetic stage of SF. The word is not meant to convey a return to aestheticism or art-for-art's sake in any traditional or regressive fashion, but rather to mark the new centrality of dilemmas of perception and representation as such: dilemmas which foreground the status of language as such, but also the problematization of the Real, as that decenters old-fashioned, formerly stable subjects in Dick, but also generates the marginalities of Delany's social world and the catastrophic instabilities of a whole global system in Ballard's aesthetics of disaster and in the relativisms to which alien visitations and cultures condemn our own parochial values. (We may then wish to posit yet a sixth stage, that of cyberpunk more generally, in the new abstractions of the computer and of globalization and finance capital from the Reagan–Thatcher era on.) We might therefore chart the various stages of SF (not forgetting that they overlap, and that each new one retains the formal acquisitions of the previous ones, and also that the dates are merely symbolic):

1. Adventure, or "space opera", which comes most immediately out of the work of Jules Verne, but could perhaps be marked in the American tradition by Edgar Rice Burroughs' *A Princess of Mars* (1917).
2. Science (or at least the mimesis of science), which might classically be dated from the first SF pulps in Gernsbach's *Amazing Stories*, beginning in 1926.
3. Sociology, or, better still, social satire or "cultural critique", which it is conventional to attribute to the innovation of Pohl and Kornbluth's *Space Merchants* (1953).
4. Subjectivity, or the 1960s: Philip K. Dick's ten great novels are, for example, all written in the concentrated period from 1961 to 1968.
5. Aesthetics, or "speculative fiction", conventionally associated with Michael Moorcock's journal *New Worlds*, which ran from 1964 to 1977; but which in the US is associated with the work of Samuel Delany (1942–).
6. Cyberpunk, which opens with a bang with William Gibson's *Neuromancer* (1984): a general period break which is also consistent, not only with the neo-conservative revolution and globalization, but also with the rise of commercial fantasy as a generic competitor and ultimate victor in the field of mass culture.

But the fourth category, of subjectivity and representation, must also be enlarged to make a place for a second wave of feminism from 1969 onwards, which not only produces a whole new generation of women writers in the SF field, but even more significantly determines a whole renewal and reinvention of the Utopian text itself. In hindsight, then, this new determinant or causal line might well encourage us to rewrite our synchronic system of this fourth or representational stage as an imperative to think all these features together in some new way which makes a central space for gender as such (along with the anthropological aftereffects of the various Third World revolutions during the same period).

Asimov's creative life in fact spanned all these periods, and we should there-fore not be surprised to discover at work within his more youthful productions subordinate elements destined to become the dominants of a later system. Thus the climax of "Nightfall" turns out to have the literal force of the word *aesthetic* – in Greek designating perception as such – and to provide, as the unexpected consequence of Asimov's scientific premise, a dazzling, well-nigh blinding visuality:

> Not Earth's feeble thirty-six hundred Stars visible to the eye – Lagash was in the center of a giant cluster. Thirty thousand mighty suns shone down in a soul-searing splendor that was more frighteningly cold in its awful indiffer-ence than the bitter wind that shivered across the cold, horribly bleak world.[14]

So it is that the meaning of the otherwise incomprehensible word "stars" is revealed every second millennium to the inhabitants of Lagash; and the aes-thetic bonus of pleasure in this seemingly science-oriented puzzle is given in the spectacle at which we stare avidly even as it drives the subjects of the planet mad: the *jouissance* of imaginary excess (and of multiplicity as well).

Galactic visuality is one of the earliest human aesthetics, extending back in time well before its formalization in the zodiac and constellations. In a beauti-ful passage of *Aesthetic Theory*,[15] Adorno singles out fireworks as the very prototype of art's temporality, its fleeting existence as sheer apparition, a dazzling that fades out of being. The stars in the night sky are just such an apparition suspended in time, a multiplicity stretched immobile across space, whose other face is that firmament as the scroll of which Apocalypse tells us that it will be rolled up in the last days. The first forms of perception and artic-ulation impose themselves as the staring light of the planets, the slow separation from each other of those lights from the wheeling rise and fall of the thronged numbers behind them. What defines this perception, however, is a reversal of vision in which it is the stars that look down on us and hold us in their blinding field of vision. This is the fear so uncannily represented by Asimov, that as individuals and as a whole living species we are caught and immobilized in this

14 "Nightfall", p. 410.
15 T.W. Adorno, *Aesthetic Theory* (1997), p. 81.

remorseless gaze of the heavens, very much in the spirit of Sartre and Lacan.[16] It is a primal terror quite unlike the effect of the moon, whose presence is a Utopian promise, as in Le Guin's *Dispossessed* where the orb of Urras means indescribably human and natural richness to the settlers of Anarres, on which on the contrary the lonely emissary gazes with longing and nostalgia.

But we cannot leave "Nightfall" behind us without following up the problem with which we began and interrogating the thread which, if at all, links the two incommunicable worlds of the before and after of this unhappy planet. That thread is religion: the Cultists retain a knowledge of the catastrophe which the most advanced scientists are only now, on its very eve, in the process of discovering. We thus witness a peculiar alliance between two enemies, religion and Enlightenment, against the popular masses who are suspicious of both. But this combination reflects a dialectic: for the two forces constitute the fundamental opposition of the Enlightenment paradigm itself: religion and superstition versus scientific progress. The latter will then provide the *Bildungsroman* narrative of what I have called anthropological SF, which traces the rise of "civilization" across the historical ages; while the other pole of religion will eventually as we have seen migrate into fantasy and provide the Enlightenment paradigm's mirror image: history as the loss of magic and the decline of the "old world" of the village and the order of the sacred.

In SF, however, religion is a kind of mediatory space; it is the black box in which infrastructure and superstructure mysteriously intermingle and celebrate an enigmatic identity – at one with mode of production and culture alike (both of whose concepts it ambiguously anticipates). Religion was perhaps the most ancient organizing concept in the emergence of anthropology as a discipline: the ultimately determining instance for national or racial character, the ultimate source of cultural difference itself, the marker of the individuality of the various peoples in history (a role it still plays in Hegel and whose revival today we can witness in ideologues like Samuel Huntington). It can thus provide the most facile solutions for SF, as a kind of ready-made thought of the other; and at the same time stage the most interesting conceptual dilemmas and form-problems. In a moment we will see it reduced to a more readily manageable and identifiable motif.

But first we need to find translations of Asimov's historical and cyclical figures into some of SF's other modes: here we have the quintessential narrative of one closed system followed by another with which it cannot overlap, and whose problematical continuity with its predecessor is in many ways the central exhibit of the tale, its basic formal effect or paradox. For this story will look rather different when translated into the realm of subjectivity and of

---

16 J.-P. Sartre, *Being and Nothingness* (New York, 1966 [1943]), "The Look"; Jacques Lacan, *Le Séminaire*, Vol. XI (Paris, 1973 [1967]), pp. 70–72.

humanist psychology, where the narrative must find its figuration in terms of individuals rather than long and legendary historical chronologies.

Thus nothing seems quite so remote from the Golden Age-type galactic and historical speculation than Philip K. Dick's world of hallucination and drug-induced vision, or the claustrophobia of his post-historical landscapes, the dreary and artificial off-worlds to which the post-catastrophe earth-dwellers have been forced to emigrate, and whose sensory and experiential impoverishment makes a recourse to pharmacological illusion only too comprehensible. In the episode I wish to use here as a kind of anecdotal epigraph,[17] the recent immigrant to Mars attempts to use the "layout" (as this imaginary Barbie-doll drug setting is commercially termed) as an occasion for an adulterous fling with a neighboring wife, but is too distracted by the imaginary pre-catastrophe landscape – an idyllic beach scene – to make his move. We once again therefore confront two sealed worlds without contact with one another: the real life of an ungrateful Mars and the seamless and timeless dream life of Perky Pat and Walt. Here the problem of a connection between the two – in Asimov figured in terms of religion and tradition – becomes the fateful question of memory: can it be prevented, can it be falsified, how to kick-start it into functioning again? In this case, the bridge across the abyss will take the form of a reminder, a lipstick scrawl by the protagonist to himself on the bathroom mirror, urging him to hurry up. The derisory upshot is that by this time all the other neighbors, male and female alike, have joined the collective fantasy and are only too willing to urge him on: a parody of Utopian collectivity if there ever was one. Sexual disgust is not the only disillusionment such an outcome holds in store for Dick's protagonists, who can also know the inverse state of a nightmarish solipsism in the course of their drugged and schizophrenic hallucinations, the latter now constituting a synchronic system or state from which no escape is possible or even imaginable.

Translated into a more dignified and humanist idiom, however, the dilemmas of memory present a more recognizably SF narrative: as in Le Guin's early *City of Illusions* (1967), where the protagonist suffers an induced amnesia which is designed to prevent him from carrying out his world-salvational mission. Falk is indeed for the moment stranded without an identity or a past on a tribal world terrorized by distant alien conquerors known as the Shing. Something tells him he must undertake the journey to their transcontinental capital (probably the former Denver) in order to recover his memory and remember his mission. The paradigmatic journey across a North America which has regressed to pre-industrial conditions and what are essentially Native American social forms (always Le Guin's Utopian ideal) rehearses her fundamental narrative form without much distinction or interest. It would indeed seem to account for the author's justified dissatisfaction with this particular

17 Philip K. Dick, *The Three Stigmata of Palmer Eldritch* (New York, 1965).

work, which she wrongly attributes to its mingling of fantasy and SF, of Tolkien-inspired elements with the post-atomic technologies of the latter. In fact, we find this same "inadmissible" combination in one of her most significant and successful late works, *Always Coming Home* (1985), with its marriage of tribal organization and cybernetic infrastructure. The more plausibly indicted formal flaw might well lie in the attempt to combine the geographical plot with the kind of psychological denouement we are discussing here.

The novel finds its resolution, at any rate, in introspection and a properly psychological discovery: Falk is himself a descendant of those original settlers who had to flee Earth at the time of the Shing invasion. As his people have lost touch with their ancient homeland, and more particularly as they have not yet acquired the wonder-working technology of the ansible – that instrument of simultaneous galactic intercommunication invented by Shevek in *The Dispossessed* and in one way or another the symbolic and ideological center of Le Guin's cosmos, here present by way of its very absence – they must send an agent back to reconnoiter, and that agent is none other than Falk himself. It would be tedious to try to explain why the Shing find themselves obliged to wipe his previous memory without altogether destroying it (in fact, they need him to find their pathway to destroy their ancient enemies, now somewhere in outer space); but the premise of the restoration of the previous memory and identity is the total obliteration of the present one. It is thus between these two equally intolerable alternatives that Falk finds himself poised: the loss of his present identity or the permanent eclipse of the old one. This figuration then, far more powerfully than Asimov's cyclical chronology, allows us to glimpse again that fundamental anxiety of Utopia, to which we will return in greater detail later on, namely the fear of losing that familiar world in which all our vices and virtues are rooted (very much including the very longing for Utopia itself) in exchange for a world in which all these things and experiences – positive as well as negative – will have been obliterated. "My project", as Sartre puts it, "is a rendezvous I give myself on the other side of time, and my freedom is the fear of not finding myself there, and of not even wanting to find myself there any longer."[18] What is then so often identified as Utopian boredom corresponds to this withdrawal of cathexis from what are no longer seen as "my own" projects or "my own" daily life. This is meanwhile the sense in which depersonalization as such becomes a fundamental or constituent feature of Utopia as such.[19]

18 Sartre, *Being and Nothingness*, p. 73.
19 See my *A Singular Modernity* (London, 2003) for a discussion of depersonalization as a "fundamental tendency" in modern philosophy in general: I might have added that (famously since Keats and "negative capability") it is also very central indeed in modernist aesthetics and in particular in modern poetry: thus, Fernando Pessoa's "Degrees of Lyric Poetry" (five in number) are all intensifying forms of depersonalization (see Irene Ramalho Santos' *Atlantic Poets* [Dartmouth, 2003], pp. 14, 77–78).

But for the moment it is the narrative solution to this dilemma, rather than the dilemma itself, which interests us:

> to escape the utter panic welling up in him he looked around for any object to fix on, reverting to early trance-discipline, the Outcome technique of fixing on one concrete thing to build up the world from once more ... The book: he held it in his hands ... Columns of beautiful meaningless patterns, lines of half-comprehensible script, changed from the letters he had learned long ago in the First Analect, deviant, bewildering. He stared at them and could not read them, and a word of which he did not know the meaning rose up from them, the first word:
>
> The way ...[20]

The "Way" is of course the Tao, the central reality of Le Guin's metaphysics, which presides over all her work just as it benevolently offers George Orr a transcendental bridge across the convulsions of diachrony. But Le Guin did not bother to invent so cumbersome a psychological apparatus to explain how Orr managed to hold a fading memory of the past together with the newly wished (and often catastrophically different) present. Meanwhile, one feels that the Tao here, in *Planet of Exile*, is little more than contingent content, a pretext for endowing the mechanisms of memory with meaning (or as the Russian Formalists might put it, with "motivating" it): would not any printed text have done as well, or are we to grasp some unique power in the single word, the single syllable, the single character? I feel that it is neither superfluous nor gratuitous to recall at this point Brecht's great poem on the writing down of the *Tao Te Ching* – and to commemorate the customs officer, who has the merit of asking the Master what he meant and requesting a written version, before the sage on his buffalo and his little helper disappear forever around the bend into the forest and into legend:

> Sprach der Knabe: "Dass das weiche Wasser in Bewegung
> Mit der Zeit den machtigen Stein besiegt.
> Du verstehst, das Härte unterliegt."

Said the boy: "He taught how quite soft water, by attrition over the years will grind strong rocks away. In other words, that hardness must lose the day."[21]

Such is the democratic teaching of Brecht's Lao-tse, which still retains and envelops the more mystical sense of the rhythms of time.

---

20 Ursula K. Le Guin, *Planet of Exile* (New York, 1966), p. 138.
21 Bertolt Brecht, "Legend of the Origin of the Book Tao-te-ching on Lao tse's Road to Exile", *Poems 1913–1956* (New York, 1976), pp. 314–316; "Legende von der Entstehung des Buches Taoteking auf dem Weg des Laotse in die Emigration", *Werke* (Frankfurt, 1988), XII, 33.

What the Brecht reference makes clear, however, is that in all these cases we have to do with writing and with script. If the psychologists continue to talk about "memory traces", the expression, in the continuing absence of any genuinely physical referent, remains a figural one in which the memory of a past event is compared to a "trace", that is to say, to a kind of writing. But Asimov's millenarian religious cult also, like all religious traditions, includes within itself as its fundamental instrument of transmission a sacred scripture of some kind; while even Dick's lipstick scrawl on the mirror remains a form of *écriture*, reminding us dimly of those desperate messages left by serial killers at the scene of their crime.

We do not need to plunge into the intricacies of Derrida's early work to agree that the seemingly very different concepts of writing and time are in reality profoundly complicitous and interrelated: whether the very idea of language is the result of an incapacity to think time coherently or the other way round, we do not have to decide. But that both are secretly inhabited by a humanistic (or metaphysical) illusion is symbolically revealed by the very conception of the ansible and by the ideology of some simultaneous communication in the present which it promises and embodies, while the unique value of the Utopian text also lies in its function as a memory trace, but as a message from the future, something foreshadowed in distorted form by all the great scriptures, which give themselves as messages of otherness, but transmitted in the past.

These incomprehensible written messages have their archaeological analogies, particularly in the potsherds and cultural fragments of the museum as such, which becomes a kind of vast message written in an unknown language of objects. Inevitably the museum makes its paradigmatic appearance in the foundational text of modern Science Fiction:

> I found the Palace of Green Porcelain, when we approached it about noon, deserted and falling into ruin … Within the big valves of the door – which were open and broken – we found, instead of the customary hall, a long gallery lit by many side windows. At the first glance, I was reminded of a museum. The tiled floor was thick with dust, and a remarkable array of miscellaneous objects was shrouded in the same grey covering … Going towards the side I found what appeared to be sloping shelves, and clearing away the thick dust, I found the old familiar glass cases of our own time …[22]

Yet Wells' museum registers our own earthly future as a past which is the sorry history of human devolution: a prophetic archaeology whose time paradox consists in the reversal of the one that interests us here, and secures its shock – like the encounter on the beach at the end of *Planet of the Apes* (1968) – by

---

22 H.G. Wells, *The Time Machine*, in *The Time Machine/War of the Worlds* (Greenwich, CT, 1968 [1895, 1898]), pp. 75–76.

demonstrating that difference is identity, and that these alien artifacts are in fact relics of our own future, and transform a break into a grim continuity. In fact, the Time Traveler learns nothing from them, save a gloomy *fin de siècle* vision of entropy, and ends up ransacking this museum for possible weapons, as do those later castaways in *The Mote in God's Eye* (1974), who, like visitors to Asimov's Lagash, are able to read a sorry history of cyclical catastrophe and resurrection in the weapons they find there.[23]

The Strugatskys' Zone is a rather different kind of museum, whose objects tell us nothing about its alien visitors or their history, but emit powerful signals of sheer otherness. So also the strange object with which Ian Macauley is confronted on his arrival on Sigma Draconis III:

> A sort of pear-shaped thing here, with a hook on the narrow end, about a metre and a half long … and next a cluster of five corroded bars, like the frame of a child's swing … and next a sort of plate, a concave shallow disk with four large and four small protuberances spaced equidistantly around its circumference …[24]

This particular archaeologist is also a linguist, as is appropriate for the philological work that seeks to reconstruct alien life as a whole (and in particular to search for the secret of its decline and extinction). Asimov's scriptural trace gives way, in Brunner, to a whole collection of enigmatic objects, which the linguist–archaeologist must read like a detective deciphering clues; and indeed at this point the SF novel of alien reconstruction asymptotically approaches that of the detective story as such.

Unfortunately for these galactic detectives, however, no Rosetta Stone can be imagined for such a language:

> In the case of Earthly languages, however dead, there is always the chance of finding a living language, or a dead language already deciphered, that bears some relationship to it, however faint. Failing that, there is at least the fact that any Earthly language was written by human beings with human ways of thought. That makes a starting point, however feeble. None of this is the case with the para-symbols [alien writing], so that they constitute a problem that clearly has no solution.[25]

This is indeed what will bring Stanislaw Lem to the conclusion that alien life is radically unknowable, as we shall see in the next chapter. Still these SF linguists

---

23 Another interesting Motie museum will be referred to in Chapter 9: a historical museum in which commemorative paintings of the past speak, and exhibits from various historical epochs are inhabited by living specimen creatures.

24 John Brunner, *Total Eclipse* (New York, 1974), p. 50.

25 Isaac Asimov, *The Gods Themselves* (New York, 1972), pp. 35–36.

of the future, who have naturally already solved the mysteries of Mohenjo-Daro and of the Etruscans, are only too eager to confront the puzzle of alien language and life, thereby placing their creators in the even more uncomfortable situation of having to invent the latter out of whole cloth in the first place.

The SF novelist thus shares, but to a metaphysically far greater degree, that problem of the construction of a "double inscription" which marks the vocation of the mystery writer: namely that of inventing some first narrative which is to be hypothetically reconstructed as "fact" in the second or properly narrative time of the detective himself. It is a distinction that goes back to Aristotle's differentiation of myth and plot – the original legend, rearranged on stage into dramatic episodes by the playwright; and then reinvented by the Russian Formalists (fable and "suzhet"), and after them Genette. "Who cares who killed Roger Ackroyd?" Edmund Wilson famously wondered; and perhaps it is less the solution than the very deductive process itself which is the true focus of our interest and fascination. Even the Great Detective, with all his eccentricities, is only as charismatic as his Great Deductions. The consequence is unhappily not unlike the phenomenologists' account of the act – serving a tennis ball, for example – which must fail in order for us to become conscious of it. So the Great Deduction must always be just slightly skewed or flawed in order for us to grasp it as such; and in order to distract us from a solution which would inevitably fall beneath the Wilsonian judgment. Thus the grandeur of George C. Scott's supreme act of intellection in *The List of Adrian Messenger* (John Huston, 1963) consisted in the properly linguistic flair with which this amateur detective construed the victim's delirious ravings, as reported by a French witness: "the last brush: no more brushes! all gone!" Scott conjectures that in reality the dying man had pronounced a synonym of the English "brush", namely the word "broom", itself a homonym of the name of the family – Brougham – whose heirs are in the process of being successively eliminated. The flaw lies in the supposition that the Frenchman's unconscious would have known English well enough to have been capable of making this mistake: on the other hand, it seems possible that only a foreign speaker would have been tempted to do so; and this slight hesitation between plausibility and improbability endows the Great Deduction with its electrifying and paradigmatic value.

Seen in this way, it becomes clear that the SF author is placed in a position of divine creation well beyond anything Agatha Christie or even Aristotle might have imagined; rather than inventing a crime of some sort, the SF writer is obliged to invent an entire universe, an entire ontology, another world altogether – very precisely that system of radical difference with which we associate the imagination of Utopia.

Now it is true that Ian Macauley's Great Deduction benefits from a few previous findings and in particular from prior knowledge of the Draconians themselves:

We know, roughly, what they looked like – bodies like two matching crab shells one above the other, four short walking limbs, two grasping limbs, all tipped with tubular claws down which ran nerve channels, and composed of a modified version of their hidelike skin, as are human nails. We know, or think we know, that they are possessed of a sense we don't have, though many fishes do: the ability to perceive electromagnetic fields. We suspect the many crystals we've found still impregnated with such fields, after the manner of a tape recording, were their counterpart of inscriptions.[26]

The electromagnetic nature of the aliens' language, or at least of their sensibility, along with his knowledge of the rather unstable weather of Sigma Draconis III, enables Ian to conjecture a keen interest of its inhabitants in the passage of electrical storms and to complete his Great Deduction of the function of the mysterious object we have already mentioned (it is a barometer). This achievement then sets up the even greater problem for us of the nature of the crystals, conjectured to be a form of writing, and beyond that, the reason for the extinction of the alien civilization itself.

This larger puzzle then makes up the topical relevance of John Brunner's beautiful and melancholy fable *Total Eclipse* (1974), which is allegorical on both levels of its "double inscription": the reconstructed history of the extinction poses the question – "is the same [fate, namely extinction] likely to happen to us?";[27] while the history of its reconstruction asks the rather different allegorical question of how we can possibly understand radical difference, whether it is the difference of this alien civilization or that of Utopia itself. The first question is then redoubled within the work itself, for the Earth from which the archaeologist-explorers have come is racked with atomic warfare and famine (and without the benefit of an ansible), thereby imperiling the very survival of the human colony on Sigma Draconis III itself.

Most SF Great Deductions skip over the linguistic dilemmas – which involve something perhaps even more momentous than the invention of another world, namely the invention of another, and non-human, language – either by omitting the intricacies of linguistic categories as such, or by having the aliens learn English instead (as in *The Mote in God's Eye*). Ian Macauley's solution involves a rather different and non-linguistic method, one which indeed takes us back to fundamental nineteenth-century debates on historiography and properly historical forms of understanding. Of particular relevance is Dilthey's distinction between *Erklären* and *Verstehen*, or Explanation and Understanding respectively: two modes of thinking which distinguished the procedures of the hard or natural sciences from the *Geisteswissenschaften* (imperfectly translated as "the human sciences"). This is a belated rehearsal

26 *Total Eclipse*, p. 3.
27 Ibid., p. 12.

of Vico's great *verum factum* principle, according to which we can truly under-stand only what we have ourselves made, or in other words history; but not what God has made, or nature. Dilthey's distinction supplements this one by stipulating that we can formulate laws for nature, or in other words *explain* the latter's dynamics and operations; but that we cannot *understand* those opera-tions in the way in which we understand other human beings, their acts and motivations, and even the historical processes that emerge from them.

Yet there is here yet a further underlying premise, concerning the way in which we are able to "understand" other people. "Empathy" (*Einfühlung*) is a late nineteenth-century specification of the much older notion of sympathy, by which our possibility of "putting ourselves in the other person's place" is named and supposedly conceptualized. We do this, Dilthey thought, by reading cultural codes but above all by way of expressivity, which offers something like a mold into which our sympathies with the other can flow and become crystallized. The fascination with the varieties of human facial expressions and gesturality did not begin with Darwin's great compilation, nor did it end with the James–Lange theory of emotion (which posits the priority of the physiologi-cal "expression" over its lived experience). Modern theories of communication are no doubt still refinements of this essentially humanist conception of inter-personal relations, which necessarily comes to grief on sheer otherness and the problem of the radically alien.

Yet the great detectives have often made a fetish of empathy (or "intu-ition"), most dramatically in Georges Simenon's Maigret novels, in which the inspector always imaginatively places himself in the criminals' shoes (just as this unbelievably productive novelist does in his characters').[28] It is thus alto-gether fitting that Brunner's archaeological detective-linguist should espouse the same method, and fashion a model of the Draconian body large enough to contain the investigator himself, and to allow him the freedom, but also the constraints, of the characteristic movements of this species. Various pros-theses are evolved in order to adapt human kinetics to Draconian: one for the manipulation of the four running limbs, one to convey approximations of the electro-magnetic signals; while this imaginary identification is rein-forced by heavy doses of hypnotism. Ian's plan is to spend a month living the life of a Draconian in the various cities and buildings which have already been excavated on the planet, at the end of which he promises himself a leap of illumination and understanding (which the novel does in fact provide). A certain number of shortcuts may strike the reader as cheating: it is for example hard to imagine how he would have made his Great Deduction without the existence of a variety of distantly related (non-sentient) animal cousins to the aliens, or, even more specifically, without the prior knowledge (perhaps gleaned from those related species) that Draconian individuals all go through

28   See my *The Prison-House of Language* (Princeton, 1972), pp. 204–205.

a sexual cycle, in which "infancy was a neuter stage; there followed a male stage; and after that a comparatively short female stage prior to the infertility of old age".[29]

After the rigor of Brunner's construction, it may seem frivolous to return to Asimov, this time a late work which usefully brings us back to the representational problem which was central for us here, namely the possibilities of communication between two alternate and utterly separate worlds or systems. *The Gods Themselves* (1972), to be sure, does not bring much imaginative energy to bear on the problem of communication as such; and this is probably why this interesting novel does not constitute any very durable addition to the canon. Indeed, its premise remains very much within the form we have attributed to the Golden Age, the matching of a scientific riddle (how there could be such a thing as Plutonium 186) against this or that viable narrative content of a different type.

The work is in fact a triptych which deploys interesting (but equally unrealized) generic discontinuities: a drama of academic politics, followed by a pale *symboliste* fable about aliens; and on into a conclusion heavily orchestrated with the physical details of human life on the moon, the effects of lowered gravity on the body, and so forth. In a schematic way, we can say that the second and third parts offer two distinct othernesses (or negations) to the first or human realistic representation: for Part II is a non-human para-Universe; while Part III offers a kind of synthesis of otherness and familiarity, still human but (perhaps) post-human in physical and even mental ways.

Yet all this is premised on the initial contact between two simultaneous alternate worlds; and one can appreciate Asimov's inventiveness by observing his extrapolation of an impossible chemical isotope into the idea of a barely perceptible leak between the two sealed universes. With this extraordinary and unparalleled event, the narrative dynamic is given and a first mechanism is constructed to facilitate the exchange:

> The plutonium/tungsten can make its cycle endlessly back and forth between Universe and para-Universe, yielding energy first in one and then in another, with the net effect being a transfer of twenty electrons from our Universe to theirs per each nucleus cycled. Both sides can gain energy from what is, in effect, an Inter-Universe Electron Pump.[30]

Not only is communication here modeled on market exchange (at least the Structuralists were decent enough to interpose Mauss' anthropological thesis of the gift between their concept of the exchange of signs and the cruder contemporary forms of market capitalism), but it seems to corroborate the

---

29 *Total Eclipse*, p. 40.
30 *The Gods Themselves*, p. 27.

most deliriously optimistic claims of free-market rhetoric, where everybody profits and nobody loses anything: "a road", as one of the characters puts it, "that is downhill both ways".[31] Indeed, the laws in each Universe are sufficiently different for the necessary technical loss in each to amount to a gain (I omit the scientific "explanations"). This is communicational immediacy with a vengeance – a coexistence of radically distinct systems which, whatever its hard science, appears to fly in the face of the physics of imperialism or even the simplest mechanics of social class.

Needless to say, it is also an illusion; and each world proves to be menaced in its very existence by an ongoing transmission that heats up one Universe and cools the other off to dangerous proportions. This is also the moment in which real communication between the universes begins, and the dissidents on each side attempt to publicize the dangers involved in what are for the power structures and the populations at large simply a miraculous source of free energy (their social effects on the two universes are never really explored). Here the potentiality of this text for some properly Utopian figuration is replaced by a host of more conventional political parallels, at which point, predictably, a happy ending and the prospect of liberal pluralism reappears. It turns out that there are still more alternate Universes, exchange with which can modify the perilous long-term effects of the merely dual (or unilateral) contact: the critique of economic liberalism is thereby canceled by an enlargement of the network to what we might anachronistically call global dimensions. But it is less Asimov's personal ideology which is at issue here than the way in which this outcome once again corroborates the view that political and social experience both enable and limit scientific research and invention, rather than the other way round, as most intellectual histories presuppose. A new form must first emerge in the concrete realm of social relations before it can be transferred to more specialized domains of intellectual and productive life: this is in effect the deeper meaning of Marx's observation that human history only confronts its subjects with such problems as they can already solve.

In that spirit, what the sixties does seem to have enabled Asimov to think and to express in a new way is feminism, which is not only to be detected in the embarrassingly jocular and awkward newly found "sexual freedoms" of the text, but above all in the identification of the dissidents in both universes as female. Gender in fact unexpectedly becomes the central theme of this novel, by way of the para-Universe, which turns out to include inhabitants with three different genders, along with a mysterious non- or post-sexual type of being (the so-called Hard Ones, as opposed to the tripartite Soft Ones). Shades of Brunner's androgynous Draconians! We will come back to this unexpected turn in a later chapter. For the moment it is sufficient to underscore

31 Ibid., p. 47.

our findings in this one, namely that temporal questions – the diachrony of synchrony, the matter of the transition to Utopia, the representational dilemmas in thinking historical time itself – seem fatally to lead in almost all cases to the rather different problem of whether alien life, radically different sentient beings, can be imagined at all. Swift could only imagine a Utopian existence by populating it with non-human forms, which he nonetheless represented under the guise of earthly animals. Withdrawing from human society, his returning narrator prefers to spend the best part of his time in the barn:

> My Horses understand me tolerably well; I converse with them at least four Hours every Day. They are strangers to Bridle or Saddle; they live in great Amity with me, and Friendship to each other.[32]

In much the same way, we also must now spend time with the aliens before confronting Utopia directly.

---

32 Jonathan Swift, *A Selection of His Works* (New York, 1965), p. 280.

8

The Unknowability Thesis

But before doing so, we need to set in place an implacably negative and skeptical position, that of the great Polish novelist Stanislaw Lem (1921–), which is however not without its own concomitant ethical imperative, as we shall see. Here the problem of diachrony and its possible continuities is once again transferred to the question of synchronous systems (as we have observed happening in the development of the preceding chapter). Yet Lem constitutes an intermediate stage between the system and the alien, insofar as his enigmatic beings are both all at once; and the problem of representation is resolved by the relatively more modernist position that it is in any case impossible. We need to set in place one remarkable foreshadowing of Lem's doctrine: and that is the intricate and unresolvable puzzle Arthur C. Clarke sets out for us in his *Rendezvous with Rama* (1972), one of the permanently fascinating texts in the canon, whose luster was not dimmed by a series of meretricious sequels.[1] Rama, a mysterious object entering the solar system, proves to be an artificial construction which seems to be waiting for the life form for which it has presumably been prepared. Its human explorers are therefore able to establish the presence of a mystery to be solved, without being able to solve it before the artifact is again flung beyond our solar system by the sun's gravity, on a course that has evidently been plotted well in advance. Clarke's alien mystery story is somehow uniquely more satisfying than any of those with solutions (including his own later sequels) and suggests that God's creation is best imitated by the invention of questions rather than of answers.

If Clarke was agnostic in his representation of alien otherness, Stanislaw Lem is resolutely atheist. Three works centrally document this position, which may be said to be an offshoot of his more general scientific and Enlightenment philosophy, as outlined in his non-fictional computer treatises and those more

---

1 Arthur C. Clarke (1917–) is one of the major figures of British SF, uniting a serious commitment to space technology and speculative science with an idiosyncratic mysticism, a combination epitomized by the concluding "Star Child" episode of the film *2001* (1968), on which he collaborated with Stanley Kubrick.

humorous tales which form something like a Lewis Carroll or Deleuzian compendium of scientific paradox, as well as in his skepticism with respect to the possibilities of the science-fictional genre itself. Perversely, this Science Fiction is designed to demonstrate, in some Kantian way, its own absolute limits. Here *His Master's Voice* (1968) stands as the bitter paradigm case of the impossibility of understanding the Other (unless one also wants to adduce the fiasco of the grim later novel of that name [1986]): a signal from outer space that can never • be deciphered, yet which stands as a pretext for the most ingenious human conjectures (as does the science of Solaristics in the related novel we will examine shortly) and also offers a projective screen for revealing the most toxic impulses and energies of that planet-bound human race which we are. The narrator of this novel is no doubt Lem's most fully realized or "realistic" character, with a psychology as interesting as any in post-Dostoeyevskian fiction, and one of the most repulsive as well, a "genius" seething with ressentiment and with a self-loathing that expands to include the race of which he is a member. Here Lem's skepticism breaks the conventional form of storytelling, insofar as the narrative of successive failures leads nowhere, its litany of frustrations even formally unsatisfying as a parodic cancellation of the "grand narrative" of scientific discovery and ultimate problem-solving. As such *His Master's Voice* becomes Lem's most fascinating and dislikable work, whose empty lesson we need to supplement with two other more rewarding (and famous) novels.

As is well-known, *Solaris* (1961) rewrites the skepticism into a more viable fable, in which a uniquely single and singular alien being – the human observers assimilate it to an ocean that covers the entirety of a remote planet bearing the title name – resists scientific inquiry with all the serene tenacity of the godhead itself (as which, indeed, certain schools of thought interrogate it). Precise measurements document the slight, barely perceptible deviation of the planet's movements from all known natural laws, and reinforce the general consensus that its "ocean" is in fact a sentient being. A bravura section on Solaristics anticipates Lem's passion for writing reviews of non-existent and imaginary books by projecting a whole library of all possible approaches to the study of this unknown.

The theories recapitulate the development and eventual stagnation of each new line of scientific inquiry in turn; and indeed, in the immense logical variety of the theories and schools and the extraordinary ingenuity and mental energy invested in them, Lem has given us a virtual representation of science itself, "hard" science and not just knowledge, with a miniature sociology of the scientists, a history of their funding, and an account of the role of experimentation and of scientific publication as well. This history of an imaginary science – worth any number of realistic novels on the subject – extends the drama and implications of this particular "first contact" far beyond an ingenious contribution to that particular sub-genre of SF and makes it over into a metaphysical parable of the epistemological relation of the human race to its not-I in general: where that not-I is not merely nature, but another living being.

Meanwhile, the being in question is described and yields clues and hints of its own (some of which the reader is allowed to develop independently). Thus, we are given to understand that what is peculiar about the immense and unique solitary being is the result of the mediate position of its planet between two stars, in a situation in which life is not supposed to be able to develop at all: this situation determines an unstable trajectory which the sentient being has seemingly come into existence to correct (whence the initial data which failed to correspond to the physical laws governing inert matter). This initial datum sets in place a radical difference in the situation faced by this life form, a situation for which human beings have no equivalent and which they are unable to imagine. Yet did not human intelligence itself (or consciousness) develop as an analogous response to an unresolvable structural dilemma of this kind, a permanent state of tension and danger for which no instinctual solution was found?

Meanwhile, however, the ocean conveniently provides its own material for study and scientific investigation. Seemingly indifferent to the presence of these minute human life forms (it is itself even bigger than the whole of Earth's surface), and as though dreaming, or reflecting on its own thoughts, it periodically throws up immense spatial phenomena, sometimes of more stable appearance and indeterminate duration: mountains, islands, fantastic architecture, expressive forms of all kinds, which have been classified into three general groups: the extensors, the mimoids, and the symmetriads – themselves for over a century the object of the most intense and systematic study and scientific fascination. This is as it were the aesthetic production of Solaris, and it yields no result save to confirm Kant's doctrine that art is a production without a concept.[2] The fatal accidents that accompany scientific interrogation of these formations only appear in one specific instance (when a pilot falls directly into the ocean

---

2 Stanislaw Lem, *Solaris* (New York, 1970 [1961]), pp. 121–122: "The human mind is only capable of absorbing a few things at a time. We see what is taking place in front of us in the here and now, and cannot envisage simultaneously a succession of processes, no matter how integrated and complementary. Our faculties of perception are consequently limited even as regards fairly simple phenomena. The fate of a single man can be rich with significance, that of a few hundred less or so, but the history of thousands and millions of men does not mean anything at all, in any adequate sense of the word. The symmetriad is a million – a billion, rather – raised to the power of N: it is incomprehensible. We pass through the vast halls, each with a capacity of ten Kronecker units, and creep like so many ants clinging to the folds of breathing vaults and craning to watch the flight of soaring girders, opalescent in the glare of searchlights, and elastic domes which criss-cross and balance each other unerringly, the perfection of a moment, since everything here passes and fades. The essence of this architecture is movement synchronized towards a precise objective. We observe a fraction of the process, like hearing the vibration of a single string in an orchestra of supergiants. We know, but cannot grasp, that above and below, beyond the limits of perception or imagination, thousands and millions of simultaneous transformations are at work, interlinked like a musical score by mathematical counterpoint. It has been described as a symphony in geometry, but we lack the ears to hear it." See also note 8, below.

itself) to betray any awareness of these systematic explorations and probes by another life form (the pilot's child later rises up in a gigantic simulacrum).

This lack of specific attention to humans may be assumed to have come to an end shortly before the protagonist's arrival on the planet: in exasperation at its silence, the ocean's surface has been subjected by its explorers to intense x-ray bombardment (the dose is scarcely lethal, but can nonetheless be ranged under that typically human option of destroying the planet and its life form altogether). This is the point at which "visitors" appear, strange yet familiar human figures without memory, which seem to have emerged out of some nameless guilt in the various scientists' past (one of whom at length commits suicide). The subjective life of these visitors, if one can call it that, seems to be limited to a determination to keep their host present and visible at all times; thus serving as something of an objective correlative for the intolerable exasperation often felt by a lover's overwhelming possessiveness.[3] Kelvin's own visitation by a lover for whose death he was responsible becomes a drama of neurotic dependency which results in one of the most remarkable scenes in the novel, when the "visitor", a frail and beautiful girl, feels some nameless anxiety at his apparent absence (he has inadvertently pushed the bathroom door closed behind him):

> I heard the sound of running water, the clinking of bottles; then, suddenly, all sound ceased. I waited, my jaw clenched, my hands gripping the door handle, but with little hope of holding it shut. It was nearly torn from my grasp by a savage jerk. But the door did not open; it shook and vibrated from top to bottom. Dazed, I let go of the handle and stepped back. The panel, made of some plastic material, caved in as though an invisible person at my side had tried to break into the room. The steel frame bent further and further inwards and the paint was cracking. Suddenly I understood: instead of pushing the door, which opened outwards, Rheya was trying to open it by pulling it towards her. The reflection of the lighting strip in the ceiling was distorted in the white-painted door-panel; there was a resounding crack and the panel, forced beyond its limits, gave way. Simultaneously the handle vanished, torn from its mounting. Two bloodstained hands appeared, thrusting through the opening and smearing the white paint with blood. The door split in two, the broken halves hanging askew on their hinges. First a face appeared, deathly pale, then a wild-looking apparition, dressed in an orange and black bathrobe, flung itself sobbing upon my chest.[4]

---

3 An unhappy situation paradigmatically dramatized in Robert Hichens' classic ghost story, "How Love Came to Professor Guildea", in *Great Tales of Terror and the Supernatural*, ed. P.C. Wagner and Herbert Wise (New York, 1994). Proust also insists on the way in which the lover is often insufferable to the beloved, who (as is customary in Proust) responds with cruelty.

4 *Solaris*, pp. 93–94.

The problem of the visitors is both a clue to the "thinking" of the sentient ocean and something of a diversion from that "purer" science-fictional problem, in the sense in which it introduces questions of the personal or private meaning of the apparitions, whose origin seems to lie simply in the intensity with which they have registered on the memory (either consciously or unconsciously) and not with any other feature of the putative relationship (even though guilt is of course the most obvious magnifier of the trace in question). It is, however, henceforth proven to everyone's satisfaction that the ocean is not only sentient but also the cause and origin of the material hallucinations, which can be seen as a kind of reverse experiment it has undertaken on the human investigators whose presence it has just become aware of.

Is the ocean punishing or torturing its guests? The suggestion shows that even now, faced with this overwhelming new information about Solaris, humans remain the prisoners of an anthropomorphic philosophical system. They seem unable to judge Solaris according to any other coordinates than those of Carl Schmitt – friend or foe – and of Kant himself – pleasure or pain. The conceptual limitation then confirms Lem's ultimate message here, namely that in imagining ourselves to be attempting contact with the radically Other, we are in reality merely looking in a mirror and "searching for an ideal image of our own world".[5] This is why there is a way in which the operation is not merely self-defeating but even suicidal, for in order to strip away the anthropomorphism, we must somehow do away with ourselves: "Where there are no men, there cannot be motives accessible to men. Before we can proceed with our research, either our own thoughts or their materialized forms must be destroyed."[6] The ultimate conclusion, then, and Lem's fundamental lesson in all these parables, is that there can be no

> "question of 'contact' between mankind and any non-human civilization …."
> Grastrom pointed out correspondences with the human body – the projections of our senses, the structure of our physical organization, and the physiological limitations of man – in the equations of the theory of relativity, the theorem of magnetic fields, and the various unified field theories.[7]

Solaris is thus the negative proof of our thesis about writing: for here there is no writing, no message, and the ocean has merely activated traces within our own brain and projected them back to us; nor are its private "expressions" – the mimoids, the extensors – an aesthetic that has anything to do with art as we know it, even though we can find a strange pleasure in these peculiar

---

5 Ibid., p. 72.
6 Ibid., p. 134.
7 Ibid., p. 170.

formations. (Tarkovsky, indeed, exploits them for a more Proustian purpose, housing within the mimoid a representation of the house of Kelvin's childhood, and of the parents he will never again, owing to the temporal disparities of space travel, see in this life.)[8]

Yet oddly enough, the balance sheet is not wholly negative. The religious figuration of *Solaris* turns out to be as much an allegory of the scientific process – the final discovery of its nature serving the narrative of the revelation of the Absolute – as a projection of our perplexity before a closed and conscious monadic single-celled being (indeed, some of Kelvin's nightmares seem to betray his attempt to feel his way, by empathy, into the "skin" of such an impossible being).[9] And yet there remains the possibility that, like us, Solaris is itself an imperfect being, an imperfect or sick god,[10] like that insane deity of Schelling who has to create the world in order to cure himself:[11] in that case, we understand Solaris better than we know.

But there is the other possibility: the "experiment" is not a torture but rather a groping and clumsy attempt to wish us well, to please us, even to give us happiness.[12] Such is the indefinitely suspended and unresolved possibility of meaning of the interspecies "handshake" that concludes the novel:

> I went closer, and when the next wave came I held out my hand … the wave
> hesitated, recoiled, and then enveloped my hand without touching it, so that
> a thin covering of "air" separated my glove inside a cavity which had been
> fluent a moment previously, and now had a flesh consistency.[13]

Still, we have thus far only illustrated one face or dimension of Lem's doctrine, and for the complementary one we need to turn (far more briefly) to another of the novels of his major period, *The Invincible* (1964), so named after the starship (in search of a missing space vessel) whose landing on an unregistered planet triggers the events of interest to us and in particular the "contact" with a radically alien form of being.

Here we find the portrayal of a non-organic and non-sentient being, which is however superimposed on all the familiar kinds already present in Lem. The eponymous starship in fact navigates through a constellation in which there has already existed an alien life form, that of the Lyrians, which is presumed

---

8 In my opinion, an even more crucial moment differentiating Tarkovsky's film from Lem's original is to be found in the scene in which the ocean, by way of its surrogate creature Rheya, inspects a reproduction of Breughel's *Fall of Icarus* and begins to grasp the alien nature of human aesthetics.

9 *Solaris*, pp. 90, 178.

10 Ibid., p. 197.

11 Slavoj Žižek, *The Indivisible Remainder* (London, 1996), pp. 35–46.

12 *Solaris*, p. 193.

13 Ibid., pp. 202–203; and see Kelvin's dream, p. 179.

to have become extinct owing to the explosion of its own sun. Nothing is left of this alien civilization save the conviction that it must have been radically different from our own (and therefore, according to the principle established in *Solaris* and maintained throughout Lem's life work, unknowable to us). Indeed, there are hypothetical hints of this unknowability and they consist in the presumption that Lyrian society has attempted to escape its own system and to colonize another distant planet – Regis III, on which the Invincible is in the process of landing. The attempt having been unsuccessful and the living Lyrians having perished, only their machines remained, which however on hypothetical reconstruction prove to have been so different from our own as also to "prove" that the aliens on Lyre were radically different from us in all the senses of those words. Meanwhile, it even seems possible that Regis III itself contained yet another and different form of organic or alien life (saurians? intelligent or not?), which has also been exterminated. But let us leave these questions aside for a moment.

No novel of Lem is heavier with machinery than this one. An interest in scientific technology we certainly find throughout his work, with special emphasis on the paradoxes inherent in computer operations; but if anything, the paradoxes are hyperintellectual and scarcely serve to dramatize the weight of matter itself. Here, however, enormous machinery fills the diegetic space, and it does not only have to do with the phallic monumentality of "the twenty-storey high ship which was profiled against the waning sky so majestic in its immobility that it really did seem invincible".[14] Rather, it is the entire novel which is filled to the breaking point with enormous robots, an inexhaustible supply of cumbersome vehicles with their various safety shields projected from carefully calculated surrounding stationary positions, small space exploration vessels as well, including a host of exploratory spy satellites fired off at intervals, and finally, most menacing of all, the eighty-ton superweapon called the Cyclops, which includes an anti-matter weapon of enormous power, an electronic brain, a telescopic "hand", the capacity to levitate several meters above the ground surface, etc., etc. It will be said that in the era of miniaturization and small-scale computer hardware all these machines seem incredibly cumbersome and out-of-date, something which does not deprive the novel of its power (since we still inhabit a world in which there are also large machines). But I will wish to observe, in reply, that Lem's imagination knows this in advance and anticipates the very theme of miniaturization by way of his counterforce itself.

The latter – the "cloud of flies" or black cloud – very precisely constitutes such a final stage of miniaturization. We have to do here with a swarm of "smart" crystals, able to arouse and combine at moments of danger, and to organize themselves into a strategically and tactically superior mass (they finally

14 Stanislaw Lem, *The Invincible* (New York, 1973 [1964]), p. 234.

defeat the very Cyclops itself, as we shall see), and then to sink back into an inert multiplicity, leaving stray individual crystals littered across the terrain. This is, then, a new form of the alien: the intelligent non-organic. What does this new kind of alien contribute to the unknowability thesis advanced in *Solaris*?

We are all familiar with the paradigm of the attack on us of our own machinery in some later evolutionary stage, forgetting that in an older robotic tradition, that of Asimov's "three robotic laws" in *I, Robot* (1950), special mechanisms were designed and inserted in order to ensure the harmlessness of the new beings and in particular the priority of their commitment to human life, even at the cost of their own survival.[15] In Dick, however, a bifurcation appears, in which benign helper figures such as the "Lincoln" and the "Stanton" in *We Can Build You* (1962/1969) are shadowed by the more sinister figures of *Do Androids Dream of Electric Sheep?* (1968), whose even more frightening filmic avatars are familiar from Ridley Scott's version of the novel in *Blade Runner* (1982). The transition seems to have taken place at the moment in which the purely mechanical robot is transformed into the at least partially organic android.[16]

At any rate, from the 1960s onwards, the possibility of the cybernetic combines with the requirement of organic material, and the machine seems less and less likely to be content with the benevolent role of the classic "Robbie the Robot" (*Forbidden Planet*, 1956). James Cameron's classic *Terminator* (1984) is only the best of these later stories, in which our own war machinery begins to function for itself, computer intelligence now turning against the human intelligence which once constructed it and, in its autonomy, turning against the human beings which are now its enemy. The story of HAL, in Kubrick's *2001* (1968), makes this motivation clear enough: the humans still have the power to turn the machinery off, and the latter's new "instinct" of self-preservation requires it to destroy that danger, and presumably to go on to eradicate anything which might evolve back into it, namely organic life itself.

But in *Terminator*, and even in the case of HAL, a process is at work which removes a good deal of the scientific and philosophical interest of the narrative and turns it back into a conventional struggle between armies or matched forces of some kind: this is the inevitable tendency of anthropomorphism

15 I quote Asimov's three robotic laws:
    1. A robot may not harm a human being, or, through inaction, allow a human being to come to harm.
    2. A robot must obey the orders given to it by the human beings, except where such orders would conflict with the First Law.
    3. A robot must protect its own existence, as long as such protection does not conflict with the First or Second Law.

16 The classic text on the cyborg is Donna Haraway's "Manifesto for Cyborgs", *Socialist Review*, No. 80 (March/April 1985). For a further discussion of the android in Dick, and in particular what I call the "android cogito", see "History and Salvation in Philip K. Dick", in Part Two, Essay 10, below.

which we have already found to have been indicted in *Solaris*, but which in the films mentioned is rendered inescapable by the human forms taken by these robots or androids (in *2001*, the name and the observing eye of the computer are enough to restore the semblance of another subject).

In *The Invincible*, however, we have to do with a swarm of crystals which can in no case be reduced to the subjectivity of a human character. And the absence of human form is doubled by the multiplicity of these elements, a second non-human characteristic which individual biological organisms cannot understand or grasp by way of projection, even though the analogies of bee and insect colonies are there to reinforce it, and to endow the multiple with a dystopian dimension ideologically calculated to make the political flesh creep and to indict social systems allegedly devoid of individuality. It is interesting to note that as with Solaris, and therefore in the dialectics both of the One and of the Many, segments removed from the central mass simply disintegrate or become inert shards of matter.

As the history of the swarm is gradually reconstructed – yet another archaeological mystery, but a more urgent and dangerous one – the hypothesis emerges that these mechanisms originated from the crash of the Lyrian starship many centuries earlier, whose technology alone continued to function, and indeed to evolve, in a fashion distantly analogous to biological evolution on earth. Regis III is assumed to have once had atmosphere, and even vegetation and lower forms of animal life: all of which (save for what remains untouched beneath the surface of the sea) has by now been eradicated by the crystals, in a kind of non-instinctual strategy of self-defense and self-preservation.

This is then the hostile world on which Invincible's missing sister ship has unwittingly landed, with grim results for the entire crew; and it is perfectly in keeping with the structure of the crystals that the landing of the new vessel should trigger one long war between the animate and the inanimate. But it is a "war" based on a fundamental misunderstanding, and on the anthropomorphic projection of hostility and antagonism – human traits, emotions, and projects – onto beings which, not being alive, are not even conscious in the enigmatic and alien sense in which the sentient ocean of *Solaris* is judged to be conscious in a way incomprehensible to us.

There are however some fundamental representational problems here, and we may again invoke Vico to grasp them. The "crystals", whatever their complex evolution (and the very nature of non-organic "evolution" itself), are far back in time somehow nonetheless the result of production and labor. They are very distant descendants of machines whose first generations were made by sentient beings, albeit for specifically alien purposes. Like Vico's history, then, we can understand them, that is to say, we can hypothetically reconstruct their history, and form various plausible theories of their formation and their function. We have seen that in the case of Solaris this was impossible, and the proliferation of theories – from the scientific to the religious – runs wild in the void, since the ocean is not a human creation and can therefore by definition in advance not be understood. Here, ambiguously, the impossibility of anthropomorphism is displaced back onto the alien being of the original Lyrian inventors themselves.

The moral question at stake has here nonetheless been reversed. It is in reality the peculiar experience of the humans on Solaris Station which is a struggle, if not an overt war, since it involves episodes of a contact in which there are two sides and in which each party is presumably seeking to assert an advantage if not a mastery (taking the very problem of understanding itself as an instance of Foucauldian power/knowledge). But no such struggle exists in the case of the crystals since there are neither two sides nor two adversaries. Thus, as dangerous and lethal as the alien swarm may be in contrast with the relatively benign ocean of Solaris, the solution which consists in eradicating the former with superior firepower is in some respects comparable to the ethical problem of whether the last surviving smallpox viruses in the world should be destroyed. We do not belong here, the human characters repeat over and over again, we have no business here and the idea of destroying this peculiar constellation of non-organic forces is as sensible as Voltaire's condemnation of the Lisbon earthquake. Indeed, our project to destroy this "enemy" is as reasonable as Xerxes' flagellation of the sea; such a project is ethically even more reprehensible than the genocide planned for Solaris, insofar as it reinforces and plunges us ever deeper into that anthropomorphism which is the most dangerous form of ignorance and error. A similar ethical problem is raised by the opponents of terraforming in *Red Mars*: where the "red ecologists" base their radical politics on a defense of nature dialectically opposed to the spirit of the ecological movement on earth, inasmuch as the "nature" of Mars is to be preserved by resisting the implantation of organic life, atmosphere, and the like.

In *The Invincible*, then, the unknowability thesis is replaced by a different but related one: namely the imperative of anthropocentrism, or of maintaining what Lem calls the "geocentric attitude", which is both a paradoxical reversal and logical corollary of the first thesis. The latter was a principle of *méconnaissance*, something like Lacan's ego (linked to be sure to the mirror stage and narcissism), in which the self intervenes between ourselves and any more "scientific" knowledge of the Real, just as the categories of human understanding (derived from the unique functions of the human body and thus from its relationship to its own unique eco-system) fatally incline all speculation about the Other in the direction of the human.

But is this not precisely what has just been denounced for its anthropomorphism?

> [The geocentric attitude] consists not only in alone seeking out beings comparable to ourselves and in understanding those alone, but should also dictate

our non-involvement in things which do not concern us at all since they are non-human. To conquer the desert? Of course, why not? But not to attack what exists and has over millions of years created its own equilibrium, which is dependent on nothing and no one outside itself save for the effects of radiation and physical bodies. And this persistent equilibrium is active and a form of agency, neither worse nor better than that of the albuminous compounds which are called animals or men.[17]

If now we grasp even the intent to understand as an intrusive and aggressive power, we may abandon the Other – even this constructed and non-natural Other – to "be in its being" as Heidegger might say: abandon it to some complete isolation as sealed and seamless as the future itself or even that radically different system we call Utopia. But the limit of ethics lies in the fact that even this solution is closed to us, insofar as we now know about the possibility and thus cannot go back behind that knowledge (which condemns us to the impossible and to an insoluble contradiction) and recover an innocent state of ignorance.

It is worth concluding this story of failure with a limited success: the deduction that it is brainwaves and analogous vibrations that trigger the lethal hostility of the crystal swarm. The protagonist (Rohan) then wears a low-voltage apparatus on his head in order to disguise these otherwise fatal emanations: the scene in which a swarm of "flies" hovers uncertainly over him (the hypothesis having not yet been tested) has some distant kinship with Ripley's confrontation with the alien monster who will be her mate (in *Alien 3*). What is almost more serious, however, is that the swarm can also detect the presence of computer operations within machinery: not only does it thus incapacitate the Cyclops and turn it into a wandering and semi-autistic robot of enormous killing power (which might well be directed against the Invincible itself), this capability also menaces all the high-powered technology on which the human crew relied for protection. Thus Rohan's lone victory over the swarm does not in any way portend a victory for the Invincible, which has no option but to take off into outer space once again, leaving Regis III forever behind it.

Both of these fables then, *Solaris* as well as *The Invincible*, in their different ways signify non-communicability between the absolutely alien and Other, and thus an airtight barrier between the systems to which they belong, whether in space or in time, in simultaneity or in chronological succession. In Chapter 7 we observed the chronological problem give way to that of language itself, as the fundamental mode whereby we imagine communication with another system. It will be argued that in these two extreme cases (in which paradoxically an impossible historical relationship is dramatized under the sign of First Contact and its dilemmas) the memory traces of Solaris become a kind of

17 *The Invincible*, p. 183.

language, as though the ocean used the humans themselves and their desires and experiences as signifiers in some new language enabling it to communicate to them, however painfully and imperfectly; while the very inorganic crystals themselves in *The Invincible* stand as the most obvious incarnation of writing and of letters themselves, particularly when we remember the origin of cuneiform in those little cubes designated to inventory the harvest and the surplus stock in the granary. But each of these versions is ironic: the ocean falling into the fundamental philosophical mistake of the belief in the immediacy of face-to-face communication, and writing becoming the most incomprehensible of marks and unintelligible traces (and, distantly beyond that, perhaps embodying Lévi-Strauss' notion of the link between writing and power in the most horrifying way).[18] But even more alarming is the fact that the crystals leave no physical traces on their victims, whom they destroy by obliterating their mental functions or their energy systems: the traces the Invincible finds at the disastrous site of the first exploratory vessel to Regis III (which it has in fact come to investigate) are the marks of human teeth on bars of soap – shades of the horror film! Yet in both cases it is the human body which is called upon to register the alien interaction with its own emotions and physical spasms: language and expression seeming only to belong to the human side of the mutual opposition. What, then, if the alien body were little more than a distorted expression of Utopian possibilities? If its otherness were unknowable because it signified a radical otherness latent in human history and human praxis, rather than the not-I of a physical nature?

18   The reference is to Claude Lévi-Strauss, *Tristes tropiques* (New York, 1974), the chapter called "The Writing Lesson".

9

The Alien Body

The Nordic language recognizes four orders of foreignness. The first is the otherlander, or utlänning, *the stranger that we recognize as being a human of our world, but of another city or country. The second is the* framling – *Demosthenes merely drops the accent from the Nordic* främling. *This is the stranger that we recognize as human, but of another world. The third is the* raman, *the stranger that we recognize as human, but of another species. The fourth is the true alien, the* varelse, *which includes all the animals, for with them no conversation is possible. They live, but we cannot guess what purposes or causes make them act. They might be intelligent, they might be self-aware, but we cannot know it.*[1]

The turn from the nature and comprehensibility of other worlds to the representation (and representability) of alien life may be said to mark a passage through Montesquieu's discoveries. The founder of a certain tradition of political science, indeed, marked the mediation between an abstract political system and the palpable and physical, sensory, qualities of region and landscape. So it is, for example, that on a rudimentary basis the invention of another world ought to involve the production of new qualities, such as for example new colors:

What was peculiar about [a large feathery ball floating in the air] was its color. It was an entirely new color – not a new shade or combination, but a new primary color, as vivid as blue, red, or yellow, but quite different. When he inquired, she told him that it was known as "ulfire". Presently he met with a second new color. This she designated "jale". The sense impressions caused in Maskull by these two additional primary colors can only be vaguely hinted at by analogy. Just as blue is delicate and mysterious, yellow clear and unsubtle, and red sanguine and passionate, so he felt ulfire to be wild and painful, and jale dreamlike, devilish and voluptuous.[2]

---

1 Orson Scott Card, *Speaker for the Dead* (New York, 1986), p. 38.
2 David Lindsay, *Voyage to Arcturus* (New York, 1963 [1920]), p. 53.

It would be churlish to suggest that Lindsay is cheating here, and that the new colors are in reality simply new words, which are then taken in tow by a series of sensory adjectives. In reality we are here also at one of those forks in the generic path from which fantasy begins to split off from SF and go its own way. Yet surely it is a very exciting project indeed, and one which offers representation its ultimate Utopian challenge: to imagine a new heaven and a new earth! At the very least we may posit an allegorical relationship between the two: to be able to imagine a new color is allegorical of the possibility of imagining a whole new social world. In fantasy, as we have already seen, this possibility will be deployed in the form of new powers: so that the very power of the writer himself to convey the new is a form of magic, or perhaps we should rather say that magic in the content signifies this power in the form.

From the standpoint of SF, however, the new sensory phenomena will not be reified at the level of innovation: rather they lead us back to the other representational questions, which are somehow prior to the purely sensory ones, those which are etymologically aesthetic. For a new quality already begins to demand a new kind of perception, and that new perception in turn a new organ of perception, and thus ultimately a new kind of body. The "error" in Lindsay (which distinguishes fantasy from SF) lies in the attributing of a new perception of new color to a body (Maskull's) which remains the same as our own. For SF the representationally productive questions set in at that point: not whether we as readers are able to imagine the new color, but whether we can imagine the new sense organ and the new body that corresponds to it. But such representational queries always come in one way or another up against the Chimera problem dear to British empiricism: namely, whether we can really imagine anything that is not *prius in sensu*, that is not already, in other words, derived from sensory knowledge (and a sensory knowledge which is that of our own ordinary human body and world). There are two recurrent answers to this question: in the one the "Chimera", the allegedly new thing, will be an ingeniously cobbled together object in which secondary features of our own world are primary in the new one; or else the new object will be pseudo-sensory alone, and in reality put together out of so many abstract intellectual semes which are somehow able to pass themselves off as sensory. (And of course, in the long run, there is always Hegel on sense certainty to fall back on as well as Derrida's dictum: "there is no such thing as sense perception").[3]

An example of the first strategy will surely be that of the electrical or electromagnetic sense, which we find everywhere as a new possibility throughout SF: no doubt there are new technological innovations, such as x-rays and the like (as well as special camera effects) which permit us to begin minimally imagining what living would be like in such a world; yet it is interesting to

---

3 See Jacques Derrida, "Structure, Sign and Play"; discussion in *The Structuralist Controversy*, ed. Richard Macksey and Eugenio Donato (Baltimore, 1972), p. 272.

observe the degree to which this "new sense" often begins to shade over into the representation of a new kind of language and a new kind of communication, which surely mixes the pre-givens, the already existing human data, in a rather different way. In the long run, all of these fail to solve the fundamental problem which they hand on back to yet another one, namely the alien body itself, the external fact of the new sense organs and how we are to imagine them.

For both solutions, indeed, we may return to Stanislaw Lem and a leisurely extract from his other great alien novel, *Eden* (1959). Here the novelist has assigned himself the rigorous task of imagining new forms of plant life as well as new forms of industrial production:

> It was hot. Their shadows grew shorter the farther they walked. Their boots sank in the sand, and the only sounds were their footsteps and their breathing. As they approached one of the slender shapes that in the twilight had resembled trees, they slackened their pace. Out of the buff-colored soil rose a perpendicular trunk, as gray as an elephant's hide and with a faint metallic luster. The trunk, no thicker at the base than a man's arm, developed, at the top, into a flattened cup-shaped structure some seven feet above the ground. It was impossible to see whether or not the calyx was open at the top. It was completely motionless. The men stopped about twenty feet from this extraordinary growth, but the Engineer continued toward it and was lifting his hand to touch the "trunk" when the Doctor cried, "Stop!"
>
> The Engineer drew back reflexively. The Doctor pulled him away by the arm, then picked up a small stone and tossed it high into the air. The stone described the steep arc and dropped straight into the flattened top of the calyx. They all gave a start, so sudden and unexpected was the reaction. The calyx began undulating and closed; there was a brief hissing sound, like gas escaping, and the whole grayish column, now trembling feverishly, sank into the earth as if sucked in. The hole that was created was instantly filled by a greasy, foaming brown substance. Then particles of sand began to float on the surface, the coating of sand became thicker, and in a few seconds no trace of the hole remained: the ground was smooth and unbroken.[4]

These clearly alien forms do not, in this work, lead us into the epistemological riddles we have confronted in *Solaris* and *The Invincible*, but take us resolutely forward to the act of imagining the alien body as such. We may conjecture that the possibilities for such an imagining are probably limited by the variety of flora and fauna offered by earth itself, and that the number of possibilities of the former are more or less determined by the latter (and their various combinations). Suffice it to say that Lem here plays honestly and boldly and

4 Stanislaw Lem, *Eden* (New York, 1989), pp. 27–28.

openly forms his image of the Other on the basis of the body itself: an enormous hulk from which, as from a kangaroo's pouch, a tiny humanoid body partially emerges. The first inspection is that of a corpse:

> As from a gigantic, elongated oyster, a small two-armed trunk emerged between the thick, fleshy folds that closed winglike around it; dangling, its knotty fingers touched the floor. The thing, no bigger than a child's head, swayed back and forth, slower and slower, suspended from pale-yellow ligament membranes, until finally it came to rest. The Doctor was the first to pluck up the courage to approach it. He grasped the end of a limp, multi-jointed arm, and the small veined torso turned, revealing a flat, eyeless face, with gaping nostrils and something jagged, like a tongue bitten in two, in the place where a man's mouth would be.[5]

Not all "doubles", as the crew begins to call them, are without eyes; indeed one of the problems of the explorers is that they come upon mass graves of these beings, as well as strange museums, in which a variety of skeletal configurations is exhibited. At length they are able to meet an alien fellow scientist, who both explains the historical causes of much of what they have seen and also practices and exemplifies the communication by electricity (and by electrical "writing") which is that of the bodies in question. Certainly Lem has not exhausted the possibilities of the electromagnetic; we may compare Brunner's Draconian space, organized not visually but by the sensing of various spatial fields:

> His eyes were still shut, but he could discern the change from interior to exterior very clearly. Overhead, a vast nothing; underfoot, another tingling surface, but different in character from what he had awoken to … to right, left, and in front, other walls, also with gaps where streets/alleys ran … casting back at him a sort of radar echo … except that it was not a pulse-emitted-echo-received sensation, it was a there-it-is sensation, perfectly continuous … People. Instead of a clear signal of that distant wall, a multiple hum of pressure (as it were) moving and intertwining … good, yes, must have been a bit like that. (A flicker in his mind, based on the tingling of his skin, making a pattern that hinted at comprehensibility.)[6]

At the outer limit of this particular sensory model we touch on telepathy as such (now posited as an additional sense); and we find the new mode conveyed negatively, either in the destructive impact human thoughts and feelings have on the Pe-Ellians (in Phillip Mann's remarkable *Eye of the Queen* [1983];

5 Ibid., p. 58
6 Brunner, *Total Eclipse*, pp. 118–119.

or indeed in the unenviable human telepath in Silverberg's nightmarish *Dying Inside* [1972]). But these negative renderings draw less on representation as such than on taboo, the fear of violation, for example, or distaste at overpossessiveness.

Returning to Lem for one last moment, we may observe how he ingeniously covers his tracks by adding to this first puzzle a second one, namely that of the mass graves, the malfunctioning of factories, the collective terror of the nighttime crowds in the city of the doubles, etc. Here, it is as though he once again returns our anthropomorphism to us as a question and a riddle, rather than a mere projection: it is as though, the novel suggests, any conventional anthropological exploration of another society posits it in functionalist terms as a structure or machine whose dynamic principles are to be discovered. But suppose the machine is malfunctioning: suppose the structure has deteriorated, perhaps by reason of underpopulation, or of conquest or military defeat? At that point the system cannot be observed directly, it will have to be reconstructed out of rudimentary clues which may themselves be misleading. The society in question may in other words be in the condition of a biological sport, of a malformed organism, of a teratological formation of some kind which can scarcely yield any clues as to the healthy organism it replaces. The discipline of anthropology is in other words necessarily normative, and reestablishes the model of a norm even there where it is unthinkable: only Colin Turnbull, in *The Mountain People*, and Lévi-Strauss himself, in *Tristes tropiques*, have reflected on the frustration involved in coming upon a society not merely in decline but in utter collapse.[7]

Still, anthropology (and SF itself) have a conventional context with which to domesticate such phenomena, and it is that projected by the Second Law of Thermodynamics and indeed by Wells' *Time Machine* (if not by Spengler): namely the grand narrative of entropy and devolution. This then returns a meaning to the diseased symptoms and reconfers an order and kind of evolutionary or devolutionary normative on the aberrant objects of study.

But Lem clearly wishes to go further than this, or rather to replace the normative model with contingency as such. As in the Strugatskys' *Hard to Be a God* (1964), that contingency is fascism: here figured as a series of incomprehensible genetic experiments which have eventually taken their toll of the population of Eden and resulted in some mysterious planetary dictatorship. It is as though alien anthropologists, on their first visit to earth, landed in Auschwitz, and attempted to construct a rational model of human society on the basis of what they found there. The eugenic and genetic model is then pressed back into service in explaining the factory system as such in all its aberrant productivity, and finally the strange plant formations on which life in Eden along with its production is ultimately based. There is thus here an unresolved tension

7 Colin Turnbull, *The Mountain People* (New York, 1972), and Lévi-Strauss, *Triste tropiques*.

between the production of vivid and sensory images, radical differences (differences which in the light of modern human history are perhaps in reality not so radical after all), and the abstract philosophical explanations and structural principles which these images are supposed to illustrate and of which they are examples and test cases. If we emphasize the latter side of the tension, we then begin to tilt back towards the notion that genuine difference, genuine alienness or otherness, is impossible and unachievable, and that even there where it seems to have been successfully represented, in reality we find the mere structural play of purely human themes and topics. But this necessarily leads us squarely to the work of one of SF's most remarkable creators.

One cannot study the representation of alien life forms without making a special place for Olaf Stapledon (1886–1950), who is in many ways the Fourier of SF just as he is the Dante Alighieri of Utopias. Indeed, not the least of his similarities with Fourier is the literal naïveté of his imagination and the heavy-handedness of his style, which seems incapable of discriminating between opinion and "Utopian knowledge", between the unselfconscious expression of crude personal thoughts on this or that and the crystallization of the insight or the leap of imagination. Exasperation (and occasional embarrassment) are the price one pays for contact with this strange mind, seemingly English-provincial in its limits, and yet as odd and unparalled as anything he himself dreamt up on his alternate worlds (or indeed in the far future of this one).

There can be no doubt that *Star Maker* (1937) is so idiosyncratic that it seems to have no genre, not even those of SF or Utopian literature, and that it is a somehow unique and unclassifiable work, repulsive to some readers or even without interest, for others as fascinating as natural patterns that have no relationship to our visual or artistic traditions. Indeed, this lack of fit between our genres and our art and this peculiar text suggests some line of approach to what we may call the R.C. Elliott question about art in utopia itself.[8] But when one thinks that the entire work is a kind of non-figurative play between several oppositions keenly central to Utopia, as we shall see in a moment, and when one remembers the cosmological sweep of this immense imaginary epic history, as well as its quasi-religious solemnity (although radically atheist), we may be reminded of a few of those books which have been central to our own earth and our own traditions. Indeed, we may posit that in an achieved utopia, one become unimaginably real and distinct from us in whatever far future or galactic space, the question of art would already have been answered, and *Star Maker* would have turned out to be the *Divine Comedy* of that realized new world, returning to us as a sacred text or scripture mysteriously catapulted from out of the future into our own fallen present, as though it were indeed the enigmatic writing destined to secure a continuity

8 Elliott proposed to judge the quality of a given Utopia on the basis of the art its creator attributed to his imaginary society. See Elliott's *Shape of Utopia* (Chicago, 1970).

across the barrier of time and historical transformation. It is a situation which reverses Ernst Bloch's interpretation of the absent work of art at the center of the artist-novel as a hole in the present which marks the place of a Utopian future to come. With *Star Maker* we have the work, and only its Utopian social context is missing. Meanwhile an immense galactic Spinozan vision completes philosophy as well, endowing Marxism with its appropriate metaphysic, and realizing philosophy by abolishing it.

Yet, as has already been observed when we have to do with fantasy – that is to say, with daydreaming in the Freudian sense – it is important to distinguish the quotient of ideology involved, and to separate the expression of opinion from the operation of deeper structural mechanisms. There is no mystery about Stapledon's ideology: it is resolutely left-wing, and his admiration for the Soviet Union (he was a lifelong fellow traveler) makes him representative of a whole thirties Left ideology. His profound distrust of Americanization may prove relatively more prophetic however, than his Stalinism, although *Brave New World* and related texts in Europe suggest that here too his positions were relatively characteristic, and that we need to separate this particular fear of Americanization (modernization in the media, and consumerism) from the more political fear of American power after the Second World War. At any rate, Stapledon, uniquely among SF writers, had an authentic sense of the inevitability of class inequality and the omnipresence of class struggle.

Leslie Fiedler provides a dismal catalogue of the failures of Stapledon's political forecasts (mainly in the *Last and First Men* [1931]) in order to demonstrate the sterility of this naïve and pro-Stalinist set of opinions.[9] But I think that these failures are better dealt with in narrative terms as a kind of imitation of historical discourse: "It was after an unusually long period of eclipse that the spirit of the third human species attained its greatest brilliance"; "for a million terrestrial years these long-armed hairless beings were spreading their wicker huts and bone implements over the great northern continents, and for many more millions they remained in possession without making further cultural progress; for evolution, both biological and cultural, was indeed slow on Neptune".[10] It is a language Stapledon's readers must learn to enjoy, if they are not to find the doors of his work closing to them: but this does not necessarily mean that we have to admire its stylistic qualities. What we do need to do is to specify its function and the content related to that function.

What accounts for the sterility of the earlier forecasts is that here the historical-narrative mode is running on empty, and thus gives itself the content of mere opinion. Indeed, any analysis of Stapledon's style would want to register two distinct forms: on the one hand there is certainly a will to convey the

9 Leslie Fiedler, *Olaf Stapledon*, (Oxford, 1983), pp. 31–36, 67–72. And see also the Stapledon special issue of *Science Fiction Studies*, No. 28, Vol. IX, Part 3 (November, 1982).

10 Olaf Stapledon, *Last and First Men / Star Maker* (New York, 1968), pp. 151, 209.

impression of enormous temporalities, of the passing of geological rhythms and eons of time. It may be thought that this is something only the cumulative effect of the pages of a very long book – Proust or Mann – can end up conveying (in fact, in Proust, it is the absence of time passing that the narrator's perpetual present registers); but this is precisely the problem that Stapledon, who does not want to waste voluminous pages on an effect that he in fact intends to presuppose, wants to overcome. The model is no doubt the immense range of temporalities of Well's *Time Machine*, but there clearly the effect is uniquely dependent on the machine itself, and on the montage of the various ages: it is the radical difference (and identity) of the Morlocks or the Eloi with our own human present that does the job of suggesting an immense temporal gap. But Stapledon wants to show the tendencies at work within this passing time; and he is therefore reduced to the most childish reiteration of large numbers ("for close on a hundred million terrestrial years this aerial society endured with little change"),[11] quantities which virtually by definition the reader cannot feel or estimate, and which in any case end up fatiguing the mind.

Along with that empty temporality – which in fact leaves the basic structure of the sentence unchanged, so that we attempt to combine it with the content of quite ordinary narratives – there is from time to time the Verne-like *fait divers*: "by one of those rare tricks of fortune, which are as often favourable as hostile to humanity, an Arctic exploration ship had recently been embedded in the pack ice for a long drift across the Polar sea",[12] etc. Yet such anecdotes become ever more infrequent as we are progressively distanced from any recognizable humanity (by "hundreds of millions of years"). They are then replaced by what we may call more social ones: "It was while they were struggling in the grip of this vast social melancholy … that the Fifth Men were confronted with a most unexpected physical crisis"[13] (in this case, the immanent explosion of the sun).

Yet both of these narrative forms are to be distinguished by the rhythms of progress and decline profoundly embedded in Stapledon's imagination; and which are reinforced by the music of a well-nigh Heideggerian *Stimmung*, that of the "vast social melancholy" alluded to in the earlier quotation, which alternates with a joy of existence and productive activity. Yet it is the melancholy mood which is far and away the most striking emotional ground-tone of these works, and something for which it is otherwise difficult to imagine any acceptable "objective correlative" (it is worth remembering that Eliot's invention of the concept[14] also has to do with melancholy and the loathing of existence – in this case, that of Hamlet – and that he described his own inspiration for

---

11 Ibid., p. 199.
12 Ibid., p. 90; and compare the episode of the "Divine Boy", pp. 80ff.
13 Ibid., p. 185.
14 T.S. Eliot, "Hamlet and His Problems", in *Selected Essays* (New York, 1950).

The Waste Land in just such terms as well). But Stapledon's fantastic "motivation of the device" is distinct from either Eliot's subjective version (Hamlet's Oedipal feelings) or the ideological pathos of the so-called decline of the West (in Spengler).

Star Maker retains the narrative dynamic of entropy but to a very different effect, for it aims at exploring the consequences of a new kind of frame; namely the peculiarities of new life forms rather than the ultimate destiny of our own. Two overarching formal properties of the narrative are retained: the daydreaming narrative will always combine the requirements of both success and failure: it will in other words unite the two antithetical characteristics of the bourgeois ideology of progress and entropy as it emerged in the nineteenth century and was preeminently expressed by Wells (who also saw both poles, but embodied them in distinct works, rather than combining them into one). Thus, Stapledon insists on the modernization or Whig paradigm, progress in everything, and above all in industrialization; followed by the corresponding late nineteenth-century entropy paradigm, in which devolution and decay result from social success itself ("in Bvalltu's view man had climbed approximately to the same height time after time, only to be undone by some hidden consequence of his own achievement").[15] This is the external narrative constraint common to the various alien galactic histories, which individually turn on a number of other categorical positions we examine in a moment.

But what needs to be insisted on now is the relationship between a fantasizing temporal narrative and the as it were structural frame (a physical one) which enables it and limits it all at once. Meanwhile we need to distinguish between the categorical oppositions, the thematics of the frames in question – which is to say the antithesis according to which we interrogate and evaluate these visions – and the semic material, the bodies and life forms, out of which their variety is constructed. Of the former, as will be seen, I will isolate the categories of the one and the many, of industrialization (that is to say, the artificial or prosthetic versus the natural) and that of class antagonism versus social equality (the conventional SF opposition between country and city seems to play a fairly insignificant role here, except when combined with one of the previous categories, such as industrialization or class conflict). We will leave these aside for the moment.

The variety of the life forms draws on a quite different combination scheme; and it is probably worth stressing the Fourieresque aesthetic pleasure inherent in the production of this variety. For does not Stapledon himself say, of the Second Men, that

> around the ancient core of delight in physical and mental contact with the
> opposite sex there now appeared a kind of innately sublimated, and no less

15 Stapledon, *Star Maker*, p. 290.

poignant, appreciation of the unique physical and mental forms of all kinds of live things. It is difficult for less ample natures to imagine this expansion of the innate sexual interest; for to them it is not apparent that the lusty admiration which at first directs itself solely on the opposite sex is the appropriate attitude to all the beauties of flesh and spirit in beast and bird and plant.[16]

We must now develop this attitude in ourselves as readers of Stapledon (never forgetting that the argument can be maliciously reversed, reducing all the variety of his SF and Utopian fantasy to scarcely disguised sexual fantasies from the very outset).

We will now examine this seeming variety in that unequaled section of *Star Maker* which runs from the discovery of the Other Earth all the way to the leap beyond life forms to the secret life of inorganic beings and finally of the stars themselves. We here encounter four basic forms (with a good deal of secondary variation and elaboration), among which still recognizably humanoid figures of the Other Earth, whose fate loosely approximates Stapledon's usual forecasts of the doom of our own contemporary civilization, give way to beings as unlike the anthropomorphic as can be imagined. It is, indeed, the principle of that imagining we must first seek, on the structural premise that where the greatest differences are to be generated, they are necessarily generated along axes of opposition; and tend to be negations or inversions of one kind or another, rather than radically new and unrelated phenomena. Difference, in other words, necessarily posits for its recognition what Greimas would call an *isotopie* (or Hegel an inner identity of identity and difference). The conventional presupposition is not only that in that sense the new is impossible, but also that Utopia is just as unimaginable, its images always reflecting a kind of anthropomorphic projection which we may now limit by recognizing them as the projections of our own society and its parochial obsessions. It is equally clear that Stapledon wishes to disprove these presuppositions by the very variety of his invention, from which we may now isolate the four principal varieties of biological and civilizational difference: the nautiloids (a species of "living ships"); the symbiotic race, in which ichthyoids (intelligent fish-like creatures) live in close biological combination with arachnoids (crustacean or spider-like beings); the intelligent swarm of avian beings; and finally, the plant men, released from their roots to move about and work at night, passing the day rooted in a meditative ecstasy of solar absorption.

It will already be observed that these various life forms between them exhaust three of the four traditional elements: water, air and earth. As fantasy has long conjectured the existence of fire beings – salamanders, the inhabitants of the sun – the absence of the fourth element is an interesting mystery.

16 Stapledon, *Last and First Men*, p. 101.

I cannot particularly defend my intuition that Stapledon associates it with industrialization, always one of the perilous critical points of his imagined societies; but perhaps, on the other hand, its place is taken by the stars themselves as hostile beings.

Yet other categories offer better ways to grasp Stapledon's principle of differentiation than these as it were primal and pre-Socratic physical elements. We have so far been working with the obvious thematic opposition between the One and the Many, between individuality and the collective: a crucial ideological motif on which Stapledon insists over and over again in dialectical fashion, positing the principle that it is necessary to insist on the values of individualism when a society has gone too far in the direction of the collective and the conformist; and by the same token necessary to insist on the values of the collective when a society, such as our own, has gone too far in the way of individualism.[17]

Yet on the deeper level of structure this ideological opposition is criss-crossed by a completely different motif, which although it can also be expressed in terms of numbers ought rather to be grasped as coming from a different realm altogether. This is the motif of dualism, which can first be discerned in the way in which the star-traveling narrative consciousness is at the very outset counterposed against the home and the family unit (and its peculiar domestic problems and anxieties). This is a duality incommensurable with the notion of individualism deployed in the previous tension of the One and the Many. To be sure, the married unit is in some sense the product of individualism; and the collective being of groups like the avian swarm will invent other relationships (even of a sexual kind) which completely replace monogamy. Yet the duality of marriage stands in a different kind of opposition to the collective than does individualism: we have to do here with the dual negatives of the contradictory and contrary (in both traditional logic and the Greimas square), which may be associated with Plato's differentiation in *The Sophist* between "it is not" and "it is not the same as", between absolute negation and differentiation, or Hegel's distinction between opposition and simple difference.[18]

At any rate, it is this transversality of the dual with the opposition One/Many that seems finally to make up the richness of Stapledon's alien forms. Here, indeed, we find the presence of at least two kinds of dualisms, as over against the physical simplicity of the individual one of nautiloid existence – the shiplike creature – and the equally emblematic multiplicity of the avian horde (among which we may count the swarm of crystals in Lem's *Invincible*). The first and most striking is of course the symbiotic form, in which the two species – one fish-like and the other a more crustacean-cum-insect and

17 *Star Maker*, pp. 330–331.
18 Plato, *Complete Works: The Sophist*; and G.F.W. Hegel, *Encyclopedia Logic*. And see Chapter 12, below, for a further discussion of marriage and the family in Utopia.

therefore more amphibious structure – first combine a general sympathy and then develop a ritual (non-sexual, non-reproductive) pairing between their individual members: "the ordinary partnership was at once more intimate than human marriage and far more enlarging to the individual than any friendship between members of distinct human races".[19] At length it is this partnership which enables the symbiotic pair to liberate itself from the purely material constraints of its planet, by way of telepathy: thus, the immensely intelligent fish-like beings continue to swim in the latter's home waters, while the arachnoids develop space travel and colonize the nearby regions of the galaxy. Meanwhile, industrialism also rears its ugly head, by way of new drugs which allow the arachnoids to live independently of their partners, with whom they subsequently develop a class antagonism, with disastrous consequences.

At one level this duality clearly expresses the mind/body problem, and is no doubt Stapledon's way of attempting to restructure a structural constraint that cannot really be done away with. We must also take into consideration the possibility that mind/body dualism here also either expresses, or is expressed in, the gender dualism: active/passive is certainly an operative feature of the symbiotic description. In another sense the symbiotic race is a kind of ideal synthesis since it envelops all three of the dominant elements: the ichthyoids that of water, and the arachnoids a combination of *terra firma* and air. But they cannot particularly be seen as a resolution of the One/Many distinction.

The symbiotics are, however, only the external form taken by dualism in this production of variety. We must also notice that dualism is internalized in what looks like either the most individualistic, or even better the most pre-individualistic life form, namely that of the plant people, who cyclically divide their time between an active nocturnal existence and a daytime contemplative and rooted one: both ichthyoid and arachnid all at once and in the same individual tree trunk.

We may therefore organize these semes in diagrammatic form (see figure). The point of this discussion is not to exhaust the very peculiar and idiosyncratic richness of Stapledon's work, but rather to show how the variety of his alien life forms is determined by semic oppositions which seek (structurally and narratively, which is to say unconsciously) to resolve social contradictions. His ideologies are in their own way also attempts to resolve (or at least to express) those contradictions; but in this unique case it is easy enough to peel the opinion away from the structure and to rephrase the findings in a more cognitive way.

Thus, there is a kind of philosophy of history at work here, one which is ultimately based on mortality and on the impending extinction of the human race (or even of the universe itself) in ten billion years. This is to be contemplated with a kind of tragic ecstasy, and Fiedler is especially good on the

19 *Star Maker*, p. 322.

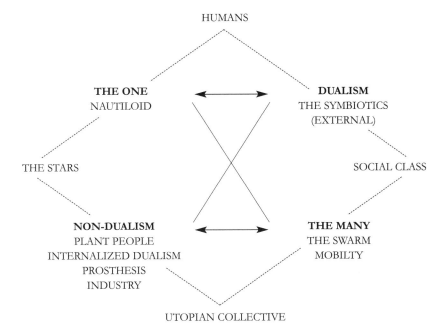

ambivalence of this metaphysical feeling *par excellence*, this ecstatic resignation to defeat and death – which is to say an apprehension of the Starmaker as being beyond sympathy, casting a glacial vision down on phenomenal events.

There is a Spinozan accent to such moments, one somehow always the complement or the completion of any truly dialectical philosophy; as in Bvalltu's praise song:

> Oh, Star Maker, even if you destroy me, I must praise you. Even if you torture my dearest. Even if you torment and waste all your lovely worlds, the little figments of your imagination, yet must I praise you. For if you do so, it must be right. In me it would be wrong, but in you it *must* be right … And if, after all, there is no Star Maker … even so, I must praise. But if there is no Star Maker, what can it be that I praise? I do not know. I will call it only the sharp tang and savor of existence.[20]

The cyclical rhythms of social rise and fall which determine such mysteries transcend the ideologies of entropy even in the moment in which they give dramatic expression to its truth, inscribing the for and against, the failure inherent in every historical success along with the return of new Utopian possibilities. The multiplicity of his worlds allows Stapledon to have all conceivable outcomes simultaneously.

20 Ibid., p. 291.

But there is yet another historical force at work here, which is less the expression of metaphysics of history than that of the mode of social and cultural critique: this is that denunciation of industrialization and its noxious and "dehumanizing" consequences which is reiterated throughout the tragic destinies of Stapledon's multiple societies. In particular, industrialization is grasped as a temptation for most of them to shortcircuit nature and to destroy everything positive about their achievements in the name of some short-term advantage. The sad story of the Other Earth – a Huxleyan dystopia in which people are immobilized by their media satisfactions and spend their lives in what is called bed-ecstasy, artificially imbibing media pleasures (which are here those of taste and smell, of earth sensations) – is perhaps not so convincing as the drugs which enable the symbiotic culture to separate itself again into two races, or the tree people to do without their sun stasis. In both these cases, industrialism is what destroys a successful balance, what ruins an enviable Utopian disposition. There is here, in Stapledon's passionate indignation about the waste of possibilities, an ideological return to that spirit of tragedy tran-scended in the vision of the Star Maker, and a regression to those anti-industrial Romantic motifs which preceded Marxism and its denunciation of class exploitation (which Stapledon also shares).

For the most part, conventional SF representations of the social contradic-tions of alien life fall short of either diagnosis – of the condemnation of industrial waste and abuse à la Ruskin, or of Marxian class consciousness. More frequently, such accounts of the fatal crisis of alien societies turn on features enumerated by Stapledon in his vast compilation of social fatalities (but in him secondary to the contradictions of class and industrial modernity), and in particular on religion and on biological destiny.

It is indeed ironic, but perhaps significant, that the best of all alien repre-sentations – Heinlein called it the finest SF novel ever written – should have been composed in a resolutely Cold War spirit, and designed to preach an unremitting vigilance and hostility to the newly discovered alien species as a scarcely disguised foreign policy lesson, not particularly liberalized by its prediction of a convergent American–Soviet military Empire of the galactic future. The banner year 1974 not only saw the publication of Brunner's *Total Eclipse* and Le Guin's *Dispossessed* (*Roadside Picnic* and *Rendezvous with Rama* preceded them by only two years), but also that of Niven and Pournelle's *The Mote in God's Eye*, which can be taken as a kind of military utopia (the delight in castes, corporations and aristocracies, male bonding, the non-profit ideolo-gies of warfare and technology, which hard-science SF tends to reproduce at a lower level of political intensity): such right-wing Utopias are quite unlike the free-enterprise, neo-conservative celebrations of present-day cyberpunk; nor do they reproduce the fascist themes of inferior races, ressentiment, physical prowess and the like, more often to be found in fantasy (and of which Adolf Hitler's well-known "novel" *Lord of the Swastika* is the most famous exemplar).[21] Indeed, it is tempting to assign the years around 1974 (the oil crisis, the end of the Vietnam War) as the closing of a Utopian period which began in that other banner year 1968, only to be replaced by a second Cold War.

At any rate, the Moties are certainly not an inferior race and the authors' political agenda requires them to play the game honestly, and to endow their aliens with superior intelligence and productivity and with a history of progress and modernization much older than the human, but fully a match for the latter. This ambitious representation of alien life and society thus eschews the malignancy of comic-book villains as well as the theological evil of more religiously inspired revelations, such as those of Clarke's *Childhood's End* (1953) or Blish's *A Case of Conscience* (1959) (or the more recent *Sparrow* by Mary Doria Russell [1996]). A few atavistic gothic features are to be sure glimpsed in military situations, mostly in order to generate serious debate on alien intentions and on the foreign policy to be pursued in the new post-First-Contact outer space.

Yet the debate remains necessarily premised on some fundamental species difference; and the intelligent aliens of Mote Prime are organized into what we would probably think of as castes on the basis of variations in a body type rather different from that of earthly human beings:

> There were two slender right arms ending in delicate hands, four fingers and two opposed thumbs on each. On the left side was a single massive arm, virtually a club of flesh, easily bigger than both right arms combined. Its hand was three thick fingers closed like a vise … There was no neck. The massive muscles of the left shoulder sloped smoothly up to the top of the alien's head. The left side of the skull blended into the left shoulder and was much larger than the right. There was no left ear and no room for one. A great membranous goblin's ear decorated the right side …[22]

Otherwise, following the principle of empirical selectivity, one is tempted to visualize these beings as a kind of combination of those "tribbles" of a famous Star Trek episode with earthly felines of some sort. The Moties' art – uncompromisingly realistic and representational –sheds a more historical light on these physiognomies:

---

21 See Norman Spinrad, *The Iron Dream* (New York, 1972), in which we read the life and works of an unsuccessful Austrian painter who emigrates to the New World before the First World War and becomes a successful pulp novelist.

22 Larry Niven and Jerry Pournelle, *The Mote in God's Eye* (New York, 1974), p. 78. Larry Niven (1938–), the author of an inventive galactic series on "Known Space", is perhaps best known for his vision of the unique system called *Ringworld* (1970), which has been suggestive for any number of subsequent authors. His collaboraion with Jerry Pournelle (1933–), a practitioner of more military and hawkish SF, produced distinctive work rather different from their individual styles.

Here a Brown-and-white had climbed on a car and was apparently harangu-ing a swarm of Browns and Brown-and-whites, while behind him the sky burned sunset-red … a quasi-Motie, tall and thin, small-headed, long-legged … was running out of a forest, at the viewer. Its breath trailed smoky-white behind it. "The Message Carrier", Hardy's Motie called it.[23]

The combination of the legendary with the caricatural strikes me as project-ing cartoon qualities, amateurish figures whose design is itself part of the subject matter and the meaning. In Thurber in particular the arms are always rounded and boneless, like a kitten's arms; this peculiar impression is corrob-orated by the importance of a structural difference between bones, and in particular the intricacy of the human backbone (in which the Moties are greatly interested) and their own unbending and club-like appendages. Insistence on this eclectic empiricism is not meant to denigrate the authors' imagination: how could that be the case, when this principle virtually cancels the demiur-gic powers of all imagination in the first place? Indeed, we observe the same play of stereotypes in the human characters, in which (again, shades of *Star Trek*) the engineer is a Scot, and the trader a polyglot Levantine (at least he is not yet a "terrorist"). In a formulaic literature, the art lies not in invention but in combination, and this is particularly interesting matter when we have to do, as in the literature of aliens and First Contact, with what I have been appar-ently celebrating as an extreme effort of the Utopian imagination as such. What then is the Utopian imagination? (But we should not leave Motie art without adding the SF dimension of these alien works, as disappointing to their human visitors as is, no doubt, SF itself to a readership of modernists: for there is a twist, and a secret SF ingredient – they are also apprehended telepathically: heard dramas emerge from them, which remind us of nothing in Western art quite so much as those friezes in *Purgatorio* in contemplating which the divine pilgrims actually *hear* music.)[24]

We also need in passing to add to our previous enumeration another museum on the Mote planet, one in which the biological inhabitants of various moments of Mote history (a very long history indeed, as the reader will recall) are preserved – alive, and not merely by holograph – in their original climatic surroundings, including a burning city with rat-like Motie animal cousins, along with various live-stock relatives. This is a rather different kind of institution designed to combine the zoo and the historical museum, or in other words to associate biology with history far more closely than is the case with the human species; and to develop an attention to the alien body of a sociological and

23   Ibid., p. 260.
24   Dante, *Purgatorio* (Singleton; Princeton, 1973), Canto X, pp. 102–105, lines 55–96; to this I am tempted to add the lone painting in the Strugatskys' *Snail on a Slope* (1966–1968): "a large picture of pathfinder Selivan's exploit: Selivan with arms upraised was turning into a jumping tree before the eyes of his stunned comrades" (New York, 1980, p. 105).

not merely an evolutionary kind. The risk is that the causal priorities can be reversed in such an arrangement; and where human evolution serves as a kind of limit to historical and social possibility, to view the alien anatomy as a historical destiny and a historical doom.

At any rate, *The Mote in God's Eye* is one of the few SF novels to "include" production and the mode of production as such (as Pound might have put it), in ways that expand a Utopian consciousness for its human readers. The caste system is to be sure already familiar from human history, although on Mote Prime (unlike what happens in Stapledon or in earthly human history) it does not finally move towards a dichotomous class system as its climax and fulfillment. What is relatively more unique here is however the development – seemingly a feat of genetic engineering – of a caste of intellectuals as such: the so-called mediators, who come into being to deal with everything from languages and translation to the settlement of labor disputes and other kinds of conflicts. It is a concept which allows a plausible representation of alien language, and also a plausible version of the distances and indirections involved in diplomatic and anthropological contact; and even in tourism – the mediators constituting a kind of Intourist for the human visitors, both monitoring their contacts and offering semi-official explanations for unfamiliar practices and institutions. But only certain types of academic specialization prepare us for the unique mediatory relationship designated as that of the "fyunch-(click)", which is the one-on-one assignment attachment of the individual mediator to its human posting:

> "I'm Fyunch(click) to you. It means considerably more than just *guide* …. I am assigned to you. You are a project, a masterwork. I am to learn as much about you as there is to know. I am to become an expert on you … and you are to become a field of study to me."[25]

This socio-biological category is then evidently credited with a degree of intimacy that far outstrips the various conceivable earthly varieties, producing comical misunderstandings on the order of the mock pathetic cry, in the midst of the human-Motie military crisis, "A man does not lie to his Fyunch-(click)!" These mediators not only resolve domestic clashes, they also go a long way towards overcoming that fundamental dilemma of SF representation we have called Lem's unknowability thesis.

Another caste, that of the workman or handyman, the so-called brown, articulates the peculiarities of the Motie anatomy, and in particular the triple arms, at the same time that it illuminates the deeper mysteries of Motie production as such. The specificity here is not only the extraordinary capacity of these single-minded intelligences to improve any conceivable (human) design, but

25 *The Mote in God's Eye*, p. 216.

above all the object world generated by such "improvements", which are ongoing and universal. But this means a very different relationship to objects than our own: the latter presupposes a certain temporal permanence, not merely in our tools and appliances, but in our very spaces themselves, in our habitat and our architecture:

> We now think that every structure is only temporary to them. They must have had high-gee couches at takeoff, but they're gone now. They arrived with no fuel to take them home. They almost certainly redesigned their life-support system for free fall in the three hours following their arrival … It's a major departure from human psychology …. Perhaps a Motie would never try to design anything permanent at all. There will be no sphinx, no pyramids, no Washington Monument, no Lenin's Tomb.[26]

Meanwhile, the "hotel" in which the human visitors are housed on Mote Prime has been built especially for that purpose, and will disappear overnight when the purpose has been fulfilled: something which accounts for the perfunctory evocation of the alien cityscape here, just about the only aspect of the genre which is neglected in this remarkable novel.

But the unique characterization of Motie production is significant, not for its testimony as to the authors' talent or ingenuity and imagination, but rather for the way in which it projects a solution to a fundamental human opposition, namely that between handicraft production of an individual type or style and industrial mass production of serial objects and items. In this new world, where the large holding arm is answered by two small and instrumental ones, after the fashion of a lathe, a missing form is abstractly generated in which the tailor-made is somehow industrial and produced with the rapidity and precision of the assembly line. The Browns thus dramatize not only the extraordinary skill at repairing and even at inventing new technological devices, they also project a wholly original idea of industrial design as such (which is in fact and in hindsight an anticipation of the newer possibilities in so-called CNC, or computer-numerically-controlled, production).[27]

A similarly unique combination of features – about which it is not clear whether it is regressive or Utopian – can be observed on a social level, where the definition of this particular mode of production – *industrial feudalism* [28] – also synthesizes two antithetical modes and socio-economic arrangements, in which a decentralized clan system, with competing overlords, is combined

---

26 Ibid., p. 213.

27 I am indebted to Michael Speaks for an explanation of this numerated process, on the occasion of a visit to Gregg Lynn's studio in Venice, California.

28 *The Mote in God's Eye*, p. 356. But perhaps we are still in a situation of industrial feudalism today, if one considers Max Horkheimer's theory of "rackets" as a description of corruption organized into a clan system: *Gesammelte Schriften*, vol. 12, pp. 287–291.

with factories (themselves constantly in the process of transformation and restructuration) and has reached an extraordinarily high degree of scientific and technological knowledge (probably greater than that on Earth). It then becomes clear that the gap or contradiction which cannot be filled in by the earthly mind – the absence of any centralized or coordinated government for a population of this size and a social life of this complexity – is very precisely overcome by the existence of the caste of mediators we have already described: better still, the latter have been invented to solve the problem of the former.

It now remains to inspect the fly in the ointment, and to identify the form these novel combinations take on when projected onto the individual or existential level. The Utopia, we said, was a text in which the relations between the individual and the collectivity are substituted for the dual relations between two or small numbers of individuals which make up the existential or social life of the self. That more purely existential, or personal level, is here constituted by gender and gender relations, on which once again the fact of the body and of biology and anatomy can be seen more directly to determine large-scale social structures.

By definition, these gender relations are at one with the structure of marriages, families, inheritance law and the like: insofar as discovering the former allows the explorers to provide something fundamental and characteristic about the alien society, which a few stray cases of deviancy will not do. Thus, subversion of the norm – if there is any, and, after the sixties, SF tends conventionally to include a sporadic rehearsal of such aesthetic and existential revolts – will come by way of the defamiliarization of those human norms and customs which the alien gender arrangement may provoke. Asimov's triple marriages may be taken as an example of this peculiar effect: in *The Gods Themselves* a fairly conventional image of an alien society and alien norms can be seen to be rather scandalous if translated into human and earthly terms. It is precisely this reverse Gestalt-structure that plays into the hands of SF's realist and psychoanalytic critics, who, insensitive to alien, let alone Utopian, figuration, retranslate these fantasies back to normal human neuroses, if not psychoses (remember the properly science-fictional cosmic fantasies of President Schreber, whose literary value Freud and Lacan both deny absolutely). One tends to feel that feminist critiques of the new alien worlds are more relevant, particularly since the freedom to project different alien worlds structured by feminist principles or values is there maintained (the Utopias of Charlotte Perkins Gilman, Joanna Russ or Marge Piercy are only the most dramatic of those realizations).

At any rate, the female sex (or gender) is certainly placed at some disadvantage in the figuration of Motie biology, in which the individual begins as a male and then changes sex in the development period:

"Every variant of my species has to be made pregnant after she's been female for a while. Child, male, female, pregnancy, male, female, pregnancy, 'round and 'round. If she doesn't get pregnant in time, she dies. Even us. And we Mediators *can't* get pregnant. We're mules, sterile hybrids."[29]

There is also the suggestion that in the past some of the great feudal barons have been able to become sterile males, thus putting them in a different and more advantageous position of power, one from which a single centralized Empire might eventually be expected to develop: here a faint dialectical possibility is put in place that a manipulation of newer biological techniques biology or anatomy might ultimately enable a political and even a socio-economic transformation of the mode of production. But the reality of Motie history is a constant pressure of overpopulation, leading to periodic crises and the cyclical breakdown of civilization and its constraints: horrendous wars, times of troubles, the reversion to Neolithic conditions and the long climb back into Enlightenment science and technology again and their destructive capacity. This historical destiny both reflects a human one (the fact of overpopulation itself) and differentiates itself by the absence of any possible medical or political controls. We may well feel that the authors have cheated a bit here, and that androgyny (compare *The Left Hand of Darkness*) need not necessarily lead to the xenophobic prospect of the "Motie peril" and of waves of Motie hordes likely to pour out of the transfer point and overwhelm the human empire of the galaxy. But the raw Utopian nerve which is touched here is the capacity of the generations of human society to succeed themselves in the post-historical Utopian framework (which a new generation may no longer wish to accept); just as the nightmare image of overpopulation itself symptomatizes the end of the individualistic subject and the immense global appearance of a multiplicity of subjects in the postmodern era.

As for gender, it is curious and suggestive that in the same year in which *The Mote in God's Eye* appeared (1974), another SF work was published, one already introduced in an earlier chapter and which replicates the sexual dynamics of the Niven/Pournelle scheme in the intent of making a similar world-historical statement, although this one is scarcely a Cold War message and sounds instead the pessimism of something like a dawning catastrophe for the human race as a whole. Indeed, John Brunner's late sixties works, most notably *Stand on Zanzibar* (1968), notoriously took up these issues from what we might call a "realistic" SF near-future or dystopian perspective. What is surprising about his *Total Eclipse* is not their return, in the more poetic form of a kind of fable, but rather the climactic discovery of a peculiar historical fatality in Draconian gender and marriage arrangements.

29 *The Mote in God's Eye*, p. 340.

We have already mentioned the androgyny which this species shares with the Moties: unlike the latter, however, that of the Draconians is not cyclical, but rather dooms the individual to an immobilized ("sessile") final stage of life:

> Their culture must have been as influenced as all human cultures have always been by sex …. Both sexes coexisted in the same individual. Infancy was a neuter stage; there followed a male stage; and after that there was a comparatively short female stage prior to the infertility of old age.[30]

The technological novelties of Draconian culture (the central focus from which it was disseminated, the discovery of only one prototype of the various high-technological inventions, such as airplanes) are not related to this gender rhythm as closely as was the case in Niven and Pournelle. But on the other hand, the existential outcome of Draconian existence is lived and felt far more intensely by Ian in his mimetic–empathetic mode:

> I know who I am. Suddenly I'm quite sure who I am. I'm neuter. No wonder my friends won't talk to me right now.
>   I've lived the active part of my life. What I was able to do, with complete mobility, is done. I am growing slower and more awkward in my movements (I feel I move awkwardly, there are deep aches, deep as my bones, penetrating me like blades) in spite of …
>   As though resigned already to completing his life in a stiff sessile mode, he spent long hours at the side of the dry empty river, among no-longer-existent plants that clung to its muddy banks, feeling the soothing caress of the current by force of will, groping, creeping, striving towards acceptance of senility … but not that yet. Between now and then some climax, some repayment for the sacrifice of activity, some reward, some – something.[31]

The riddle of the extinction of the Draconians is then quickly solved: these aged sterile Draconian survivors spend their last years amassing a kind of genetic "insurance": the hieroglyphic crystals are the record of these legally binding "sexual favors" which constitute the wealth of the various clans, but end up condemning the race itself to in-breeding and genetic degeneration. The archaeologists deliver an apocalyptic vision of a kind of Draconian Pompeii, an endgame in which deformed and misshapen Draconian skeletons huddle, as if in the Wellsian final evening of their history, around a tomb crowned with statues of the rulers of yesteryear, Draconian forms in the flush of health and power.

---

30 *Total Eclipse*, pp. 39–40.
31 Ibid., pp. 121–122.

All of this suggests an unhappy outcome for the Utopian and SF genre itself, whose lines of exploration and invention have now been rerouted and deviated along the lines of gender and sexuality, rather than those of class dynamics and the mode of production. Where the latter categories have been maintained they are expressed as a reversion to older modes of production in which filiation and inheritance were fundamental determinant mechanisms. Perhaps the dynamics of class and class struggle – as exemplified in Stapledon for example – do not admit of as much interesting and exotic variation and differentiation as do gender phenomena (as for race, its thematic is relatively neutralized by the presupposition of alien life in the first place – which can, to be sure, stand as the allegory of race, as in Octavia Butler – although it can also return, within an alien world, as the representation of interspecies coexistence and rivalry, as in Aldiss' *Helliconia Spring* [1982]). Are we then to follow Louis Marin's rather pessimistic prognosis, that the invention of Utopia takes place within the still empty space that later a "science of society" (Marxism) will fill, thus rendering this genre henceforth unnecessary? At the very least, the gender turn of the Utopian imagination is the sign of a waning of the Utopian imagination in the post-Cold-War period, in which the socialist model seems to have been discredited by Stalinism and the excesses and dysfunctionality of the newer global capitalist system have not yet begun fully to appear.

I believe that the representation of alien existence, that is to say, of the imagination of radical otherness, can be seen to have passed through several distinct stages on its way to the contemporary period (where the alien and the other has once again reverted to magic and to dragons).[32] The rich and varied account of alien species and their bodily and social dispositions, something like the Golden Age of that sub-tradition of SF centering on aliens, belongs to the texts we have been considering here, which essentially flourish in the sixties and seventies.

The succession of Ridley Scott's two filmic masterpieces, *Alien* (1979) and *Blade Runner* (1982), may be said symbolically to mark a transition. *Alien* draws some unexpected consequences from Lem's unknowability lesson: one of the unique formal features of this film is that we never see the alien completely at any stage of its growth and development, and thus in a way can never really know it. Meanwhile, although it is supposedly even more intelligent than human beings, its Van Vogtian malignancy[33] is such that it can never be "empathized" from within and by imitation or mimicry, as we have seen to be the case for most representations of the *Verstehen* of otherness, and indeed it is also represented as having no language. But this film, which one might have expected to offer a renewed Cold War fable, turns into a welcome and timely

32 See the discussion of dragons in Chapter 5.
33 See Essay 6, "The Space of SF: Narrative in Van Vogt", in Part Two.

attack on the corporations and multinationals, and includes a vivid picture of human class structure.

Blade Runner then signals the passage from the classic or exotic alien to the representation of the alien other as the same, namely the android, whose differentiation from the earlier robot secures a necessarily humanoid form. This may be said to be the moment of a kind of Hegelian self-consciousness or reflexivity in the genre, in which our attention and preoccupation as readers turn inward, and meditate on the "android cogito",[34] which is to say on the gap or flaw in the self as such.

But the moment of the android is also the moment of the emergence or intervention of a new narrative twist or fold, namely that of the love interest between human and alien. It is this which will be perpetuated in the third moment I hypothesize here, when in the mid-eighties (Mann, *The Eye of the Queen*) or in the nineties (Gwyneth Jones, *White Queen* [1991]) the SF plot veers into perversion, and sexual intercourse with the alien becomes a figure for everything non-normative or deviant or taboo in human society. This is perhaps the place to mention what is to my mind Samuel Delany's finest novel, *Stars in My Pockets Like Grains of Sand* (1984), a unique compendium of distinct forms of otherness:

> One of his chief characters is, to begin with, the victim of radical brain mutilation, and then the sole survivor of a planetary holocaust. The other, a male homosexual human cathected to lovers with either savagely chewed fingernails or strong claws (depending on the species), shares an extended-familial and sexual life with intelligent, six limbed lizards … The most audacious and challenging affront to the schemata we have been socially constructed to read as pre-eminently natural is the Web's gender convention. In its universal though always locally variable language Arachnia, all conscious beings are "women", whatever their gender or species, taking the pronouns "she" and "her" except when the entity referred to by an individual is an object of "her" sexual excitement, when "he" is appropriate.[35]

Yet paradoxically, now that most such taboos have been exhausted, this forbidden contact with the radical other is more reminiscent of incest – the most ancient and fundamental of all the taboos – than of other garden-variety perversions and substitutions. It is a significant development, whose future cannot now be predicted. Ultimately perhaps, as in that other SF filmic masterpiece *The Man Who Fell to Earth* (1976), the alien, fully assimilated, its Difference transmuted into Identity, will simply become a capitalist like the rest of us.

---

34 See Essay 10, "History and Salvation in Philip K. Dick", in Part Two.
35 Broderick, pp. 142–143; Broderick's Delany chapters are highly to be recommended.

10

Utopia and its Antinomies

But the debate over Utopia's representability or not, indeed over its imagin-ability and conceptualization, does not threaten to put an end to Utopian speculation altogether and to return us sagely to the here and now and our own empirical and historical limits. Rather such debates find themselves drawn inside the Utopian text, thereby becoming occasions for further Utopian pro-ductivity. And this seems to be the case for a wide variety of negations which are not reducible to a single logical form: thus the "unknowability thesis" whereby so radically different a society cannot even be imagined is a rather different proposition from the anti-Utopian one according to which attempts to realize Utopia necessarily end up in violence and totalitarianism. Meanwhile, the theory that Utopia is necessarily a negative and critical construction and can never generate any positive or substantive representation or vision is a global denial which has little enough in common with the fights within the Utopian tradition that oppose rural to urban visions, for example, let alone those which seek to replace the supreme Utopian value of happiness with that of freedom.

As a practical matter of Utopian studies, all these categories need to be dealt with separately. As a theoretical matter, on the other hand, it would be of interest to sort them into so many varieties of the negative and negation, which might well be accommodated into a Greimas square or semiotic rec-tangle, but which are all of them included in what we call the dialectic. Attacks on the latter, largely based on Kant's early essay on negative quantities, and most comprehensively staged in Deleuze's *Difference and Repetition*,[1] generally identify the dialectic with a single one of these negations, which it is accused of conflating with one or more of the other formal varieties. But the dialec-tic is in reality the study of all these types of negation together (along with

1 Kant's 1763 essay is entitled "Attempt to introduce the concept of negative magnitudes into philosophy"; Lucio Coletti's arguments (they are essentially attacks on Hegel's concept of neg-ativity) are to be found in *From Rousseau to Lenin* (New York, 1972); Deleuze's classic work is, of course, *Différence et répétition* (Paris, 1968); and see also Ernesto Laclau and Chantal Mouffe, *Hegemony and Socialist Strategy* (London, 1985), Chapter 3.

their contradictions with each other): thus, it includes both contrariety and contradiction (the two negative axes of the Greimas square), but also the logical difference between them (a difference which is at once both contrariety and contradiction, a sublation of both which is at one and the same time their synthesis and their differentiation). This is the place not to pursue such a theoretical argument further, but merely to observe that our four final chapters will try to sort out these types of negation insofar as they concern Utopia: the present one and its sequel dealing with characterizations of Utopia in opposition to each other (the city Utopia versus the country Utopia for example); the penultimate one addressing that seemingly absolute negation of Utopia which is the anti-Utopia; and the concluding chapter a discussion of Utopia as radical or absolute difference from the present as such.

As far as the oppositions within Utopia are concerned, it is worth recalling that one of the unique features of the Utopian tradition consists in the way in which the form itself seems to interiorize differences which generally remain implicit in literary history (thereby paradoxically remaining external to the literary works themselves). High-literary writers may therefore write against each other, or they may be interpreted as writing against each other by literary critics and historians; but the autonomy of (modernist) literary form tends to project each individual work as a kind of absolute in its own right, which can only be reduced to an opinion and a polemic stance in some ongoing Bakhtinian argument by a violent shift in perspective from the text to a historical construction and indeed to a literary-historical narrative substituted for it. To paraphrase Hegel, each work, each style, seeks the death of all the others: a proposition subsequently demonstrated in Malraux's *Voices of Silence* (1946) and philosophically affirmed as recently as Adorno's *Aesthetic Theory* (1970).

But what in literature or art remains an irreconcilable existence of so many absolutes, on the order of the various religions, becomes in the Utopian tradition a Bakhtinian dialogue or argument between positions which claim the status of the absolute but are willing to descend into the field of struggle of representability and desire in order to win their case and convert their readership. And, inasmuch as the practice of the genre necessarily includes a generic reference to More's foundational text, history and the succession of Utopian generations become themselves interiorized within the later Utopias and variously incorporated into the Utopian argument (much as philosophical texts are obliged to take positions on the entire history of philosophy that preceded and enabled them).[2]

Some of these Utopian arguments are explicit public debates, as in the eternal pair of Bellamy and Morris, the latter's *News from Nowhere* (1890) being

---

2   See Richard Rorty, *Philosophy and the Mirror of Nature* (Princeton, 1979), in which the very notion of a "history of philosophy" is demonstrated to be a construction (that is to say: it is a "constructed", and not a natural continuity).

an explicit response to the former's *Looking Backward* (1888).[3] Here the essential differences are twofold: Bellamy's industrial state (modeled on the army) is refuted by the anarchistic "withering away" of the state in Morris, while the account of labor in *Looking Backward* (something like Marx's "realm of necessity" opposed to the "realm of freedom" of non-work and leisure time)[4] is challenged by Morris' notion of a non-alienated labor which has become a form of aesthetic production.

Meanwhile, the "ambiguous Utopia" of Ursula Le Guin's *Dispossessed* (1974) was famously challenged by the "ambiguous heterotopia" of Samuel Delany's *Trouble on Triton* (1976), presumably on the grounds that Le Guin's Marxist view of the modes of production did not, despite its allusions to a revised position on homosexuality in the communist world, sufficiently address the countercultural issues that arose in the "new social movements" of the 1960s and 1970s. But where Morris answered one Utopia with another, Delany's subtitle seems to propose a wholesale refusal of the form itself, in favor of a Foucauldian alternative of Utopian spaces and enclaves within the reigning dystopia of the system: thus, *Triton* includes just such a space in its picture of the "unlicensed sector" in which, as in Rabelais or Sade, anything and everything is permitted (see below); just as the galactic war in which his Utopian planet is embroiled could stand as a comment on the violence implicit in Utopian closure as such. But the novel has nonetheless generally been read as a Utopian answer to another Utopia, rather than as an anti-Utopia of the more

3 The seismic effect of Bellamy's virtual reinvention of Utopia cannot be underestimated: it electrified a variety of cultures in ways comparable only to Chernyshevsky's impact on the more local area of Russia (there were at least six different Chinese translations, for example). Meanwhile, the productive reactions go well beyond Morris' socialist/anarchist reply; *Looking Backward* may also be said to have generated the first genuine totalitarian dystopia – Ignatius Donnelly's *Caesar's Column* (1890), which preceded Jack London's *Iron Heel* by seventeen years. The ferment aroused in feminist Utopias is documented in Dolores Hayden, *The Grand Domestic Revolution* (Cambridge, MA, 1981). One may, to be sure, credit the age rather than the Utopian visionaries it produced: for behind the bourgeois progressivism of the period whose monument was the pragmatist movement in philosophy there lay the immense forces of populism itself: see Lawrence Goodwin, *Democratic Promise: The Populist Moment in America* (New York, 1976).

4 Karl Marx, *Capital*, Volume III (London, 1981), pp. 958–959: "The realm of freedom really begins only where labour determined by necessity and external expediency ends; it lies by its very nature beyond the sphere of material production proper. Just as the savage must wrestle with nature to satisfy his needs, to maintain and reproduce his life, so must civilized man, and he must do so in all forms of society and under all possible modes of production. This realm of natural necessity expands with his development, because his needs do too; but the productive forces to satisfy these expand at the same time. Freedom, in this sphere, can consist only in this, that socialized man, the associated producers, govern the human metabolism with nature in a rational way, bringing it under their collective control instead of being dominated by it as a blind power; accomplishing it with the least expenditure of energy and in conditions most worthy and appropriate for their human nature. But this always remains a realm of necessity. The true realm of freedom, the development of human powers as an end in itself, begins beyond it, though it can only flourish with this realm of necessity as its basis. The reduction of the working day is the basic prerequisite."

familiar Cold War type (something Le Guin's novel approaches more closely in its view of the repressive conformism of Anarresti society than anything in Delany) or even the explicitly anti-Utopian denunciations of Chernyshevsky and of Paxton's Utopian Crystal Palace in Dostoyevsky (not normally considered a writer in the Utopian tradition at all, but see Chapter 11).

Whether this increasingly reflexive development of the Utopian form as such portends its imminent mutation or transformation will be considered in a concluding chapter. Its history, at any rate, has certainly been characterized by substantive oppositions of the kind just touched on; and it is time to take a brief inventory of the latter, an exercise which requires at least one preliminary philosophical warning. It would be tempting, and probably even possible, to fold such a list of oppositions into each other, thereby producing a single primordial antithesis of which each is only a local embodiment or specification. The result would be to ontologize solutions to specific historical situations in the form of some timeless metaphysical dualism such as that between materialism and idealism. It is, for example, enough to reflect on the status of the body in the various textual Utopias from Thomas More all the way to Le Guin and Delany to become aware of the feasibility of such a project, and also, I hope, of the way in which it would relentlessly psychologize the various Utopian options as a matter of ascetic or hedonistic temperament. To be sure, all the Utopian options in question must involve existential commitment and visceral participation, even where – especially where – one particular vision is rejected with passion or revulsion. At the same time, on both existential and social levels, there is bound to be a thematic interrelationship between the various options, which involve topics such as work and leisure, laws and behavior, uniformity and individual difference, sexuality and the family – topics which any Utopian proposal would necessarily have to address in one way or another. Yet as we have suggested in an earlier chapter, the grand Utopian idea or wish – the abolition of property, the complementarity of desires, non alienated labor, the equality of the sexes – is always conceived as a situation-specific resolution of a concrete historical dilemma. The viability of the Utopian fantasy assuredly finds its test and its verification in the way in which it promises to solve all the other concomitant problems as well. But each of these will reshuffle its primary and secondary terms, its dominants and its subordinates, its combined practice of Imagination and Fancy, in structurally original ways. It is best to hold to the specific historical focus, to the central thematic of the new social proposal, which makes its own unique trajectory of the links between the problems to be solved, rather than to reduce the texts to this or that world-view, let alone to assimilate them all to the mentality detected and diagnosed by a far more homogeneous anti-Utopian ideology: we thus now shift from a focus on Utopian form and the structure of wish-fulfillment to an examination of Utopian content.

We may begin our inventory in a relatively random way, by citing the excellent summaries of Goodwin and Taylor:

> Among the supposedly disjunctive categories of analysis which commentators have found fruitful are the ascetic/abundant (indulgent), aesthetic/functional, scientific/primitivist, sensual/spiritual and religious/secular. Most recently the introduction of the term "sexist" to academic circles has given rise to analysis of the role of women and the function of the family in utopias. From the standpoint of political thought today, the following dichotomies are the most important: egalitarian/inegalitarian (or elitist), "open"/totalitarian, libertarian/coercive, democratic/undemocratic and optimistic (with regard to human nature)/pessimistic …[5]

And in another chapter, they thematize the strategic dilemmas of modern Utopias in the following terms: industrialism versus anti-industrialism; private property versus common ownership; religion versus secularization; revolution versus gradualism; statism versus communitarianism; and democratic versus authoritarian organization.[6] The disparity between these lists, not entirely attributable to the laudable aim of transcending the opposition between humanist and social-scientific approaches to Utopia, would probably open up interesting new problems, but also lead us back to current events (and, as we shall see later on, to ideologies). Thus, the at first surprising presence of religion in these oppositions – after More's religious tolerance, it does not seem to play much of a role in the principal written Utopias, even down through the 1960s – can be validated today in terms of something like an opposition between fundamentalism and Western political tolerance (or, in other words, between Rawls and Islam). The open/totalitarian opposition is surely a Cold War reflex; while the double opposition between asceticism and sensuality, somewhat moot in the 1960s, has taken a new lease on life with AIDS and contemporary neo-Confucianism; yet this timely reminder warns that it also needs to be reformulated in feminist terms (themselves enfeebled since the 1960s and 1970s). Such oppositions have certainly not gone away; but the historical movement from the 1960s to the moralizing of the free-market era dramatizes the ways in which they find themselves rethematized by historical modifications in our own "context".

I wish to approach the issue of Utopian antinomies from a rather different, and more purely philosophical standpoint, while at the same time acknowledging the significance of just such historical or contextual analyses of individual or textual Utopian expressions. It would be a pity, indeed, if such analysis led us to believe that the now more purely historical perspective

---

5 Barbara Goodwin and Keith Taylor, *The Politics of Utopia* (New York, 1983), p. 59.
6 Ibid., pp. 129–137.

on such debates has made a whole range of Utopian issues, and perhaps even Utopia itself, a purely antiquarian matter. Yet (as has already been said) it would be equally unsatisfactory to frame the debates in purely philosophical or metaphysical fashion. But before addressing this question more directly, let's look at a series of oppositions, which will in part overlap with Taylor and Goodwin's.

I

We may begin with the question of work or labor, a significant absence from their lists, but an inevitable issue in our current world, menaced both within the nation-state and on a global scale with both alienated, oppressive labor, and massive and permanent structural unemployment. At once, then, we can observe this seemingly simple theme separate into two kinds of questions, one on the nature of work or labor and the status of leisure, the other on full employment as such. At length, however, these issues will meet and become a single topic once again.

Few Utopian fantasies are quite so practical and potentially revolutionary in their effects as the demand for full employment, for if there is any program that could not be realized without transforming the system beyond recognition and which would at once usher in a society structurally distinct from this one in every conceivable way, from the psychological to the sociological, from the cultural to the political, it would be the demand for universal full employment in all the countries of the globe, full employment at a living wage. As all the economic apologists for the system today have tirelessly instructed us, capitalism cannot flourish under full employment; it requires a reserve army of the unemployed in order to function. This first monkey wrench would be compounded by the universality of the requirement, inasmuch as capitalism also requires a frontier and the possibility of perpetual expansion in order to go on existing and to sustain its inner dynamic. But at this point the Utopianism of the demand becomes circular, for it is also clear, not only that the establishment of full employment would transform the system, but also that the system would already have to have been transformed, in advance, in order for full employment to be established. I would not call this a vicious circle, exactly; but it certainly reveals the space of a Utopian leap, between our empirical present and the Utopian arrangements of this imaginary future.

Yet about such a future, imaginary or not, I would also wish to note that it returns upon our present to play a diagnostic and a critical-substantive role: to foreground full employment in this way, as the fundamental Utopian requirement, then allows us to return to concrete circumstances and situations and to read their dark spots and pathological dimensions as so many symptoms and effects of unemployment. Crime, war, degraded mass culture, drugs, violence, boredom, the lust for power, the lust for distraction, the lust for nirvana, sexism, racism – all can be diagnosed as so many results of a society unable to accommodate the productiveness of all of its citizens. At this point, then, Utopian circularity becomes both a political vision and program, and a critical and diagnostic instrument.

This particular theme also strikes a mortal blow at a system which, by virtue of the elective affinity between developing automation and a market ideology intent on profits rather than on production and rapidly evolving into the stage of finance capital, has produced a universal imperative of downsizing and a notion of efficiency based on the requirement of the least possible number of employees. The new imperative is then enforced by the banks (and internationally by their supranational projection in the IMF), who are able to refuse investment and loans to corporations which do not "balance their budgets", that is to say, do not show the will to dismiss as many workers (from all classes, white-collar fully as much as blue-collar) as possible. The mechanism therefore effectively generates its own crisis in a historic reversal of Henry Ford's strategy of creating enough lower-class consumers to buy up his products. Here a population is generated who are no longer able to afford the products of the system. Meanwhile, however, the living standard of the advanced countries is too high for their industries to compete with cheap labor elsewhere in the world, and so these remnants of industrial production move, first to Mexico, and then to China, while waiting for wages in the adopted environment to rise and our own living standards to drop, so that we can begin the production cycle here all over again from rock bottom.

The Utopia of full employment cuts across these dilemmas without solving them; in effect, it presupposes that the system has already been transformed in such a way as once more to permit full employment. At the same time, as a resolution, it mobilizes deep-seated existential anxieties: for, despite the likelihood that most of the readers of this book are still employed, we are all of us familiar with the fear of unemployment, and not unacquainted with the psychic misery involved in chronic unemployment, the demoralization, the morbid effects of boredom and the waste of vital energies and the absence of productivity (and this, even if we tend to grasp such things in bourgeois and introspective ways).

Now, however, we need to see how this particular Utopian figure generates its own opposite: for insofar as the emphasis is placed on the search for a solution to the disaster of permanent unemployment, a rather different one also lies to hand, and that is the guaranteed minimum wage, something which has occasionally been proposed by elements of the Left, but which would seem to constitute a more classically right-wing, not to say, fascist solution, in the Roman style of bread and circuses. Here the excess of wealth of the state and its patrons is sensibly and tactically motivated in order to produce the consumers required to keep the system functioning and to absorb production. It is a solution that has also had its Utopian advocates, and seems redolent of all the voluntary-labor

Utopias which boast the realization of the ultimate communist motto, "to each according to his needs". These Utopias are not generally obliged to enforce work in Draconian ways: ostracism (as in Le Guin's *Dispossessed*), along with desperate ecological crisis, is enough. Or else the society is fantasized as being at such a high state of production – and automation! – that machinery produces the required abundance with only a minimum of human labor, variously estimated at anything from two to six hours a day,[7] and this owing in some cases to the reduction of luxuries and consumption, and the "reeducation of desire", the retraining of the population in basic needs (Morris, Callenbach). But that retraining, and its possibility, implies a fundamental presupposition which has not gone unchallenged and which we will examine in a moment.

For the rest, the Utopia of abundance and absolute leisure is an ancient one: the famous *pays de Cockaygne* indeed reflects a peasant ideology in the combination of hunger and back-breaking toil it fantasizes away.

> Ah! those chambers and those halls!
> All of pastries stand the walls,
> Of fish and flesh and all rich meat,
> The tastiest that men can eat.
> Wheaten cakes the shingles all,
> Of church, of cloister, bower and hall.
> The pinnacles are fat puddings,
> Good food for princes or for kings.
> Every man takes what he will,
> As of right, to eat his fill.
> All is common to young and old,
> To stout and strong, to meek and bold.
>
> Yet this wonder add to it –
> That geese fly roasted on the spit,
> As God's my witness, to that spot,
> Crying out, "Geese, all hot, all hot!"
> Every goose in garlic drest,
> Of all food the seemliest.
> And the larks that are so couth
> Fly right down into man's mouth,
> Smothered in stew, and thereupon
> Piles of powdered cinnamon.
> Every man may drink his fill
> And needn't sweat to pay the bill.[8]

---

7   Marcuse, *Eros and Civilization* (1955) and Rudolph Bahro, *The Alternative* (London, 1978 [1977]).
8   Quoted by J.C. Davis, *Utopia and the Ideal Society* (Cambridge, 1981), p. 21.

In our time, in societies of high productivity, it also encourages fantasies of enclave life, as in the 1960s American counterculture, in which a bare minimum is necessary to survive and lead a different kind of Utopian life within standard American capitalist affluence. These Utopias are to be sure explicitly or implicitly collective in their nature: the medieval ones obviously taking the village and the older collectivities for granted, while contemporary versions presuppose a kind of secret underground network within the official state, so many clandestine communities of a hidden Utopian nature flourishing beyond the latter's reach and invisible to the latter's organs of surveillance. "Crime" is here what is defined by the law and legality of that official state, which can be ignored in the name of clan loyalty but which also, in a kind of dialectical reversal and paradox, can offer a new form of collective labor.[9]

Yet was not the whole purpose of the great socialist movements precisely to get rid of labor in the first place? And is it not something of a contradiction – if not, indeed, an outright admission of defeat – when such movements call for universal employment and wage labor generalized around the globe? Indeed, did not Marx's own son-in-law write a famous pamphlet entitled *Le Droit à la paresse* (*The Right to Idleness*);[10] and have not the most consequent contemporary socialist theoreticians contemplated at some length the ambivalence of the "jobless future" which is both a nightmare and a "promesse de bonheur" all at once.[11]

Surely, however, the simple distinction between alienated and non-alienated labor[12] is enough to cut this Gordian knot and resolve what seems to be a fundamental contradiction between the proponents of work and the proponents of a realm, if not of freedom, then at least of free time. But I fear that the contradiction runs deeper than this, and that the distinction afforded by the concept of alienation is not enough to paper over these deeper warring ideological impulses.

There is indeed here a valorization of production and of modern conceptions of productivity which is clearly incompatible with the Rousseau revival and with images such as those Marshall Sahlins offers us of the "first affluent society":

---

9 I might as well here cite my unpublished paper on the Utopian aspects of the heist or caper film.

10 Paul Lafargue, *Le Droit à la paresse* (Paris, 1883); Lafargue is arguing against the misuse of the rhetoric of the "dignity of labor" and its "ennobling" function etc. by the capitalists and their ideologists.

11 The reference is to *The Jobless Future* by Stanley Aronowitz and William DiFazio (Minnesota, 1994). The other fundamental contemporary discussion of labor, alienated, non-alienated and Utopian is to be found in André Gorz, *Critique of Economic Reason* (London, 1989); but see also Bahro, note 7, and Moishe Postone, *Time, Labor, and Social Domination* (Cambridge, 1996).

12 First elaborated in Marx's 1844 manuscripts. And, indeed, see Marx himself on the "realm of freedom", above, note 4.

When Herskovits was writing his *Economic Anthropology* (1958), it was common anthropological practice to take the Bushmen or the native Australians as "a classic illustration of a people whose economic resources are of the scantiest", so precariously situated that "only the most intense application makes survival possible". Today the "classic" understanding can be fairly reversed – on evidence largely from these two groups. A good case can be made that hunters and gatherers work less than we do; and, rather than a continuous travail, the food quest is intermittent, leisure abundant, and there is a greater amount of sleep in the daytime per capita per year than in any other condition of society.[13]

In the 1960s, this incompatibility was expressed in the increasingly widespread characterization of Marxism as a productivist ideology which combined the most intense versions of Max Weber's "Protestant" work ethic (the admiration of Lenin and Gramsci for Taylorism and Fordism is frequently recalled) with a more properly "Promethean" domination of nature.[14] There are, to be sure, other and very different Marxisms (which also include the Utopian strains within Soviet Marxism itself);[15] but our interest here lies, not in the accuracy of either interpretive position, but rather in their deeper motivations and fantasy structure.

One could, indeed, go on to identify a Christian and ascetic, self-punishing and guilt-ridden impulse in that requirement of work specified in many early Utopias; an impulse – the curse of the lost garden, the punishment of the "sweat of your brow" – that seems richly to validate Weber's religious specification of his modern work ethic. As has been mentioned in an earlier chapter, even the official Epicureanism of More's imaginary society is somewhat tarnished by his philosophical idealism as well as his nostalgia for monasticism and by the famous hairshirt (the date at which he began to wear it is, to be sure, unknown). Yet one can also adduce very different explanations for such "productionism" (and even, perhaps, for the religious traditions thus alleged to motivate it). Indeed, any inspection of contemporary right-wing materials often enough betrays the deepest anxieties as to what might happen to the social order if its institutions of repression and discipline, of obligatory labor, were to be relaxed; while any alert Lacanian will readily observe that envy of

13   Marshall Sahlins, "The First Affluent Society", in *Stone Age Economics*, p. 14. The essay is of a piece with Baudrillard and Pierre Clastres; see also note 14 in Chapter 2.

14   See for a paradigmatic expression, Jean Baudrillard, *The Mirror of Production* (Paris, 1973).

15   Sheila Kirkpatrick's assertion that there was such a thing as "daily life under Stalinism" has aroused the indignation of Cold War veterans. Yet, leaving aside Günter Grass' monumental *Ein weites Feld*, it might be best to leave the word to the Easterners themselves: see Slavoj Žižek, "When the Party Commits Suicide" (*New Left Review*, No. 238, November–December 1999); and for other expressions of what has come to be called *Ostalgie*, see Charity Scribner, "From the Collective to the Collection", *New Left Review*, No. 237 (September–October, 1999).

the *jouissance* of others, of the slackers and the allegedly "non-productive" members of society, is an explosive force indeed.[16]

Now we may perhaps return to the distinction between alienated and non-alienated labor in a new way by coming at its genealogy. Marx's 1844 innovation was indeed to have supplied a fourfold account of the nature of alienation itself (the worker is alienated from his tools, from his product, from his pro-ductive activity, and from his species-being as such, or in other words his fellow workers). But this concrete account of alienation leaves us at best with a more psychological and reactive picture of what non-alienated labor might be: a control over the production process, for example; a share of the product; a sol-idarity with fellow workers; and perhaps an innovative replacement of the static conception of property implied in the negative description by a new one organ-ized around the experience of process and the categories of collectivity.

Yet the motivation for the new account of alienation – for which Marx drew significantly on Hegel – is to be found in an earlier moment in German idealism, namely in Schiller's theorization of play (*Spiel*) as a transcendence of Kant's division of the faculties.[17] Schiller indeed attempts politically and socially to complete that interpretive movement whereby Kant's *Critique of Judgment* was grasped as the link between the two other Critiques, and the latter's aesthetics seen as a bridge between his critique of epistemology and his ethics. The attempt thereby testifies to the temptation of an aesthetic solution to the dilemmas of what will only later be identified as alienation; and Schiller's concept of play – a very different kind of idea from anything to be found in either Kant's or Hegel's aesthetics – becomes the predecessor of the aesthetic politics of Ruskin, and following him of Morris: one in which non-alienated labor can finally find a positive analogue in art as such, it being understood that for both later theoreticians aesthetics finds its paradigm in architecture and construction (and in Morris' case in design) rather than in the more indi-vidualistic arts. This is a valorization of production which will return in the 1960s in Herbert Marcuse's Utopian vision, inspired by the contemporaneous "happenings", of the aesthetization of everyday life as such. And this is also perhaps the moment to observe the way in which aesthetic theories seem to shadow Utopian ones at every turn, and to make themselves available for plau-sible resolutions of otherwise contradictory Utopian dilemmas.

For the moment, however, it is important to note that both Ruskin's and Marcuse's aesthetic politics are responses to a historically new development in the social situations addressed by earlier Utopian thinkers, and that is the emergence of industrial technology. In particular, Marcuse's Utopian vision is

16 Slavoj Žižek, "The 'Theft of Enjoyment'", in *Tarrying with the Negative* (Durham, NC, 2003), pp. 201–205.

17 Friedrich Schiller, *Letters on the Aesthetic Education of Mankind* (Cambridge, 1967 [1795]), and also Georg Lukács' remarkable essay on Schiller's role in the Marxist tradition, in *Beiträge zur Geschichte der Aesthetik* (Berlin, 1954).

explicitly enabled by his conviction that the state of productivity attained in the 1960s was capable, when organized and managed properly, of feeding the entire population of the world and abolishing hunger and want.[18] This technological optimism, which seems to have lasted until the end of the 1970s, at least in the US, was then brutally effaced by the neo-conservative revolution and its accompanying effects – the debt, population explosion, the failure of modernization – in the Third and later in the Second Worlds.

The separation of the theme of technology and invention from the "ugliness" of factory and industrial work as such can thus sometimes offer the relief of a *deus ex machina* to more modern Utopian dilemmas: witness those mysterious "force vehicles" which provide for the transport of goods in the "Nowhere" of the otherwise anti-technological Morris.[19] Witness also the computers which organize labor assignments in Le Guin's *Dispossessed* and the *heyimas* or communications center which more paradoxically takes charge of the dynamics of her pre-modern, proto-Indian villages in *Always Coming Home*.[20]

But these are still relatively primitive computers; and it does seem fair to me to suggest that the new wave of Utopian production in the late 1960s stops short of the cybernetic age, and fails to exploit its new and properly Utopian resources. The latter are certainly expressed, as a Utopian impulse, in movements like that of cyberpunk and in all kinds of Utopian fantasies associated with the Internet;[21] but the principal result so far seems less to have been the production of new visions of social organization and of social relations than the rendering anachronistic and insipid of the older industrial notions of non-alienated labor as such.[22]

---

18   Marcuse, *Eros and Civilization*, p. 84.

19   William Morris, *News from Nowhere and Other Writings* (London, 1993), p. 186.

20   Ursula Le Guin, *Always Coming Home* (New York, 1985), p. 48.

21   *Wired* magazine is, I believe, the homeland for such Utopian fantasies about the Internet.

22   But even if the computer age is a "brave new world" whose Utopian or dystopian valences remain to be measured, the Utopian propaganda for cybernetics (or indeed for globalization itself) has exploited what is essentially its cultural or communicational dimension. Books like Thomas L. Friedman's *The World Is Flat* (New York, 2005), however, make it plain (whether explicitly or implicitly) that there is a whole business infrastructure whose communicational infrastructure would demand a very different representation than what is offered in the usual rhetoric of informational and communicational democracy (which has also been the underlying ideological theme of contemporary philosophy, from structuralism to Habermas). Indeed, the literary Utopists have scarcely kept pace with the businessmen in the process of imagination and construction, pursuing various forms of globalized Fancy and ignoring a global infrastructural deployment in which, from this quite different perspective, the Walmart celebrated by Friedman becomes the very anticipatory prototype of some new form of socialism for which the reproach of centralization now proves historically misplaced and irrelevant. It is in any case certainly a revolutionary reorganization of capitalist production, and some acknowledgement such as "Waltonism" or "Walmartification" would be a more appropriate name for this new stage than vacuous terms such as "post-Fordism" or "flexible capitalism", which are merely privative or reactive.

The negative affect of the older images persists, however, and has been displaced from the realm of industrial to that of informational production, as befits a cybernetic age. But at this point, rather than evoking alienated labor, we might rather speak of alienated leisure. For we here encounter that dimension of industrial production henceforth known as the media (a term which spans a whole range of communicational phenomena from automobiles and superhighways to radio and television): and it is in this area that industrial and post-industrial Utopias confront their gravest challenge. Morris did not indeed have to worry much about mass culture, which he expected gradually to be effaced by the new social relations and the return of handicraft and genuinely aesthetic work satisfaction.

Indeed, it is first on the Right that the political and social anxieties associated with "the masses" takes on a properly cultural dimension. For now the free time More provided his Utopians for spiritual and intellectual pursuits has been transformed into the commodity of "leisure" and is rapidly colonized by the entertainment industry. The resultant right-wing critiques of a "degraded mass culture" (in Heidegger, T.S. Eliot, Ortega y Gasset) are characterized by the omission of any discussions of capitalism and the eventual transfer of this particular form of entropy to this or that dystopian system, of which, to be sure, Huxley's *Brave New World* (1932) is the epic poem.[23] On the Left, similar anxieties are expressed in Stapledon's picture in *Star Maker* (1937) of his "other world", whose inhabitants become so addicted to the technological bliss of their telephonic taste system that they end up passing their whole lives in bed. The "culture industry" (1947) of Adorno and Horkheimer then theorizes the structure of the commodification of culture and provides a powerful dystopian vision of the alienation of leisure under capitalism which is not particularly relieved by any alternative accounts of a socialist (and mostly Stalinist) culture, and which hands its dystopian torch down to more contemporary critical theories, such as that found in Debord's *Society of the Spectacle* (1968) and in Baudrillard, where the final stage of commodity reification is famously discovered to be the image, and ultimately the simulacrum.

The image indeed abolishes that older distinction between mind and body, between intellectual and manual labor, on which the philosophical humanism of the theory of non-alienated labor was predicated. Commodified mass culture is indeed superstructure and infrastructure all at once; its consumption, according to Adorno and Horkheimer, is just as much a matter of production as it is of consumption ("the technology of the culture industry confines itself to standardization and mass production and sacrifices what

---

23 The term dystopia has traditionally been used (as it is here) to designate representations of the future best characterized as "new maps of hell" (Kingsley Amis, 1960), and such predictions have loosely been grasped as anti-Utopias. Tom Moylan's work (Chapter 12, note 31) forces us to rethink this stereotype, as we shall see shortly.

once distinguished the logic of the work from that of society").[24] The Utopian return to the old Platonic distinction between true and false happiness, as in Marcuse, is now denounced as humanism by a mass culture flowering into full postmodernity, and unmasked as the elitism of intellectuals attempting to pass themselves off as philosopher-kings. Meanwhile, in the nightmare of social life as one long televised orgy (in Brian Aldiss' *Helliconia* trilogy [1982–85]) the opposition between puritanism and hedonism returns with a vengeance, suggesting that the Utopia of full employment and even of non-alienated labor as such is motivated by an idealism unwilling to trust a sinful human race with the poisoned gift of free time.

II

Such, then, are the dilemmas and contradictions of a Utopian meditation on production; but the same themes are to be found, rearranged in a somewhat different trajectory, in any meditation on Utopian consumption, let alone in that inspired by the question of distribution. For the dystopias of mass culture we have just touched on are merely the face of consumption glimpsed, as it were, from the realm of production itself. When we turn to the former more directly, the antithesis with which we are confronted is better formulated as one between abundance and poverty. But here poverty sheds the overtones of repression and Puritanism associated with the various labor debates and takes on something of the luminosity of a more joyous and Franciscan vision, of the light of the desert or the serenity that comes with fasting. But it is important to realize that neither of these poles – abundance and Franciscan poverty alike – exists in our world. Both are Utopian: the vision of abundance developing out of the Marcusean fantasy of high productivity, while the choice of poverty is constituted out of a radical aesthetic simplification of our everyday life in the present, a reduction of desire to the limits of need which has as little to do with moderation as a rather miserable class virtue as it does with real misery and the suffering of real hunger and destitution.

This is precisely what makes up the hidden imbalance or dissymmetry of Le Guin's wonderful juxtaposition of these two states of being in the twin planets of Urras and Anarres in *The Dispossessed*, whose very ecologies become expressions of their ideological antagonism. To be sure, the writer has attempted to transcend local Cold War stereotypes by making her communists over into anarchists, with overtones of Taoism: yet well before Stalin and his repressive industrialization, Morris had also distanced his own communism from a centralizing state socialism in advance (that particular revolution having failed, he tells us, and given way to the one portrayed in *News from Nowhere*).[25] Indeed, a

---

24 T.W. Adorno and Max Horkheimer, *Dialectic of Enlightenment* (Palo Alto, 2002), pp. 95, 104.
25 Morris, *News*, pp. 140ff.

conventional state socialism (also present in *The Dispossessed* in the neighboring country of Thu) can easily be accommodated by convergence theory, which saw capitalism and Stalinist industrialization as two faces of the more general process of modernization. No such resolution can be imagined for the decentralization of Anarres, which is incompatible with the various Urras systems (the latter conveniently enough already representing First, Second and Third Worlds).

Yet a stereotypical anti-socialist (or anarchist) convention is reproduced, as it were for even-handedness, in the emphasis on conformity in Anarres, on a kind of small-town bigotry which is conveniently allied to the accompanying stereotype of bureaucracy and its alleged jealousies and repression of innovation (Shevek's superior tries to take credit for his scientific discoveries, while the populace denounces his travel to Urras as treason in a prototypical mob scene). But the contrasting portrait of Urras (the two planets are assigned alternating chapters, in a bravura form in which Shevek's prehistory develops alongside the story of his decisive journey) does not offer a complementary critique of the political and social drawbacks of capitalism as a mode of production and regulation: rather it emphasizes the phenomenon of consumption as such, thereby both reproducing and critically estranging the classic dissymmetry of Western Cold War rhetoric, in which political objections (freedom) are enlisted against an anti-capitalist economic system. But in Le Guin no objections are implied against the Anarresti collectivist mode of production as such. Meanwhile, the political structures of domination and exploitation in Urras are withheld (we do not even know how A-Io is governed) until the climactic strike and repression, in contrast to the lynch mob on Anarres with which the book begins.

So it is that the narrative "rhetoric" of this "ambiguous Utopia" is on both sides of the diptych displaced onto the theme of consumption, which is calculated to estrange or defamiliarize our habitual perceptions and to shock us into some fresh awareness of everything nauseating about our own current wealth and our own rich commodity system (the subliminal images of food and eating are everywhere here, Shevek emblematically vomits at one point, and the word "rich" obviously carries nauseous culinary overtones with it). Commodity reification and consumerism then become vivid exemplifications of what Odo denounced as excess and excrement; but at this point the reproach of Left puritanism takes on plausibility again, while the very concept of reification, in which the religious overtones of the fetishized object are repudiated in the name of need and simple functionality, is seen as having a more suspicious motivation than that of simple materialism as such, which could always be reformulated in terms of the *pays de Cockaygne* and of physical pleasure.

Another way of grasping the new objection is to reformulate it in terms of aesthetics, or rather as a repudiation of aesthetics and art, even including the Morris–Ruskin celebration of beauty. For is not art in fact excess *par excellence*, the superfluous above and beyond sheer physical subsistence? Is it not decoration (also denounced by Odo, along with ornament in the spirit of Adolf Loos) that adds something to human mere animal existence? Nor is Shevek insensible to this sensory and aesthetic splendor, which he finds in the land-scape,[26] but above all in the magnificent fabrics, which adorn the rooms but are also suggestive of clothing, bodies and sexuality (even comfort is redolent of sexuality),[27] as are finally the commodities themselves: "The air of the shop was sweet and warm, as if all the perfumes of the spring were crowded into it. Shevek stood there amidst the cases of pretty luxuries, tall, heavy, dreamy, like heavy animals in their pens, the rams and bulls stupefied by the yearning warmth of spring."[28]

Yet it is not the minimalism of Anarresti art (see Chapter 12) which is opposed to the aesthetics of consumption on Urras: an opposition which would reassimilate this opposition to our own art history and the more familiar supercession of an aesthetic of beauty by a modernist aesthetic of the sublime. Poverty on Anarres is not to be identified with that sobriety of white walls and streamlining with which Le Corbusier and Loos rebuked a decadent nine-teenth-century bourgeois taste: an aesthetic of the cold shower and of rigorous hygiene, a kind of reeducation of desire for the machine age, in which a new kind of athletic libidinal investment ultimately triumphs over its overstuffed predecessor.

Here we may rather speak of something like a displacement from aesthetic consumption as such to a transformation of everyday life. Ironically, however, the Ruskin prescription for such a transformation, in which the ugliness of the factory world was to be replaced by nature and a return to medieval hand-icraft, is as it were itself inverted, the new system demanding a libidinal dissociation from the consumption of individual objects or works, and a pro-jection of these impulses onto social and collective relations generally. In Anarres, then, social relations, both private and public, are cathected with all the energies released by the abolition of property.

It is a transformation now surcharged and overlaid by another opposition, one of the most fundamental in all Utopian thought, namely the opposition between city and country, a Utopian antinomy which is now expressed within the realm of space as such, and which also tends to modulate our attention from consumption to production and distribution. For now Abbenay is char-acterized in terms of transparency, a rather different ideologeme associated with the reification debates, and tending to displace the suspicions of puri-tanism. Here what is definitional about the commodity is not so much its religious or spiritual "fetishistic" value, as rather its function as a disguise of labor. The fetishized commodity indeed interrupts the transparency of the

---

26   Ursula Le Guin, *The Dispossessed* (New York, 1974), p. 82.
27   Ibid., p. 18.
28   Ibid., p. 211.

process of production and exchange: it inserts a sham materiality into something which is originally (and remains beneath the surface) a social relation, a
relationship between people. In that allegedly original (and no doubt Utopian)
relationship, the human labor that gives an object its value is visible to the
consumer, as is that of the object it is exchanged for. In the process of consumption we have here preeminently to do with labor time and with a
reciprocity of work, a primordial division of labor in which it is not the talents
of the respective workers which is at stake but simply their mutual complementarity. With the developing inequality of human relations, however,
consumption risks being burdened with guilt, as we glimpse the expense of
toil and labor time which has gone into the production of what becomes for
us a luxury: thus the materiality of the object itself is summoned to veil the
human relationship and to give it the appearance of a relation between things.
This is the analysis which the development of reification theory in recent times
(in France and in Germany alike, with *Tel Quel* as much as with Adorno) has
crystallized in a striking motto, namely, that reification can be defined as the
effacement of the traces of production on the object.

The description of Abbenay draws on this conception of reification in
terms of transparency and opacity:

> Abbenay was poisonless: a bare city, bright, the colors light and hard, the air
> pure. It was quiet. You could see it all, laid out as plain as spilt salt.
>
>   Nothing was hidden … The activity going on in each place was fascinat-
> ing, and mostly out in full view … No doors were locked, few shut. There
> were no disguises and no advertisements. It was all there, all the work, all the
> life of the city, open to the eye and to the hand.[29]

Transparency becomes here a vehicle for the collective totality, which is able
to grasp how the specialized work of each group is necessary for the whole.
In principle it is this transparency then, this grasp of the social totality, which
serves as the "moral incentive" on Anarres, and which replaces the profit
motive (the catch being the pressure of conformity and group intolerance
which confronts Shevek in this Utopia's "ambiguity"). It will also be noted
that the hostility to commodity reification and consumerism is reproduced in
the hostility to commerce as such: here the "advertisements" become bad aesthetic excess, and when Shevek is asked on Urras, "Is there anything you
aren't?" with some wonderment at the variety of trades he has practiced, he
decisively replies "A salesman."[30]

Unsurprisingly, then, the counterimage of Urras will take the form of the
commodity and its aesthetic excess. This image in fact sums up Shevek's

29 Ibid., pp. 98–99.
30 Ibid., p. 216.

experience of the capital city, A-Io, which unlike Abbenay does turn out to have concealments and the "mystères" traditionally associated with the city as such: hiding places (let us remember that these are denounced in a peculiar and memorable passage of Thomas More: "nullae latebratae"),[31] places of conspiracy (and sexual excess) and of refuge against the state and its power. For Shevek must himself hide out in such a place during the revolutionary insurrection, accompanied by a wounded participant who dies during the concealment. It is an experience which accounts for Shevek's final characterization of Urras to the Hainish ambassador:

> It is a box – Urras is a box, a package, with all the beautiful wrapping of blue sky and meadows and forests and great cities. And you open the box and what is inside it? A black cellar full of dust, and a dead man.[32]

What is, however, paradoxical about all this is the appeal to nature imagery to characterize the aesthetic illusions of Urras, Anarres being itself a barren desert for which none of these evocations of nature are appropriate.

But this is not normally the way in which Le Guin positions herself on the Utopian spectrum: indeed we have already identified her emblematically as the prototype of a Utopian commitment to the countryside and the village, to agriculture and small face-to-face groups, as opposed to the urban celebrations of a Delany: the commitment of a pastoral Morris, as opposed to the industrial Bellamy. Indeed, the opposition probably becomes meaningful only after industrialization in the nineteenth and twentieth centuries. One would not, for example, consider Hythloday's account of Amarautum as the expression of any particularly urban ideology (despite More's own identification with London, or the setting of *Utopia* in Antwerp); nor would one characterize Fourier's phalansteries as being particularly expressive of any great commitment to the land and the soil.

But it is clear enough that Delany's *Triton* takes up the challenge, and celebrates precisely those "latebratae" forbidden by More and lived as nightmarish by Le Guin's Shevek. This is indeed the sense of the so-called unlicensed sector within the official Utopia of Delany's novel:

---

31 See More, *Works*, Volume IV, pp. 146–147: "Now you can see how nowhere is there any license to waste time, nowhere any pretext to evade work – no wine shop, no alehouse, no brothel anywhere, no opportunity for corruption, no lurking hole, no secret meeting place. On the contrary, being under the eyes of all, people are bound either to be performing the usual labor or to be enjoying their leisure in a fashion not without decency."

32 *The Dispossessed*, p. 347. It is only fair to add that Le Guin uses the same figure in her decidedly anti-Utopian attack on socialism called "The Ones Who Walk Away From Omelas" (*The Wind's Twelve Corners*, New York, 1975); and see the special issue of *Utopian Studies* on this text: Volume 2, Nos 1 and 2 (1991).

At founding, each Outer Satellite city had set aside a city sector where no law officially held – since, as the Mars sociologist who first advocated it had first pointed out, most cities develop, of necessity, such a neighborhood anyway. These sectors fulfilled a complex range of functions in the cities' psychological, political, and economic ecology. Problems a few conservative Earth-bound thinkers feared must come, didn't: the interface between official law and official lawlessness produced some remarkably stable unofficial laws throughout the no-law sector …[33]

But caught up in perpetual warfare and organized around total informational surveillance, Triton is the repressive side of Utopia, into which, as a rectification and a kind of supplement of freedom, the unlicensed zone has been introduced: something like the Sade Utopia ("Français, encore un effort"), where anything goes and indeed the law requires everything to be permissible (under pain of death); except that here the "anything" is carefully limited, thereby replicating and reproducing that peculiar phenomenon of the boundary and the limit which inaugurates Utopian closure in the first place, something like Carl Schmitt's "amity line",[34] and introduces all the ambiguities of secession and imperialism we shall deal with below.

The unlicensed zone is thus the city's ironic commentary on the freedom which ostensibly defines it in the first place. "The freedom of the city" – *Luft der Städte*: the "licensed" city is preeminently the place, in the Middle Ages, of refuge and sanctuary: the end of the underground railway, the space which releases the landed peasant or serf from bondage to his lord and from servile status; which releases him, indeed, from Marx's "rural idiocy", from the bigotry of village life, where envy and the baleful spells and witchcraft of the sorcerer neighbors reign supreme.

This political or social freedom is then, in the imaginary of the city, redoubled by another, which reinforces it with *jouissance*, namely the freedom of sexual encounter celebrated most openly by Baudelaire:

> Moi, je buvais, crispé comme un extravagant,
> Dans son oeil, ciel livide où germe l'ouragon,
> La douceur qui fascine et le plaisir qui tue.

> ("A une passante")

But this "freedom" invested in the urban term of our opposition is most often incarnated in the problematical third term, which, as distribution, should

33 Delany, *Trouble on Triton* (Middletown, CT, 1996) the title was changed from the original *Triton* [1976], p. 8.
34 See Carl Schmitt's discussion of the "amity line" in the *Nomos der Erde* (Berlin, 1950), pp. 60–69: a boundary beyond which "anything goes" between states officially at peace.

in principle function as the liaison between city and country; and that is commerce. The association of the city with business is doubly paradoxical, given the way in which, for most Utopias, money has been an irritant and a foreign body which the new Utopian arrangements and organization are generally concerned to regulate and control, if not to banish altogether. The city, which as a mythic image oscillates back and forth between the New Jerusalem and Dis or Satan's city Pandemonium, is thus available for anti-Utopian and dystopian functions fully as much as for more properly Utopian ones.

Indeed, when we reach late or postmodern capitalism – that stage of finance capital in which Utopian impulses and alternatives have been stifled and suppressed as much as possible – some of those energies seep into what used to be dystopian figures; and cyberpunk revels in the demonic energies of the "sprawl" and of metropolitan excess in ways that are certainly celebratory and often proto-Utopian. Everything depends, here, on how the opposite of a potentially Utopian freedom is conceived; and also, and fundamentally, to what degree nature and the natural are still able to be grasped and articulated as positive terms and forces, and their opposite as artifice, the unnatural, the toxic and poisonous, as in Stapledon's vision of the technologies that blast the healthy "natural" development of a given society. The nature into which Ridley Scott's blade runner and his android lover flee, the intact and inhuman Mars on which Robinson's "first hundred" land, are a good deal more forbidding than the fields tilled by Le Guin's First and Last Americans; while the alien agriculture glimpsed in Lem too insistently reminds us of agriculture's artificial origins to be able to function in any ideologically organic way.

III

At this point, however, semiotic oppositions have crystallized which can be abstracted from their original economic contexts – those of production, consumption and distribution – and transferred onto a range of other Utopian polemics, most notably those in which the political itself makes its intermittent and conjunctural appearances. I am tempted to assert that the political is always a category mistake which arises at moments of crisis or deeper contradiction, and takes its form of appearance from the nature of the crisis itself. It would be tempting, but facile, simply to observe that the very space of the political itself (and of power) varies so completely with the mode of production of which it is a function that it cannot be generalized and resists all definitional conceptualization. To put it another way; the source of the political – Schmitt's state of exception,[35] Negri's constituent power[36] – is always outside conceptualization and codification, so that it brings with it a kind of

---

35 Carl Schmitt, *Political Theology* (Chicago, 1996).
36 Antonio Negri, *Insurgencies* (Minnesota, 1999), p. 324.

inverted Gödel's law where the foundation is always open and indeterminable.

So it is that the political formulations we begin to approach by way of a Utopian antinomy between city and country are never autonomous: and this is most striking in the case of what may be the most recent or postcontemporary opposition to emerge from the Utopian debates, namely that between complexity and simplicity. The new positive or substantive term, which finds a host of equivalents in related areas – such as the popular characterization of late capitalism as a "flexible" kind (in opposition to the presumably more rigid Fordism – "any color you like as long as it's black") – can also be identified as the sequel to older slogans, and in particular to the notion of decentralization, once popular on a Left-liberal agenda. This older version had the advantage of projecting a powerful negative term in the form of a bad and tyrannical centralization, which overrode local differences and autonomies and ruthlessly standardized its field of power. Decentralization could then be an appeal to local democracy and pluralism and some initial affirmation of what will later come to be valorized as Difference.

It might be thought that in the economic area the agenda of decentralization would offer an advantageous space for the critique of monopoly and multinational "giants"; unfortunately the alternative – presumably small business, entrepreneurship and invention – no longer strikes anyone as a viable one, but rather as a species on its way to extinction. In this situation, flexible capitalism can arrogate the virtues of multiplicity and difference to itself, in the way in which computerization enables niche production and the systematic variation of products, while so-called postmodern marketing supplies globalized corporations with the rhetoric and imagery of multicultural adaptability and the contextualization of their products around the world.

Under these postmodern conditions, and in the discursive struggles that are appropriate to them, it is difficult for the earlier positive term to win back much credibility: how many people today are willing to shoulder the banner of centralization, for example, let alone the rigid standardizations of Fordism? As for the socialist equivalent, the valorization of the Plan, now burdened with the epithet of "central" planning, the excitement it generated in the 1920s and 1930s, at the beginning of the Soviet experiment, has been completely forgotten, and that exultation of human power and collective control has been transmuted into the standard dystopian lust for power, itself by now become an utterly antiquated caricature. Meanwhile, the alternative version of the return to simplicity – in the face of the aesthetically more stimulating appeal of the various forms of "complexity" on offer – yields an odor of nostalgia: the simple life, indeed, regressive images of village culture, whether in the sixties communes or the hunters-and-gatherers of tribal societies, seeming less and less plausible in the era of world-wide ecological disaster and global warming. The semiotic content shared by both centralization and anti-complexity is then energetically unmasked as that bad old metaphysical entity

Nature itself. Even Raymond Williams' argument that socialism would not be simpler, but far more complex, than capitalism,[37] a shrewd intervention in a discursive field increasingly dominated by Thatcherism and Reaganism, is suspected of harboring regressive sympathies for nature and the yeoman farmer; while the concomitant conception of a "human" nature – already denounced as "humanism" by the Althusserians of the 1960s – is readily dispatched as essentialism and foundationalism: while Delany's prosthetics – the optional antlers and extra arms and organs of the earlier novels, culminating in the sex changes of *Triton* – are fundamental exhibits in the new post-human lifestyles[38] designed to replace the older natural ones (the related case of the infamous centered subject will be discussed in the final chapters).

This is the point at which the currently enfeebled Utopian debates reach all kinds of interesting contradictions and dialectical reversals. Complexity (Luhmann's favorite word, adopted by Giddens and "Third Way" theorists) is certainly a slogan which can triumphantly accommodate the market and money, particularly in its current post-monetary forms: the mediation is secured by cybernetics and the computer, without which the new transnational finance capitalism would be impossible. But what becomes, in that context, of the polemics explicitly waged against socialist planning (let alone of that much more immediate version directed against the planning of the Welfare State)? Here the anti-Utopian arguments revert to Edmund Burke, whose attacks on revolutionary hybris and on the catastrophic results of Jacobin constructionism and planning were very much staged in terms of nature: the slow growth of institutions and indeed (in the most literal sense) of "culture" itself. This strategy is then reproduced in the contemporary debate, which, following some of the most ancient defenses and apologias for capitalism, argues that the market is grounded in human nature, and that it is precisely the effort to remove it which is unnatural and which leads to violence.

But the appeal to human nature is no longer plausible in the postmodern and constructivist spirit of late capitalism and its ideologies. This is indeed the ambiguity of postmodernism as a philosophy, that its progressive endorsement of anti-essentialist multiplicity and perspectivism also replicates the very rhetoric of the late-capitalist marketplace as such. As for planning, socialist or otherwise, what could be more complexly post-human than the attempt to direct the multiplicities of contemporary production and consumption, of the labor market, of investment and ecology? Clearly, it is the computer which is central to this version of imaginary economics: what Soviet planning so desperately lacked, finance capital can be said to have diverted for its own unproductive purposes. But then in a final turn of the screw the computer

---

37 Raymond Williams, *Politics and Letters* (London, 1979), p. 433.
38 The various current conceptions of the post-human presumably spring from Donna Haraway's "Manifesto for Cyborgs" (see Chapter 8, note 16).

has also been celebrated as *natural*, by virtue of its derivation from the even more complex human brain itself.

It has already been observed that none of the now classic Utopias of the 1960s were able to confront the realities of the computer and the Internet: and that even Le Guin's proposals for a Utopian use of cybernetics, in *The Dispossessed* and *Always Coming Home*, are timid and discreetly self-effacing in comparison to a delirious contemporary rhetoric about which it is difficult to decide to what degree it is really Utopian – the Internet as an immense collectivity – or merely a substitute for and a displacement of the Utopian: we thereby find ourselves replaced in that alternation between the Utopian program and the Utopian impulse with which we began.

From another, political rather than economic, standpoint the question about the Internet resolves itself into a familiar and ancient philosophical antinomy: does it relate or does it separate and disperse? Is it the sign of identity or of multiplicity? In politics that centralization mostly today repudiated in the name of a decentralization now associated with democracy was not always oppressive: the local, in feudalism, was rather itself the locus of repression and domination, from which an appeal to the center and the monarch was often the only resort. Meanwhile Rousseau's notion of the unanimity of the general will is incompatible with decentralization (and has been denounced as Jacobin and totalitarian), despite Rousseau's own utopian preference for the village or the commune as over against the corrupt big city.

The Utopians have been divided on the matter: More's fifty-four cities are all alike "insofar as the terrain permits",[39] while Bellamy's industrial system ("nationalism") is resolutely centralized. This is the sense in which centralization can be inflected either in an economic or a political direction: for it can designate unanimity in Rousseau's sense fully as much as an organized locus of state power or industrial production; Yugoslavian workers' self-government ("autogestion") was an old symbol of this combination, to which ideological lip service is still sometimes paid. But today the presence to hand of the computer has blurred the economic issues, allowing one to assume that decentralization can now magically be achieved by the new technology, and thus flattening out and defusing the contradiction which Utopian solutions were one called into being to resolve, at least in the imagination.

It is not so easy to fantasize away the political ones, however, where the antithesis between this or that avatar of the state and the radical grassroots democratic process generally invoked by the Left remains a dilemma: is it really so, as the conservatives argue,[40] that the more genuine democracy is achieved on that grassroots level, the more ungovernable a country becomes?

---

39   More, *Works*, Volume IV, p. 117.
40   Samuel Huntington's famous remark, elaborated in M. Crozier, S. Huntington and J. Watanuke, *The Crisis of Democracy* (New York, 1975).

Certainly the American experience of these matters offers a perpetual history of sectarianism, marked by schism and secession, a fission process leading to smaller and smaller and more and more impotent groups and groupuscules. The model of direct democracy, however, which Marx and Lenin admired in the Paris Commune, and which several American states, most notably California, have since written into their constitutions – the well-known processes of referendum and recall – tends to be based on a Rousseauian idea of unanimity and the general will. (And obviously the more Utopian American projects of this kind were devised before the emergence of the media and its current monopolies on information: although the Internet has even more recently seemed to offer – at least in fantasy – a counterweight to the media problem.)

For the Utopian hostility to "democracy" in its current populist formulations needs to be properly situated. In More as well as in Rousseau, it is inspired by the fear of factionalism, a classical concept subsuming groups ranging from political parties as such all the way down to ethnicities and lobbies of various kinds. It is in order to discourage the emergence of factions, for example, that More forbids political discussions, a law which sounds ominous indeed to modern ears: "To take counsel on matters of common interest outside the senate or popular assembly is considered a capital offense".[41] *Red Mars*, on the other hand, is richly informed by the omnipresence of factions and the political problems they present (which are, to be sure, unified by the outside threat of an armed takeover by Earth). The status of politics in Utopia is in any case bound up with this issue of factions: the party constituting the unthinkable concept lying mid way between the individual and the social totality.

IV

But I hope some readers will want to take the position that postmodernism in economics is not at all the same as postmodernism in thinking or in philosophy; and that a principled rejection of the old "centered subject" (whether in psychology or in ethics) ought not to be discredited by the replication of its form in globalization, in business and in finance. This is an awkward historical situation, and it is by no means always cheap invective and mud-slinging to argue, as some of us have from time to time, that such replication is exceedingly suspicious and testifies to the way in which postmodern or decentered thinking and art reinforce the new social and economic forms of late capitalism more than they undermine it. The new values thus often seem to offer training in a new logic, and thereby to strengthen and perpetuate trends in the infrastructure in such a way as to cast doubt on all the older programs of critique and critical distance.

41 More, *Works*, Volume IV, p. 125.

Meanwhile, even if we divest such arguments of their invective and their personal reference, and transform the debunking stance and the accusation of ideological intention into some more neutral historical description, a fear remains which is now that of ·the *Zeitgeist*: some immense historical process and mutation whereby everything from the economic to the philosophical is stamped with the same forms and logic irrespective of political and ideological commitment. Indeed, the presumption of the existence of something like postmodernity was always based on the evidence of those thoroughgoing modifications of all the levels of the system which we call late capitalism. The issue here then becomes that of the nature and structure of historical transitions from one stage or period to another.

We may, however, also observe that the homology of forms and structures between the various socio-economic and cultural levels is itself a function of increasing abstraction: so it is that forms of complexity which develop within concrete economic institutions slowly become divorced from their substance or content and as free-floating patterns migrate to other areas and become available for quite different uses and applications – in design fully as much as in the allegorical organization of scientific propositions, or the newer systems of conceptuality. We may even be tempted to reverse the thrust of the argument and to suggest that the deployment of such forms in the economic realm is itself the result of their concrete emergence in newer kinds of social life (let alone in new discoveries in the scientific realm).

But this leaves the political question intact: namely, whether resistance is still possible under such a regime of replication. It remains a theoretical question: whether homologies can generate oppositions or negations; as well as a historical one: what kind of system it is in which such structural standardization or contamination is possible in the first place. But perhaps it is in terms of our previous Utopian oppositions that the whole problem needs to be restaged: as the return of that old opposition of difference and identity between which Utopianism has oscillated throughout history – More's (and indeed Plato's) commitment to identity coming to seem rather dystopian to us today.

I believe, however, that it is best to consider this particular dilemma as part of a Utopian debate in a new sector of thematics which we have not yet touched on, namely that of subjectivity. For even the premise of some fundamental Utopian depersonalization takes a position on subjectivity and individualism, a position which is indeed more closely allied with postmodern thought and its decentering of consciousness than with more bourgeois and humanist notions, even though More's external social forms seem to reflect a logic of identity at odds with postmodern Difference.

But the more fundamental categories for any discussion of Utopia and subjectivity would rather seem to me to be those of pedagogy and of transition: or in other words, the question of the formation of subjectivities, and that of the problems posed by their death and succession, by the generations and the relationship of the later classes of subjects to the institutions of Utopia laid in place by their predecessors. To put it this way is to realize that in socialism both of these poles are subsumed under the notion of cultural revolution: the collective pedagogy of subjects to be formed or reformed for life and activity in the new mode of production – a process which is then supposed to secure the social reproduction of the new social world across a number of generations, if not indefinitely.

This is probably the area in which the modern concern with freedom, which replaces the older Utopian preoccupation with happiness, can most adequately be grasped. Although conveniently transferable to the political field and available for all kinds of ideological exploitations, the demand for freedom in the Utopian tradition seems more plausibly read as an irritation and an impatience with pedagogy – with the philosopher-king, with the state and its ideological apparatuses, with Skinner, with More, with theories of pedagogy in general; as well as a resistance to older generations. It seems on the face of it unlikely that early modern experiences of the state could be direct or immediate enough to have a formative influence on values so existentially and passionately held as those that resonate in words and concepts like "freedom": the exception would no doubt be that of life under foreign or domestic military (or police) occupation. This is not to abandon the priority of a political unconscious over a Freudian one: Sartre once very sensibly observed that both acknowledge the family as the first structure through which classes and the social are learned along with the structures of desire.[42] In any case both the family and the official world of the state and of society are subsumed under the mode of production itself. As always, determinism here, and causality as such, are more a matter of determination and its limits, that is to say, of the availability of certain structures and their content or on the other hand the historical non-existence of such possibilities.

Thus, any number of models of a complex and decentered system seem to have emerged in recent times, of which older versions, such as Leibniz's monadology, seem but clumsy and pre-technological fantasies or anticipations. Clearly the evolution of cybernetic systems has enlarged what can be imagined, that is to say, what can be schematized: yet this is not to say that it is the new technology itself which has in the last instance enabled the emergence of such schematizations and their application to a wide range of other areas. That application exists, to be sure, only in fantasy in any number of cases: thus I have tried to show, in another place, that much of so-called cognitive philosophy – the attempt to "explain" consciousness on the basis of hypotheses about the decentered functioning of the brain – functions in reality as a political allegory and offers pseudo-scientific models of what are

---

42 Jean-Paul Sartre, *Search for a Method* (New York, 1963), pp. 61, 100–101.

actually political systems. Such scientific and philosophical speculations, whatever other value they may have and however testable or falsifiable in the laboratory, are also ideological constructs designed to ground a particular political system in biological nature.[42]

This brings us to what is perhaps the fundamental Utopian dispute about subjectivity, namely whether the Utopia in question proposes the kind of radical transformation of subjectivity presupposed by most revolutions, a mutation in human nature and the emergence of whole new beings; or whether the impulse to Utopia is not already grounded in human nature, its persistence readily explained by deeper needs and desires which the present has merely repressed and distorted. As we have implied in some of the preceding chapters, this is a tension which is not merely inescapable; its resolution in either direction would be fatal for the existence of Utopia itself. If absolute difference is achieved, in other words, we find ourselves in a science-fictional world such as those of Stapledon, in which human beings can scarcely even recognize themselves any longer (and which would need to be allegorized, as we have tried to do so in Chapter 9, in order to bring such figuration back to any viable anthropomorphic and Utopian function). On the other hand, if Utopia is drawn too close to current everyday realities, and its subject begins too closely to approximate our neighbors and our politically misguided fellow citizens, then we slowly find ourselves back in a garden-variety reformist or social-democratic politics which may well be Utopian in another sense but which has forfeited its claim to any radical transformation of the system itself.

As for that achievement of a radical impersonality in Utopia, the effacement of the private property of the self and the emergence of some new decentered and collective practice of social and individual relations, it would in the best of cases scarcely correspond to an abolition of subjectivity but rather merely to a new form of the latter, in which bourgeois individualism – another name for the old humanist "centered subject" under attack by contemporary theory – has been replaced by the "multiple subject positions" of postmodernity and late capitalism. Once again the notion of the replication of the system becomes the final form of conspiracy theory, and the concept of a Utopian transformation becomes an additional resource in the warehouse of late capitalism's ruses and lures.

But it is time to conclude this interminable inventory, and to observe that even though each of these oppositions seems to confront us with a fundamental choice and a fundamental decision about the very nature of Utopia – even though, indeed, the very reading or construction of utopias remains a dead letter if the text in question fails to challenge us in this well-nigh visceral

---

43 I must here refer to an unpublished analysis of Daniel Dennett's *Consciousness Explained*, which will appear in Volume II of *The Poetics of Social Forms*, on allegory.

way – it may well be misguided to respond to the challenge on its own terms; and even more misguided to attempt its resolution by way of this or that compromise, combination or synthesis. How this new problem is to be met will be addressed in the following chapter.

II

Synthesis, Irony, Neutralization and the Moment of Truth

Why each of the options offered by our pairs of opposites should not have its moment of truth – a question which leads at once to the great relativist question in philosophy, to the bemused contemplation of warring and incompatible Absolutes or of the multiplicity of "truth-events"[1] – is a perplexity only apparently resolved by historicism, with its many truths succeeding each other throughout the historical succession of radically different modes of production in time. How much the more perplexing then will not the inversion of the same question be, which inquires as to the truth content of not-yet-being, and the effectivity of the various Utopian futures of the past?

It is a problem perhaps best produced by a comprehensive notion of ideology, in which the inevitability of the latter results from our inescapable situatedness:[2] situatedness in class, race and gender, in nationality, in history – in short, in all kinds of determinations, which no biological individual can evade and which only a few belated idealisms or the most incorrigibly rationalist and universalist Enlightenment philosophy conceived of transcending.

But the argument can also be pitched at a lower level, in terms of representation as such: if there is nothing in the mind which was not already transmitted by the senses, according to the old empiricist motto, we are also generally inclined to think today that there is nothing in our possible representations which was not somehow already in our historical experience. The latter necessarily clothes all our imaginings, it furnishes the content for the expression and figuration of the most abstract thoughts, the most disembodied longings or premonitions. Indeed, that content is itself already ideological in the sense outlined above, it is always situated and drawn from the contextually concrete, even where (especially where) we attempt to project a vision absolutely independent of ourselves and a form of otherness as alien to our own background as possible.

Here, indeed, the old dialectic of identity and difference inevitably returns with a vengeance, and nothing is quite so ideological and self-bound as my

---

1 A concept at the center of Alain Badiou's philosophy.
2 See David Simpson, *Situatedness* (Durham, NC, 2003).

desperate attempt to escape my situation in thought and to imagine what is farthest from me and most alien: the poverty of those images is the tell-tale indication of my limited experience and of my inability to imagine anything outside myself. Alas, that intellectual whom the Utopian must also be – forever shackled by the determinants of race and class, of language and childhood, of gender and situation-specific knowledge – is also burdened by the constitutional commitment to the abstract and to the universal, which is to say to the inveterate professional effacement, in advance and by definition, of all these concrete determinants of a properly Utopian ideology: but it is an effacement which is a repression rather than a working through.[3] How could it then be otherwise with Utopia in general, and the attempt to imagine the most fundamental difference of all and to project ourselves into the Novum of a new mode of production?

This is why all of our images of Utopia, all possible images of Utopia, will always be ideological and distorted by a point of view which cannot be corrected or even accounted for, as when we observe that this or that Utopian could not have been aware of later social developments (like Aristotle and the limits of slavery),[4] or that a given problem was alien to his experience. All these rectifications, as though traveling blind by compass or sextant, presuppose that there is ultimately somewhere a correct view of Utopia which is to be attained by allowing for the author's partiality or even by triangulating a variety of different Utopias in order to determine their common emplacement. But there is no such correct Utopia; and all the familiar ones we have are irredeemably class-based. More is marked not only by his status as lawyer and a Londoner, a humanist close to Henry VIII's court; he is also marked by the ambiguities of that transitional period between the medieval dispensation and the emergent absolute monarchy. His very possibility of imagining or fantasizing the Utopia we have is absolutely determined by these seeming limitations or specifications.

In the same way, Campanella is marked by the culture of the church; Fourier by all kinds of petty bourgeois fantasies and by the traveling salesman's view of society and human nature he can hardly have been expected to shake off; Bellamy is a typical small-town middle-class American from the age of the inventions, a Thomas Edison or a Ford of the industrial Utopia to come (just as Fourier wished to be its Newton, with all the naïveté of the autodidact); and so on down the line, eventually adding race and gender into the profile.

Yet this interminable historicism – once we are aware of its dynamic – demonstrates its ultimate sterility by depriving us of any possibility of our

---

3 This critique of intellectuals and their professional idealism seems to me to have been the driving force in Pierre Bourdieu's work. The role of anti-intellectualism in anti-Utopianism should not be underestimated.

4 See Marx on Aristotle, in *Capital*, Volume I (London, 1976), pp. 151–152.

own Utopian construction, now that we know it will inevitably reflect little more than our own class position. Whatever the persistence of the Utopian form, then, its content comes to seem irredeemably tainted, and we come to wonder whether any Utopianism is possible which is not some mere projection of our own situation. Does this mean that there cannot even be a minimum formulation of Utopian demands which might somehow retain effective universality? Can we not envision some zero-degree Utopia, a Utopia in which content was reduced to its most undeniable validity for all societies?

It was always Adorno's merit usefully to complicate the simple problems, while brutally simplifying the complicated ones: slashing through antinomies and productively using idealism and materialism against each other in the movement of a thought thereby released from its paralysis. It is thus not surprising that we owe just such a minimalist Utopian proposal to this thinker, a proposal calculated to clarify our own options in the present situation:

> He who asks what is the goal of an emancipated society is given answers such as the fulfillment of human possibilities or the richness of life. Just as the inevitable question is illegitimate, so inevitable is the repellent assurance of the answer, calling to mind the social-democratic ideal of the personality expounded by the heavily bearded Naturalists of the 1890s, who wanted to live a good life. Genuine feeling is only to be found in the crudest response: that no one shall go hungry any more. Every other answer substitutes, for a condition that should only have been defined by human needs, the habits of a system organized around production as an end in itself.[5]

One's ready assent to this proposition can only properly be understood if we take into account the target it is meant to criticize. It is no longer very clear which Second International Utopians Adorno had in mind here: let's hope they did not include the grand figure of Morris himself! At any rate, it seems obvious enough that the diatribe is directed at Utopian fantasies organized around pleasure or enjoyment. Adorno was indeed himself a philosopher (and an aesthetician) whose central organizing preoccupation lay in suffering, in irreparable pain as such. He therefore had little tolerance for hedonism,[6] and the passage suggests that for him the attempt to replace suffering with pleasure is to be denounced as frivolous and insulting to the victims.

We may also be tempted to conclude that he had little use for the very activity of Utopian fantasizing, whose reveling in details can only, from the standpoint of mass starvation, constitute a reprehensible luxury. (He thereby

---

5 T.W. Adorno, *Minima Moralia* (London, 1974 [1951]), pp. 15–156, translation modified.
6 As Rose Subotnik pertinently observes, he never mentions Haydn (*Developing Variations* [Minneapolis, 1991] p. 50).

reproduces one of the paradoxes with which we began, namely the seeming incompatibility, in the classical Utopist, between social indignation or prophetic rage and the handicraft delectation of the Utopian hobby.) We may even wonder whether this particular denunciation does not imply a repudiation of narrative as such, particularly when the latter promises to reorganize the Utopian impulse as a field and to inaugurate Utopia as a genre. From the standpoint of narrative, indeed, Adorno's fascination with the formal *tour de force* of Beckett's *Endgame* brings us as close as we can get to non-narrative, while still remaining within the realm of the aesthetic (for Adorno an absolute requirement). Utopia is to be sure itself a mixed form: but its so-called non-narrative portions – the long-winded tours of the new Utopian landscape, along with all manner of Skinnerian trays – still constitute forms of content and modes of figuration (unlike the cancellations whereby Beckett artfully neutralizes the content of every possible situation and event, of every possible act). The aesthetic itself may certainly be considered a Utopian enclave in Adorno's world, but it is a peculiarly transitory and fleeting space, a line of flight which can last but a moment, before being reabsorbed into that nightmarish real world of suffering against which it was an ephemeral protest, and of which it is the briefest dissonant expression.

To be sure, the aversion to hedonism does not, in Adorno, exclude the valorization of happiness, but happiness precisely as just such a fleeting and ephemeral moment:

> *Rien faire comme une bête*, lying on water and looking peacefully at the sky, "being, nothing else, without any further specification or fulfillment" – this might indeed take the place of process, act, satisfaction, and thereby keep the promise of the dialectic eventually to flow back into its origin.[7]

Yet here too it is against society's "blind fury of activity" that the possibility is evoked; and like all clever philosophers Adorno evades a theory which would give content to happiness, or lend it thematization (as though, like Lacan's Real, happiness were something "that resists symbolization absolutely"). Happiness cannot, in other words, become an end in its own right, without being sucked back into that Weberian system of means and ends from which it was to have been an escape in the first place. Happiness is thus at one with the refusal of content, an intransigence not to be sullied by nostalgia for archaic systems like the gift, nor by the futurist visions concocted by bearded socialists either. The claims of need are to remain absolute and apodictic: the resultant guilt will then reincorporate that of the Holocaust and intimidate Utopians of Left and Right alike: "cleaving", as Adorno liked to say, "to the determinate negation".[8]

---

7 *Minima Moralia*, p. 156.
8 T.W. Adorno, *Philosophie der neuen Musik* (Frankfurt, 1958 [1948]), p. 33.

Adorno's positions on Utopianism, however, go even further than this, for they imply a fundamental stance on the nightmare of human history as such, here depicted as a ceaseless and frantic activity of which capitalism is only the latest and most frenetic stage. Here natural history intersects and overrules the purely human kind, and this immemorial story of interminable struggles and mutual aggressivity, inevitable misery and unwarranted triumph, is seen to be grounded in the seemingly biological and Darwinian instinct of self-preservation.[9]

The philosophical subtext of this startling suggestion lies in the proposition that "self-preservation" is not an instinct at all, but rather something like an ideology, or at the very least an ideological mechanism. All human societies, necessarily organized around scarcity and power, have had to program their subjects in such a way as to construct some seemingly primordial effort to preserve one's self at all costs, which is to say at the cost of other people. This "self", which one then jealously hoards and protects against incursion, is something like a form of property, the very first form, perhaps, around which all our personal and social struggles are organized. Adorno's speculations thereby unexpectedly renew their ties with the oldest and most tenaciously rooted Utopian traditions: to abolish private property. Yet it is now the private property of the self which is to be abolished, with the equally unexpected result that death itself – the most private of all experiences, about which Heidegger affirms that it is "je mein eigener", that only I can experience – loses its sting, no longer divesting us of what is most precious.

Yet would not this relinquishment of the ultimate form of private property leave us in a state no longer recognizably human? It is a consequence Adorno was willing to contemplate, as his only partly ironic ethical ideal testifies: "to live like good animals".[10] Utopia, then, the falling away of the "instinct" of self-preservation, would emerge as a state in which, as with animals, a life in the pure present would become conceivable, a life divested of all those fears of survival and anxieties about the future, all that endless tactical and strategic struggle and worry – *Sorge!* – which makes up human history or pre-history, and in whose absence some altogether unrecognizable "human nature" would take the place of this one. It is a frightening thought, to the degree to which it posits the ultimate radical otherness and encourages visions of the far future in which we will have lost almost everything that makes us identifiable to ourselves as human: a vision of a population of sentient beings grazing in the eternal present of a garden without aggressivity or want. In such a future, indeed, we will truly have become aliens in the science-fictional sense, a

---

9 T.W. Adorno and Max Horkheimer, *Dialectic of Enlightenment* (Palo Alto, 2002 [1947]), pp. 22–23.

10 T.W. Adorno, *Negative Dialectics* (New York, 1973 [1966]), p. 299.

perspective calculated, as we have already seen, to reawaken all the most classical fears of Utopia as such.

Adorno's minimal Utopian demand, therefore, far from being purely formal and without ideological content, vehiculates the most complexly historical themes and undertones. On the one hand, the irredeemable guilt of the human condition returns again and again to the primacy of suffering, crying out, with Dostoyevsky and Sartre, that Utopia and art are worthless compared to the pain of a single child; while on the other an old longing for the serenity of animals or the simple-minded, from Wordsworth, Flaubert and Whitman down to modern times, astonishingly reappears in this hyperintellectual thinker, generally so resistant to nostalgia. Ange ou bête? It is probably on the side of the imagining of the post-human and even the angelic that Utopian otherness is likely to find its productivity.

We must therefore conclude that the search for a minimal Utopian demand, a universally acknowledged zero degree of Utopian realization – even so seemingly obvious one as "that no one shall go hungry any more" – cannot escape the force field of ideology and class-situatedness. The fallback position, then, confronted with the multiplicity of Utopian concerns which we have discovered to be in violent opposition to each other, is evidently the pluralist one, in which we acknowledge the authenticity of the Utopian impulse invested in each option, no matter how distorted it may be, while at the same time seeking to identify its "moment of truth" and to isolate and appropriate its specific Utopian energy.

Yet this apparent capitulation to common sense and liberal or humanist pluralism may demand a more complicated method then the usual non-dialectical sorting out and picking and choosing. What changes everything is the way in which truth and its "moment" are conceived; and in which a substantive vision of the latter inevitably generates something like a feeling of progress; the whole movement crowned by a nascent reflexivity, a coming to self-consciousness, of the Utopian process itself. Such a method of evaluation smacks of bad caricatures of Hegelianism and offers the usual targets for anti-historicist critique. The mistake is, however, to imagine that non-error, truth, even whatever minimal truth is alleged to persist in the so-called "moment of truth", is a positive phenomenon. We do not use this concept properly unless we grasp its critical negativity as a conceptual instrument designed, not to produce some full representation, but rather to discredit and demystify the claims to full representation of its opposite number. The "moment of truth" is thus not a substantive one, not some conceptual nugget we can extract and store away, with a view towards using it as a building block of some future system. Rather its function lies not in itself, but in its capability radically to negate its alternative.

Thus, the moment of truth of Le Guin's pastoral vision, of her Utopian advocacy of the countryside and the village, has nothing to do with the attractiveness of these ideological illusions, except insofar as it is that very attractiveness which gives her moment of truth its critical power and sharpens its cutting edge. Rather, the radical function of her vision lies in its demysti-fication and negation of Delany's equally ideological vision of the Utopian city. And, as might have been expected, the converse is also true, and it is in Delany's urban fantasy that we find the means to disqualify Le Guin's idyllic countryside (which of course also includes the warrior technology that brutally interrupts it). The "unlicensed zone" rebukes everything that is complacent and specious, celebratory and deluded, about ideologies of nature; while the serenity of the village casts the silence of an equally final judgment on a febrile urban agitation.

I can make the consequences of this method clearer and more specific by comparing it to a critical proposition with which it apparently has a kinship. I refer to Gary Saul Morson's interesting 1981 *The Boundaries of Genre*,[11] which combines an analysis of Dostoyevsky's *Writer's Diary* – a Menippean text if there ever was one, even more significantly so when one considers it as Morson does as a single organically unified work – with a theory of utopias and in par-ticular of the Utopian genre. His position is that Dostoyevsky was nowhere nearly so fundamentalist a reactionary as we have always thought (or perhaps, since he so obviously was a reactionary, it might be better to substitute the expression anti-Utopian for that term). This is to be demonstrated by the exis-tence – alongside such openly anti-Utopian texts as the *Notes from Underground*, the "Grand Inquisitor" episode in *The Brothers Karamazov*, and *The Devils* – of more positively Utopian pieces ("The Dream of a Ridiculous Man"), or more accurately of the coexistence, within the *Writer's Diary* itself, of both Utopian and anti-Utopian texts and features side by side. But this would so far merely testify to some fundamental political ambivalence on Dostoyevsky's part, to be resolved, perhaps, by chronology or by the unevenly varying political context.

Morson's argument is, however, a good deal more interesting than this, since as his title suggests, he here wishes to invoke a whole dialectic of genre: not merely to anchor the Utopian genre in a conception of parody derived from Russian Formalism but also to suggest a way in which the parodic system produces generic variations out of itself. Thus a genre identified as anti-Utopia will turn out to be a "parody" (in Morson's now complex and idiosyncratic sense of the word) of the original Utopian genre itself – feigning to take it seriously *à la* Swift or even Orwell, only the better to show how implausible, not to say how undesirable, it ends up being. But now, in two important and complex readings, he goes on to show that several of the traditional exem-plars of these two generic categories are in fact on closer inspection to be ranged under the other category as well. Thus, one of the classic anti-Utopias,

11   Gary Saul Morson, *The Boundaries of Genre* (Austin, Texas, 1981).

Zamyatin's *We*, turns out also to be an example of the Utopian genre itself,[12] while, in some final turn of the screw of the dialectic, the very foundational text of the Utopian genre as such, Thomas More's eponymous work, proves to contain, alongside its Utopian ingredients, all the makings of an anti-Utopia and a parody or satire of itself. This is an argument which solves a number of problems in the history of the reception of More's little book; it is also at least implicitly an enlargement of Bakhtin's dialogism to include dissent and dis-agreement not merely among the official discussants (More and Hythloday) but within the very structure of the text itself.

This is not, however, the stopping point of Morson's argument, which goes on to posit yet a third form, the meta-parody or meta-Utopia, which turns out to include both the Utopia and its generic adversary, and then also serves to explicate everything otherwise puzzling and incoherent or contradictory about *The Writer's Diary* as well. Is this a satisfying solution, or are we not tempted to evoke the unnecessary multiplication of imaginary entities, in this case genres, in a discussion which freely admits that if we do not consciously acknowledge the existence of the new third form the text in question may well appear a chaotic failure?

This is not to disregard the dialectical quality of all this, nor to ignore the place it makes for oppositions and negations. I merely want to introduce another set of coordinates, namely that of modernism and postmodernism, and to observe that as Morson formulates it, his argument is still very much offered within a modernist literary framework which evokes "the complex issues involved in literary interpretation"[13] and is based on a whole rhetoric of literary reflexivity: "Its margins play on their own marginality", "the frames ... become part of a literary work that self-consciously includes what might otherwise not be taken as part of the work proper".[14] The *Quijote* remains a central reference, as the meta-Utopia comes to approach a mod-ernist value as such, that of self-consciousness or reflexivity. If so, then the theory can quickly be identified and folded back into one of the supreme literary values and concepts of that era, namely Irony. For it is in Irony that we are able to have our cake both ways and deny what we affirm, while affirming what we deny. Irony is indeed the synthesis of opposites prescribed in the modernist period; and as a supreme modernist value (from Thomas Mann to Paul de Man)[15] it is both distinct from and documented by all the specific individual ironies of the text (Morson refers to two of them: the

12 See Chapter 2, note 21.

13 Morson, *Boundaries of Genre*, p. 174.

14 Ibid., p. 167.

15 Paul de Man's affirmation of Schlegel's "irony of ironies" (*Blindness and Insight* [Minneapolis, 1997]), pp. 221–222: "Mit der Ironie ist durchaus nicht zu scherzen," etc.) is a defining moment. And see my discussion of de Man in *A Singular Modernity*, pp. 106–118; see also *Postmodernism* (Durham, NC, 1991) pp. 258–9.

"irony of origins" or perspectivism,[16] and the use of irony in a purely anti-Utopian way).[17]

It is at this point that I am finally in a position to clarify the stubborn negativity which has always puzzled readers of Louis Marin's *Utopiques*, and also to explain myself to Utopians who have felt that some of the formulations I have proposed in earlier studies[18] were depressingly self-defeating if not indeed positively defeatist (Utopia as a necessary failure of imagination). But the clarification can only be achieved at the price of a resolute hostility to Irony (very much in a postmodern spirit), and in the spirit of a principled repudiation of the modernist value of reflexivity. Only this negative specification will allow us to stake out a position distinct from Morson's yet related to it. In order to do so we have every interest in returning to Marin and his use of the Greimas semiotic scheme, which, as will be recalled, differentiates the contradiction of a given term from its logical contrary.

Insofar as a contradiction can also logically be posited of the latter, this yields a diagram with four basic positions. It would indeed seem ironic to identify the so-called complex term as a form of Irony, when for most people "irony" consists in taking no fundamental position, in being neither for nor against, to use our characterization of its opposite number, the neutral term.

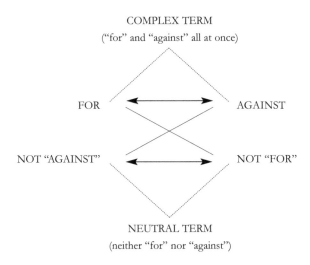

COMPLEX TERM
("for" and "against" all at once)

FOR   AGAINST

NOT "AGAINST"   NOT "FOR"

NEUTRAL TERM
(neither "for" nor "against")

---

16 Morson, p. 77.

17 Ibid., p. 155.

18 See below, in Part Two, Essay 4: "Progress versus Utopia, or, Can We Imagine the Future?"
As this essay has been much referenced, and despite the modification of its positions the reader
will observe in the present work (particularly here and in Chapters 4 and 6), I have reproduced
the original without changes.

Yet the complex term in fact seeks to have it both ways, and to define itself by exploiting everything supposedly positive about both poles of the opposition. If this combination is Utopian, as many people have suggested, then it is precisely a bad Utopianism, founded on the illusions of representation and of affirmative content; and modernist irony shares those illusions in a specifically aesthetic and aestheticizing fashion, valorizing art as the space in which the incompatibles can reach a positive kind of fullness. Thus the traditional caricature of Hegel and dialectical philosophy posits the unification of the two major terms as a "synthesis" (in Greimas the "complex" term). Not only is this very much the kind of spurious resolution we have denounced in our inventory of Utopian oppositions above; it is also the space of the modernist value of Irony, which promises if not to reconcile the fundamental opposition in question (Art and Life, Private and Public, City and Country, Mind and Body) then at least to allow us to think and practice both at the same time. Irony is thus also a way of unifying opposites; and with it you can at one and the same time believe in the importance of politics and embrace everything we might lose if we indulged in political practice. Thomas Mann is famously, and on his own admission,[19] the practitioner of these interminable ironies (indeed, he revels in them), which taken from another perspective are also the very medium of modernist reflexivity and self-consciousness, since they allow us to be in two places at once – within the act or commitment, and outside it in some more disembodied way in the quite different space of reflexive awareness of it and of ourselves.

At any rate, I believe that this is also the emplacement mapped out by Morson's notion of the meta-genre and the meta-Utopia, which *par excellence* allows us to be Utopian and anti-Utopian all at once, and to hover for one last moment in that suspended space in which we are both and neither, in which the die is not yet cast (and never will be). Irony is, as I have argued elsewhere, the quintessential expression of late modernism and of the ideology of the modern as that was developed during the Cold War (whose traces and impasses it bears like a stigmata).

To put it in yet another, more methodological way, we may say that Irony still believes in content; and that its squaring of the circle fails to escape the impasse in which the attempt to evaluate the various forms of Utopian content has left us. The problem that now confronts us is how to return to the formalism (the absolute formalism) of our earlier chapters; and how to invent such a formalism, not by spurious syntheses or the ironic superposition of our opposites, but rather by going all the way through that contradictory content and emerging on the other side. It is precisely this possibility which the semiotic square seems to promise.

For now our scheme allows us, following Marin's guidance, to identify another possible position, namely that "synthesis" of the two negations which

---

19 See Thomas Mann, *Betrachtungen eines Unpolitischen*, 1918 (and everywhere else).

Greimas named the "neutral" term. Not both at once, but neither one nor the other, without any third possibility in sight. This neutral position does not seek to hold two substantive features, two positivities, together in the mind at once, but rather attempts to retain two negative or privative ones, along with their mutual negation of each other. It is no less demanding an exercise, and its relationship to postmodern cynicism needs to be explored and to be juxtaposed with that equally ideological modernist aestheticism which emerges from Irony and reflexivity; but it will at least clarify the approach to Utopian oppositions proposed here. They must neither be combined in some humanist organic synthesis, nor effaced and abandoned altogether: but retained and sharpened, made more virulent, their incompatibility and indeed their incommensurability a scandal for the mind, but a scandal that remains vivid and alive, and that cannot be thought away, either by resolving it or eliminating it: the biblical stumbling block, which gives Utopia its savor and its bitter freshness, when the thought of Utopias is still possible.

Another way of coming at all this has to do with what Paul de Man liked to call "thematization"; this is, as it were, a conceptual cousin of reification and a way of linguistically designating the temptations of positivity in a dialectical world in which (using Saussure's famous formulation) "there are no positive terms, but only differences".[20] Thematization, in other words, means assigning a stable figuration or symbolic expression to a system in motion; it suggests a dogmatism of the signifier for which meanings are fixed and stable, and are assigned definitive content. At this point the linguistic or deconstructive perspective rejoins the ideological one outlined above. Any positive or substantive terms in which Utopia is thematized will in other words reflect the class ideology of its deviser (and its public).

The diagram opposite suggests, then, the spirit in which, for example, the contradiction between the Utopia of the city and that of the country might more productively be mapped out.

This still seems to leave us in a very unpromising place indeed, one in which no substantive or positive vision of Utopia can be accepted; in which all the concrete specifications of Utopia must be challenged, in a process reminiscent of what Adorno's negative dialectic offered to do for philosophy and its propositions (and what Derridean deconstruction also does in so thoroughgoing a way that unlike Adorno it even refuses any positive or substantive concept of its own negative method, and indeed of method as such[21]). In a final chapter we will see whether anything Utopian is still to be achieved under such circumstances and such restrictions. But we must first confront a very different kind of negation, one which aims to cancel the Utopian form altogether and as such.

20 See my *The Prison-House of Language*, p. 15.
21 I refer to "classical" rather than the current "positive" deconstruction.

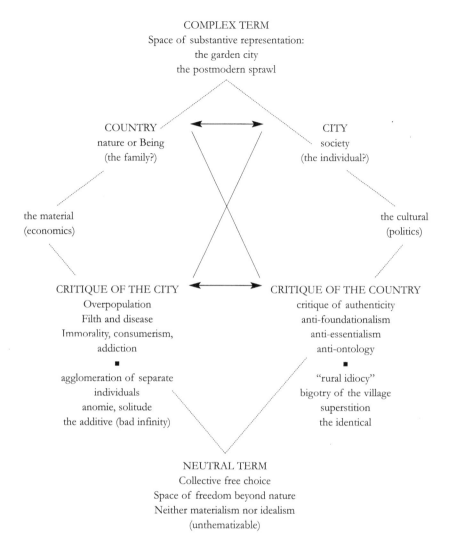

COMPLEX TERM
Space of substantive representation:
the garden city
the postmodern sprawl

COUNTRY
nature or Being
(the family?)

CITY
society
(the individual?)

the material
(economics)

the cultural
(politics)

CRITIQUE OF THE CITY
Overpopulation
Filth and disease
Immorality, consumerism,
addiction

■

agglomeration of separate
individuals
anomie, solitude
the additive (bad infinity)

CRITIQUE OF THE COUNTRY
critique of authenticity
anti-foundationalism
anti-essentialism
anti-ontology

■

"rural idiocy"
bigotry of the village
superstition
the identical

NEUTRAL TERM
Collective free choice
Space of freedom beyond nature
Neither materialism nor idealism
(unthematizable)

12

Journey into Fear

I

Readers have a right to wonder what they will find to read in Utopia, the unspoken thought being that a society without conflict is unlikely to produce exciting stories. Some of the Utopians themselves worry about this: Bellamy's narrator reads the "masterpiece" by the greatest writer of the future age and observes the following:

> Let no admirer of the great romancer of the twentieth century resent my saying that at the first reading what most impressed me was not so much what was in the book as what was left out of it. The story writers of my day would have deemed the making of bricks without straw a light task compared with the construction of a romance from which should be excluded all effects drawn from the contrasts of wealth and poverty, education and ignorance, coarseness and refinement, high and low, all motives drawn from social pride and ambition, the desire of being richer or the fear of being poorer, together with sordid anxieties of any sort of one's self or others; a romance in which there should indeed be love galore, but love unfretted by artificial barriers created by differences of station or possessions, owning no other law than that of the heart.[1]

Yet the imaginary novel evidently succeeds in conveying "something like a general impression of the social aspect of the twentieth century", something apparently less arduous to convey in the absence of the above-listed evils, of which only the battle of the sexes seems to have survived (as witness its title, *Penthesilea*). Skinner takes a different tack: "we shall never produce so satisfying a world", says his Utopian demiurge, "that there will be no place for art",[2] a remark that seems to stress the conventional association of unhappiness and artistic creation.

But his argument is of a more sociological type; stressing the financial support and leisure Walden offers:

---

1 Edward Bellamy, *Looking Backward* (New York, 1986 [1888]), pp. 133–134.
2 Skinner, *Walden Two*, p. 126.

Why shouldn't our civilization [the post-war US] produce art as abundantly as it produces science and technology? Obviously because the right conditions are lacking. That's where Walden Two comes in … What you need is a culture. You need a real opportunity for young artists … A great productive culture must stimulate large numbers of the young and untried … Don't expect a Golden Age …[3]

And he shows us a collection of promising paintings, about which it is not clear whether they are figurative or modernist (or in other words, whether this particular Utopia has yet begun to confront the crisis of representation). But it is obvious that the visual arts, and architecture and music, perhaps not even omitting a lyric poetry essentially devoted to the "eternal human" themes, will offer less problematical possibilities than the novel as such (or even filmic narrative, which few of the contemporary Utopians ever get around to).

Indeed, we seem in many of these Utopias to approach that condition famously prophesied by Hegel as "the end of art", by which he meant the supersession of art, as an approach to the Absolute, by philosophy. He apparently did not, however, foresee the end of all artistic production but only of the kind of works we would today associate with modernism, namely those with philosophical aspirations.[4] Essentially decorative artistic production would persist in Hegel's philosophical Utopia – he explicitly mentions Dutch genre painting – and this seems to hold for Skinner's Utopia as well, where now the personal taste and aesthetic ideology of the Utopian writer himself comes back into play with a vengeance and, like Thomas More's preference for Romanesque architecture, determines the incidental details.

Only in Morris do we find a vigorous revision of these attitudes, for in the thick of Ruskin's Gothic revival – with what we call modern art still a few decades in the future – the repudiation of the art of his own contemporaries changes the picture altogether:

It is true that in the nineteenth century, when there was so little art and so much talk about it, there was a theory that art and imaginative literature ought to deal with contemporary life; but they never did so; for, if there was any pretence of it, the author always took care … to disguise, or exaggerate, or idealize, and in some way or another make it strange [sic!]; so that, for all the verisimilitude there was, he might just as well have dealt with the times of the Pharaohs.[5]

The reproach is a dual one, and suggests that class ideology intervenes to prevent any accurate representations of the miseries of contemporary society;

---

3 Ibid., p. 89.

4 See my essay "'End of Art', or 'End of History'?" in *The Cultural Turn* (London, 1998); and also the discussion of Marcuse above. I am grateful to Peter Bürger for this insight.

5 Morris, *News from Nowhere*, p. 131.

while at the same time it implies that there is something ill-conceived in the first place about an aesthetic that would wish to provide a mimesis of contemporary life. This attack strikes at the novel as a form (apart from the Utopian texts, Morris' literary work consisted in poetic romances), and in fact shifts the aesthetic center of gravity from literature as such to architecture (and design) very much in the spirit of his master Ruskin. Yet in the case of Morris it would be paradoxical to evoke the "end of art", since his fundamental Utopian (and practical-political) program lies in the transformation of alienated labor into the quest for beauty as such:

> The loss of the competitive spur to exertion had not, indeed, done anything to interfere with the necessary production of the community, but how if it should make men dull by giving them too much time for thought or idle musing? … The remedy was … the production of what used to be called art, but which has no name amongst us now, because it has become a necessary part of the labor of every man who produces.[6]

Art can thus be said to disappear from this Utopia only in the sense in which, as with Marcuse and the Utopians of the 1960s, it is realized, and generalized throughout society as the very aesthetization of daily life (in Morris very specifically becoming the term for non-alienated labor as such).

In this passage, however, we feel the stirrings of a fear already implicit in the conception of art in the other Utopian texts we have touched on, a fear that will develop into a gale-force wind in the anti-Utopians: it is simply the fear of boredom. Bellamy's hesitations about the novel of the future – which seems to make a place only for the pangs of love (it will be remembered that a tragic love passion is also the *fait divers* inserted at the center of *News from Nowhere*) – suggest, as do Skinner's energetic reassurances, that a social order incapable of producing interesting and exciting stories will not necessarily be itself either uninteresting or tedious. (As for Callenbach's contribution to all this – which might well be characterized as something of a Silicon Valley aesthetics of invention and entrepreneurialism – Morris throws cold water on it in advance by dryly observing, of his own "epoch of rest", that "this is not an age of inventions".)[7]

Art thus becomes one crucial symptom, if not of the quality of daily life in Utopia, then at least of what people fear it might turn out to be; and the artistic representation of the Event – from the mere prospect of interesting things happening all the way to the availability of struggle and conflict, and beyond them, of History itself – turns into the experimental laboratory in which Utopia is itself probed for the satisfactions it can afford modern subjects. The work

6 Ibid., pp. 159–160.
7 Ibid., p. 192.

of art within the work of art, Gide's *mise en abyme* (Bloch's empty hole of the work of art within the artist-novel) thus itself becomes the miniature glass in which Utopia's most glaring absences are thus reproduced with minute clarity; and what was able to conceal them at an external level of political and social argument, of economic production, is now, by the purely aesthetic, suspended. Indeed, in a world in which production has itself become purely aesthetic, in which the political has withered away, and History has come to a rather different kind of end than the one predicted, with mixed feelings, by Alexandre Kojève – in such a world only the end of art itself can save the beholder from a disabused revelation of everything we might miss.

Many features of daily life seem to be lacking here, and the return to the village, for all its sociability, by omitting all those piquant features and dissonances of modernity that modernism has taught us to appreciate and to read with delectation, discloses their deep inextricable kinship with capitalism itself (which has now, as in Bellamy, vanished like a dream). What remains is then given over to a strange kind of dialectical indeterminacy: is this materialist new world of the body and the epoch of rest, for example, to be understood as a place of sexlessness, as in Boorman's *Zardoz* (1974) or Shaw's *Back to Methusaleh* (1921); or is it not on the contrary, as in Aldiss' nightmare vision in the *Helliconia* trilogy (1982–1985), a place of absolute excess, a perpetual orgy multiplied by the omnipresent media and figuring everything post-human that can be attributed to a realm beyond necessity? The end of art here designates, not its desperate lack of appropriate content, so much as the superfluousness of the individual artwork or object in a world which has become completely aestheticized. And does such a Utopia not simply complete that process of the reduction to the present and the abolition of past and future which has been diagnosed and seen to be at work in our own current postmodernity?[8] Yet the Utopia of excess, fully as much as the Utopia of privation, is calculated to arouse the anxieties of even the most postmodern of Utopian readers, and to betray the deeper fears awakened and aroused by this form.

Struggle and conflict, meanwhile, have become so closely identified with competition and the anxieties of survival under capitalism (in all its stages) that their absence brings too sudden and abrupt a stillness for us to analyze the loss. Callenbach's War Games are no doubt also a way of providing a periodic substitution for our freedom from conflicts that are exhilarating for ambitious and active personalities (work having already been made pleasurable by the aesthetization of production as such). A world of purely interpersonal relationships without the so-called responsibilities of position and earning a "living" may well strike today's capitalist adults as regressive. We have already seen Kim Stanley Robinson's analysis of the Utopian enclave of

---

8 See my essay "The End of Temporality", in *Critical Inquiry*, Volume XXIX, No. 4 (2003).

the scientific collective; here is a useful evocation of the Utopian features of the former "actually existing socialism":

> Yet, at least for the intelligentsia, life in the fin de siècle USSR had its com-
> pensations. No one had very much money, but no one had to do very much
> work, either. The result was a whole society that acted as if it had never left
> college: intense, emotional, time-consuming friendships; endless hours spent
> drinking tea or vodka and discussing the meaning of life; the avid pursuit of
> esoteric spiritual or creative interests. If middle-class Russians sometimes seem
> perversely nostalgic for the Soviet Union, one reason is that the collapse of
> communism forced them horribly and abruptly to grow up.[9]

Infantilism is also a Utopian trait, as attractive as it is alarming; and this ambivalence can be traced into the visions of interpersonality itself, which range from overpopulation and the sprawl, awakening the usual fears of the non-West or of Koolhaas' "culture of congestion", to carefully manicured visions of Proustian elites and a sociability in some virtually pure state, uncontaminated by material worries or physical hardship (the idylls of colonial nostalgia are not unrelated to these, reminding us that the original Utopia was in fact a settler colony). These are all states in which Nature (and Nature's God) have been transcended, leaving us alone with ourselves and our purely existential concerns: states in which anxious meditations on the Event and its nature and possibility return with a vengeance.

Nowhere is this more apparent than in the Utopian relationship to History itself; and if for many of us Utopia is grasped as a political fulfillment of History, we tend to overlook an "end of history" internal to the Utopian texts themselves and not unrelated to the crisis in their aesthetic production within Utopia. For those, for example, who misunderstand Ruskin's Gothic program as a historical revival of some kind, Morris' outright antipathy to history will come as a surprise:

> As for your books [Clara explains to the visitor], they were well enough for
> times when intelligent people had but little else in which they could take
> pleasure, and when they must needs supplement the sordid miseries of their
> own lives with imaginations of the lives of other people. But I say flatly that
> in spite of all their cleverness and vigor, and capacity for storytelling, there is
> something loathsome about them. Some of them, indeed, do here and there
> show some feeling for those whom the history-books call "poor", and of the
> misery of whose lives we have some inkling; but presently they give it up, and
> towards the end of the story we must be contented to see the hero and heroine
> living happily in an island of bliss on other people's troubles ...[10]

9   Chrystia Freeman, *Sale of the Century* (New York, 2000), p. 114.
10 Morris, *News from Nowhere*, pp. 175–176.

And speaking of history itself as a field of study, the Utopian explainer observes frankly, "Some don't care about it; in fact, I don't think many do. I have heard my great-grandfather say that it is mostly in periods of turmoil and strife and confusion that people care much about history."[11] Skinner's Frazier is even more blunt: "We don't teach history ... We don't keep our young people ignorant of it, any more than we keep them ignorant of mythology, or any other subject. They may read all the history they like. But we don't regard it as essential in their education."[12] Bellamy is more discreet on the matter of schooling, but after all it is his time-traveler himself who is the great history lesson; the Utopians already live in blissful ignorance of this past, as their preacher tells us: "Already we have well-nigh forgotten, except when it is especially called to our minds by some occasion like the present, that it was not always with men as it is now. It is a strain on our imaginations to conceive the social arrangements of our immediate ancestors."[13] To this picture of the "end of history" as a pedagogical requirement, it remains only to add the feeling of Morris' Utopians about the future: "Meantime, my friend, you must know that we are too happy, both individually and collectively, to trouble ourselves about what is to come hereafter;"[14] and our impression of Utopia as an enclave outside of historical time is complete. Even Hythloday's box of Greek classics merely confirms the original Utopians in their commitment to the here and now. All of which is very much in the spirit of John Boone's "attempt to inspire the people on [Mars] to figure out a way to forget history"[15] (as we shall see, a very different relationship to the past, and to our own present of history, is affirmed by Marge Piercy's Mattapoisett Utopians, but they are after all time-travelers in the other direction).

Meanwhile, if History is a matter of the succession of generations, we have not yet identified the intersection of the Utopian and the generational (see below) but it is clear enough that narrative cannot really deal with generations either, or with generational time; and as for the Event, it does indeed get registered, but as the mythic beginning of Utopian time, the moment of foundation or inauguration, the moment of revolutionary transition. All of diachronic time is compressed into this single apocalyptic instant, which the narrative relates as the memory of old people. Novels have indeed invented various strategies for suggesting *durée* or the passage of time (in their systems of verbal tenses but also by way of the length of their books); but except for the occasional look backwards, novelistic characters cannot serve particularly efficiently as registering apparatuses for the slow changes in historical time.

11 Ibid., p. 67.
12 Skinner, *Walden Two*, pp. 237–238.
13 Bellamy, *Looking Backward*, p. 205.
14 Morris, *News from Nowhere*, p. 132.
15 Kim Stanley Robinson, *Red Mars*, pp. 255–256.

Kim Stanley Robinson's Martians are particularly instructive in this respect, as he is obliged to invent a longevity treatment for them in order to equip them with an experience of history unavailable within our own biological limits (and, as already mentioned above, has recourse to reincarnation in order to render that even longer alternate world history which is the narrative of *Days of Rice and Salt*).

All of which suggests an intimate relationship, within the Utopian framework, between the anonymity of the generations and depersonalization or death itself; and furthermore, between that fundamental anxiety and the seeming absence of events or actions in Utopia, the latter being able to be registered historically (as in Robinson) only by characters who in one way or another transcend the normal life span. But the absence of these great historical events can be said itself formally to be little more than the reflection of the absence of the smaller events of everyday life, along with the absence of action that seems to characterize most traditional Utopias, reduced to little more than perfunctory love stories in the course of the Utopian tour. Yet such absences, which can be justified by the specificity of Utopian form, will also put us on the track of that reproach of boredom which is in reality one of the deepest fears motivating political anti-Utopianism: namely that Marx's "end of prehistory" will usher in a world in which little more exists than "birth, copulation and death".

There would thus seem to be a fundamental contradiction between the timeless placidity of the achieved Utopias and the enormity of the social ills and evils that lends the Utopian solution its urgency and its passion. At least two kinds of historical events seem to have been excluded in advance from the Utopian framework: the convulsions of the various dystopias in store for our own world, and the systemic transformation or revolution that ushers in Utopia itself. It is as though the Utopian end of history has canceled the very category of events to which these collective experiences belong, leaving only that daily life to which Barthes claimed the Utopian form was reduced in the first place.[16]

Perhaps indeed it was the relative absence of those life-and-death issues in postwar America that lent *Walden Two* its frankness and thoughtfulness about just such no longer trivial topics and objections. So it is that the crucial issue is posed with acuity by one of Frazier's more astute critics:

> What you lack, compared with the world at large, is the opportunity to make long-term plans. The scientist has them. An experiment which answers an isolated question is of little interest. Even the artist has them. If he's a good artist or a good composer, he isn't concerned with the single picture on his easel or the composition on his piano. He wants to feel that all his pictures or compositions

16 Barthes, *Sade, Fourier, Loyola* (Paris, 1971), p. 23.

are saying something – are all part of a broader movement. The mere joy in running a race or painting a picture, or weaving a rug, isn't enough. Your good man must be working on a theory or a new style or an improved technique.[17]

It is an extraordinary objection, which not only raises questions but reveals contradictions and paradoxes. Callenbach will work hard to insist on the permanent presence and shaping power of invention in his Utopia: something which Skinner's lunch tray suggests will also be appealed to in the various Waldens Three, Four and Five. But at that point it can be sensed that these Utopian inventions slip onto the side of daily life and cease to carry the whole force and weight of the existential act, the momentous decision, the anxiety of heroic choice and of genuine historical praxis.

It is the very sense of the Novum which has been modified here; although the discussion itself suggests that the Utopias in question still emerge from a force field of modernism in which very precisely the issue of the New is paramount, and its seeming loss in Utopia a matter of mourning and need. Was this so in the classical Utopias? After all, More's text very centrally theorized the great transition from the feudal to the modern-capitalist; and the very spirit of Rabelais, for instance – the first books are more or less contemporaneous with More's own death – is one of euphoria at the new age: "Les grands ages sont révolus" – even though this cry is formulated in terms of the rediscovery of the past, rather than (as in the Brechtian version – the processions in *Galileo*) of the future.

Yet to put it this way is also to remember the expansion of the great Soviet Utopias out into space (Efremov's *Andromeda* [1958]), and their displacement of the imperialist impulses of capitalism into scientific progress on the one hand and the exploration of the galaxies on the other: which may in this context also be seen as a projection onto the cosmos of the gamble of the Stalinist aesthetic of socialist realism, namely the hope that a narrative of collective production could not only be possible as such, but also exciting and aesthetically satisfying. Meanwhile, we also need to register Skinner's own answer to the objection, which has to do with the momentous historical event of imperialist expansion of Utopia itself, the systematic spreading of the Walden experiments throughout the country, and indeed presumably around the globe.

But these ambitious possibilities do little more than to replace us in the period before Utopia, in which it is the founding of Utopia that constitutes the supreme Event, if not the last. Indeed, this lone axial Event, which seems henceforth to abolish events as such in the placidity of Utopian daily life, is also the source of a very different ambivalence and a very different anti-Utopian fear: that of the founder of Utopia himself, of this enigmatic being of whom Rousseau said that he must at one and the same time be more and

17 Skinner, *Walden Two*, pp. 166–167.

less than human all at once. Indeed, we here return to that question of art in Utopia with which we began this chapter, inasmuch as the founder of Utopia himself becomes the supreme artist who makes all other art superfluous and whose masterwork is very precisely the Utopian system as such. It was indeed a remarkable act of interpretation by Boris Groys to identify Stalinism and artistic modernism and to grasp Stalin himself as the supreme embodiment of the modernist artist as such, the seer, whose relationship to the Absolute is peremptory and dictatorial: the Master, the *sujet supposé savoir*, the Big Other in person (it will be remembered that Malevich's ambition for suprematism was no less than to take over and supplant the Party itself).[18] The anti-Utopian fear of state power and dictatorship is a very basic one, to which we will return in a moment. At this point, however, it is perhaps enough to identify a certain popular philistinism at work within the fear of Utopia, the hatred of modern art and its visionary artists, and beyond them the hatred of intellectuals in general, as whom (not wrongly, at least in the early years) the Party as such is identified. For a class-conscious and anti-intellectual populism, it is clear that Utopia as a work of art is an invention of intellectuals designed to use the masses as its raw material, its noble political and social ideals simply masking its contempt for ordinary people and their daily lives, which are to be trans-figured by the Utopian project.

Meanwhile, the reproach of boredom so often addressed to Utopias envelops both form and content: the former on the grounds that by definition nothing but the guided tour can really happen in these books, the latter owing precisely to our own existential reluctance imaginatively to embrace such a life. Three tendencies converge on this reaction and give it its unquestionable power. The first is the old aesthetic conviction that happiness is not the appro-priate content for any interesting work of art: the obvious line of inquiry to be pursued here is then the attempt to define happiness in the first place (or to deconstruct its stereotype). We will go no further than that here.[19]

The second line of inquiry has to do with precisely that world reduced to daily life as such, that village world, in which only the everyday exists, without great projects or indeed any very substantial relationship to the future and to action, a world in which we can very well imagine more vigorous and ambitious temperaments to chafe and pine. Risk-takers, indeed, entrepreneurs and busi-nessmen, will not be likely to find the same satisfactions in these more risk-free worlds as the inventor might or the social reformer: yet *Ecotopia* already set the example of the Utopian impulse capable of investing entrepreneurial commerce, so that we need not be surprised to find, in its full-blown develop-ment in the cyberpunk of the 1980s and 1990s, something like the Utopian expression of late or finance capital as such. So it would seem that the Utopian

18 Boris Groys, see Introduction, note 1.
19 But see the discussion of Adorno in the previous chapter.

form is far from being absolutely restricted by its own limits, is capable of mutation and of the seemingly unlimited reflexive reincorporation of anti-Utopian positions and impulses which on the face of it negate the form as such.

II

Yet there remains a third approach to Utopian boredom which has to do with the construction of its subjectivity. I believe that the concept of boredom is initially a theological one, and that it retains this character not merely from Augustine to Pascal, but on down to present-day existentialism. The religious provenance can be identified by its privative definition, and the way in which the temporal misery of human beings is attributed to their status as a secondary created nature, as opposed to the plenitude of the creator, and also to their sinfulness and corruption, as over against the angelic if not the divine itself. To attribute boredom to Utopia is thus paradoxical, for this new state omits all notions of sin, while its materialism presumably precludes concepts of creation as well (although as we have seen some temporal notion of a foundational event is still retained). From any religious perspective, therefore, the very idea of Utopia is sacrilegious (no matter how many priests and secular religious are included); and it is presumably the expression of a hubris whose historical and political form is no doubt the belief in perfectibility itself, implicit in Enlightenment revolutionary movements. Yet most Utopias bring their anti-social elements under control by way of that radical depersonalization we have already touched on, and which would seem to return us to more pious, if not Buddhist, values of selflessness and psychic renunciation: a notion of the abandonment of the private property of the self which is grasped as something positive rather than as asceticism and repression.

Probably it is precisely this depersonalization that explains the affective strand of anti-Utopianism presently under consideration. Falk's dilemma (see Chapter 7) is indeed the most acute expression of the existential fear of Utopia insofar as it raises the possibility of a loss of self so complete that the surviving consciousness cannot but seem an other to ourselves, new-born in the worst sense, in which we have lost even that private unhappiness, that boredom and existential misery ("je mein eigenes", as Heidegger might say), which constituted our identity in the first place. Here, truly, Utopia would be the place of radical difference indeed, and ourselves the most unimaginable aliens; while non-alienated life might prove to be the most alienating of all.

But we need to pursue these existential paradoxes a bit further; and it is worth considering for a moment those anti-Utopian positions that emerged from psychoanalysis and that, enveloping Marxism itself as their target, were based on a homology between the individual subject and the social totality as such. Thus, the fundamental principle of Lacanian psychoanalysis – that the "centered" subject is a mirage, that subjectivity is always split and divided,

192 ARCHAEOLOGIES OF THE FUTURE

never unifiable – is echoed on the level of the social by the Laclau–Mouffe emphasis on "antagonism", which persists in all social formations and renders any idea of social unification or harmony illusory, along with the revolutionary programs which hold out such tempting images of the social "totality" and its possible transformations. Lacan's fallen subject comes to us (via Sartre) from the old religious traditions mentioned above; the discomfort with totalizing political programs is clearly a more modern reaction against communism as such, if not, indeed, against Jacobinism. Žižek's gloss on both these positions (which do not have to be homologous with each other, in my opinion) predicates the critique as an attack on that whole range of fundamentalisms, beginning with the Marxian denunciation of capital, which offer to solve all social problems by addressing a single reified theme (which does not have to be this or that version of the Marxian one):

> We have, for example, feminist fundamentalism (no global liberation without the emancipation of women, without the abolition of sexism); democratic fundamentalism (democracy as the fundamental value of Western civilization; all other struggles – economic, feminist, of minorities, and so on – are simply further applications of the basic democratic, egalitarian principle); ecological fundamentalism (ecological deadlock as the fundamental problem of mankind); and – why not? – also psychoanalytic fundamentalism as articulated in Marcuse's *Eros and Civilization* (the key to liberation lies in changing the repressive libidinal structure) …[20]

One only wishes here to observe that the individual subject ("post-Marxist" or not) is in fact all these things at once, and is equally activated by issues of class, of gender and race, or equality, of ecology, and of the instincts. The discovery of so-called post-Marxism is, then, not that current society is a space in which various groups (the new social movements) compete with each other in flying their different thematic banners; but rather that we are multiply interpellated (to use the Althusserian formula) by the identities that all these groups presuppose, and that we necessarily respond to all these interpellations even when we refuse to repress them – our passionate prejudices are acknowledgments fully as much as our envies and our enthusiastic identifications.[21]

---

20 Slavoj Žižek, *The Sublime Object of Ideology* (London, 1989), p. 6.
21 But perhaps it would be more appropriate to offer some properly science-fictional versions of these well-known post-Lacanian "multiple subject positions":
    "Human contacts were parcellated, to use a term from brain science or systems theory; parceled out … One could therefore:
    1. pursue a project in paleolithic living,
    2. change the weather,
    3. attempt to restructure your profession, and
    4. be happy,

Yet I cannot but feel that behind these very pertinent and timely critiques there also lies a more metaphysical and Nietzschean resistance to promises about the future, in which all problems will have been solved and all cares wiped away. Here, Utopia is explicitly identified with religious transcendence and denounced in an uncompromisingly Enlightenment spirit, which turns out to include the Enlightenment itself in its Utopian target. Yet the "thought of the Other" which is here arraigned is in fact little more than that dilemma we have first confronted in the situation of Falk: for in effect it is presupposed that what the misguided and fundamentalist Utopians are mesmerized by an image of the future whose structural defect lies in the omission of their own existence as such. No wonder these harmonious pictures of the future society are so appealing: their attraction lies not so much in all the concrete problems they may have triumphantly solved, but in the construction of an optical image from which existence itself – the miseries of the self and of existential temporality, that condemnation to freedom we each must live and which, far more than death, is the Heideggerian "je mein eigenes" – all that has been removed by a sleight of hand, a masterful feat of ideological prestidigitation. This particular anti-Utopianism is therefore a lesson in existentialism and an injunction to put the self back into political prognoses, if not to admit that political change never solves personal problems. That may well be; but when the existential lesson is transferred to the political level, it simply becomes one more political ideology as such among others, this particular version of Nietzsche turning out to be the equally aberrant vision of an eternal present where nothing ever changes and unhappiness is always with us.[22] No wonder the desire called Utopia becomes the most dangerous political enemy, the one most worthy – despite its seeming insubstantiality – of persistent and vigilant critique. Nonetheless we will try to retain something of this existential insight when we come to discuss that formal closure which seems to be essential in the very construction of Utopias and which alone can account for the optical illusion denounced by these particular anti-Utopians.

Still, it remains paradoxical to assert that such dissatisfactions are at the very root of the fear aroused by Utopia, inasmuch as for people programmed by the Cold War, it is rather a *1984*-style vision of dictatorship, enhanced with the philosophical ingredients of Dostoyevsky's Grand Inquisitor, which

---

all at once, although not simultaneously, but moving from one thing to another, among differing populations; behaving as if a different person in each situation. It could be done, because there were no witnesses. No one saw enough to witness your life and put it all together ...."
(K.S. Robinson, *Fifty Degrees Below*, New York, 2005, pp. 68–69).

22 See, for example, Jean-François Lyotard, *Économie libidinale* (Paris, 1974), p. 155: "non, décidément, il faut le dire clairement: *Il n'y a pas* du tout de sociétés primitives ou sauvages, nous sommes tous des sauvages, tous les sauvages sont des capitalistes-capitalisés."

conflates Utopia as such with Stalinism and tends to identify Utopian projects with a will to power and with an evil or corruption inherent in human nature which are presumably anything but boring.[23]

Only *Walden Two*, written before the onset of the Cold War, and betraying some sympathy with the Soviet experiment, attempts to face this reproach head on with its portrait of Frazier, the megalomaniac founder of the community, who consciously improves on God's creation,[24] fantasizes his own crucifixion,[25] and yet passes utterly unrecognized and uninfluential among the inhabitants of his own Utopia. In most of the other texts it is the temporal gap between the old and the new, and the radical nature of the Utopian transition, which places the great founders like Lycurgus and Solon – so admired by Rousseau[26] – out of reach of anything like the dictatorial exercise of old-fashioned power. And clearly, before the existence of a professional police force, and even of professional armies, the "state" itself could not be felt as an autonomous force (or "subject of history"), but was rather confronted in seemingly unrelated encounters with tax collectors, the enforcers of the big landlords (or feudal barons), various passing troops of mercenaries – in short, of punctual violence, but probably not as any even intermittent yet truly systemic constraint. At any rate it seems clear enough that the earlier or more traditional Utopias are far more concerned with happiness than with freedom: unless, to be sure, one replaces this last in the context of the specific unfreedoms of feudalism as such, without anachronistically attributing to them the anxieties of dictatorship and bureaucracy that haunt the bourgeois world. Even the traditional preoccupation with the older category of tyranny, which presupposes individual usurpation rather than any structural defect, weighs less in the balance than specifically feudal abuses as such: as witness More's whole social panorama in Book One of the foundational text. There, it is clearly as much from feudal arrogance and corruption, as from the miseries of enclosure and the disorder of banditry and lawlessness (signs of the impending "transition to capitalism"), that Utopia provides deliverence and relief.

Indeed, it is worth remembering that More's text itself springs from the horror of repression, and in particular from the extraordinarily disproportionate system of punishments and penalties in effect in the England of his own time. Book One recapitulates a litany of petty offenses for which capital punishment is prescribed; and the thefts thought to warrant this momentous retribution lead us on to a consideration of crime in general and its relationship to private property, in such a way that the very institutions of Utopia (in Book Two) can be grasped as a creative response to such repression and a

23 Goebbels is said to have cried, after the Night of Broken Glass, "Now no one can say that we Nazis are not *interesting!*"
24 Skinner, *Walden Two*, p. 267.
25 Ibid., p. 295.
26 See the discussion in Chapter 2.

systemic rebuke to "law and order" as such. Even Rousseau's idea of freedom – whose ringing tones are now confounded in historical memory with those of the French Revolution itself – had the literal sense of independence, of disengagement from feudal hierarchies, from patronage and servitude, and from the status of the retainer or the protégé.

It is evident that the emergence of the employee, and of large-scale industrial institutions, must radically alter this meaning if it does not render it outmoded as an ideal. There can be no doubt that for the most part later Utopias have embraced the collective institutional conditions imposed by industrial capitalism, and have in effect participated in the creation of new ideologies for the wage-working part of the population, in a situation in which the hegemonic ideologies of the owners projected new forms of entrepreneurial individualism and individuality.

The wild card in all this, leaving aside the hegemonic power of individualism and its media contamination of lower-class points of view, must be identified as the state and its historically original forms of power, to which ideology and Utopia alike have been compelled to respond. Here, clearly enough, anti-Utopian anxieties about freedom and the power of the state have been able, within Utopian production itself, to develop into complicated arguments, from Bellamy and Morris on, about the presence of the state in future Utopian societies. The Utopian genre, however, which has its own capacities for appropriation, has been able to draw even the anti-Utopian fears of the Utopian state back inside itself in the form of revolutions against Utopia which themselves inevitably take on Utopian characteristics, from *The Moon Is a Harsh Mistress* (Heinlein, 1966) to Kim Stanley Robinson's Mars trilogy. Yet it should be noted that both of these paradigmatic texts are essentially anticolonialist (in the spirit of the American revolution), just as it should also be specified that the earlier visions of Utopian revolt are revolts against state socialism[27] rather than against socialism itself.

It is clear, then, that anti-Utopian fears and anxieties will vary according to the forms of state power with which this or that historical society is confronted: at certain moments (the French Revolution, the New Deal) the state can seem to embody progressive forces and is indeed no longer considered an alien power but rather the expression of popular forces themselves. At other moments, its subsumption under the interests of a ruling class or oligarchy is not only visible but leaves its mark on people's experience and daily life. Bureaucracy is subject to much the same fluctuation in value: and the heroic moments of impersonal state service, the great literacy campaigns of *instituteurs*, the expansion of welfare programs and social workers let alone of committed revolutionary cadres, remind us that this stigmatized dimension of the state does not always have to be the object of generalized hostility.

27 Morris, *News from Nowhere*, pp. 135–136.

In the next and final chapter, we will want to examine more closely what is certainly the central Left political tension in the present situation: the opposition between Marxism and a resurgent anarchism, in which the former is belabored with all the affective associations attached to state power and centralization. The anarchist repudiation of the ideologeme of statism, however, serves as an interesting testing ground for the new postmodern dictum that the distinction between Left and Right no longer exists in late capitalism.

For it would seem important to distinguish between the anarchism (and sometimes even the anti-communism) of the new anti-globalization movements and the more middle-class ideologies and attitudes of a libertarianism which can sometimes be intensified into the neo-fascism of militia groups (themselves no doubt Utopian formations) but draw the line at anti-capitalism. Whatever the problems raised by the term *socialism*, it is important to remember that both Marxism and anarchism are socialist or Left revolutionary movements – people of the Book, as it were – and that Bakunin had an intellectual and philosophical relationship to Marx's *Capital* analogous to Mohammed's relationship to the Old and New Testaments. Ideology becomes visible, indeed, not necessarily in political and social attitudes, but rather in that ultimate visceral commitment which turns on capitalism itself.

This is, no doubt, to jump the gun and to presuppose answered in advance the more postmodern generic question of whether Utopia must always be at one with socialism. To be sure, the gradual assimilation of socialism by Utopia (and vice versa) was a historical development, which need not seem permanent in the face of a new stage of capitalism and a new kind of cybernetic production: in that case, the anarchist revival seemed to offer the promise of a dissociation between the two visionary concepts, if not indeed a new liberation of the form itself. But in postmodernity we have merely reached a new stage in the expansion and reorganization of capital itself, and not, as ideologues speculated in the 1950s and 1960s, a new mode of production altogether (the most widespread version of such speculations was Daniel Bell's "postindustrial society", which posited a new ruling class of scientists and technicians, and which distantly echoed the "new class" speculations contemporaneous in Eastern Europe). This paradoxically marked a return to Plato's Utopia of the Guardians, but has not been confirmed by the fate of science itself, increasingly pressed into the service of capitalism and profit in recent years.

The Utopian impulses of recent literature, however, enthusiastically affirm the *jouissance* of money making and the externalization of capitalism; and thereby express either the privileged stratum of US class polarization today, or, more symbolically, the "blindness of the center" and the indifference of the superstate generally to the state of the newly globalized world outside its borders. I conclude, at any rate, that it is still difficult to see how future Utopias could ever be imagined in any absolute dissociation from socialism in its larger sense of anti-capitalism; dissociated, that is to say, from the values of social and economic equality and the universal right to food, lodging, medicine, education and work (in other words, to put the proposition in representational rather than ideological terms, no modern Utopia is plausible which does not address, along with its other inventions, the economic problems caused by industrial capitalism). The proof is that even the neo-conservative fundamentalisms of the day continue to promise eventual satisfaction in all these areas, in that rising tide of universal prosperity and development to which they claim to add the elusive thing called freedom, as well as the imaginary thing called modernity.

Yet it is certain that the Cold War immensely complicated the problems of Utopian representation by foregrounding the ideological ambiguity of the modern state as such, in ways that reshuffled the dialectic of Identity (or uniformity) and Difference and that still live on into the post-Cold War period (or in other words, into postmodernity). The existence of the Soviet Union, indeed, produced a new kind of ideological object, positive and negative all at once: an anti-systemic movement directed against intolerable class oppression, which seemed to transform itself under our very eyes into a form of state power more oppressive than the tyrannical feudal structures it was called into being to sweep away. Alongside the historiographic problems raised by Stalinism, in other words, we must acknowledge the extraordinary opportunities it offered for new ideological production and for the invention of all kinds of new and complex fantasy investments which this historically unique situation calls into being: historical analogies drawn from "oriental despotism", and from ancient forms of tyranny, all the way to propositions about the transformation of bureaucracy into a "new class"; and innumerable constellations of paranoia and conspiracy theory, in which, as with anti-semitism, the dimly apprehended forms of capitalist organization are projected onto its enemies or victims.

My favorite allegorical narrative of the process is Bakhtin's notion of the *carnivalesque*,[28] in which the moment of carnival itself – revolution, very much including cultural revolution – constitutes the break between a traditional oppressive social system – Roman Catholicism, standing for the Czarist ancient regime – and its more modern replacement in Baroque state power (which figures Stalinism): in this ingenious narrative, which has no more historical relevance than any other ideological fantasy, we can observe the advantages of a Utopian position from which both bourgeois society (evolving under the Czar) and communism, both Right and Left, can be denounced, but at a heavy price, namely the ephemerality of the moment of carnival itself, however cyclical it may be conceived to be. Yet here the Utopian impulse is placed under a great strain, inasmuch as it constitutes a kind of vanishing mediator

28 Mikhail Bakhtin, *Rabelais and His World* (Bloomington, 1984 [1965]), pp. 274–277.

after whose disappearance order is to be sure restored; but an order of a different and more effective type, which may be able some day to do without the safety valve of carnival altogether.

Bakhtin's is however a double negation, and this is surely the moment to remind ourselves of a program which set out to distinguish various kinds of negativity from one another, as in just such a critique of the old order which is also a prophetic warning about the new repressivities of what replaces it. Are both to be considered then, in the light of carnival's moment of freedom, dystopias?

As has been suggested in passing in the previous chapter, this word is laden with dangerous and misleading ambiguities, which are not diminished by the recent coinage of this neologism (whose wider currency dates, we are told,[29] from the 1950s – in other words, from the Cold War). As our own practice has testified, it is not easy to change one's linguistic habits when it comes to a word like this, which obviously began to fill a palpable collective need. Still, there would seem to be a real gap between the two negations in question. The dystopian tetralogy of John Brunner, for example,[30] is the classic exemplification of a principle designated by the title of a famous 1940 Heinlein story: "if this goes on …". Overpopulation, pollution, an inhuman rate of technological change – these are then extrapolated into what are certainly in Brunner "new maps of hell", maps frequently (and not incorrectly) characterized as dystopian. But is the same principle at work in Orwell's nightmare vision in *1984*? The affirmation that Orwell conceived of the "creeping totalitarianism" of contemporary politics – whether that of Labour Britain or of the USSR – in the mode of the "if this goes on" principle remains a mere biographical affirmation. Surely, the force of the text (and of *Animal Farm*) springs from a conviction about human nature itself, whose corruption and lust for power are inevitable, and not to be remedied by new social measures or programs, nor by heightened consciousness of the impending dangers.

Tom Moylan's proposal for a generic conception of the "critical dystopia" clarifies this difference.[31] The critical dystopia is a negative cousin of the Utopia proper, for it is in the light of some positive conception of human social possibilities that its effects are generated and from Utopian ideals its politically enabling stance derives. Yet if one reserves the term dystopia for works of this kind, then Orwell's works must be characterized in a markedly different way and by a distinctive generic terminology: I propose to characterize them as anti-

29 John Clute and Peter Nicholls, *Encylopedia of Science Fiction*, p. 360.
30 See Chapter 5, note 3, above.
31 See Moylan, *Scraps of the Untainted Sky* (Westport, CT, 2001), along with the discussions in Moylan and Raffaella Baccolini, eds, *Dark Horizons* (New York, 2003). Perhaps the notion of the "critical dystopia" corresponds to R.C. Elliott's conception of satire as a kind of generic opposite number to Utopia: see Chapter 3, note 3, above, and R.C. Elliott, *The Power of Satire* (Princeton, 1960).

Utopian, given the way in which they are informed by a central passion to denounce and to warn against Utopian programs in the political realm. This passion, which is of course at one with Burke's denunciation of the French Revolution as well as with more contemporary anti-communisms and anti-socialisms, is clearly quite distinct from the monitory fears and passions that drive the critical dystopia, whose affiliations are feminist and ecological as much as they are Left-political.

In that case, a fourth term or generic category would seem desirable. If it is so, as someone has observed, that it is easier to imagine the end of the world than the end of capitalism, we probably need another term to characterize the increasingly popular visions of total destruction and of the extinction of life on Earth which seem more plausible than the Utopian vision of the new Jerusalem but also rather different from the various catastophes (including the old ban-the-bomb anxieties of the 1950s) prefigured in the critical dystopias. The term apocalyptic may serve to differentiate this narrative genre from the anti-Utopia as well, since we do not sense in it any commitment to disabuse its readership of the political illusions an Orwell sought to combat, but whose very existence the apocalyptic narrative no longer acknowledges. Yet this new term oddly enough brings us around to our starting point again, inasmuch as the original Apocalypse includes both catastophe and fulfillment, the end of the world and the inauguration of the reign of Christ on earth, Utopia and the extinction of the human race all at once. Yet if the Apocalypse is neither dialectical (in the sense of including its Utopian "opposite") nor some mere psychological projection,[32] to be deciphered in historical or ideological terms, then it is probably to be grasped as metaphysical or religious, in which case its secret Utopian vocation consists in assembling a new community of readers and believers around itself.

---

32 In his classic work on the subject, *The Sense of an Ending* (Oxford, 1966), Frank Kermode associates the apocalyptic with two distinct (yet perhaps related) sources: a projection of existential fears of death, and a formal consequence of the structural requirement that narrative have some kind of ending. But as with Freud's reading of dreams about one's own death, the end of the world may simply be the cover for a very different and more properly Utopian wish-fulfillment: as when (in John Wyndam's novels, for example) the protagonist and a small band of other survivors of the catastrophe go on to found some smaller and more livable collectivity after the end of modernity and capitalism. Or else we follow Kermode's passing remark – "even in Jewish thought there was no true apocalyptic until the prophecy failed" (p. 5) – and construe certain kinds of apocalypse as the expression of the melancholy and trauma of the historical experience of defeat. *Paradise Lost* comes to mind, but also recent historical novels, such as Vargas Llosa's *Guerra de fin del mundo* (Barcelona, 1981) or Luther Blissett's *Q* (Turin, 2000). Nor does it seem out of place to interpret the immense eschatological *jouissance* of the greatest of modern apocalyptic writers, J.G. Ballard (1930–), as the expression of his experience of the end of the British Empire in the Second World War (see *The Empire of the Sun* [1984]).

III

One has indeed a peculiar reaction today to the classic Cold War dystopia, whose Manichaean emergence in everything from horror films to respectable literary and philosophical achievements marks it as an essentially mass-cultural and ideological phenomenon. Leaving the conventional trappings of villainy out of it, several symptomatic and paradoxical features of Orwell's *1984* thrust themselves forward insistently. The central contradiction of the novel's framework lies, as I have argued elsewhere, in the inconsistency between the advanced technology of the all-seeing and infallible surveillance systems and the repeated assurances that science cannot function under totalitarianism (an assurance reinforced by the shabbiness of Oceania itself). Orwell's linguistic anxieties are ecumenical, combining a critique of the dialectic (the original double-speak, in which any utterance can have two diametrically opposed meanings) with a sense of the impoverishment likely to result from the intensification of common-language philosophy, Basic English, and the Wittgensteinian ethos: this is truly a convergence theory in which Stalinism and Anglo-Saxon commercialism and empiricism are sent off back to back!

But the most haunting feature of *1984* is the elegiac sense of the loss of the past, and the uncertainty of memory. The rewriting of political history in Oceania is assimilated to the personal dreams of a lost childhood: Winston's mother and baby sister "were down in some subterranean place – the bottom of a well, for instance, or a very deep grave – but it was a place which, already far below him, was itself moving downwards".[33] These lyrical fragments of unreliable childhood memories recall nothing quite so much as the haunting nostalgia of Chris Marker's *La Jetée* (1964), filmed in a series of photographic stills and equally assimilating a personal trauma to the post-atomic devastation and underground scientific dictatorship that follows the end of the world. But *La Jetée* is also a film about temporality as such, where the impulse that drives the Orwellian unconscious is foregrounded and raised into the light of a remorseless analysis and an incomparably stark desolation of feeling.

The mystery of Orwell in fact requires us to distinguish three levels of his work: first, that articulation of the history of Stalinism which he observed and experienced empirically, on the level of contingent events; then its ahistorical universalization into a baleful vision of human nature as an insatiable and lucid hunger for power and its exercise; and finally the truly pathological and obsessive fixation on this conjuncture as a solution to his own existence, its conversion into a life passion. The haggard and implacable elaboration of this passion has certainly become the face of anti-Utopianism in our own time, and as a representation it can scarcely be argued away. But is it historical or universal? Did anti-Utopianism always take forms like this, indeed, did it even exist as such in earlier moments of history? To what degree does Orwell's

---

33 George Orwell, *1984* (New York, 1961 [1949]), p. 28.

obsession betray some conviction as to the inevitability of Utopia (and thus, the urgency to warn vainly of its imminence)? Can we separate anti-Utopianism in Orwell from anti-communism? Or in other words, is his work a testimony to the inextricable ways in which these two phenomena have become conflated (or at least were historically conflated, beginning with Marx and reaching indistinguishability in the era of Stalin)? If Orwell's sad passion stands as a paradigmatic expression of the Cold War, has it become anachronistic in globalization? (One thinks of the cry of *Barbarella*'s villain, as he sinks into the magma: "Earth, you have lost your last Great Dictator!") Finally, if Orwell's nightmare is a specific expression of modernism, what can survive of it in the postmodern age?

At this point a final difficulty remains, which is that of the very status of the fear so deeply embedded in the dystopias, and of which Orwell seems the most authentic and original expression. This is not a personal or psychoanalytic question, although clearly enough such biographical questions are of the greatest interest and hypothetical answers to them deserve scrutiny in their own right.

But equally clearly the fear – acknowledged not only by a whole Cold War public but reaching back into the eighteenth-century European readership as well, with their gothic nightmares of imprisonment and of evil monks or nuns – is not at all a private matter but a collective phenomenon of no little historical interest. Our immediate methodological or hermeneutic quandary is, then, why such a primordial affect should not merit the same privilege we have accorded to the Utopian impulse, of which we have insisted that it is primary, and not to be reduced – via pop-psychological notions of sublimation – to the mere disguised expression of other impulses such as those of sexuality (or even personal frustration). Why should Orwell's terror not equally be exempted from such reductive diagnoses?

Certainly it mobilizes all the resources of self-preservation, if the latter be considered to be an instinct. (In a grand Utopian moment, as we have already seen in a previous chapter, Adorno suggested that Utopia was constituted by the very falling away of this "instinct", which he saw as the specific defense mechanism generated by class society as such, or in other words by all previous social orders up to and including our own.) In that case, one must add that societies (or to be more precise, modes of production) also know a collective instinct of self-preservation which is awakened in moments of mortal danger. Significantly, both of the dystopian awakenings mentioned above are collective responses of the bourgeoisie: the first in its struggle against feudal absolutism and arbitrary tyranny, the second in its reaction to the possibility of a workers' state. This terror clearly overrides that other collective impulse which is the Utopian one, which, however, as irrepressible as the libido, continues to find its secret investments in what seems most fundamentally to rebuke and deny it: thus the projected oppressors, whether of clerical or party-bureaucratic nature, are fantasized as collectivities which distantly reproduce a Utopian structure, the difference being that I am included in the Utopian structure but excluded from the oppressors. But at this point, the dynamic has become that of group behavior, with its cultural envy and its accompanying identity politics and racisms.

As for Zamyatin's *We*, it is ambiguous in a rather different way, as we have already observed.[34] Here it is not the personal and the political that are confused but rather aesthetics and bureaucracy. Both are human productions after all, and the engineer Zamyatin is a true constructivist whose World State is decidedly a work of art of the epoch of Malevich and El Lissitsky: that he should have mixed feelings about it is not to be held against him. After all it was only a generation earlier that Worringer associated abstraction with the death drive, in a supremely influential statement.[35] Zamyatin's Benefactor is not Big Brother, but rather a peremptory *chef d'école* like Breton or indeed Malevich himself (an aesthetic dictatorship Groys will much later on re-identify with Stalin). *We*'s revolutionaries are iconoclasts rather than freedom fighters, and the sexual repression of the state is closer to Loos' condemnation of ornament and Le Corbusier's hygienic spaces than to Puritan settlements or Roman Catholic monasteries. At any rate *We* is a true anti-Utopia in which the Utopian impulse is still at work, with whatever ambivalence: unlike Orwell's dispirited reaction to postwar Labour Britain, which is itself a depressive symptom of revolutionary discouragement.[36]

But both these works make it clear that their allegedly anti-Utopian fears are not to be taken at face value. This is the point at which I wish to dissociate such psychological considerations from a very different source of Utopian fear which I will derive from the formal properties of this genre, and in particular from that closure on which we have so often insisted: closure in space, closure in time, the closure of the Utopian community and its position beyond history, or at least beyond Marx's "pre-history" as we know it.

IV

For it is this seamless closure of the new system that renders it alien and existentially threatening, and which clothes the radically New in the lineaments of a sublime terror before which we necessarily pause and hesitate, or draw back.

---

34 See Chapter 2, note 21.
35 The reference is to Wilhelm Worringer's essay "Abstraction and Empathy", written in 1907.
36 *Brave New World* (1932), which makes up the third of the canonical dystopian trilogy, is very much an aristocratic critique of the media and mass culture, rather than of any Orwellian "totalitarianism" (and on this last, by all means see Slavoj Žižek, *Did Somebody Say Totalitarian?* [London, 2001]).

It is therefore worth returning to a more formalistic examination of precisely those narrative constraints or limits likely to arouse negative political reactions along with aesthetic ones and capable of stimulating that very anti-Utopianism which is the deepest enemy of this peculiar form.

A beginning can be made in this formalist exploration by reflecting on the nature of narrative itself, whose limits are coterminous with some fundamental conceptual antinomies (probably owing to the fact that these last are also secretly narrative in their dynamics). Thus, that familiar and utterly ideological and stereotypical humanist "theme" of the opposition between the individual and society can be approached from a philosophical standpoint, by pointing out the obvious, namely that the "individual" is also a social category not necessarily present in all kinds of societies. But it can also be repositioned within the machinery of narrative or storytelling and the latter's capacities.

In this respect, it is crucial to note that narrative has only one actantial category: what we generally identify as the "character" or speaking more technically the "actant". All forms of collective action – whether they are identified as the nation or the people, or an ethnic group of some kind, or even a small face-to-face team, let alone a pair – must be somehow accommodated in this single category of the actant. Thus, Stapledon's imaginary histories frequently move whole societies around as though they were characters; while in More it is the Utopians as an identical population who replace either the nation at one end of the spectrum or the individual at the other.

It may be instructive to observe this formal shortage or deficiency at work in conceptual thought as well. It is enough to think of Rousseau's embarrassment in *The Social Contract*, where no entities can be located beyond the individual: all social multiplicities are thereby equally assimilated to collectivities of homogeneous and equal units, whatever their dimensions and their ontological status (which on other accounts might vary from the organic to the serial, or the nation to the ethnic). Rousseau thereby finds himself obliged, very much in science-fictional or Utopian terms, to invent a new entity distinct from all these, in which the social also exists in a new and hitherto unidentified form imaginable only as the unanimity of those individuals (and distinct from their additive totality): it is this new category he calls the General Will. But the fortunes of this idea are such as to cast doubt on the viability of this representational innovation. The attempt to represent Utopia will face similar difficulties and dilemmas, which are, as I've suggested above, essentially narrative problems, dysfunctions of a narrative nature.

We may now look at some of those, the local effects produced by this more general structure of the narrative machinery. First and foremost in almost all respects comes the requirement already mentioned for system as such, at first epitomized by spatial closure, a permanent structural feature of the genre only moderately disguised when, with capitalism and historicity, this imaginary no-place migrates from the south seas or the north or south pole to the future and becomes accessible only by time travel, if not in some outer space which itself lies for all practical purposes in the future.

Closure is initially motivated by secession and the preservation of radical difference (as well as the fear of contamination from the outside and from the past or history). Utopus' great trench, which makes all Utopias over into islands, is paradigmatic of Ecotopia's secession from the US (ratified by the "helicopter war" and the subsequent Cuba-style blockade, initiated from within fully as much as from without). It is already refigured for the present by the flight of the Odonians in antiquated spaceships to Urras' barren moon, where secession is dramatized as a substitute for violent revolution on the home planet: something not avoided in the Mars trilogy, despite the even more formidable intervening gap. The Utopias of Fourier and Skinner, situated in their respective countrysides and less obviously extraterritorial, are no less quarantined, according to the wishes of the Utopians themselves; but they also articulate that other narrative possibility inherent in this enclave reality which is that of an outward or imperializing influence and as it were Utopian contamination of the surrounding area.

Thus both Fourier and Skinner foresee the spread of their model, and the implantation of Utopian colonies everywhere; Bellamy and Morris, who finesse the initial problem by positing the conversion of the whole world to their Utopian schemes, nonetheless also tell the story of its gradual spread in terms of emulation and relatively peaceful persuasion. Such was also to have been the triumph of Winstanley's commons, which, having abolished wage work, could expect gradually to draw all of the former laborers elsewhere into its orbit and to leave the rich estates of the feudal barons to wither on the vine.[37] The tragic outcome in real life, namely the extinction of the Utopian enclave by the landowners, testifies to the wisdom of Utopian secession in the first place.

Secession can today be seen to have its own internal momentum, however, and the turbulent breakdown of federations all over the world (not even to go back as far as the American Civil War) suggests that this particular right to self-determination is by no means a value shared universally. But if the perspective on closure is reversed, this formal requirement takes on an even more sinister dimension, something also observable at once in More himself. For this author was not for nothing the contemporary of Machiavelli and a witness to the emergence of *Realpolitik* and the absolute monarchy or nation-state: as we have already observed, the cold-blooded dealings of his Utopians with their neighbors is as cynical as anything in *The Prince*, and as remorseless.

---

37 See J.C. Davis' illuminating discussion of Winstanley, in *Utopia and the Ideal Society*, pp. 183–188.

Then too, we do well to remember (as Balasopoulos reminds us)[38] that Utopia is very much the prototype of the settler colony, and the forerunner of modern imperialism (at least in its North American, apartheid, or Zionist forms – "the people without land" supposedly meeting "the land without people"). That Utopias should turn out to be one of the privileged literary expressions of the Spanish empire (whose subject Campanella also was) is thus equally significant: the predestined harmony between a form without content and a content without form. My own feeling is that the colonial violence thus inherent in the very form or genre itself is a more serious reproach than anything having to do with the authoritarian discipline and conformity that may hold for the society within Utopia's borders. All of which goes a long way towards justifying Barthes' structuralist comment that closure alone allows system to come into being,[39] or in other words enables the deployment of genuine systemic difference. Closure thereby operates on a conceptual or categorical level fully as much as in international relations, and it may also determine the emergence of those abstract ideals of purity and unanimity, of identity on all levels, that have inspired the enemies of Utopia to associate it with racism and other forms of political compulsiveness.

For the Utopians themselves, however, a rather different rationale for these oppressive forms of unanimity seems to have imposed itself. Nor should we forget the context of religious warfare in More's own century, and the divisive function of religion ever after and down to our own time. Indeed, to the ideological secession from just such realities corresponds the obligatory tolerance that reigns within Utopia and frowns on the over-zealous and on proselytism.

Here we return to our earlier discussion about freedom, but now from a formalistic or narratological perspective, one in which slowly but surely the whole vexed issue of the relationship between Utopia and politics (which has been with us since the beginning of this discussion) can be expected to return with a vengeance. For it is now a question of trying to see, from within the constraints of the form, why the earlier Utopians should have known such unanimity on the need to exclude political discussion and the development of any form of local difference, and not only the religious kind. As we have shown above, there is a systemic perspective for which it is obvious that whatever threatens the system as such must be excluded: this is indeed the basic premise of all modern anti-Utopias from Dostoyevsky to Orwell and beyond, namely that the system develops its own instinct for self-preservation and learns ruthlessly to eliminate anything menacing its continuing existence without regard for individual life.

But, as we have already observed, it is precisely in terms of anti-systemic tendencies that the formation of smaller groups and movements within

38 See Antonis Balasopoulos, "Unworldly Worldliness: America and the Trajectory of Utopian Expansionism", *Utopian Studies*, Vol. 15, No. 2 (Winter 2004).
39 See Chapter 1, note 6.

Utopian society was seen and pronounced to be undesirable: the period word for such formations being *factionalism* and very much including political parties as well as smaller kinds of associations. As we have already observed, this principle defines one of the great dividing lines between so-called traditional Utopias and modern ones, insofar as contemporary democratic and anarchist currents aim precisely at asserting the viability of a host of factions within the state (or against the state). The oppressive unanimities of the older state-Utopia do not seem to have generated any original narrative reactions against what seems to us today an unbearably conformist and standardized environment. Eighteenth-century affirmations of freedom, as in Godwin's *Caleb Williams* (1794), still identify feudal arbitrariness as their target, while the lack of freedom is identified by Jean-Jacques as dependency and as a quasi-feudal servitude at the mercy of another's will. In that situation, the state as the unanimity of Utopia spells my release from hierarchy and service to particulars; whereas in modern industrial times, in which the state has itself become a character or individual, freedom is redefined as release from the oppression of state power itself, a release that can take the form of existential pathos, as with the dilemmas of the individual rebel or anti-hero, but which now, after the end of individualism, seems to take the form of identification with small groups.

From our present standpoint, however, which is a narratological one, it would seem that these small groups fall precisely into that no-man's-land between the individual *actant* and the social totality which can only be imagined or given figuration as yet another individual *actant*, or in other words a hyper-organism. But the intermediate small groups, or the parties, the factions, the warring communities of belief, fall into neither one of these categories, which they implicitly correct and cancel all at once. The philosophical analysis of the small face-to-face group – most elaborately pursued by Sartre in *The Critique of Dialectical Reason*[40] – tends desperately and in vain to reconcile the categorial opposition of the individual to the agglomeration by a process of mutual or dialectical negation not too different from what was outlined for other issues in the preceding chapter: were Sartre's effort an ontology, indeed, I would characterize its solution as the fitful and necessarily ephemeral emergence of a different kind of collective being. But perhaps this is only to endow the still missing new concept in advance with a nimbus of quasi-sacred legitimacy.

V

There is, however, one particular small group whose existence cannot be banned from Utopia or successfully forbidden and expelled by the supreme

---

40 J.-P. Sartre, *The Critique of Dialectical Reason*, Volume I (London, 2004 [1960]); and see my Introduction to this volume.

operation of Utopian unanimity: this is the family itself. It persists like a foreign body within the new society, and that persistence, secured no doubt by biology, threatens the geometrical Utopian diamond with a flaw in the form that cannot be corrected or fantasized away, however much Utopian ingenuity is expended on doing so. It is as though Utopian form itself, the machinery of representation, repeated André Gide's famous cry: "Familles, je vous hais!" – a cry of impotence, rather than the declaration of a war that could be won.

This paradoxical proposition, which is meant in part to account for the inveterate incompleteness of the Utopian form and its structural failure to achieve closure, can perhaps be clarified from several standpoints. The first has to do with the identification of the family as the fundamental building block of that mode of production from which modern capitalism sought to escape: indeed More's own period is precisely that epoch of transition in which the newer nation-states seek convulsively to liberate themselves from the feudal clan system and the extended family units of the great barons and landowners. The nuclear family, however, is not the solution of this struggle, but only a side effect of a process in which absolute monarchy and central-ization succeed in substituting themselves for the dispersal of the feudal manors. Indeed, even the attempts to celebrate the nuclear family in bourgeois literature and in eighteenth- and nineteenth-century realism have a certain pathos, while complaints about its asphyxiating framework grow ever more insistent in the twentieth, from Gide to the schizogenetic family dear to anti-psychiatry. The obligatory romance motif that seems an inevitable component of the Utopian text from the nineteenth century on can be seen as a compen-sation for this unresolvable problem and a displacement of its status from that of a social institution to one of sexuality and individual relationships. Modern feminism is only the latest Utopian effort to bypass the bourgeois family in the direction of group marriage or single-gender systems; the post-human movement adds a new wrinkle in the form of the "optional kinship system" of misfits and monsters.[41]

Perhaps another perspective may also be helpful here. A number of years ago Bourdieu and his team published a wonderful collective volume on the sociology of amateur photography:[42] two of its findings may be retained (only the second of which interests us directly). The first is the ideological need to justify this practice for which society had not yet produced any codified role or status: the amateur photographers did so by borrowing the aesthetic dis-course of a nobler art, namely painting, and by reproducing painting's apologia

---

41 See Phillip Wegner's remarkable essay, "'We're Family': Kinship, Fidelity, and Revolution in *Buffy the Vampire Slayer*", in *Living Between Two Deaths: Periodizing US Culture, 1989–2001* (Durham, NC, forthcoming).

42 Pierre Bourdieu et al., *Un art moyen* (Paris, 1965).

in all its variants. The experience of postmodernism, not yet registered in the Bourdieu investigation, and in which photography has precisely become a major art in its own right (with utterly different theoretical self-justifications derived from the newly emergent "society of the spectacle"), gives us a certain distance from this once marginal social practice and the ways in which it then sought to rationalize its existence.

It is a marginality which then becomes inescapable in Bourdieu's second finding, namely that whatever the aesthetic chosen by these amateur photographers, they were all unanimous in excluding family photographs from a practice they wished to be "artistic". Bourdieu concludes that amateur photography was invented as a disguised and seemingly acceptable way of escaping the bourgeois family as such, of getting out of the house, of creating a space from which the family was utterly absent. We may here recall Jean Borie's suggestive idea that the nineteenth-century novel was itself an "art de célibataire", and that even when technically married, the great nineteenth-century novelists were all bourgeois bachelors in spirit, placing themselves in some freer social space from which to look back and to pass judgment on a society precisely dominated by the bourgeois nuclear family itself[43] (the judgments of course are the novels themselves, which after Jane Austen's achievement – yet another bachelor! – are uniformly negative on the subject).

We may also explore this incompatibility between Utopian form and the family as such by reflecting on the destiny of the family in that related discourse which is political theory. Either society as such is assimilated to the form of the family, as in Confucian patriarchy (or perhaps one should phrase it the other way around and see the state coopting the appearance of family structure for its own purposes); or else, after some initial consideration of the *oikos*, political philosophers follow Aristotle in dissociating this structure (which of course includes the governing of slaves and servants) from the state as such. Indeed, Aristotle startles us by observing that "the state is by nature clearly prior to the family and to the individual, since the whole is of necessity prior to the part".[44] On the other hand, all such theorists have made a distinct place, alongside monarchy and democracy, for oligarchy, which most often strikes one as preeminently an association of great families or clans.

But what is merely a problem for political philosophy becomes a mission for Utopia as a form: even where the family is not legislated out of existence altogether, stringent management and reform tend to reduce it to the biological and non-social fact of the couple, following the classic Utopian example of Sparta, where men and women live apart and only meet clandestinely, the resultant offspring taking their place in a communal nursery. Nor do the Jesuit

---

43 Jean Borie, *Le Célibataire français* (Paris, 1976); and now see Eve Sedgewick, *Between Men* (New York, 1992).
44 Aristotle, *Politics*, paragraph 1253, line 19.

Utopias in Paraguay, in which a bell was rung at night to summon couples to their conjugal duties, offer a convincing version of some new transformation of the family altogether.[45]

The persistence of the bourgeois family in Bellamy is certainly one of the features of this influential book that has not worn well: I believe that it is more objectionable to modern tastes than the much-maligned Industrial Army. Yet at the same time Bellamy includes an antidote which he fails to develop (perhaps out of Victorian timidity: Skinner's reticence on the subject is also noteworthy, and explainable by American social values). This is what is probably, more than child-rearing, the centerpiece of all Utopian feminism, namely the communal kitchen and dining room, which effectively abolish one of the two fundamental aspects of woman's function in securing social reproduction, the communal nursery effectively removing the other.[46]

Anxieties about the family in Utopia, then – which seem to come in the antithetical forms of the fear that it will disappear altogether, or, alternatively, that it will still be there – have their deeper logic in that inevitable structure of Utopian closure which has reemerged so often in this discussion and which probably also offers the deeper narrative meaning of the anxieties about freedom itself. Thus a deep-structural formal contradiction projects itself into the manifest content, not just of one symptomal thematic, but of layered and surcharged combinations of fantasies. Here, for example, the anxiety about the family combines with the great political issues of gender on the one hand, and more obscure fears about sexuality on the other, while laterally linking up with patriarchal images and narative fragments whose final form is the nightmarish Big Other of the anti-utopias as such.

Such constellations of highly charged libidinal themes, cathected or anti-cathected, are thus readily awakened by Utopian form as such, which at once challenges everything in our experience, from personal existence to institutional habits and social fantasies on other levels. The Utopian thematics of the body, indeed, proved particularly auspicious for the new issues of the countercultural 1960s, when indeed Utopias began to flourish again, until brought prematurely to a halt by the emergence of the new political category of the small group (ethnic or identity-oriented), which, as was suggested above, does not seem to have accommodated itself to the narrative apparatus of the classical Utopia.

45 See on other Latin American Utopias, Fernando Gomez, *Good Places and Non-Places in Colonial Mexico* (Lenham, Maryland, 2001); Alicia M. Barabas, *Utopias indias* (Quito, 1989) and Michael Ennis, "Historicizing Nahua Utopias" (PhD thesis, Duke University 2005).
46 Lyman Tower Sargent has made a comprehensive survey of the forms taken by the family in Utopian (or "intentional") communities: see "Utopia and the Family: A Note on the Family in Political Thought", in *Dissent and Affirmation: Essays in Honor of Mulford Q. Sibley*, ed. Arthur L. Kalleburg, J. Donald Moon and Daniel L. Sabia Jr (Bowling Green, OH: Bowling Green University Popular Press, 1983), pp. 106–117, 256–259.

Meanwhile, another crisis in the form is determined by the seeming distance between these libidinal materials and the nature of current or infrastructural organization, itself significantly modified since the onset of third-stage or neo-liberal capitalism, whose content seems itself to bifurcate between faceless conspiracies on the one hand (rather than the great dictators of yesteryear) and the cyberspace of business innovation and its commodification of consumption. Nonetheless, narrative analysis seems the most reliable guide to these dilemmas, demonstrating in passing how all the political and conceptual polemics around "totalization" were in reality so many arguments about narrative closure.

13

The Future as Disruption

Let's recapitulate our findings at this eleventh hour. We have come laboriously to the conclusion that all ostensible Utopian content was ideological, and that the proper function of its themes lay in critical negativity, that is, in their function to demystify their opposite numbers. The examination of the anti-Utopia, then, of the fear of Utopia, has led us to identity a fundamental source in the very form of Utopia itself, in the formal necessity of Utopian closure. In addition we have been plagued by the perpetual reversion of difference and otherness into the same, and the discovery that our most energetic imaginative leaps into radical alternatives were little more than the projections of our own social moment and historical or subjective situation: the post-human thereby seeming more distant and impossible than ever!

Indeed, when we formulate the topic in terms of the fate of Utopia, of its future, or better still its relationship to our future, all the old ambiguities of form and content resurface and it is no longer clear whether the future we have in mind is the future of a literary genre, so often pronounced dead in the course of history, so often miraculously resurrected in moments of need and crisis, much like a literary Golem; or whether we mean the thing itself, the political program, whose very excess and commitment to the absolute and to the absolutely unrealizable and impossible, has paradoxically so often had a concrete impact on the merely practical and on the praxis of politics itself. At this point, then, the inquiry splits into two separate paths, about which one can only hope that like Proust's Swann and Guermantes ways they will eventually rejoin each other and prove to have been the same all along.

I

The first of these ways, then, is that of the evolution of the Utopian form, of which Perry Anderson has said that *Woman on the Edge of Time* (1976) marks a fundamental break,[1] but which on other accounts is still very much alive and

---

1 Perry Anderson, "The River of Time", in *New Left Review*, No. 26 (March/April, 2004), p. 71. And on feminist utopias, see Peter Fitting, "So We All Became Mothers': New Roles for

productive of new kinds of texts that transform their own generic tradition (as new texts always must virtually by definition). The other question has to do with Utopian thinking and radical social alternatives, about which Mrs Thatcher has so famously affirmed that none exist, but which so many political movements around the world today are energetically attempting to reinvent. Do not the answers to these two distinct inquiries necessarily involve very different kinds of discourse: on the one hand, formal proposals which somehow offer a way out of the ideological impasses of Utopian content we have rehearsed at such length above; on the other hand, economic explorations and novel political schemes which, roughly divided according to what we have called Utopian Imagination and Utopian Fancy, cannot escape the status of content (however formalistic an exercise the writing of constitutions has always seemed to be)? We have not yet been able to suggest any practical use for the neutralization structure outlined in Chapter 11, whether envisaged as the possibility of new Utopian literary production or as some political scheme for accommodating a variety of ideologies without lapsing into the pious hopes of this or that liberal pluralism or multiculturalism. What may at least be affirmed at this stage is that the solution will have to be a resolutely formalist one: which is to say an absolute formalism, in which the new content emerges itself from the form and is a projection of it. Indeed in the absence of reliable content only form can fill the bill. Form becomes content – in that overarching plan which is the Imagination – while the formerly tainted sets of opposites sink to the level of decoration or Fancy.

What we have perhaps not yet sufficiently emphasized is the relationship of this seemingly political crisis of Utopia (generally attributed to the fall of the communist parties and their substitution by the new social movements and anarchist currents) to a more general crisis of representation attributed to the advent of postmodernity. This last must not of course be confused with modernism's own relationship to a crisis of representation, which the older movement attempted to overcome by way of heroic formal invention and the grandiose prophetic visions of the modernist seers. In postmodernity representation is not conceived as a dilemma but an impossibility, and what can be termed a kind of cynical reason in the realm of art displaces it by way of a multiplicity of images, none of which corresponds to "truth". I have argued elsewhere that such alleged relativism offers new and productive paths to history and to praxis; and there is no reason to fear that postmodern Utopias will not be as energizing in their new historical context as the older ones were in previous centuries. The more immediate doubt lies in the differentiation of the newer Utopias from their modernist predecessors. I have already warned

Men in Recent Utopian Fiction", in *Science Fiction Studies*, 12 (1985), pp. 156–183; and "The Turn from Utopia in Recent Feminist Fiction", in Libby Falk Jones and Sarah Webster Goodwin, eds, *Feminism, Utopia and Narrative* (Knoxville, TN, 1990), pp. 141–158.

of the dangers of applying a properly modernist conception of Irony to any new Utopian forms: to that warning I must now add that other fundamental modernist determinant called "reflexivity". We have observed the operation of reflexivity, for example, in Chapter 6, in which the structure of the Utopian wish-fulfillment itself slowly swung about into its object, form thereby becoming content and transforming the Utopian wish into a wish to wish in the first place. But if this is what we now, in postmodernity, mean by an absolute formalism, then we will have so far done little more than offer a tired and henceforth conventional (modernist) solution for a new and historically original problem.

The argument is in fact also one between daily life and the great collective project, most often (and too rapidly) assimilated to the difference between anarchism and Marxism. A certain anarchism, indeed, by emphasizing a freedom from state power which does not so much involve a seizure and destruction of the latter as the exploration of zones and enclaves beyond its reach, would seem to valorize a life in the present and in the everyday, a conception of temporality rather different from the strategies of large-scale anti-capitalist struggle as the perspective of *Capital* would seem to impose them. Such differences come to a head around the now problematical idea of revolution: its crisis is not only the practical one, namely the absence of agency and indeed of any conception of what "coming to power" might mean for movements which are not parties and in a situation in which power is a network of cybernetic grids. It is a crisis centering on the very notion of time itself, an opposition between the here and now of perpetual revolt – indeed, of daily life itself as revolt and permanent revolution – and the old Left tradition of the Day, Sorel's myth of the general strike, the dawning of Year I, the axial Event, the break that inaugurates a new era (of cultural revolution, of socialist construction, etc.).

But this is an opposition between temporalities which also seems to characterize Utopias as well: Utopus' inaugural gesture as opposed to that daily Utopian life beyond the end of history which lies at the center of the form itself. This is in fact a narrative opposition: between the time of events that could be emplotted, organized into one story in its various versions, and the seemingly non-narrative guided tour, in which the features of daily life and of the everyday institutions are lovingly enumerated.[2] In terms of subjectivity, it would also seem that the opposition involves a distinction between consciousness – as an impersonal presence to the world which is always with us as long as we exist – and the self, which is so often an object of consciousness, but also of biography and its stories, of fantasy and trauma, of "personal" ambitions and private life, in short, of narrative as such. Consciousness is in that

---

2 Callenbach has actually written both versions; his "prequel" *Ecotopia Emerging* (New York, 1981) tells the story of the war of independence of Ecotopia from the United States.

sense the realm of the existential; the self is the domain of history, personal or otherwise. But here again the old opposition between Fancy and Imagination reemerges: Imagination being the domain of shaping form and narrative *par excellence*, while Fancy governs the detail, on which it dwells, and to which it brings a different quality of attention, sensuous and obsessive all at once, and with no impatience or regard for haste or time. In literature, we may say that these two dimensions are the distinct levels of plot and of style, which can never really be reunited; but it is clear that it is an opposition which runs through everything else, valorizing narrative at the same moment that it calls its primacy into question, and surfacing as a crisis in the political at the same time that it calls all the older ethical formulas into doubt, along with the newer psychoanalytic ones.

It is not a matter of solving this dilemma or of resolving its fundamental antinomy: but rather of producing new versions of those tensions, new ratios between the two terms, which disrupt the older ones (including those invented in the modern period) and make of the antinomy itself the central structure and the beating heart of Utopia as such.

II

Any new formal solution will, then, need to take into account both the historic originalities of late capitalism – its cybernetic technology as well as its globalizing dynamics – and the emergence, as well, of new subjectivities such as the surcharge of multiple or "parcellated" subject positions characteristic of postmodernity and touched on in the previous chapter, according to which we are black in one context, and intellectual in another, a woman in another, an English speaker in another, and a middle-class or bourgeois subject in yet a fifth: it being understood that the "contexts" also overlap, indeed that our unique historical and national situation is defined very precisely by the conjuncture of all these contexts or collective framings, which are overdetermined but not at all indeterminate. The collectivity is thus inside of us, fully as much as it is outside us, in the multiple social worlds we also inhabit all at once. But if Utopias can correspond to this kind of multiplicity, then they will assuredly be Delanyian ones, a Bakhtinian polyphony run wild, as with that hyperactive DJ husband of Oedipa Maas of whom his friends say that when he comes through a door, "the room is suddenly fully of people".[3] One thinks irresistibly of Flaubert's great political gatherings in *L'Éducation sentimentale*, in which hosts of political crackpots interminably express their opinions and schemes in a very Babel which is able to convey revulsion at Utopias, intellectuals and the mob all at the same time: so easy is it to pass from a model of the psyche to that of the commonwealth.

3 Thomas Pynchon, *The Crying of Lot 49* (New York, 1967), p. 104.

Indeed, that more sober political model of this pluralism of the subject positions of the psyche which corresponds to a rhetoric of decentralization seems to have lost its political charge on both the Left and the Right (the latter once evoking states' rights, the former defending local self-determination). Paradoxically, what has displaced both ideals is none other than globalization itself, which can indeed pass effortlessly from a dystopian vision of world control to the celebration of world multiculturalism with the mere changing of a valence.

On this political or macro level, then, the ideological opposition between the centered subject and its other has been replaced by the differentiation between the global and the local: as though any kind of local unit, from city to nation-state, and passing through whatever variety of provincial forms one can imagine, could possibly resist the overwhelming power of the global market forces, let alone delink from the latter and reconquer its autonomy and self-sufficiency. The latter was systematically dismantled by the global division of labor forcibly set in place by the new world system: self-sufficient local industries are driven into bankruptcy by huge international corporations, which then move in to fill those needs at higher prices.[4] It is difficult to imagine a situation in which the older forms of national self-subsistence could be reconstructed, short of a revolution that had indigenous capital resources available to it.

As for the autonomy of the local in matters of culture, two phenomena make this kind of traditionalism improbable. One is tourism, on which the local, in all its forms today, is preeminently dependent, as its own national industries gradually disappear. Tourist art is certainly a new space of creation and production,[5] but scarcely a form through which an older national or local culture is produced and reproduced. The other is of course Disneyfication, another word for postmodernity and its simulacra: for Disneyfication, as at EPCOT,[6] is the process whereby inherited cultural images are now artificially reproduced, as in all those lovingly rebuilt city centers which are "authentic" reproductions of their former selves: in Japan, it is said, the wooden temples are rebuilt board by board every fifty years in their entirety, conserving a spiritual identity through all the changes in material, just as our own bodies renew themselves and replace all the old cells over determinate cycles of time. But this is not quite the same as simulation, which as its name suggests is rather more comparable to forgery and the systematic "reproduction" of a period in lavish costume-drama movie sets: gentrification, Disneyfication, must also be seen as components in that land speculation which, along with financial

4 See Stefanie Black's admirable documentary on Jamaica, *Life and Debt* (2001).

5 See Peter Wollen's chapter on "tourist art" in *Raiding the Icebox* (London, 1993); and also Nestor Garcia-Cancilini, *Culturas Hibridas* (Mexico, 1989).

6 I have heard Reyner Banham express his respect for the historical and stylistic accuracy of its Disney architects.

capital, also centrally defines postmodernity (or late capitalism). At any rate, none of these processes is very reassuring as to the future of the local: tourism and Disneyfication being the twin faces of that future as it gazes first at Third and then at First Worlds.

We may thus suppose that the opposition between global and local is an ideological dualism which generates not only false problems, but false solutions as well: pluralism and multiculturalism are the twin offspring of this dualism when it wishes to synthesize its good features into one complex term or image of resolution. Multiplicity becomes the central theme of this imaginary resolution, whose conceptual dilemma remains that of closure. Yet we may well suppose that this new development will have had some impact on the Utopian form itself, accounting for the seeming extinction of its classical varieties and the emergence of newer, more reflexive forms.

III

The older texts seemed indeed to offer blueprints for change, building plans for new societies, and validating themselves by offering guided tours, systematic descriptions of the new institutions and explanations and arguments for their superiority. This is the sense in which Anderson was right, and the great feminist Utopias of the 1960s and 1970s were somehow the last traditional ones. Paradoxically, the anti-Utopias also thrived on these substantive (not to say essentialist) visions, these narrative thematizations, which they had only to invert, changing the valences from positive to negative. A kind of break can then be posited for the emergence of Thatcherism and the crisis of socialism, the emergence of a world-wide late capitalism from its modernist integument, from which it bursts in the form of full-blown globalization and postmodernity. For whatever reason, after this moment of convulsive transition, traditional Utopian production seems to have come to a halt.

Yet Kim Stanley Robinson's monumental Mars trilogy (1993–1996) is only one example of a new formal tendency, in which it is not the representation of Utopia, but rather the conflict of all possible Utopias, and the arguments about the nature and desirability of Utopia as such, which move to the center of attention. Here the new form seems to reach back and to incorporate within itself all the oppositions and antinomies we have identified in an earlier chapter; to reorganize itself around the increasingly palpable fact and situation of ideological multiplicity and radical difference in the field of desire. Utopia now begins to include all those bitter disputes around alternative diagnoses of social miseries and the solutions proposed to overcome them; and the formal center of gravity then begins to shift precisely to the question of those differences, which are in Robinson incorporated in the major figures of the "First Hundred" settlers of Mars – those for and against terra-forming, for example; those for and against business investment; those for and against small closed communities or clans, etc.[7] What is Utopian becomes, then, not the commitment to a specific machinery or blueprint, but rather the commitment to imagining possible Utopias as such, in their greatest variety of forms. Utopian is no longer the invention and defense of a specific floorplan, but rather the story of all the arguments about how Utopia should be constructed in the first place. It is no longer the exhibit of an achieved Utopian construct, but rather the story of its production and of the very process of construction as such.

This is indeed the thoughtful assessment of Robert Nozick after he has logically computed the different personality traits of all the very different people to whom any given Utopia would be required to appeal:

> The conclusion to draw is that there will not be *one* community existing and one kind of life led in Utopia. Utopia will consist of utopias, of many different and divergent communities in which people lead different kinds of lives under different institutions. Some kinds of communities will be more attractive to most than others; communities will wax and wane. People will leave some for others or spend their whole lives in one. Utopia is a framework for utopias, a place where people are at liberty to join together voluntarily to pursue and attempt to realize their own vision of the good life in the ideal community but where no one can *impose* his own utopian vision upon others. The utopian society is the society of utopianism ... utopia is meta-utopia ...[8]

This is a plausible view, which accurately reproduces precisely that feeling of the *Zeitgeist* discussed above, namely that pluralisms are the answer to repressive unities and identities of all kinds.

Yet the program is undermined by a certain number of modernist categories which stand as symptoms of its failure fully to address the Novum of postmodernity or to rise to the level of its new problems. Foremost among these modernist symptoms is our old friend, the category of reflexivity, which constituted one of the fundamental "solutions" of the modern as far back as one wishes to go: whether in the standard view of historiography (that the modern begins with this or that form of self-consciousness, whether this is located in Descartes or in Luther, or in modern science), or in the history of art, in which unfailingly all modernisms of whatever type are endowed with reflexivity and self-designation. Nozick's use of the formula of the "meta" is

---

7 See the reading of Kim Stanley Robinson in Part Two, Essay 12, below. Meanwhile, the decision of the "jati" not to forget its previous incarnations may be said to constitute the "reflexive" moment of historical evolution in *Years of Rice and Salt* (New York, 2002), pp. 338–339.

8 Robert Nozick, *Anarchy, the State and Utopia* (New York, 1974), pp. 311–312. Nozick neglects Fourier's grand solution of the harmony of the passions, or libidinal *combinatoire*; more serious, but customary in all such political or cultural theories of Utopia, is the absence of the question that ought to have been unavoidable since Marx and Marxism, namely that of economic organization.

shorthand for this modernist *deus ex machina*, and his more substantive notion of difference would be better served by some other line of thought: true believers can, in other words, be exceedingly intelligent, historicist and reflexive, without ceasing to be fanatics. The commitment to the Absolute is an act of will, and not always hospitable to pluralist fairness.

IV

It would seem more productive to reformulate our problem in terms of the dualism of Fancy and Imagination which has so often been appealed to here: the *studium* and *punctum*, so to speak, of the Utopian image. Would it then not be appropriate to characterize the current situation of Utopian production as the supercession of the Utopian Imagination by Utopian Fancy, of the submersion of some overarching or structural Utopian vision by the delectation of a swarm of individual Utopian details, which correspond to the parcellization and thematization of so many individual Utopian opinions and personal or life-style fantasies? This is not to underestimate the worth of the immense energies of Utopian Fancy generated all around the world today like alternate fuel-sources, in an attempt to bring inventiveness and ingenuity to bear on a tangle of problems, seemingly as unresolvable individually as they are inseparable in the first place. The Tobin tax is one of these, which can perhaps better be appreciated as a properly Utopian defamiliarization of a dilemma than as a practical political program. We may also reiterate the value of Barbara Goodwin's lottery society, in which chance, rather than the logic of social class, dictates the contingent distribution of advantages and prevents the crystallization of economic inequality and its perpetuation.[9] Meanwhile the framework of crisis and catastophe which structures so many of Kim Stanley Robinson's novels enables the deployment of an immense variety of ingenious and often Utopian solutions, which merit study in their own right.

Might it then not be advisable to substitute, for that working opposition, some more unified concept of a Utopian mechanism as such, which both excludes the numerous ills of present-day late capitalist globaliztion, at the same time that it forestalls the devolution of such a Utopia as well as its disintegration into an anarchic "time of troubles"? For an illustration of just such a possible mechanism I turn to a neglected and still suggestive Utopian proposal from the 1960s – Yona Friedman's *Utopies réalisables* (1975). Friedman's is a singularly abstract yet powerfully argued set of demonstrations, in which the various Utopian options are sorted out and their conditions of possibility articulated. This analytic asceticism at length gives way to the indulgence of a global vision of Utopia, which has its family likeness with those familiar from the period, such as Buckminster Fuller, Kenneth Boulding, and Lefebvre's world

---

9 Barbara Goodwin, *Justice by Lottery* (Chicago, 2001).

city: here the globe itself offers the Utopian closure, and its ecological requirements already spell a set of limits which define Utopian possibilities.

But it is not the period qualities of this vision that interest me here: rather I want to point out a fundamental distinction between the mechanisms Friedman will propose and those of the political theoreticians. It lies in the principled and absolute separation of the economic from the political, or in other words of the infrastructure from the political (and other) superstructures. This separation is very much in keeping with my own feeling that Marxism posits the primacy of the economic (and that its neglect of political theory is no accident but rather a happy consequence); as well as accounting for that suspicion of the political if not the end or abolition of politics which has seemed endemic to the Utopian form.

We may now interrogate Nozick's proposal for a pluralism of Utopias in the light of Friedman's multiplicity of Utopian communities scattered across the globe, about which he insists – and quite against the spirit of Nozick's reflexivity – that they are non-communicating, each with its own culture and local politics (or the absence of it), each following its own Absolute. Thus, unlike so many Utopian thinkers of the period, Friedman absolutely repudiates any conception of a world state or of some higher-level United Nations or *ekumen* which would somehow unify mankind (and thus, as in the Sartre/Le Guin argument, require an eternal enemy against whom to perform this fusion of humanity as a whole). The various closed Utopias are not combined by way of the political but related by the infrastructure, that is to say, by way of the globe itself and its materiality:

> Infrastructure means the *material* support of the various projects, utopias, modes of utilization, behavioral norms, etc. … If a world state, an organization of arbitration and enforcement, is unrealizable, an organization of world management is on the contrary perfectly feasible, provided it is limited to the maintenance of access routes connecting the various territories with each other and providing for the exchange of means of survival.[10]

But we have not yet enunciated the two fundamental mechanisms of this new global Utopian system, its Utopian *punctum* as it were: these are the right of migration and the abolition of taxes. The right of migration answers the nagging question often labeled totalitarian; or, in other words, what to do about Utopias one personally finds unpleasant and suffocating, if not fear-inspiring: the unanimity or majority question, the one on which so many dystopias fasten as their definitive refutation of the whole idea. A plurality of Utopias? But what if one misguided group embraces patriarchy, or something even worse?

---

10 Yona Friedman, *Utopies réalisables* (Paris, 1975), p. 275. A vigorous review and critique of the whole range of anti-statist Utopias in this period is to be found in Boris Frankel, *The Post-Industrial Utopias* (Madison, 1987).

According to this fundamental principle, you simply leave, and go to another Utopia, one in which strict religious doctrine is maintained, like Geneva, or secular republicanism, in imitation of the Roman Republic, or simple hedonism and licentiousness, or a traditional clan structure (into which you would probably have to intermarry or enter as a dependant or a slave). The resemblance to the Mars trilogy is inescapable.

What is ingenious about this proposition is that it serves two distinct functions, one of which we have just expounded and has to do with what used to be called freedom (as over against this or that type of state or system). The other is the less obvious corollary that this principle ensures the existence of multiple, decentered, and indeed (as Friedman puts it) non-communicating communities. If you are to be able to move around in this way, and exchange one absolute for another, then obviously there must be a variety of them on offer, and they must be relatively autonomous, and unable unduly to influence each other. We'll come back to that part of the picture in a moment.

Now for the other principle: in which the state is deprived of its taxes. That, of course, we have already, since one of the most ingenious mechanisms in the neo-liberal (or neo-conservative) dissolution of the welfare state was simply to reduce the taxes on the wealthy to the point where the state was no longer able to afford its social services, and was also placed, by the sensitivity of the matter of taxation itself, in a position where it could not turn back the political clock barring the kind of universal cataclysm (like depression) which had once led to the founding of the welfare state in the first place. (It seems that not even war today, however expensive, constitutes such a cataclysm, at least in the US.)

But neo-conservatism does not include the verso of this proposition, namely that the moneys normally available from taxation are to be replaced by the public work of the citizens themselves: something Rudolf Bahro had envisaged at much the same time in his Utopian vision of the transformation of the Eastern European system (*The Alternative* [1977]): everyone will do some civic and even manual labor. There will be volunteer police duty, garbage collection, hydraulic projects, road-building and the like. Systems of exchange and barter will supplement this "withering away" of taxes and state surplus; and little by little it becomes clear that the result – if you like, the second function, besides the political one of reducing the state itself – will also be to displace the centrality of money in the economy. The thrust of the principle can perhaps be extended to strike all possibilities of building up a "standing reserve" of wealth, and to reduce money once again to the more limited function of exchange.

Finally, it should be noted that both these principles are anti-capitalist (without for all that being necessarily or overtly socialist): the first makes the enlargement and expansion necessary to capital impossible; the second removes the medium whereby capital is accumulated.

Friedman's Utopia has the signal merit of shifting the emphasis from the communicational ideologies celebrating the new global system to its possible material or economic infrastructure. But this also means a move from difference to identity and from a plurality of detail to the closure of the whole. It also raises questions about the representability of this new global Utopia; and representability, or the possibility of mapping, is a very significant matter for practical politics, as we shall see shortly.

I therefore propose a more accessible or visualizable form of this imagined global system, about which we must remember that its novelty as a Utopian mechanism consisted in the non-communicability or antagonism inherent in its component parts, a novelty which had the immediate effect of excluding rhetorics of communication, multiculturalism and even empire (in the recent sense of Americanization). In this spirit, I propose to think of our autonomous and non-communicating Utopias – which can range from wandering tribes and settled villages all the way to great city-states or regional ecologies – as so many islands: a Utopian archipelago, islands in the net, a constellation of discontinuous centers, themselves internally decentered. At once this metaphorical perspective begins to suggest a range of possible analogies, which combine the properties of isolation with those of relationship. For it is indeed as a Utopia of structural relationality that we must grasp the present proposal: "differences without positive terms" was Saussure's inaugural formulation, which may be seen in some deeper way to characterize all of modern thought as it moves away from Aristotelian substance to modern conceptions of process.

Perhaps no one thought more deeply about islands than Fernand Braudel, in his monumental history of the Mediterranean; and we can therefore do no better initially than to follow the movement of his thought as it works its way through the geographical characteristics of the great inland sea: isolating enclaves such as mountain villages, and then the fertile valleys that appear between them; coming at length down to the plains, ungrateful owing to marshes and malaria; and finally to the ports, often cut off from their hinterlands by a mountain range descending to the coast. Thus slowly collective life is turned in the direction of the sea, as is the historian's imagination.

Now as the sea encroaches on all these areas and opens up links between them, he leaps, in his mind's eye, out to the islands themselves, as they form the stations of the great trade routes, or, like Sardinia, vegetate in a rather barren isolation; or finally, form a whole system in their own multiplicity, like the Greek archipelago: "A precarious, restricted, and threatened life, such was the lot of the islands, their domestic life at any rate. But their external life, the role they have played in the forefront of history, far exceeds what might be expected from such poor territories. The events of history often lead to the islands."[11]

---

11 Fernand Braudel, *The Mediterranean and the Mediterranean World in the Age of Philip II* (New York, 1972 [1949]), Volume I, p. 154.

But now, little by little – fascinated by the dialectic of these enclaves, objects of colonization fully as much as subjects of history in their own right, at least for some brief period, and indeed their fortunes characterized by that fundamental temporal variability and mutability that characterizes the history of the inland sea as a whole – Braudel extends the figure:

> Islands that the sea does not surround. In this Mediterranean world, excessively compartmented as it was, where human occupation had left vast stretches unfilled, not counting the seas, one might argue that there were places that were fully as much islands as those surrounded by the sea, isolated places, peninsulas – the word itself is significant – like Greece or other regions which were cut off on the mainland side and for whom the sea was the only means of communication. Bounded to the north by the mountain barrier marking its frontier with Rome, the kingdom of Naples could be called an island in this sense. In the textbooks we find mention of the "island" of the Maghreb, Djezirat el Moghrab, the Island of the Setting Sun, between the Atlantic, the Mediterranean, the Sea of the Syrtes, and the Sahara – a world of sudden contrasts.[12]

But now Braudel's imagination grows flushed and kindled by this new idea. *Il s'échauffe*: islands not surrounded by the sea: "One might say that Lombardy ... It would hardly be an exaggeration to say that Portugal, Andalusia, Valencia and Catalunia ... And as for Spain itself ... At the other, eastern end of the Mediterranean, Syria was another island, a halfway house between sea and desert ... etc."[13] Now the falling cadence, the time for reflection:

> We are now taking great liberties with the concept of insularity, of course, but in the interests of a better explanation. The Mediterranean lands were a series of regions isolated from one another, yet trying to make contact with one another. So in spite of the days of travel on foot or by boat that separated them, there was a perpetual coming and going between them, which was encouraged by the nomadic tendencies of some of the populations. But the contacts they did establish were like electric charges, violent and without continuity. Like an enlarged photograph the history of the islands affords one of the most rewarding ways of approaching an explanation of this violent Mediterranean life. It may make it easier to understand how it is that each Mediterranean province has been able to preserve its own irreducible character, its own violently regional flavor in the midst of such an extraordinary mixture of races, religions, customs, and civilizations.[14]

12 Ibid., pp. 160–161.
13 Ibid., p. 161.
14 Ibid.

This is, then, the deeper truth of the "local": not cities attempting to revive their enfeebled existence by way of tourism, gentrification, Disneyfication, or the Olympics; not fantasies of high-tech industries and the renewal of urban property by way of the magical power of micro-chips; nor even the Left fantasy of delinking, in which a local socialism or progressive nationalism heroically breaks with the great global networks and goes it alone.

Indeed, the structural combination scheme is itself the truth of Utopia and perhaps even of democracy itself: here we have the ultimate rebuke of the centered subject and the full deployment of the great maxim that "difference relates" – one of the most vivid images of the collective in all its productive inner conflicts and compacts or conspiracies. This is the great lesson of Fourier; and it is also the source of the deeper libidinal attraction of free-market propaganda, and, indeed, of the figure of exchange itself; the squaring of the circle of the old paradoxes of the one and the many, the autonomous and the dependent; perhaps even the resolution of Sartre's dilemma as to whether the truly collective does not require an external enemy to come into existence. Here (as indeed with his own fused micro-group) the parts of the collective can interiorize their own threats to each other, productive of ephemeral solidarities and constellations of shifting inner alliances. Here too the play of that supreme social force of envy lights up mobile relations as it generates a warm narcissism from point to point (Žižek has indeed described the way that the violence and ethnic hatreds of the so-called nationalities took the form, before the civil wars, of the most affectionate ethnic jokes, of envious racist slurs and insults that bound people together in the Freudian Eros, before their energies were dispersed in Thanatos).[15]

This vision of shifting inner patterns of relationship goes a long way, I feel, towards palliating the objections to the closure of the system as a whole; at the same time that it guarantees on a permanent or structural basis that inner gap or béance in the subject which is normally overlooked or misrecognized and repressed in standard ideologies of the subject as a full substance: for whatever the play of interrelationships they must always project a spark across the poles and live in the permanent sense of insecurity and incompleteness. As for the other objection, that of the irreducible core, or kernel of excess that cannot be assimilated – as fundamental contingencies of the social and of history are often figured – it is also presumably given in the gaps between the enclaves and the insatiable hunger that unites them without driving them outwards towards imperial conquest, since on the level of globalization on which we are now posing the political problem there is no outside and nothing left to conquer or to colonize. Yet the whole function of a system like this is to compensate the ecological differences between the regions: mineral extraction in the one being balanced by specialized industry in another, and

---

15 Slavoj Žižek, *Revolution at the Gates* (London, 2002), pp. 202–203.

agriculture by other kinds of production, as in the older ideal of a federal system.[16]

Indeed, if it were not so outworn and potentially misleading a term, federalism would be an excellent name for the political dimensions of this Utopian figure, until we have a better one. But it will not come into focus until we realize on the one hand that the United States cannot be considered a federal system (at least since the ratification of the American constitution), inasmuch as the new and unforeseen power of standardization of the media has made the superstate into one immense experiment in social and ideological leveling (without any accompanying economic equality). It would also be necessary to understand the failure of the Soviet Union in a different way, as the collapse, not of a communism or socialism, but of the federal project as such which it presupposed. This is not the place to make that seemingly perverse argument, but enough to point to the example of that even more dramatic experiment in socialist federalism which was the "former" Yugoslavia: here historians have convincingly demonstrated that the fundamental cause of the collapse of this admirable system was not the death of Tito, or even the allegedly age-old racial and ethnic enmities of the partners, but rather the usual suspect, namely globalization itself and the policies of the IMF and World Bank, which systematically and deliberately undermined the federal system.[17] Nor do we

---

16   The "former Yugoslavia" provides an excellent example of the federal process thus envisaged. See Susan Woodward, *Balkan Tragedy*, pp. 36–38: "The concept of constituent nation can be seen as an accommodation to this reality. Individuals retained their national right to self-governance lived outside their home nation's republic …

"Federal institutions were based on the cooperative idea of government based on councils (*saveti*) in which representatives from the republics and provinces (in the parliament, executive branch, central bank, collective state presidency, and so forth) were consulted, deliberated, and made decisions on the basis of consensus. The system of parity representation of nations and of consensus aimed to prevent any single national group from gaining political dominance over the state. It was designed by numerically smaller nations (especially Slovenes and Croats) explicitly in reaction to the interwar political dominance of the Serbian state apparatus (1919–41). Therefore, all federal policy depended on cooperation from republican leaders, who could veto any decision.

"The country had a mixed economy, in which economic coordination occurred through a hybrid of instruments. Free prices regulated retail markets, but bilateral supply contracts governed most transactions between public enterprises or between processing firms and private farmers. Corporatist negotiations between unions, business chambers, and governments set rules over wages and benefits for firms. An indicative social plan similar to the French system of planning, gave information about future trends in government preferences on credit policy. The plan was based on wide consultation of firms, localities, republics, producers' associations, and civil servants, and approved by the federal parliament, not on the ministerial hierarchy of central planning. Most economic decisions were a matter of wide consultation, debate, and participation."

17   Ibid., p. 61: "When the IMF program and economic reform began to legislate reforms in banking, foreign economic relations, and the monetary system, and when political contests arose over cuts in the federal budget, the rights to foreign exchange earnings, and wage controls, they shifted to a more radical confederalist position. The safeguards of the present constitution were

have to go very far in the contemporary world to find examples of the fragility of federalism today: Canada and Spain are characteristic; while all the civil wars and breakaway movements around the globe (often of areas much too small to be viable in their own right, if such a judgment makes any sense after the implantation of the new global system) are vivid testimony to the extreme sensitivity of the federal project, which is a more urgent task for political theorization today than democracy itself: unless indeed one wants to grasp the problem of democracy (which also scarcely exists anywhere in the world today) as an allegory and a microcosm of that of federalism as such – the coexistence and interrelationship of semi-autonomous and multiple units in such a way that the tension between whole and part is never resolved (to the benefit of either side).

We can no doubt already sense figures of the emergence of such federalisms in various zones of the contemporary world: I think of Europe itself as such a would-be federal association, which cannot quite make its mind up about its dimensions; I think of Southeast Asia, as a set of wildly varying cultures and languages whose states have come to interrelate on a commercial and a political basis. And we may also find the symptomal traces of these emergent forms in thought as well: Braudel's own masterpiece, composed in the prison camp during the German caricature of European federalism, is already an anticipation of the future Europe (very precisely in the passage I have quoted); while his later work on technology may be seen as symptomizing the onset of globalization itself. Meanwhile Deleuze's revival of Leibniz's monadology, that immense federal network of overlapping monads, is also an anticipation of this political figure. The possibility of a new union of likeminded Latin American states, or the possibility of a Brazilian leadership of a community of states around the world intent on forging a resistance to US globalization, would be other possible figures of the invention of collective entities beyond either empire or secession.

V

But the failure of federalism to become completely Utopian lies not only in its practical realisability: the moment in which it becomes "only that", descending from a transcendental ideal into a contingent set of empirical arrangements. It lies above all in the absence from it of representation, that is, of the possibility of any powerful libidinal cathexis. Federalism cannot be invested with the desire associated with the lost, indeed the impossible object: the blue

---

no longer sufficient; their economic independence required further political protections. This meant eliminating the remaining political functions of the central government – the federal courts, police, army, procedural rules, and the fund for development assistance that bound the republics and provinces together – in favor of republican sovereignty."

flower, that "mass of sweet rolls" about which the dreaming Dvanov agonizes in *Chevengur*,[18] groping about in the dark feverishly, murmuring to himself, "But where then is socialism?" Here the collective ideal becomes incorporated into a kind of object, which the dreamer longs for, and which lends the driest and most lucid political thoughts a density of passion and a force to compel action, and collective action at that. Federalism would seem to lack that passionate investment which nationalism preeminently possesses: that "remainder of some *real*, nondiscursive kernel of enjoyment which must be present for the Nation qua discursive entity-effect to achieve its ontological consistency".[19] Indeed, it would be a matter of great political interest to make an inventory not only of the various lost objects the modern nationalist passions have posited, but also of what happens when federalism works, at least for a time, as in the "former" Yugoslavia. Meanwhile many of the successful socialisms have combined with the energies of nationalism to produce even stronger collective visions; nor is it clear what role nationalism plays in the political mass movements that have identified themselves as religious, and that have claimed to rise above race and nation or *ethnie*. Nationalism is at the very least the most dramatic and successful operative paradigm of a great collective project and of collective movements and politics: this is by no means to endorse it as a political idea, but rather a reason to utilize it as an instrument for measuring other collective possibilities.

From some purely intellectual and theoretical–nostalgic standpoint, Braudel's Mediterranean presents some analogies: the enthusiasm for the Mediterranean idea, for the concept of the Mediterranean as a unique structural collective object. For the struggle for control between the Spanish and the Ottoman empires constitutes it as an object of desire and indeed constructs it as such, energy then flowing back out of this system as the center of the world is gradually displaced onto the Atlantic: desire's entropy and the disinvestment of the object itself.

Here, then, closure remains a feature of the system of desire, constituting the object as such, no matter how vast or minute, isolating it within a perceptual field in which it can be *named* – surely the first and fundamental requirement for any object of desire lost or found. So for that incomparably larger mass which is Kim Stanley Robinson's Mars: earth only becoming a comparable object of desire by way of loss or subtraction (a catastrophe often figured in SF versions of a human diaspora scattered throughout galactic space), one-world humanisms being generally too feeble to generate these energies, like pacifism confronted with war, or democracy in the face of the Leader, even though such confrontations are calculated to revive and energize both sides.

18 Jameson, *The Seeds of Time*, pp. 197–198.
19 Slavoj Žižek, *Tarrying with the Negative* (Durham, NC, 1993), p. 202.

Our question is, however, whether Utopia in any form could become such an object and awaken these passions, which the religious millenarianisms reveal, but which, as a historical matter, only Bellamy's *Looking Backward* seems to have generated in the real social life of the nations, producing a political movement in the United States (significantly named "nationalist"), and scores of translations into other languages. It is not enough to say that Bellamy seemed to provide some answers for this raw industrializing situation and its laboring masses, as well as its respectable middle strata. His book is certainly a fundamental illustration of the Laclau–Mouffe analysis of the empty signifier and its political power to create alliances. But the enigma of desire remains, and we are no longer very well placed to appreciate Bellamy's secret.

But we must end this line of discussion with a return to the concept of the Utopian mechanism, which it now seems appropriate to reevaluate in the light of the opposition between Fancy and Imagination. The idea of mechanism seems to have demonstrated the necessity of an interplay or cooperation between the division of labor of these two powers: on the one hand calling strongly on the wit and ingenuity of the Utopian, and on the other, demonstrating that what was called the Imagination turned out to have much to do, not only with the closure of the system, but also with its nameability, that is to say with its chances for representation (and, thereby, for libidinal investment). At the same time, the concept of a mechanism, which already contains process or activity within itself as method or virtuality, tends to obscure that fundamental structural characteristic of Utopia, which defines and enables it fully as much as it passes judgment on it, namely, the omission of agency: the obligation for Utopia to remain an unrealizable fantasy.

VI

What can, then, today be the function of so ambiguous an entity as Utopia, if not as a forecast of political and empirical possibilities? Can this function also be sought and identified formally without adducting this or that local content?

In a splendid interpretation of Walter Benjamin's critique of progress in the "Theses on History", Habermas has offered a startling characterization of the practical-political effects Benjamin expected such a critique to have (it should be noted that Habermas here uses the word "utopian" in its old negative sense):

> The notion of progress served not only to render eschatological hopes profane and to open up the horizon of expectation in a utopian fashion [*sic*], but also to close off the future as a *source* of disruption with the aid of teleological constructions of history. Benjamin's polemic against the social-evolutionary leveling

off of the historical materialist conception of history is aimed at just such a degeneration of modernity's consciousness of time open towards the future.[20]

We may leave modernity out of it, while noting the clarification that this reading brings to the critique of progress. The latter is now seen as an attempt to colonize the future, to draw the unforeseeable back into tangible realities, in which one can invest and on which one can bank, very much in the spirit of stockmarket "futures". It is also useful to turn to a rather different meditation on temporality (equally inspired by the Frankfurt School) – that of Tafuri and Cacciari, who see this neutralized future as a form of insurance and of planning and investment, a kind of new actuarial colonization of the unknown.[21] It is thus not merely to deprive the future of its explosiveness that is wanted, but also to annex the future as a new area for investment and for colonization by capitalism. Where Benjamin observed that "not even the past will be safe" from the conquerors, we may now add that the future is not safe either, and that it is compared to that leveling of the land speculators and builder-investors, whose bulldozers destroy all the site-specific properties of a terrain in order to clear it and make it fungible for any kind of future investment, so that one can build on it whatever the market demands.[22] This is the future prepared by the elimination of historicity, its neutralization by way of progress and technological evolution: it is the future of globalization, in which nothing remains in its particularity, and everything is now fair game for profits and the introduction of the wage-labor system. If in fact globalization in space means the abandonment of these terrains after a brief period of heavy exploitation, presumably the same prospect awaits the future, large zones of which are already consigned to rubble and sterility owing to the systematic neutralization in them of trends and tendencies that might otherwise have produced very different outcomes.

But it is crucial (in my opinion) not to confuse Habermas' ideal of the "time open to the future" with notions of indeterminacy or even unpredictability. No doubt Benjamin had the Second International idea of "inevitability" in mind as one of the expressions of some bad (bourgeois) notion of progress. But Habermas' wording is a good deal more precise and powerful: the future as *disruption* (*Beunruhigung*) of the present, and as a radical and systemic break with even that predicted and colonized future which is simply a prolongation of our capitalist present. Was this not, indeed, the very weakness of the "federal" Utopia sketched out in the last selection? Yet this is the point to

20 Jürgen Habermas, *Philosophical Discourse of Modernity* (Cambridge, MA, 1987), p. 12.
21 See Manfredo Tafuri, *Architecture and Utopia* (Cambridge, MA, 1976 [1973]); and also Negri's study of Keynes (in *Insurgencies*).
22 A figure used in *Architecture and Utopia*, p. 70: "All the work of demolition served to prepare a clean-swept platform from which to depart in discovery of the new 'historic tasks' of intellectual work."

observe that, whatever else the latter may be, it also clearly registers the operation of what we have called Utopian Fancy: the archipelago as ornament and
spatial decoration. Not only does our old dualism return in force here – tactics
versus strategy, socialism versus communism – but its fundamental enigma –
the mystery of the Novum, the content of a truly Utopian Imagination –
remains in full force.

This is indeed the force of More's original Utopian starting point, and the
grandest of all the ruptures effectuated by the Utopian Imagination: namely,
the thought of abolishing money and private property. Indeed, this ancient
Utopian program may not be without its uses even in the thick of a finance
capitalism in which currency has receded in significance in the face of more
and more abstract transactions. Still, the older anathemata pronounced on gold
and riches can once again make visible that fundamental alienation in which
money as such consists. All the nations of the world today, which have experienced in one way or another the impact of late capitalism – from Russia to
Latin America, from England to India, and China to the United States itself
– complain not only of the end of traditional values (of which few enough
survived modernity in their earlier forms), but of the end of all values, and
their wholesale replacement by money as such. What we call cynical reason is
simply the empty ideology that accompanies the practices of profit and money
making, and that has (and needs) no content to disguise itself. Money does
not, of course, have any content: it is not a code, to use Deleuze's useful terminology, but an axiomatic; numbers have no content, and Weber's older
religious justifications (Calvinism, hard work, saving) are no longer necessary.
Cynical reason is simply this recognition, and it is therefore a new form of
ideology or if you prefer a new ideological process rather than a new ideology
as such. It is not disguise and rationalization, but rather clarity and frank
acknowledgement: as such it exists in the pure present, without the requirement of some great ideological project for the future, since money making is
not a project but an immanent activity. Big business, the so-called ruling class,
has projects and ideologies: political plans for future change, in the spirit of
privatization and the free market. But the mass of people who either desperately need money or are in a position to make some and to invest, do not
themselves have to believe in any hegemonic ideology of the system, but only
to be convinced of its permanence.

In this situation, a return to More's foundational Utopian principle – the
abolition of money as such, by no means an original solution with him, but
passing back through Plato into the mists of time – paradoxically demonstrates
the force of a genuinely radical disruption even in the complex financial environment of postmodernity. Meanwhile, the proposal to abolish money not
merely gives content to the larger project of eliminating private property itself:
it also dramatically regrounds the prospect of that abolition of the market of
which it is an allegorical expression, while renewing and estranging, reinventing,

the passions that are the ultimate sources of both these ideas. Money is, to be sure, not the same as capital, as Marx tirelessly and vigorously reminds us, not without some asperity; but for the moment it is the ideological and Utopian effect of this vision of its disappearance that interests us; along with the suspicion that everything operative and unreal about Utopia may well be bound up with this fundamental representational mistake about money itself.

For now the multiple fantasies that cluster around money begin to become visible and to make it seem desirable to imagine a world in which it no longer exists. Now indeed the various critical dystopias begin to appear, ranging from satiric exaggerations of our current world all the way to the most grotesque distentions and extrapolations of what the persistence of money and commodification holds in store for us in the far future.

The Utopian thought experiment, then, which abruptly removes money from the field, brings an aesthetic relief that unexpectedly foregrounds all kinds of new individual, social and ontological relationships. It is as if suddenly the Utopian strategy had been transformed back into the Utopian impulse as such, unmasking the Utopian dimensions of a range of activities hitherto distorted and disguised by the abstractions of value. Non-alienated enclaves suddenly light up in our hitherto contaminated environment – such as Kim Stanley Robinson's research laboratories (see Chapter 2) – thereby converting Utopian representation into a critical and analytical method, whereby the constraints of commodification are measured, along with the multiple developments released by its absence.

Meanwhile, thus renewed, the Utopian impulse wanders the gamut from dual relationships of all kinds, relationships to things fully as much as to other people, all the way to an unsuspected variety of new collective combinations. And insofar as our own society has trained us to believe that true disalienation or authenticity only exists in the private or individual realm, it may well be this revelation of collective solidarity which is the freshest one and the most startlingly and overtly Utopian: in Utopia, the ruse of representation whereby the Utopian impulse colonizes purely private fantasy spaces is by definition undone and socialized by their very realization.

Now, however, Utopian Fancy sets itself on the move, searching for implementations of the new principle. These are probably not yet formulas for getting rid of money as such, not yet practical political programs. Its abolition is presupposed at this point, and what is sought is rather a series of substitutions for the operations (and even the satisfactions) that money once offered. Here substitutes for the wage relationship emerge, in the form of labor chits and work certificates; and also for market exchange and its modalities. Questions about consumption and its addictions, and also about labor satisfaction, loom down the road for any contemporary Utopist; and the competition of this Utopian principle of the abolition of money with rival schemes and alternate diagnoses begins in earnest, at the same time that blueprints of the social order emerge, along with tracings of the model factory, and indeed new efforts to replace archaic Utopian pictures of cottage or industrial labor with cybernetic processes and problems.

But in this new situation, in which money, as an object or even a substitute for an object, has become as volatile as finance capital itself, the question begins to pose itself whether money has not in fact already abolished itself, by the very movement of capital as such; and therefore whether the original starting point was really a historically viable one after all, a doubt which leads on to other Utopian themes and possibilities, and sets in motion a restless and speculative Utopian search for other fundamental principles and other contents on which the Utopian Imagination, as opposed to Utopian Fancy, may set to work.

Thus the revival of the old Utopian dream of abolishing money, and of imagining a life without it, is nothing short of precisely that dramatic rupture we have evoked. As a vision, it solicits a return to all those older, often religious, anti-capitalist ideologies which denounced money and interest and the like; but as none of those are alive and viable any longer in global late capitalism, and the search for an ideological justification for the abolition of money proves fruitless, this path leads to a decisionism in which we are forced to invent new Utopian ideologies for this seemingly archaic program, and in which we are thrown forward into the future in the attempt to invent new reasons. The lived misery of money, the desperation of poorer societies, the pitiful media spectacles of the rich ones, is palpable to everyone. It is the decision to abandon money, to place this demand at the forefront of a political program, that marks the rupture and opens up a space into which Utopia may enter, like Benjamin's Messiah, unannounced, unprepared by events, and laterally, as if into a present randomly chosen but utterly transfigured by the new element.

This is indeed how Utopia recovers its vocation at the very moment where the undesirability of change is everywhere dogmatically affirmed, as with Samuel Huntington's warning, on the political level, that genuine democracy is ungovernable and that therefore Utopian demands for absolute political freedom and "radical democracy" are also to be eschewed. So successful have such positions been in contemporary ideological "discursive struggle" that most of us are probably unconsciously convinced of these principles, and of the eternity of the system, and incapacitated to imagine anything else in any way that carries conviction and satisfies that "reality principle" of fantasy we have identified above.

Disruption is, then, the name for a new discursive strategy, and Utopia is the form such disruption necessarily takes. And this is now the temporal situation in which the Utopian form proper – the radical closure of a system of difference in time, the experience of the total formal break and discontinuity – has its political role to play, and in fact becomes a new kind of content in its own right. For it is the very principle of the radical break as such, its possibility, which is reinforced by the Utopian form, which insists that its radical difference is possible and that a break is necessary. The Utopian form itself is the answer to the universal ideological conviction that no alternative is possible, that there is no alternative to the system. But it asserts this by forcing us to think the break itself, and not by offering a more traditional picture of what things would be like after the break.[23]

Paradoxically, therefore, this increasing inability to imagine a different future enhances rather than diminishes the appeal and also the function of Utopia. The very political weakness of Utopia in previous generations – namely that it furnished nothing like an account of agency, nor did it have a coherent historical and practical-political picture of transition – now becomes a strength in a situation in which neither of these problems seems currently to offer candidates for a solution. The radical break or secession of Utopia from political possibilities as well as from reality itself now more accurately reflects our current ideological state of mind. Lukács once said, in the 1960s, that we had been thrown back historically before the Utopian socialists, that even those elements of a vision of the future still lay before us, yet to be reinvented, before we would ever reach an articulated stage of pre-revolutionary awareness and potentiality such as that expressed in 1848 (immediately before that revolution) by the *Manifesto*.[24] How much the more true is this of the current period in which capitalism has, as in the industrializing period immediately following the revolution of 1848, expanded tremendously and generated a wealth calculated to smother the perception of its flaws and incapacities for a time?

Utopia thus now better expresses our relationship to a genuinely political future than any current program of action, where we are for the moment only at the stage of massive protests and demonstrations, without any conception of how a globalized transformation might then proceed. But at this same time, Utopia also serves a vital political function today which goes well beyond mere ideological expression or replication. The formal flaw – how to articulate the Utopian break in such a way that it is transformed into a practical-political transition – now becomes a rhetorical and political strength – in that it forces us precisely to concentrate on the break itself: a meditation on the impossible, on the unrealizable in its own right. This is very far from a liberal capitulation

23 Is it necessary to add that "disruption" here is not a code word for so-called terrorism? Of course; and it is therefore also necessary to add three points on violence, in order to distinguish it from disruption as Novum, as restructuration and the unexpected blasting open of habits, as that lateral side-door which suddenly opens onto a new world of transformed human beings. The points are these: (1) violence is an ideology, constructed around the structural omission of state power and physical oppression authorized by the "law"; (2) violence is always initiated by the Right and by conservative or counterrevolutionary repression, to which Left violence is then a response; (3) political violence is self-defeating, and dialectically strengthens its opposite number: thus, US expansionism generates al Qaeda, whose growth then encourages the development of an American police state, which may well in turn sussicate new forms of resistance.
24 Hans Heinz Holz, Leo Kofler and Wolfgang Abendroth, ed. Theo Pinkus, *Conversations with Lukács* (Cambridge, MA, 1975).

to the necessity of capitalism, however; it is quite the opposite, a rattling of the bars and an intense spiritual concentration and preparation for another stage which has not yet arrived.

Perhaps indeed we need to develop an anxiety about losing the future which is analogous to Orwell's anxiety about the loss of the past and of memory and childhood. This would be a good deal more intense than the usual rhetoric about "our children" (keeping the environment clean for future generations, not burdening them with heavy debt, etc.); it would be a fear that locates the loss of the future and futuricity, of historicity itself, within the existential dimension of time and indeed within ourselves. This is a relationship to a menaced future everywhere dramatized in SF, particularly in time travel, where a different choice in the present suddenly obliterates a whole alternate future, with everyone in it – a genocide comparable to wiping out another planet, or indeed whole other species, something we still seem all too capable of doing. It is perhaps in Marge Piercy's time travelers (in *Woman on the Edge of Time*) that one finds the strongest and most poignant expression of this fear, as well as of the uncertainties that make it up. The protagonist Connie is indeed a battered psyche, heavily oversedated and diagnosed as schizophrenic by the medical power establishment: who is to say that her visitors from the future are not hallucinations and the wish-fulfillments of a troubled and well-nigh terminal case? But of course, as we have shown, Utopias are also very much wish-fulfillments, and hallucinatory visions in desperate times. Connie's Utopian visitors are doubly menaced: on the one hand, as in the most realistic of the classic Utopias, their fragile society is threatened by all the non- and anti-Utopian forces of the outside world, in that never-ending war that rages around all Utopian enclaves, in real history and outside it as well.

On the other hand, as in the standard SF time-traveling paradigm, the Mattapoisett Utopians are also threatened by the present, of which they constitute an alternate history which may never come into being in the first place. As in *La Jetée*, but in a very different spirit, they have come to enlist the present in their struggle to exist; yet they can only appear to those already in need of Utopia. The appeal of Piercy's characters to Connie (and to us) is, then, the secret message of all Utopias, present, past, and future:

"Are you really in danger?"

"Yes." His big head nodded in cordial agreement. "You may fail us."

"Me? How?"

"You of your time. You individually may fail to understand us or to struggle in your own life and time. You of your time may fail to struggle altogether ... We must fight to exist, to remain in existence, to be the future that happens. That's why we reached you."[25]

25 Marge Piercy, *Woman on the Edge of Time* (New York, 1976), pp. 197–198.

PART TWO

AS FAR AS THOUGHT CAN REACH

I

Fourier, or, Ontology and Utopia

The time-honored French way of introducing a subject like Fourier (the English equivalent is not so pointed) is the formula "*actualité de* ": which sets us in a more historicist and relativist frame of mind than some more Crocean "what is living and what is dead in". The actuality approach supposes a rotating conception of the work which sets off gleams and strikes different sparks from age to age, while "what is living" suggests a hodgepodge of residual and emergent, from which the outmoded has carefully been extracted piece by piece. Neither formula turns out to be particularly viable in a situation in which the work in question was never completely known in the first place: half unpublished, mostly unread except for anecdotal plot summaries in surveys, utterly unclassical and probably uncanonizable as well owing to its textual peculiarities and generic irregularity. But this is Fourier's case today and tomorrow: I am tempted to add, not despite, but rather also because of, Jonathan Beecher's first-rate biography, which is a model of discreet psychological and socio-historical analysis and an eloquent and persuasive introduction to the works themselves.[1] We must be more than usually grateful for a study of this rare distinction at the same time that we understand how its very merits inevitably turn it into a substitute for those works, which are thereby likely to become even less read at first hand at the very moment in which they have become more accessible. At any rate, in what follows I want to say something about Fourier's "contribution" to only a very few limited yet important fields: literary history, the politics of groups, and the apparently unavoidable question of desire that constitutes the unique aureole of this particular Utopia.

Yet the matter of literary history may seem extraneous to the Fourier question and a problem for French departments more than it can be for Utopians and the other sympathizers and fellow-travelers. Perhaps it does not need to be argued exclusively in terms of national glory, however, but rather in those of representativity if not of classicality (I'm not sure that the related

---

1   J. Beecher, *Charles Fourier: The Visionary and His World* (Berkeley, 1986), henceforth referred to in the text as Beecher.

issue of canonicity applies here in the same way): for it is a peculiar problem in the unfolding of the premier European literature which, unlike the uneven development and historical spurts and irregularities of the other national literatures, regularly if dialectically produces crucial cultural documents in every generation. There is no particular mystery about this, since the French language had already been acknowledged as their literate *lingua franca* by the other traditions from the Renaissance onward, and since the ever more obvious subordination to England in a power struggle that had begun in the seventeenth century determined the strategic and symbolic restructuration across the Channel of that same struggle in cultural terms in which the French tended to be winners across the board, from gastronomy to literary movements, from interior decoration to clothing fashion and perfume. The mystery is rather the gap of Romanticism, or if you prefer, what the standard histories typically negotiate as the thirty-years' lag, the incomprehensible lapse between the "great" romanticisms of the Germans and the English and the "battle of Hernani" on the eve of the revolution of 1830.

Nor is this a question of a mere statistical anomaly, like the skipped beat of a cardiograph: rather it concerns the most truly significant moment in the emergence and formation of modernity and engages unique and historical breakthroughs in form as well as conceptuality, in the poetic ontology of the English fully as much as the absolute systematicity of the Germans. Few other moments in modern times witness the exfoliation of a Novum of this magnitude, and the reader confined to purely literary and intellectual histories is certainly entitled to a more than ordinary perplexity at the contemplation of that blank – as peremptory as anything on the period maps of Africa – that stretches between the execution of André Chénier and the first lyrics of Lamartine, and is not "properly" filled by the more doubtful productions of either Chateaubriand or Madame de Staël, both of them rehearsing foreign scenes and experiences: the one ideologically unsound, while the "evaluation" of the other has from that time to this been given over to all the vagaries and undecidabilities of the "gendered text". (Indeed, it could be argued that the essential "foreignness" of both these writers is an allegorical acknowledgement of the displacement of some fundamental poetic center of gravity abroad, and a first, none too concealed, form of cultural envy.)

The primacy of the ontological, in the Romantic period, has something to do, surely, with the drawing back of the curtains of tradition and the customary, of the sacred and its conventions, of what seemed to derive a meaning from other spaces than those of human praxis and construction. Now, for a brief period, something like a "window" of the ontological, Being in all its meaninglessness and calm persistence becomes visible, like the ocean floor or the bottom of a lake, before bourgeois conventionality and a whole new system of artificial "values" come to obscure it again. Is it possible that the less social countries, those in which conversation and social relations have been less privileged, in which silence and solitude are not thought of as guilty symptoms (think of the remark that determined the break between Diderot and Rousseau!) – is it possible that it is alone in such less socialized and societalized modes of production (the one, industrial, in advance of the French, the other "undeveloped" and lagging significantly behind it) that the "ground of being" lets itself be briefly glimpsed, as Nature in England, as cosmology and system, as the Absolute, in the German territories? (and in both, as Language, and as national, or natural, language at that – neither French nor Latin …).

To think of this ephemeral historical opening – in Europe – is, then, to think of the other reason everyone knows (and that Hegel virtually builds into his system), that has to do with the emergence of History and the unleashing and reinvestment of historical energies. The French are too busy for literature, or too preoccupied: hard to touch bottom ontologically when every passing year brings a new political system, a new set of worries as well as opportunities. Whatever the French Revolution was able to be for a Hölderlin or a Wordsworth, at distance and within the shaping Imagination, it is harder to conceive of the organic power of composition and of primal language in slow development under Robespierre, or in the rather different corruptions of the Directory (so much like our own frenzied "market" period), or in the sublimer imperialisms of the great Napoleonic conquests. Only the repressive provincial boredom of the Restauration can hatch "the dream bird of narrative" (Benjamin), and even here the story of its release (told above all by Stendhal) is a complex trajectory very much more mediated than in the great English or German poets. Repression, sublimation, gratification: it is already a well-nigh Freudian account that Hegel gives of German underdevelopment (politically, they are too immature to sustain the unique adventure of the French, whose revolution sets an end to accumulated millennia of *anciens régimes* of all kinds), and thereby of the historical luck he himself has of replicating the concrete praxis across the Rhine: Napoleon, the "world soul on horseback", within the mind, as a philosophical system. Perhaps this sublimation also demands political mixed feelings: the excitement and enthusiasm of the revolutionary fellow-traveler – Wordsworth, as well as Hegel or Hölderlin – along with the partially counterrevolutionary withdrawal, the liberal afterthoughts in the face of the Terror: whether these keep faith with a certain revolutionary ideal as such, as with the *feuillant* Hegel, or determine apostasy, as with the first generation of the English revolutionaries.

It is a plausible narrative to which we must, however, bid farewell, for it depends on strategic omissions from the French record, which only looks empty when you wear certain kinds of glasses or blinkers. To be sure, Chateaubriand and Madame de Staël are born in 1768 and 1766 respectively, a year or two before Hegel and Wordsworth (1770), let alone Coleridge (1772) or the remarkably precocious Schelling (1775): but evidently the chronological index finger has paused too soon, overleaping a momentous event (which the reader will have guessed to be none other than the birth of our subject). In effect, missing from all these accounts is the appearance of François-Marie-Charles Fourier (born 1772), the French equivalent of Hegel and Wordsworth. (The comparison with Hegel, to be sure, is scarcely new with me: Raymond Queneau projects it in several suggestive articles on the dialectic and early nineteenth-century mathematics, in which, if anything, the "mathematical" series of Fourier [for example, 5–36–9–27–4 (= 81)] are more complex than anything in the greater *Logic.*) As for England and nature, one would wish to affirm that Fourier's relationship to the gamut of human passions, obsessions, vices and manias is at least as ontological as anything in Marxism, about which no less an authority than Heidegger himself observed that it is also a fundamental relationship to Being and a reflection on ontology itself. As Beecher so plausibly asserts, the cosmological side of Fourier (which has embarrassed so many generations of would-be readers; see Beecher 349) is something like the formal and ontological completion of his great vision: it necessarily comes, like a transfigured Nature, to crown and to confirm the great reorganization of human relations of the phalange by the reaching down and internal restructuration of the otherness of Nature itself and of the cosmos by human praxis. (I will come back to the connections with a Marxian ontology later.)

As for literature, however, it is not merely the poetic and the ontological which have been obscured or occulted by the generic confusion of Utopian discourse in Fourier, which the older modes of literary history seemed unable to process or classify: it is also Literature in its more conventional forms, where "any ass but a detective" (Mark Twain) ought at once to have grasped the developmental logic of Fourier's position at the virtual mid-point between Molière and Balzac, that is to say, between moral satire and social history. Fourier in fact recapitulates the great tables and typologies of manias and obsessions in Molière (and flings the there residual doctrine of the humors onto some unimaginably higher well-nigh psychoanalytic plane), at the same time that as a *commis voyageur* mesmerized by commerce and its iniquitous dynamics he already rehearses much of the in-group-lore of Balzac and the insider know-how so ostentatiously paraded at every opportunity by the no less systemic or even cosmological inventor of the *Comédie humaine.* Everyone has heard of the pastoral scenes and masques that interrupt Fourier's properly interminable texts, ostensibly to furnish illustrations of his social arrangements, but in fact fully as much to indulge some *avant-goût* of pleasure, both in the arrangements themselves and in the formal ingenuity of their composition and projection. As is well known, Barthes compared such moments to the ritual scenes and tableaux in Sade, and to the visionary images, the scenes for meditation, in Loyola: the word *écriture* which he famously applied to all three textual curiosities is perhaps no longer comprehensible in his sense since the Derridean appropriation – it means construction and even constructivism, as opposed to the merely verbal euphorias of something like style. Still, one wants to retain a certain number of these moments, saturated with Balzacian wish-fulfillment: the great war *des petits patés*,[2] which reaches Rabelaisian proportions; the judgment of the love court on Fakma (*NMA* 174–201); any number of daily *emplois du temps*, which we will perhaps have occasion to examine later on; the incessant botanizing, whose combinations virtually by definition transcend the daydreaming ruminations of Rousseau's solitary, and also "bear fruit" in the quite utilitarian production of specific yet extraordinarily varied comestibles; and so forth. Such set pieces are no more unreadable than much else that has acceded to the manuals of literary history (if sometimes no less so either).

In his "delicious" essay on Fourier (to be found in the most delicious of all his books, the one called *Sade, Fourier, Loyola*), Barthes takes it out on Marxism for the rudeness, in May 1968, of his students, who were not interested in looking more closely into Fourier and his "bourgeois ideology". Certainly Fourier was counterrevolutionary in the literal sense (he despised the Jacobins and deplored the violence of the Great Revolution), without being monarchist or reactionary: if, as de Gaulle liked to say, the communists were neither Left nor Right but east, then Fourier was in some more vertical and elevated place from all this: but it is probably not right, either, to associate Marxism with that "politics" that is excluded from the Fourierist Utopia, where the state and the political have already withered away. The argument is twofold, namely that Marx is in this sense not political either, but rather economic (just like Fourier himself); but then also that Fourier is profoundly political after all, and that it would involve a fundamental misreading and misunderstanding to insist on a Fourier of desire in the place of a political Fourier. (Which is no doubt what Barthes does in the more conventional framework of his essay, going on however to repair the stereotype of Marxism with the notion that their relationship – that of Marx and Fourier – "is not complementary but supplementary: each is something like the excess [*le trop*] of the other. Excessive: what can't be swallowed. So from our vantage point today (*after* Marx), politics is the obligatory laxative; then Fourier is the child who won't take it, who vomits it back up."[3])

But if politics means getting any group of people to agree to something and to act together, if it means encouraging individuals to speak their minds and to come to enjoy doing so, at the same time that you find a way to bring them to fall silent without discouragement, and with a certain confidence that so much virtually ontological disagreement will nonetheless generate action rather than paralysis – then Fourier is political and understood very well that the "theory of attraction" was his great intervention into political theory and philosophy as such:

2 Charles Fourier, *Nouveau Monde amoureux*, ed., S. Debout-Oleszkiewicz (Paris, 1967), pp. 339ff., afterwards *NMA* in text.

3 R. Barthes, *Sade, Fourier, Loyola* (Paris, 1971), p. 93.

Et comme les Séries passionnées ne se composent que de groupes, il faut, avant tout, apprendre à former les groupes.

"Ha! ha! les groupes, c'est un sujet plaisant que les groupes: ça doit être amusant les groupes!"

Ainsi raisonnent les beaux esprits quand on parle de groupes: il faut d'abord essuyer d'eux une bordée de fades équivoques; mais que le sujet soit plaisant ou non, il est certain qu'on ne connaît rien aux groupes, et qu'on ne sait pas même former un groupe régulier de trois personnes, encore moins de trente.

Cependant nous avons de nombreux traités sur l'étude de l'homme: quelles notions peuvent-ils nous donner sur ce sujet, s'ils négligent la partie élémentaire, l'analyse des groupes? Toutes nos relations ne tendent qu'à former des groupes, et ils n'ont jamais été l'objet d'aucune étude.[4]

We must take this assertion seriously, I believe, and review the lengthy history of (at least Western) political philosophy in the light of its fundamental presupposition, namely that the central problem of all political philosophy (or later on, of all political science) is the constitution of the group. If so, three consequences become immediately obvious. First, the abstract or fig-leaf slogan "democracy" is in reality the designation of a problem or dilemma disguised as a "value" or ideal: democracy can scarcely mean anything other than the dynamics of the group, whose solution it presupposes in advance of any empirical investigations. Second, such investigations are, however, in our time seriously mystified by the emergence of a pseudo-science which offers to subsume them, namely so-called social psychology, which, incorporating all the data relevant to group dynamics as such, confiscates it all to the benefit of that anti-revolutionary ideology that emerged from the terror of the "mob" in the French Revolution and reaches a kind of climax in Gustave LeBon at the end of the nineteenth century (thence passed on to Freud but also to any number of other liberal or conservative counterrevolutionary ideologists). This powerful ideologeme seeks to document the sheer irrationality of all group action and to warn of the ways in which the individual identity and rational consciousness are only too easily submerged in its intoxicating appeal. There can indeed have been few such cases in modern times in which an essential "scientism" (going so far as to endow a whole new academic discipline as such) is so immediately identified with outright and shameless ideological content.

This development then suggests, third, that the two tendencies which unevenly come asunder in the ancient development of political "philosophy" and the only too modern development of social psychology – preeminently "two halves that don't add up" (Adorno) – project the unfulfilled idea of some more concrete thinking of the group in which the conceptual insufficiencies

---

4   Charles Fourier, *Nouveau Monde industriel* (Paris, 1973), p. 99, afterwards *NMI* in text.

of "value" and empirical dynamics – of the "individual" and "society" – cancel each other out: this is the space colonized with incomparable intelligence and confidence by Fourier himself. It has no name; but in its light we can now systematically reevaluate the Western tradition and grasp the new fact that most "contributions" to political science from Plato on are in reality the inverse or photographic negative of this one. "Sovereignty" is thus what whips an unworthy or fallen collectivity into line, and tries to bring about some genuine group cohesion by fiat: such are the violences of Plato's guardians or Machiavelli's Prince (even still residually of Gramsci's "modern" Prince). Nothing is meanwhile more wholesome than Fourier's nausea for the family structure appealed to by the "organic" successors of Aristotle all the way down to the ethnics or nationals of our own time; while the constitutional theorists of citizenship and "civil society" all know in their heart of hearts that they are cleaving to a second-best, mainly intent on hedging their practical recipes with ingenious preventive mechanisms inspired by ideological anxiety if not the outright fear of groups as such.

On my view (about which I would be glad to stand corrected) only two other theories have had the intellectual boldness to replace the problem of groups and their constitution back in the very center of what need no longer be called political theory: these are Sartre's *Critique of Dialectical Reason* on the one hand, and Laclau and Mouffe's *Hegemony and Socialist Strategy* on the other, both of which we will find it profitable to confront with the *fons et origo* (which neither mentions).

Both are inspired by a very modern anxiety which seems alien to Fourier: namely what might be called psychic centralization, and what it is easy to identify (in both cases) as part of the hangover of the Stalinist centralized party. And in both cases it is perhaps less a question of representing an ideal than it is of arguing for the very possibility of a radically different kind of organization than the one identified as Stalinist. But these arguments take place on very different levels, Sartre's on that of concrete social relations, Laclau and Mouffe's on that of culture (that is, of the slogans and issues around which a collective politics can best crystallize).

Sartre's is both a synchronic and a diachronic argument, in that he will both demonstrate that a non-centralized collective or group dynamic is possible, and show its historical transformation into a different form (in the event, precisely the Stalinist form of centralized "sovereignty" which presides over this theory like its nightmare). Sartre's group ontology predicates a process of group formation rather than an achieved structure: such a process begins, somewhat like the small eddy which precedes a whirlpool, within that larger amorphous agglomeration of individuals he calls "seriality" (which has its own specific laws, whose formulation in the *Critique of Dialectical Reason* is not its least interesting feature). Indeed, as a way of distinguishing seriality from the group, where the center is omnipresent, seriality may be defined as a collective situation in which the center is always elsewhere. The group (or more properly the "group-in-fusion") is then a system in which, by virtue of a constant rotation, everyone is the center in turn and there are no privileged positions, not because the latter have been eliminated (by puritanism or envy, by *ressentiment* or edict) but rather by virtue of the omnipresence of such "privilege" which is passed from one participant to the next like the magic objects of myth or legend. This reflects a situation in which not only does everyone have a right to speak, but the individual utterance, like a perpetual present, is always influential, momentarily sweeping all before it (at least until the next one): on the other hand, and by the same token, no one's idea draws persuasive power from the identity of the speaker, but rather the other way round, the speaker's power rises and falls with the faithfulness with which the speech reflects everyone else's feelings. This ebb and flow of prestige is not the same as, but comparable to, the multiplication of a more eighteenth-century style of titles, ranks and privileges in Fourier, which offer a supplementary gratification in a situation in which there is no correlation between standing and social function. Everyone can see, however, that the Sartrean description corresponds to a particularly fluid moment in the life, and in particular in the emergence of groups, in which a general collective direction or project is clear, but no specific leadership has solidified. The formation process itself, however, patterned in a mythic way on the initial and formative events of the French Revolution – threat from the outside, tennis-court oath, terror, etc. – is cyclical, and has very little in common with Fourier's conception of history (which is couched in terms of great moments or stages – what we might call modes of production – rather than of contingent events).

The figures at work in the Sartrean conception of the group are relatively complex and abstract: they can be characterized as a perpetual interference between figures of structure and figures of process: they are thus a little more than Sartre's reply to Lévi-Strauss and emergent structuralism (although that is a component of the *Critique* and its motivation), and amount to an incorporation of structural concepts with a view towards the latter's transcendence if not neutralization.

The figure at work in Laclau and Mouffe is more easily identifiable as a structural one, since it is effectively borrowed (without being acknowledged as such) from Roman Jakobson's influential "definition" of poetry as the projection of the axis of simultaneity upon that of contiguity (for example, rhyme would be the phenomenon constituted by an identity – the sound endings – redistributed in the successive time of the lines themselves). The "problem" Laclau and Mouffe have set for themselves can in effect be described as that of constructing a "party line" for an alliance of different groups in which it is urgent that the line or interest of no single one predominates over the others as the "party line" of the Stalinist experience was thought to have done. Yet these different aims and interests cannot persist in simple autonomy or independence from one another either, in an agglomeration in which each group supports the position of the other without any real passion or identification, simply in order to buy support in turn for its own particular concerns. Rather, a relationship must be developed in which the various slogans or aims become at least momentarily identified with each other; and this is clearly a poetic relationship, in which a literal signifier for one group will be figurally projected onto another group and adopted, as it were, in a rather different tropological spirit. Thus, one can imagine a situation in which the literal cause of one group – in, let us say, effective administrative control over its own part of the city – is adopted as a figural abstraction (autonomy, democracy) by another group which has a different conception of autonomy.

But what is here limited to its specifically political and cultural dimension, as a "cause" or an ideal, even a "subject position" (although this last would seem to fix and determine small-group politics in a far more definitive and lasting way than Laclau and Mouffe have in mind), is in Fourier a matter of temperament and passion. He had already identified the phenomenon they characterize as a projection of one axis upon another, and had characteristically named it as "repercussion harmonique", where passions maintain as it were musical overtones into the dominance of quite different activities, but also where various specific forms of repression can invert beneficent passions into toxic ones (*NMI* 462ff.).

The fundamental difference, however, remains the one I have suggested as obtaining between a conception of culture and one of temperament or passion: Laclau and Mouffe's imperfectly developed notion of the "group subject position" would presumably offer a mediation between these two levels, the one of language, the other of interpersonal relationship, except that, as has been suggested, too strong a theory of the individual subject position would tend to anchor the group into this or that psychology, this or that value or obsession, with a permanency all of these theories have desperately attempted to avoid. In fact, Fourier's conception of group dynamics can from our standpoint be approached as something like a synthesis *avant la lettre* between Sartre on the one hand and Laclau and Mouffe on the other: for on the one hand he theorizes the actual positioning of the members of the group, and their possible combinations, with a virtuosity that extends far beyond the bounds of the Sartrean guerrilla unit; while on the other he evolves a remarkably fluid and mobile conception of the content of group activities and of the changing patterns of interests which the various groups and the various members of an individual group end up pursuing.

What I have designated by the word *ontological* in Fourier is, then, precisely this coordination of base and superstructure, so to speak: in other words the ways in which the individual passions (cultural) themselves take charge of and organize the figures of the mode of production itself (the "infrastructure" or shape, size and dynamic of the various groups). The terminology of figuration is preeminently appropriate for Fourier, whose anticipation of modern typologies and combination schemes is essentially based on a range of figures, such as those of geometry (*NMI* 367: "major passions: friendship – the circle; ambition – the hyperbola; minor passions: love – the ellipse; paternity – the parabola").

But Fourier is non-structuralist (and his schemes tend more to the Sartrean side of things) to the degree to which he feels the need and urgency of mechanisms that set the group in motion, that encourage the proliferation of new combinations and thus use structure (or figure) as a mere static point of departure for unforeseeable events and adventures: it being understood that we are here literally in a Hegelian end of History, and that such events, combinations, episodes and algorithms can no longer be historical, that is to say, they can no longer bring about structural change or evolution or development in the "mode of production" itself, but are rather internal to that and themselves components of the play of its various mechanisms.

How to achieve such an ideal combination of structure and event? Clearly, this can only be imagined by building eventfulness into the structure itself, and once again it is this identification of the two fundamental levels of being – extension and thought, for Spinoza; or substance and subject, in Hegel; or even the tension between World and Earth, in Heidegger – that marks Fourier's vision as an ontological one. The trick is turned by including among the fundamental passions – alongside the first five, which correspond to the five senses; and the four forms of social attraction, listed above as major and minor passions – three more whose very internal drives are in one way or another combinational. These three "distributive" or "mechanizing" passions have often been admired as among the most subtle and inventive conceptions of Fourier's unique genius in the imagination of social figures and the material of human relationships: they are, to be sure, the famous cabalistic, butterfly and composite passions, which between them lend an exhaustive impulsion to the creation of the desirable range of interpersonal relations and group structures (sometimes estimated at the number of 1,620, by calculations I am unable to verify).

The nature of these three passions, however, underscores the fundamental difference between Fourier and most of those who have meditated in one way or another about groups (including Sartre and Laclau/Mouffe): for the latter, perhaps drawing on the powerful anti-collective ideologies of the late nineteenth century, tend to think in spite of themselves of groups as homogeneous and homogenizing forces that tend towards identity and reinforce unities of various kinds. Their effort, in the theorizing of groups, has traditionally involved the imagining of just such unifying group mechanisms which would nonetheless allow for a certain minimal variety (or freedom, or democracy, or whatever value term you prefer), a variety produced by the group-unifying mechanism itself (the turning mechanism of the Sartrean group, the projective articulation and identification of the Laclau–Mouffe alliance).

Fourier's conviction, however, excludes this baleful momentum of group unification (perhaps because he knows, as an isolated intellectual in the first formative period of modern French political life, how difficult it is to bring a genuine group or party together in the first place); rather, it presupposes the need, within unifying groups or groups-in-fusion, for fundamental internal dissonances and contradictions. Fourier's three "pivotal" passions, the three passions he will call upon to cement group relations and stimulate internal group dynamics, are all in one way or another anti-social passions of the sort that organizers and administrators are normally concerned to neutralize or eliminate ("ces trois passions titrées de vice, quoique chacun en soit idolâtre, sont réellement des sources de vice en civilisation, où elles ne peuvent opérer que sur des familles et des corporations; Dieu les a créées pour opérer sur des séries de groupes contrastés" [*NMI* 92]).

Nowhere is this quite so obvious as in the "cabalistic" passion, the passion for intrigue and dissension, *l'esprit de parti* and calculation: "even in a gesture or a wink, everything is calculated yet swift and instantaneous" (*NMI* 112). The cabalistic passion may be seen as Fourier's substitute for the market, in current free-enterprise ideology. It is an interpretation that cuts deep, particularly when you understand everything that Fourier's experience owes to private business, as a clerk and then a *commis voyageur*, as an observer obsessed by the vices and corruptions of a business world that has nonetheless formed his imagination. Fourier comes to his critique of nascent capitalism by way of commerce, where Engels comes to his by way of factory production. The former's incisive analyses of a whole range of commercial phenomena, including market crises (see Beecher's discussion of Fourier's anticipation of the very concept of financial crisis as such), have often been admired; yet the ambiguous relationship of his Utopian vision to the commercial dynamics of his day demands clarification, particularly in our own time, where the market has been celebrated as an autonomous and totalizing system which necessarily ends up drawing everything else into itself. Marxism, with its emphasis on production over distribution and consumption, has seemed exempt from the corruptions of the market and of the commodity form; but it has bought this exemption with an appearance of puritanism and renunciation which scarcely affords it much flexibility in dealing with the omnipresent consumerist mentalities of what is now a virtual world public. Fourier is thus better placed to separate out alternate possibilities from the market psychologies of his own period. Thus, the emphasis of contemporary ideologues on the virtues of competition, which they attribute to the market as such as a beneficent mechanism which is also deeply embedded in human nature, is in the Fourier vision of things displaced, and very precisely secured by the cabalistic passion for intrigue, which includes emulation along with productive jealousies and envies. This passion – which it would be best not too hastily to characterize in purely psychological terms, as we shall see shortly – can thus survive the capitalist market system as such (just as money and inequalities of wealth survive it, and become something like the status and rank distinctions which for their part outlive the *ancien régime* and are also pressed into active service in the new Utopian order). Meanwhile, even culturally, we are better placed than many of Fourier's contemporaries (with the obvious exceptions of Balzac and the emergent technicians of the novel) to grasp everything that is already profoundly Utopian about gossip itself (in both Proust and Joyce the very motor force at work in human sociability and storytelling); while Fourier himself explicitly underscores the de-provincializing function of intrigue, which exposes a somnolent population to new rumors and possibilities, and stimulates a productive lust for action and for the trammeling of new projects. Nothing is more remarkable, among the multitudinous slogans this Utopia floats from its banner-head, than this positioning of the conspiratorial schemer at the heroic center of social construction itself; and nothing better illustrates the sublime indifference of Fourier to conventional moral judgments (and not only the usual sexual ones).

The composite passion is somewhat more obscure, if only because, unlike the preceding rubric, it attempts to name something of which we are not conventionally aware in current society, and which Fourier begins by defining as a hitherto illicit commingling of material and spiritual interests and excitements. The eighteenth century knew this passion under its stigmatized name of "enthusiasm", so that Fourier's own nomenclature is by way of being an analysis of enthusiasm fully as much as a socialization of it. In effect, to use an even more modern terminology, he seems here to project a role, in the interests and the passions, for what we might call "fetishism", that is to say, for an undue intellectualization of what might otherwise pass as a more inoffensively material pleasure (or vice versa: a relatively ordinary spiritual passion might be unduly and in appearance unhealthily associated with a material object). Or, the composite in Fourier might well be assigned the philosophical role of reflexivity and self-consciousness (a rather different and unexpected link to his German idealist contemporaries): as a function whereby material activities are somehow doubled by their intellectual and spiritual focus, creating something like a stereoptic passion which would thus alone generate the violence of enthusiasm as such. To take a relatively prosaic example, one may contrast the pleasures of the table with a composite version of this last in which gastronomy – Fourier calls its heightened version gastrosophy! – absorbs a whole range of philosophical interests and concepts and becomes something like a master passion in which the cosmos is itself at stake: it is then clear that something as comprehensive as this second or composite relationship to eating will encourage a fetishism and an energetic and vigorously rationalized commitment that its simple or material version does not (and need not) involve.

If the cabalistic passion generated relations outside a given activity, and determined as it were a wealth of lateral connections between its practice by my group and that of other groups, as well as between its practice and different kinds of practices, then the composite passion may be grasped as it were vertically, as the subsumption within a given activity of a whole range of material and psychic or spiritual and intellectual investments. It thickens such practices and as it were allegorizes them: for Fourier's indebtedness to Schelling's notion of analogy (see for example *NMI* 49) is not only to be observed in his cosmological fantasies but also here in this conception of libidinal investment and sublimation which is as anticipatory as his analyses of repression.

The third passion – the butterfly passion – then sets these two preceding ones in motion and as it were develops and enriches them over time: projecting a conception of human activity more French and social than the austere Faustian one, at the same time that it offers a rather different way out of the Hegelian alternative of objectification and alienation than anything in the dialectical tradition (although the famous Utopian reflection of Marx and Engels themselves about fishing in the morning and theorizing at night is immediately Fourierist in spirit as well as in inspiration). The fundamental idea behind the butterfly passion is the conviction that human beings cannot pursue any activity profitably and pleasurably for much longer than two hours at a time (even sleep is drastically reduced to three or four hours in this Utopia, while the life span is immeasurably extended). It is clear that besides the variety of activities the butterfly rhythm necessarily calls for, and the complexity of production arrangement it demands (one recalls Raymond Williams' wonderful remark that socialism will not be simpler than capitalism but immeasurably more complex), it also offers a variety of pleasures and gratifications which the following "parcours" or schedule of gratifications may serve to suggest:

> Leandre has just succeeded with the woman he was courting. This is a composite pleasure, for senses and soul alike. Immediately thereafter she gave him a lucrative patent title he had been seeking; it's a 2nd pleasure. Fifteen minutes later, she takes him into the salon, where he meets some happy surprises, in particular the meeting with a friend thought to be deceased; 3rd pleasure. Shortly thereafter, there enters a famous man, Buffon or Corneille, whom he always wanted to know and who is dining with them; 4th pleasure. Then an exquisite meal; 5th pleasure. Leandre is seated beside a powerful man who can help him and promises to do so; 6th pleasure. In the course of the dinner a message is delivered notifying him that he has just won a lawsuit; 7th pleasure. (*NMI* 404–405)

Few passages so clearly mark the difference between the Utopian text and literature itself (or at least what we call narrative): far from demanding the concrete representation of our wish fulfilled, this retrospective agenda asks us to desire it as though it were a cherished blueprint of our own future. Not realization but the resurrection of the wish itself, such is the joyousness of

Fourier's dream pictures, rather more eighteenth-century and Mozartian in spirit than in that of the contingencies of being of the nineteenth-century realist novel. Beecher has well insisted on the revulsion of Fourier for the tragic, his implacable insistence on the happy end, on perpetual and universal resolution, along with infinite gratification: it is a note that escapes literary forms by the measure in which it transcends both the Frye/White categories of comedy and romance; nor can it philosophically be thought of as anything quite so shallow as optimism either, since this particular will to optimism (which to that degree has something in common with the Nietzschean will), by willing to will itself, reaches down into inorganic nature in order to lift everything that is to its own height. For at the same time this particular consciousness has unwittingly learned the deeper secret of wish-fulfillment, namely that it demands conditions of possibility in order to be dreamed or fantasized in the first place. In Fourier, however, the fantasy is so peremptory and deep-lunged that all of nature must be summoned forth as its condition of possibility.

The Nietzschean comparison perhaps yields another secret of Fourier's success, namely, that if you seek gratification in everything, you must affirm everything: at which point the Utopian transformation can take place. But that transformation must be total and systemic, it cannot nibble away at the real in piecemeal changes, which are the stuff of moralism. Indeed, Fourier's loathing for the moralists and for ethics as such is even more glorious than his will to gratification and his repudiation of the tragic sense of life; and it is better to say it this way than to evoke his detestation of morality as such, or better still, of "bourgeois morality", a feeling which is cheap enough for everyone to share. No, it is rather those who moralize and take the ethical view who are suspect here, at a moment in which Fourier rejoins the deeper motivations of the dialectic itself: Hegel's repudiation of Kant and the Kantian *Sollen* (or ethical imperative) in the name of a well-nigh Spinozian totality of being (where "what is, is rational" and vice versa) – and beyond that the complexly motivated set of Marx himself towards virtuality and immanence (Lukács will himself go back to Hegel's position in order to attack the Kantian and ethical way the Second International rewrote Marx and sought to stage socialism as a purely ethical project for changing the world). For, once again, Marx is ontological in the way in which he grasps the collective forms as already latent in the capitalist present: they are not merely desirable (or ethical), nor even possible, but also and above all inevitable, provided we understand the bringing to emergence of that inevitability as a collective human task and project (it must be understood that for Marx the opposite of inevitability in this sense is universal catastrophe and destruction: socialism may well never come into being, but in that case nothing else will come into being either as an alternative – "the mutual ruin of the contending forces").

It is true that Fourier also grasps moralizing as a form of repression ("la méthode répressive dite morale", *NMI* 207), thus completing the dialectical objection to *Sollen* or ethical "will-power" with a Freudian and a Nietzschean analysis. Ethics, "l'antipode de la nature", undermines the three fundamental passions of combination (see above) by its disapprovals (*NMI* 119), but it also deforms the Utopian impulse itself by sheer infiltration, by a deflection whereby sham Utopias of work slavery such as those he denounces in Saint-Simon and Owen come into being. Moralizing is indeed at one with civilization itself (as Freud will in effect say in *Civilization and Its Discontents*), and Fourier's scorn for this last can be read over and over again from the satirical passages, such as the rare sarcasm of this one:

> Nous n'avons eu cette année que 17 traités de morale, disait un journal de 1803, qui s'apitoyait sur la modicité de cette récolte. Il ne parlait que de la France: en y ajoutant les autres Etats, etc., etc. (*NMI* 207)

It is important to realize that one of Fourier's signal originalities is to have included the family in this diatribe, in that utterly dissimilar to all those of an either reactionary or radical disposition who have sought to model their ideal groups on the family structure as such or to have reinvented an organic equivalent for it on a larger scale. The phalange is not an extended family or manor writ even larger, but rather an anti-family (something, as he liked to point out, that we are tempted to confuse with the family only because we live in a fallen and degenerate period in which we can scarcely imagine anything else).

The ethical or moralizing habit is above all what resists the great thought of immanence, what hankers after the luxury of picking and choosing among existents: and this pantheistic affirmation (in our own time more immediately associated with Spinoza than with Hegel and Marx, for historical reasons) is then the way into Fourier's doctrine of the passions and the libido as well. It would be extraordinarily old-fashioned, in this day and age, to celebrate Fourier's "extraordinary" libidinal insights, which presumably raise him to the prophetic level of a Krafft-Ebing or a Havelock Ellis, wherever that might be. Not even the mention of Lacan is appropriate here, unless it be in terms of a rather different notion of the psychoanalytic "cure" than the one that has passed into popular (and in particular into popular North American) folklore, namely as a well-nigh religious form of redemption in which the entire personality is somehow transfigured. The spirit of the Lacanian (but probably also the classic or authentic Freudian) cure is better afforded by Slavoj Žižek's jubilant formula: Enjoy your symptom! which implies that the change, if change there is, lies not in the structure of one's character or the impulses to which one is victim, but rather in the nature of one's relationship to those impulses, which are now chosen and affirmed, rather than resisted in an in any case vain and impossible negation (and the language here may also remind us that a similar wisdom was present in Sartrean or existential psychology as well).

Whence in Fourier the affirmation of all the "vices" and perversions, along with all the other accredited and respectable impulses as well: sublimation is now too limited a concept for the way in which a material consent to all these drives, and an opening up of social space towards their practical gratification, transform them utterly. Nothing in Fourier has indeed been more often quoted than the fable of the sadistic Russian lady (*NMA* 390–392); to which we might add, Fourier's own fondness for lesbians; the utilitarian cooptation of children's love for filth and garbage in the "little hordes" who will take care of that particular labor in Utopia; and last but not least the great amorous contests and jousts, in which the needs of the ugly and elderly will be taken care of by young and beautiful "saints" whose philanthropic prostitution is a matter of public celebration and a distribution of prizes and titles. Any proper introduction to Fourier contains these materials; I recall them here in order to dramatize the ontological structure of this Utopia, in which what already is, or what is virtual, latent, at the level of fantasy or half-formed wish or inclination, is also the rockbed of the social structure itself. Fourier's libidinal realism lies in constructing society on what it contains already (just as Marx's argument aimed to show the emergence of collective or proto-socialist relations within capital itself).

Does this embrace of immanence then also imply, as in Hegel, an end of art, that is, a withering away of the various distances from the real (which may be compensatory or critical, affirmative or anticipatory) that the aesthetic always necessarily entertains with its social context? To a certain degree: opera will be, we are told, a perpetual occupation of Fourier's Utopians (but one can also imagine, as in Adorno, something like a mutation in the function of music itself, which, becoming part of life, will somehow cease to be its formal substitute). What we call charades – including the great sexual jousts and contests referred to above, and even the planned orgies (as orderly and symmetrical, as Barthes observes, as anything in Sade) – are here everywhere mobilized to turn life into sheer play: but it was that already, since work has now been organized in the form of playful gratification. Finally, there is eating in Fourier: and it is clear that that proto-aesthetic, whereby a base natural function is converted into a well-nigh structuralist *combinatoire* of tastes and flavor modes, becomes something like the very figure or emblem of the transformation of matter in Utopia – gastrosophy thus (once again?) becomes the highest form of art, in a way that perhaps reflects back on our contemporary aesthetic practices and suggests new ways to reevaluate them.

It would be depressing to conclude with Barthes' disabused observation that what is prophetic or anticipatory in Fourier's vision is the outline it contains of a tourist industry to come, on a global scale about which postmodernity perhaps reserves surprises for us. (One would in that case have to apply the counterpoison of a Bloch, who already reminded us that the tourist industry is also a foretaste of Utopia.) Better, perhaps, to conclude with the

Romantic Fourier – halfway between Wordsworth's non-figurality and the virtually medieval emblems and alchemical codes of a Philipp Otto Runge – who can still cry out:

> Sans l'analogie, la nature n'est qu'un vaste champ de ronces; les 73 systèmes de botanique ne sont que 73 tiges de chardon. Rousseau les a bien qualifiés de science rebutante, qui vient cracher du grec et du latin au nez des dames. Dites aux dames, pour les intéresser, que tel effet de passions est dépeint dans tel végétal; montrez-leur les variétés de l'amour dans l'iris, la tubéreuse, l'oeillet, la jacinthe, la pêche, l'abricot, le pigeon et le coq … (*NMI* 526)

1994

2

Generic Discontinuities in SF:
Brian Aldiss' *Starship*

The theme or narrative convention of the lost-spaceship-as-universe offers a particularly striking occasion to observe the differences between the so-called old and new waves in SF, since Aldiss' *Starship* (1958) was preceded by a fine treatment of the same material by Robert A. Heinlein in *Orphans of the Sky* (serialized in 1941 as "Universe" and "Common Sense").[1] Taken together, the versions of the two writers give us a synoptic view of the basic narrative line that describes the experiences of the hero as he ventures beyond the claustrophobic limits of his home territory into other compartments of a world peopled by strangers and mutants. He comes at length to understand that the space through which he moves is not the universe but simply a gigantic ship in transit through the galaxy; and this discovery – which may be said to have in such a context all the momentous scientific consequences that the discoveries of Copernicus and Einstein had in our own – takes the twin form of text and secret chamber. On the one hand, the hero learns to read the enigmatic "Manual of Electric Circuits of Starship", a manual of his own cosmos, supplemented by the ship's log with its record of the ancient catastrophe – mutiny and natural disaster as Genesis and Fall – which broke the link between future generations of the ship's inhabitants and all knowledge of their origins; and on the other, he makes his way to the ship's long-vacant control room and there comes to know, for the first time, the shattering experience of deep space and the terror of the stars. The narrative then terminates with the arrival of the ship – against all expectation – at its immemorial and long-forgotten destination and with the end of what some indigenous starship-philosopher would no doubt have called the "prehistory" of the inhabitants.

But this series of events constitutes only what might be called the horizontal dimension of the thematic material in question. On its basis a kind of vertical structure is erected which amounts to an account of the customs and culture that have evolved within the sealed realm of the lost ship. Both Heinlein

---

1 *Starship* (New York, 1958) was entitled *Non-Stop* in Britain; page references to this edition along with the book version of *Orphans of the Sky* (New York, 1964), are given within the text.

and Aldiss, indeed, take anthropological pains to note the peculiar native religion of the ship, oriented around its mythical founders, its codified survival-ethic, whose concepts of good and evil are derived from the tradition of the great mutiny as from some primal disobedience of man, along with its characteristic figures of speech and ritualistic formulas similarly originating in long-forgotten and incomprehensible events and situations ("Take a journey!" = "Drop dead!"; "By Huff!" = "What the devil!" in allusion to the ringleader of the mutiny; and so on). With this anthropological dimension of the narrative, the two books may be said to fulfill one of the supreme functions of SF as a genre, namely the "estrangement", in the Brechtian sense,[2] of our culture and institutions – a shocked renewal of our vision such that once again, and as though for the first time, we are able to perceive their historicity and their arbitrariness, their profound dependency on the accidents of man's historical adventure.

Indeed, I propose to reverse the traditional order of aesthetic priorities and to suggest that this whole theme is nothing but a pretext for the spectacle of the artificial formation of a culture within the closed situation of the lost ship. Such a hypothesis demands a closer look at the role of the *artificial* in these narratives, which takes at least two distinct forms. First, there is the artificiality of the mile-long spaceship as a human construct used as an instrument in a human project. Here the reader is oppressed by the substitution of culture for nature (a substitution dramatically and unexpectedly extended by Aldiss in the twist ending that I shall speak of later). Accustomed to the idea that human history and culture obey a kind of organic and natural rhythm in their evolution, emerging slowly within a determinate geographical and climatic situation under the shaping forces of events (invasions, inventions, economic developments) that are themselves felt to have some inner or "natural" logic, he feels the supreme influence of the ship's environment as a cruel and unnatural joke. The replacement of the forests and plains in which men have evolved by the artificial compartments of the spaceship is in itself only the external and stifling symbol of the original man-made decision (a grim caricature of God's gesture of creation) which sent man on such a fatal mission and which was at the source of this new and artificial culture. Somehow the decisive moments of real human history (Caesar at the Rubicon, Lenin on the eve of the October Revolution) do not come before us with this irrevocable force, for they are reabsorbed into the web of subsequent events and "alienated" by the collective existence of society as a whole. But the inauguratory act of the launchers of the spaceship implies a terrible and godlike responsibility which is not without serious political overtones and to which we will return. For the present let me suggest that the estrangement effect inherent in such a

---

2 See Bertolt Brecht, *Brecht on Theater*, edited and translated by John Willett (US 1964), especially pp. 191–193.

substitution of culture for nature would seem to involve two apparently contradictory impulses: on the one hand, it causes us obscurely to doubt whether our own institutions are quite as natural as we supposed, and whether our "real" open-air environment may not itself be as confining and constricting as the closed world of the ship; on the other hand, it casts uncertainty on the principle of the "natural" itself, which as a conceptual category no longer seems quite so self-justifying and commonsensical.

The other sense in which the artificial plays a crucial role in the spaceship-as-universe narrative has to do with the author himself, who is called on, as it were, to reinvent history out of whole cloth, and to devise, out of his own individual imagination, institutions and cultural phenomena which in real life come into being only over great stretches of time and only as a result of collective processes. Historical truth is always stranger and more unpredictable, more unimaginable, than any fiction: whatever the talent of the novelist, his inventions must always of necessity spring from extrapolation of or analogy with the real, and this law emerges with particular force and visibility in SF with its generic attachment to "future history". This is to say that the cultural traits invented by Aldiss and Heinlein always come before us as *signs*: they ask us to take them as equivalents for the cultural habits of our own daily lives, they beg to be judged on their intention rather than by what they actually realize, to be read with complicity rather than for the impoverished literal content. But this apparently inevitable failure of the imagination is not so disastrous aesthetically as one might expect: on the contrary, it projects an estrangement effect of its own, and our reaction is not so much disappointment at the imaginative lapses of Aldiss and Heinlein as rather bemusement with the limits of human vision. Such details cause us to measure the distance between the creative power of the individual mind and the unforeseeable, inexhaustible fullness of history as the collective human adventure. So this ultimate inability of the writer to create a genuinely alternate universe only returns us the more surely to this one.

So much for the similarities between these two books, and for the narrative structure which they share. Their differences begin to emerge when we observe the way in which each deals with the principal strategic problem of such a narrative, namely the degree to which the reader is to be held, along with the hero, in ignorance of the basic facts about the lost ship. Now it will be said that both books give their secret away at the very outset – Aldiss with his title, and Heinlein with the initial but retrospective "historical" motto which recounts the disappearance of the ship in outer space. Apparently, therefore, we have to do in both cases with an adventure story in which the hero discovers something we know already, rather than with a cognitive or puzzle-solving form in which we ourselves come to learn something new. Yet the closing episodes of the two books are different enough to suggest some significant structural distinctions between them. In Heinlein's story, indeed,

the lost ship ultimately *lands*, and the identity of the destination is not so important as the finality of the landing itself, which has the effect of satisfying our
aesthetic expectations with a full stop. Of course, the book could have ended
in any one of a number of other ways: the ship might have crashed, the hero
might have been killed by his enemies, the inhabitants might all have died and
sailed on, embalmed, into intergalactic space like the characters in Martinson's
poem and Blomdahl's opera *Aniara*. The point is that such alternate endings
do not in themselves call into question the basic category of an ending or plot
resolution; rather, they reconfirm the convention of the linear narrative with
its beginning (*in medias res* or *navigationis*), middle and end.

The twist ending of Aldiss' novel, on the other hand, turns the whole
concept of such a plot inside out like a glove. It shows us that there was a
mystery or puzzle to be solved after all, but not where we thought it was; as it
were a second-degree puzzle, a mystery to the second power, transcending the
question of the world as ship which we as readers had taken for granted from
the outset. The twist ending, therefore, returns upon the opening pages to transform the very generic expectations aroused there. It suddenly reidentifies the
category of the narrative in a wholly unexpected way, and shows us that we
have been reading a very different type of book than the one we started out
with. In comparison with anything to be found in the Heinlein story, where all
the discoveries take place *within*, and are predicated on the existence and stability of, the narrative frame, the new information furnished us by Aldiss in his
closing pages has structural consequences of a far more thoroughgoing kind.

The notion of *generic expectations*[3] may now serve as our primary tool for the
analysis of *Starship* – at the same time that such a reading will define and illustrate this notion more concretely. I suppose that the reader who comes to
Aldiss from Heinlein is impressed first of all by the incomparably more vivid
"physiological" density of Aldiss' style. In spite of everything the title tells us
of the world we are about to enter, the reader of *Starship*, in its opening pages,
finds himself exploring a mystery into which he is plunged up to the very
limits of his senses. In particular, he must find some way of reconciling, in
his own mind, the two contradictory terminological and conceptual fields
which I have already discussed under the headings of nature and culture: on

---

3 Any reflection on genre today owes a debt – sometimes an unwilling one – to Northrop
Frye's *Anatomy of Criticism* (1957); I should also mention, in the renewal of this field of study,
the Chicago neo-Aristotelians represented in R.S. Crane's anthology *Critics and Criticism* (1952).
For a recent survey of recent theories, see Paul Hernadi, *Beyond Genre* (1972), and for the latest
discussion of "generic expectations", E.D. Hirsch Jr, *Validity in Interpretation* (1967). On SF as a
genre, the essential statement is of course Darko Suvin's "On the Poetics of the Science Fiction
Genre", *College English*, December 1972; while the seminal investigation of the relationship
between genre and social experience remains that of Georg Lukács (see for example his *Writer
and Critic* [1970] and *The Historical Novel* [new edn 1969] or, for a more general discussion, my
"Case for Georg Lukács", in *Marxism and Form* [1972]).

the one hand, indications of the presence of a "deck", with its "compartments", "barricades" and "wooden partitions", and on the other hand, the
organic growth of "ponic tangle" through which the tribe slowly hacks its way
as through a jungle, "thrusting forward the leading barricade, and moving up
the rear ones, at the other end of Quarters, a corresponding distance" (14).
Such an apparently unimaginable interpenetration of the natural and the artificial is underscored by a sentence like the following: "The hardest job in the
task of clearing ponics was breaking up the interlacing root structure, which
lay like a steel mesh under the grit, its tower tendrils biting deep into the deck"
(14). Such a sentence is an invitation to "rêverie" in Gaston Bachelard's sense
of the imaginative exploration of the properties and elements of space
through language: it exercises the function of poetry as Heidegger conceives
it, as a non-conceptualized meditation on the very mysteries of our being-in-
the-world. Its force springs, however, from its internal contradictions, from
the incomprehensible conflict between natural and artificial imagery, which
arouses and stimulates our perceptual faculties at the same time that it seems
to block their full unfolding. We can appreciate this mechanism more accurately in juxtaposition with a later book by Aldiss himself, *Hothouse* (1962), in
which a post-civilized Earth offers only the most abundant and riotous purely
organic imagery, the cultural and artificial with few exceptions having long
since vanished.[4]

   This is not to say that Heinlein's book does not have analogous moments
of mystery, but they are of a narrative rather than descriptive kind. I think,
for example, of the episode near the beginning of "Universe" in which Hugh
and his companion, lost in a strange part of the ship, sight a "farmer":

   "Hey! Shipmate! Where are we?"
       The peasant looked them over slowly, then directed them in reluctant
   monosyllables to the main passageway which would lead them back to their
   own village.
       A brisk walk of a mile and a half down a wide tunnel moderately crowded
   with traffic-travelers, porters, an occasional pushcart, a dignified scientist
   swinging in a litter borne by four husky orderlies and preceded by his master-
   at-arms to clear the common crew out of the way – a mile and a half of this
   brought them to the common of their own village, a spacious compartment
   three decks high and perhaps ten times as wide. (12–13)

One thinks of Lucian, or of Rabelais' narrator climbing down into Pantagruel's
throat and chatting with the peasant he finds there planting cabbage; and it
ought to be said, in Heinlein's defense, that the purely descriptive intensity of
Aldiss' pages should be considered a late phenomenon stylistically, one which

4 Brian Aldiss' *Hothuse* (London, 1962) was published in the US as *The Long Afternoon of Earth*.

reflects the breakdown of plot and the failure of some genuinely narrative gesture, subverting the classical storytelling function of novels into an illicit poetic one which substitutes objects and atmosphere for events and actions. On the other hand, it is true that what characterizes a writer like Aldiss – and in the largest sense the writer of the "new novel" generally – is precisely that he writes *after* the "old novel" and presupposes the latter's existence. In an Hegelian sense one can say that such "poetic" writing includes the older narrative within itself as it were canceled and raised up into a new type of structure.

Yet the point I want to make is that the Aldiss material determines generic expectations in a way in which the Heinlein episode does not. The latter is merely one more event among others, whereas Aldiss' pages programme the reader for a particular type of reading, for the physiological or Bachelardian exploration, through style, of the properties of a peculiar and fascinating world. That such phenomenological attention is for the moment primary may be judged by our distance from Complain, the main character, who in this first section of the book may be said to serve as a mere pretext for our perceptions of this strange new space, and in fact to amount, with his unaccountable longings and rages, to little other than one more curious object within it, which we observe in ethnological dispassion from the outside. Indeed, the shifting in our distance from the characters, the transformations of the very categories through which we perceive characters, are among the most important indices of what we have called generic expectation. This concept may now perhaps be more clearly illustrated if we note that the opening pages of *Starship* (roughly to the point where Complain is drawn into Marapper's plot to explore the ship) project a type of narrative or genre which is not subsequently executed. *Hothouse*, indeed, provides a very useful comparison in this context, for it may be seen as a book-length fulfillment of the kind of generic expectation aroused in this first section of *Starship*. *Hothouse* is precisely, from start to finish, a Bachelardian narrative of the type which *Starship* ceases to be after Complain leaves his tribe, and is for this reason a more homogeneous product than *Starship*, more prodigious in its stylistic invention, but by the same token more monotonous and less interesting formally.

For the predominant formal characteristic of *Starship* is the way in which each new section projects a different kind of novel or narrative, a fresh generic expectation broken off unfulfilled and replaced in its turn by a new and seemingly unrelated one. Such divisions are of course approximative and must be mapped out by each reader according to his own responses. My own feeling is that with the onset of Marapper's plot, the novel is transformed into a kind of *adventure story* of the hostile-territory or jungle-exploration type, in which the hero and his companions, in their search for the ship's control room, begin to grapple with geographical obstacles, hostile tribes, alien beings and internal dissension. In this section, lasting for some twenty pages, the reader's attention is focused on the success or failure of the expedition, and on the problems of its organization and leadership.

With the discovery, in the middle of the night, of the immense Swimming Pool – a sight as astounding, for the travelers, as the Europeans' first glimpse of Lake Victoria and the source of the Nile – our interest again shifts subtly, returning to the structure of the ship itself, with its numbered decks through which the men slowly make their way. The questions and expectations now aroused seem once more to be of a *cognitive* type, and suggest that the mere certainty of being in a spaceship does not begin to solve all the problems we may have about it, and in particular does not explain why it is that the ship, thus mysteriously abandoned to its destiny, continues to *run* (for example, its generators still produce electricity for the lighting system).

But the result of this new kind of attention to the physical environment is yet another shift in tone or narrative convention. For the unexpected appearance of hitherto unknown beings – the Giants and the army of intelligent mind-probing rats – seems to plunge us for the moment into a storyline of almost supernatural cast. With the rats in particular we feel ourselves dangerously close to the transition from SF to fairy tale or fantasy literature in general, amid visions of the *Nutcracker* or even the comic-book variety. (This new shift, incidentally, is proof of the immense gulf which separates SF from fantasy and which might therefore also be described in terms of generic expectations.)

With the entry of the explorers into the higher civilization of the Forwards area, Marapper's plot proves a failure, and once again a new generic expectation replaces the earlier one: with the enlargement of the focus, we find, ourselves in the midst of a collective-catastrophe novel, for now we have a beleaguered society struggling for its life against real and imagined enemies: the Outsiders, the Giants, the rats and the lower barbarians of the Deadways. Once again the generic shift is signalled by a change in our distance from Complain, who from a mere team member is promoted to romantic hero through his love affair with Vyann, one of the political leaders of the Forwards state. Our new proximity to and identification with Complain is reinforced by his discovery that the chieftain of the barbarian guerrilla force is none other than his long-missing brother (a discovery which perhaps sets in motion minor generic expectations of its own, recalling last-minute denouements of the Hellenistic story *à la* Heliodorus, or family reunions in orphan or foundling plots, as in *Tom Jones* or *Cymbeline*).

At length, in the apocalyptic chaos with which the novel ends, the fires and mêlées, the invasion of the rats, the breakdown of the electrical system and impending destruction of the ship itself, we reach the twist ending already mentioned. Here the supernatural elements are, as it were, reabsorbed into the SF (one is tempted to say, the realistic) plot structure, for we discover that the Giants and Outsiders actually exist and can be rationally explained. The mechanism of this final generic transformation is a physical enlargement of the context in which the action is taking place: for the first time the inner environment of the ship ceases to be the outer limit of our experience. The ship acquires an outer surface, and a position in outer space; what has hitherto been a complete world in its own right is now retransformed into an immense vessel floating within an even larger system of stable and external coordinates. At the same time, the very function of the ship is altered, for with the momentous final discovery, the endless, aimless journey through space proves to have been an illusion, and the inhabitants discover themselves to be in orbit around the earth. It is an orbit that has been maintained for generations, so that the discovery returns upon the past to transform it as well and to turn the "tragic" history of the ship into a sort of grisly masquerade. So at length we learn that the main characters in the story, the characters with whom we have identified, are mutants administered "for their own good" by a scientific commission from Earth, a commission whose representatives the ship-dwellers have instinctively identified as Giants or Outsiders.

Thus in its final avatar, *Starship* is transformed, from a pseudo-cosmological adventure story of explorations within the strange world of the ship, to a *political fable* of man's manipulation of his fellow man. This ultimate genre to which the book is shown to belong leads our attention not into the immensities of interstellar space, but rather back to the human intentions underlying the ghastly paternalism which was responsible for the incarceration within the ship, over so many generations, of the descendants of the original crew. If my reading is correct, the twist ending involved here is not simply the solution to a puzzle confronted unsuccessfully since the opening pages of the book; rather, the puzzle at the heart of the work is only now for the first time revealed, by being unwittingly solved.

This revelation has the effect of discrediting all our previous modes of reading, or generic expectations. Over and above the story of the characters and of the fate of the ship, one is tempted to posit the existence of a second plot or narrative line in that very different set of purely formal events which govern our reading: our groping and tentative efforts to identify, during the course of the reading, the type of book being read, and our ultimate solution to the puzzle with the discovery of its social or political character.

Such a description will not surprise anyone familiar with the aesthetics of modernism and aware of the degree to which modern writers in general have taken the artistic process itself as their "subject matter", assigning themselves the task of foregrounding, not the objects perceived, not the *content* of the work, but rather the very act of aesthetic reception and perception. This is achieved on the whole by tampering with the perceptual apparatus or the frame, and the notion of generic discontinuity suggests that in *Starship* the basic storyline may be varied as much by shifts in our receptive stance as by internal modifications of the content. One recalls the well-known Kuleshov experiment, in the early days of Soviet film, in which a single shot of an actor's face seemed to express now joy, now irony, now hunger, now sadness, depending on the context developed by the shots with which it was juxtaposed. Indeed the very notion of generic expectation requires us to distinguish between the sense of the individual sentences and our assessment of the whole to which we assign them as parts and which dictates our interpretation of them (a process often described as the "hermeneutic circle"). Aldiss' *Starship* confirms such a notion by showing the results of a systematic variation and subversion of narrative context; and that such a structure is not merely an aesthetic freak, but stands rather in the mainstream of literary experimentation, may be demonstrated by a comparison with the structure of the French *nouveau roman*, and particularly with the stylistic and compositional devices of Alain Robbe-Grillet, whose work Aldiss has himself ranged in the SF category, speaking of *"L'Année dernière à Marienbad,* where the gilded hotel with its endless corridors – *énormes, sompleux, baroques, lugubres* – stands more vividly as a symbol of isolation from the currents of life than any spaceship, simply by virtue of being more dreadfully accessible to our imaginations."[5]

What Aldiss does not say is that such symbols are the end-product of a whole artistic method or procedure: in the narrative of Robbe-Grillet, for instance, our reading of the words is sapped at the very base: as the narrative eye crawls slowly along the contours of the objects so minutely described, we begin to feel a profound uncertainty as to the very possibilities of physical description through language.[6] Indeed, what happens is that the words remain the same while their referents shift without warning: the bare names of the objects are insufficient to convey the unique identity of a single time and place, and the reader is constantly forced to reevaluate the coordinates of the table, the rocking chair, the eraser in question, just as in Resnais' film the same events appear to take place over and over again, but at different times and in different settings. Such effects are quite different from what happens in dream or surrealist literature, where it is the object itself that is transformed before our eyes, and where the power of language to register the most grotesque metamorphoses is reaffirmed: thus in Ovid, language is called upon to express the well-nigh inexpressible and to articulate in all their fullness things that we doubt our real eyes could ever see. In the *nouveau roman,* on the contrary, and in those SF works related to it (for example, the hallucinatory scenes in such Philip K. Dick novels as *The Three Stigmata of Palmer Eldritch*), it is the expressive capacity of words and names that is called into question and subverted, and this is not from within but from without, by imperceptible but momentous shifts in the context of the description.

Yet there is a way in which the characteristic material of SF enjoys a privileged relationship with such effects, which seem to be common to modernist

---

5 Harry Harrison and Brian W. Aldiss, eds, *Best SF: 1969* (New York, 1970), p. 217.

6 I have discussed this phenomenon from a different point of view in "Seriality in Modern Literature", *Bucknell Review*, Spring 1970.

literature in general. One would like to avoid, in this connection, a replay of the well-worn and tiresome controversies over literary realism. Perhaps it would be enough to suggest that, in so-called realistic works, the reference to some shared or "real" objective outside world serves the basic structural function of unifying the work from without. Whatever the heterogeneity of its materials, the unity of the "realistic" work is thus assured *a priori* by the unity of its referent. It follows then that when, as in SF, such a referent is abandoned, the fundamental formal problem posed by plot construction will be that of finding some new principle of unity. Of course, one way in which this can be achieved is by taking over some ready-made formal unity existing in the tradition itself, and this seems to be the path taken by so-called mythical SF, which finds a spurious comfort in the predetermined unity of the myth or legend which serves it as an organizational device. (This procedure goes back, of course, to Joyce's *Ulysses*, but I am tempted to claim that the incomparable greatness of this literary predecessor comes from its *incomplete* use of myth: Joyce lets us see that the "myth" is nothing but an organizational device, and his subject is not some fictive unity of experience which the myth is supposed to guarantee, but rather that fragmentation of life in the modern world which called for such reunification in the first place.)

Where the mythological solution is eschewed, there remains available to SF another organizational procedure which I will call *collage*: the bringing into precarious coexistence of elements drawn from very different sources and contexts, elements which derive for the most part from older literary models and which amount to broken fragments of the outworn older genres or of the newer productions of the media (for example, comic strips). At its worst, collage results in a kind of desperate pasting together of whatever lies to hand; at its best, however, it operates a kind of foregrounding of the older generic models themselves, a kind of estrangement effect practiced on our own generic receptivity. Something like this is what I have sought to describe in my reading of *Starship.*

But the arbitrariness of collage as a form has the further result of intensifying, and indeed transforming, the structural function of the author himself, who is now felt to be the supreme source and origin of whatever unity can be maintained in the work. The reader then submits to the authority of the author in a rather different way than in the conventions of realistic narrative: it is, if you will, the difference between asking to be manipulated and agreeing to pretend that no human agency is present in the first place.

It would be possible to show, I think (and here the works of Philip K. Dick would serve as the principal exhibits), that the thematic obsession, in SF, with manipulation as social phenomenon and nightmare all in one may be understood as a projection of the form of SF into its content. This is not to say that the theme of manipulation is not, given the kind of world we live in, eminently self-explanatory in terms of its own urgency, but only that there is a kind of privileged relationship, a pre-established harmony, between this theme and the literary structures which characterize SF. To restrict our generalization for the moment to *Starship* itself, it seems to me no accident that the fundamental social issue in a book in which the author toys with the reader, constantly shifting direction, baffling the latter's expectations, issuing false generic clues, and in general using his official plot as a pretext for the manipulation of the reader's reactions, should be the problem of the manipulation of man by other men. And with this we touch upon the point at which form and content, in *Starship*, become one, and at which the fundamental identity between the narrative structure previously analyzed and the political problem raised by the book's ending, stands revealed.

That Brian Aldiss is well aware of the ultimate political character of his novel is evident, not only from his Preface, but also from occasional reflections throughout the book. But it seems clear from his remarks that he understands his fable – which illustrates the disastrous effects of larger-scale social decisions upon individual life – to have an anti-bureaucratic and anti-socialist thrust (bureaucracy being the way socialism is conceived by those it threatens). "Nothing", he tells us, "but the full flowering of a technological age, such as the Twenty-fourth Century knew, could have launched this miraculous ship; yet the miracle was sterile, cruel. Only a technological age could condemn unborn generations to exist in it, as if man were mere protoplasm, without emotion or aspiration" (162). And his Preface underscores the point even further: "An idea, which is man-conceived, unlike most of the myriad effects which comprise our universe, is seldom balanced … The idea, as ideas will, had gone wrong and gobbled up their real lives" (9). We glimpse here the familiar outlines of that most influential of all counterrevolutionary positions, first and most fully worked out by Edmund Burke in his *Reflections on the French Revolution*, for which human reason, in its fundamental imperfection, is incapable of substituting itself and its own powers for the organic, natural growth of community and tradition. Such an ideology finds confirmation in the revolutionary Terror (itself generally, it should be added, a response of the revolution to external and internal threats), which thus appears as the humiliation of man's revolutionary hubris, of his presumption at usurping the place of nature and traditional authority.

But this reading by Aldiss of his own fable is not necessarily the only interpretation open to us. I would myself associate it rather with a whole group of SF narratives which explicitly or implicitly raise a political and social issue of a quite different kind, which may be characterized as belonging to the ethical problems of utopia, or to the political dilemmas of a future in which politics has once again become ethics. This issue turns essentially on the so-called Prime Directive, in other words, on the right of advanced civilizations or cultures to intervene into the lower forms of social life with which they come into contact. (The qualifications of higher and lower, or advanced and underdeveloped, are here clearly to be understood in a historical rather than a purely qualitative sense.) This problem has of course been a thematic concern of SF since its inception: witness H.G. Wells' *War of the Worlds*, patently a guilt fantasy on the part of Victorian man who wonders whether the brutality with which he has used the colonial peoples (the extinction of the Tasmanians) may not be visited on him by some more advanced race intent, in its turn, on his destruction. In our time, however, such a theme tends to be reformulated in positive terms that lend it a new originality. That the destruction of less advanced societies is wrong and inhuman is no longer, surely, a matter for intelligent debate. What is at issue is the degree to which even benign and well-intentioned intervention of higher into lower cultures may not be ultimately destructive in its results. Although the conventions of SF may dramatize this issue in terms of galactic encounters, the concern clearly has a very terrestrial source in the relations between industrialized and so-called underdeveloped societies of our own planet.

During the 1950s and early 1960s, a safe liberal anti-colonialism, analogous to the US condemnation of the decaying British and French colonial empires, seems to have been quite fashionable in American SF. In one whole wing of it (*Star Trek*), interstellar law prohibiting the establishment of colonies on planets already inhabited by an intelligent species became an accepted convention. However, the full implications of this theme, with a few exceptions such as Ursula Le Guin's *The Left Hand of Darkness* (1969), were explored only in the SF written within socialist horizons, in particular in the works of Stanislav Lem and in the Strugatsky Brothers' *Hard to Be a God* (1964). In Western SF, this theme is present mainly as a cliché or as an unconscious preoccupation, and manifests itself in peculiarly formalized ways. So I would suggest that visions of extragalactic intervention, such as Arthur C. Clarke's *Childhood's End*, belong in this category, as well as many of the intricate paradoxes of time travel, where the hero's unexpected appearance in the distant past arouses the fear that he may alter the course of history in such a way as to prevent himself from being born in the first place. In all these traits of Western SF one detects the presence, it seems to me, of a virtual *repression* of the ethico-political motif in question, although it should be made clear that it is a repression which SF shares with most cultural and artistic activities pursued in the West. Indeed, such unconscious concealment of the underlying socio-economic or material bases of life, with a concomitant concentration on purely spiritual activities, is responsible for the ways of thinking which classical Marxist theory designates as *idealism*. It amounts to a refusal to connect existential or personal experience, the experience of our individual private life, with the system and suprapersonal organization of monopoly capitalism as an all-pervasive whole.

In the present instance – to restrict ourselves to that alone – it is our wilful ignorance of the inherent structural relationship between that economic system and the neocolonialistic exploitation of the Third World which prevents any realistic view or concept of the correct relationship between two distinct national or social groupings. Thus we tend to think of the relations between countries in ethical terms, in terms of cruelty or philanthrophy, with the result that Western business investments come to appear to us as the bearers of progress and "development" in backward areas. The real questions – whether "progress" is desirable and if so which kind of progress, whether a country has the right to opt out of the international circuit, whether a more advanced country has the right to intervene, even benignly, in the historical evolution of a less advanced country; in sum, the general relationship between indigenous culture and industrialization – are historical and political in character. For our literature to be able to raise them, it would be necessary to ask ourselves a good many more probing and difficult questions about our own system than we are presently willing to do. I should add that this comparison between the formal capacities of Western and Soviet SF is not intended to imply that the Soviet Union has in any sense solved the above problems, but merely that for the Soviet Union such problems have arisen in an explicit and fully conscious, indeed agonizing fashion, and that it is from the experience of such dilemmas and contradictions that its best literature is being fashioned.[7]

The thematic interest of *Starship* lies precisely in the approach of such a dilemma to the threshold of consciousness, in the way in which the theme of intercultural influence or manipulation is raised almost to explicit thematization. In this sense, it makes little difference whether the reader chooses to take Aldiss' own rather reactionary political interjections at face value, or to substitute for them the historical interpretation suggested above; the crucial fact remains that the political reemerges in the closing pages of the book. The structural inability of such material to stay buried, its irrepressible tendency to reveal itself in its most fundamental historical being, generically transforms the novel into that political fable which was latent in it all along, without our knowing it. So it is that *en route* to space and to galactic escapism, we find ourselves locked in the force field of very earthly political realities.

1973

---

7 Written in 1973.

3

World Reduction in Le Guin

Huddled forms wrapped in furs, packed snow and sweaty faces, torches by day, a ceremonial trowel and a cornerstone swung into place ... Such is our entry into the other world of *The Left Hand of Darkness* (*LHD*), a world which, like all invented ones, awakens irresistible reminiscences of this the real one – here less Eisenstein's Muscovy, perhaps, than some Eskimo High Middle Ages. Yet this surface exoticism conceals a series of what may be called "generic discontinuities",[1] and the novel can be shown to be constructed from a heterogeneous group of narrative modes artfully superimposed and inter-twined, thereby constituting a virtual anthology of narrative strands of different kinds. So we find here intermingled: the travel narrative (with anthro-pological data), the pastiche of myth, the political novel (in the restricted sense of the drama of court intrigue), straight SF (the Hainish colonization, the spaceship in orbit around Gethen's sun), Orwellian dystopia (the imprison-ment on the Voluntary Farm and Resettlement Agency), adventure story (the flight across the glacier), and finally even, perhaps, something like a multiracial love story (the drama of communication between the two cultures and species).

Such structural discontinuities, while accounting for the effectiveness of *LHD* by comparison with books that can do only one or two of these things, at once raise the basic question of the novel's ultimate unity. In what follows, I want to make a case for a thematic coherence which has little enough to do with plot as such, but which would seem to shed some light on the process of world construction in fictional narratives in general. Thematically, we may distinguish four different types of material in the novel, the most striking and obvious being that of the hermaphroditic sexuality of the inhabitants of Gethen. The "official" message of the book, however, would seem to be rather different than this, involving a social and historical meditation on the in-stitutions of Karhide and the capacity of that or any other society to mount full-scale organized warfare. After this, we would surely want to mention the

---

1 See the preceding essay.

peculiar ecology, which, along with the way of life it imposes, makes of *LHD* something like an anti-*Dune*; and, finally, the myths and religious practices of the planet, which give the book its title.

The question is now whether we can find something that all these themes have in common, or better still, whether we can isolate some essential structural homology between them. To begin with the climate of Gethen (known to the Ekumen as Winter), the first Investigator supplies an initial interpretation of it in terms of the resistance of this ice-age environment to human life:

> The weather of Winter is so relentless, so near the limit of tolerability even to them with all their cold-adaptations, that perhaps they use up their fighting spirit fighting the cold. The marginal peoples, the races that just get by, are rarely the warriors. And in the end, the dominant factor in Gethenian life is not sex or any other human being: it is their environment, their cold world. Here man has a crueler enemy even than himself.[2]

However, this is not the only connotation that extreme cold may have; the motif may have some other, deeper, disguised symbolic meaning that can perhaps best be illustrated by the related symbolism of the tropics in recent SF, particularly in the novels of J.G. Ballard. Heat is here conveyed as a kind of dissolution of the body into the outside world, a loss of that clean separation from clothes and external objects that gives you your autonomy and allows you to move about freely, a sense of increasing contamination and stickiness in the contact between your physical organism and the surfaces around it, the wet air in which it bathes, the fronds that slap against it. So it is that the jungle itself, with its non- or anti-Wordsworthian nature, is felt to be some immense and alien organism into which our bodies run the risk of being absorbed, the most alarming expression of this anxiety in SF being perhaps that terrible scene in Robert Silverberg's *Downward to Earth* in which the protagonist discovers a human couple who have become hosts to some unknown parasitic larvae that stir inside their still-living torsos like monstrous foetuses.

This loss of physical autonomy – dramatized by the total environment of the jungle into which the European dissolves – is then understood as a figure for the loss of psychic autonomy, of which the utter demoralization, the colonial whisky-drinking and general deterioration of the tropical hero is the canonical paradigm in literature. (Even more relevant to the present study is the relationship between extreme heat and sexual anxiety – a theme particularly visible in the non-SF treatments of similar material by Catholic novelists like Graham Greene and François Mauriac, for whom the identification of

---

2 Ursula Le Guin's *Left Hand of Darkness* (New York, 1976 [1969]), p. 96; all further references to this and other editions given within the text.

heat and adolescent sexual torment provides ample motivation for the subsequent desexualization experienced by the main characters.)

Ballard's work is suggestive in the way in which he translates both physical
and moral dissolution into the great ideological myth of entropy, in which the
historic collapse of the British Empire is projected outwards into some
immense cosmic deceleration of the universe itself as well as of its molecular building blocks.[3] This kind of ideological message makes it hard to escape
the feeling that the heat symbolism in question here is a peculiarly Western
and ethnocentric one. Witness, if proof be needed, Vonnegut's *Cat's Cradle*,
where the systematic displacement of the action from upstate New York to
the Caribbean, from dehumanized American scientists to the joyous and skeptical religious practices of Bokononism, suggests a scarcely disguised
meditation on the relationship between American power and the Third World,
between repression and scientific knowledge in the capitalist world, and a nostalgic and primitivistic evocation of the more genuine human possibilities
available in an older and simpler culture. The preoccupation with heat, the
fear of sweating as of some dissolution of our very being, would then be tan-
tamount to an unconscious anxiety about tropical field-labor (an analogous
cultural symbolism can be found in the historical echo of Northern factory
work in the blue jeans and work shirts of our own affluent society). The nightmare of the tropics thus expresses a disguised terror at the inconceivable and
unformulable threat posed by the masses of the Third World to our own prosperity and privilege, and suggests a new and unexpected framework in which
to interpret the icy climate of Le Guin's Gethen.

In such a reading the cold weather of the planet Winter must be understood, first and foremost, not so much as a rude environment, inhospitable
to human life, as rather a symbolic affirmation of the autonomy of the
organism, and a fantasy realization of some virtually total disengagement of
the body from its environment or eco-system. Cold isolates, and the cold of
Gethen is what brings home to the characters (and the reader) their physical
detachment, their freestanding isolation as separate individuals, goose-flesh
transforming the skin itself into some outer envelope, the sub-zero temper-
atures of the planet forcing the organism back on its own inner resources
and making of each a kind of self-sufficient blast furnace. Gethen thus stands
as an attempt to imagine an experimental landscape in which our being-in-
the-world is simplified to the extreme, and in which our sensory links with
the multiple and shifting perceptual fields around us are abstracted so radically as to vouchsafe, perhaps, some new glimpse as to the ultimate nature
of human reality.

---

3 Entropy is of course a very characteristic late nineteenth-century bourgeois myth (e.g.,
Henry Adams, Wells, Zola). See, for further justification of this type of interpretation, my
"In Retrospect", *Science-Fiction Studies*, 1 (1974), pp. 272–276.

It seems to me important to insist on this cognitive and experimental function of the narrative in order to distinguish it from other, more nightmarish representations of the sealing off of consciousness from the external world (as, for example, in the "half-life" of the dead in Philip K. Dick's *Ubik*). One of the most significant potentialities of SF as a form is precisely this capacity to provide something like an experimental variation on our own empirical universe; and Le Guin has herself described her invention of Gethenian sexuality along the lines of just such a "thought experiment" in the tradition of the great physicists: "Einstein shoots a light-ray through a moving elevator; Schrödinger puts a cat in a box. There is no elevator, no cat, no box. The experiment is performed, the question is asked, in the mind."[4] Only one would like to recall that "high literature" once also affirmed such aims. As antiquated as Zola's notions of heredity and as naïve as his fascination with Claude Bernard's account of experimental research may have been, the naturalist concept of the experimental novel amounted, on the eve of the emergence of modernism, to just such a reassertion of literature's cognitive function. That this assertion no longer seems believable merely suggests that our own particular environment – the total system of late monopoly capital and of the consumer society – feels so massively in place and its reification so overwhelming and impenetrable, that the serious artist is no longer free to tinker with it or to project experimental variations.[5] The historical opportunities of SF as a literary form are intimately related to this paralysis of so-called high literature. The officially "non-serious" or pulp character of SF is an indispensable feature in its capacity to relax that tyrannical "reality principle" which functions as a crippling censorship over high art, and to allow the "para-literary" form thereby to inherit the vocation of giving us alternate versions of a world that has elsewhere seemed to resist even imagined change. (This account of the transfer of one of the most vital traditional functions of literature to SF would seem to be confirmed by the increasing efforts of present-day "art literature" – for example, Thomas Pynchon – to reincorporate those formal capacities back into the literary novel.)

The principal techniques of such narrative experimentation – of the systematic variation, by SF, of the empirical and historical world around us – have been most conveniently codified under the twin headings of *analogy* and *extrapolation*.[6] The reading we have proposed of Le Guin's experimental ecology suggests, however, the existence of yet a third and quite distinct

---

4 Ursula K. Le Guin, "Is Gender Necessary?", in *Aurora: Beyond Equality*, ed. Susan J. Anderson and Vonda McIntyre (Greenwich, CT, 1976).

5 I have tried to argue an analogous reduction of possibilities for the historical novel in *Marxism and Form* (Princeton, 1971), pp. 248–252.

6 See Darko Suvin, "On the Poetics of the Science Fiction Genre", *College English*, No. 34 (1972), pp. 372–382, and "Science Fiction and the Genological Jungle", *Genre*, 6 (1973), pp. 251–273.

technique of variation which it will be the task of the remainder of this analysis to describe. It would certainly be possible to see the Gethenian environment as extrapolating one of our own Earth seasons, in an extrapolation developed according to its own inner logic and pushed to its ultimate conclusions – as, for example, when Pohl and Kornbluth project out onto a planetary scale, in *The Space Merchants*, huckstering trends already becoming visible in the nascent consumer society of 1952; or when Brunner, in *The Sheep Look Up*, catastrophically speeds up the environmental pollution already under way. Yet this strikes me as being the least interesting thing about Le Guin's experiment, which is based on a principle of systematic exclusion, a kind of surgical excision of empirical reality, something like a process of ontological attenuation in which the sheer teeming multiplicity of what exists, of what we call reality, is deliberately thinned and weeded out through an operation of radical abstraction and simplification which I will henceforth term *world reduction*. And once we grasp the nature of this technique, its effects in the other thematic areas of the novel become inescapable, as for instance in the conspicuous absence of other animal species on Gethen. The omission of a whole gridwork of evolutionary phyla can, of course, be accounted for by the hypothesis that the colonization of Gethen, and the anomalous sexuality of its inhabitants, were the result of some forgotten biological experiment by the original Hainish civilization, but it does not make that lack any less disquieting: "There are no communal insects on Winter. Gethenians do not share their earth as Terrans do with those older societies, those innumerable cities of little sexless workers possessing no instinct but that of obedience to the group, the whole" (178).

But it is in Le Guin's later novel, *The Dispossessed* (*TD*, 1974) that this situation is pushed to its ultimate consequences, providing the spectacle of a planet (Anarres) in which human life is virtually without biological partners:

> It's a queer situation, biologically speaking. We Anarresti are unnaturally isolated. On the old World there are eighteen phyla of land animal; there are classes, like the insects, that have so many species they've never been able to count them, and some of these species have populations of billions. Think of it: everywhere you looked animals, other creatures, sharing the earth and air with you. You'd feel so much more a *part*. (186)

Hence Shevek's astonishment, when, on his arrival in Urras, he is observed by a face "not like any human face … as long as his arm, and ghastly white. Breath jetted in vapor from what must be nostrils, and terrible, unmistakable, there was an eye" (22). Yet the absence, from the Anarres of *TD*, of large animals such as the donkey which here startles Shevek, is the negative obverse of a far more positive omission, namely that of the Darwinian life-cycle itself, with its predators and victims alike: it is the sign that human beings have surmounted historical determinism, and have been left alone with themselves to invent their own destinies. In *TD*, then, the principle of world reduction has become an instrument in the conscious elaboration of a utopia. On Gethen, however, its effects remain more tragic, and the Hainish experiment has resulted in the unwitting evolution of test-tube subjects rather than in some great and self-conscious social laboratory of revolution and collective self-determination:

> Your race is appallingly alone in its world. No other mammalian species. No other ambisexual species. No animal intelligent enough even to domesticate as pets. It must color your thinking, this uniqueness ... to be so solitary, in so hostile a world: it must affect your entire outlook. (233)

Still, the deeper import of such details, and of the constructional principle at work in them, will become clear only after we observe similar patterns in other thematic areas of the novel, as, for instance, in Gethenian religion. In keeping with the book's antithetical composition, to the two principal national units, Karhide and Orgoreyn, correspond two appropriately antithetical religious cults: the Orgota one of Meshe being something like a heresy or offshoot of the original Karhidish Handdara in much the same way that Christianity was the issue of Judaism. Meshe's religion of total knowledge reflects the mystical experience from which it sprang and in which all of time and history became blindingly co-present: the emphasis on knowing, however, suggests a positivistic bias which is as appropriate to the commercial society of Orgoreyn, one would think, as was Protestantism to the nascent capitalism of Western Europe. It is, however, the other religion, that of Karhide, which is most relevant to our present argument: the Handdara is, in antithesis to the later sect, precisely a mystique of darkness, a cult of non-knowledge parallel to the drastic reductionism of the Gethenian climate. The aim of its spiritual practice is to strip the mind of its non-essentials and to reduce it to some quintessentially simplified function:

> The Handdara discipline of Presence ... is a kind of trance – the Handdarate, given to negatives, call it an untrance – involving self-loss (self-augmentation?) through extreme sensual receptiveness and awareness. Though the technique is the exact opposite of most techniques of mysticism it probably is a mystical discipline, tending towards the experience of Immanence. (57–58)

Thus the fundamental purpose of the ritual practice of the foretelling – dramatized in one of the most remarkable chapters of the novel – is, by answering answerable questions about the future, "to exhibit the perfect uselessness of knowing the answer to the wrong question", and indeed, ultimately, of the activity of asking questions in general. What the real meaning of these wrong or unanswerable questions may be, we will try to say later on; but this mystical valorization of ignorance is certainly quite different from the brash commercial curiosity with which the Envoy is so pleasantly surprised on his arrival in Orgoreyn.

Now we must test our hypothesis about the basic constructional principle of *LHD* against that picture of an ambisexual species – indeed, an ambisexual society – which is its most striking and original feature. The obvious defamiliarization with which such a picture confronts the *lecteur moyen sensuel* is not exactly that of the permissive and countercultural tradition of male SF writing, as in Farmer or Sturgeon. Rather than a stand in favor of a wider tolerance for all kinds of sexual behaviour, it seems more appropriate to insist (as does Le Guin herself elsewhere) on the feminist dimension of her novel, and on its demystification of the sex roles themselves. The basic point about Gethenian sexuality is that the sex role does not color everything else in life, as is the case with us, but is rather contained and defused, reduced to that brief period of the monthly cycle when, as with our animal species, the Gethenians are in "heat" or "kemmer". So the first Investigator sent by the Ekumen underscores this basic "estrangement effect" of Gethen on "normally" sexed beings:

> The First Mobile, if one is sent, must be warned that unless he is very self-assured, or senile, his pride will suffer. A man wants his virility regarded, a woman wants her femininity appreciated, however indirect and subtle the indications of regard and appreciation. On Winter they will not exist. One is respected and judged only as a human being. It is an appalling experience. (95)

That there are difficulties in such a representation (for example, the unavoidable designation of gender by English pronouns), the author is frank to admit in the article referred to.[7] Still, the reader's failures are not all her own, and the inveterate tendency of students to describe the Gethenians as "sexless" says something about the limits imposed by stereotypes of gender on their own imaginations. Far from eliminating sex, indeed, Gethenian biology has the result of eliminating sexual repression:

> Being so strictly defined and limited by nature, the sexual urge of Gethenians is really not much interfered with by society: there is less coding, channeling, and repressing of sex than in any bisexual society I know of. Abstinence is entirely voluntary; indulgence is entirely acceptable. Sexual fear and sexual frustration are both extremely rare. (177)

---

7 See note 4. Some problems Le Guin does not notice – e.g., synchronization of kemmer and continuity of sex roles between love partners – are pointed out by the relentlessly logical Stanislaw Lem in "Lost Opportunities", *SF Commentary*, No. 24, pp. 22–24.

The author was in fact most careful not merely to say that these people are not eunuchs, but also – in a particularly terrifying episode, that of the penal farm with its anti-kemmer drugs – to show by contrast what eunuchs in this society would look like.

Indeed, the vision of public kemmer-houses (along with the sexual license of utopia in *TD*) ought to earn the enthusiasm of the most hard-core Fourierist or sexual libertarian. If it does not quite do that, it is because there is another, rather different sense in which my students were not wrong to react as they did and in which we meet, once again, the phenomenon we have called world reduction. For if Le Guin's Gethen does not do away with sex, it may be suggested that it does away with everything that is problematical about it. Essentially, Gethenian physiology solves the problem of sex, and that is surely something no human being of our type has ever been able to do owing largely to the non-biological nature of human desire as opposed to "natural" or instinctual animal need. Desire is permanently scandalous precisely because it admits of no "solution" – promiscuity, repression, or the couple all being equally intolerable. Only a makeup of the Gethenian type, with its limitation of desire to a few days of the monthly cycle, could possibly curb the problem. Such a makeup suggests that sexual desire is something that can be completely removed from other human activities, allowing us to see them in some more fundamental, unmixed fashion. Here again, then, in the construction of this particular projection of desire which is Gethenian ambisexuality we find a process at work which is structurally analogous to that operation of world reduction or ontological attenuation we have described above: the experimental production of an imaginary situation by excision of the real, by a radical suppression of features of human sexuality which cannot but carry a powerful fantasy-investment in its own right. The dream of some scarcely imaginable freedom from sex, indeed, is a very ancient human fantasy, almost as powerful in its own way as the outright sexual wish-fulfillments themselves. What its more general symbolic meaning in *LHD* might be, we can only discover by grasping its relationship to that other major theme of the novel which is the nature of Gethenian social systems, and in particular, their respective capacities to wage war.

It would seem on first glance that the parallelism here is obvious and that, on this particular level, the object of what we have been calling world re-duction can only be institutional warfare itself, which has not yet developed in Karhide's feudal system. Certainly Le Guin's work as a whole is strongly pacifistic, and her novella "The Word for World Is Forest" is (along with Aldiss' *Dark Light-Years*) one of the major SF denunciations of the American geno-cide in Vietnam. Yet it remains an ethical, rather than a socio-economic, vision of imperialism, and its last line extends the guilt of violence to even that war of national liberation of which it has just shown the triumph: "'Maybe after I die people will be as they were before I was born, and before you came. But I do not think so.'" Yet if there is no righteous violence, then the long afternoon and twilight of Earth will turn out to be just that onerous dystopia SF writers have always expected it would.

This properly liberal, rather than radical, position in Le Guin seems to be underscored by her predilection for quietistic heroes and her valorization of an anti-political, anti-activist stance, whether it be in the religion of Karhide, in the peaceable traditions of the "creechies", or in Shevek's own reflective temperament. What makes her position more ambiguous and more interesting, however, is that Le Guin's works reject the institutionalization of violence rather than violence itself: nothing is more shocking in *TD* than the scene in which Shevek is beaten into unconsciousness by a man who is irritated by the similarity between their names:

> "You're one of those little profiteers who goes to school to keep his hands clean," the man said. "I've always wanted to knock the shit out of one of you." "Don't call me profiteer!" Shevek said, but this wasn't a verbal battle. Shevet knocked him double. He got in several return blows, having long arms and more temper than his opponent expected: but he was outmatched. Several people paused to watch, saw that it was a fair fight but not an interesting one, and went on. They were neither offended nor attracted by simple violence. Shevek did not call for help, so it was nobody's business but his own. When he came to he was lying on his back on the dark ground between two tents. (50–51)

In other words, Utopia is not a place in which humanity is freed from violence, but rather one in which it is released from the multiple determinisms (economic, political, social) of history itself: in which it settles its accounts with its ancient collective fatalisms, precisely in order to be free to do whatever it wants with its interpersonal relationships – whether for violence, love, hate, sex or whatever. All of that is raw and strong, and goes farther towards authenticating Le Guin's vision – as a return to fundamentals rather than some beautification of existence   than any of the explanations of economic and social organization which *TD* provides.

What looks like conventional liberalism in Le Guin (and is of course still ideologically dubious to the very degree that it continues to "look like" liberalism) is in reality itself a use of the Jeffersonian and Thoreauvian tradition against important political features of that imperializing liberalism which is the dominant ideology of the United States today – as her one contemporary novel, *The Lathe of Heaven* (1971), makes plain. This is surely the meaning of the temperamental opposition between the Tao-like passivity of Orr and the obsession of Haber with apparently reforming and ameliorative projects of all kinds:

> The quality of the will to power is, precisely, growth. Achievement is its cancellation. To be, the will to power must increase with each fulfillment, making the fulfillment only a step to a further one. The vaster the power gained, the vaster

the appetite for more. As there was no visible limit to the power Haber wielded through Orr's dreams, so there was no end to his determination to improve the world. (128)

The pacifist bias of *LHD* is thus part of a more general refusal of the growth-oriented power dynamics of present-day American liberalism, even where the correlations it suggests between institutionalized warfare, centralization and psychic aggression may strike us as preoccupations of a characteristically liberal type.

I would suggest, however, that beneath this official theme of warfare, there are details scattered here and there throughout the novel which suggest the presence of some more fundamental attempt to reimagine history. What reader has not indeed been struck – without perhaps quite knowing why – by descriptions such as that of the opening cornerstone ceremony: "Masons below have set an electric winch going, and as the king mounts higher the keystone of the arch goes up past him in its sling, is raised, settled, and fitted almost soundlessly, great ton-weight block though it is, into the gap between the two piers, making them one, one thing, an arch" (4–5); or of the departure of the first spring caravan towards the fastnesses of the North: "twenty bulky, quiet-running, barge-like trucks on caterpillar treads, going single file down the deep streets of Erhenrang through the shadows of morning" (49)? Of course, the concept of *extrapolation* in SF means nothing if it does not designate just such details as these, in which heterogenous or contradictory elements of the empirical real world are juxtaposed and recombined into piquant montages. Here the premise is clearly that of a feudal or medieval culture that knows electricity and machine technology. However, the machines do not have the same results as in our own world: "The mechanical-industrial Age of Invention in Karhide is at least three thousand years old, and during those thirty centuries they have developed excellent and economical central-heating devices using steam, electricity, and other principles; but they do not install them in their houses" (28). What makes all this more complicated than the usual extrapolative projection is, it seems to me, the immense time span involved, and the great antiquity of Karhide's science and technology, which tends to emphasize not so much what happens when we thus combine or amalgamate different historical stages of our own empirical Earth history, but rather precisely *what does not happen*. That is, indeed, what is most significant about the example of Karhide: namely that *nothing* happens, an immemorial social order remains exactly as it was, and the introduction of electrical power fails – quite unaccountably and astonishingly to us – to make any impact whatsoever on the stability of a basically static, unhistorical society.

Now there is surely room for debate as to the role of science and technology in the evolution of the so-called West (that is, the capitalist countries of

Western Europe and North America). For Marxists, science developed as a result both of contradictions in production and of the quantifying thought-modes inherent in the emergent market system; while an anti-Marxist historiography stresses the fundamental role played by technology and inventions in what now becomes strategically known as the Industrial Revolution (rather than capitalism). Such a dispute would in any case be inconceivable were not technology and capitalism so inextricably intertwined in our own history. What Le Guin has done in her projection of Karhide is to sunder the two in peremptory and dramatic fashion:

> Along in those four millennia the electric engine was developed, radios and power looms and power vehicles and farm machinery and all the rest began to be used, and a Machine Age got going, gradually, without any industrial revolution, without any revolution at all. (98–99)

What is this to say but that Karhide is an attempt to imagine something like a West which would never have known capitalism? The existence of modern technology in the midst of an essentially feudal order is the sign of this imaginative operation as well as the gauge by which its success can be measured: the miraculous presence, among all those furs and feudal *shiftgrethor*, of this emblematically quiet, peacefully humming technology is the proof that in Karhide we have to do not with one more specimen of feudal SF, but rather precisely with an alternate world to our own, one in which – by what strange quirk of fate? – capitalism never happened.

It becomes difficult to escape the conclusion that this attempt to rethink Western history without capitalism is of a piece, structurally and in its general spirit, with the attempt to imagine human biology without desire which I have described above; for it is essentially the inner dynamic of the market system which introduces into the chronicle-like and seasonal, cyclical, tempo of pre-capitalist societies the fever and ferment of what we used to call progress. The underlying identification between sex as an intolerable, well-nigh gratuitous complication of existence, and capitalism as a disease of change and meaningless evolutionary momentum, is thus powerfully underscored by the very technique – that of world reduction – whose mission is the utopian exclusion of both phenomena.

Karhide is, of course, not a utopia, and *LHD* is not in that sense a genuinely utopian work. Indeed, it is now clear that the earlier novel served as something like a proving ground for techniques that are not consciously employed in the construction of a utopia until *TD*. It is in the latter novel that the device of world reduction becomes transformed into a socio-political hypothesis about the inseparability of utopia and scarcity. The Odonian colonization of barren Anarres offers thus the most thoroughgoing literary application of the technique, at the same time that it constitutes a powerful and timely rebuke to present-day attempts to parlay American abundance and consumer goods into some ultimate vision of the "great society."[8]

I would not want to suggest that all of the great historical utopias have been constructed around the imaginative operation I have called world reduction. It seems possible, indeed, that it is the massive commodity environment of late capitalism that has called up this particular literary and imaginative strategy, which would then amount to a political stance as well. So in William Morris' *News from Nowhere*, the hero – a nineteenth-century visitor to the future – is astonished to watch the lineaments of nature reappear beneath the fading inscription of the grim industrial metropolis, the old names on the river themselves transfigured from dreary slang into the evocation of meadow landscapes, the slopes and streams, so long stifled beneath the pavements of tenement buildings and channeled into sewage gutters, now reemergent in the light of day:

> London, which – which I have read about as the modern Babylon of civilization, seems to have disappeared ... As to the big murky places which were once, as we know, the centres of manufacture, they have, like the brick and mortar desert of London, disappeared; only, since they were centres of nothing but "manufacture", and served no purpose but that of the gambling market, they have left less signs of their existence than London ... On the contrary, there has been but little clearance, though much rebuilding, in the smaller towns. Their suburbs, indeed, when they had any, have melted away into the general country, and space and elbow-room has been got in their centres; but there are the towns still with their streets and squares and market-places; so that it is by means of these smaller towns that we of today can get some kind of idea of what the towns of the older world were like, – I mean to say, at their best.[9]

Morris' utopia is the very prototype of an aesthetically and libidinally oriented social vision, as opposed to the technological and engineering-oriented type of Bellamy's *Looking Backward* – a vision thus in the line of Fourier rather than Saint Simon, and more prophetic of the values of the New Left than those of Soviet centralism, a vision in which we find this same process of weeding out the immense waste-and-junk landscape of capitalism and an artisanal

---

8 Inasmuch as *The Dispossessed* – surely the most important utopia since Skinner's *Walden Two* – seems certain to play a significant part in political reflection, it seems important to question her qualification of Anarres as an "anarchist" Utopia. Thereby she doubtless intends to differentiate its decentralized organization from the classical Soviet model, without taking into account the importance of the "withering away of the state" in Marxism also – a political goal most recently underscored by the Cultural Revolution and the experimental communes in China and the various types of workers' self-management elsewhere.

9 William Morris, *News from Nowhere* (London, 1903), pp. 91, 95, 96.

gratification in the systematic excision of masses of buildings from a clogged urban geography. Does such an imaginative projection imply and support a militant political stance? Certainly it did so in Morris' case; but the issue in our time is that of the militancy of ecological politics generally. I would be inclined to suggest that such "no-places" offer little more than a breathing space, a momentary relief from the overwhelming presence of late capitalism. Their idyllic, yet elegiac, sweetness, their pastel tones, the rather, pathetic withdrawal they offer from grimier Victorian realities, seems most aptly characterized by Morris' subtitle to *News from Nowhere: "An Epoch of Rest"*. It is as though – after the immense struggle to free ourselves, even in imagination, from the infection of our very minds and values and habits by an omnipresent consumer capitalism – on emerging suddenly and against all expectation into a narrative space radically other, uncontaminated by all those properties of the old lives and the old preoccupations, the spirit could only lie there gasping in the fresh silence, too weak, too new, to do more than gaze wanly about it at a world remade.

Something of the fascination of *LHD* – as well as the ambiguity of its ultimate message – surely derives from the subterranean drive within it towards a utopian "rest" of this kind, towards some ultimate "no-place" of a collectivity untormented by sex or history, by cultural superfluities or an object-world irrelevant to human life. Yet we must not conclude without observing that in this respect the novel includes its own critique as well.

It is indeed a tribute to the rigor with which the framework has been imagined that history has no sooner, within it, been dispelled, than it sets fatally in again; that Karhide, projected as a social order without development, begins to develop with the onset of the narrative itself. This is, it seems to me, the ultimate meaning of that motif of right and wrong questions mentioned above and resumed as follows: "to learn which questions are unanswerable, and not *to answer them*: this skill is most needful in times of stress and darkness." It is no accident that this maxim follows hard upon another, far more practical discussion about politics and historical problems:

> To be sure, if you turn your back on Mishnory and walk away from it, you are still on the Mishnory road ... You must go somewhere else; you must have another goal; then you walk a different road. Yegey in the Hall of the Thirty-Three today: "I unalterably oppose this blockade of grain-exports to Karhide and the spirit of competition which motivates it." Right enough, but he will not get off the Mishnory road going that way. He must offer an alternative. Orgoreyn and Karhide both must stop following the road they're on, in either direction; they must go somewhere else, and break the circle. (153)

But, of course, the real alternative to this dilemma, the only conceivable way of breaking out of that vicious circle which is the option between feudalism and capitalism, is a quite different one from the liberal "solution" – the Ekumen as a kind of galactic United Nations – offered by the writer and her heroes. One is tempted to wonder whether the strategy of *not* asking questions ("Mankind", according to Marx, "always [taking] up only such problems as it can solve")[10] is not the way in which the utopian imagination protects itself against a fatal return to just those historical contradictions from which it was supposed to provide relief. In that case, the deepest subject of Le Guin's *LHD* would not be utopia as such, but rather our own incapacity to conceive it in the first place.

1975

---

10 Karl Marx and Friedrich Engels, *Basic Writings on Politics and Philosophy*, ed. Lewis S. Feuer (Garden City, New York, 1959), p. 44.

4

Progress versus Utopia, or, Can We Imagine the Future?

It will then turn out that the world has long dreamt of that of which it had only to have a clear idea to possess it really.

Karl Marx to Arnold Ruge (1843)

A storm is blowing from Paradise; it has got caught in his wings with such violence that the angel can no longer close them. The storm irresistibly propels him into the future to which his back is turned, while the pile of debris before him grows skyward. This storm is what we call progress.

Walter Benjamin, *Theses on the Philosophy of History* (1939)

What if the "idea" of progress were not an idea at all but rather the symptom of something else? This is the perspective suggested, not merely by the interrogation of cultural texts, such as SF, but by the contemporary discovery of the Symbolic in general. Indeed, following the emergence of psychoanalysis, of structuralism in linguistics and anthropology, of semiotics together with its new field of "narratology", of communications theory, and even of such events as the emergence of a politics of surplus consciousness" (Rudolf Bahro) in the 1960s, we have come to feel that abstract ideas and concepts are not necessarily intelligible entities in their own right. This was of course already the thrust of Marx's discovery of the dynamics of ideology; but while the older terms in which that discovery was traditionally formulated –"false consciousness" versus "science"– remain generally true, the Marxian approach to ideology, itself fed by all the discoveries enumerated above, has also become a far more sophisticated and non-reductive form of analysis than the classical opposition tends to suggest.

From the older standpoint of a traditional "history of ideas", however, ideology was essentially grasped as so many *opinions* vehiculated by a narrative text such as an SF novel, from which, as Lionel Trilling once put it, like so many raisins and currants they are picked out and exhibited in isolation. Thus

Verne is thought to have "believed" in progress,[1] while the originality of Wells was to have entertained an ambivalent and agonizing love–hate relationship with this "value", now affirmed and now denounced in the course of his complex artistic trajectory.[2]

The discovery of the Symbolic, however, suggests that for the individual subject as well as for groups, collectivities and social classes, abstract opinion is but a symptom or an index of some vaster *pensée sauvage* about history itself, whether personal or collective. This thinking, in which a particular conceptual enunciation such as the "idea" of progress finds its structural intelligibility, may be said to be of a more properly *narrative* kind, analogous in that respect to the constitutive role played by master-fantasies in the Freudian model in the unconscious. Nevertheless, the analogy is misleading to the degree to which it may awaken older attitudes about objective truth and subjective or psycho-logical "projection" which are explicitly overcome and transcended by the notion of the Symbolic itself. In other words, we must resist the reflex which concludes that the narrative fantasies which a collectivity entertains about its past and its future are "merely" mythical, archaetypal and projective, as opposed to "concepts" like progress or cyclical return, which can somehow be tested for their objective or even scientific validity. This reflex is itself the last symptom of that dissociation of the private and the public, the subject and the object, the personal and the political, which has characterized the social life of capitalism. A theory of some narrative *pensée sauvage* – what I have else-where termed the political unconscious[3] – will, on the contrary, want to affirm the epistemological priority of such "fantasy" in theory and praxis alike.

The task of such a theory would then be to detect and to reveal – behind such written *traces* of the political unconscious as the narrative texts of high or mass culture, but also behind those other symptoms or traces which are opinion, ideology, and even philosophical systems – the outlines of some deeper and vaster narrative movement in which the groups of a given collectivity at a certain historical conjuncture anxiously interrogate their fate, and explore it with hope or dread. Yet the nature of this vaster collective sub-text, with its specific struc-tural limits and permutations, will be registered above all in terms of properly narrative categories: closure, recontainment, the production of episodes, and the like. Once again, a crude analogy with the dynamics of the individual unconscious may be useful. Proust's restriction to the windless cork-lined room, for instance, the emblematic eclipse of his own possible relationships to any concrete personal or historical future, determines the formal innovations and

1   See, on Verne, Pierre Macherey's stimulating chapter in *Pour une théorie de la production littéraire* (Paris, 1966).

2   The literature on Wells is enormous: see, for an introduction and select bibliography, Darko Suvin, *Metamorphoses of Science Fiction* (New Haven, 1979). This work is a pioneering theoretical and structural analysis of the genre to which I owe a great deal.

3   See my *The Political Unconscious* (Ithaca, NY, 1981).

wondrous structural subterfuges of his now exclusively retrospective narrative production. Yet such narrative categories are themselves fraught with contradiction: in order for narrative to project some sense of a totality of experience in space and time, it must surely know some closure (a narrative must have an ending, even if it is ingeniously organized around the structural repression of endings as such). At the same time, however, closure or the narrative ending is the mark of that boundary or limit beyond which thought cannot go. The merit of SF is to dramatize this contradiction on the level of plot itself, since the vision of future history cannot know any punctual ending of this kind, at the same time that its novelistic expression demands some such ending. Thus Asimov has consistently refused to complete or terminate his *Foundation* series; while the most obvious ways in which an SF novel can wrap its story up – as in an atomic explosion that destroys the universe, or the static image of some future totalitarian world state – are also clearly the places in which our own ideological limits are the most surely inscribed.

It will, I trust, already have become clear that this ultimate "text" or object of study – the master-narratives of the political unconscious – is a *construct*: it exists nowhere in "empirical" form, and therefore must be re-constructed on the basis of empirical "texts" of all sorts, in much the same way that the master-fantasies of the individual unconscious are reconstructed through the fragmentary and symptomatic "texts" of dreams, values, behavior, verbal free association, and the like. This is to say that we must necessarily make a place for the formal and textual *mediations* through which such deeper narratives find a partial articulation. No serious literary critic today would suggest that content – whether social or psychoanalytic – inscribes itself immediately and transparently on the works of "high" literature: instead, the latter find themselves inserted in a complex and semi-autonomous dynamic of their own – the history of forms – which has its own logic and whose relationship to content per se is necessarily mediated, complex and indirect (and takes very different structural paths at different moments of formal as well as social development). It is perhaps less widely accepted that the forms and texts of mass culture are fully as mediated as this: and that, here too, collective and political fantasies do not find some simple transparent expression in this or that film or TV show. It would in my opinion be a mistake to make the "apologia" for SF in terms of specifically "high" literary values – to try, in other words, to recuperate this or that major text as exceptional, in much the same way as some literary critics have tried to recuperate Hammett or Chandler for the lineage of Dostoyevsky, say, or Faulkner. SF is a sub-genre with a complex and interesting formal history of its own, and with its own dynamic, which is not that of high culture, but which stands in a complementary and dialectical relationship to high culture or modernism as such. We must therefore first make a detour through the dynamics of this specific form, with a view to grasping its emergence as a formal and historical event.

I

Whatever its illustrious precursors, it is a commonplace of the history of SF that it emerged, virtually full-blown, with Jules Verne and H.G. Wells, during the second half of the nineteenth century, a period also characterized by the production of a host of utopias of a more classical type. It would seem appropriate to register this generic emergence as the symptom of a mutation in our relationship to historical time itself: but this is a more complex proposition than it may seem, and demands to be argued in a more theoretical way.

I will suggest that the model for this kind of analysis, which grasps an entire genre as a symptom and reflex of historical change, may be found in Georg Lukács' classical study *The Historical Novel* (1936). Lukács began with an observation that should not have been particularly surprising: it was no accident, he said, that the period which knew the emergence of historical thinking, of historicism in its peculiarly modern sense – the late eighteenth and early nineteenth centuries – should also have witnessed, in the work of Sir Walter Scott, the emergence of a narrative form peculiarly restructured to express that new consciousness. Just as modern historical consciousness was preceded by other, for us now archaic, forms of historiography – the chronicle or the annals – so the historical novel in its modern sense was certainly preceded by literary works which evoked the past and recreated historical settings of one kind or another: the history plays of Shakespeare or Corneille, *La Princesse de Clèves*, even Arthurian romance: yet all these works in their various ways affirm the past as being essentially the same as the present, and do not yet confront the great discovery of the modern historical sensibility, that the past, the various pasts, are culturally original, and radically distinct from our own experience of the object-world of the present. That discovery may now be seen as part of what may in the largest sense be called the *bourgeois cultural revolution*, the process whereby the definitive establishment of a properly capitalist mode of production as it were reprograms and utterly restructures the values, life rhythms, cultural habits and temporal sense of its subjects. Capitalism demands in this sense a different experience of temporality from what was appropriate to a feudal or tribal system, to the *polis* or to the forbidden city of the sacred despot: it demands a *memory* of qualitative social change, a concrete vision of the past which we may expect to find completed by that far more abstract and empty conception of some future terminus which we sometimes call "progress". Sir Walter Scott can in retrospect be seen to have been uniquely positioned for the creative opening of literary and narrative form to this new experience: on the very meeting place between two modes of production, the commercial activity of the Lowlands and the archaic, virtually tribal system of the surviving Highlanders, he is able to take a distanced and marginal view of the emergent dynamics of capitalism in the neighboring nation-state from the vantage point of a national experience – that of Scotland – which was the last arrival to capitalism and the first semi-peripheral zone of a foreign capitalism all at once.[4]

What is original about Lukács' book is not merely this sense of the historical meaning of the emergence of this new genre, but also and above all a more difficult perception: namely, of the profound historicity of the genre itself, its increasing incapacity to register its content, the way in which, with Flaubert's *Salammbô* in the mid-nineteenth century, it becomes emptied of its vitality and survives as a dead form, a museum piece, as "archaeological" as its own raw materials, yet resplendent with technical virtuosity. A contemporary example may dramatize this curious destiny: Stanley Kubrick's *Barry Lyndon*, with its remarkable reconstruction of a whole vanished eighteenth-century past. The paradox, the historical mystery of the devitalization of form, will be felt by those for whom this film, with its brilliant images and extraordinary acting, is somehow profoundly *gratuitous*, an object floating in the void which could just as easily not have existed, its technical intensities far too great for any merely formal exercise, yet somehow profoundly and disturbingly unmotivated. This is to say something rather different from impugning the content of the Kubrick film: it would be easy to imagine any number of discussions of the vivid picture of eighteenth-century war, for example, or of the grisly instrumentality of human relationships, which might establish the relevance and the claims of this narrative on us today. It is rather the relationship to the past which is at issue, and the feeling that any other moment of the past would have done just as well. The sense that this determinate moment of history is, of organic necessity, precursor to the present has vanished into the pluralism of the Imaginary Museum, the wealth and endless variety of culturally or temporally distinct forms, all of which are now rigorously equivalent. Flaubert's Carthage and Kubrick's eighteenthth century, but also the industrial turn of the century or the nostalgic 1930s or 1950s of the American experience, find themselves emptied of their necessity, and reduced to pretexts for so many glossy images. In its (post-) contemporary form, this replacement of the historical by the nostalgic, this volatilization of what was once a *national* past, in the moment of emergence of the nation-states and of nationalism itself, is of course at one with the disappearance of historicity from consumer society today, with its rapid media exhaustion of yesterday's events and of the day-before-yesterday's star players (who was Hitler anyway? who was Kennedy? who, finally, was Nixon?).

The moment of Flaubert, which Lukács saw as the beginning of this process, and the moment in which the historical novel as a genre ceases to be functional, is also the moment of the emergence of SF, with the first novels of Jules Verne. We are therefore entitled to complete Lukács' account of the

---

4 An important discussion of Scotland's unique place in the development of capitalism can be found in Tom Nairn, *The Break-Up of Britain* (London, 1977).

historical novel with the counter-panel of its opposite number, the emergence of the new genre of SF as a form which now registers some nascent sense of the future, and does so in the space on which a sense of the past had once been inscribed. It is time to examine more closely the seemingly transparent ways in which SF registers fantasies about the future.

II

The common-sense position on the anticipatory nature of SF as a genre is what we would call a *representational* one. These narratives are evidently for the most part not modernizing, not reflexive and self-undermining and deconstructing affairs. They go about their business with the full baggage and paraphernalia of a conventional realism, with this one difference: that the full "presence" – the settings and actions to be "rendered" – are the merely possible and conceivable ones of a near or far future. Whence the canonical defense of the genre: in a moment in which technological change has reached a dizzying tempo, in which so-called "future shock" is a daily experience, such narratives have the social function of accustoming their readers to rapid innovation, of preparing our consciousness and our habits for the otherwise demoralizing impact of change itself. They train our organisms to expect the unexpected and thereby insulate us, in much the same way that, for Walter Benjamin, the big-city modernism of Baudelaire provided an elaborate shock-absorbing mechanism for the otherwise bewildered visitor to the new world of the great nineteenth-century industrial city.

If I cannot accept this account of SF, it is at least in part because it seems to me that, for all kinds of reasons, we no longer entertain such visions of wonder-working, properly "science-fictional" futures of technological automation. These visions are themselves now historical and dated – streamlined cities of the future on peeling murals – while our lived experience of our greatest metropolises is one of urban decay and blight. That particular Utopian future has in other words turned out to have been merely the future of one moment of what is now our own past. Yet, even if this is the case, it might at best signal a transformation in the historical function of present-day SF.

In reality, the relationship of this form of representation, this specific narrative apparatus, to its ostensible content – the future – has always been more complex than this. For the apparent realism, or representationality, of SF has concealed another, far more complex temporal structure: not to give us "images" of the future – whatever such images might mean for a reader who will necessarily predecease their "materialization" – but rather to defamiliarize and restructure our experience of our own *present*, and to do so in specific ways distinct from all other forms of defamiliarization. From the great intergalactic empires of an Asimov, or the devastated and sterile Earth of the post-catastrophe novels of a John Wyndham, all the way back in time to the nearer future of the organ banks and space miners of a Larry Niven, or the conapts, autofabs, or psycho-suitcases of the universe of Philip K. Dick, all such apparently full representations function in a process of distraction and displacement, repression and lateral perceptual renewal, which has its analogies in other forms of contemporary culture. Proust was only the most monumental "high" literary expression of this discovery: that the present – in this society, and in the physical and psychic dissociation of the human subjects who inhabit it – is inaccessible directly, is numb, habituated, empty of affect. Elaborate strategies of indirection are therefore necessary if we are somehow to break through our monadic insulation and to "experience", for some first and real time, this "present", which is after all all we have. In Proust, the retrospective fiction of memory and rewriting after the fact is mobilized in order for the intensity of a now merely remembered present to be experienced in some time-released and utterly unexpected posthumous actuality.

Elsewhere, with reference to another sub-genre or mass-cultural form, the detective story, I have tried to show that at its most original, in writers like Raymond Chandler, the ostensible plots of this peculiar form have an analogous function.[5] What interested Chandler was the here and now of the daily experience of the now historical Los Angeles: the stucco dwellings, cracked sidewalks, tarnished sunlight, and roadsters in which the curiously isolated yet typical specimens of an unimaginable Southern Californian social flora and fauna ride in the monadic half-light of their dashboards. Chandler's problem was that his readers – ourselves – desperately needed not to see that reality: humankind, as T.S. Eliot's magical bird sang, is able to bear very little of the unmediated, unfiltered experience of the daily life of capitalism. So, by a dialectical sleight-of-hand, Chandler formally mobilized an "entertainment" genre to distract us in a very special sense: not from the real life of private and public worries in general, but very precisely from our own defense mechanisms against that reality. The excitement of the mystery-story plot is, then, a blind, fixing our attention on its own ostensible but in reality quite trivial puzzles and suspense in such a way that the intolerable space of Southern California can enter the eye laterally, with its intensity undiminished.

It is an analogous strategy of indirection that SF now brings to bear on the ultimate object and ground of all human life, History itself. How to fix this intolerable present of history with the naked eye? We have seen that in the moment of the emergence of capitalism the present could be intensified, and prepared for individual perception, by the construction of a historical past from which as a process it could be felt to issue slowly forth, like the growth of an organism. But today the past is dead, transformed into a packet of well-worn and thumbed glossy images. As for the future, which may still be alive in some small heroic collectivities on the Earth's surface, it is for us either

---

5   Fredric Jameson, "On Raymond Chandler", *Southern Review*, 6 (Summer 1970), pp. 624–650.

irrelevant or unthinkable. Let the Wagnerian and Spenglerian world-dissolutions of J.G. Ballard stand as exemplary illustrations of the ways in which the imagination of a dying class – in this case the canceled future of a vanished colonial and imperial destiny – seeks to intoxicate itself with images of death that range from the destruction of the world by fire, water and ice to lengthening sleep or the berserk orgies of high-rise buildings or superhighways reverting to barbarism.

Ballard's work – so rich and corrupt – testifies powerfully to the contradictions of a properly representational attempt to grasp the future directly. I would argue, however, that the most characteristic SF does not seriously attempt to imagine the "real" future of our social system. Rather, its multiple mock futures serve the quite different function of transforming our own present into the determinate past of something yet to come. It is this present moment – unavailable to us for contemplation in its own right because the sheer quantitative immensity of objects and individual lives it comprises is untotalizable and hence unimaginable, and also because it is occluded by the density of our private fantasies as well as of the proliferating stereotypes of a media culture that penetrates every remote zone of our existence – that upon our return from the imaginary constructs of SF is offered to us in the form of some future world's remote past, as if posthumous and as though collectively remembered. Nor is this only an exercise in historical melancholy: there is, indeed, something also at least vaguely comforting and reassuring in the renewed sense that the great supermarkets and shopping centers, the garish fast-food stores and ever more swiftly remodeled shops and store-front businesses of the near future of Chandler's now historic Los Angeles, the burnt-out-center cities of small Midwestern towns, nay even the Pentagon itself and the vast underground networks of rocket-launching pads in the picture-postcard isolation of once characteristic North American "natural" splendor, along with the already cracked and crumbling futuristic architecture of newly built atomic power plants – that all these things are not seized, immobile forever, in some "end of history", but move steadily in time towards some unimaginable yet inevitable "real" future. SF thus enacts and enables a structurally unique "method" for apprehending the present as history, and this is so irrespective of the "pessimism" or "optimism" of the imaginary future world which is the pretext for that defamiliarization. The present is in fact no less a past if its destination prove to be the technological marvels of Verne or, on the contrary, the shabby and maimed automata of P.K. Dick's near future.

We must therefore now return to the relationship of SF and future history and reverse the stereotypical description of this genre: what is indeed authentic about it, as a mode of narrative and a form of knowledge, is not at all its capacity to keep the future alive, even in imagination. On the contrary, its deepest vocation is over and over again to demonstrate and to dramatize our incapacity to imagine the future, to body forth, through apparently full representations which prove on closer inspection to be structurally and constitutively impoverished, the atrophy in our time of what Marcuse has called the *utopian imagination*, the imagination of otherness and radical difference; to succeed by failure, and to serve as unwitting and even unwilling vehicles for a meditation, which, setting forth for the unknown, finds itself irrevocably mired in the all-too-familiar, and thereby becomes unexpectedly transformed into a contemplation of our own absolute limits.

This is indeed, since I have pronounced the word, the unexpected rediscovery of the nature of utopia as a genre in our own time.[6] The overt utopian text or discourse has been seen as a sub-variety of SF in general. What is paradoxical is that at the very moment in which utopias were supposed to have come to an end, and in which that asphyxiation of the utopian impulse alluded to above is everywhere more and more tangible, SF has in recent years rediscovered its own utopian vocation, and given rise to a whole series of powerful new works – utopian and SF all at once – of which Ursula Le Guin's *The Dispossessed*, Joanna Russ' *The Female Man*, Marge Piercy's *Woman on the Edge of Time*, and Samuel Delany's *Triton* are only the most remarkable monuments. A few final remarks are necessary, therefore, on the proper use of these texts, and the ways in which their relationship to social history is to be interrogated and decoded.

III

After what has been said about SF in general, the related proposition on the nature and the political function of the utopian genre will come as no particular surprise: namely, that its deepest vocation is to bring home, in local and determinate ways and with a fullness of concrete detail, our constitutional inability to imagine Utopia itself: and this, not owing to any individual failure of imagination but as the result of the systemic, cultural and ideological closure of which we are all in one way or another prisoners. This proposition, however, now needs to be demonstrated in a more concrete analytical way, with reference to the texts themselves.

It is fitting that such a demonstration should take as its occasion not American SF, whose affinities with the dystopia rather than the utopia, with fantasies of cyclical regression or totalitarian empires of the future, have until recently been marked (for all the obvious political reasons); but rather Soviet SF, whose dignity as a "high" literary genre and whose social functionality within a socialist system

---

6 A fuller discussion of these propositions and some closer analyses of More's *Utopia* in particular, will be found in my review article of Louis Mann's *Utopiques* (which also see!), "Of Islands and Trenches", *Diacritics*, 7 (June 1977), pp. 2–21. See also the related discussion in "World Reduction in Le Guin", Part Two, Essay 3, above. (And of course see Part One, and, in particular Chapter 11.)

have been, in contrast, equally predictable and no less ideological. The renewal of the twin Soviet traditions of Utopia and SF may very precisely be dated from the publication of Efremov's *Andromeda* (1958), and from the ensuing public debate over a work which surely, for all its naïveté, is one of the most single-minded and extreme attempts to produce a full representation of a future, classless, harmonious, world-wide utopian society. We may measure our own resistance to the utopian impulse by means of the boredom the American reader instinctively feels for Efremov's culturally alien "libidinal apparatus":

> "We began," continued the beautiful historian, "with the complete redistrib-ution of Earth's surface into dwelling and industrial zones.
>
> "The brown stripes running between thirty and forty degrees of North and South latitude represent the unbroken chain of urban settlements built on the shores of warm seas with a mild climate and no winters. Mankind no longer spends huge quantities of energy warming houses in winter and making himself clumsy clothing. The greatest concentration of people is around the cradle of human civilization, the Mediterranean Sea. The subtropical belt was doubled in breadth after the ice on the polar caps had melted. To the north of the zone of habitation lie prairies and meadows where countless herds of domestic animals graze …
>
> "One of man's greatest pleasures is travel, an urge to move from place to place that we have inherited from our distant forefathers, the wandering hunters and gatherers of scanty food. Today the entire planet is encircled by the Spiral Way whose gigantic bridges link all the continents … Electric trains move along the Spiral Way all the time and hundreds and thousands of people can leave the inhabited zone very speedily for the prairies, open fields, moun-tains or forests."[7]

The question one must address to such a work – the analytical way into the utopian text in general from Thomas More all the way down to this histori-cally significant Soviet novel – turns on the status of the negative in what is given as an effort to imagine a world without negativity. The repression of the negative, the place of that repression, will then allow us to formulate the essen-tial contradiction of such texts, which we have expressed in a more abstract fashion above, as the dialectical reversal of intent, the inversion of represen-tation , the "ruse of history" whereby the effort to imagine utopia ends up betraying the impossibility of doing so. The content of such repressed "semes" of negativity will then serve as an indicator of the ways in which a narrative's contradiction or antimony is to be formulated and reconstructed.

Efremov's novel is predictably enough organized around the most obvious dilemma the negative poses for a utopian vision: namely, the irreducible fact

7 Ivan Efremov, *Andromeda* (Moscow, 1959), pp. 54–55.

of death. But equally characteristically, the anxiety of individual death is here "recontained" as a collective destiny, the loss of the starship *Parvus*, easily assimilable to a whole rhetoric of collective sacrifice in the service of mankind. I would suggest that this facile *topos* functions to displace two other, more acute and disturbing, forms of negativity. One is the emotional fatigue and deep psychic depression of the administrator Darr Veter, "cured" by a period of physical labor in the isolation of an ocean laboratory; the other is the hubris and crime of his successor, Mven Mass, whose personal involvement with an ambitious new energy program results in a catastrophic accident and loss of life. Mven Mass is "rehabilitated" after a stay on "the island of oblivion", a kind of idyllic Ceylonese Gulag on which deviants and anti-socials are released to work out their salvation in any way they choose. We will say that these two episodes are the nodal points or symptoms at which deeper contradictions of the psychiatric and the penal, respectively, interrupt the narrative functioning of the Soviet Utopian Imagination. Nor is it any accident that these narrative symptoms take spatial and geographical form. Already in Thomas More, the imagining of Utopia is constitutively related to the possibility of establishing some spatial *closure* (the digging of the great trench which turns "Utopia" into a self-contained island).[8] The lonely oceanographic station and the penal island thus mark the return of devices of spatial closure and separation which, formally required for the establishment of some "pure" and positive utopian space, thus always tend to betray the ultimate contradictions in the production of utopian figures and narratives.

Other people's ideologies always being more self-evident than our own, it is not hard to grasp the ideological function of this kind of non-conflictual utopia in a Soviet Union in which, according to Stalin's canonical formula, class struggle was at the moment of "socialism" supposed to have come to an end. Is it necessary to add that no intelligent Marxist today can believe such a thing, and that the process of the class struggle is if anything exacerbated precisely in the moment of socialist construction, with its "primacy of the political"? I will nevertheless complicate this diagnosis with the suggestion that what is ideological for the Soviet reader may well be Utopian for us. We may indeed want to take into account the possibility that, alongside the obvious qualitative differences between our First World culture (with its dialectic of modernism and mass culture) and that of the Third World, we may want to make a place for a specific and original culture of the Second World, whose artifacts (generally in the form of Soviet and East European novels and films) have generally produced the unformulated and disquieting impression on the Western reader or spectator of a simplicity indistinguishable from naïve sentimentalism. Such a renewed confrontation with Second World culture would have to take into account something it is hard for us to remember within the ahistorical closure

8 Compare "Of Islands and Trenches" (see note 6).

of our own "*société de consommation*": the radical strangeness and freshness of human existence and of its object-world in a non-commodity atmosphere, in a space from which that prodigious saturation of messages, advertisements, and packaged libidinal fantasies of all kinds, which characterizes our own daily experience, is suddenly and unexpectedly stilled. We receive this culture with all the perplexed exasperation of the city-dweller condemned to insomnia by the oppressive silence of the countryside at night; for us, then, it can serve the defamiliarizing function of those wondrous words which William Morris inscribed under the title of his own great Utopia, "an epoch of rest".

All of this can be said in another way by showing that, if Soviet images of Utopia are ideological, our own characteristically Western images of *dystopia* are no less so, and fraught with equally virulent contradictions.[9] George Orwell's classical and virtually inaugural work in this sub-genre, *1984*, can serve as a textbook exhibit for this proposition, even if we leave aside its more obviously pathological features. Orwell's novel, indeed, set out explicitly to dramatize the tyrannical omnipotence of a bureaucratic elite, with its perfected and omnipresent technological control, yet the narrative, seeking to reinforce this already oppressive closure, subsequently overstates its case in a manner which specifically undermines its first ideological proposition. For, drawing on another topos of counterrevolutionary ideology, Orwell then sets out to show how, without freedom of thought, no science or scientific progress is possible, a thesis vividly reinforced by images of squalor and decaying buildings. The contradiction lies of course in the logical impossibility of reconciling these two propositions: if science is rudimentary, then the technological power of the dystopian bureaucracy vanishes along with it and "totalitarianism" ceases to be a dystopia in Orwell's sense. Or the reverse: if these Stalinist masters dispose of some perfected scientific and technological power, then genuine freedom of inquiry must exist *somewhere* within this state, which was precisely what was not to have been demonstrated.

IV

The thesis concerning the structural Impossibility of utopian representation outlined above now suggests some unexpected consequences in the aesthetic realm. It is by now, I hope, a commonplace that the very thrust of literary modernism – with its *public introuvable* and the breakdown of traditional cultural institutions, in particular the social "contract" between writer and reader – has had as one significant structural consequence the transformation of the cultural text into an *auto-referential* discourse, whose content is a perpetual interrogation of its own conditions of possibility.[10] We may now show that this is

9 In other words, to adapt Claudel's favorite proverb, "le pire n'est pas toujours sûr".
10 See my *The Prison–House of Language* (Princeton, 1972), pp. 203–205.

no less the case with the utopian text. Indeed, in the light of everything that has been said, it will not be surprising to discover that as the true vocation of the utopian narrative begins to rise to the surface – to confront us with our incapacity to imagine Utopia – the center of gravity of such narratives shifts towards an auto-referentiality of a specific, but far more concrete type: such texts then explicitly or implicitly, and as it were against their own will, find their deepest "subjects" in the possibility of their own production, in the interrogation of the dilemmas involved in their own emergence as utopian texts.

Ursula Le Guin's only "contemporary" SF novel, the underrated *Lathe of Heaven* (1971), may serve as documentation for this more general proposition. In this novel, which establishes Le Guin's home city of Portland, Oregon, alongside Berkeley and Los Angeles, as one of the legendary spaces of contemporary SF, a hapless young man finds himself tormented by the unwanted power to dream "effective dreams", those which in other words change external reality itself, and reconstruct the latter's historical past in such a way that the previous "reality" disappears without a trace. He places himself in the hands of an ambitious psychiatrist, who then sets out to use his enormous proxy power to change the world for the benefit of mankind. But reality is a seamless web: change one detail and unexpected, sometimes monstrous transformations occur in other apparently unrelated zones of life, as in the classical time-travel stories where one contemporary artifact, left behind by accident in a trip to the Jurassic age, transforms human history like a thunderclap. The other archaetypal reference is the dialectic of "wishes" in fairy tales, where one gratification is accompanied with a most unwanted secondary effect, which must then be wished away in its turn (its removal bringing yet another undesirable consequence, and so forth).

The ideological content of Le Guin's novel is clear, although its political resonance is ambiguous: from the central position of her mystical Taoism, the effort to "reform" and to ameliorate, to transform society in a liberal or revolutionary way is seen, after the fashion of Edmund Burke, as a dangerous expression of individual hubris and a destructive tampering with the rhythms of "nature". Politically, of course, this ideological message may be read either as the liberal's anxiety in the face of a genuinely revolutionary transformation of society or as the expression of more conservative misgivings about the New Deal-type reformism and do-goodism of the welfare state.[11]

On the aesthetic level, however – which is what concerns us here – the deeper subject of this fascinating work can only be the dangers of imagining Utopia and more specifically of writing the utopian text itself. More transparently than much other SF, this book is "about" its own process of production,

---

11 That the author of *The Dispossessed* is also capable of indulging in a classical Dostoyevskian and counterrevolutionary anti–utopianism may be documented by her nasty little fable "The Ones Who Walk Away from Omelas", in *The Wind's Twelve Quarters* (New York, 1975), pp. 275–284.

which is recognized as impossible: George Orr cannot dream Utopia; yet in the very process of exploring the contradictions of that production, the narrative gets written, and "Utopia" is "produced" in the very movement by which we are shown that an "achieved" Utopia – a full representation – is a contradiction in terms. We may thus apply to *The Lathe of Heaven* those prophetic words of Roland Barthes about the dynamics of modernism generally, that the latter's monuments "linger as long as possible, in a sort of miraculous suspension, on the threshold of Literature itself [read, in this context: Utopia], in this anticipatory situation in which the density of life is given and developed without yet being destroyed through its consecration as an [institutionalised] sign system."[12]

It is, however, more fitting to close this discussion with another SF–Utopian text from the Second World, one of the most glorious of all contemporary Utopias, the Strugatsky Brothers' astonishing *Roadside Picnic* (1977; first serialized in 1972).[13] This text moves in a space beyond the facile and obligatory references to the two rival social systems; and it cannot be coherently decoded as yet another *samizdat* message or expression of liberal political protest by Soviet dissidents.[14] Nor, although its figural material is accessible and rewritable in a way familiar to readers who live within the rather different constraints of either of the two industrial and bureaucratic systems, is it an affirmation or demonstration of what is today called "convergence" theory. Finally, while the narrative turns on the mixed blessings of wonder-working technology, this novel does not seem to me to be programmed by the category of "technological determinism" in either the Western or the Eastern style: that is, it is locked neither into a Western notion of infinite industrial progress of a non-political type, nor into the Stalinist notion of socialism as the "development of the forces of production".

On the contrary, the Zone – a geographical space in which, as the result of some inexplicable alien contact, artifacts can be found whose powers transcend the explanatory capacities of human science – is at one and the same time the object of the most vicious bootlegging and military-industrial Greed, and of the purest religious – I would like to say Utopian – Hope. The "quest for narrative", to use Todorov's expression,[15] is here very specifically the quest for the Grail; and the Strugatskys' deviant hero – marginal, and as "antisocial" as one likes; the Soviet equivalent of the ghetto or countercultural anti-heroes of our own tradition – is perhaps a more sympathetic and human figure for us than Le Guin's passive-contemplative and mystical innocent. No less than

---

12 Roland Barthes, *Writing Degree Zero*, trans. Annette Lavers and Colin Smith (London, 1967), p. 39.

13 Arkady and Boris Strugatsky, *Roadside Picnic*, trans. A.W. Bouis (New York, 1977).

14 This is not to say that the Strugatskys have not had their share of personal and publishing problems.

15 Tzvetan Todorov, *Poétique de la prose* (Paris, 1971).

The Lathe of Heaven, then, *Roadside Picnic* is self-referential, its narrative production determined by the structural impossibility of producing that Utopian text which it nonetheless miraculously becomes. Yet what we must cherish in this text – a formally ingenious collage of documents, an enigmatic cross-cutting between unrelated characters in social and temporal space, a desolate reconfirmation of the inextricable relationship of the utopian quest to crime and suffering, with its climax in the simultaneous revenge-murder of an idealistic and guiltless youth and the apparition of the Grail itself – is the unexpected emergence, as it were, beyond "the nightmare of History" and from out of the most archaic longings of the human race, of the impossible and inexpressible Utopian impulse here nonetheless briefly glimpsed: "Happiness for everybody! … Free! … As much as you want! … Everybody come here! … HAPPINESS FOR EVERYBODY, FREE, AND NO ONE WILL GO AWAY UNSATISFIED!"

1982

Science Fiction as a Spatial Genre: Vonda McIntyre's *The Exile Waiting*

I

SF seems particularly well-suited – or should I say vulnerable? – to paraphrase. Not that this stigmatized operation is utterly absent from the criticism of other kinds of literary texts. Surely we have paraphrase when a seemingly realistic novel is read, and thereby rewritten, in terms of a psychological experience, of which the "events" are then seen as the *expression* (of pathological melancholy and fear of death in the case of Zola's *La Joie de vivre*, for example); and the same thing happens when a symbolic or modernizing narrative is read in terms of a concrete historical situation (that is, rewritten as realism, as when Kafka's novels become symbolic representations of phenomena connected with the Austro-Hungarian monarchy). Still, the results for SF narratives seem likely to be often far more disastrous than this, since the operation of paraphrasing tends here to call into question the very genre itself, whose specific conventions now become so much external decoration, mere optional clothing for content whose plain and unvarnished reality looks very different indeed, although not necessarily more noble and lofty.

So one initially wants to resist rewriting that splendid novel, *The Exile Waiting*,[1] in terms of the soap operas it sometimes seems distantly to recall. Consider this: two protagonists who do not yet know each other, the one – Jan – a rather passive son of a dissatisfied father (the son is a blond Japanese, something even more disturbing for a wealthy father whose fantasy life is lived out in twelfth-century Japan, in a simulacrum of Lady Murasaki's court), the other a sensitive girl – Mischa – whose idolized older brother is a kind of junky, her younger sister a mental defective, and an even younger maimed and deformed sibling lost in the dispersal of the family (shades of Byzantine romance or the dispatching of British children to the countryside in the Second World War). These two figures will ultimately and predictably join forces, not before the violent intervention of a third narrative vector in the person of two genetically engineered but temperamentally unlike "pseudosibs", Subtwo

---

1 Vonda N. McIntyre, *The Exile Waiting* (Greenwich, CT, 1975): page references to this edition henceforth given within the text.

and Subone, who lead a party of raiders from space to invade and conquer the underground "Center" of old Earth which is the vivid setting of this SF representation. The two sibs are held together telepathically in an antagonistic relationship in which Subtwo, one of the central protagonists, represents engineering and technological wizardry as well as responsibility and organization, where Subone is little more than a brutal and egoistical thug. The complex relationships of these figures to one another (and to themselves) is a tangible refutation of the stereotype of SF as lacking introspection and the subtle characterizations we expect in high literature. At the same time their interplay, which, as I will show in a moment, recalls the rhythms of the soap opera (in · as contemporary a form as you like), threatens to take on the interminability of the serial form as such, in which the longing for closure is tantalizingly reawakened and perpetually frustrated. The desire of the main protagonists to leave Earth once and for all no doubt steers in the direction of an ending, but it will be paid for, as we shall see, with a radical shift to a completely different diegetic mode, one we will characterize as spatial: a brutal modulation from interpersonality to geography, from interrelationship to what Kenneth Burke would have called "scene".

Still it follows from what I have called "generic discontinuities" that we cannot fairly summarize an SF plot in this fashion, since each moment of the narrative tends to project its own fresh generic framework, in a perpetual process of restructuration not unlike the model of reading projected by Stanley Fish, in which each segment of an ongoing sentence opens up a range of possibilities and uncertainties then unexpectedly redirected by the next choice in line. In this instance we are dealing with a fiction which, diachronically considered, only becomes a chase-and-pursuit paradigm in its later stages, and we should respect that reading experience as we explore some of the synchronic complexities of the SF narrative.

II

The reading signals of soap opera are mainly triggered by the presentation of each of the major figures as the bearer of what used to be called a "personal problem", a 1950s pop-psychological American term that designated neurotic paralysis and the hangups that prevent people from functioning. The category sets the terms of narrative in terms of development rather than morality: the physical escape from Earth is the figure for release from the prison of neurotic repetition. Meanwhile, it seems clear that what marks the three main characters out as protagonists, as *interesting* figures, over against the secondary characters whose meaning is decided in advance (the self-indulgence of Subone, or of the planet's "tyrant" Blaisse, or the revolt of the mutants and misfits), has little to do with positivity or negativity: Jan is too passive to be a real hero, Subtwo occupies the position of the villain but is obviously recuperable. Instead, it is a very special "personal problem" which, as with the soaps and with certain kinds of bestsellers, marks all three as appropriate raw material: the two strongest ones, indeed – Mischa and Subtwo – are very specifically flawed and strategically weakened by their unwanted sensitivity to a more vulnerable or more degenerate sibling figure who weighs each of them down like a ball-and-chain and debilitates each, always intervening to complicate vigorous and independent decisions and to throw the actions of each off course. This – something like a tragedy of altruism – can perhaps be differentiated from the previous category by means of the specific form of helplessness it involves: where the "personal problem" – Freud's "character is destiny" – somehow projected the fatality of the self (from the presence of this or that annoying character trait all the way to alcoholism, homosexuality, suicidal depression, and the like), this more recent form suggests that it is the fidelity to an other which is the problem (that *other* then being understood along the lines of the older category of the "personal problem", so that there is virtually a diachronic progression in these stereotypes, the more recent building on and enveloping the older, and now dated, kind of psychology). Jan, with his lack of energy and initiative and a detached and aesthetic view of the world around him which finally comes to seem pathological in its own way, is still the closest to the older model and to some more classical Oedipal paralysis: perhaps that is why the author has had to vary this particular figure in a particularly striking way, by including his erotic devotion to the elderly, half-blind navigator (the young man's affair with this dying older woman presents an interesting gender variant, one which strikes me as rather different from the traditional romantic–sentimental educations and one which, even in today's youth cult, may sound an interestingly transgressive note). Still, this situation is no more than a background motif which enriches and complicates the dominant one of alienating devotion in a merely secondary way (Jan is obliged to bury the dead navigator–poetess on "Earth").

Nor do I want to suggest that there is anything especially wrong or tainted about the human raw material I have just described: we might think in particular of the forbidding Heideggerian ethic – let the other *be* in his or her *being* – with its Nietzschean presupposition that charity is aggression and that devotion of this kind may well be the worst possible service to the loved one, especially to the loved one! I cannot think what kind of historical or social situation would tend to generate and develop an art with such thematic concerns (for example, is it really desirable to be one's brother's keeper?); nor can I think of any *a priori* grounds on which a novel, play, or film on this subject would be doomed in advance to sentimentalism or to mediocrity. But while I can imagine an authentic work of art on such themes, to be authentic it would have to develop such situations afresh, from zero, and would be concerned to foreground and to interrogate the various categories (otherness, devotion, suffering, the "personal problem", etc.) through which we normally think them. *The Exile Waiting*, however – in this exactly like the "soaps" – takes such categories as givens, as structures of the real world, rather than historically determinant ideas about the real world, and as the basis or precondition for plot development rather than its thematic aim and center. This should be enough to vitiate the novel and to stamp it as a meretricious product whose function – like that of the more degraded forms of mass culture – lies in playing with and building on our psychological and social stereotypes rather than in criticizing and subverting them.

That is, however – at least in my opinion – not quite the case: the raw materials of McIntyre's novel share a certain kind of naïveté with those of Le Guin (to whom it is dedicated). But as this last name suggests, naïveté of a sociopolitical and psychological kind has not been incompatible with wide influence, historical importance (the reinvention of utopia), and artistic quality and value. If this is so, then the problem is reversed, whereupon we should inquire whether the formal possibility of a certain kind of aesthetic and narrative value may not rather *presuppose* and be dialectically related to just such otherwise seemingly oversimplified content.

Our investigation here will nevertheless take another direction: we will seek to determine whether there may not be something in the very nature of the structure of SF as a genre which "redeems" precisely such stereotypes (which we have observed are of one substance with the soaps).

III

If indeed the psychological attitudes and interpretations, the characterological schematism described above, are rather something like the raw material on which the form of SF narrative works, then we must add that it transforms them, by way of its own unique production process, into *something else*: something which in the case of *Exile*, has a different kind of aesthetic value than would be observable even in the best "psychological" art. That this production process, this transformation of raw materials, is at one with a play of figuration specific to this genre is apparent at once, since the psychic devotion and dependency I have tried to characterize in an everyday psychological way (as it might, more "realistically", be shown in the soaps) is here "rendered' in terms of telepathy. We are therefore at once beyond mere translation from one medium to another as we confront a convention with a long history of its own. The production process is therefore twofold: it takes us from psychological content, with its own terms and language, to a reified figure, and from the immediacy of a certain kind of experience to a historical motif in which a given treatment or inflection will always be seen as a variation of pre-existent treatments of the same theme and as an implicit commentary on the history of the theme itself.

What must be added, however, is the reminder that, like the elements of language itself, such "themes" have their own meaning, often concealed and sedimented within them, as an etymology is buried within the structure of the ostensible word – so that the variation on the theme is also, implicitly, a commentary on that deeper meaning as well. In this case – the theme of telepathy – the material signifier expresses and conceals the utopian fantasy of a genuinely collective set of social relationships, in which the individual subject or ego – a historical result of the development of commerce and capitalism – is again dissolved in its monadic isolation and returned to its ground as a nexus of human relationships and a transmission point for collective relationships.

To put it this way is to realize the degree to which this collective theme is for the most part reduced in *Exile* to kinship or consanguine relationships and to the family as a natural unit (Mischa and her siblings, the attempt at an artificial family in the case of the pseudosibs, and finally, although telepathy plays no part in it, the Oedipal background of Jan's situation – which has at least the merit of suggesting that here the parental axis is being displaced in favor of the horizontal axis of brothers and sisters). The one exception is Mischa's thieving (but the sexual overtones of burglary-penetration, violation, defilement, etc. – have often been noted).

Socially, these restrictions are more plausible: what is left on "Earth", for the most part underground (particularly during the uninhabitable winters), is in a state of degenerescence of a feudal type, dominated by the Families, into whose system an individual tyrant has inserted himself, his function being the control of "foreign relations" – that is, the relations with spacecraft, which can in any case not land during the great storms of the winter months. It is the eccentric spatial relations generated by this anomalous situation which Subtwo is then able to appropriate; and in any case the conquest by the pseudosibs (something like barbarian tribes taking over an empire in full decadence) is itself the result of this seasonal rhythm – no one expects a spaceship to be able to land in winter, and the inner city and palace are defenseless (much like Singapore during the Second World War, when the Japanese penetrated the peninsula's jungle side, towards which no guns pointed).

This kind of far-future reversion to a galactic Middle Ages is of course only too familiar, as is its cause (nuclear holocaust); but in terms of the family thematics outlined above, the feudal setting now suggests that Mischa's dilemma is to be read as part of the process of the liquidation of just such family and blood ties, which have become almost physically oppressive (and not only in her case). There seems to be a thematic progression in this respect, since Subtwo's similar "problem" no longer involves a real brother (although Subone is distantly related genetically), and the genetic engineering of which he is the result is felt to be rational, scientific, and very different from what still regressively holds for Center ("Earth's" central cave):

As Blaisse explained, Subtwo slowly understood that he did not mean "blood" but genetics, and biological and social relationships. It was a most ridiculous way of forming alliances, though perhaps no more ridiculous than some he had witnessed. It was the way Center was ruled. (52)

For the novel to be read this way, however, its conclusion would have had to have been heightened and intensified by some more dramatic representation of the well-nigh cloacal explosion of the lower depths, the emergence of the mutants and misfits out of the deepest caverns into the "light of day" of what remains of civilization (and of state power) – as the triumphant mutant army pursues the remnants of the pseudosibs' strike force. Were it a matter of "performing" the novel by way of a certain kind of reading, and of organizing the narrative into a certain rhythm, of plotting the slow narrative curve of a certain kind of development, then one would have wanted this emergence to come with something of the force of the appearance, on the seashore, of the rebel army in Pontecorvo's film *Burn!* (1968): the ragtag and bobtail of the ragged fighters on foot or mounted, with their camp followers and carts, and, as they come riding and marching into view, stretching as far as the eye can see. That expanse, however – and the extraordinary prospect of a march on the beach, through the sand, by the sea (as also in the first glimpse of the mounted riders in the film version of *Planet of the Apes* (1968) – obviously offers a very different kind of space from what is constructed for us in *Exile* (see below); and there is in any case in my mind some question as to whether the SF novelist can plan architectonic effects of this kind, in the way a conventional novelist – for example, the Flaubert of *Salammbô* – can, building carefully to an experience of proportion and time carefully blocked out by number of pages, by overexposure to sensory detail, and above all relying on a certain set of univocal reading directions which seem to me inconsistent and even incompatible with the play of generic discontinuities in SF.[2] And this is not only a matter of "description" versus "narration" in Lukács' sense of that opposition, but has to do with our relatively greater freedom, in such SF novels, to readjust thematic and narrative developments according to our own inclinations.

Still, what seems minimally incontrovertible is that *Exile* displaces kinship relations with more essentially political forms of community and collectivity, not to say social class itself. All of this is beautifully rendered, in particular through Val's hostility to the injured Jan (who is otherwise physically and psychically normal, and thus not eligible for the deep-underground fellowship of oppression and deformation, as well as of enforced exile, of the physical or psychic mutants, who are at once exposed and banished into the tunnels beyond the Center).

2 For more on "generic discontinuities", see my remarks on *Starship*, Essay 2 above.

Mischa's "telepathy" is obviously just such a form of mutation (although she has not been caught and identified as a mutant); but the mode of representation of this telepathy seems to me generically original and to have little enough in common with some of the more standard versions of this theme (for example, Wyndham's *Rebirth* [1955]). In Subtwo's case, the telepathic link is seen as interfering with the development of normal human relations with other people (on the order of Lévi-Strauss' interpretation in his *Elementary Structures of Kinship* of the incest taboo – to keep fresh blood but also fresh experience and new people coming into the tribe):

> Time and again he had asked Subone to communicate his wishes verbally, normally, instead of relying on the artificial bio-mechanical link between them. The link was no longer dependable, for which Subtwo was glad: he only wished it would finish dying and dissolve completely. Something must be wrong: he and Subone should have been free of 'one another long before this. But as they remained, they would always be too concerned each with the other; they would continue to have difficulty dealing with ordinary human beings, who could not and would never know automatically what another person was thinking. (43)

Here is the most obvious restriction on the telepathy motif as it is traditionally dealt with, a restriction which will subsequently also become visible in the working out of the Mischa story (even though she is officially supposed to be receptive to *all* other minds, not merely those of her family). For Subtwo's sensitivity is to a single other consciousness, something which prevents the "gift" from being expanded into a more generalized personality trait, as in Bester's classic *The Demolished Man* (1951): "The essence of the Esper [Extra Sensory Perceiver] is his responsiveness. His personality always takes color from his surroundings" (*TDM* 31). Meanwhile, *Exile* also tends to limit the development of the telepathy motif in Mischa to a few other characters as well: the ill-fated older brother, the deformed younger one, but above all the younger sister, whose thought appeals – implacable and virtually impossible to ignore or disobey – are among the most original features of the work:

> Gemmi expanded through Mischa's consciousness, laughing with delight despite having been forced to seek her out. Mischa cringed. "No," she said softly. "Not now. Go away." But she was speaking to herself, not to Gemmi. Gemmi could not understand. (121)

This mixture of bubbling laughter and childish or properly infantile delight, followed by the screams that greet refusal or hesitation and that stab the brain with a well-nigh physical Pavlovian shock not unlike the defense mechanism of the normal human baby, offers a far more gruesome dependency situation than does Subtwo's perpetual awareness of someone who is a normal mature male and uses the link for merely rational exploitative purposes. The thematic variation here, however, seems to me essentially to involve a generic borrowing or graft, or at least to be reinforced by one: I am thinking of several classic ghost stories, whose horror results precisely from the idiocy of the haunting and the cloying and imbecilic fawning of the ghost upon the consciousness of the straightlaced Victorian and professional male thereby victimized (see the much-anthologized "How Love Came for Professor Guildea" [1900] by Robert Hitchens, and above all, "The Beckoning Fair One" [1911], the classic tale by Oliver Onions, often rated as the finest ghost story ever written).[3]

IV

I have elsewhere made some suggestions as to the social meaning of the genre of the ghost story, at least in its middle-class form (the hold of the past, through the house itself, a possession by History – "le mort saisit le vif!" to quote one of Marx's favorite sayings – which can stretch all the way back to precapitalism and the feudal aristocracy and which will know a somewhat different (Irish) figuration in Bram Stoker's *Dracula* [1897]). It seems to me that the peculiar sense of history dramatized by the ghost story is a compensatory product, a reaction–formation triggered in resistance to the more general social development of a society without a historical memory, a society reduced, in other words, to an aggregate of nuclear families from which little by little the very storytelling of the past slips away and for which, therefore, the art–novella ghost story comes as something of the "return of the repressed". The ghost story would then be a relatively minor generic symptom in the period between the emergence of the historical novel (the strong form of the bourgeois consciousness of its past) and that of SF (more mixed and ambiguous in its visions of the mortality of bourgeois society but also of the historical future figured in terms of catastrophe, the end of the world, or the dawn of something else). The distinction between the meaning of the genre (as a "social equivalent") and its ideological function is clear in just such Victorian ghost stories (with their palpable fear of the breakdown of bourgeois decorum, alongside which it seems possible that they also faintly register the tremors of late-nineteenth-century feminism, as depicted in women's own writing (in Charlotte Perkins Gilman's *The Yellow Wallpaper* [1892], for example) and in such novels as Gissing's *The Odd Women* [1893]). Nor would we expect the same motif, displaced to contemporary SF (and feminist SF, at that!), to bear the same ideological charge of essentially masculine anxieties, although it might plausibly still vehiculate the same residual

---

3 Onions' story can be found reprinted in the numerous editions of *Great Tales of Terror and the Supernatural*, ed. Herbert A. Wise and Phyllis Fraser. See also Part One, Chapter 8, note 3, above.

meaning. In that case, the deeper meaning of the ghost story proper – the contemplation of a non-bourgeois past, the nagging sense of a radically different historical dynamic and relationship to generations and to the dead – is in *Exile* permuted and structurally repositioned in terms of the fate of the older nuclear family, the pathological morbidity of its protective survival as a "haven in a heartless world," and the well-nigh explicit juxtaposition of psychological and genetic ties against the alternative of a militant group politics.

Yet whatever the meaning of such motifs (that is to say, whatever "social equivalent" may be found or proposed for them), they also raise the issue of figuration itself, something that has been implicit since the beginning of this discussion. The figural "bonus", the difference between the conventional–realistic psychological drama of altruism and dependency and the SF retelling of this narrative material in terms of telepathy, the passage through figuration–this will evidently be crucial, not merely in determining the specificity of SF in general as a genre and a narrative medium, but also in estimating the aesthetic value of texts such as the one presently under consideration.

V

We can begin with a fairly crude way of formulating the problem: What can be said or shown in the figural (SF) narrative which it is impossible to encode in the psychological language of the realistic one? Are there specifically figural *events* of a type unavailable in the language of the psychological narrative (it always being understood that a seemingly abstract paragraph of "psychological analysis" is likely to be itself a kind of micro-narrative in which the psychological abstractions tend to play an allegorical, yet diegetic role)? Or, reversing this, what can be achieved in the realistic text which escapes the register of the SF mode?

A single illustration or experimental case will have to suffice here, but it is in many ways the very climax of the telepathy plot: the "cure" of Mischa, her liberation from the cloying or shrilling possessiveness of Gemmi.

> Mischa let him draw on the power of her fury, and reach out – as if his spirit were shaped like his body, with sharp claws. He pulled her with him until she could see Gemmi more clearly than she ever had or wished to; in that split second Mischa could see all that Gemmi could see: a mosaic of every consciousness in Center. But neither she nor Crab could stand it. They drew back and the total melding was over. But Crab stayed near Gemmi; Mischa saw what he was searching for and pointed it out. He reached for it. "Wait, no," Mischa said, "That one first." He reached through a maze of connections and snapped a single thread. Gemini's pain vanished with the destroyed synapse … Crab cut the second synapse, and Gemmi disappeared. (204)

This particular "link", severed by the deformed younger brother (Crab), is very precisely a figural event, in the sense in which what is diegetic in it can be derived immediately from the reactivation of dead figures in the language (in such terms as "link" or "sever", which have been seen used abstractly in the present sentence). The new figural event will then soak up and absorb a mass of affect loosely floating about such neutralized or deadened figures – for example, notions of cords or threads, umbilical, electric, or whatever, and notions of instruments of disjunction, scissors, clips, and the like. Such figures are often invested with psychoanalytic and libidinal or corporeal over- and under-tones which, as a supplement come to enrich the event itself, now taken as a mere plot mechanism or general background situation (Gemmi's dependency on Mischa and the latter's guilt); the latter is much easier to paraphrase "realistically" or to "translate", than is the textual resolution, which one could, nonetheless, imagine as the supportiveness of a younger crippled brother which gradually diverts the infirm sister away from the heroine. But the SF "event" is clearly far more economical than our paraphrase, and that in a twofold way.

The story of Crab himself was a component of the novel's presentation of its underclasses: the child sold to Hugoesque beggar-entrepreneurs, who exploit his mutilation in the interests of horrible, quasi-medieval spectacles (for profit). The mutilation explains the name (although Crab's first appearance is preceded by an auditory warning, "a soft clicking sound", etc.):

> The creature …was barely recognizable as human, in his form, his body wide and flat, hunched over short, bowed legs, his head hardly distinct from his shoulders. His eyes protruded. He raised his hands – his claws – and clicked horny digits together: only his thumbs were distinct; all his fingers were fused into one. His skin was thick and scaly. (156)

Crab is, however, also a psychic mutant (with heightened telepathic powers) and thus signifies the entire range of this underclass (slaves, deformed beggars, mutants driven further underground). In the SF tradition, moreover, one strong "classical" overtone is quite unavoidable – namely the giant decapods in the closing pages of *The Time Machine* (1895), last living beings on the shell of Earth's final twilight – a form which does not tend to be the most frequent envelope for SF versions of the Other or the Alien.

What must be noted, however, is that the crab-like extremity, the very emblem which seals the horror of this vision of the maiming and exploitation of children, is also – in the second plot line – the key instrument and emblem of deliverance. What in the system of images of the human body is a powerful condensation of negative imagery (of which the fear of castration is the obvious dominant) becomes in the resolution of the Gemmi narrative an active and positive instrument – the figural materialization of the "cutting of the knot", but also a well-nigh machine-like engineering tool, whose operation (reaching in among the tangled wires, finding the correct one) evokes home mechanics and the building or repair of appliances – in short, a whole code system of work, praxis and human artifice and know-how very distinct from the disturbing sub-organic nature imagery of the crustaceans themselves. Both are "condensed" elegantly in the figure of Crab, and the figural event takes place at the coincidence of the two narrative paths in question (the underclass, Mischa's "problem").

It should also be added that the final, intolerable vision of a total melding ("a mosaic of every consciousness in the center") suggests a rather different but no less topical ideological reading of this particular theme of *Exile,* connecting it with the more familiar overtones of a present-day suspicion of concepts of "totality". The family unit (by kinship or genetic engineering) is presented as being too small and asphyxiating; the collective revolt of the mutants seems to offer a larger and more viable form of community, that of the oppressed; while the prospect of some vaster collectivity that might include every living human being within itself once again inspires anxiety and raises fresh doubts.

VI

Still, as a way of translating a feature or conceptual trait into something visually representable, and beyond that, as a ground for forming and embodying a new type of *event*, such punctual forms of figuration seem relatively distinct from another whole area or element of figurability, I am referring to the use and representation, in virtually all types of SF, of *space*, whose deeply constitutive relationship with the genre remains to be worked out. Spatial representation wholly enables, and serves as a pretext for, the more punctual figures, devices and gimmicks touched on above: but it also somehow transcends the SF plot interest in a significantly more general way. The hypothesis is then that, whatever our immediate narrative interest in *this* particular SF plot and its res-olutions, we also attend to and derive a readerly gratification from the development of space in SF worlds, in general, a gratification not noticeably damaged by awkwardnesses in the handling of the plot proper. (Indeed, we might well want to consider the possibility that the two levels of reading interest are in some ultimate way incompatible, and that attention to spatial representation in SF may well – virtually *a priori* – exclude the achievement of well-formed plots of the type writers in other genres and media have aspired to and sometimes devised.[4])

Although there exists a surface world in *The Exile Waiting*, it is virtually impenetrable during the winter months; and the fiction's dominant space is therefore the inner space of the underground, with its enormous hollowed

---

4 See, for a different version of this problem, my essay "On Raymond Chandler", *Southern Review,* 6 (1970), pp. 624–650.

plazas, the rooms within rooms of its inner buildings, and finally the artificial and natural caverns and caves beneath. There *is* an exterior, or out-of-doors, here, but it is in Jan's memory and on another planet – his homeland of the Japan-like Koen, with its scarlet forests and gardens. We are therefore in *Exile* explicitly condemned to a certain experience of closed, perhaps even claustrophobic space, which it is interesting to compare to that of the sealed spaceship in Aldiss' *Starship* (see Essay 2). That closed space, however, was a projectile on its way somewhere (even if we cannot sight the goal beyond sealed windows); this one is the space of exploration, whose *scène à faire* will, on the paradigm of Verne's *Journey to the Center of the Earth* (1864) or Wells' *The First Men in the Moon* (1901), be the discovery of three unexpected inner toxic chambers in the "Earth's" depths which involve the same curious symbiosis of the organic and the artificial we find in Aldiss' inner environment, but which in McIntyre raise ecological issues rather than those of political exploitation and control.[5]

Our first exposure to this inner space is, however, the space of the Center itself (or of the city), that of the plaza before the palace, but also of the shanty-town of private dwellings all around it:

> Light-tubes spread across the ceiling like the gills of a mushroom. The instantaneous impression was one of chaos, of tiny gray projections climbing each other to reach the ceiling, spotted here and there with color or movement. Mischa knew the city well enough to see the underlying order: five parallel spiral ramps leading up the walls at a low pitch, giving access to the stacked dwellings. The helices were almost obliterated by years of building-over, use, and neglect. The walls of the cavern, crowded with single-unit box-houses piled against the stone, looked like shattered honeycombs. To Mischa's left, and below her, Stone Palace was an empty blotch of bare gray rock on the mural of disorder. (18)

Whatever the conceptual messages and overtones of a passage like this (urbanism, shoddy zoning laws, etc.), it seems to me that the mental operation demanded by the description has a somewhat different meaning in its own right. There is here a doll-house quality which has something to do with sheer reduction or minaturization (no normal human city or village can be "taken in" at a glance in this way). It has something to do as well with historical representation, the notion of rebuilding after catastrophe, the absence of the (perhaps sham) depth of human artifacts which have seemingly grown over time and are therefore somehow instinctively felt to be "natural". But as Brecht taught us, whatever has been *constructed* at once forfeits the mesmerizing (and crippling) prestige of the natural: it can be changed. Many SF

---

5 Cf. my remarks on Aldiss' *Starship*; and see on this tradition Peter Fitting, ed., *Subterranean Worlds* (Middletown, CT, 2004).

cityscapes and utopias seem to me to participate in this curious paradox: that what signals the constructed, invented, artificial nature of SF as a genre – the palpable fact that an author has strained her or his invention to contrive some near or far future city (and to make it somehow distinctive and different from those of rivals or predecessors) – that very lack of ontological density for the reader, that very artifice and unbelievability which are surely disastrous in most realistic novels, is here an unexpected source of strength, feeding into the more traditional SF estrangement effects in a curiously formal, reflexive and overdetermined way. Brecht was accustomed to associate understanding with praxis (as in Vico), and to use these two as powerful, aggressive and rather un-Viconian weapons against the ideological mystification of the "natural", or of "naturality" (Roland Barthes' explicitly Brechtian neologism). In other words, if you can tinker with it and take it apart like a radio set or an automobile engine, you are freed from all the paralyses of nature and being and in the realm of at least symbolic political praxis and change. The very homemade qualities and amateurishness of certain SF constructions have, I think, similar effects, which are supplementary to whatever they set forth to do on the level of content with respect to existing human institutions. I have said this negatively in connection with contemporary utopias: that their shallowness is not the mark of their failure of imagination, but rather very precisely their political function on the formal level – namely, to bring the reader up short against the atrophy of the utopian imagination and of the political vision in our own society.[6] In an inverse way, McIntyre's private vision of a beehive cluster of shacks applied by the writer's imagination in one great lump to a stony inner cavern of enormous size perhaps recovers some of the active power of human praxis.

This larger generic effect – it is something like the content of the form, or the ideological meaning or social equivalent of the specific mental operations determined by this feature of the form – can be contrasted with more local and punctual estrangement effects on the level of content proper. An instance of the latter is Subtwo's malaise with the organic irregularities of the inner space of the subterranean dwellings: "nothing in this place was composed of straight lines. The curtains fell in waving gathers. The rooms were round, or irregular, or, worst, *almost* square. The angles were slightly flawed, the lines slightly crooked, the floors slightly uneven"(56). The feeling is perhaps linked to Subtwo's horror of waste in human arrangements, most particularly in the institution of slavery. On the other hand, as a spatial and emotional reaction it is also very clearly a sign of Subtwo's technocratic and scientist world-view. The fact that within this Gaudi-like disorder and proliferation he can build himself a calm haven of well nigh Bauhaus geometrical

---

6 See, further, my argument in "Of Islands and Trenches" (in *Ideologies of Theory*) and "Progress versus Utopia", above, Essay 4.

order ("lines straight and angles square … pleasing rectangular shapes and volumes … proportions … geometrically and aesthetically perfect …" [69]) shows that one can actively *change* this space, or better still, produce radically new types of space altogether. What is dialectical about the shock of contact between feudal regression and scientific and technological manipulation is that, unlike perspectives such as those found in the Strugatsky Brothers' *Hard to Be a God* (1964), neither type of space is valorized and both are ideologically and emotionally flawed.

VII

Both of the experiences of space in *Exile* thus stand in sharp contrast to the flight to the center of the "Earth" and the more "natural" experiences there awaiting the protagonists (experiences to which Subtwo predictably responds with horror and nausea). But it is worth first pausing over the insertion into the narrative of two curious episodes which prove to be emblems of reading or condensed allegories of the spatial dominants projected by this particular novel. Indeed, without some such interpretation, episodes like this stand out a little like Aldiss' telepathic rats, as though intrusions from some other generic convention, if not mere anti-mimetic or anti-realistic signals or reflexes without further interest. In this case, however, the spatial content of each of these details is suggestive. In the first episode, Mischa is sealed in what seems to be an elaborate new version of handcuffs or of a straitjacket:

> Her eyes were closed and she could not open them. The darkness was the scarlet of her body heat, veined with images of capillaries – in her eyelids, holding nothing but fog beyond. She floated in an environment that lacked gravity, pressure, and light, surrounded by something that soaked up everything she could see or hear or touch or smell … Her fingertip touched a minuscule irregularity of the matrix that bound her … She probed the imperfection, wishing she could grasp and tear it. Her nail slipped beneath it … the flaw grew … (36–37)

The motif of total submersion, which aroused interest at the same time when sensory deprivation experiments were fashionable and has been figurally developed in a number of ways (in Ballard, in Paddy Chayevsky and Ken Russell's *Altered States* [1978], and so forth), has perhaps less rarely been used as the paradigm for the straitjacket. As such in *Exile* it fairly effectively conditions our sense of the dialectic of inside and outside, reducing this dialectic (which might also have meant warmth and shelter, say, or miniature comforts after the terror of infinite spaces) to an asphyxiated condition from which one must escape at all costs. I would argue that the function of this kind of episode is precisely to inflect our reading of space, and to program us (or cue us) to the desired system of responses (in this case, emergence into the open is positive, while the logic of the closed or the interior entails [psychological] shrinkage, contraction and constraint). I am assuming then that there are no "natural" responses to or evaluations of space; that it is not nature, but culture and history, which determine the reading of the inside/outside dialectic at any given moment (but this is why, in a complex and sedimented historical culture like our own, the writer has to have a formal freedom to nudge us this way rather than that).

The other version of this same motif – and the episode is otherwise so gratuitous as to demand structural explanation in terms of this first one – seems to involve a movement of reversal and inversion. Whereas Mischa's experience went from the sealed to the liberation of the open via the tiniest rent of her smallest fingernail, the death of her brother Chris literally offers the spectacle of a body gradually closed in and sealed over, by way of a mysterious black sphere which, shattering, releases a "black fluid" that "spread slowly across Chris's chest, flowing first over the wound and then beneath the bandages": "The black shell grew, sucking warmth from him, from the air, from Mischa ... The black plastic helmeted Chris's hair ... sealed itself over Chris's eyes ... Chris lay shrouded in the dark and she could do nothing more" (146–148). It must be understood that the plastic film has anaesthetic qualities, and that this seemingly nightmarish process is in reality a euthanasia, a gift designed to reduce Chris' sufferings and to speed the inevitable. What is negative about the image of envelopment must therefore be qualified by that positive feature; the movement is otherwise quite compatible symbolically with the earlier episode.

To be sure, this claustrophobic envelopment is itself a concentration of the claustrophobia of the novel's closed space in general, and a prolongation of its intensifying and ever more contracting dimensions, as the underground beneath this underground city is probed by the fleeing protagonists, in tunnels which shrink alarmingly as they descend. There would be more to say about the way in which this particularly spatial anxiety of contraction and suffocation offers its own *jouissance* and even its own possibility of Utopian investment: it is a figure which invites both bodily and semiotic readings, reflecting back to the "civilized" inhabitants of the Center their own undisguised truth as creatures of a burrow (it is in fact a former underground missile site of the now uninhabitable Earth).

What must now in addition be reckoned with is a further dimension of symbolic reference which I will rapidly (and perhaps a little over-dogmatically) characterize in terms of reading itself. I suspect that most kinds of texts – and in particular those of mass culture – include within themselves not merely directions about the reading process and the way in which its operations are to be performed, but also symbolic references to that process itself. It would be too ambitious to try to document this hypothesis in detail; so I will merely remind the reader of detective stories of the moments of calm in which the harried detective or policeman returns to his own home and relaxes by reading a book (most generally, of course, a detective story). The apartment, the room, as retreat, as withdrawal, as solitude – this charged figure is, I believe, very often the way in which a certain ideology of reading is passed off on readers and developed in them. (It should be understood that this kind of symbolism is situation- and text-specific: the "room" is not some eternal Jungian representation of the reading process, if only because the latter is itself a historical phenomenon.)

The so-called sub-genres of paraliterature are, however, clearly far from being equivalent in their social function. Thus we would not expect the fairly straightforward signals of the detective story to be reproduced in the same way in SF, let alone in the kind of late, sophisticated auto-referential SF of the type under discussion here. What is striking about these figures for the reading process (if I am right in so identifying them) is the implicit association of reading a book alone in a room with physical asphyxiation and with it a range of associations generally felt to be privative or negative. At the same time, we must also underscore *Exile*'s structural implication: that reading (like escaping from the body-seal or, on the contrary, being enveloped in it) is very precisely a process – that it involves accumulations, dialectical transformations, and so forth – and not some static act of contemplation. I am therefore tempted to see the conception of "generic discontinuities" inscribed here in the very symbol of the reading process itself – and inscribed with a certain anxiety, a certain ambivalence, as if the outcome were uncertain or even unknown, as though the reader hesitated on the point of surrendering her or his reading body to this unpredictable dialectical experiment.

VIII

Returning now to the ultimate voyage into the bowels of Mcintyre's "Earth" – that is, literally into the "inside" of what has already been given to us as an "inside"– we can see the semic terms for the new experience realized and given figuration in ways distinct from the older spatial aesthetics of "round" versus "square" that aroused Subtwo's anxieties. Now the content of this opposition becomes far more clearly specified as organic versus inorganic. Indeed, the protagonists make two great discoveries: first, a treacherous forest of crystal shards (in which Jan is wounded), and second, the final terminus of the burial rituals of the planet, a sump of rotting corpses and decayed organic matter. Whatever analogies are possible between this and the round/square opposition, the new one marks a heightened involvement of the bodily senses (and their modes of evaluation – agreeable, disgusting, and the like) by comparison with the relatively visual aesthetic distance of the earlier experiences. Yet in this case the two distinct types of content – the brittleness of crystal, the loathsome sponginess of the pool – are semically marked as being the same:

the crystals are themselves poisonous and the result of centuries of toxic waste and nuclear damage on the "Earth's" outer surface. What this identification does on the more immediate level of the plot is not only to drive the characters back to the "surface" (that is, the Center), but also, by discrediting all forms of closed space, to blast them off "Earth" altogether (in what thereby becomes a happy ending).

But besides not visibly solving the problem of figuration with which we began, this interpretation presents us with a new one: that of closure generally in SF. Not only is the future open by definition; collective narratives – those of SF generally – cannot be expected to have endings, particularly happy endings, of the same type as individual narratives. The format of the "classical" SF novel (180 pages paperback) made this plain. Everyone has known the peculiar "formal feeling" of the end of a Dick novel, say, in which nothing can be said to be concluded: having laid out the essentials and presented them to us, the author now, like Molière or Shakespeare, concerns himself with wrapping up his production as expeditiously as possible. The action, in other words, can hardly be said to be complete in the Aristotelian sense; but the book has somehow been ended. The newer format of the great four- or five-volume series (not all of them fantasy, as Aldiss' ambitious new "Helliconia" series testifies, but all of them incorporating historical modifications of the older SF format) merely confirms this proposition by eliminating the formal gesture of the technical ending and assimilating completed action, wherever necessary, to global history, the history of the species.

On my reading of McIntyre, it is spatial experience which allows her to endow the dénouement of her narrative strands with a force and definition they might not otherwise have – a proposition which also suggests a hypothetical and provisional answer to the initial question raised here, that of the translatability of SF back into other, more "realistic" (and sometimes more meretricious) narratives. Here, too, I want to suggest that in a book like *Exile* we can observe a significant displacement in our reading interest from narrative in that sense, with its linear causality, toward spatial experience as such. In fact, the processes of figuration discussed above (in which the "psychological" content is transformed into bodily emblems) are both covered and subsumed by that greater displacement and given legitimacy by it. If, as I believe, all SF of the more "classical" type is "about" containment, closure, the dialectic of inside and outside, then the generic distinction between those texts and others that have come to be called "fantasy" (for example, Mcintyre's own *Dreamsnake* [1978]) will also be a spatial one, in which these last are seen as open-air meadow texts of various kinds. Meanwhile the more deliberate move, which we can witness everywhere in the genre today, from "individual" SF to great SF epic histories of a new type, is less a matter of the extrapolation of forms of individual destiny onto collective history (where "peoples" or "races" or "species" would also be seen as knowing success or failure, etc.) than it is of the mediation of space itself; and the collective adventure accordingly becomes less that of a character (individual or collective) than that of a planet, a climate, a weather and a system of landscapes – in short, a map. We need to explore the proposition that the distinctiveness of SF as a genre has less to do with time (history, past, future) than with space.

1987

6

The Space of Science Fiction:
Narrative in Van Vogt

I want to tell you about the first Science Fiction story I ever read – or at least remember reading – as a pre-teen. It told the story of a panther-like monster of preternatural intelligence and strength, discovered among the ruins of a long-dead alien civilization. The monster lived on a substance described as "organic id", while its human adversaries fought among themselves as to the appropriate strategies. I was very proud indeed, at that time and age, to have produced what I thought a powerful interpretation, in the form of an allegory of the psychic functions – an allegory somewhat more Jungian than Freudian as it turned out – not realizing that the author himself had very baldly and crudely slapped those clues in place, having an explicit and didactic interest in just such theories of the psychic division of labor and how to overcome it. My interpretation therefore simply consisted in uncovering the author's intentions, much as I had been meant to do. The interpretation I mean to offer to you today will hopefully be of a somewhat different, "symptomal" type.

My own discovery, through this story, of the peculiar powers of Science Fiction as a genre, turns out to have been something a little more than an accident of personal history. In fact, this story, entitled "Black Destroyer" and published in the July 1939 issue of *Astounding Science Fiction*, was not only A.E. Van Vogt's first publication, but hit the then still poorly articulated field of the Science Fiction pulps like a bombshell; or, as we might put it today, constituted a narrative intervention which virtually singlehandedly restructured the dominant paradigms in the genre. "Black Destroyer" with only one stroke established its author as one of the leaders of a small group of younger writers – among them Robert Heinlein and Isaac Asimov – who were in the process of creating what is henceforth known as the Golden Age of Science Fiction: a tremendous burst of narrative production and paradigmatic innovation generally considered to have extended from the end of the 1930s to the beginning of the 1950s. Indeed, some have gone even farther, and see in "Black Destroyer" the very opening salvo of the Golden Age itself. These historical observations would then need to be completed by the reminder of John Campbell's unique role as the editor of *Astounding* and as the critic and

sometimes the virtual collaborator of all the writers of this younger generation: the Golden Age is synonymous with *Astounding* and its impulses are quite
incomprehensible unless Campbell's role is appreciated. There are few enough
high-literary equivalents of this role, although the activity of the manifesto-
producing leader of the vanguard cultural group – Breton and the surrealists,
for instance – offers some distant analogies.

There are also few high-literary analogies for the subsequent career of the
author of "Black Destroyer". Over the next ten years or so, he will know a
prodigious period of creativity, publishing 900,000 words in *Astounding* in the
form of a series of henceforth classical stories and novels. It is, incidentally,
also appropriate to remind you that A.E. Van Vogt, one of the two or three
stars of the American Golden Age, was a Canadian, raised in Manitoba, who
wrote his greatest works there and in Ottawa, before moving, like so many
others, to southern California. It will also be appropriate to note that, according to a general consensus of critics and readers, something happens to the
quality of this production after the late 1940s: Van Vogt continued to publish
extensively, perhaps too extensively, over the next thirty years, but little of that
production has the electrifying excitement of the production of the first period
or manner. One explanation which has frequently been offered for this drop
in quality and inventiveness will also be familiar to students of literary history
(and I pass it on without either endorsing or repudiating it): towards the end
of the 1940s Van Vogt discovered the Truth, in the form of Dianetics (subsequently renamed Scientology), the invention of another Science Fiction writer,
L. Ron Hubbard. Thank God, Gide says somewhere, Balzac never discovered
the truth or system he had been looking for all his life! Van Vogt discovered
the truth, the system: it is in fact a system with which we may have some distant
sympathy today, since it argues for a deconstruction of millenial Aristotelian
logic and Occidental "common sense" in the name of new Utopian and I dare
say dialectical thought patterns (something very much in the air in that period,
and also visible, quite differently, in Asimov). On the other hand, the notion
that conceptuality in general and the adoption of philosophical systems in particular are harmful to the workings of genius, creativity and inspiration – that
notion strikes me as a Romantic or a high modernist cliché about which we
may well want to preserve some informed suspicion. At any rate, I will have
little more to say here, either about Dianetics, or about the later Van Vogt,
however theoretically interesting those problems may be. I will add only one
further piece of information to this literary–historical sketch of the situation
of this genre called Science Fiction, and it is this: that Van Vogt's work clearly
prepares the way for that of the greatest of all Science Fiction writers, Philip
K. Dick, whose extraordinary novels and stories are inconceivable without the
opening onto that play of unconscious materials and fantasy dynamics released
by Van Vogt, and very different in spirit from the more hard-science aesthetic
ideologies of his contemporaries (from Campbell to Heinlein).

This final observation, however, suggests another basic qualification before we begin our work in earnest. I am very anxious that the texts I am going to be dealing with not be simply assimilated to the paradigms of high culture or of the literary institution. (Even one's critical and interpretive practice threatens to have this fatal effect, like the framing operations of film: the focus on the text, its critical and analytical dismantling, seems automatically to confer a certain high-literary dignity on the object.) These stories, however, emerge from the world of the pulps and of commercial culture whose conventions remain intimately linked to their narrative intelligibility. They cannot be read as Literature: not merely because they include much that is trash and what Adorno would have called easy reading; but above all, because their strongest effects are distinct from those of high literature, are specific to the genre, and finally are enabled only by precisely those sub-literary conventions of the genre which are unassimilable to high culture. One cannot, in other words, select out a few intense "literary" effects and canonize those, since their conditions of possibility are very precisely pulp conventions. Something analogous could be said for the often strange and fascinating effects of the non-auteur film, the whole commercial underclass of the B movie.

In the case of Van Vogt, however, we can sharpen this warning and this dilemma in a very precise and concrete way. The working habits of this author, indeed, present some striking analogies with procedures long since on the books of high culture. This is the way Van Vogt describes his methods in his autobiography:

> I dream my story ideas in my sleep. I don't say that I get all my ideas by dreaming, but it is how I get aspects of them. I'm writing a story, for example, and I suddenly realize I don't know what comes next – you see, I have no endings for my stories when I start them … just a thought and something that excites me. I get some picture that is very interesting and I write it. But I don't know where it's going to go next. So then I sleep on it, and keep waking up thinking, "Well, now, I need a lift here of some kind." Then, I fall asleep, you see, even as I put that thought into my mind. Then I wake up again and repeat that, just run through the thought. If I can't do this, if I sleep all through the night, the next day I just wander around with ideas. Generally, either in a dream or about ten o'clock in the morning – bang! – an idea comes and it will be something in a sense non-sequitur, yet a growth from the story. I've gotten my most original stories that way; these ideas made the story different every ten pages.[1]

Elsewhere he confides that in fact he wakes up, or has himself woken up, every ninety minutes throughout the night.

1 *Reflections of A.E. Van Vogt* (Lakemont, Georgia, 1975), pp. 78–79.

"Le poète travaille." The parallel to surrealist procedures is inescapable; and one is tempted to wonder what kind of Science Fiction might have emerged from the inaugural surrealist phrase, "un homme coupé en deux par la fenêtre". Breton's passion for B movies and for the most garish and vulgar kinds of cultural junk and paraliterature is also most relevant here. My point, however, is that we must not read Van Vogt as a surrealist writer, despite the extraordinary fantasy logic of his tales, which as he himself points out rebound in the most shocking and unexpected new directions every ten pages. The stunning and depressing historical irony of the surrealist movement was that this preeminent anti-aesthetic vanguard movement, which despised Literature and aimed at the radical transformation of daily life itself, became the very paradigm of Literature and literary production in the Western mainstream high-cultural tradition. To grasp the movement of a Van Vogt narrative as virtual dream, as the logic of fantasy, as unconscious free association and projection, as sheer subjectivity, is in other words to "contain" those narratives and reduce them to a manageable literary operation already classified and catalogued in advance. In this sense, the very category of the "irrational" or the "subjective-unconscious" is a category in the service of instrumental reason itself, and a way of defusing and marginalizing otherwise aberrant, dangerous and subversive cultural phenomena. I would like to suggest that your or our resistance to the pulp conventions in such writers is the privileged form of censorship, and is itself the supreme symptom of the approach of a whole range of cultural and psychological defenses.

With these preliminaries out of the way, I want to touch briefly on three features of Van Vogt's work, three formal peculiarities of his narratives, which can perhaps initially be previewed under the headings of space, the subject and the Other. The discussion will be provisional, not only because of the constraints of time, but also because, as you will see shortly, it suggests a whole project of research and analysis.

As far as space is concerned, however, it is at once clear that Van Vogt's stories and novels all have something of that very special sense of place which also characterizes his contemporaries in the detective-story tradition (Chandler above all) and in *film noir*: a certain kind of run-down urban space, impersonal yet threatening alike, which is not incompatible with a specific, but historically determinant, experience of the countryside into which from time to time the city-dweller adventures. It will be difficult enough to convey this succinctly; but perhaps the following description of the initial flight of the hero of *Slan*, his first novel, will give some feeling for the Van Vogt cityscape:

> Then he was on a vacant lot, beyond which towered a long series of black-ened brick and concrete buildings, the beginning of the wholesale and factory district ... He scrambled up some steps into an open doorway, into a great, dark-lit warehouse ... a dull light-world of looming box shapes, and floors

that stretched into the remote semi-darkness ... He paused and peered out of the door. He was staring into a street vastly different from Capitol Avenue. It was a dingy street of cracked pavement, the opposite side lined with houses that had been built of plastic a hundred or more years before. Made of virtually unbreakable materials, their imperishable colors basically as fresh and bright as on the day of construction, they nevertheless showed the marks of time. Dust and soot had fastened leechlike upon the glistening stuff. Lawns were ill-tended, and piles of debris lay around.[2]

Only the final detail – plastic houses of the future, brightly colored, pristine, unbreakable, but worn out all at the same time – marks this urban description off from a Chandler cityscape; and I stress this point at some length because I will undoubtedly want to propose that we define our larger corpus as including a range of different sub-genres and media production from this general period which runs from the years immediately preceding the Second World War to the beginnings of the Cold War.

Now, however, we must look at less familiar types of spatial relationships: doors in particular are rather alarming in this world. A woman is wounded in her own bedroom; she awakens in a strange functional laboratory room; mounting a stairway, she opens a metal door and steps out onto a jungle pathway.

A brilliant sun was shining down on a hilltop clearing a few feet away. She climbed toward it, reached it, and stood briefly paralyzed by what she saw ... She was on an island, an atoll green with jungle, and surrounded by a blue ocean that extended on every side as far as the eye could see ... Dizzy, she turned to look at the door through which she had come. She expected to see a building, but there wasn't any. Undergrowth spread in a thick tangle all around where the building should have been. Even the open door was half-hidden by lichens that intertwined cunningly all over the exposed metal face of the door.[3]

In this story, such spatial disjunction is still minimally explained in terms of Science Fiction conventions, that is, of powers attributed explicitly to the characters (not magical powers, to be sure, which would place us in the domain of fantasy, but what we may call "hyperscientific" ones). I will call explanations of that type a kind of containment, in that – always within the conventions of the genre – they still tend to explain away the effect, or to rationalize it, thereby attenuating its force. I should add that we never find in Van Vogt the strong, rationalized SF convention often used in such juxtapositions of different space, namely teleportation, which is of course a virtually "realistic" form of containment.

---

2 A.E. Van Vogt, *Slan* (New York, 1982 [1940]), pp. 9–10.
3 A.E. Van Vogt, *The Worlds of A.E. Van Vogt* (New York, 1974), "The Purpose" (1945), pp. 61–62.

But often the explanation, the containment strategy, fades to the point at which such spatial passages are allowed to emerge with all of their originary force and scandalousness. In one of Van Vogt's most famous stories, for example, "The Weapons Shop", we have first of all the appearance, overnight, of a brand-new building in someone's backyard, the emporium of the title: this is the inversion of the effect we have been considering, the sudden intrusion, into normal everyday space, of a new object, whose inner volume does seem distinct from the outside world, but not yet altogether abnormally so. At the climax of the story, the protagonist is invited to leave the store through a side door:

> He could see flowers beyond the opening; without a word he walked toward them. He was outside almost before he realized it … He turned leftward to go to the front of the weapons store. Vagueness transformed into a shocked, startled sound. For he was not in Glay, and the weapon shop wasn't where it had been. In its place … A dozen men brushed past Fara to join a long line of men further along … But Fara's very being was concentrating on the section of machine that stood where the weapon shop had been. A machine, oh, a machine … His brain lifted up, up in his effort to grasp the tremendousness of the dull-metalled immensity of what was spread here under a summer sun beneath a sky as blue as a remote southern sea. The machine towered into the heavens, five great tiers of metal, each a hundred foot high …[4]

A final example from another one of the great stories, called "The Search", a narrative too intricate to summarize but which includes interesting rural landscapes. The protagonist is forced into a car, at a certain point, by one of his enigmatic but cosmic adversaries, yet instead of finding himself within the "long gleamy-hooded car"

> he was lying on his back on a hard floor. Drake opened his eyes and for a blank moment stared at a domed ceiling two hundred feet above him … For a moment then his mind wouldn't accept what his eyes saw. There was no end to that corridor. It stretched until it became a blur of grey marble and grey light.[5]

Along the walls, there are a number of doors, behind which Drake finds sumptuous but empty offices. In the distance, in the middle of the corridor, is a door of a very different type:

---

4 "The Weapons Shop", in Raymond J. Healy and J. Francis McComas, eds, *Famous Science-Fiction Stories* (New York, 1957), p. 768

5 A.E. Van Vogt, *Destination: Universe* (New York, 1952), p. 147.

At first, it was only a brightness. It took on glittering contours, became an enormous glass affair set in a framework of multitinted windows. The door was easily fifty feet in height. When he peered through its transparent panes, he could see great white steps leading down into a mist that thickened after about twenty feet, so that the lower steps were not visible.[6]

The steps, as you may imagine, prove to be endless, stretching down into an eternal void.

So much for the most striking examples: doors that literally open onto other worlds, that connect radically distinct types of space whose difference can range from worldly to otherworldly. Now, were we to accept at face value the verb "connect", we might be tempted to describe all this in terms of some unusual syntactical relationship: a spatial syntax, in which two distinct spatial substantives are articulated by means of that spatial verb which is the door. Yet in the strongest form of such effects, the two spaces are really not related; nor are they inertly juxtaposed in their radical difference, as in a collage. The passage through these doors is certainly an act or an event, but an unthinkable one, and thereby, one would also suppose, an unspeakable one, one which somehow sets us at the limits of what articulated language can do.

The field of linguistics is indeed ultimately constituted by the sentence itself as the object of study (the alternate formulations – the proposition or the speech act – seem to me variations on that more fundamental object). What then logically follows seems to have been historically the case, namely that linguistics is unable to break out of the bounds of the sentence. I quote Leonard Bloomfield: "Each sentence is an independent linguistic form, not included by virtue of any grammatical construction in any larger linguistic form. Whatever practical connection there may be between [the various sentences that make up some larger utterance], there is no grammatical arrangement uniting them into one larger form ... "[7] This point is to my mind confirmed rather than refuted by the efforts of various text grammars to propose larger units which subsume separate and individual sentences; however stimulating and suggestive such efforts have been, I cannot feel that any of them ultimately carry conviction or can be said to have achieved the program or project they often eloquently spell out.

Turning now to space, which is to say, to architecture, the question will be whether there is anything in that particular language which corresponds to the form of the sentence in speech (or in linguistics). That cannot, surely, be the building, that is, the overall architectural text. But I have been struck by a curious phenomenon: in all the extraordinary wealth of architectural and formal innovation in what is sometimes called postmodernism today, there is

6 Ibid., p. 148.
7 Leonard Bloomfield, *Language* (Chicago, 1961), p. 170.

one basic form which does not seem to have changed, which resists innovation, and which sometimes condemns such efforts to a peculiar inconsequence and a socially as well as aesthetically disappointing sterility: no one has been able to invent a new, a radically new form for what we will call the *room*. It is as though the room itself, the basic interior unit, the very space of dwelling, had persisted with very little modification from prehistoric times. We dwell within its walls, whether those are fourfold or manifold, and in whatever shape. The most powerful objection to this proposition surely comes from the innovations of modernism, where the so-called free plan of Le Corbusier aims at just such a radical break with the tradition and its conventional rooms and separations. Yet I am tempted to wonder whether this innovation might not be compared to certain historically new forms of the sentence, in particular so-called *style indirect libre*, what Ann Banfield has called the "unspeakable sentence".[8] The sentence there is indeed maintained, but transformed and refunctioned in a most curious and original way. Yet perhaps when the free plan is perceived as being successful, success simply means that this space has again been reassimilated to the age-old category of the room proper. When it is not successful, it ceases to be perceived as a form at all, and falls to the level of that dead empty institutional space so omnipresent in our larger contemporary buildings: that is to say that its syntax fails, and that, instead of producing a sentence, the architect has only succeeded in muttering nonsense, fragments, schizophrenic discourse.

At any rate, this peculiar parallel between the sentence and the room sheds some light on the Van Vogt spatial effect considered earlier. Van Vogt is then also something like a text grammar: not a theory but a mystery. His two distinct spaces are like the juxtaposition of two sentences from utterances absolutely distinct and heterogeneous. The mysterious door (which obviously has its earlier analogues in fairy tales and magical literature of all kinds) is then the sheer operator of this juxtaposition and the unthinkable sign of the operation itself. Yet at this point the analysis remains descriptive, and gives us no clues at all as to any possible interpretation of the process.

I therefore now move on to my second topic in order to see whether it may not retrospectively offer any interpretive clues: this was a peculiar effect of the subject to be found here and there in Van Vogt's corpus. One of the more characteristic Van Vogt narrative lines runs something like this: a protagonist operating within the now classical "realistic" *film noir* cityscape, on which we have already commented, suddenly finds himself intercepted by preternatural beings with ordinary human bodies. Most frequently these disguised aliens are part of a vast network or conspiracy in process somewhere within that familiar "realistic" environment; sometimes indeed the bewildered protagonist slowly comes to understand that he is in the presence of two

8 Ann Banfield, *Unspeakable Sentences* (London, 1982).

such networks in competition or struggle with each other – a benevolent and a malevolent alien underground – a situation which as you may imagine makes for plots whose intricacy is beyond all summary. At the climax of the story, however – and this is the feature I want to dwell on – the hero sheds his recognizable human consciousness and identity and realizes that he is himself precisely one of those aliens (the benevolent kind, needless to say). In order to fulfill his function in the conspiracy, however, he has had to undergo amnesia and to put on or wear a human consciousness – an operation so successfully executed that he believes it himself during the early parts of the story, whence his (and our) confusion. I have felt that a plot of this kind is to be grasped as what I will call a historical ideologeme: a specific narrative unit which in and of itself – in its own formal language – transmits a historical or a social message or meaning. It is a proposition which can be "verified" by finding the same ideologeme at work in other genres and other media during the same general period. If therefore we are able to detect the presence of this narrative unit at work beneath the different narrative and formal conventions of some of the other sub-genres, then we may feel ourselves on somewhat firmer ground in advancing the hypothesis that such a narrative motif has a certain autonomy of its own and knows a certain independence from any of the individual texts in which it can be discovered.

I will therefore suggest that the identity transformation designated in Van Vogt's Science Fiction can also be found, in very different manifestations, or narrative realizations, in the detective stories of the period, as well as in *film noir*. But here it is not to Chandler that one would turn, but rather to one of the most successful writers of thrillers in this general period (from the late 1930s to the late 1940s), a writer since largely forgotten but who seems presently to be enjoying a revival of interest: I am referring to Cornell Woolrich, who also wrote under the name William Irish (if that name is unfamiliar, you will at least recognize two classic film versions of his work, Truffaut's *The Bride Wore Black* and Hitchcock's *Rear Window*). I would not rule out the possibility of locating this ideologeme in high or serious literature, either (although here we would have to establish some much more complicated generic categories before proceeding): the example which here springs to mind is Richard Wright's strange and uncharacteristic novel *Savage Holiday*. But it is in *film noir* that we find the most "realistic" development of the narrative unit in question, a development which offers some useful clues as to its ultimate historical meaning or content: I'm thinking, for example, of the great Bogart film, *Dead Reckoning* (John Cromwell, 1947), in which the protagonist, a veteran returning from the war, finds himself in familiar surroundings which have undergone bewildering and incomprehensible modifications no less striking than in Van Vogt's Science Fiction. That the narrative should here find its most satisfactory organization around the figure of the returning Second World War veteran is to my mind the first, essential clue: my own point of departure for some eventual interpretation, that is, for a decoding of the social and historical content of the ideologeme, would then be the wartime situation itself, with its tremendous dislocations and relocations, first with the draft and the continent-wide migration to the new wartime industries, and then with the return of men who carry in their heads the memory of other continents and other worlds and who fail to recognize their home cities, families, wives and friends. I want to stress the obvious, namely that this hypothesis is only a point of departure, and that it ought not to exclude the exploration of a wide variety of other possible meanings; while the whole matter of causality and expression (does the lived situation cause the emergence of the new paradigm, or does the latter preexist it and articulate the existential?) is theoretical problem of the greatest interest indeed. If, however, this hypothesis carries any conviction or can be felt to have any plausibility, we may well be tempted to transfer some of its force back to our first narrative effect, where the door between two worlds can now be read as a virtual allegory of the brutal and abrupt world-displacements of Americans at war (we may also suppose that Van Vogt's own biographical displacements, from western Canada to the capital, and thence to Los Angeles, sensitized him in advance to this kind of logic of sheer juxtaposition).

I come now to my final observation about Van Vogt's work, which bears on the narrative status of the Other – a category conventionally figured in Science Fiction under the time-honored motif of the alien. You may be aware that it is only during the period of the emergence of SF into intellectual maturity in the 1960s, that the initial focus of Golden Age and pre-Golden Age narratives on space adventure and technology or science is displaced by and expanded to a larger concern with sociological and anthropological issues. This can be seen vividly in the history of the motif of the alien, which in the earlier period (and in the great B Science Fiction and horror films of the 1950s) remains an isolated monster, a kind of life aberration. It is not until the late 1960s that the representation of the alien comes to include a much more interesting ambition: the attempt to represent entire alien cultures or societies, to imagine what a whole alternative form of collective life might be like. It is the difference and the distance between brain-eating pod people or carnivorous vegetables and the anthropological visions of a Le Guin or of Niven and Pournelle's classic novel, *The Mote in God's Eye* (1974).

Van Vogt's aliens and monsters belong, of course, in the first of these periods, but with a peculiar twist or wrinkle which seems to me of the greatest significance. Let us return for a moment to Coeurl, the preternatural and baleful feline monster of the inaugural story, "Black Destroyer". Coeurl is a good deal more intelligent and *sympathique* than your run-of-the-mill garden-variety pod person, but nonetheless still clearly belongs to that general genus of the species monster. Yet it will be remembered that this formidable alien was encountered during the exploration, by an interplanetary human expedition, of the ruins of an alien culture. Reflection on this fact brought me to what I felt to be a momentous discovery, which I have been able abundantly to confirm throughout Van Vogt's other work, and it is this: "Black Destroyer" is not in fact a conventional alien narrative, although everything in it is organized to leave that impression with the reader. In fact, it is a quite distinct narrative paradigm, which one is tempted to call the two-alien situation. The point is that Coeurl is not a descendant of the extinct alien race which built the city under exploration: he is of a different alien species, and from a different point in the galaxy (or outside of it). We therefore have one living and terrifying monster superimposed upon the traces and archaeological remains of what we can only suppose to have been very different monsters either from Coeurl or from *Homo sapiens*. The situation is a curious one, since it is, from a practical storytelling standpoint, gratuitous: the plot line would not have been materially altered had the space explorers found Coeurl on a vacant planet.

Or so it would seem: yet it is the presence of just such seemingly gratuitous details which make up the charm and the mystery of narrative texts of this kind, or, to speak a different language, which demand a semiotic analysis that can account for the signifying effectivity of features which are not technically narrative units. The obvious objection would be that we have to do here with something which should be considered in terms of scene, setting and description as such. Yet this apparent scene – the ruined city – is in fact the trace of an absent character; but a character who plays no part whatsoever in the narrative.

I have said that the two-alien situation can be found everywhere in Van Vogt's work, although I hesitate to attribute to him its outright invention. It seemed to me useful, however, to show this same narrative paradigm at work in a recent and very popular film by one of the most interesting contemporary directors, namely, *Alien* (1979) by Ridley Scott.

While it bears some resemblance – taking into account the vast difference between the 1950s and the 1970s – to the old-fashioned monster movies (Scott's monster is if anything more ferocious and horrifying than anything the 1950s Bs were able to realize technically), it is in fact a far more complicated, sophisticated and interesting artifact. More significant than that for our purposes, *Alien*, like the Van Vogt stories, does not derive from the monster paradigm at all, but rather from that distinct form I have been calling the two-alien situation.[9] You remember how the monster hatches from a collection of hideous, leathery, mushroom-type eggs discovered on a distant planet by the crew of the mining vessel Nostromo. This industrial spaceship, however, was attracted to the planet by a mysterious signal, which turns out to have been a

9 On this point I am indebted to Peter Fitting. See his contribution to "Symposium on *Alien*", in *Science-Fiction Studies*, No. 22 (Vol. 7 pt. 3), November 1980.

warning code. What the crew discovers is in fact the wreckage of an alien spaceship, along with a single mummified body of one of its crew. The eggs are then found to have been deposited in its hold; meanwhile the mummy of the alien navigator is found to have been horribly mutilated, its ribcage virtually exploded from within. The spectator able to think back over these details at the end of the film will come to the obvious conclusion: the eponymous character, the monster of the film's title, is distinct from the aliens who once manned the alien ship. Meanwhile, subsequent events will have made clear that what happened to the alien ship and its crew must have been the same fate visited on the crew of the Nostromo – namely death and destruction at the hands of the shape-shifting monster. Besides that, as with the builders of Van Vogt's ruined city, we know nothing further about these second aliens, save that they had a high degree of civilization, and became extinct long before the beginning of the narrative, serving no function in that except to attract the new human crew or prey down to this terrible planet. *Alien* is thus virtually a film version or translation of "Black Destroyer". (Van Vogt is not credited, and as it turns out he sued the film-makers for plagiarism; the latter settling out of court.)

Now is all this some mere narrative curiosity or does the two-alien situation conceal some significance of wider interest? I would first of all point out that this situation superimposes very precisely the two types of representation of aliens I mentioned before, in a more historical context. The monster is the old biological alien, the aberrant and omnivorous form of a life energy that is virtually animalistic, and that, no matter how numerous these creatures, seems to lead an isolated and purely individual existence. The second alien, on the other hand, testifies in its absence to a whole alternative culture and society, and has left the traces of alien social relationships – a city and sophisticated technology, all of which presuppose language.

I believe that we have here a very special case of what Freud called splitting; you will remember that this concept is introduced in his well-known essay on Hoffman's story *The Sandman,* and designates a way of handling the ambivalence of the Oedipal relationship. The father is the object of socially obligatory love and also of deep unconscious hostility and aggressivity: he can take the form, therefore, either of paternal and protective benevolence, or of the terror and menace of the ogre. The neurotic hero of *The Sandman* splits this ambivalent figure in two, so that alongside the kindly but ineffectual father we also confront the diabolical father, the devil, the malignancy of evil. It is clear enough that our two aliens fall back into this general ethical polarization of good and evil, baleful and benign; can we go any farther than this in describing the transfer of the operation of splitting from the Freudian or Oedipal framework to that of the category of the Other in general?

I want, in conclusion, to cast a glance back at the inaugural text of modern anthropology, since anthropology can be considered that discipline governed *par excellence* by the category of the Other and which explicitly takes the Other as its object of study. (My own interest in this text is also determined by its very special place in the Marxist tradition.) I am referring to Lewis Henry Morgan's classic book *Ancient Society* (1877), the conceptual structure of which is organized around a tripartite classification of societies, which seems to derive from eighteenth-century Danish archaeology, but whose diffusion we owe essentially to Morgan, namely the distinction between savagery, barbarism and civilization. Although Morgan's differentials are primarily technological (including the technology of writing), the classification is an evaluative and judgmental one. Thus, civilization, which begins with writing, is here assimilated to what will become capitalism, and is therefore negatively positioned. The word *barbarism*, on the other hand, far from carrying the usual stigma, designates what is for Morgan the most glorious form of human social organization, as realized in the *gens* – his central illustration being the Iroquois Confederacy, of which he was himself an honorary member.

Here we evidently have again the Rousseauism of the noble primitive and the nostalgia for a form of human social organization on the scale of human life as it ought to be lived. But this is a tripartite and not a dual schema, which raises the interesting question of what the concept "savagery" means for Morgan. What we find is that there is little to be said of this earliest social form, since what gives a social order its lawfulness and articulation (among other things, one would today underscore the role of the incest taboo) is there not yet in existence: "low down in savagery the community of husbands and wives, within prescribed limits, was the central principle of the social system".[10] Elsewhere this system is always designated by the fateful terms "this stupendous system of promiscuity", where the adjective is obviously to be taken as that which strikes the mind with stupor and disbelief. Clearly then, in the very night of time, the first social formation of human history is also evaluated negatively, like the most recent one, although for very different reasons.

I believe that Morgan's tripartite scheme can be grasped as yet another, but if you like a fundamental, version of the two-alien narrative, since the third form, "civilization", is our own standpoint as readers. Civilization thus knows not one, but two contraries: a "stupendous" and frightening or taboo form, that of the primal horde and of the promiscuity of the original savages; and a glorious and heroic one, endowed with all the kinship legalities, yet on the proper scale for human life, to the point where at the very climax of his work, Morgan will call for the restoration of the *gens* (and an abolition of civilization or capitalism), very much in the spirit of Marx himself:

> The dissolution of society bids fair to become the termination of a career of which property is the end and aim; because such a career contains the elements

---

10 Lewis Henry Morgan, *Ancient Society* (Palo Alto, 1975 [1877]), p. 49.

of self-destruction. Democracy in government, brotherhood in society, equality in rights and privileges, and universal education, foreshadow the next higher plane of society to which experience, intelligence and knowledge are steadily tending. It will be a revival, in a higher form, of the liberty, equality and fraternity of the ancient gentes.[11]

But in the case of Morgan we possess some of the elements of a possible explanation and interpretation of our strange paradigm, in which an evil alien form – without sociality, but invested with the most frightening forms of desire – is juxtaposed alongside a good alien form in which the lineaments of an alternate social organization become visible. Lewis Henry Morgan was a complex and contradictory individual, in whom passionate fascination with the forms of American Indian life is linked to the career of one of the founders of the Republican Party and a lawyer for the lumber trusts, and that career in turn punctuated by passionate enthusiasm for the short-lived Paris Commune of 1871. But Morgan was also a Victorian gentleman, endowed with the arche-typal Victorian spouse (and future *veuve abusive*, of the type of Mark Twain's or Richard Burton's wives), his best friend a respected Presbyterian minister on the Princeton faculty. He must therefore somehow manage a passionate and libidinal primitivism which offers certain dangers in the Victorian context; and it is clear that he does so by performing an act of Freudian splitting, *avant la lettre*. Sexually tabooed features will therefore be disjoined, and allowed to reorganize themselves in the independent figure of the savage, that is to say, the abomination of promiscuity; at which point the second alien emerges in all its glory, as a heroic form of existence which can now safely be celebrated in public, in and for itself. We must not, however, content ourselves with some merely psychoanalytic diagnosis of this operation as sheer work on the phantasm: its mystery lies in the result, that the act of splitting also serves to found a "scientific" analysis of modern capitalism which is itself no mere phantasm, but work on the Real.

Indeed, if we recall that the scheme in effect posits not three but four terms – savagery, barbarism, civilization and that "next higher plane of society" which is the future, and which, far from marking some merely cyclical return of the gens and of "barbarism", portends a wholly new and Utopian form – we may well wish to grasp the two-alien narrative as a novel instrument for generating the future. The two negative terms it deploys – contradiction versus contrariety – are intensified by that syntactic door which opens onto the blinding otherness of a new world and a new self. It is a door which Van Vogt succeeded in opening for a time.

1984

---

11 Ibid., p. 552.

7

Longevity as Class Struggle

The topic of this essay and volume is also a matter of some personal gratification because it allows me to indulge in the chance to talk about one my
favorite books from very long ago – an occasion that might never have arisen
otherwise, at least in the normal span of our current lifetimes. George Bernard
Shaw's *Back to Methuselah* was published in 1921, at about the same time as
Karel Čapek's unrelated *The Makropoulos Secret*. Meanwhile, one character in
Shaw observes in passing that H.G. Wells "lent me five pounds once which I
never repaid; and it still troubles my conscience".[1] We are, with Shaw and
perhaps even with the "nonsynchronously synchronous" Čapek, still in the
afterwash of that late Victorian age in which science, doubt and vitalistic
philosophy met to produce the very first modern Science Fiction; and I might
say, as someone who has always spoken against the legitimization of popular
sub-genres by high-literary respectability (that is, Dashiell Hammett compared
to Dostoyevsky), that on the other hand there are genuinely science-fictional
pleasures coursing through the epic text of Shaw's "metabiological pentateuch" which some might still be tempted to identify with the canon.

It is questionable, however, whether the canon is yet ready to return to
Shaw; or whether Michael Holroyd's immense biographical efforts, or the
current Irish revival – more specifically the Oscar Wilde revival – or even the
heliotropic turning of the collective imagination back to the *belle epoque* and
the age of the Second International are sufficient to make Shaw's art again
available to us. This is to say that we may still harbor some deeper doubts or
hesitations about the cryogenic revival of this figure, just as we may entertain
them about Robert A. Heinlein, whose garrulous and didactic longevity has
so much in common with that of the socialist playwright. To acknowledge
Shaw as our Bertold Brecht (although for the poetic drama it is rather
W.H. Auden one would like to acknowledge as Brecht's English-language
approximation) is then to reckon in another way with the possibility that after

---

1 George Bernard Shaw, *Back to Methuselah* (New York, 1921), p. 131. Later page references
in the text preceded by *BM* are to this edition.

Brecht we may no longer need a Shaw. Still, in the uniquely apolitical atmosphere of Anglo-American literature (where the other rival for some genuinely Brechtian intellectual and artistic-activist role may well turn out to be T.S. Eliot himself), it is always instructive to examine the extraordinarily rich practice of one of the few great political artists of modern times. It has been said, indeed, that few things contributed so fundamentally to the cultural preparation for the Labour Party's victory in 1945 as Shaw's tireless propaganda for socialism, which took the form of secondary figures in the great plays whose tirades gradually domesticated, respectabilized and legitimized that terrifying ideology for the British middle classes.

Back to Methuselah, though, makes it clear that the implacable critique of middle-class hypocrisy in general and the English national character in particular (which an Anglo-Irishman was particularly well placed to articulate) was also a fundamental cultural and political act: something we can perhaps appreciate all the more in the superstate today, from which all lingering and nagging or garbled approaches to some self-knowledge about American vices of national character, let alone original sin, have been triumphantly expunged. One must also appreciate the fable whereby the last genuine remnants of true ethnic or group consciousness – the Irish and the Jews – abolish themselves as cultures on the shattering contact with the long-lived, whose proximity and existence – this is one of the fundamental themes of the play – inspire a well-nigh fatal "discouragement" in normal short-lifers like ourselves. But this running political commentary – including a great deal more on the British parliamentary system, which is no longer necessarily of interest to us, along with some remarkable developments on war and aggressiveness from Cain to Ozymandias and the Napoleons of the far future – can serve to illustrate the formal and structural peculiarities of the Shavian play, where much can be added in passing of a seemingly extraneous or digressive nature, and the mesmerizing experience of sheer unbridled talk itself can laterally, as it were, allow any number of supplementary topics to be carried into the spectatorial consciousness along with the official subject of the play. "There has to be something to eat and drink on every page," Flaubert once said by way of characterizing the drive for heterogeneity he felt at work within his own will to style.

Meanwhile, the all-inclusive nature of the monuments of high modernism – their vocation to become the Book of the World – also seems echoed, but idiosyncratically, in this Shavian method, which seems to consist in affirming a whole list of his own idiosyncrasies, of which the ideal Shavian spectator expects – nay, demands – a full recapitulation in every new play.

We are not interested in those idiosyncrasies today (too bad for us!), but it is worth underscoring a single extraordinary moment in *Back to Methuselah*, what Brecht might have called a *gestus* – the shaping of an act or an event into a gestural form that speaks in its own new language – before using this particular fantasy about longevity or immortality to gauge and bring out the specificities and the differences of the other, more modern versions we will have to deal with later on. As any schoolchild knows, *Back to Methuselah* begins in the Garden of Eden. From there, four additional full-length plays (a cycle that evidently owes something to Wagner) lead us to the Utopian condition of a "summer afternoon in the year 31,920 AD", or, following the title of this concluding play in the cycle, "As Far as Thought Can Reach". Not the least fascinating aspect of its dramaturgy – occasionally the cycle is actually performed – is the suggestion of recurrence implicit in the use of the same actors for later and later roles, so that the first family of Eden turns up in the proper nonconformist British drawing room of the 1920s, the still exceedingly British world government of the twenty-second century, the world of AD 3000 dominated by powerful and mysterious long-lifers who have segregated the short-term people in other parts of the globe and serve as their oracles, and on into some ultimate Utopian state in which sexual relations have ceased and humans are born fully grown from eggs, and with but three or four years to live a normal, "childish" life before acceding to the unlovely isolation and wisdom of the condition of the Ancients, who long only to do away with their bodies altogether and attain the immortality of pure thought. One may incidentally feel that Shaw's physical puritanism is not much more repellant than Heinlein's hearty and obligatory hedonism; maybe neither value has that much to do with sex after all. Indeed, I am going to argue that as a general rule, at least in these works, the official subjects can mask a less obvious but deeper one, which it is the task of the critic and the interpretative process to draw out.

Shaw takes what one may want to call a Christian Scientist attitude toward biology, and perhaps even toward politics and metaphysics as such: in these last areas, it would be easy to diagnose his attitude as the expression of a kind of Fabian or social-democratic idealism, which would reflect a characteristic overestimation of reason and persuasion and an equally characteristic underestimation of ideology, unconscious drive and the rule of violence in human history. That is just the kind of idealism one would expect to find as the working ideology and legitimation of the practice of one of the great political orators of the twentieth century; but in Shaw it is by no means as one-dimensional an idealism as this account might suggest. Indeed, his view of choice dovetails well with the requirements of a theatrical aesthetic (with its structural premium placed on speech amid dialogue) and opens a mediatory dimension between base and superstructure of a more distinctive and unique kind.

For Adam "decides" to live for a thousand years at the moment when words and concepts are being invented for the first time: his freedom to choose his own life span is part of that first unnamed freshness of the universe, and incidentally coordinates the theme of longevity with that of language and figuration, as we shall see below. But it is with the second moment in the process that we are most concerned here. For in the most characteristically Shavian fashion this first play or moment of the pentateuch, in the Garden of Eden before the Fall and then several centuries later, is succeeded by a new moment staged in the quintessential British drawing room, on Hampstead Heath, peopled by the two cranks of the title ("The Gospel of the Brothers Barnabas") along with their families and assorted typical British politicians of the interwar period. It is indeed the conviction of the brothers that politics, as it is still practiced despite its disastrous consequences in the Great War a few years earlier, can only be reformed by biology, but of an unusual kind: "Our program is only that the term of human life shall be extended to three hundred years," and "our election cry", the flapper spokesperson adds, "is 'Back to Methuselah'" (*BM* 77).

Faced with this possibility, the politicians rearrange their platforms and electoral strategies and the curtain falls. It is about the next evening that I want to talk primarily and to some purpose. This play, or subplay, is significantly entitled "The Thing Happens": a description that parlays the immediate representational motif – in this case whether people will live longer, or indeed forever – onto a higher level of symbolic abstraction. As far as the longevity motif is concerned, it always involves a basic representational dilemma: How can you show that people have begun to live longer? At what point can longevity become visible in the narrative itself? It is all very well for us to look back across Lazarus Long's long life. From the outset, virtually by definition, we know that the "thing" has happened to him. But we and the writer are more often in the unhappy position of Emperor Rudolph II of Bohemia, who first tries the Makropoulos secret out on the inventor's daughter in 1600 and then goes mad. "How," as she puts it three centuries later on the modern stage, "how could he be sure I was going to live for three hundred years? So he put my father in a tower as a fraud and I ran away with everything he had written to Hungary or to Turkey, I don't remember which."[2]

How indeed? How do you make an event out of such a condition, whose features consist in suddenly beginning one day to wonder why after so many years a friend or acquaintance has not seemed even to begin to change or grow old? It is by comparing newsreels of the drownings of a number of famous people that Shaw's short-lifers discover their astonishing physical similarity, much as though we were to discover that Alexander the Great, Christopher Marlowe and, say, James Dean all looked suspiciously like the same person. At the very least this would tend to convert the immortality or longevity drama back into a kind of detective story – something it most notably is in Čapek's play. In a moment, I want to trace the consequences of this representational problem or dilemma out in two different directions: namely, on the one hand, the reason why the long-lifers feel the need to disguise their unusual destinies;

2 Karel Čapek, *The Makropoulos Secret* (Boston, 1975 [1922]), p. 81.

and, on the other hand, the question of time itself, not merely how one might represent an expanse of human time of this magnitude but what it would feel like existentially and to what degree the inner experience of the long-lived might be imagined to be radically and qualitatively different from that of the normally mortal – would there, for example, be many more volumes full of Proustian *madeleines* and *souvenirs involontaires*?

But this particular representational problem – the palpable difficulty in finding an objective correlative or narrative figuration for the disclosure of longevity or immortality – suggests some more fundamental interpretative and hermeneutic lesson. In the following pages we will act methodologically as though a principle exists according to which the ostensible content, the manifest topic or subject matter, always masks a deeper one of an entirely different nature. Some such principle is probably always at work in the hermeneutic process since interpretation would not be required if the work always said exactly what it meant. Interpretation seems called for in the present instance by the nagging suspicion that the longevity motif may be a cover or blind for something else.

This is a point that might be illustrated the other way around by the thematics of death, more specifically by meditations on its meaning: Simone de Beauvoir (but also Ernst Bloch, I believe, in a very different philosophical context from Sartrean existentialism) has argued that since death is meaningless in the first place, such meditations, despite their evident charge of affect, cannot be expected to lead anywhere; they are reveries in a void that in reality capture and express feelings and anxieties of a very different (non-existential) kind. The interpretative hypothesis would then suggest that the theme of death – thinking about it, experiencing the death anxiety – invariably serves as a cover and vehicle for deploying the fear of something else (for de Beauvoir, the fear of having wasted one's life, regret at not having lived).

What we must now conjecture is whether something similar could be advanced for the immortality or longevity plot: whether its anxieties too might stand, in the conscious mind, as substitutes for some more concrete and fundamental worry and fear – some deeper contradiction – at issue in the unconscious. With the possibility of such a hermeneutic reversal, I come back to the most stunning development in Shaw's narrative. In "The Thing Happens", set in AD 2170 in the office of the president of the world system, which is located in the British Isles, members of that government – some of whom look suspiciously like the politicians in the previous twentieth-century governmental system and are indeed their descendants – slowly discover that two of their number, the Archbishop of York and the Domestic Minister, Mrs Lutestring, are in reality very different from themselves and prove to have lived for over two hundred years. Who are these two people? They are evidently not the political leaders (whose descendants we have actually witnessed here, still in charge of the ship of state after so many generations), nor even the great-grandchildren of the original "inventors", if one may put it that way. They are, in fact, the parlormaid of the house and the fatuous young tennis-playing cleric we remember to have courted the brothers' daughter (or niece), and who offered singularly pure specimens of a witless leisured class in its most marginal and secondary manifestations. These, and not the protagonists, the main characters or stars, are those whom the lightning somehow struck. They merely overheard the good tidings, which were meant for a more important public. When Mrs Lutestring is asked what set her thinking about the new idea of longevity, she replies:

> Conrad Barnabas' book. Your wife told me it was more wonderful than Napoleon's Book of Fate and Old Moore's Almanac, which Cook and I used to read. I was very ignorant; it did not seem so impossible to me as to an educated woman. Yet I forgot all about it, and married and drudged as a poor man's wife, and brought up children, and looked twenty years older than I really was, until one day, long after my husband died and the children were out in the world working for themselves, I noticed that I looked twenty years younger than I really was. The truth came to me in a flash. (*BM* 135–136)

And for the Mozartian accents of Shaw's instrumentality, the pathos more delicate than anything in Čapek or Heinlein, there is also a brief expression of regret, in a play whose ruthless indifference to death matches its idealism: "There was one daughter who was the child of my very heart. Some years after my first drowning I learnt that she had lost her sight. I went to her. She was an old woman of ninety-six, blind. She asked me to sit and talk with her because my voice was like the voice of her dead mother" *(BM* 135).

Radical chains, the weakest link, the meek shall inherit the earth – such are some of the more ancient cultural stereotypes that cross the mind confronted with this remarkable development, so unsuspected as to offer the very figure of sheer unforeseeability and unexpectability as such and in itself. I will use the *gestus* of this twist in two ways, the first of which has to do with the nature of causality here proposed to us. It should be clear that in Shaw, as has already been observed, a kind of Christian Science version of the "life force" replaces the machinery of the modern or postcontemporary "rejuvenation" technology. What happens when all that is reckoned back into the contemporary SF narratives we will see in a moment; but it seems unsatisfactory to attribute the new development to mere voluntarism or a boundless Enlightenment belief in the power of the conscious mind or of Reason as such. On the contrary, Shaw here offers us an infinitely more flexible and subtle vision of the unconscious mind – perhaps even the unconscious collective mind – than we are used to dealing with. Indeed, if you take the whole stage of part two (in which the "gospel" of the Brothers Barnabas is promulgated) as an allegorical representation of that psyche itself, we have one conscious will –

the brothers – earnestly conveying its message to corrupt listeners only too eager for their own part to exploit its possibilities, while elsewhere in the drawing room distracted secondary minds catch bits of the freighted rigmarole in passing and a servant passes in and out of the central stage carrying a tea tray and intent on more menial business, storing up pieces of conversation for future use. There is a family likeness here to Proustian involuntary memory, which has no use for overly conscious acts of attention of the will but takes in its bounty of experience laterally, as it were, and by way of afterthought: indeed, Proust also promises a kind of increase of life, but by adding to the conscious life span all those secondary lives we had no time to notice we were also living simultaneously with the first, official one. Walter Benjamin's notion of distraction and Brecht's idea of the musing, reflective distance of the judicious, smoking theater spectators of his pedagogical dramas (from which Benjamin's idea developed) also merit a mention here, for future comparison. So also do current neo-pragmatist reflections about belief itself and the peculiar level at which it operates: a postmodern substitute for the roles played by the more modernist Freudian notion of the unconscious and the Marxist notion of ideology.

Another figure from the 1920s, though, seems closer to Shaw's intricate conjuncture of the unpredictable and unforeseeable with the inevitable, and it will move us on to the second remark I had in mind to make about this episode. This is the famous image, which we owe to Victor Shklovsky, of the "knight's gambit", the knight's non-linear jump across the chessboard that awkwardly seems to rebuke, in a vaguely premonitory or Utopian fashion, the more traditionally graceful yet prosaic moves of the other pieces. The most richly inventive of the Russian Formalists, Shklovsky wanted to dramatize by this figure an idea that was dear to all of them and had to do essentially with literary history – namely, that this last does not proceed from father to son (nor even, one supposes, from mother to daughter) but rather from uncle to nephew. The development of forms and genres is thus discontinuous and teleological all at once: when one is brought to fullest development (and by definition exhausted), what takes its place is not the successor or epigone but rather a marginalized and hitherto popular form that springs into place as a new space for formal and artistic development and evolution. So also with Shaw's characters: it is not the ruling class or its politicians but the poor, ignorant and undeveloped who are the recipients of the new message. "I was too ignorant to understand the thing was impossible," the former chambermaid tells us. And in some similar fashion Georg Lukács, also in *History and Class Consciousness* (but following the first published articles of Marx himself), posits the richer human and intellectual and cultural potential of people who have been denuded of everything, who have not inherited the standard culture or undergone the standard educational formation – indeed, who have become little better than commodities themselves, reduced to selling their own labor-power.

I mention these parallels in order to complete the second move demanded by this interpretative process, which is to suggest that, at least in this case, the longevity drama is not "really" about longevity at all, but rather about something else, which can a little more rapidly be identified as History. It is History as such (not merely literary history) whose *telos* moves according to the knight's gambit; and the power of Shaw's play is to have given body to that within the extraordinarily limited and genteel confines of the bourgeois drama and the bourgeois drawing room. The title of this episode, "The Thing Happens", then, can already be seen in advance to fling the whole drama of unexpected longevity onto a higher plane of abstraction, where it stands for the Event itself, the Event in collective history, that radical act we often, for want of a better term, call revolution – a sudden collective movement of the people that can never be predicted in advance, that strikes the least likely place and the least likely collective agents or actors, that cannot be prepared by arrangements of the conscious will, but that is surely prepared in other subterranean if not unconscious ways. Benjamin sought a different kind of figuration for this ultimate Event of our collective social life, this ultimate mystery, when he had recourse to the language of the messianic, trying thereby to convey – against linear notions of historical accumulation and progress (which he attributed to the Second and Third Internationals fully as much as bourgeois thinking) – the way in which the Messiah arrives at the most unexpected moment, through some small lateral door in the historical present. It is a supreme event that has nothing whatsoever to do with anything that went before, or even anything that transpired in the seconds immediately preceding the sudden apparition of this utterly new reality. In Shaw, the break is less absolute. There is preparation of a cultural and intellectual kind; seeds are sown, but the thing happens in seeming independence of all that. I want to explore the possibility that the longevity plot is always a figure and a disguise for that rather different one which is historical change, for radical mutations in society and collective life itself.

As to why this is so, why everything has to mean something else, in this particular case the hermeneutic principle – for this is ultimately at stake in allegorical interpretation as such – can be defended locally in terms of the experience of longevity itself, about which our books tell us uniformly that nothing whatsoever is to be said. This emptying out of the very figure of long life, the absence of content at the core of the narratives we are examining, can be said, if you do not mind a rather different philosophical reference, to exemplify a fundamental Nietzschean doctrine about the irreducibility of the present. We will let Heinlein field this one, which is the discovery by the short-lived Dora, who is if anyone the principal woman protagonist of *Time Enough for Love*:

> Long ago, three or four years at least, shortly after I figured out that you were a Howard, I also figured out that Howards don't really live any longer than we ordinaries do … We all have the past and the present and the future. The past

is just memory, and I can't remember when I began, I can't remember when I wasn't ... So we're even on that. I suppose your memories are richer; you are older than I am. But it's past. The future? It hasn't happened yet, and nobody knows. You may outlive me ... or I may outlive you. Or we might happen to be killed at the same time. We can't know and *I* don't want to know. What we both have is *now*.[3]

It is a discovery that, later on, Lazarus Long will summarize as follows: "Each individual lives her life in *now* independently of how others may measure that life in years" (*TEL* 398). One may wish to nuance the account and point out that, typically for the bourgeois philosophical position, Dora overestimates the past and underestimates the future, something Shaw's next evening, or subplay ("The Tragedy of an Elderly Gentleman"), makes clear. "It is not", Zoo tells the elderly gentleman in question (a short-lifer, or ordinary), "the number of years we have behind us, but the number we have before us, that makes us careful and responsible and determined to find out the truth about everything" (*BM* 183). And indeed, Shaw insists over and over again on the idea that not the accumulation of past memories and experiences piling up, but rather the perspective of having to live for several hundred years more makes up the difference and "wisdom" of the long-lived. We will return to this difference when we raise the issue of the psychological, and in particular the issue of boredom versus "discouragement".

For the moment, however, it is the narrative consequences of the matter that I want to underscore: for if Dora is right, then from any existential point of view there can be no essential difference between the experience of the short-lifers and that of the long-lived, and the Emperor Rudolph was quite right to go insane, like a theatergoer who is told he will have to wait another thirty years for the play to be finished. This is why the sheer experience of the present – which Heinlein discovers and reinvents in the passages I have quoted – can play no part whatsoever in his novel and occupies less than one page out of six hundred. Longevity is thus, as I have tried to suggest, a pretext for doing something else: in Heinlein's case, among other things, it serves first as a structural frame for interpolated stories – just as the Russian Formalists claimed about *Don Quixote* years ago. Don Quixote, Shklovsky argued, is not a character but the "motivation of a device", the pretext for stringing together a host of interpolated stories, novellas and anecdotes, in the process of which this pretext is reified and turned into a character in its own right. So also Lazarus Long, who may then be looked at from two different perspectives. From one standpoint, indeed, the project may be seen as the equivalent of a modernist one for Heinlein. That is to say, and whatever the differences, this

---

3 Robert A. Heinlein, *Time Enough for Love* (New York, 1973), 283. A later page reference in the text preceded by *TEL* is to this edition.

ultimate project is designed to be all-inclusive and interminable in the most literal sense, and it thus fulfills the existential requirement and function of the archetypal modernist projects in Mallarmé or Joyce or Proust: that they completely absorb everything contingent about human existence, that they give you something to do for the rest of your life and thereby make every accident and every stray moment of that otherwise uneven and unjustifiable sequence of days and years supremely meaningful, by virtue of the project into which it can be incorporated (not necessarily in any basely autobiographical way). The theme of boredom that I anticipated above – the boredom of Utopia, the tedium or acedia of the long-lifer – now acquires a somewhat different and unexpected resonance, as that which threatens the modernist project and risks falling out of it into a random unjustifiability that the project cannot redeem or transform. The banal form of this is, then, the possibility for Heinlein to fill up book after book of Lazarus Long stories.

The content of those stories, however, moves us on to a somewhat different aspect of the matter, which is the pedagogical strain Heinlein shares with Shaw, but which in the American is more fundamentally related to a kind of cult of experience (in Shaw it is based on an impertinent assumption of difference and sheer genius). As is the case with the oldest realists in the tradition, much story-telling in Heinlein (or at least much of the later storytelling) seems to be based on the pleasure of sheer know-how, from which there flows the more multiple pleasures of sheer explanation (how to set up camp in the wilderness, how to outsmart your enemies, how to invest in galactic stocks, be an interplanetary trader, raise a family, and so forth). All of this can perhaps be resumed under the notion of assuming the paternal function – or better still, of combining that function with primal narcissism. It explains why, if Shaw's parable is really about History, Heinlein's is about the Family (and I do not mean to deny the link he makes between rejuvenation and the starting up of multiple new families).

But all of that in turn is based on what Jean-Paul Sartre long ago in *Nausea* denounced as the "ideology of experience", the idea that we learn from the past and that the older we are and the more experiences we are supposed to have had, the more we know and the more suitable we become for occupying a paternal function that consists in explaining things interminably and in showing off our infinite know-how. Late Heinlein, then, confronts us with the interesting question of what narrative really is: not so much what storytelling really is as what the story in storytelling might or might not be. When I show someone how to repair a car engine or put up a tent, is that a story or the material for a story? The answer must be that the lesson becomes a story only when I am able to show myself in the act of giving the lesson in the first place. Longevity is then the excuse, not for lots of lessons so much as for lots of stories about those lessons.

But early Heinlein was clearer about another displacement or consequence of the longevity plot, which we already encountered in Shaw at the end of

"The Thing Happens" and with a certain reversal then in full force in the next drama of the pentateuch, "The Tragedy of an Elderly Gentleman", to which I have already referred. The motif of longevity or immortality, I have suggested, must always necessarily mean something else to acquire narrative content; but there is a second set of consequences that flows from the choice of the cover motif itself. This new set of narrative consequences has to do with the coexistence of long-living characters with the older, shorter-lived kind, so that the new, semiautonomous, independent story that coexistence begins to tell, in all the versions that are conveniently consulted under the rubric of immortality or longevity, becomes a story that can only be identified as that of class struggle.

What immediately happens in Shaw, for example, is that on discovering long-lifers in their midst, the politicians of the world state make plans to kill them all. Heinlein's *Methuselah's Children* (1958) is then the classic story of this persecution. In it, group fear and envy transcend the dynamics we generally associate with the backlash against race or gender or ethnic markings and attain the proportions of a kind of existential panic very similar to class panic itself. For now it is not merely that the *jouissance* of the alien group – its collective cohesion, the intensity of libidinal gratification this cohesion produces – seems far greater than my own and incites me to the kind of envy that, as Slavoj Žižek has shown,[4] underlies the various backlash formations. Now in the case of long life itself, my very existence as an individual and a group is called into question, and a political mobilization of a necessarily more cynical or lucid kind results, one that cannot be disguised, legitimized, or mythologized by fantasies about race or gender. This development can be seen, if you like, as the coming to the surface of that deeper historical content we first posited: if the longevity plot is really about radical social change, then its working out is bound to involve the violence and collective convulsion of just such struggles as we begin to find inscribed here in a second moment. The modern developments of the genre then show the narrative consequences and possibilities of this content, as we will see.

But it is perhaps worth concluding with Shaw at this point, using a few final observations about *Back to Methuselah*, to develop another motif neglected until now: namely, the matter of the boredom of eternity. *Time Enough for Love* begins indeed with Lazarus' well-nigh terminal depression at the thought that as he had already done everything conceivable (in a life span of some two thousand years) there was no point to living any longer. It is something that the novel then seeks energetically to cancel: narratively, by way of the frontier motif itself; formally, by way of the *Thousand and One Nights* compendium; and libidinally, by fantasies about clones (and probably about bisexuality). The biographical old age of Shaw himself, who, haunted by Jonathan Swift's Struldbruggs, longed

---

4   See Slavoj Žižek, *For They Know Not What They Do* (London, 1991).

to die as passionately as T.S. Eliot's Cumaean Sybil, would seem to document the plausibility of the complaint. But we must decline to endorse this stereotypical wisdom and must rather insist that boredom itself, like the fear of death, is always the disguised expression of something else. This becomes much clearer when we adjust the valences from the individual to the collective, when the complaint about the boredom of Utopias can much more clearly be seen to be so much propaganda for the excitement of market competition.

What is more interesting in Shaw's play is the displacement or inflection of the boredom motif toward what he calls discouragement, the morbid and suicidal quasi-physical feeling short-lifers experience in the presence of the long-lived, who have by now become, in the fourth play of the pentateuch, virtually a different species and are in the last play, or ultimate Utopia ("As Far as Thought Can Reach"), transformed into an oviparous life form that sheds most of its bodily, formerly human, interests after the fourth year (the "boredom" of this now being remotivated as a kind of childishness). Discouragement, however, marks a kind of reversal of the power relations not unlike the great "thought-experiment" of H.G. Wells' *The War of the Worlds* (1898), in which the genocides of colonial peoples are redirected on Europe itself so that the "civilized" can learn what it feels like for a change. Here too the short-lifers – our own species, like the Neanderthals – have lost the class struggle with the alternate society and the alternate Utopian beings; and the cultural envy of the traditional ruling classes has given way to the experience of defeat and the pain of the vanquished. It is the obverse of Shaw's picture of lateral or preconscious conversion; here too discouragement is both physical and a matter of deeper preconscious awareness and conviction that has little enough to do with the conscious mind. It is indeed one of the grand and dramatic merits of SF as a form that it can thus win back from the sheerly psychological or subjective such expressive powers of pathology – depression, melancholy, morbid passion – and place this material in the service of collective drama; but it may not be so important to insist, for insiders, on what must be stressed for the benefit of outsiders to SF as such: namely, that the unique new possibilities of this representational discourse – which has come to occupy something of the functions of the historical novel in the beginning of the bourgeois age – are social, political and historical far more than they are technological or narrowly scientific.

Still, it is in the direction of science and technology that the longevity plot leads in our own time, and I will conclude with a few comments on the distinctiveness of the latest, post-Heinlein, fortunes of the genre – a characterization I scarcely mean to be understood in purely chronological terms, since books like Robert Sheckley's *Immortality, Inc.* (1958), Clifford D. Simak's *Why Call Them Back from Heaven?* (1967) and Robert Silverberg's *To Live Again* (1969) – all from the 1950s or 1960s – precede *Time Enough for Love* in linear time at the same time that they largely anticipate and foreshadow a novel like

Joe Haldeman's *Buying Time* (1989), which I take to be characteristic of current contemporary or postcontemporary works in this particular form.

Paradoxically, the new narrative mutation is now far better equipped to navigate the problem of representing longevity as an event by the way in which the question regarding the appropriate contemporary technology is appealed to as a stand-in or substitute for the thing itself. Thus, in Haldeman, the rejuvenation process itself, which might be expected to entail the corniest battery of traditional SF wonder-working medicines and machinery, is displaced by two innovations: it needs to be renewed every so often, and at each renewal one's entire fortune must be given to the corporation (a development from which an interesting subplot of an investment nature emerges). The absence of medical and technological details is motivated, however, as it already was in Heinlein (whose delight in village explanations did not that way lie), in this manner: the whole thing is so agonizingly painful that the subject represses all memory of it. I suppose that the most graphic way of handling this properly technological moment is the idea of changing bodies, as in Sheckley (or even, secondarily, in Silverberg); but that brings us close to fantasy and the occult, as indeed the survival of the category of zombies, poltergeists, and the like in Sheckley's novel testifies (in a virtually autoreferential comment). The most chilling representation of the subject is therefore one in which the camera ensures a kind of documentary objectivity: I refer to John Frankenheimer's great film *Seconds* (1966), in which the embarrassing political questions – Where do the new bodies come from? How is the organization itself structured? – receive the grimmest answers. But there can be no doubt that the ultimate displacement is one in which longevity and immortality are represented by their opposite, and the virtually non-narrative idea of living forever is made into a story you can tell by way of the deep freeze that precedes it (sleep or suspension now taking the place of living as a narratable event). It remained for Philip K. Dick's *Ubik* (1969) to produce in advance something like the metanarrative of this now conventional narrative and raise visceral questions about our vulnerability during this half-life condition, questions that are themselves, as we shall see, displaced political ones.

For it is finally the political overtones that save the new paradigm from regressing into some older science-and-technology SF paraphernalia of an outmoded Golden Age type. The idea that, in the deepening conservatism of the Reagan years and beyond, SF has reverted to more exclusively scientific interests (or, better still, that, in a kind of Eliot-like dissociation of sensibility, its energies have been divided between just such a return to science, on the one hand, and a surrender to multivolume fantasy production, on the other) seems a plausible enough assertion, which it would nonetheless be advisable to nuance. For I think that the contemporary fascination with hard science tends to be as sociological as it is epistemological, and this not least because of the massive cooptation of pure science in the

United States by business and defense research of all kinds. But this means that if we are interested in contemporary science, it is not only in the theories but in the very mechanics of experimentation – the grant procedures, the lobbying whereby the necessary laboratories (which can range from a giant celestial telescope to expensive underground shooting ranges for rare electrons) are funded. And this leads on finally to an interest (still sociological) in the psychology of the newer scientists who have, perhaps since *The Double Helix*, begun to replace traditional artists as the characterological disguises and distorted expressions of the representation of what Utopian, non-alienated work might look like. But, clearly enough, in the moment we become interested in scientific activity as a collective or guild matter, in terms of professionalism and socially determined psychological dispositions and aptitudes – in other words, in yuppie science, if I dare put it that way – in that moment we are not far from the convulsive reappearance of general politics as such.

How could it be otherwise in a situation in which the most intimate psychological problems of geriatric care and contraceptive medicine, amid the still exceedingly physical matters of the homeless as well as of the massive and systematic administration of drugs to elderly and psychiatric patients, are everyday media concerns; in which the salaries of what are euphemistically called health-care providers are debated with as much acrimony as the yearly bonuses of the great business executives; in which the privatization of hospitals becomes a matter of profit and business, and investment is solicited for the so-called health industries as a whole? In this atmosphere, not only are the arrangements of all professional guilds, including those of the scientists, drawn back into an instant micropolitics, but the kinds of political privilege specifically suggested by health care can only be magnified to panic levels by the addition of the chance that one might be selected to live forever, presumably on the basis of a cash down payment.

It has been said that one of the most remarkable political revolutions, one of the grandest moments in the history of human freedom, occurred on that day in the Egyptian Fifth Dynasty (in the third millennium BC) when eternal life, hitherto the privilege of the elite, was extended to the Egyptian population as a whole. If this is so far a phantasm, so will it be for a scientific fantasy in which the representation of long life for a few is bound to raise the inevitable issue – a most embarrassing one ideologically, but a happy, welcome and productive one on the level of narrative construction and storytelling – of the attitude of all the others to this ultimate form of special privilege. Free-enterprise ideology in the United States was always stimulated by the fantasy that under the rules of the game you (or your children) had the outside chance to strike it rich; but the new fantasy of extended life can no longer be used that way. It now serves a divisive ideological function of excluding the anonymous demographies of the only-too-mortal.

For fantasy is also a harsh mistress and includes its own ironclad reality principle. You cannot satisfactorily daydream about living forever without first settling the practical matter of how those who do not live forever are going to be handled: fantasy demands a certain realism in order to gain even provisional or ephemeral libidinal and aesthetic credit, and this is indeed the deeper truth-mechanism of narrative itself (and the source of the adage about trusting the tale rather than the teller and his own personal ideology). However a story may originate in private wish-fulfillment, it must end up disguising its private subjectivity and repairing all the non-functioning machinery,[5] building a village behind the Potemkin façade, dealing with the sheerly logical contradictions the unconscious has left behind it in its haste – in short, shifting the attention of the aesthetic spectator from the gratification of the wish to its far less appealing preconditions in the Real, and thereby becoming in the process transformed from the expression of an ideology to its implicit critique.

In the case of longevity or immortality, I would not want this critique to be taken in any moralizing sense. I am indeed astonished and appalled at the degree of residual moralism still inherent in this topic. It surely has some relationship to the traditional anti-Utopian motif of ultimate boredom I referred to, although the scarcely veiled motivation of this is political and thereby a little less complicated than the insistence of so many writers on the subject that it would be evil to live forever, that true human existence requires a consent to mortality, if only to make room for our children's children; that hubris and egotism are to be denounced as prime elements in this particular fantasy about the supreme private property, not merely of having a self but of having it live forever. All that may be so, but I would be very embarrassed to argue it this way, and there is certainly an aroma of *ressentiment* or sour grapes to be detected in this extraordinary puritanism, which may simply reflect the greater facility accorded to writers by simple religious and ethical paradigms, as opposed to the more strenuous business of imagining the social itself.

I conclude by suggesting two levels of the political in recent SF longevity paradigms: on the more global level, what is reflected is clearly the increasing class polarization of the advanced countries of late capitalism (in the United States, we are told, 1 percent of the population now owns 80 percent of the wealth). On this level, it does not seem farfetched to argue that the motif of some special privilege of long life offers a dramatic and concentrated symbolic expression of class disparity itself and a way to express conveniently the passions that it cannot but arouse. But here one would want to add in something of the history of the form and suggest that the new paradigm marks a modification of the older, only-too-familiar near-future

---

5   The classic analysis remains Sigmund Freud's "Creative Writers and Day-Dreaming" (1908), *Standard Edition*, Vol. IX, pp. 141–153. (And see Part One, Chapter 4, in this volume.)

paradigms of overpopulation, ecological disaster, and the like. The longevity novel would thus stand as an enlargement of the possibilities of the near-future sub-genre, deploying the attempt to imagine future technologies in the service of the expression of deeper and more obscure fears and anxieties.

The hermeneutic model I have proposed above – deeper meaning hidden within the text, behind, below the surface, like an "unconscious" of the text that needs to be interpreted out – is no longer a very popular one in this age of surfaces and decentered, textualized consciousness. Another model may therefore also be suggested, namely that of allegory: a structure in which a more obscure train of thinking attaches itself parasitically to a second, an other (*allos/agoreuein*) line of figuration, through which it attempts to think its own, impossible, as yet only dimly figured thought. So it was by way of death and existential anxiety, along with the fantasy of living forever, that Shaw's play tried to think through its imperial content, at the very moment of the agony of the British Empire itself: it was by way of similar affective content, but at another time and in another place, that Heinlein invoked fantasies of the disappearing family and the disappearing frontier, and attempted to produce high-technological and far-future images of both as viable forms. In the most recent SF texts on longevity, however, what seems to be the deeper secondary line of reflection and allegorical intellection is the increasing institutionalization and collectivization of late modern or postmodern social life, as that seems primarily embodied in the vast transnational corporation, bigger than most governments, and virtually impossible to modify or control politically.

In this material, for the moment at least, the political dilemma is at one with the representational one: the problem of bringing the great corporations under political control is the same as the problem of mapping their presence in our daily lives, of perceiving them, of giving them expression and articulation, of a narrative as well as a cognitive type. In earlier periods of SF (to limit ourselves to that prescient registering apparatus), the great corporations coexisted with small businesses and their more humane ethos, as in Philip K. Dick for example, or else called forth over against themselves individualistic rebels and heroes of a classic populist-style revolt, as in Frederik Pohl and C.M. Kornbluth's *The Space Merchants* (1953). In our particular longevity sub-genre, it is surely Norman Spinrad's remarkable *Bug Jack Barron* (1969) – a high point of a certain 1960s narrative ethos and still full of surprising vitality – that marks the exhaustion of the paradigm of heroic revolt, beyond which there stretches the faceless anonymous longevity of the multinational or trans-national corporation of the present day, as that began to emerge after the winding down of the Vietnam War (in the Allende coup, for example).

But it is precisely that anonymity that poses questions not merely for narrative – problems of agency and *actant*, of anthropomorphism and personification, indeed of event and diegetic change – but also questions for political praxis as well. The transnational structures have of course found a different kind of expression in the sheer euphoria and delirium of cyberpunk, where their cybernetic networks are affirmed with all the excitement of the high and the nonstop production of new language and new figuration. It may not be inappropriate, then, in closing, to see the new longevity narrative as the other face of that, the bad trip, the obscure and deep-rooted depression in the face of an uncertain future, in which the function of immortality is only to revivify images of transnational eternities.

1996

8

Philip K. Dick, In Memoriam

Philip K. Dick, who died in March at 53, was the Shakespeare of Science Fiction. Thirty odd novels over as many years made his name as familiar to SF enthusiasts as it was unknown in English departments, although he became a cult figure among French intellectuals. The most ineffectual way to argue Dick's greatness, however, is to claim his books as high literature (as when enthusiasts pass off Hammett or Chandler, say, for Dostoyevsky). A mass-cultural sub-genre like SF has different (and stricter) laws than high culture, and can sometimes express realities and dimensions that escape high literature.

Consider Dick's capacity to render history. Consumer society, media society, the "society of the spectacle", late capitalism – whatever one wants to call his moment – is striking in its loss of a sense of the historical past and of historical futures. This incapacity to imagine historical difference – what Marcuse called the atrophy of the Utopian imagination – is a far more significant pathological symptom of late capitalism than features like "narcissism". "Nostalgia art" from *American Graffiti* to Doctorow's (otherwise fine) novels testifies not to an interest in the past but rather to its transformation into sheer stereotypes. Even the lessons of older revolutionary theory and practice are often vitiated by historical nostalgia (*Reds* is also nostalgia a film, alas!).

Science Fiction is generally understood as the attempt to imagine unimaginable futures. But its deepest subject may in fact be our own historical present. The future of Dick's novels renders our present historical by turning it into the past of a fantasized future, as in the most electrifying episodes of his books. In one of the finest and most somber of his novels, *Ubik*, hapless protagonist Joe Chip is desperately trying to reach Des Moines and must travel across a landscape whose objects are rapidly decaying in time. In a first ominous note he finds that the coin-operated refrigerator of his own 1992 present begins to refuse money that has reverted to 1970s coinage.

The great airports are also presumably reverting (is there still a "New York Airport" in the late 1930s? he wonders), while even the ground transportation to get him across the island begins to become obsolete, the flapples and helicopter taxis of his own day replaced by a classic museum-piece 1939 LaSalle. When he finally manages to rent a Curtiss-Wright biplane theoretically capable of reaching Des Moines sometime tomorrow afternoon (the LaSalle has in the meantime reverted to a 1929 Model A Ford), there is no guarantee the process will not regress beyond the age of aviation altogether.

In *Now Wait for Last Year* this quest for an impossible past takes the form of a complex that a senile tycoon builds on his private asteroid, a complex that reproduces with loving authenticity the Washington, DC, of his 1935 boyhood, 120 years earlier. Employees work overtime on the search for period artifacts to furnish this simulation of the past, unearthing such priceless treasures as an old package of Lucky Strike *with the green*, a radio recording of the soap opera *Betty and Bob* or of Alexander Woolcolt's "Town Crier".

In his most famous novel, *The Man in the High Castle*, Dick unfolds an alternate history in which the Germans and the Japanese won the Second World War and occupy and administer the two halves of the continental US between them. But while the Nazis (Hitler long since dead of syphilitic paresis, the succession having passed to Baldur von Schirach) have completed the genocide of Africa and are on their way to colonize the moon, the milder and more aesthetic Japanese have developed a passionate fad for genuine pre-war American artifacts.

Kipple and Biltong

The Dick future is no less peculiar than its collectable pasts – a bureaucratic world in which creditors' jet-balloons humiliate hapless debtors by hovering overhead and blaring out their financial standing to the surrounding crowds, in which the coin-op door of your own apartment refuses to let you out when (like Joe Chip) you never have any loose change on you, and automated cabs offer comments and advice more exasperatingly than any contemporary taxi driver.

In some of these near-futures an even more ominous phenomenon, kipple, makes its appearance. This is Dick's personal vision of entropy, in which objects lose their form and "merge faceless and identical, mere pudding-like kipple piled to the ceiling of each apartment" (from *Do Androids Dream of Electric Sheep?* filmed as *Blade Runner*). This late twentieth-century object-world (unlike the gleaming technological futures of Verne or Wells) tends to disintegrate under its own momentum, disengaging films of dust over all its surfaces, growing spongy, tearing apart like rotten cloth or becoming as unreliable as a floorboard you put your foot through.

Hence the obsessive compensatory theme of reproduction. In one of his most alarming fables, "Pay for the Printer", Dick imagines a steadily deteriorating post-atomic universe momentarily rescued by the arrival of a curious blob-like species, the Biltong, who appeared "in the closing days of the War, attracted by the H-bomb flashes" (Dick's work includes whole boarding houses full of benevolent and likeable aliens). The Biltong can reproduce perfectly any item or object set before them. But with old age and exhaustion, their prints become blurred and lose definition – whiskey tastes like anti-freeze, doors rip off cars, houses collapse. At length, a population that has forgotten how to produce anything lynches its dying benefactors.

This post-catastrophe perspective may explain why in Dick's novels, as in other kinds of populism, handicraft skill (especially potting) becomes the privileged form of productive labor. Yet it is the related theme of reproduction and of the production of copies that makes Dick's work one of the most powerful expressions of the society of spectacle and pseudo-event, in which "the image is the final form of commodity reification", as Guy Debord puts it in *The Society of the Spectacle*. For Dick was also the epic poet of drugs and schizophrenia of a 1960s counterculture (not excluding the gnostic mysticism that he propounded insistently in his final years, after the renunciation of the drug culture in *A Scanner Darkly*, in 1977).

This is the Dick of *The Three Stigmata of Palmer Eldritch* (a sardonic commentary on Bradbury's idyllic *Martian Chronicles*), where conscript settlers on a barren Mars seek distraction from their deformed vegetables by a collective drug ritual in which they transubstantiate into the figures of a Barbie-doll-type lay-out, enjoying the proxy pleasures of a vanished jet-set Earth, driving Jaguar XXB sports ships over still pristine Californian beaches and making imaginary love with each other while their bodies lie immobile in Martian hovels.

End to individualism

But Dick was more than a supreme embodiment of 1960s countercultural themes. This is, for instance, a literature about business, and in particular the sector of image and illusion production. Its "average heroes" – an older, populist, Capraesque type of small employees such as record salesmen, self-employed mechanics and petty bureaucrats – are caught in the convulsive struggles of monopoly corporations and now galactic and intergalactic multinationals, rather than in the *Star Wars* feudal or imperial battles.

It is a literature in which the collective makes a fitful and disturbing reappearance, most often in a paralyzed community of the dead or the stricken, their brains wired together in a nightmarish attempt to find out why their familiar small-town worlds are lacking in depth or solidity, only to discover that they are "in reality" all immobilized together in some cryogenic half-life.

It is, finally, a literature of the so-called "death of the subject", of an end to individualism so absolute as to call into question the last glimmers of the ego, as when, in one of Dick's most chilling stories, an executive in an android-producing firm makes the shattering discovery that he is himself an android. "We didn't want you to know," his fellow employees console him gently, "we didn't want to tell you."

It may be the very conventionality, the inauthenticity, the formal stereotyping of Science Fiction that gives it one signal advantage over modernist high literature. The latter can show us everything about the individual psyche and its subjective experience and alienation, save the essential – the logic of stereotypes, reproductions and depersonalization in which the individual is held in our own time, "like a bird caught in cobwebs" (*Ubik*). Dick's work does that. It is a virtual "art of the fugue" of storytelling, narrative pyrotechnics that unravel themselves in delirium and can stand as a critique of representation itself.

1982

9

After Armageddon:
Character Systems in
Dr Bloodmoney

Dick's voluminous work can be seen as falling into various distinct thematic groups or cycles:[1] there is, for instance, the early Van Vogtian game-playing cycle, the Nazi cycle (for example, *The Man in the High Castle*, *The Unteleported Man*), a relatively minor Jungian cycle (of which the best effort is undoubtedly *Galactic Pot-Healer*) and, of course, the late "metaphysical" cycle which includes his most striking novels, *Ubik* and *The Three Stigmata of Palmer Eldritch*. On such a view, *Dr Bloodmoney* (1965) can be assigned to a small but crucial middle group of eschatological novels, along with its less successful companion piece, *The Simulacra*. In these two works, for the first time, there emerges that bewildering and kaleidoscopic plot structure we associate with Dick's mature production. At the same time, this cycle helps us to understand the origins and the function of this sudden and alarming proliferation of sub-plots, minor characters and exuberantly episodic digressions, for both of these works dramatize the utopian purgation of a fallen and historically corrupted world by some final climactic overloading, some ultimate explosion beyond which the outlines of a new and simpler social order emerge. But in the two cases the "coding" of the evil, as well as its exorcism, is different: in *The Simulacra* (1964), this is political and economic, and it is a big-corporation but also entertainment-industry-type power elite which invites purgation, while in *Dr Bloodmoney* the historical crisis is expressed in terms of the familiar counterculture denunciation of an evil or perverted science (compare Vonnegut in *Cat's Cradle*), only too emblematically exposed by the invention of the atomic bomb.

In this particular book, indeed, for the first and last time in the Dick canon, we are given to witness an event which serves in one way or another as the precondition and the premise of other books but which already lies in the past by the time most of the latter begin: the atomic cataclysm, World War Three, the holocaust from which all the peculiar Dick near-futures spring and in which they find their historical sustenance. Here alone are we able to see the bombs actually fall and the towers topple; indeed, an untypical flashback isolates the

1 For the chronology, see note 1 of the next essay.

moment itself and draws our attention to it with hallucinatory intensity. So we would want to ask, at the outset, why such a vision of catastrophe, on which other SF writers have not shown the same reluctance to dwell, should be so infrequently represented by a writer not otherwise known for his squeamishness; or, to reverse the order of priorities, what in the construction of *Dr Bloodmoney* enables it to present this vision.

In the context of Dick's world, for his aesthetic and that narrative line that is so unmistakably his own, the raw material of atomic destruction presents artistic problems unlike any other, problems of a delicate and strategic kind, that involve the very scaffolding of Dick's novelistic construction. Nowhere else, indeed, is the fundamental ambivalence of his imagination revealed so clearly, an ambivalence which is, however, the very source of his strength elsewhere and the formative mechanism of his invention. For the point about the atomic cataclysm in *Dr Bloodmoney* is not merely that Bluthgeld takes it to be a projection of his own psychic powers, but that, as the book continues, we are ourselves less and less able to distinguish between what I am forced to call "real" explosions, and those that take place within the psyche. Every reader of Dick is familiar with this nightmarish uncertainty, this reality fluctuation, sometimes accounted for by drugs, sometimes by schizophrenia, and sometimes by new SF powers, in which the psychic world as it were goes outside, and reappears in the form of simulacra or of some photographically cunning reproduction of the external. In general, the effect of these passages, in which the narrative line comes unstuck from its referent and begins to enjoy the bewildering autonomy of a kind of temporal Moebius strip, is to efface the boundary between real and hallucinatory altogether, and to discredit the reader's otherwise inevitable question as to which of the events witnessed is to be considered "true".

In such moments, Dick's work transcends the opposition between the subjective and the objective, and thereby confronts the dilemma which in one way or another characterizes all modern literature of any consequence: the intolerable and yet unavoidable choice between a literature of the self and a language of some impersonal exteriority, between the subjectivism of private languages and case histories and that nostalgia for the objective that leads outside the realm of individual or existential experience into some reassuringly stable place of common sense and statistics. Dick's force lies in the effort to retain possession and use of both apparently contradictory, mutually exclusive subjective and objective explanation systems all at once. The causal attribution, then, of the hallucinatory experiences to drugs, to schizophrenia or to the half-life, is not so much a concession to the demands of the older kind of reading or explanation as it is a refusal of that first, now archaic solution of symbolism and modernism: the sheer fantasy and dream narrative. To attribute his nightmares to drugs, schizophrenia or half-life is thus a way of affirming their reality and rescuing their intolerable experiences from being defused as an unthreatening surrealism; a way of preserving the resistance and the density of the subjective moment, of emphasizing the commitment of his work to this very alternation itself as its basic content. And this discontinuity is at one with our fragmented existence under capitalism; it dramatizes our simultaneous presence in the separate compartments of private and public worlds, our twin condemnation to both history and psychology in scandalous concurrence.

Now, however, it becomes apparent what is unique about the atomic blast as a literary event in such a world: for with it the question about the referent, about the truth value of the narrative, returns in force. It becomes impossible for Dick to do what he is able to do elsewhere: to prevent the reestablishment of the reality principle and the reconstitution of experience into the twin airtight domains of the objective and the subjective. For unlike the time warps and the time sags, the hallucinations and the four-dimensional mirages of the other books, atomic holocaust is a collective event about whose reality the reader cannot but decide. Dick's narrative ambiguity can accommodate individual experience, but runs greater risks in evoking the materials of world history, the flat yes or no of the mushroom cloud. And behind this difficulty, perhaps, lies the feeling that America itself and its institutions are so massively in place, so unshakeable, so unchangeable (save by total destruction), that the partial modification available in private life through drugs and analogous devices is here unconvincing and ineffectual. How, then, does *Dr Bloodmoney* manage to assimilate something which apparently by definition lies outside the range of Dick's aesthetic possibilities?

The overall plot of the novel is rather conventional: we follow several survivors of the blast in their various post-atomic adventures which all appear to reach some climax in the death of Bluthgeld (the Dr Bloodmoney of the title, supposedly referring to Edward Teller), and which all have a kind of coda in the return to Berkeley as to a gradual reemergence of civilization. Yet it seems to me that the content of the individual adventures, and the detail of the novel, cannot really be understood until we become aware of the operative presence within it of a certain number of systems of which the surface events are now seen as so many combinations and articulations.

Chief among these, as is so often the case in non-realistic narratives, narratives not dependent on common-sense presuppositions and habituated perceptions, is that formed by a whole constellation of peculiar characters. The revelation – made in passing, without any great flourishes – that the initial point-of-view figure (Stuart) happens to be black has the function of staging the appearance of the first really unusual figure – the thalidomide *cul-de-jatte* or phocomelus Hoppy Harrington – in the still fairly "realistic" and everyday perspective of social stigma: both work for a businessman who prides himself on providing jobs for people otherwise excluded from the normal white American society with which we are all familiar. It is only later on, after the bomb blast, that the real mutants begin to flourish; yet it seems to me that these opening pages have the function of slowly beginning to separate us from our ordinary characterology, and of deprogramming our typological reactions, preparing us for a narrative space in which new and unfamiliar systems of classifying characters can operate at full throttle, unimpeded by cultural and personal presuppositions on the part of the reader.

A first hint that these various characters do not exist as mere isolated curiosities, as unrelated monsters of various kinds, is provided by the fate of the "first man on Mars", immobilized in eternal orbit by the outbreak of the war and circling Earth henceforth as a kind of celestial vaguely leftist disk jockey whose task it is to provide a communications relay between the stricken areas over which he passes, and otherwise to play hours of taped music and read aloud the few available surviving texts – Somerset Maugham's *Of Human Bondage*, for instance – which remain of the cultural patrimony at the dawn of these new dark ages. Dangerfield is, of course, a more or less ordinary human being, yet aspects of his situation slowly – and improbably – begin to impose an analogy with Hoppy's. Consider, for instance, Stuart's reflection on the latter character: "Now, of course, one sees many phoces, and almost all of them on their 'mobiles', exactly as Hoppy had been, placed dead center each in his own little universe, like an armless, legless god".[2] This image might also characterize Dangerfield's sacred isolation as he circles the earth; but a childhood memory of Hoppy's reinforces the parallel: "'One time a ram butted me and I flew through the air. Like a ball.' … They all laughed, now, himself and Fergesson and the two repairmen; they imagined how it looked, Hoppy Harrington, seven years old, with no arms and legs, only a torso and a head, rolling over the ground, howling with fright and pain – but it was funny; he knew it"(18–19). This power of Hoppy's to project bodies into the air like soccer balls later becomes lethal (the death of Bluthgeld), but it suggests a kinesthetic affinity for Dangerfield's fate as well – the live being housed in a cylindrical unit rolling through empty space. And when it is remembered that this plot line reaches its climax in Hoppy's attempt to substitute himself, through his own voice and powers of mimicry, for the ailing Dangerfield, the analogy between the two positions becomes unmistakable.

Yet they are not exactly symmetrical. Subsequent events, and the introduction of newer and even stranger characters, seem to make the point that Hoppy is, if anything, insufficiently like Dangerfield. At this stage, indeed, in the increasing post-atomic prosperity of the West Marin collective, it is as though Hoppy, with his complicated prostheses and his remarkable skills in repair and invention, has become far too active a figure to maintain the analogy with the imprisoned disk jockey. The episode-producing mechanism of the novel then produces a new being, a more monstrous and more adequate replica

2 P.K. Dick, *Dr Bloodmoney, or How We Got Along After the Bomb* (New York, 1965), p. 96 (all further references given in the text).

in the form of the homunculus Bill, carried around inside his sister's body and emitting messages to her and to others on the outside, but as decisively insulated from the world as Dangerfield himself.

Indeed, it may be suggested that the entire action of the novel is organized around this sudden shift in relationships, this sudden rotation of the axis of the book's characterological system on the introduction of the new being. We may describe it as a problem of substitutions: Hoppy's error is to believe that he is Dangerfield's opposite number, and, as such, destined in some way to replace him. In fact, however, his mission in the plot is quite different, for he is called upon to eliminate the ominous Bluthgeld, who has not yet figured in our account and whose anomaly (schizophrenic paranoia) would not seem to be a physical disability of the type exemplified by Hoppy or Bill, or, by metaphoric extension, by Dangerfield himself.

But before trying to integrate Bluthgeld into our scheme, let us first rapidly enumerate the other freaks or anomalous beings that people this extravagant work. We have omitted, for one thing, the realm of the dead themselves, to which Bill has special access – "trillions and trillions of them and they're all different ... Down in the ground" (136). Here then, already the half-life world of *Ubik* is beginning to take shape; yet as entities the dead are quite distinct from either Bill or Dangerfield in that, equally isolated, they have no mode of action or influence on the outside world, and cannot even, as do the former, emit messages to it: "After a point the dead people down below weren't very interesting because they never did anything, they just waited around. Some of them, like Mr Blaine, thought all the time about killing and others just mooned like vegetables" (155).

Finally, among the extreme varieties of mutant fauna in the post-atomic landscape, we must not forget to mention the so-called "brilliant animals", creatures with speech and organizational ability, like Bluthgeld's talking dog or the touching subjects of the following anecdotes: "'Listen, my friend,' the veteran said, 'I got a pet rat lives under the pilings with me? He's smart; he can play the flute, I'm not putting you under an illusion, it's true. I made a little wooden flute and he plays it through his nose' ... 'Let me tell you about a rat I once saw that did a heroic deed,' the veteran began, but Stuart cut him off" (98–99). These gifted animals, indeed, provide Stuart with his livelihood, the sale of Hardy's Homeostatic Vermin Traps, mechanical contrivances scarcely less intelligent than the prey they are designed to hunt down, and which may therefore lay some equal claim to being yet another variety of new creature.

I will now suggest that all of these beings, taken together, organize themselves into systematic permutations of a fairly limited complex of ideas or characteristics which turns around the notion of *organism and organs*, of mechanical contrivances, and (in the case of the phocomelus) of prostheses. But the results of these combinations are a good deal more complicated than a simple opposition between the organic and the mechanical, and A.J. Greimas' semantic rectangle³ allows us to map the various possibilities inherent in the system as shown in the diagram.

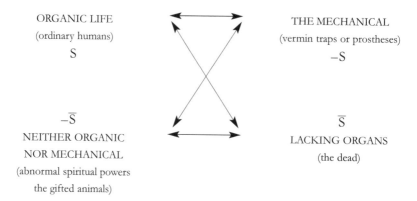

ORGANIC LIFE

(ordinary humans)

S

THE MECHANICAL

(vermin traps or prostheses)

–S

–S̄

NEITHER ORGANIC

NOR MECHANICAL

(abnormal spiritual powers

the gifted animals)

S̄

LACKING ORGANS

(the dead)

The four self-generating terms of the graph represent the simplest atomic units of the characterological system of *Dr Bloodmoney*. Yet it will be noted that, with the possible exception of S itself (or, in other words, of all the *normal* human characters in the book), all are in another sense merely part of the background of the work, providing a kind of strange new living environment for the action in it, and marking out the life coordinates of this post-atomic universe, fixing the limits within which the plot will unfold, without themselves really participating in it. In particular, it will have become clear that none of the really aberrant characters described above can be accommodated neatly within any given one of the four basic terms.

Yet the generative capacity of the semantic rectangle is not exhausted with these four primary elements. On the contrary, its specific mode of conceptual production is to construct a host of complex entities out of the various new combinations logically obtainable between the simple terms. These new and more complicated, synthetic concepts correspond to the various sides of the semantic rectangle, so that the complex term designates an idea or a phenomenon able to unite in itself both terms of the initial opposition S and –S, while the neutral term accordingly governs the negatives of both, a synthesis of the bottom terms –S̄ and S̄. The respective combinations of the left-hand

3 This forbidding apparatus is based on the idea that concepts do not exist in isolation but are defined in opposition to each other, in relatively organized clusters; and on the further refinement that there is a basic distinction between the opposite, or contrary, of a contradictory, S. Thus if S is the Good, then –S is Evil, while S̄ is that somewhat different category of things "not good" in general. The determination of the negative of –S is more complicated, as I show in the text; and as is also demonstrated further on, there is the further possibility of more complicated terms which unite these simple ones in various ways. See, for further discussion of this schema, A.J. Greimas, "The Interaction of Semiotic Constraints", *Yale French Studies*, No. 41, 1968; and also my *Prison-House of Language* (Princeton, 1972), pp. 162–168, as well as my Introduction to Greimas, *On Meaning* (Minneapolis, 1987).

and right-hand sides of the rectangle are technically known as the positive and negative implications respectively, while the diagonals are designated as the deictic axes. A little experimentation now shows that these four combinations correspond exactly to the four principal anomalous characters or actors of the book.

The complex term, for instance, a being which would unite a normal human body (S) with a machine or mechanical prostheses (–S), can only be Dangerfield himself, as he circles the Earth forever united to his satellite. The negative implication which emerges from the union of a prosthesis with a crippled being (S + $\overline{\text{S}}$ lacking organs) is of course Hoppy Harrington, the phocomelus. The neutral presents perhaps greater problems, insofar as it involves the enigmatic fourth position, $-\overline{\text{S}}$ + $\overline{\text{S}}$, itself the negation of a negation and thus apparently devoid of any positive content. Yet if we read this particular term, which is neither an organism nor a machine, as something on the order of a *spiritual* prosthesis, a kind of supplement to either organic or mechanical existence which is qualitatively different from either, then we sense the presence of that familiar realm in Dick's works in which, under the stimulus of drugs or schizophrenic disorder, vision, second sight, precognition, hallucination, are all possible. If this reading is accepted, then the neutral term would be understood as a combination between just such a spiritual prosthesis or supplementary power and a being lacking organs; and it becomes clear that what is thus designated can only be the homunculus Bill, with his access to the realm of the dead and his absence from the world of physical existence. Our scheme has the added advantage of allowing us now to integrate Bluthgeld himself into a more generalized system of anomalous characters. As long as our basic traits or characteristics were limited to the opposition of organic and mechanical, the system seemed to bear no particular relevance to the figure of Bluthgeld. With the idea of spiritual powers, his position with relation to the other characters is now more easily defined, and it would seem appropriate to assign him the as yet unfilled function of the so-called positive implication, or, in other words, the synthesis of S (ordinary human) and $-\overline{\text{S}}$ (spiritual prosthesis). Now his privileged relationship to Hoppy Harrington also becomes comprehensible: to the phocomelus alone will fall the power to destroy Bluthgeld, because Hoppy is the latter's reverse or mirror-image. Indeed, their relationship is still more complicated than this; for in appearance Hoppy is Bluthgeld's creature, and the other characters believe him to be the genetic result of the notorious 1972 fall-out catastrophe for which the scientist was responsible. In reality, however, he is a thalidomide birth from an earlier period – 1964 – and owes nothing to Bluthgeld, whom he is thus free to annihilate.

We may now articulate this new system of combinations diagrammatically. Not only does this scheme permit us to account for the construction of the main characters of *Dr Bloodmoney* and to understand their relationship to each other, it provides us with material for grasping their symbolic value as well,

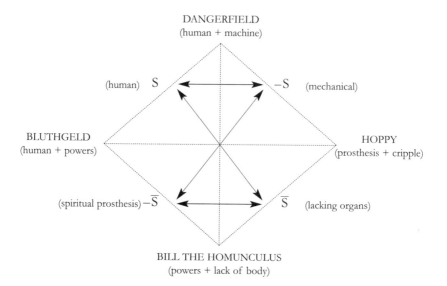

and thus eventually for an interpretation of the bizarre events which the novel recounts. The systematic arrangement here proposed, for instance, suggests that the four characters are distinguished by distinct functions or realms of activity and competency. If, for example, we take *knowledge* as a theme, and interrogate the various positions accordingly, we find that each corresponds to a different and specific type of cognitive power: Hoppy thus possesses knowledge about the future as well as a practical kinaesthetic knowledge and control of inorganic matter; Bill the homunculus possesses (verbal) knowledge about the dead and kinaesthetic knowledge/control of organic matter. Meanwhile, the final long-distance psychoanalysis of the ailing Dangerfield suggests that the particular type of knowledge associated with him is (verbal or theoretical) knowledge of the past, and he is, of course, the guardian of an almost annihilated Earthly culture. As for Bluthgeld, his province is surely Knowledge in general, the theoretical secrets of inorganic matter (and kinaesthetic control of it), that is, of the universe itself.

But as we enrich the thematic content of the four positions, it seems possible to characterize them in a more general way, one which may ultimately allow us to see them in terms of some basic overriding thematic opposition. So to each position or combination would seem to correspond a particular type of professional activity as well: Dangerfield is thus, as we already noted, a kind of celestial DJ, one version among many of the characteristic Dick entertainment celebrity, whose most recent incarnation is the Jason of *Flow My Tears, The Policeman Said*. Opposed to this valorization of the word, Hoppy takes his place as an embodiment of the other characteristic form of creative activity in Dick's world, namely the practical handiman or artisan-inventor. The other two figures do not at first glance appear to fit very neatly into this scheme of things: Bluthgeld is of course the prototypical mad scientist, but more directly, during the course of the book's action, the psychotic and visionary; while Bill – judging from the endless conversations carried on with him by his sister Edie, much to the dismay of her elders – would seem best described as an imaginary playmate.

Still, even these approximations suggest some larger thematic oppositions: there is a sense in which both Hoppy and Bluthgeld have as their privileged object the world of things, which they divide up between them along the traditional and familiar axis of contemplative and active attitudes. Bluthgeld, whether as a scientist or a madman, sees into the structure of the world in a contemplative fashion; and this suggests that his great sin was to have passed, whether voluntarily or inadvertently, from the realm of contemplation to that of action (the fall-out from the tests of 1972, World War Three itself). As for Hoppy, his knowledge of the future is, like his mechanical skill, simply part of the equipment necessary for survival; but his increasing psychic powers suggest an abuse of his particular position not unlike that of Bluthgeld's, and fraught with similar dangers.

Insofar as he forms a structural pendant to Dangerfield, I am tempted to describe the homunculus Bill in terms of the well-known axis that information theory provides between sender and receiver. Bill sends messages also, to be sure, but in relationship to the realm of the dead his principal function is surely that of receiving them, that of the absent listener to imaginary conversations, that open slot which is the function of the interlocutor in all discourse, even that of absolute solitude. There thus is articulated around the character of Bill the whole communicational syntax of interpersonal relationships, so that at this point the vertical axis which includes the positions of both Bill and Dangerfield seems by its linguistic emphasis quite sharply distinguished from the other axis which governs the world of objects (see figure).

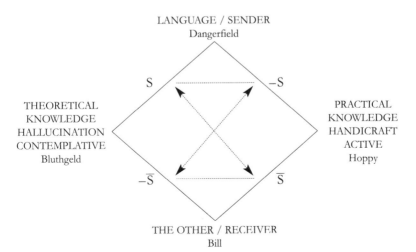

The verbal axis which includes the positions of Bill and Dangerfield is now seen to be primarily a linguistic one, and sharply distinguished from the horizontal axis which includes the positions of Bluthgeld and Hoppy and which is concerned with physics. Furthermore, the vertical Bill–Dangerfield axis is one of the use of knowledge for community well-being (prefigured in the "just" killing for the community's sake), whereas the horizontal Bluthgeld–Happy axis is one of the perversion of knowledge or its manipulation (even literally in the case of Hoppy's "handling" at a distance), which threatens to destroy the human community. The organic or communicational Bill–Dangerfield axis bringing together the past and the present, the living and the dead, is thus the locus and bearer of life-enhancing activities in the novel, whereas the inorganic or physical Bluthgeld–Hoppy axis is the locus of individualistic madness which would, if unchecked, certainly enslave and most probably destroy human life on Earth. Clearly, Dick's solution of the fundamental politico-existential problems facing humanity is here slanted toward art and language rather than toward an explicit scientific diagnosis which would meet the political problem head on. Nonetheless, Dick seems to realize that the verbal, linguistic or communicational field cannot by itself provide a solution. The playful character of Bill rises therefore, by his at least approximate synthesis of verbal and kinaesthetic powers, of communications and active physical intervention, to the status of final mediator, arbiter and one could almost say saviour in the microcosm of *Dr Bloodmoney*.

With the characterological systems of the book thus revealed, we may now perhaps attempt a reading of its action as a whole. Briefly, it may be suggested that the book is organized around two narrative lines, one following Bluthgeld himself and the people who knew him, the other involving Hoppy Harrington and his respective acquaintances. The privileged narrator or "point of view" for the first plot is Bonnie, that of the second Stuart McConchie. Hence the arrival of Stuart in the West Marin County commune where Bonnie lives and where Bluthgeld is in hiding serves to trigger off the explosive interaction between the two plot lines, the lethal encounter between Hoppy and Bluthgeld, and the final dénouement.

The end or object of the action's development is evidently the neutralization of the dangerous and sinister Bluthgeld and his removal from the human scene in general; the complexity of the intrigue results from the difficulty of accomplishing this. For Bluthgeld is after all seen as the cause, in person, of World War Three; yet this personalized and Manichaean view of history involves us in some curious conceptual antinomies which the narrative may be seen as a symbolic attempt to work through. It would seem appropriate, then, here to follow the example of Lévi-Strauss[4] in his analysis of myth

---

4 See Claude Lévi-Strauss, "The Structural Study of Myth", in *Structural Anthropology* (New York, 1967), pp. 202–228.

as a narrative construction of symbolic mediations or syntheses whose purpose is the resolution, in story form, of a contradiction which the culture in question is unable to solve in reality. In the present context, this contradiction may be formulated as follows: How can you get rid of the cause of something as devastating as atomic war, when – in order to function as its cause in the first place – that ultimate causal determinant must be all-powerful and thus by definition impossible to get rid of? To put it in terms of the plot, the only way that an isolated individual like Bluthgeld can be imagined to be the "cause" of World War Three is by endowing him with a power so immense that it is thereafter impossible to imagine any other power capable of matching him. If you like, the contradiction is more one inherent in liberal thought than in reality: if world politics is seen, not as the expression of class and national politico-economic dynamics which have an inner logic of their own, but rather as the result of the decisions of free conscious agents, some of whom are good (us) and some of whom are evil (the enemy, whoever he happens to be), then it is clear that the problem of the evil adversary's sources of power will return again and again with a kind of agonizing and incomprehensible persistence. Like any good American "leftist", of course, Dick sees the enemy as the American power elite and in particular its nuclear physicists; yet that point of view, as attractive as it may be, remains a prisoner of the same basic contradictions as the liberal ideology it imagines itself to be opposing.

In the novel itself, the solution lies in the development of a counterforce, an adversary powerful enough to neutralize Bluthgeld's magic and thus to destroy him. This is Hoppy Harrington's role, and the phocomelus grows in power as the book continues – objectively because the needs of the new post-atomic community encourage the growth and diversification of his special talents, and subjectively insofar as his self-confidence keeps pace with the immense range of new contrivances and weapons he has been able to evolve (some of them psychic). Along with this new self-confidence, however, his resentment has intensified as well. By the time of the confrontation with Bluthgeld, Hoppy is himself a dangerously paranoid figure, potentially as harmful to the community as the man he is now able to destroy. Thus a kind of interminable regression is at work here, in which any adversary powerful enough to blast the evil at its source becomes then sufficiently dangerous to call forth a nemesis in his own right, and so forth (see Dick's early novel *Vulcan's Hammer*). The basic contradiction, in other words, has not been solved at all, but merely displaced onto the mechanism devised to remove it, where it continues to function without any prospect of resolution.

The elegance of Dick's solution to this apparently insoluble dilemma makes of his novel a kind of textbook illustration of that mechanism which structuralism has taken as its privileged object of study and which has seemed to underscore a basic parallelism between the workings of kinship systems and those of language, between the rules governing gift-giving in primitive societies and those at work in the market system, between the mechanisms of political and historical development and those of plot. This is the phenomenon of *exchange*, and nowhere is the flash between contrary poles quite so dramatic as in the moment in *Dr Bloodmoney* when the circle is squared and the mind of the homunculus is substituted for that of the malevolent Hoppy, on the point of taking over the world: "'I'm the same; I'm Bill Keller,' the phocomelus said. 'Not Hoppy Harrington.' With his right manual extensor he pointed. 'There's Hoppy. That's him from now on.'– In the corner lay a shriveled dough-like object several inches long; its mouth gaped in congealed emptiness. It had a human-like quality to it, and Stockstill went over to pick it up" (211–212). What makes the exchange possible is the peculiar status of the homunculus' body, both in and outside the world; Bill was attached to something real, a foetal body which died rapidly on exposure to the atmosphere; but in another sense, he was the only one of the four characters to be *without* a body and thus able to switch places without the development of an elaborate counterforce which might then – as in the infinite regression described above – become a threat in its own right. Hoppy fights Bluthgeld, in other words, on the latter's own terms, while Bill's replacement of Hoppy amounts to a shift from that system to a new one; and this is made possible by Hoppy's own violation of his particular system and powers. For he meant to replace Dangerfield by mimicry, that is, by the use of a verbal and linguistic skill quite different from the kinaesthetic one with which he had beaten Bluthgeld. But at this point, then, he is vulnerable to the superior use of the same purely verbal power by Bill, who intimidates and demoralizes him by his own use of the voices of the dead, and then finishes him off by wholesale personality transference – combining verbal and kinaesthetic power.

The basic shift in question we are now able to understand as a substitution of one axis for another, of that of Dangerfield and the homunculus for that of Bluthgeld and Hoppy, of that of language for that of existence – either practical or contemplative – in the world of objects. The latter axis – the horizontal one, in our schematic representation above – is of course marked negatively, both of its extremes being evil or malevolent in terms of the narrative. It does not, however, follow that the other axis is in contrast completely positive: in fact, in most of the novel both Bill and Dangerfield are immobilized or paralyzed. Even at the end, both remain under a depressing restriction in mobility and human potentialities in general, which serves to deprive the novel's resolution of tones that might otherwise be complacent or unacceptably aestheticizing.

For it seems clear that the basic event envisaged by *Dr Bloodmoney* is the substitution of the realm of language for the realm of things, the replacement of the older, compromised world of empirical activity, capitalist everyday work and scientific knowledge, by that newer one of communication and of messages of all kinds with which we are only too familiar in this consumer and service era. In reality, this shift seems to me to contain many negative and doubtful elements, and to welcome too unqualifiedly developments which are not necessarily an unmixed blessing. It is of course the very distinctness of these two axes – itself predicated on the "fact" of atomic war – that allows the exchange in *Dr Bloodmoney* to take place in so striking and exemplary a fashion. But even in this novel, there is a hint of fusing concern about language and concern about objects in Bill, so that the exchange solution is only a provisional one, and relatively unstable. I would want at this point to return from this novel to Dick's other works in order to determine whether the priority of language over objects is there maintained. It would seem, for instance, that in some of the other works (*Galactic Pot-Healer*, for example, or most recently *Flow My Tears, The Policeman Said*), handicrafts, and particularly pot-making, are understood as a different kind of synthesis between art and work, developing more explicitly the trend in the present book.

Our analysis is in any case not complete until we return from this as it were super-human level of the narrative – the interactions between the various synthetic or complex terms of the characterological system – to the more pedestrian reality of the ordinary human characters like Bonnie or Stuart, who constitute, as I have suggested earlier, merely one simple term among others in the original system. Now it can be confidently asserted, it seems to me, that what held for the other simple terms (machines, the dead, the animals) holds true for the human population of *Dr Bloodmoney* as well, namely that they provide the background and furnish the spectators and onlookers for a drama largely transcending them in significance. Thus the novel betrays a formal kinship with earlier works of Dick, such as the deservedly forgotten *Cosmic Puppets*, in which ordinary humans are the playthings of cosmic forces of some mythological type: the difference being that here those forces are not theological or Jungian in content but correspond to the very realities of modern history itself (scientific technique on the one hand and the communicational network on the other).

As far as the ordinary human characters of the book are concerned, then, the drama enacted not so much above as among them amounts to a purification of society and its reestablishment, to the rebirth of some new and utopian Berkeley on the ruins of the old one in whose streets ominous Bluthgelds might have from time to time been glimpsed (and surely the choice of the site of that dress rehearsal of May 1968 which was the Free Speech Berkeley of 1963 – two years before the publication of Dick's novel – is no accident and has historical implications that largely transcend whatever autobiographical motives may also be involved). To say that the social form to which Dick's work corresponds is the small town would convey something anachronistic in the present social context; or at any rate, we should add that it is to be understood as the university town which never knew the provincialism nor the claustrophobia of the classical Main Streets of the American

Middle West. Nor is Dick's pastoral a purely agricultural one, like that achieved in a kind of desperate exhilaration by the survivors of John Wyndham's various universal cataclysms. As different from the latter, or from the small-town pastoral in the best works of Ray Bradbury and Clifford Simak, it is an artisanal world against the scarcity of which the various commodities once more recover their true taste and reassert a use value to which the jaded sensibilities of the affluent society, brainwashed by advertising, had become insensitive: so now there is something precious about the individual cigarette, made of real tobacco, and the glass of real pre-war Scotch, while even the language of Somerset Maugham becomes something we have to treasure. The vision of freshening our own stale and fallen universe, of a utopian revitalization of the tired goods and services all around us, their projection into some genuinely Jeffersonian commonwealth beyond the bomb, is the ultimate recompense for all those complicated struggles and interchanges we have been describing; and they go far towards compensating for what we would otherwise have to see as an ideological imbalance in Dick's work in general, a status defense on the part of the artist and an idealistic overemphasis on language and art in the place of political action. The typically American and "liberal" hostility to politics is outweighed, it seems to me, by just such glimpses into a reestablished collectivity, glimpses which, at the heart of all Dick's obligatory happy endings, mark him as an anti-Vonnegut, as the unseasonable spokesman for a historical (and Utopian) consciousness distinct from and superior to that limited dystopian and apocalyptic vision so fashionable in Western SF today.

1975

10

History and Salvation in Philip K. Dick

I want to propose two principles for dealing with a writer like Philip K. Dick: they seem to me to have the merit of dislodging or displacing stubbornly gripped and traditional false problems. The first of these principles suggests that we regroup this voluminous work in the form of cycles. Leaving out the trash and the hack work, I propose three: the so-called mainstream novels, from 1955 to 1960 (some seven novels that we still have); the Science Fiction period, from 1961 to 1968 (I include ten novels, from *The Man in the High Castle* to *A Maze of Death*; we could argue about these and also set the dates a little earlier or a little later[1]); and finally the religious novels, from 1973 to 1981 (some five works). One of the things I hope this can accomplish (without quite believing that it will) is, as you might already have guessed, to disconnect the religious thematics from the earlier works.[2]

But let us move on to the second principle, and this is to treat all the works of a given cycle as though they were variants of one single work and to attempt to produce what I have called a "synoptic" reading of them. The synoptic gospels, you recall, are those reconstructed and recombined narratives which cut the four gospels up into episodes and try to paste them all together into a single book. Sometimes the episodes overlap and get pasted on top of each other with only minor variants. Sometimes an episode appears which does not figure in the other gospels. Sometimes the accounts differ radically and we get two (or even four) distinct accounts of what happened. I found this method

---

1 The following is a list of novels and editions used (page references in text) with dates of both publication and composition (following Lawrence Surin's chronology in *Divine Invasions*, New York, 1989, pp. 290–312): 1961: *The Man in the High Castle* (New York, 1985, orig. 1962), 1962: *We Can Build You* (New York, 1994, orig. 1972), 1962: *Martian Time-Slip* (New York, 1964), 1963: *Dr Bloodmoney* (New York, 1965), 1963: *Now Wait for Last Year* (New York, 1981, orig. 1966), 1963–1964: *Clans of the Alphane Moon* (New York, 1984, orig. 1964), 1964: *The Three Stigmata of Palmer Eldritch* (New York, 1977, orig. 1965), 1966: *Do Androids Dream of Electric Sheep?* (New York, 1984, orig. 1968), 1966: *Ubik* (New York, 1991, orig. 1969), 1968: *A Maze of Death* (New York, 1971). Page references within the text are to these editions.

2 But see, for an attempt to integrate the last novels into the earlier corpus, Kim Stanley Robinson, *The Novels of Philip K. Dick* (New York, 1984).

useful in exploring Raymond Chandler's novels: their material basis, as with Dick's, lies in the world of the pulps in which something that saw life initially as a short story is then expanded into a whole novel, or is reduced to being an episode in a novel.[3]

There is another rationale to this procedure, which lies in the premise that novels are combinations of heterogeneous kinds of raw material. The novel is an omnibus form in which various types of generic discourse are amalgamated, their seams or geological layers then effaced in an act of attempted synthesis which purports to unify the generically disparate and most often at least serves to conceal the variety of the novel's sources. To be sure, one can also insist on the creative power of this act of unification, even if it does not succeed. I take it that it was Macherey's lesson that the deeper significance of a given work lay precisely in the contradiction between the various types of generic raw material.[4]

At any rate the "synoptic" method can serve as a beginning for that interpretive move insofar as it aims to sort the various narrative substances out and to classify them. This will produce continuities in some cases and radical disidentifications in others; thus the paradigm of the unhappy marriage, which dominates the mainstream novels, will leave its traces throughout in the form of the threatening or aggressive woman (often with recurrent names), whose pointed breasts so often aim at the hapless male protagonist like missiles (*sic*). On the other hand, what is often loosely called religion here seems to involve a variety of different motifs and realities: the obsession with conversion that dominates the last or late cycle – it being understood that for Dick obsession and conversion are one and the same thing, so that it would be equally meaningful to talk about the conversion to obsession – is not at all the same thing as the consolation of Mercer rising out of the tomb world (in *Do Androids Dream of Electric Sheep?*). Meanwhile the theological preoccupations of *Ubik* are yet again something else: representational dilemmas, which rehearse the impossible dialectic of the letter and the spirit and its interminable paradoxes (of which the theological tradition offers one of the richest explorations). All these narrative elements or substances need to be separated out from each other, and the range and variety of the raw material assessed and inventoried, before we proceed to any rash and premature, necessarily speculative, interpretive act.

Let us continue with the matter of what is lumped together as religion, for some of those motifs constitute one of the four general categories we need, in some preliminary way, to sort Dick's work into. These motifs will not necessarily exhaust the matter of the late work, which I have excluded from the present discussion but which returns in the incitement it offers critics to reread the

---

3 See my "On Raymond Chandler", in *Southern Review*, No. 6 (1970), pp. 624–650; and its companion piece, "The Synoptic Chandler", in *Shades of Noir*, ed. Joan Copjec (London, 1993).
4 See Pierre Macherey *A Theory of Literary Production* (London, 1978).

central novels in terms of the gnosis of new age spirituality and exotic theologies, and in short to seek Dick's "actuality" in terms of current pseudo-religious modes and fashions. To be sure, it would be more important to try to grasp the later "mystical" turn in purely formal and narrative terms, as an attempt to solve problems of content with which the Science Fiction matrix could no longer deal (just as it would be important to grasp the shift from the period of the "mainstream novel" in the same formal and formalizing terms). An absolute formalism, indeed, offers the only really satisfactory way of approaching the writer's concrete social and psychic content, by way of demonstrating the latter's unique and uniquely historical demands on representation. We cannot go so far here, as I have said; but the formalist approach to whatever motifs in our corpus present a religious appearance or religious associations – that is to say, an approach to these motifs as solutions to problems of representation inherent in their content – will be productive in a variety of ways.

First of all, it may help to discredit the facile word *theme* which seems at one and the same time methodologically unavoidable and overly humanistic or anthropomorphic: the "theme", in other words, seems to promise a meaning and to offer a general category that can range all the way from images to ideas. (I hasten to add that the term *motif*, used above, is not much better, but at least underscores the purely formal nature of the entity, at the expense of alleged meanings.)

Thus "empathy" is one of those motifs, and finds itself written into many of the early novels of our cycle as a constituent part of the plot (the empathy tests, which certify androidhood or schizophrenia), all the while seeming to offer a philosophical concept of some kind, saying something about human warmth or coldness in interpersonal relationships and sometimes (as in *Do Androids Dream of Electric Sheep?*) even parading itself as a kind of privileged key to the novel's meaning or message. But it is precisely that notion of a meaning or message that (in the wake of so much modern theory, from the formalists onward) I would want to challenge here, and this with two remarks.

The first is a simple reminder of what so many critics since Shklovsky have maintained, namely that the "meanings" of a work, its ideas, its conceptual content, all of this is to be seen fully as much a part of the work's raw materials as everything more tangible (setting, psychological character traits, etc.). An absolute formalism demands a bracketing as radical as Husserl's in phenomenology, after which the various kinds of conceptual content, such as precisely this pop-psychological or pop-psychoanalytic notion of "empathy" in Dick, are to be seen as specific building blocks. From the perspective of a formalist bracketing, then, the work has no meaning of that humanistic kind (whatever Dick himself might have thought). To be sure, it has an utterly different kind of meaning as a historical symptom and as a socially symbolic representational structure. But in that case "ideas" like empathy are merely elements in that symptom or structure. They document Dick's intellectual involvement (however naïve) in the pop-cultural debates of the period (something Anthony Wolk's research on his readings in psychiatric literature usefully underscores).

But this leads us to a second parenthetical remark, which may be termed the Angenot dilemma: indeed, in *1889* as well as in a host of other fundamental historical-archival inquiries, Marc Angenot demonstrates how the acquisition of information about a work's context stands in inverse proportion to the assessment of its value.[5] "Context" is in this sense more a matter of journalistic fashion than it is a function of that nobler and more democratic thing called the public sphere or civil society: it consists in making an inventory of everything "people" were talking about in the media and its real-life commentaries (kitchen, barber shop, bars and taverns) at any given time. Angenot shows us how even the most celebrated works can disintegrate into a tissue of allusions, gossip, trendy thoughts and "problems" when the informational context is restored with a certain degree of abundance and complexity. His example is Zola, but it might just as well be Shakespeare; and we may expect future scholarship to yield a volume of information about current events in the American 1950s and early 1960s which threaten our appreciation of Dick's inventiveness and "thinking" in much the same way, turning "engagement" into name-dropping and giving a novel twist to the classical notion of the artist as the "antennae of the race" (Pound).

As for the philosophical contradictions of this "concept", we will see that its difficulties, even more fundamental in the central notion of identification than with empathy or sympathy and turning obviously enough on the problem of thinking any relationship between the other and consciousness, do in fact find themselves registered in Dick's work, but in unexpected places and as representational dilemmas, and not in the form of pseudo-psychological theorizing.

Indeed, we must admire the way Dick's imagination parleys the whole vacuous theme of empathy into a new and novel religion, or California-style religious craze, namely the consolations of Mercerism, complete with the life story of the humble savior, the delivery mechanism (the "black empathy box" with its twin handles, a kind of cousin of the Penfield mood machine, or, in another avatar, of the Dr Smile suitcase), the ritual of the "imitation", the conception of the salvational value of suffering and sacrifice, and even the emergence of a kind of "higher criticism" (the revelation that "Mercer" was in reality a down-and-out actor called Al Jarry). We may also note the character of Mercerian theology: Buddhist or nihilistic conviction that "there is no salvation", the purpose of the ritual being "to show you that you are not alone"; to which a *Bhagavadgita* moral is added, appropriately enough for the

---

5 Marc Angenot, *1889: Un état du discours social* (Montreal, 1989). And see also my essay "Marc Angenot, Literary History, and the Study of Culture in the Nineteenth Century", *Yale Journal of Criticism*, Vol. XVII, No. 2 (2004), pp. 233–253.

ethical dilemmas of this middle-class bounty-hunter: "Go and do your task, even though you know it's wrong." I think it would be overhasty to characterize this, particularly in the later stages, as some kind of parody of religion, for the parodic elements are soaked up laterally into the SF conventions and framework, while the relationship of Mercerism to suffering and to the desolation of the post-atomic landscape freezes all possible grins into some mixed tonality or nightmarish zaniness preeminently characteristic of Dick's ontological and evaluative undecideability (of which more later).

The crucial point about "empathy", however, is that in Mercerism it is enacted in the form of "fusion" with the other, or, rather, with the televisual image of the other. Philosophically, in other words, it has seemed impossible to imagine any identification with the other short of a merging together of the two subjectivities. But this opens up some novel representational perspectives or possibilities.

First of all, the fusing with Mercer is grasped in terms of landscape:

> He saw at once a famous landscape, the old, brown, barren ascent, with tufts of dried-out bonelike weeds, poking slantedly into a dim and sunless sky. One single figure, more or less human in form, toiled its way up the hillside … John Isidore gradually experienced a waning of the living room in which he stood; the dilapidated furniture and walls ebbed out and he ceased to experience them at all. He found himself, instead, as always before, entering into the landscape of drab hill, drab sky …(18)

Not only is it the landscape which is the instrument of fusion with Mercer; one can also speak of a kind of metaphoric identification, a metaphoric slippage, between the desolation of the depopulated and radioactive San Francisco of the post-World-War-Terminus years and this barren and desolate hilly landscape, which however is in no way visually similar to the wasted city. The mysteries of substitution and sacrifice thus remain, only they are transposed onto the two landscapes, about which it continues to be unclear how the desolation of the one could in any way relieve the desolation of the other.

It is also worth noting that "fusion" blurs the distinction between individual and collective in a different way, one quite distinct from the dual relationship with Mercer; but this is something best observed in a very different situation, namely that of the colonists on Mars and their pastime, the Perky Pat layout (in *The Three Stigmata of Palmer Eldritch*). Here, an even less promising landscape seems imperiously to demand some form of escape, as Barney Mayerson's arrival makes clear:

> The sand-dredge had completed its autonomic task; his possessions sat in a meager heap, and loose sand billowed across them already – if they were not taken below they would succumb to the dust and soon … The other hovelists

gathered to assist him, passing his suitcases from hand to hand, to the conveyor belt that serviced the hovel below the surface. Even if he was not interested in preserving his former goods they were; they had a knowledge superior to his ... It hadn't upset him that much, seeing the half-abandoned gardens and fully abandoned equipment, the great heaps of rotting supplies. He knew from the edu-tapes that the frontier was always like that, even on Earth; Alaska had been like that until recent times and so, except for the actual resort towns, was Antarctica right now. (140, 150)

Although it is clear enough that even Barney himself is not reassured by this final denegation, we probably need to interrogate Dick's own exhilaration with such scenes: the "kipple" of the post-atomic San Francisco of *Do Androids?* (the term designates the way in which everything solid is frittering into dust), and the sand of the as yet incompletely colonized Mars, can neither of them be taken as outright visions of horror (unlike, for instance, Mercer's tomb-world or the menace of Jory in *Ubik*). In another way they seem to rhyme with the America of the 1950s of the mainstream novels, of which the.least that can be said is that they reinvent the notion of provincial exile for the modern American tradition. It may not altogether be ineptly psychological to venture a diagnosis: if SF catastrophes are often the mere pretext for the re-invention of the small Utopian community of the future, one may perhaps hazard the guess that here Dick's own subjective malaise finds itself objec-tively (as well as collectively) motivated. Not only is it worse than any passing subjective depression, but it has to be shared and experienced by everyone else as well.

However this may be, there would seem to be little enough resemblance between the "stations-of-the-cross" agonies of identification with Mercer and the Frankie Avalon beach-movie wish-fulfillments made available to the colonists on Mars by the Perky Pat layouts:

> He was Walt. He owned a Jaguar XXB sports ship with a flat-out velocity of fifteen thousand miles an hour. His shirt came from Italy and his shoes were made in England ... Walt shut off the TV, rose, and walked barefoot to the window; he drew the shades, saw out then onto the warm, sparkling early-morning San Francisco street, the hills and white houses. This was Saturday morning and he did not have to go to his job down in Palo Alto at Ampex Corporation; instead – and this rang nicely in his mind – he had a date with his girl, Pat Christensen, who had a modern little apt over on Portero Hill.
> It was always Saturday. (44–45)

In this participatory, drug-assisted fantasy, the metaphysical complications of "fusion" are rather more comical, since any number of men can share the Walt figure, and any number of women that of Pat. Nor is the historical reference any less confusing: interactive Barbie doll accessories (the doll was pioneered in 1959), along with the very style of the beach scenes, strongly evoke the 1950s, while the futuristic equipment rather furnishes the sequence with the trappings of some SF fantasy about a Silicon Valley finance-capital future. And unlike any number of other SF or historical novelists, Dick's seeming liberties with history are never without significance. We might, for example, hypothesize the futuristic elements as precisely those essential in a fantasy dreamed in the 1950s; or yet again, we might imagine that in *Palmer Eldritch*, the novel's present (however far into our own future) is somehow homologous with our own historical 1950s.

In fact, the truth is elsewhere, and we must note that precisely these futuristic elements – notably the sports ship – are accompanied by a more alarming seepage from the outside world. This is a fantasy already tainted by the reality principle; and the beach at which Walt and Pat plan to swim on this eternal weekend that is theirs cannot be visited in the afternoons, on account of the effects of global warming. Wish-fulfillments, as Freud and the Utopians taught us alike, are not to be achieved so easily, by the mere making of a wish; they have their own specific formal demands and constraints, which betray the realities of their context even more effectively than the inversion in the content. Thus, as with the stones with which Mercer is persecuted and wounded, a dystopian and entropic world consistently threatens the thin fabric of the projective identification. But this involves a curious paradox: for in the characteristic Dick nightmare, about which the reader had always assumed that it was a matter of degradation of reality (as, physically, with kipple itself), it turns out on the contrary that it is the dreamworld or hallucinatory state which is degraded, and progressively infected by reality itself.

And this is precisely the case with Chew-Z and the far more baleful effects of the operation Palmer Eldritch lays in place to drive out the rival Perky Pat/Can-D monopoly. To be sure, the transformation of everything in the "world" into Palmer Eldritch himself – announced by the "stigmata" of the title – is a more sinister experience than anything the layouts have to offer:

Leo's office door opened. Miss Gleason, the ship-requisition papers in her hands, entered. The hand which held the papers was artificial; he made out the glint of undisguised metal and at once he raised his head to scrutinize her face, the rest of her. Neanderthal teeth, he thought; that's what those giant stainless steel molars look like. Reversion, two hundred thousand years back; revolting. And the luxvid or vidlux or whatever they were eyes; without pupils, only slits. Jensen Labs of Chicago's product, anyhow. "Goddam you, Eldritch," he said.

"I'm your pilot too," Palmer Eldritch, from within the shape of Miss Gleason, said. "And I was thinking of greeting you when you land. But that's too much, too soon." (199)

I want to suggest that the nightmare here is solipsism, the imprisonment within one's own individual consciousness, without contact with otherness or external reality. Yet Palmer Eldritch's appearance then restores that reality and stands as a form of what the Romantics technically called Irony, namely the way in which the Creator reveals himself behind and through his creation, the latter growing thin and transparent. Nor should it be thought that Eldritch is an exclusively and implacably evil force (whatever kind of alien he may be beneath his human disguise): indeed, like Stanislaw Lem's sentient ocean in *Solaris*, he would like to do something nice for human beings, only he does not understand what that might be or how to go about it.

Such references, however, and the "stigmata" in question – vidlux eyes, prosthetic hand, stainless-steel teeth – would seem to return us inescapably to the conceptuality of theology, if not, indeed, of religion itself. But this is precisely the dimension we need to interrogate at this point. For one thing, it seals the deeper and rather surprising consonance between Mercerism – a quasi-religious consolation therapy – and the seemingly utterly frivolous and escapist recourse to Perky Pat: as witness the account of the colonist Sam Regan, a habitual consumer of Can-D:

> He himself was a believer; he affirmed the miracle of translation – the near-sacred moment in which the miniature artifacts of the layout no longer merely represented Earth but *became* Earth. And he and the others, joined together in the fusion of doll-inhabitation by means of the Can-D, were transported outside of time and local space. (38)

The parody has its deeper justification in the very nature of theological speculation itself For just as the history of philosophy and its discourse consists, from the *Parmenides* to Hegel's *Logic*, in a prolonged meditation on the nature of the conceptual categories themselves, so also theology offers a thinly disguised deployment of the impasses of representation, in which the unrepresentable relationship between letter and spirit is dramatized as an incarnation, when not a relationship between body and soul, as in the mystical reunion with Perky Pat and Walt. Thus the elective affinities between Dick's writing and the most traditional theological figures and figurations need not be interpreted in any conventionally religious way, unless religion is itself nothing more than just such an intense aesthetic and formal obsession with representation as such.

But now we need to take a further step, inasmuch as theology has scarcely offered an ultimately determining instance for our interpretation. What we have until now neglected is as it were the material apparatus through which these experiences of mystical participation are transmitted: an earlier generation of Dick readers (including me) assumed that the mediation took the form of drugs or schizophrenia; but it seems time to propose a different reading for what are certainly thematic constants in Dick's work. After all here, in Mercerism as well as in the Perky Pat layouts, we have to do with an essentially interactive televisual spectacle (and perhaps the omnipresence of this communicational technology today can excuse the reminder of its novelty in Dick's 1950s, along with the cultural fears and worries it inevitably inspired, and still does). Thus, we may suggest that these episodes very much include a meditation on mass culture, a hypothesis reinforced by Cornel West's insistence that religion is also very much a form of American mass culture (whose absence from current Cultural Studies he deplored). Drugs are also, perhaps, a form of American mass culture; and certainly what is feared in all these instances is precisely a certain "fusion" with the medium and a loss of individual autonomy. Television is in any case another one of those contextual 1950s themes and current-event references which we have observed Dick's work to soak up (as with the dramatization of the then novel Barbie dolls); and it may be suggested that in Dick drugs and schizophrenia are bad, not because they provoke hallucinations, but because those hallucinations are too closely related to television.

This is, however, the point at which to observe that Dick's ethical positions – in other words, the judgments in terms of the ethical binary of good and evil – are systematically varied in a way which not only sets him "beyond good and evil" but also explains something of the realistic and non-ideological density of his work. (Perhaps we may also hazard the guess that what distinguishes the late, "religious", works is precisely the waning of this ethical alternation, and the decision to take sides once and for all.)

It is a systematic commutation we will find at work in each of the four groups of raw material (or narremes), of which this "mass-cultural" category is only the first. Clearly negative, for example, is the evidently toxic hallucinatory addiction to the drug JJ180 by Kathy Sweetscent (in *Now Wait for Last Year*), also incidentally one of those numerous points at which Dick seizes the occasion to redouble his plot structure with the obsessive "mainstream" theme of the bad marriage and the "castrating" female (another characteristic theme of the 1950s, at least in the US).

The drug in question, in keeping with the novel's thematic register, induces time travel along a proliferation of time lines and alternate futures. Yet in this connection it is worth recalling that Kathy's professional situation in Tijuana Fur and Dye Corporation consists in hunting down authentic antiques for the latter's owner, Virgil Ackerman. The nostalgic pursuit of metonymic objects from past time would then seem to constitute the positive version of the clearly negative variants of the future, so that the novel can be seen to be an intricate commutation process in which temporality is alternately shifted from baleful to salvational registers. For while it is important not prematurely to overestimate the role of nostalgia in a narrative system we have not yet completely explored, the creation of Virgil Ackerman's Wash-35 – "a painstakingly elaborate reconstruction of the specific limited universe of childhood, which Virgil had known, constantly refined and improved in matters of authenticity by his antique procurer" (21) – is surely for many of us one of Dick's most sublime inventions (about which we must also remember that the same year witnessed Dick's own childhood experience of that city):

> Several blocks away [from "the five-story brick apartment building where Virgil had lived as a boy"] lay Connecticut Avenue, and, along it, stores which Virgil remembered. Here was Gammage' s, a shop at which Virgil had bought Tip Top comics and penny candy. Next to it Eric made out the familiar shape of the People's Drugstore; the old man during his childhood had bought a cigarette lighter here once and chemicals for his Gilbert Number Five glassblowing and chemistry set. "What's the Uptown Theater showing this week?" (27)

Here, then, we have the resurrection in the flesh, if not of the dead, then at least of the past, gradually filled in with authentic objects and peopled by lifelike robots of the personnel of Virgil's childhood; and in this respect we may also remember the collectibles of *Man in the High Castle* as well as the mediation of material objects – the LP records of the various recreated classical record stores – at the heart of Dick's relationship to music.

Yet something more than the standard psychology (or psychopathology) of the collector seems at stake here: for the objects would seem to set in place what Kenneth Burke might have called the category of the "scene" as such: places lovingly devised and composed for a human activity which has disappeared, as living hosts disappear in course of the generational process, leaving their empty shells and housing behind them. Collecting in this sense then suggests a desperate repetition, which, by reconstructing the scene, struggles to restore the human acts and interpersonal events it once housed. But such an analysis immediately clarifies our earlier thematic material as well, for the layout is just such a scene, and fusion with Mercer in some sense replaces the novelty of fresh action and eventfulness with a kind of eternal return of the televisual image. In this particular semic cluster, then, a historically marked object-world joins hands with the phenomenon of 1950s media to make up the space and category of the empty scene as such; and this is something like a pure form, which can be inflected in either a negative or a positive way, and accommodate either malign or redemptive content.

Now it is time to outline the strategy of the rest of this essay which will propose to construct three more such semic clusters, on the order and model of the linked and echoing variants of this first or "scenic" one (although clearly not in the same kind of detail). In a second step, the relationship of these four semic clusters to each other will be organized according to their various oppositions with one another, which, involving the classical logician's distinction between contrary and contradictory, will take the form of the Greimas semiotic rectangle (below).

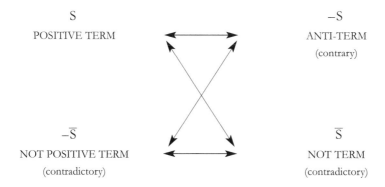

S
POSITIVE TERM

−S
ANTI-TERM
(contrary)

−S̄
NOT POSITIVE TERM
(contradictory)

S̄
NOT TERM
(contradictory)

The usefulness of this exercise (which may otherwise strike the reader as mechanical or anti-aesthetic) lies not only in its demonstration of the deeper interrelationship between the various thematic clusters, but also in the way in which it opens up the possibility of an even more ambitious (if speculative) interpretive act. For each side of the rectangle also offers the occasion for the projection of a kind of impossible synthesis, in which contraries or contradictions find some ideal solution: the hypothesis being that it is at that level alone that we will be able to surprise something of the energy and the impulsion of the work itself.

However this may be, it now seems appropriate to set the "empathy" with Mercer (whose intricate associations we have just examined at some length) in structural juxtaposition with a narrative function explicitly distinguished from it in both narrative and thematic ways, namely the absence of "empathy" in the androids themselves, alleged to lack all human warmth and sympathy in measurable quotients which show up on the Voigt–Kampff test (modeled as Anthony Wolk has shown on various 1950s psychiatric questionnaires designed to detect schizophrenia and that probably entertain connections to Soviet psychiatry and language theory which remain to be explored by Dick scholarship). Roy Baty is clearly meant, in his implacable malignancy, to dramatize this testable differentiation from the human, which, however, the novel itself refutes, by showing the very real community of interests and feelings between the rebel androids and their palpable dismay at the extermination of their fellows.

Nonetheless, the empathy question arises mainly as an attempt to distinguish androids from humans; and this shift from the Asimov robotics, with its emphasis on labor and as we may say labor laws and practices, to this mimeticism (which raises questions more closely related to the current ones around cloning), seems to have been Dick's personal achievement (although something of the currency of the term *android* must be due to the movie version of the novel in question [*Blade Runner*, Ridley Scott, 1982]). I believe, therefore, that Dick's focus is far more Cartesian than it is ethical or pop-psychological, an impression reinforced by recalling the ambiguities of Descartes' dualism, which makes him into the father of modern materialism and modern idealism alike. Animals are machines, and how do I really know that other people are not also automata? But Dick reactivates the Cartesian problem in a peculiarly virulent and modern way; and reawakens Cartesian doubt in an even more threatening and all-embracing fashion than the hypothesis of the "malignant genie". For in crucial stories like "Imposter" or "The Electric Ant" the questions now identified as involving Artificial Intelligence seep into and infect every experience of Descartes' realm of thought or consciousness, and it is no longer only the android who has to ask such autoreferential questions. What emerges at length is what I will call the "android cogito": I think, therefore I am an android. This reverses the external issue of testing into a permanent rift within self-consciousness itself; and it is symptomatic that the debates about *Blade Runner* (from which the Phil Resch episode, dramatizing the android cogito, has been removed) have slowly evolved into discussions as to whether Rick Deckard (unquestionably a human in the novel) might not be an android himself.

Yet in giving final shape to this particular thematic cluster – paradoxically organized around the philosophical problems raised by the individual consciousness, which is however (in a fashion reminiscent of the aggressivity of Lacan's mirror stage) dramatized as the enemy of humans rather than their alter ego – we must not omit to add a few other features linked to androids but also linked, at least metonymically, to the cluster itself.

One of those is surely the seme of the technological, which at once evolves in Dick's political imagination into that of the great corporations, with their monopoly on reproductive techniques and their social power (already the worry about the "organization man" and the related impersonal and anonymous business structures – monopolistic but not yet globalized – had become a popular theme of 1950s culture). At the same time we need to retain all the ambivalence of Dick's sense of this technology, most of the time mechanical, but occasionally throwing up stunningly organic images such as "Pay for the Printer", in which the alien Biltong faithfully reproduce any object set in front of them – a situation then grimly worked out for capitalism in *Now Wait for Last Year*, where the "Martian print amoeba" is made to retain its mimicry of animal furs: "the answer, developed over a period of many months, consisted in killing the amoeba during its interval of mimicry and then subjecting the cadaver to a bath of fixing-chemicals which had the capacity to lock the amoeba into that final form" (14).

In "Pay for the Printer", to be sure, the organic reproductive or mimetic technology is a kind of alien assistance in a postwar situation in which "real" human technology has been largely destroyed. But the emergence of the theme as a feature of some future postwar devastation (just like the more conventional emergence of autonomous and lethal machinery in the *Terminator*-like landscape of "Second Variety", filmed as *Screamers* [Christian Dugay, 1995]) underscores a somewhat more paradoxical association, namely the relationship of this complex of thematics to the idea of the future itself. Why should the notion of the future ever be paradoxical in a genre most often largely defined in terms of extrapolation and systematic anticipation in the first place? But I think we should not take Dick's interest in the future as a given; indeed, we will shortly find that his sense of history is unexpectedly complicated and more original than any mere futuristic exercise.

At any rate, the completion of this cluster, in which individual subjectivity and the android cogito are linked to a perspective on the future along with technology in its strongest traditional form (not yet cybernetic, yet driving the reproductive and the mimetic to its very limits), can now by a kind of thematic inversion send us on to another crucial complex of themes. We have evoked the Rosen Association of *Do Androids Dream?* as a gigantic transnational, whose business practices (providing the android workforce of the off-world factories) are reminiscent of the Nazi slave labor organizations of *The Man in the High Castle*. But we have not yet observed that the Rosen organization is itself the outgrowth, in the far future, of that small family business on whose troubles the plot of *We Can Build You* (written some four years earlier) turns. It is indeed in *We Can Build You* that the very invention of the android, or at least the emergence of the Dickian android, with all its rich associations, can be observed.

For these first androids strike one as being of a very different kind and spirit from those of Roy Baty's menacing group of predators; and indeed I am tempted to say that Dick's invention of the Lincoln and the Stanton are among the most sublime achievements of his work. In the beginning, to be sure, they are meant to be working parts of a grandiose commercial version of something like Virgil Ackerman's Wash-35: only, as Maury describes it, this project aims at nothing less than

> a ten-year-spaced-apart centennial of the U.S. Civil War, and what we do is, the Rosen factory supplies all the participants, simulacra – that's the plural, it's a Latin type word – of *everybody*. Lincoln, Stanton, Jeff Davis, Robert E. Lee, Longstreet, and around three million simple ones as soldiers we keep in stock all the time. And we have these battles fought with the participants really killed, these made-to-order simulacra blown to bits, instead of just a grade-B movie type business like a bunch of college kids doing Shakespeare. (20)

This is the resurrection of the past and the dead with a vengeance, aiming at nothing less than a lifelike and realistic second death of all those thus revived. The project (we are after all only seven years after the launching of Disneyland in 1955) would seem desperately and structurally to aim, following our format here, at supplying the empty category of the Scene with an Event, and indeed an Event of the most momentous and world-historical kind. But the event is itself a simulacrum; its choice and content are utterly contingent (Dick wrote the novel during the Civil War centennial); and finally, it is too expensive and the government will not sponsor it anyhow.

What happens is something rather different, and far from being the central actors or protagonists of a drama, these two first androids turn out to be specimens of that peculiar and distinct category of Vladimir Propp's *Morphology of the Folktale* which he terms the *adjuvant* or the *helper*. It will be seen at once that the helper is not a category of the same order as that of the protagonist (or the villain either, for that matter): not a mere secondary character (flat characters as opposed to round ones, or a part for a character actor rather than a star). The nature of the helper cannot be identified in advance (save perhaps in Propp's original folktale materials, with their magical forces and their Manichaean organization); only the function of such a figure can be described, as an agency of salvation, from whatever source and in whatever intent.

So it is that the Lincoln becomes the legal counsel for the new Rosen firm, and the Stanton its first chairman of the board; both plan out the strategy of the organization in its struggle with the rival Barrows Corporation; and indeed the professional term offers the most satisfactory clue to the function of the helper in this particular work (and in Dick generally), namely to *give counsel*. This is so, whether we have to do with something as mechanical as the suitcase containing the psychiatrist Dr Smile (in *Palmer Eldritch*); as duplicitous as the telepathic alien Lord Running Clam (in *Clans of the Alphane Moon*), or as devoted and reliable as the deceased Ella Runciter (in *Ubik*), consulted on a regular basis in her half-life by her corporate husband.

What characterizes all these figures is their essential selflessness, something readily explained by their condition, which is either that of a machine or that of the dead. Yet this does not mean that they do not, particularly in the cases of the Lincoln and the Stanton, have their own inner mode of existence. So it is that as a stereotype Lincoln stands for suffering in general (not only the war years, but also in the affair with Ann Rutledge, for which Dick drew heavily on Carl Sandburg's sentimental four-volume biography); yet this awakening into sentient android consciousness rewrites the first flickering eyelid of the Frankenstein monster's existence as some emergence into a well-nigh existential horror of existence itself:

> the black, opaque eyes rolled, focusing and yet not focusing, seeing everything and in a sense not picking out any one thing. As if it were primarily in suspension, yet waiting with such infinite reserve that I could glimpse thereby the dreadful fear it felt, fear so great that it could not be called an emotion. It was fear as absolute existence: the basis of its life. It had become separate,

yanked away from some fusion that we could not experience – at least, not now. Maybe once we all had lain quietly in that fusion. For us, the rupturing was long past; for the Lincoln it had just now occurred – was now taking place. (72–73)

Meanwhile, we must also grant the Stanton its own unique existence and individuality, even if of a very different type, namely that exasperation with other people which also characterizes Dick's interpersonal world and of which the characteristically Dickian bad marriage (with the castrating female) is only to be taken as a sub-set and not a primary form. For what marks Dick off from the high-literary writers of his period is that his protagonists have already been thrown into a human and collective, indeed a distinctively American, world; they cannot begin in subjectivism and radical isolation, as is so often the case in the paradigms of high modernism, although they can certainly regress into that state (which then is in the Dick universe identified as "schizophrenia"). But the Stanton's exasperation is of a historical kind:

> The round, wrinkled face darkened. "Mr Lincoln is dead …. You mean they are going to bring him back? … Sir, have you ever heard of Artemus Ward?" "No," I admitted.
>
> "If Mr Lincoln is revived you will be subjected to endless humorous selections from the writings of Mr Ward." Scowling, the Stanton picked up its book and once more read. Its face was red and its hands shook. (57)

I propose in any case to make a link between the function of giving counsel and the phenomenon of schizophrenia which is so often its pretext, and which we can observe here (in *We Can Build You*) as it emerges from the mainstream novels and takes on a characteristic Dickian SF value of its own. Schizophrenia is thus not merely the inversion of the individuality or the individualism of the android cogito; it is also the pretext (what the Russian Formalists would have called the "motivation of the device") for the giving of counsel in the first place, the place and appeal to the helper, the essential helplessness of the individual human being abandoned outside the great collectives of Dick's businesses and corporations.

Yet these also know a significant variation, and with this possibility of reconstructing collectivity we now come to our fourth and final thematic cluster. We have mentioned Dick's "interpersonal world" and the peculiar tonality of exasperation it seems imbued with (as with some larger family – that of *We Can Build You*, for example – in which the various members, with their ineradicable eccentricities, have begun to grate on each other ceaselessly). It remains to show how just such a world lends its features to a specific vision of small collectivities in Dick – collectivities which do not, as in much Utopian or revolutionary imagery, leap discontinuously from the bad society of the present to a radically different one; yet which also, unlike high modernism, retain the sociability in place without turning away from its alleged inauthenticity and *Gerede* (Heidegger's empty chatter of the *man* or anonymous crowd).

Most often such small collectivities – no doubt inherited in some fashion from the "mainstream novels" – are the unintended result and bonus of nuclear catastrophe, as most paradigmatically in *Dr Bloodmoney*, with its West Marin County settlement of rural refugees who cluster together in the schoolhouse to hear Walt Dangerfield's broadcasts as the satellite passes overhead.[6] Indeed, I think it is often the case that seemingly negative or destructive features of the manifest content have an utterly different function in their latent source. Freud said as much about death and dead bodies in dreams (which may have nothing whatsoever to do with those realities): in SF I am often struck – the novels of John Wyndham come to mind as evidence – by the way in which global cataclysm so often serves as a mere pretext for the dreaming of a far more positive Utopian wish-fulfillment – in that instance as in this one, the coming into being of a small community beyond big city or nation. This structure would then accommodate other, more generalized types of catastrophes, as most notably on the Mars of *Martian Time-Slip*, with its various specialized communities – labor-union-based, for example, or Zionist – in which collective solidarity goes hand in hand with a certain secessionist impulse.

But we need to isolate and underscore one persistent feature which characterizes these communities (and which can also be linked to catastrophe as to its pretext): this is the overriding necessity and omnipresence of handicraft and repairmen. Indeed the West Marin collective – with the repairman Hoppy Harrington at its center – can be seen as a virtual exfoliation and institutionalization of the TV repair shop of pre-nuclear Berkeley from which Hoppy himself emigrated. Repair thus metonymically leads us back to small business in general in Dick (the record stores and antique shops; Berkeley, California!).

The latter are specifically marked as places in which production as such does not take place; on the other hand, they are spared the opprobrium of the by-product category of mere distribution and indeed are lent a positive and well nigh Utopian dimension in their own right. The activity of repairing appliances, then, offers the synthesis between the valorization of small business on the one hand and the imperfect and exasperating attempts to keep the small communities in existence; and no doubt draws its Utopian force from the nostalgia for handicraft itself and as such. If the fans of Perky Pat (or of Mercer himself, as far as that goes) are the consumers of Dick's universe, then these repairmen are their opposite numbers and keep the machinery going, even if (unlike the Rosen Association) they do not produce it in the first place.

---

6 See my "After Armageddon: Character Systems in Dr Bloodmoney", Essay 9 in this volume.

Now we are in a position to set these four semic complexes in relation to each other according to the structure of the Greimas rectangle. We can best achieve this by concentrating the traits of each group in correlation with the others. Thus, it seems logical enough for "individual consciousness" – as the semic marker of the android group – to stand in stark opposition, as a contrary, to the seme of collectivities. Meanwhile the semic cluster that combines helpers and schizophrenia would seem to offer a fairly general negation of the android grouping, while the empty scene of the layouts and the mass culture offers an equally global negation of the collectives and small social groups of the post-atomic repair cluster. This lower level of the contradictories then offers a revision of the standard Dick thematics of drugs and schizophrenia, in which mass culture comes to stand in a certain opposition to the helpers:

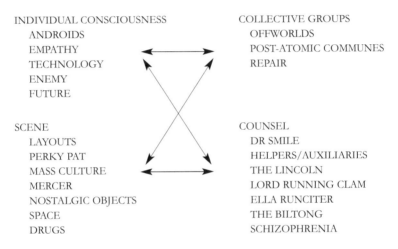

INDIVIDUAL CONSCIOUSNESS
 ANDROIDS
 EMPATHY
 TECHNOLOGY
 ENEMY
 FUTURE

COLLECTIVE GROUPS
 OFFWORLDS
 POST-ATOMIC COMMUNES
 REPAIR

SCENE
 LAYOUTS
 PERKY PAT
 MASS CULTURE
 MERCER
 NOSTALGIC OBJECTS
 SPACE
 DRUGS

COUNSEL
 DR SMILE
 HELPERS/AUXILIARIES
 THE LINCOLN
 LORD RUNNING CLAM
 ELLA RUNCITER
 THE BILTONG
 SCHIZOPHRENIA

But in this form the exercise is still a relatively idle and arbitrary one: its true interpretive interest lies in the possibility for syntheses which it now proposes, for it is these syntheses which will put us on the track of those "real toads in imaginary gardens" that are the object of any criticism which pursues the moment of truth of the work itself. "Imaginary resolutions of real contradictions" we might also have put it: in this following Lévi-Strauss' lead in his readings of myth, which also enable a properly Marxian perspective on the relationship between art and society, inasmuch as the powers of art can only extend to the articulation of real social tensions and structural contradictions by way of the imaginary production of one narrative synthesis after another (until the possibilities are exhausted), rather than any active and practical intervention within the social field as such.

Four such imaginary solutions seem to be implicit in our scheme, as the syntheses of each of the contiguous corners of the rectangle. On the side of the twin negations (the contrary and the contradictory) of collectivities and therapies, there can be little doubt that the space of this particular synthesis is occupied by a whole novel in its own right, namely *Clans of the Alphane Moon*, which then at once also assumes the position of the Utopian term in Dick's production. It will be remembered that the various small collectivities of the Alphane moon-settlements which have degenerated after the war with the Alphanes and the withdrawal of Earth forces from this outpost – are all organized around various mental disorders or, better still, around the character-types projected by various psychopathologies. Mans (manic-depressives), Heebs (hebephrenics), Skitzes (schizophrenics), Pares (paranoids), along with assorted Ob-Coms, Deps and Polys – each congregate in their own settlements, coming together uncomfortably for the occasional moon-wide assembly. This is an imperfect Utopia to say the least: a comparison with Louis Mann's scheme in *Utopics*, for instance, reminds us of the distance between his synthesis of the two neutral terms (the bottom side of the rectangle) and this combination of negative ones. Meanwhile, the example of Fourier is there to offer a radically different method for combining psychological (and even psychopathological) character types. For in Fourier these come together to complement each other, each type being assigned a task appropriate to it and one which a different type would find repugnant: it is a combination of skills and manias which *Clans* achieves only at the supreme moment of crisis. In any case, on the level of narrative, the identification of the clan dynamics with the problematic (and characteristically Dickian) Rittersdorf marriage necessarily leaves this Utopia in a very tentative and precarious space indeed.

It has often stereotypically been observed that the opposite of Utopia is history: this is at any rate what we find to be the case in our schema of the structure of Dick's work, where it is the left-hand side of the rectangle, or in other words the synthesis of the positive and non-negative terms, which witnesses the coming together of the future (the androids) and the past (the nostalgic objects and collections). In fact, not only is this the place of history as such, it is also the space of historical method, and that of one of Dick's most remarkable innovations: what I have elsewhere called "nostalgia for the present".[7] This idea, if it is one, is not a concept but rather a thinking by way of the form, a thinking in and through narrative, in the sense in which Deleuze attributed a kind of non-conceptual philosophizing to film-makers or painters. In the same way, Dick's historico-temporal perspective here constitutes a whole new way of thinking about time and history and a kind of method or organon for approaching these phenomena, which the atmospheric conditions of postmodernity seem increasingly to occlude and to render intangible and unutilizable.

For the premise of this new encounter with time is very precisely that absence of the present which was for Ernst Bloch the foundation of a whole

---

7 See my *Postmodernism, or, the Cultural Logic of Late Capitalism*, Chapter 9, "Nostalgia for the Present", esp. pp. 279–287.

new theory of the Utopian and for Proust the conditions for the grounding of a whole new aesthetic. Yet Dick's perpetual and nostalgic return to the past is anything but Proustian, since it takes place under the lowering horizon of an SF future. In Dick neither the past nor the future can become autonomous; and this is why I have wanted to argue that, whatever the post-atomic or post-catastrophic situation of the Dick world in any given novel, these conditions are not to be considered, even in *Dr Bloodmoney*, as dystopian. For one thing, the genuinely anti-utopian is always driven by the passionate desire to disprove Utopia, something utterly missing here. For another, any inveterate reader gradually comes to the conclusion that Dick revels in the misery and impoverishment of these landscapes (as the reader ultimately does as well).

Nor is the past autonomous either: the vision of Wash-35, the recovery or the resurrection of the universe of childhood, is not really the object of desire. What Dick longs for is rather the lost object as such, or in other words nostalgia for the present, something that can only be achieved when the present is transformed into a distant past by a future perspective whose true function and reason for being is merely and precisely to be the operator of just such a shift in tense perspectives. Dick thus offers us a perverse and timely instrument for grasping the present as history in a situation in which, far more than for its author, we also suffer from the hollowness of our own present or what Mallarmé already called the absence of contemporaneity.

Now we must quickly identify the final sides of the semiotic square. The union of the neutral terms, the bottom side of the rectangle, in which the empty space of the layouts meets the realm of schizophrenia, including as well that half-life within which Joe Chip is henceforth, like a Christian soul in a fallen world, condemned to do good works and to seek the salvation of his fellow dead – this place, given over to televisual addiction and the therapies, can only be the United States itself, and in particular the America of the 1950s, in which Dick's imagination is immobilized as in a time capsule (like the doomed voyagers of *Maze of Death*).

Any reading of the climactic synthesis, the complex term, in which an impossible meeting is staged between the extremes of the fundamental opposition or contradiction (here, between individual consciousness and the collective), must necessarily remain tentative and open to a variety of readings and hypotheses. Still, if it is a question of the evolutionary leap, the combination of some future android technology and the handicraft efforts of the quintessential Dick repairmen, at least one episode comes insistently to mind: it takes place near the beginning of *Now Wait for Last Year* and is triggered by the reluctance of one of Ackerman's workmen (Bruce Himmel) to discard a faulty rocketship guidance monad (the so-called Lazy Brown Dog).

"Don't melt it down," Himmel said. His unsightly body twisted with embarrassment; his arms wound themselves about, the long knobby fingers writhing

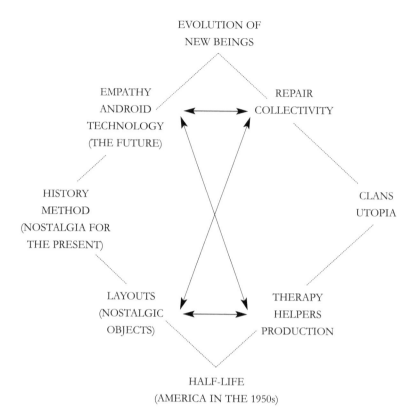

EVOLUTION OF
NEW BEINGS

EMPATHY   REPAIR
ANDROID   COLLECTIVITY
TECHNOLOGY
(THE FUTURE)

HISTORY   CLANS
METHOD   UTOPIA
(NOSTALGIA FOR
THE PRESENT)

LAYOUTS   THERAPY
(NOSTALGIC   HELPERS
OBJECTS)   PRODUCTION

HALF-LIFE
(AMERICA IN THE 1950s)

… "I – don't do that anymore." Defensively, his face dark with resentment and with the corrosive traces of deeply etched phobia anxiety, he stood aside. Within the room – a storeroom, evidently – small carts rolled about on silver-dollar-sized wheels; twenty or more of them, astutely avoiding one another in their zealous activity. On board each cart Eric saw a Lazy Brown Dog, wired in place and controlling the movements of the cart. (15)

There is something moving about this exercise of Christian charity towards defective machinery, and a very modest salvationalism in this emergence of new kinds of mechanical beings from a very imperfect landscape. But this needs to be marked as a most fragile and tentative solution indeed; and Dick's essential realism is to be gauged by the sequel, at the very end of the novel, in which Eric witnesses the evolutionary and Darwinian future of these mechanical beings, now fighting bitterly among themselves:

The cart was pursued by another of its kind. They met, in the tangle of news-papers and bottles, and then the debris trembled and bits flew everywhere as the carts fought it out, ramming each other head-on, trying for the cephalic unit mounted in each other's center, trying to knock out the Lazy Brown Dog

… Now one seemed to be triumphing. It withdrew and, like a goat, maneuvered to locate itself for the coup de grace. While it was positioning itself the damaged one, in a last burst of native wit, popped into the sanctuary of a discarded galvanized zinc bucket and was out of the fray. Protected, it became inert, prepared to wait things out, forever if necessary. (202–205)

So this potential survival of the fittest once again illustrates that variation and shifting of the valences that characterizes Dick's most energetic work, in which a given term can change from negative to positive and back without warning and without regret. We might then leave matters here, in this evolutionary suspension, in which the future is permanently in doubt.

But I prefer a somewhat different ending, in which Dick's salvational instinct finds its raw material and its nourishment in the most depressing of all his novelistic "realities", the settlements on Mars in *Martian Time-Slip*. In this episode, its climactic one, it is as though all the corners of our semiotic rectangle, all the semic clusters, are united in one final apotheosis. Here we find an android-type prosthetic being, repaired again and again, we find helpers and therapy and schizophrenia, but also that mixture of the past and future which this time breaks through a kind of televisual veil of illusion into a historically different reality. It is the fate of the virtually autistic child Manfred, whose participation in his present as a child is blocked by the reality of his bedridden old age (in one of Dick's most emblematic nightmare buildings), from which he is unexpectedly rescued in the very "time-slip" of the title:

The living room was filled with Bleekmen. And in their midst she saw part of a living creature, an old man only from the chest up; and the rest of him became a tangle of pumps and hoses and dials, machinery that clicked away, unceasingly active. It kept the old man alive; she realized that in an instant. The missing portion of him had been replaced by it. Oh, God, she thought. Who or what was it, sitting there with a smile on its withered face? Now it spoke to them.

"Jack Bolin," it rasped, and its voice issued from a mechanical speaker, out of the machinery: not from its mouth. "I am here to say goodbye to my mother." (218–219)

Here then is the collective, the primitive communism of the aboriginals, who have also become the helpers and the rescuers of the schizophrenic Manfred, himself now a new kind of prosthetic being who has emerged from out of the future of his own past, immobilized in gubbish, and about to escape, with his friends around him bearing him away, all tubes and hoses trailing behind, into the alternate dreamtime of another History and another present.

2000

11

Fear and Loathing in Globalization

Has the author of *Neuromancer* really "changed his style"? Has he even stopped writing Science Fiction, as some old-fashioned critics have put it, thinking thereby to pay him a compliment? Maybe, on the contrary, he is moving closer to that "cyberpunk" with which he is often associated, but which seems more characteristically developed in the work of his sometime collaborator Bruce Sterling? In any case, the representational apparatus of Science Fiction, here refined and transistorized in all kinds of new and productive ways, sends back more reliable information about the contemporary world than an exhausted realism (or an exhausted modernism either).

William Gibson, now the author of *Pattern Recognition*, has certainly more often illustrated that other coinage, "cyberspace" and its inner networks of global communication and information, than the object-world of late commodification through which the latest novel carefully gropes its way. To be sure, Sterling celebrated the hackers, the heroic pirates of cyberspace, but without Gibson's tragic intensity and as the oddballs and marginals of new frontiers to come; and the rush and exhilaration of his books, rather alien to the cooler Gibson, has always seemed to me to derive as much from global entrepreneurship and the excitement of the money to be made, as from paranoia.

But that excitement also expresses the truth of emergent globalization; and Sterling deserves more than a mere paragraph or parenthesis here. The novels are often episodic, but stories like those collected in *A Good Old-Fashioned Future* (New York, 1999) are authentic artifacts of postmodernity and little masterpieces in their own right, offering a Cook's tour of the new global waystations and the piquant dissonances between picturesque travellers and the future cities they suddenly find themselves in: Tokyo to be sure (Tokyo now and forever!), in which a Japanese-American federal prosecutor from Providence, Rhode Island, finds herself enveloped in a conspiracy waged with ceramic cats; but also the California of misfit inventors, in which a new process for manufacturing artificial (and aerial) jellyfish threatens to convert all the oil left in the ground in Texas into so much worthless *Urschleim*, then offering an unsurprisingly happy hunting ground for meetings between old

1960s-style terrorists and the former KGB, along with youthful and ruthless ecological nationalists, veteran international industrial spies, and an aged Finnish writer of children's books immensely popular in Japan. Meanwhile, Bollywood actors in flight from the Indian tax system have the great good luck to happen on the biggest mass grave in history, in Bolton, in an England decimated by the plague and now good only for making cheap movies on location; while, in Germany, in Düsseldorf, the new institution of the *Wende* is explored, in which, observed by a "spex" salesman from Chattanooga, periodically all the destructive collective movements of the time, from football hooligans to anti-modern moral majorities, coincide in a ritual "turbulence". Indeed, it is Chattanooga, with its burnt-out downtown future megastructure, now a rat's nest of squatters, which serves as the stage for a more complex and characteristic encounter: between a de-sexed bicycle repairman (new gender movements have proliferated in this future, including that of Sexual Deliberation, which artificially eradicates the sex drive) and the private police of a long-serving and now senile congressional stalwart, whose artificial identity replacement (the so-called mook) risks being unmasked by an unwanted package in the mail. Finally, classic Science Fiction returns with the discovery in a Central Asian desert, by twenty-first-century bounty-hunters, of an enormous artificial underground cavern, in which the Zone (the latest future form of the old East Asian Co-Prosperity Sphere, now run, to be sure, by China) has housed three world-sized sealed-off human communities as an experiment in testing the viability of 400-year-long space flights. I have only incidentally mentioned some of the wacky SF technology taken for granted in these tales: what is significant are the priorities of global cyberpunk, in which technological speculation and fantasy of the old Toeffler sort takes second place to the more historically original literary vocation of a mapping of the new geopolitical Imaginary.

This is why such Hunter Thompsonian global tourism has real epistemological value: cyberpunk constitutes a kind of laboratory experiment in which the geographical-cultural light spectrum and band-widths of the new system are registered. It is a literature of the new stereotypes thrown up by a system in full expansion, which, like the explosion of a nova, sends out a variety of uncharted signals and signs of new communities and new and artificially differentiated *ethnies*. Stereotypes are preeminently the vehicle through which we relate to other collectivities (no one has ever confronted one of the latter without their mediation); they are allegorical cartoons which no longer convey the racist contempt of the older imperialism but can often (as Žižek has observed for the racist jokes popular in the old Yugoslavia) function as affectionate forms of inclusion and of solidarity.

Indeed, an inspection of this literature already provides a first crude inventory of the new world system: the immense role, first and foremost – and very much in Gibson's evocations (all the way down to *Pattern Recognition* itself) –

of Japan as the monitory semiotic combination of First World science-and-technology with a properly Third World population explosion. Russia now also looms large, but above all in the form of its various mafias (from all the former Republics), which remind us of the anarchy and violent crime (as well as of the conspiratorial networks and jobless futures) that lurk just beneath the surface of capitalism. It also offers the more contemporary breakneck drama of the devolution of a country that had already reached parity with the First World. Europe's image ambiguity, a kind of elegant museum or tourist playground which is also an evolutionary and economic dead end, is instructive; and the absence of Islam is a welcome relief, in a moment in which it is reality rather than culture or literature which is acting on the basis of that particular stereotype.

This new geopolitical material marks a significant historical difference between such commercial adventure stories and the equally cynical gonzo journalism of an older period (indeed, the affinities and distinctions between the cultural products of the 1960s and 1970s and those of the 1990s and 2000s would be well worth exploring further). Equally significant is that these protagonists – busy as they are in locating rare products, securing secret new inventions, outsmarting rivals and trading with the natives – do not particularly need the stimulus of drugs (still a preponderant, one may even say a metaphysical, presence in so recent a world-historical expression as David Foster Wallace's *Infinite Jest*, of 1996).

But it is by way of the style that we can best measure these differences and position the new literature on some kind of time continuum; and here we may finally return to the main course, which is to be sure the distinctiveness of *Pattern Recognition*, where this style has reached a kind of classical perfection. I will define it as a kind of hyped-up name-dropping, and the description of the clothes selected by the protagonist (Cayce Pollard) for her first day in London is a reliable indicator: "a fresh Fruit T-shirt, her black Buzz Rickson's MA-1, anonymous black skirt from a Tulsa thrift, the black leggings she'd worn for Pilates, black Harajuku schoolgirl shoes. Her purse-analog is an envelope of black East German laminate, purchased on eBay – if not actual Stasi-issue then well in the ballpark."[1] I have no way of knowing whether all these items actually exist; but eBay is certainly the right word for our current collective unconscious; and it is clear that the references work, whether you know the product is real or that it has been made up by Gibson (neither being my own case). What is also clear is that the names being dropped are brandnames, names whose very dynamic conveys both instant obsolescence and the global provenance and neo-exoticism of the world market today in time and space.

---

1 William Gibson, *Pattern Recognition* (New York, 2003), p. 8 (all further pages references to this edition are given within the text).

There is a further point, namely that little by little, in the current universe, everything is slowly being named; nor does this have anything to do with the older Aristotelian universals in which the idea of a chair subsumes all its individual manifestations. Here the "high-backed workstation chair" (4) is almost of a different species than the seat in the BA 747 "that makes her think of a little boat, a coracle of Hexcel and teakfinish laminate" (122). But there are also exercise chairs, called or named "reformers": "a very long, very low, vaguely ominous and Weimar-looking piece of spring-loaded furniture" (6), which can also be translated into another language, where it becomes "a faux-classical Japanese interpretation in black-lacquered wood, upholstered with something that looks like sharkskin"(178). Each of these items is on its way to the ultimate destination of a name of its own; but not the kind we are familiar with when we speak of a "Mies chair" or a "Barcelona chair": not the origin, but rather the named image is at stake, so that an "Andy Warhol electric chair" might be a better reference.

In this postmodern nominalism, however, the name must also include the new and fashion. What is worn-out or old-fashioned is only useful as a cultural marker: "empty chrome stools of the soda-fountain spin-around kind, but very low, fronting on an equally low bar" (152), where it is the "low", the "very low" that connotes Japan. And in Moscow the table "flanked by two enormous, empty wingback armchairs" (294) only stands for backwardness. This is probably why Gibson's Russian episode is less interesting: he brings a residual Cold War mentality to this built space, "as though everything was designed by someone who'd been looking at a picture of a Western hotel room from the eighties, but without ever having seen even one example of the original" (282). Current Soviet and Eastern European nostalgia art (*Ostalgie* in German) is far more vibrant and exciting than this, and reflects the situation of an alternate universe in which a complete set of mass-produced industrial products, from toilet seats to windowpanes, from shower heads to automobiles, had been invented from scratch, altogether different from the actually existing Western inventory. It is as though the Aztecs had beaten Cortez and survived to invent their own Aztec radio and television, their own Aztec power-vehicles, their own Aztec film genres and popular culture.

At any rate, the premise here is that Russia has nothing new to offer us (the Sterling aesthetic offers much better chances of appreciating what is genuinely new, world-historically innovative in Eastern nostalgia art); and the conclusion to be drawn is that name-dropping is also a matter of knowledge and an encyclopedic familiarity with the fashions of world space as those flow back into the boutiques or flea markets of the West. What I have called name-dropping is therefore also to be grasped as in-group style: the brand names are also the wink of familiarity, to the reader in the know. Even the cynicism (taking the word in Sloterdijk's rather than in its post-Watergate sense) is a joyous badge of group adherence, the snicker as a form of hearty laughter, class status as a matter of knowing the score rather than of having the money and the power. In-group style was, I believe, the invention (or better still, the discovery) of Thomas Pynchon, as early as *V* (1963), even though Ian Fleming deserves a reference ("Thank you, Commander Bond," murmurs Cayce, as she pastes a hair across the outside apartment door [73]). But just as we no longer need drugs, so we no longer need Pynchon's staples of paranoia and conspiracy to wrap it all up for us, since global capitalism is there to do so more efficiently (or so we are told).

Nonetheless, *The Crying of Lot 49* remains a fundamental paradigm; and, as with Hunter Thompson, the differences are historically very instructive indeed. For the posthorns and the other telltale graffiti have here been replaced by something like a "work of art"; the clues point, not to some unimaginable reality in the social world, but to an (as yet) unimaginable aesthetic. It is a question of an unidentified film of some kind, which has come to be known (among insiders) as "the footage", and which shows up in stills and clips in the most unlikely places (billboards, television ads, magazines, the Internet), in "one hundred and thirty-four previously discovered fragments … endlessly collated, broken down, reassembled, by whole armies of the most fanatical investigators". Indeed, as one might expect, a whole new in-group has formed around the mysteries of the footage; we are experiencing, one of the characters observes, the "birth of a new subculture"; a world-wide confraternity comes into being, committed to this new object and passionately exchanging and arguing contradictory theories about it. The footage thus makes *Pattern Recognition* over into something like Bloch's conception of the novel of the artist, which carries the unknown unrealized work of art inside itself like a black hole, the empty present of a future indeterminacy, the absent sublime within the everyday real:

> Light and shadow. Lovers' cheekbones in the prelude to embrace.
>
> Cayce shivers.
>
> So long now, and they have not been seen to touch.
>
> Around them the absolute blackness is alleviated by texture. Concrete?
>
> They are dressed as they have always been dressed, in clothing Cayce has posted on extensively, fascinated by its timelessness, something she knows and understands.
>
> The difficulty of that. Hairstyles, too.
>
> He might be a sailor, stepping onto a submarine in 1914, or a jazz musician entering a club in 1957. There is a lack of evidence, an absence of stylistic cues, that Cayce understands to be utterly masterful. His black coat is usually read as leather, though it might be dull vinyl, or rubber. He has a way of wearing its collar up.
>
> The girl wears a longer coat, equally dark but seemingly of fabric, its shoulder-padding the subject of hundreds of posts. The architecture of

padding in a woman's coat should yield possible periods, particular decades, but there has been no agreement, only controversy.

She is hatless, which has been taken either as the clearest of signs that this is not a period piece, or simply as an indication that she is a free spirit, untrammeled by even the most basic conventions of her day. Her hair has been the subject of similar scrutiny, but nothing has ever been definitively agreed upon.

The one hundred and thirty-four previously discovered fragments, having been endlessly collated, broken down, reassembled, by whole armies of the most fanatical investigators, have yielded no period and no particular narrative direction.

Zaprudered into surreal dimensions of purest speculation, ghost-narratives have emerged and taken on shadowy but determined lives of their own, but Cayce is familiar with them all, and steers clear.

And here in Damien's flat, watching their lips meet, she knows that she knows nothing, but wants nothing more than to see the film of which this must be a part. Must be.

The problem, for the group forming around this artifact, as indeed for all group formation, is that of the contradiction between universality – in this case the universality of taste as such – and the particularity of this unique value that sets us off from all the others and defines us in our collective specificity. A political sect (as we now seem to call these things) wishes to affirm the universal relevance of its strategy and its ultimate aims, and at one and the same time to keep them for itself, to exclude the outsiders and the late-comers and those who can be suspected of insufficient commitment, insufficient passion and belief. The deeper anxiety of the practitioners of the footage website and chatroom is, in other words, simply that the footage will go public: that CNN will get wind of this interesting development; that the footage, or the completed film, the identified and reconstructed work of art, will become, as they say, the patrimony of mankind, or in other words, just another commodity. As it turns out, this fear is only too justified; but I omit the details, as I hate people who tell you the ending, except to express my mixed feeling that Pynchon's solution was perhaps the better one, namely to break off *Lot 49* on the threshold of the revelation to come, as Oedipa is on the point of entering the auction room.

After all this, it may come as something of a surprise to learn that the footage is not the central issue of this novel, even though it supplies the narrative framework. Yet it ought already to have been clear that there is a striking and dramatic contradiction between the style, as we have described it, and the footage itself, whose "absence of stylistic clues" suggests a veritable Barthesian "white writing". Indeed, it is rather this very contradiction which is the deeper subject of *Pattern Recognition*, which projects the Utopian anticipation of a new art premised on "semiotic neutrality", and on the systematic effacement of names, dates, fashions and history itself, within a context irremediably corrupted by all those things. The name-dropping in-group language of the novel thus revels in everything the footage seeks to neutralize; the work becomes a kind of quicksand, miring us ever more deeply in what we struggle to escape. Yet this is not merely an abstract interpretation, nor even an aesthetic: it is also the existential reality of the protagonist herself, and the source of the "gift" that informs her profession.

Cayce Pollard's talent, lying as it does halfway between telepathy and old-fashioned aesthetic sensibility, is in fact what suspends Gibson's novel between Science Fiction and realism and lends it its extraordinary resonance. To put it simply (as she does), Cayce's business is to "hunt cool"; or in other words, to wander through the masses of now and future consumers, through the youth crowds, the "Children's Crusade" that jams Camden High Street on weekends, the teeming multitudes of Roppongi and Shinjuku, the big-city agglomerations of every description all over the world, in order mentally to detect the first stirrings of anything likely to become a trend or a new fashion. She has in fact racked up some impressive achievements, of which my favorite, reeking somewhat of DeLillo, is the identification of the first person in the world to wear his baseball cap backwards. But these "futures" are very much a business proposition, and Cayce is something like an industrial spy of times to come. "I consult on design … Manufacturers use me to keep track of street fashion" (87); these modest formulas are a little too dry and underplay the sheer physicality of this gift, which allows her to identify a "pattern" and then to "point a commodifier at it". There is here no doubt something of the specialized training of the authenticator of paintings and the collector of antique furniture; but its uncanny temporal direction condemns Cayce irredeemably, and despite her systematically black and styleless outfit, to the larger category of fortune-tellers and soothsayers (and also occasionally puts her in real physical danger).

This new *métier* thus draws our world insensibly into some science-fictional future one, at least on the borders, where other details also fail to coincide: such as the paid job of another character to start rumors, to drop the names of products and cultural items enthusiastically in one bar after another, in order to set in motion what would in Pynchon have been a conspiracy, but what is here just another fad or craze.

But Cayce's gift is drawn back into our real (or realistic) world by the body itself; she must pay for it by nauseas and anxiety attacks, the commodity bulimia, which are the inevitable compensation for her premonitory sensibility. It is as if the other face of the "coming attraction", its reification and the dead-end product of what was once an active process of consumption and desire itself, were none other than the logo. The mediation between these two extremes of *ergon* and *energeia*, of product and process, lies no doubt in the name itself, of which we have said that in the commercial nominalism of the postmodern everything unique and interesting tends towards the proper name. Indeed, within the brand name the whole contradictory dialectic of universality and particularity is played out as a tug of war between visual recognition and what we may call the work of consumption (as Freud spoke of the work of mourning). And yet, to paraphrase Empson, the name remains, the name remains and kills; and the logo into which the brand name gradually hardens soaks up its toxicity and retains the poison.

Cayce's whole body is a resonator for these omnipresent logos, which are nonetheless louder and more oppressive in certain spaces (and places) than in others. To search for an unusual item in Harvey Nichols, for instance, is a peculiarly perilous activity:

> Down here, next to a display of Tommy Hilfiger, it's all started to go sideways on her, the trademark thing. Less warning aura than usual. Some people ingest a single peanut and their head swells like a basketball. When it happens to Cayce, it's her psyche. Tommy Hilfiger does it every time, though she'd thought she was safe now. They said he'd peaked, in New York. Like Benetton, the name would be around, but the real poison, for her, would have been drawn … This stuff is simulacra of simulacra of simulacra. A diluted tincture of Ralph Lauren, who had himself diluted the glory days of Brooks Brothers, who themselves had stepped on the product of Jermyn Street and Savile Row, flavoring their ready-to-wear with liberal lashings of polo knit and regimental stripes. But Tommy Hilfiger surely is the null point, the black hole. There must be some Tommy Hilfiger event horizon, beyond which it is impossible to be more derivative, more removed from the source, more devoid of soul. (17–18)

These nauseas are part of Cayce's navigational apparatus, and they stretch back to some of the oldest logos still extant, such as her worst nightmare, Bibendum, the Michelin Man, which is like that crack through which the Lacanian Real makes its catastrophic appearance. "National icons", on the other hand, "are always neutral for her, with the exception of Nazi Germany's … a scary excess of design talent."

Now it is a little easier to see the deeper meaning of the footage for Cayce: its utter lack of style is an ontological relief, like black-and-white film after the conventional orgies of bad Technicolor, like the silence of solitude for the telepath whose mind is jammed with noisy voices all day long. The footage is an epoch of rest, an escape from the noisy commodities themselves, which turn out, as Marx always thought they would, to be living entities preying on the humans who have to coexist with them. Unlike the footage, however, Gibson's novel gives us homeopathy rather than antidote.

It does not seem anticlimactic to return to the future and to everything also autoreferential about this novel, whose main character shares the sound of the name of that of *Neuromancer*, if not its spelling (or gender). Is it possible that Cayce's premonitions of future novelty can also stand as the allegory of some emergent "new Gibson novel" as well? *Pattern Recognition* at any rate does seem to constitute a kind of pattern recognition for Gibson as well, as indeed for Science Fiction generally.

2003

12

"If I Can Find One Good City I Will Spare the Man": Realism and Utopia in Kim Stanley Robinson's *Mars* Trilogy

Strictly speaking, Utopia is not a genre in its own right,
but rather the socio-political sub-genre of Science Fiction.

Darko Suvin[1]

For those who still think that Science Fiction is about science, the *Mars* trilogy will certainly qualify. Not only are scientists and engineers among its principal characters; pages upon pages offer pocket disquisitions on a host of topics that surely qualify as hard science, most of it relating to terraforming: such as the biochemistry of rocks and solids; the dynamics of gases and the composition of atmosphere; aquifers and the release of water and other liquids; genetically engineered micro-organisms and genetically reconstructed DNA; radiation, light and heat; the food chain; the structure of topsoil; meteorology and the dynamics of wind and climate; botanical systems and classification; "string theory" and the unified field theory in physics; the mechanics of velocity in astronomical and military situations. Robinson manages to hold the non-scientific reader's interest and attention during these brief but ludic discussions, about which one would also like to hear the scientists' opinions or to browse through a collection of essays by the experts on his treatment of these specialized matters, which I take to be a mixture of state-of-the-art conceptualization and "speculation", mainstream or otherwise. It is true that the literary critic would here interpose the reminder that the novel offers a mimesis of science and scientific activity and not the thing itself. It is an aestheticist answer, which has always aimed at separating out the literary and "imaginative" from the referential ("real" science, "real" scientific texts and so on), but which in the present context has the disadvantage of bracketing the "cognitive" as such. Still even the "verisimilitude" of imitation necessarily has something to do with outside factors, and in particular the rapidly changing configurations of these various scientific fields in the real world.

1 *Metamorphoses of Science Fiction* (New Haven, 1979), p. 61.

More pertinent is, I think, the way in which these scientific facts and findings, presuppositions and activities are themselves staged: namely, as data and raw materials for the solving of problems, rather than as abstract and contemplative features of an epistemology or scientific world picture. Not only are "problems" – crises, dilemmas, catastrophes (has Sax thought about what to do if Burroughs was flooded?) – more dramatic than classic unresolved issues in theoretical science; but they also potentially give free rein to a different kind of imagination and a wilder set of propositions and puzzle-solutions. My favourite is Art Randolph's proposal for solving the population explosion: "I would give everyone alive a birthright which entitled them to parent three-quarters of a child." He explained that every pair of parents would thus have the right to bear a child and a half; after having one, they could either sell the right to the other half, or arrange to buy a half from some other couple' etc.[2] There is thus a supplementary energy and invention to be admired in these solutions, above and beyond the "merely" scientific ones (unless indeed, the scientific ones are themselves aesthetically the result of just such ingenuity in the first place, something that non-scientists, with their reified respect for science as an absolute, are less often prepared to allow). At any rate, this kind of speculative problem-solving is obviously rather different from what one finds in a Science Fiction that offers a description of this or that kind of alien anatomy, a premise about the mechanism of this or that faster-than-light space travel, or a preview of developments in the universe several billion years from now. Indeed, the specifically SF motifs are here few and far between, and largely in the area of perception:

> To the east stood a number of rocket landing vehicles, each one a different shape and size, with the top of more sticking over the eastern horizon. All of them were crusted the same red-orange as the ground: it was an odd, thrilling sight, as if they had stumbled upon a long-abandoned alien spaceport. (R 89)

But even here the next sentence puts us on the track of an idiosyncrasy (particularly when we remember that it is a Russian member of the First Hundred who is making the observation): "Parts of Baikonur would look like this, in a million years." Leaving aside a few wonderful Stapledonian excesses (the terraforming of Venus and the train-city Terminator on Mercury in the last volume), what look like science-fictional elements here are mostly temporal inversions, parts of early Mars looking old and museum-like, the great metropolis of Burroughs drowned under water in the last volume, inverted allusions to Terran ancient history – in particular to Crete – as those rise back up in

---

2 Kim Stanley Robinson, *Green Mars* (New York, 1994), p. 69. Henceforth, all references to the trilogy – also including *Red Mars* (New York, 1993) and *Blue Mars* (New York, 1996) – are given within the text with the abbreviations R, G and B.

Mars like a "return of the repressed". Is this then to say that the *Mars* trilogy is a more realistic kind of Science Fiction than what we ordinarily associate with space travel and emigration? Perhaps: but that is not quite the notion of realism I want to propose here.

Yet one more thing needs to be said about the kind of science we find in this novel: it is related to the overall problem of terraforming Mars, no doubt, but also has more general implications. Secondary themes hint at the secret of "problem-solving" here: the mockery of Sax's "monocausotaxophilia" (or, for example, "the love of single causes that explain everything"). But Sax himself is perplexed about prediction – "the interventions that worked, the interventions that backfired – the effects unintended, unforeseen, unnoticed" – particularly as far as Martian weather is concerned: "impossible to predict, even if one froze the variables and pretended terraforming had stabilized, which it certainly had not. Over and over Sax watched a thousand years of weather, altering variables in the models, and every time a completely different millennium flitted past" (B 336).

These structural unpredictabilities, based on chaos theory, have often been taken to be so many arguments against historical determinism, and assimilated to the anti-Marxian arsenal (in the name of some "freedom" and creativity at work at the very heart of Nature itself). Yet I think that "predictability" as such was never at stake here, and that we have here rather to do with that more fundamental structure of problem-solving in the *Mars* trilogy, which is not so much to be characterized in terms of *indeterminacy* as rather in those of *overdetermination*. The Althusserian concept[3] was indeed specifically designed to name what is finally not ultimately thinkable about historical conjunctures of this kind.

In other words, if all of Mars is one gigantic laboratory (and in another way it is, and we will also have to think about the novels from that perspective), then it is a unique laboratory in which the variables can never be isolated in the ordinary ways, but always coexist in a multiplicity which can scarcely be mastered by equations let alone by the computer itself. This means that whatever the scientific theme confronted – botany, biology, geology, physics, chemistry, astronomy – the projected solution to the imaginary problem will always involve the rehearsal of a specific kind of thinking to which we are not often accustomed, namely the grappling with what Althusser calls "complex overdetermined concrete situations"[4] which he also very specifically associates with history and above all with politics. It is therefore not only about the construction of a "biotic community" in topsoils that one might be tempted to exclaim (as Nadia does): "My God, it's like trying to get this government to work" (B 269): all of the scientific problems described in the novel, without

---

3 See Louis Althusser, *For Marx* (London, 1977), trans. Ben Brewster, especially chapters 3 ("Contradiction and Overdetermination") and 6 ("On the Materialist Dialectic").

4 Ibid., p. 217: an "unevenness (in dominance) of the ever-pre-given complex whole".

exception, offer an allegory, by way of the form of overdetermination, of social, political and historical problems also faced by the inhabitants of Mars.

This is, then, the sense in which science and politics are not (or not only) two separate themes in the *Mars* trilogy, which appear to alternate from chapter to chapter of the story of the planet's development; nor is it only a question of the inevitably scientific dimensions of any politics on Mars, nor even the increasingly obvious fact that scientific research today is itself a specialized form of institutional politics, over and above its implications for the more generally social and political. Besides all this, we need to insist on the way in which any first scientific reading of the *Mars* trilogy must eventually develop into a second allegorical one, in which the hard SF content stands revealed as socio-political – that is to say, as utopian.

We have to do, in other words, with the registers of reading and inter-pretation, and the way in which a shift between these two fundamental levels of nature and human collectivities tends to problematize each one in turn, and to send us back to the other. And this interpretative alternation also explains the more horizontal alternations in the text itself, its heterogeneities and the uneven sequence of great sheets of material – now the exploration of the land-scape, now the grappling with political problems from Earth (the UN, the nation-states, the multinationals), now the brilliant set-pieces (the assassination of John Boone – "the first man on Mars" – the two revolutions, the falling of the space elevator as it wraps itself twice around the planet, great floods and fires in the tented cities, Sax's life disguised, then his rescue from the security new town, the search for Hiroko, the dramatic cures and dramatic deaths) … so many distinct reading temporalities that are carefully juxtaposed, in a kind of distant echo of the narrative heterogeneities of the classical utopias them-selves, the discovery in space or time, the encounters, then the guided tours and explanations, to which here correspond the innumerable visits to different kind of communities and settlements all over the new planet. Sheer length, sheer reading time, is crucial here in order to develop an *analogon* of historical time itself, as its overdeterminations slowly evolve across the longer Martian years, which the device of the longevity treatment prevents from forming into generations (or perhaps at best only three generations whose time is unsettled in a politically problematic way – a Bénard instability? – by the irregular immi-gration of Earth-dwellers). It is something of a scientific laboratory experiment in its own right, for human collective history knows rhythm and a logic radi-cally distinct from the normal biological life span, and its paradoxes and unknowabilities stem as much from that incommensurability as they do from the other one that opposes biological individuals to larger multiplicities. The *Mars* trilogy then experimentally extends the lives of its viewers and partici-pants in order to make them coeval with their own history, at the same time that it projects an original collectivity – the first settlers, the so-called "First Hundred" – as a collective protagonist or multiple subjects for that history itself; and this is also the moment to observe that the three books form a single narrative and constitute a single novel, rather than a genuine trilogy (like Robinson's Orange County books), let alone a series on the fantasy model. The shifting adjectives of the titles then correspond to stages in the development of the planet itself – first reddish rock, then covered by green plant life, and finally bathed in water and wrapped definitively in the great Martian oceans. (What the colours stand for here, and their political implications, we will see later.) Meanwhile, the later theme of the memory problems of the survivors, and the relationship of memory to the structure of the brain, is a kind of decorative projection of the structural or narrative device, what we will in a moment call its autoreferential inscription, and belongs to something like the modernist structural traits or features of the *Mars* trilogy.

Yet categories like "modernism" or "realism" have never seemed particularly compatible with so peculiarly generic a classification as that of Utopia (or Utopian discourse, the Utopian text), and we need to clarify them before we can work our way back to the more central issue of the relationship between Science Fiction and utopia that the *Mars* trilogy so insistently raises. One is tempted to think indeed that the hidden agenda behind predictably aimless and academic distinctions between realist and modernist utopias has more to do with the question about the possibility of a "postmodern" utopia, that is, about the possibility of utopias today as such, than it does with genre theory. In any case the classificatory categories in question themselves seem uniquely "modern", and not very relevant to More or Cyrano, let alone to the fantastic as such in general.

Rather than marshalling various traditional or *a priori* conceptions of realism, it seems best to begin with the *Mars* trilogy's own answer to this question, which can surely be glimpsed in Sax's musings about the way he thinks of science:

> I try to understand. I pay attention to things, you see, very closely. As closely as I can. Concentrating on the specificity of every moment. And I want to understand why it happens the way it does. I'm curious. And I think that everything happens for a reason. Everything. So, we ought to be able to tease those reasons out. When we can't … well, I don't like it.
>
> It vexes me. Sometimes I call it … the great unexplainable. (*G* 12)

What is important in this rambling statement is less the issue of causality (about which the question of single versus multiple causes will be crucial enough in a different context, as we have already seen above) than it is the evocation of resistance: external reality organizes itself into a problem or even, at some lower limit, into an event as such, whose nature poses a problem only insofar as it raises a question about its own coming into existence in the first place, about the very why of its happening. This problem then, in the name of external reality or the world itself, refuses an answer and eludes a solution: and I will want to suggest that it is very precisely this kind of "resistance" of a phenomenon posited as external and independent which defines the situation of literary realisms as well, and needs to be their effect when they succeed in becoming realism in the first place.

It is a "definition" which has the advantage of adapting to a variety of contents and historical situations, including the traditional ones: namely that realism has something to do with observation, with social documentation, with the rise of journalism and the "construction" of the ephemeral or actuality, and so forth. It also moves us away from the standard history-of-ideas notion of the central role of the emergence of modern science; and this is perhaps less paradoxical than it may at first seem, since the very observation about science with which we began already amounted to an attempt to describe science in terms of a whole range of other activities, or, in other words, to assimilate science to non-scientific activity and daily life as such. Science thereby becomes only one of the by-products of this increasingly specified "resistance" of reality, and not particularly even the primary agent, in a process we would do better to describe in terms of secularization.

For it is secularization as such which forestalls the easier answers of the theological or the traditional, the symbolic or the mythic; the latter's absence both confirms the autonomy of the problematic object and accounts for the creative frustration of the questions asked of it. At same time, this initial moment of secularization also precludes the development and deployment of subjectivity as such, and of the intricate dilemmas of projection and anthropomorphism, the confusions that result when we are able to begin wondering about the very source of the answers themselves: the mark of a humanization and socialization so extensive that Ann puts it, "we'll wonder … why when we look at the land we can see anything but our own faces (R 142).

Is this to say that the realistic moment must always betray a certain naïveté, a certain absence of reflexivity, an attention to the object too rapt to register the operation of our own mental categories in the process? In that case, or so the canonical account runs, realism's sequel modernism will date precisely the emergence of that new reflexivity and categorial consciousness. It is a reproach (or at least a historical diagnosis) which ought presumably also to be extended to language itself, in order to gauge the extent of this precarious situation and the fragility of the realist moment in general. For the very unexplainable, in Sax's sense, the evocation of those problematic entities outside ourselves whose density refuses to answer our questions, the crucial event or occasion of the unsolvable mystery as such – these are all constructions of the realist's language, and presumably, particularly when we have to do with a novel, stands as a human artifact constructed in advance, after the fashion of the classic mystery novelist who initially devises a sequence of events designed to be as provisionally unintelligible as possible. In that case, literary realism is a trick and a deceit, which has to collapse as soon as the idea of fiction dawns on its reader. The unexplained presumably has to lie outside of language; even if the very illusion of the unexplained and the unexplainable is itself produced by language in the first place. And this is even more visible when we come to the most philosophically ambitious fictions: the tree root, for example, in Sartre's *Nausea*[5] which is supposed to stand for the absolute Not-I, and to resist and unveil the feebleness of the adjectives with which we try to seize and evoke it. Is the existential narrative still a realism, then? I think so, but it comes at the moment in which the various initial realisms have passed over into ontology; it is an ontological realism, as we shall see in a moment.

What threatens our belief in realism today, and yet perhaps stimulates newer and even more desperate forms of realism, is our widespread conviction (which owes as much to Sartre as to anybody else) about the "constructedness" of reality as such – the constructedness of scientific fact fully as much as of social institutions, the construction of gender and of the subjective fully as much as that of the objective categories through which we intuit the allegedly still real world. In that case everything is human, and the formerly unexplainable, the formerly contingent and resistant, will recede uniformly against the horizon of a complete humanization and a complete socialization, of the awareness of the omnipresence of praxis and production in the seeming autonomy of what lies outside us.

Thus, even the tree root must wane and fade away in its Being when we incorporate the longer historical view into our dealings with nature: in particular, a knowledge of the historical invention and production of plant life by emergent human society. At that point, then, presumably, everything we have hitherto considered to be natural and organic becomes as manufactured as the cityscape itself: and this is certainly a radical defamiliarization that much of Science Fiction has attempted to convey. If the tree and its roots are not the result of such ancient domestication, as it were the dogs among plant life, then this form tends to separate itself out, not as a messenger of some unknowable Being, but rather merely as a kind of archaic symbol:

> The Mediterranean tree, the tree of the Greeks … Each tree was like an animal holding its plumage up into the wind, its knobby legs thrust into the ground. A hillside of plumage flashing under the wind's onslaught, under its fluctuating gusts and knocks and unexpected stillnesses all perfectly revealed by the feathering leaves. (*B* 187)

On the other hand, one can also evoke a more dialectical construction, a production by the negative, as when even wilderness itself – "desert" in its

---

5 Jean-Paul Sartre, *La Nausée*, in *Oeuvres romanesques* (Paris, 1981 [1938], pp. 150–160 (journal notation beginning 'Six heures du soir').

archaic sense of the emptiness of people – waste, the radically non-human in earthly nature, is itself brought into being and generated by the emergence of the fact of the human – the jar on the hill – in its midst:

> It made the slovenly wilderness
> Surround that hill.[6]

This was Marx's great reminder to Feuerbach, when he invited him to look out on to the Roman Campagna:

> So much is this activity, this unceasing sensuous labour and creation, this pro-
> duction, the foundation of the whole sensuous world as it now exists that,
> were it interrupted for only a year, Feuerbach would not only find an enormous
> change in the natural world, but would very soon find that the whole world
> of men and his own perceptive faculty, nay his own existence, were missing.[7]

Behind the theory of social construction, therefore, lies praxis and human production itself, which makes a mockery of realism's staged mystery stories, its fictive astonishment at encountering the "resistance" of a reality it has itself cooked up in another avatar. The thought then drifts across the mind, like the proverbial cloud no bigger on the horizon than a hand, and in the form of what is as yet a merely speculative perplexity, whether precisely that produc-tion and its story, the very construction of otherness itself, the history of praxis and the resistances it must transform in its turn – whether those nar-ratives at the second degree, or better still at the level of preconditions – might not yield a realism in their own right, comparable to yet different from the more familiar realisms whose secrets we have been trying to surprise. Production, praxis, even construction as such, in fact require the resistance of some initial raw material, diffused through the situation which itself takes shape only under the pickaxe of the original project: it is a formula that combines both requirements, that of the confrontation of an unyielding set of elements, to be inventoried and described, that of the human pressure that will gradually give them names and the appearance, if not yet of a city, at least of its quarry and foundation pit, an immense building site whose future skyline is still unknown.

This is, at any rate, the ambiguous space in which the *Mars* trilogy is uniquely positioned, wedged in between the moments of otherness and production, between geology and biology, rock and plant, impact crater and tented village. Time is inscribed, in this spatial novel, as the marker of "emergent properties"

---

6 Wallace Stevens, "Anecdote of the Jar", in *The Palm at the End of the Mind* (New York, 1967), ed. Holly Stevens, p. 46.

7 Karl Marx and Friedrich Engels, *The German Ideology* (Moscow, 1976 [1845–1846], p. 46.

(*B* 343), of the radically unexpected and unpredictable, which is to say of contingency and ontological resistance in the realm of temporality and of change itself; hitherto static descriptions of the outside world are thus already secretly historical:

> The flowers were mounted on little mossy cushions or florettes, or tucked among hairy leaves. All the plants hugged the dark ground, which would be markedly warmer than the air above it; nothing but grass blades stuck higher than a few centimeters off the soil. He tiptoed carefully from rock to rock, unwilling to step on even a single plant. He knelt on the gravel to inspect some of the little growths, the magnifying lenses on his face-plate at their highest power. Glowing vividly in the morning light were the classic fellfield organisms: moss campion, with its rings of tiny pink flowers on dark green pads; a phlox cushion; five-centimeter sprigs of bluegrass, like glass in the night, using the phlox taproot to anchor its own delicate roots ... there was a magenta primrose, with its yellow eye and its deep green leaves, which formed narrow troughs to channel water down into the rosette. Many of the leaves of these plants were hairy. There was an intensely blue forget-me-not, the petals so suffused with warming anthocyanins that they were nearly purple – the color that the Martian sky would achieve at around 230 millibars, according to Sax's calculations on the drive to Arena. It was surprising there was no name for that color, it was so distinctive. Perhaps that was cyanic blue. (*G* 150)

Here the very colors are events in their own right, the yellow eye of the primrose "looks back at you" (Rimbaud), the unnamed blue almost speaks to you, like a word on the tip of the tongue. Color is here on Mars already defamiliarized and made strange, pre-prepared for further dramas of meaning, as we shall see. Meanwhile, the various traits themselves hover on the strategic fault line between the symbolic and the contingent, between meaning and being: blocking off a space of undecidability which is unexpectedly narrative:

> So he dove back into studying plants. Many of the fellfield organisms he was finding had hairy leaves, and very thick leaf surfaces, which helped protect the plants from the harsh UV blast of Martian sunlight. These adaptations could very well be examples of homologies ... or they could be examples of convergence ... And these days they could also be simply the result of bioengineering ... There was a biotique lab in Elysium, led by a Harry Whitebrook, designing many of the most successful surface plants, especially the sedges and grasses, and a check in the Whitebrook catalogue often showed that his hand had been at work, in which case the similarities were often a matter of artificial convergence, Whitebrook inserting traits like hairy leaves into almost every plant he bred. (*G* 160)

Art then, rather than nature: the hairy leaves are like the traits of style of a distinctive painter, which help to authenticate this or that doubtful canvas. Now suddenly otherness falls away, and we have to do with the mediation of human artifacts, to be scrutinized not for natural laws and evolutionary processes but rather for intentions and forensic responsibility. Indeed, all this later unexpectedly comes to life in a different way, when Harry Whitebrook appears on the scene in person, in flesh and blood so to speak (B 214); he has moved on to experimentation with animal life, and rather large animal life at that, and Ann thinks of assassinating him, as one of the great criminals of terraforming. Yet the apparition has a rather different effect from this mystery-story one: rather like those rare moments in the novel when God, or the Author, make their appearance in person – the visit to the corporate office at the end of Frank Norris's *The Octopus*, or the desperate appearance in the writer's study of one of the doomed characters of Miguel de Unamuno's *Mist* – more than a mere figure in the carpet this, a kind of ultimate chance to ask the ultimate questions, to unravel the fabric of the universe by tugging on this tantalizing loose thread. It is what the Romantics called Irony, in the heightened or sublime sense of the I behind the not-I – the lantern bobbing through the woods towards the cabin in which the terrified characters of C.D. Grabbe (in *Scherz, Satire, Ironie, und tiefere Bedeutung)* attempt to hide, warning the audience, as the curtain is about to fall, that the newcomer is in fact Grabbe himself, "the author of this damned play!" Yet such Romantic Irony is rarely understood to be the logical outcome of any really consequent realism: here, I believe that its ghostly presence rather marks the fault line between realism and something else, which I will call ontology and into which the inventory of otherness and resistance can logically develop, when realism is conceived in a religious or metaphysical mode. It is an outcome which will not surprise students of film theory, where the ontological strains both in Bazin and in Kracauer have a religious solemnity and promise a "redemption of physical reality".[8]

This ontological alternative is more difficult to project and to achieve in narrative literature as such, where an approach to the visible and the tactile is mediated by language and must generally be keyed by interpretive signals (thus Heidegger's examples are mainly those of lyric poetry).[9] In the *Mars* trilogy, however, and in Science Fiction generally, it is the possibility of separating off the elements of human labor from the underlying conditions of Being itself which makes both dimensions available for celebration. Thus it has been observed about *Robinson Crusoe* that its mythical status of origins, of an absolute new beginning and the philosophical blank state of human

---

8 André Bazin, "The Ontology of the Photographic Image", in Bazin, *What Is Cinema?* trans. H. Gray (Berkeley, 1967), pp. 9–16; and Siegfried Kracauer, *Theory of Film: The Redemption of Physical Reality* (New York, 1960).

9 Martin Heidegger, *Unterwegs zur Sprache* (Pfullingen, 1959).

culture and civilization, depended on some initial prestidigitation: not only is the island occasionally visited by other people and cultures, but above all Crusoe himself is able to salvage a good deal of Europe from the shipwreck, and to stock his island refuge in advance with a variety of tools and materials, in other words with stored human labor. But this inventory is not only obvious, it is foregrounded in the *Mars* trilogy, where to the Whitmanesque list – "an Allen wrench set, some pliers, a power drill, several clamps, some hacksaws, an impact–wrench set, a brace of cold-tolerant bungie cords, etc., etc." (R 96) – a wholly different preview, a synthesizing perspective, is added: "'You know what this is,' Nadia said to Sax Russell one evening looking around her warehouse, 'it is an *entire town*, disassembled and lying in pieces'" (R 96). Crusoe's atomized individualism makes it hard for him to feel about his laden yet doomed ship what disassembling the *Ares* suggests to its settler-passengers: "like dismantling a town and flinging the houses in different directions" (R 78). Crusoe must meanwhile produce his own internal division of labor: the *Ares* brings a collective one with it, and Mars itself generates whole new kinds of tasks, competencies, métiers and vocations (my favorite is the new art of "cliffside trail-making" which Nirgal encounters in the course of his joggings and ramblings around the planet [B 368]). "Terraforming" then retroactively includes all those implements, all those receptacles of human value, and it becomes the fundamental dividing line between realism as the narrative of human praxis and ontology as the traces of Being itself: two formal or generic possibilities, which thereby reinforce each other, insofar as production requires some preexistent being on which to do its work, while Being itself can be detected only in the spaces that human praxis spares, in the evanescent chance at origins that time and history inexorably efface.

It is therefore scarcely surprising that the trilogy should inscribe this its structural condition of possibility within the narrative itself: it is something like the modernist feature of this "realistic" text, its mode of autoreferentiality in other words, of designating its own unique process of production, and reproducing the form of the text within its themes. In something of the same fashion we have already observed the way in which the theme of the longevity treatment as it were authorizes the length of the trilogy itself and replaces the latter's temporality within its narrative, in the form of memory and forgetfulness and the structure of the brain. Terraforming now finds its internal marker and as it were its interpretant and its organ of resonance in the allegorization of two specific characters, Ann and Hiroko, who become the symbols and monuments, larger than life, of the pro and the con of this new productive process. It is true that all of the central characters gradually become allegorized in similar ways – "in the arguments on Earth, many people began to use the colonists' names as a kind of shorthand for the various positions" (R 151) – so that their collective relations project the intricate political constellations and multiple oppositions of the work, while individually they survive and redouble themselves over the course of the narrative, becoming their own legends or – what is probably more significant in a work in which long-range communication is also a significant issue – their own media images. Yet perhaps some supplementary word should be offered here about the talents and "specialties" of this particular writer, whose affinity for individual sports like skiing is also evident in other works and has its bearing on the veritable anthology of physical modes of appropriating the planet here. What must also be mentioned in that respect is the unique narrative sociability he shares with Pynchon and Delany, the preference, over states of individual introspection (although not, as we have seen, of perception), for collective zaniness and the manic interaction of a host of different characters, in a gamut that ranges from the late-night party all the way to revolution itself.

At any rate, it is clear that tension between the characters is a precondition for such moments of collective euphoria and the gift of tongues.[10] Multicultural liberals (like John Boone) are opposed to Machiavellian operators (like Frank Chalmers, for whom politics "was all damage control" [G 442]), themselves both opposed to professional mediators (like Art Randolph, responsible for the original Dorsa Brevia declaration and then the first constitution itself), all of their forces and positions then recirculated through the women characters, Mars' first president and first engineer. Nadia Cherneshevsky (along with that of her eventual partner the anarchist Arkady Bogdanov, her name offers a properly utopian autoreferentiality), and the first real leader of the expedition, Maya Toitovna, whose public interventions throughout the first two hundred years offer a political fever chart of Martian history. The "semiotic rectangles"[11] with which Michel occasionally tries to sort out the "temperaments" of his patients among the First Hundred are perhaps not complicated enough to do justice to the multiple interactions between them and the constant evolution and reorganization of those interrelationships themselves at higher levels; a process which not only reconfirms the doctrine of "emergent properties" but perhaps in its own way also offers abstract cross-sections of "overdetermination" at fixed stages in its own trajectory.

The characters can also be typologized and allegorized, because their specializations are required for the novel's heterogeneity, passing from the various sciences (Sax Russell) to architectural and urban construction (Nadia) and on to politics (Maya or Frank). But the principal structural allegory develops around two central figures who are both marginal to the central historical movement of things and indispensable to the struggle over meanings which

---

10 But I must also note its opposite, in the frozen and chaotic results of the first floods: "The landscape itself was now speaking a kind of glossolalia" (R, 495).

11 See A.J. Greimas, *On Meaning* (Minneapolis, 1987).

is also a part of that movement. Both are in that sense forces of negativity, Ann Clayborne because she herself implacably personifies refusal and opposition, Hiroko because her ultimate incarnation and avatar seems to have become absence itself: she negates empirical reality in the spirit of an ideal, while Ann seeks to undermine it in the political activism of an opposition to activism and an attempt to end history itself in a different way, by bringing change and "progress" to a halt.

For terraforming ought to constitute the utopian moment *par excellence* of this grand historical adventure, a global equivalent of that "flowering tree" which signalled the passage from winter to spring in Morris' *News from Nowhere*,[12] as its protagonist woke out of the sleep of his miserable "historical" London. But even if the inspection of plant life is one of the keenest events in this trilogy, the celebration of the coming of life is scarcely unanimous. Ann is the place of this particular great refusal, which it is essential to grasp as an affirmation as well and the very space of the alternative, if not indeed the original ontology. "A mask of anger", she is also a figure of desperate mourning and silence; her misery and unhappiness persists throughout her surface activities, as geologist and also *de facto* party chief – they are the most tangible expression of the irreversible loss which is also the colonization of Mars. And it is no doubt this persistence of a grief that cannot be resolved that makes her into more than an allegory of melancholy in its most morbid Freudian sense; her gaunt and unappeasable face suggests that she is ridden and inhabited by the incubus of a characterological defect which the others want to explain psychologically: "I think it is a denial of life. A turning to rock as something she could trust. She was mistreated as a girl, did you know that?" (*B* 44). Indeed, she comes to stand for death, from which she herself escapes by merest accident ("the long runout" – *G* 100; the enforced longevity treatment – *B* 83; the emergence unscathed from the hopeless civil war – *B* 27). Yet perhaps this is to mistake the irrevocability of death for a rather different kind of historical irreversibility – the fact that Mars is henceforth tainted and can never be returned to any pristine state, no matter what conservationist movements spring up as a second best in Ann's wake.

Indeed, one's impression is that the "original" planet speaks less often directly to its settlers than their own future projects for it: it must come as a pause and a shock in order to be seen:

> truly giant walls flanked him on both sides, dark brown slabs riven by a fractal
> infinity of gullies and ridges. At the foot of the walls lay huge spills of ancient

---

12 "It was winter when I went to bed last night, and now, by witness of the riverside trees, it was summer, a beautiful bright morning seemingly of early June" (William Morris, *News from Nowhere* (London, 1970 [1890]), p. 3.

rockfall, or the broken terracing of fossil beaches. In this gap the Swiss road was a line of green transponders, snaking past mesas and arroyos, so that it looked as if Monument Valley had been relocated at the bottom of a canyon twice as deep and five times as wide as the Grand Canyon. The sight was too astonishing for John to be able to concentrate on anything else, and for the first time in his journey he drove all day with Pauline [the computer] off. (R 236)

Does this very astonishment not confirm Ann's suspicion that the First Settlers "have never even seen Mars" (R 160), but only their own faces, their own projections, even in the guise of life forms engineered and implanted by human beings? Ann's "mistake had been in coming to Mars in the first place, and then falling in love with it. Falling in love with a place everyone else wanted to destroy" (R 490). It would be wrong to think of her relationship to this planet as some purely aesthetic or contemplative one, however: for she is in a way its historian and the student of its archaic palimpsest: "To see the landscape in its history, to read it like a text, written by its own long past: that was Ann's vision, achieved by a century's close observation and study, and by her own native gift, her love for it" (B 79). Here too the romance of causation and the story of production transform so many visual and natural curiosities into deep time:

the fantastic pressures engendered by the impact had resulted in all manner of bizarre metamorphoses, the most common being giant shattercones, which were conical boulders fractured on every scale by the impact, so that some had faults you could drive into, while others were simply conical rocks on the ground, with microscopic flaws that covered every centimeter of their surfaces, like old china ... shattercones that had landed on their points and stood balanced; others that had had the softer material underneath them eroded away, until they became immense dolmens; giant rows of fangs; tall capped lingam columns, such as the one known as Big Man's Hardon; crazily stacked strata piles, the most prominent of them called Dishes in the Sink; great walls of columnar basalt, patterned in hexagons; other walls as smooth and gleaming as immense chunks of jasper. (G 421)

I think that the philosophical debate is thus poorly posed if we stage it in terms of the death wish, or of "a desperate attempt to stave off the present moment; to stave off history" (B 79), since the reading of the historical record is inscribed in such ontological meditation, and even the contemplation of Mars's pristine surface in that sense offers materials for "a poem that includes history", as Pound liked to put it. Heidegger is there, meanwhile, to show that the "opening onto Being" need not be exclusively restricted to the inorganic or to rock surfaces; although we need to juxtapose his accounts with the august later poetry of McDiarmid:

> All is lithogenesis – or lochia,
> Carpolite fruit of the forbidden tree,
> Stones blacker than any in the Caaba,
> Cream-coloured caen-stone, chatoyant pieces,
> Celadon and corbeau, bistre and beige,
> Glaucous, hoar, enfouldered, cyathiform …
> I must begin with these stones as the world began.[13]

It seems to me that the only way to do justice to this significant philosophical component of the trilogy is to grasp the anti-humanism inherent in all ontology, from the religious varieties all the way to secular ontologies like that of Heidegger. We have not done with the great debates around humanism that were conducted in the 1960s, even though such official themes seem to have receded into the archives of fashion. But we cannot yet assess this anti-humanist ontology until we take account of its great alternative, the "areophany" of Hiroko, who stands for greenness – viriditas – and life, and whose vitalism thus seems to oppose Ann's death urge in all respects: "Life is so much spirit, Hiroko used to say. It was a very strange business, the vigor of growing things, their tendency to proliferate, what Hiroko called their green surge, their viriditas" (G 153). Yet even this identification with the organic and the biological is somewhat discredited in advance by the presence of genetic engineering (just as the claim to Being of rocks was by their history).

Yet just as life does not simply run parallel to the organic and to dead matter, so also Hiroko's story is scarcely symmetrical to that of Ann; and if the latter becomes a political symbol (and a virtual allegory), Hiroko's transmutation into a virtual (Mars) goddess is both comparable and yet very different indeed. Nor does her modest first appearance as a rather withdrawn Japanese botany expert, nor even the lush arrangements of her spaceship farm (or the rumours about her "male harem", a collection of alleged sperm donations from members of the crew), presage the surprise of her disappearance, along with a whole breakaway group of followers, including a stowaway from Earth (the legendary Coyote-to-be). But the significance of this secession is enhanced by evidence of long and careful planning: caches stored around Mars' surface and undetectable from the air, and the wondrous sanctuaries underneath the ice, in which bamboo structures nestle among greenhouses ("the green world inside the white", as Nirgal thinks [G 7]), slowly project the image of a genuine alternative world ("they probably wanted to get free of us. Make something new. What you and Arkady say you want, they really wanted" [R 226]), and generate utopia within the utopia of the Mars colony. They also invest her person with an authority not far from

---

13 Hugh McDiarmid, "On a Raised Beach", in Douglas Dunn, ed., *The Faber Book of Twentieth-Century Scottish Poetry* (London, 1992), pp. 56–57.

superstition; so that the staged reappearances at crisis moments in the planet's history are politically influential as well as dramatic:

> A string of three sand-colored dirigibles floated up the slope of the volcano. They were small and antiquated, and did not answer radio inquiries ...
>
> When their gondolas popped open, and twenty or so figures in walkers stepped out, a silence fell. "That's Hiroko", Nadia said suddenly over the common band. (R 332)

Hiroko is thus the leader of a social and political sect, but also an authority figure for the larger Green movement; her well-nigh legendary status is meanwhile to be understood as the component of a cultural politics as well, as when she systematically develops and encourages a kind of Mars ritual during the great organizing congresses: "Hiroko ... seems an alien consciousness, with entirely different meanings for all the words in the language, and, despite her brilliance at ecosystem design, not really a scientist at all, but rather some kind of prophet" (G 115). Yet it is not particularly any personal ambition that is involved (we are told again and again of her impersonal relationship to her followers and her children, her relative indifference to individuals) but rather the sense, conscious or unconscious, that social cohesion is cemented, as the term suggests, by *re-ligio*, and therefore that the unique relationship the settlers need to develop to Mars must be sealed and strengthened by a ritual attachment to the planet of the type that some Terran ecological and feminist groups have tried to develop around the mythic entity of Gaea. (The appearance of a "feral" community of intentionally primitive hunters on Mars also suggests Ernest Callenbach's inclusion, in *Ecotopia*, of an archaic ritual of rivalry and physical violence as a collective steam-valve: in the *Mars* trilogy, however, the feral merely designates one alternative possibility among others, as, indeed, does Hiroko's "new religion".) All this is of course heightened by the mystery of her disappearance and presumed death in the firestorm at Sabishii; after which her reappearance, to rescue Sax in the snowstorm (B 57), is only the first in many rumored sightings, on Earth itself, back on Mars and even in the outer planets and satellites.

But it is obviously as the spiritual leader of the Greens that the figure of Hiroko takes on an ideological meaning comparable to Ann's. No doubt we need to gloss these political terms, about whose traditional Terran meanings the *Mars* trilogy has some tricks to play on us. For if Earth's ecological movements have come to be designated as Green, it takes but a little reflection to understand that the comparable movement of conservation on Mars will be called Red; and that it is Ann's extreme or radical position, that the original Mars should be maintained in its pristine shape, without breathable atmosphere or plant life, that is the truly "ecological" political ideology. On Mars, then, the "Greens" are the party of progress and as it were of development in its bad, industrial sense: they stand for the "terraforming" of the planet and the loss, as it were and as we have seen above, of its ancient Being and meaning; never mind for the moment that there are clearly a whole range of technologies available to do this, and thus a whole range of Green ideologies and Green versions of "respect for the planet" (the most frequently mentioned compromise, unacceptable to Ann herself – until the very end? – being the proposal to limit breathable atmosphere up to a certain distance alone, so that above that mark the Martian landscape will retain its original desolation and impact formations). Hiroko's notion of "viriditas" can thus be seen as a kind of ideological compensation: the construction of an image of Martian life that might win the same kind of ecological adherence and loyalty as Ann's more obvious and literal appeal to what really once was. (But it should be noted that, latterly, Ann herself feels the ideological and political need to invent a Red version of "viriditas", a viriditas of rock (*B* 558), a paradoxical concept that seemed physically realized in advance by the green glow of Uranus [*B* 434].)

Still, Ann's "Reds" are a violent bunch, whose advocacy of "armed struggle" will certainly suggest Terran analogies, while Hiroko's "Greens" remain as vitalist as any of those so designated on Earth. I think we should not exaggerate the narrative temptation to reconcile these positions in some final, ideological "happy ending": it is true that something analogous is acted out on that symbolic level of color on which we have commented, in one of the novel's most striking descriptions:

> Right next to the pond were patches of dark green succulent leaves, dark red at their edges. Where the green shaded into red was a color he couldn't name, a dark lustrous brown stuffed somehow with both its constituent colors. He would have to call up a color chart soon, it seemed; lately when looking around outdoors he found that a color chart came in handy about once a minute. Waxy almost-white flowers were tucked under some of these bicolored leaves. Farther on lay some tangles, red stalked, green-needled, like beached seaweed in miniature. Again that intermixture of red and green, right there in nature staring at him. (*B* 54)

But the name for this unnameable color is Utopia, which stares insistently back at us from the *Mars* trilogy just as it does at Sax.[14] The utopian text is not supposed to produce this synthesis all by itself or to represent it: that is a matter for human history and for collective praxis. It is supposed only to produce the requirement of the synthesis, to open the space into which it is to be imagined. And this is the spirit in which the various political "solutions"

---

14 "'But where is socialism?' Dvanov remembered, and peered into the murk of the room, searching for his thing" (Andrei Platonov, *Chevengur* [Ann Arbor, 1978 (1928–1929)], p. 79); and see the discussion in my *The Seeds of Time* (New York, 1994), pp. 73–128.

of the *Mars* trilogy are also to be evaluated: that they are numerous, and contradictory or even irreconcilable, is I believe an advantage and an achievement
in a contemporary utopia, which must also, as Darko Suvin has pointed out,
stage an implicit debate with the objections and ideological and political prejudices of its readers.

Indeed, Suvin's originality, as a theorist of both SF and utopias all at once,
is (among other things) not merely to have linked the two generically; but
also to have conjoined the SF and utopian critical tradition with the Brechtian
one, centering on estrangement (the so-called V-effect); and to have insisted
not merely on the function of SF and Utopia to "estrange", to produce a V-
effect for the reader from a normal "everyday" common-sense reality, but
also to do so "cognitively" (a no less Brechtian component of the definition).
The reassertion of the cognitive means, as we said at the outset, a refusal to
allow the (obvious) aesthetic and artistic status of the SF or utopian work to
neutralize its realistic and referential implications: so we do want to think
about "real" science when we read these pages (and not only about the
"mimesis" of science in the bad dismissive sense Plato gave that term), and
by the same token we want to be able to think about "real" politics here and
not merely about its convincing or unconvincing "representation" in these
episodes, which dramatize our ideological objections and resistances to
Utopia fully as much as they satisfy our impulses toward it. Unlike the "mono-
logical" utopias of the tradition, which needed to dramatize a single utopian
possibility strongly because of its repression from Terran history and political possibility, this more "polyphonic" one includes the struggle between a
whole range of utopian alternatives, about which it deliberately fails to
conclude.

If the *Mars* trilogy is "realistic", then, on the strength of its inner reinvention of production as such, and "modernist" insofar as it then systematically
designates that process of production as such, we must also insist on its
properly utopian structure as a kind of "world reduction" in which not merely
breathable atmosphere but custom, human relationships and finally political
choices are pared down to the essentials and represented in a kind of zero
degree. It is an argument that can be staged negatively, by an analysis of one
of the great generic set-pieces of this narrative of coexisting worlds, and one
which in genuine modernist fashion designates the utopian genre by its very
exercise, namely the obligatory return tourist trip to Earth itself (which can
be compared to the more central journey in Le Guin's *The Dispossessed*, and
also to the equivalent in Brian Aldiss' quite different and non-utopian *Helliconia*
trilogy). Here indeed, we find estrangement effects within the estrangement
effects, and as it were in a *mise en abyme* that according to Gide's formula inverts
the thematics of the surrounding work with a kind of telescopic precision.
Here "terraforming" is still central – that is to say the existence of a layer of
breathable atmosphere – yet its Terran equivalent suddenly becomes more

vivid than the not insignificant accompanying problem of gravity (into which the Mars settlers slowly seem to grow):

> The air was salty, hot, clangorous, heavy … There was a doorway glowing with light. Slightly dizzy with the effort, [Nirgal] walked out into a blinding glare. Pure whiteness. It reeked of salt, fish, leaves, tar, shit, spices: like a greenhouse gone mad. (B 139)

A landing in the Caribbean is evidently calculated to enhance the senses in general, assaulting them with the masks and costumes of Carnival and the sound of steel bands, and also with the lushness of green vegetation; yet the most "bodily" of all the senses seems the most strategically symbolic in its dominance:

> the rank stench was suddenly cut by the smell of tar on the wind … The sweet scent [of a flower necklace] clashed with the stinging salt haze. Perfume and incense, chased by the hot vegetable wind, tarred and spiced…The stench was of a greenhouse gone bad, things rotting, a hot wet press of air and everything blazing in a talcum of light. (B 140)

This sensorium acts out the coexistence of multiplicities, and heightens the existential shock and conjunction of simultaneities that in the thinner, poorer air of Mars are carefully separated out from one another: as a figure for earth's population crisis, it also emits a utopian afterimage of some Martian solution. At any rate, it is aesthetically as well as politically unsurprising that it is precisely this structural parallelism that Nirgal should point out in his first address to the Terran welcomers:

> "Mars is a mirror", he said in the microphone, "in which Terra sees its own essence. The move to Mars was a purifying voyage, stripping away all but the most important things. What happened in the end was Terran through and through … we can most help the home planet by serving as a way for you to see yourselves. As a way to map out an unimaginable immensity." (B 141)

It should be added that this position is by no means shared by all the parties on Mars itself; and also that the theme of "immensity" is itself something of a defamiliarization, since so much about Mars – "Olympus Mons, the tallest mountain in the solar system" (R 86) or the canyons we have already seen which dwarf our own Grand Canyon – has been evoked in gigantistic terms (along with the accompanying mythologies of Big Man and Paul Bunyan, and, by inversion, the "little red people"). Now, however, unexpectedly, Nirgal in the Alps comes to "the sudden knowledge that Earth was so vast that in its variety it had regions that even out-Marsed Mars itself – that among all the ways that it was greater, *it was greater even at being Martian*" (B 159). These spatial and dimensional paradoxes are also, I think, hints about the peculiar reading methods we need to develop in order to navigate the structural peculiarities of utopian estrangement, which must separate us decisively from Earth before returning us to it.

Indeed, if it were not too clever by half it could be suggested that the other fundamental political preoccupation of the work is in this respect itself rather autoreferential. For it is important to understand that the debate over terra-forming, and the symbolic opposition between Ann and Hiroko, is only one of the political axes around which the social and revolutionary drama of the book is fought: the other having to do with the independence of Mars from Earth, a durable Heinlein or SF theme[15] which is deepened here by the more utopian consideration of a whole change of self and the emergence of a New Martian on the order of Soviet New Man – the issue, in other words, of a cultural as well as a political revolution.

We must indeed here recall the structural precondition of that social "blank slate" upon which traditional utopias wrote their text: the radical separation of Utopia from historical reality, whether in the "great trench" dug by More's Utopus, or the ancient, now forgotten bloody revolution which ended capitalism long before the beginning of Morris' *News from Nowhere*, or even the planetary flight that, in a few dilapidated spaceships ferries Odo's followers across to the unpromising twin planet Anarres. But in the *Mars* trilogy this gesture remains suspended and incomplete: and the space elevator – brought down in one of the most spectacular revolutionary episodes (it wraps itself twice around the planet like a broken necklace) and then perpetually rebuilt, in Robinson's answer to Niven's Ringworld and so many other "floating islands" – is the persistent emblem of the threat of Terran politics and intervention, and the dilemmas of autonomy and "delinking" on Mars as well. In the traditional utopia it was the emblematic trench which "ended History"; here it is the attempt repeatedly to begin history over again which is the very subject of the work, and the other issue on which the various political parties and movements (some twenty are listed at B 100) must necessarily take a stand. There is thus material here for any number of combinations, so that in the long run the Greimas rectangle would seem to be more appropriate, after all, than dualisms of the Red/Green type (or even of Nirgal's green/white distinction: "in archetypal terminologies we might call green and white the Mystic and the Scientist ... but what we need, if you ask me, is a combination of the two, which we call *the Alchemist*"(G 13). What complicates all these logically possible combination and permutation schemes is the movement of History itself, which slowly modifies the fundamental situations and crises themselves. On the one hand, the issues surrounding terraforming are themselves transformed

---

15 As, classically, in Robert A. Heinlein, *The Moon Is a Harsh Mistress* (New York, 1966).

when a minimal atmosphere is acquired and a botanical biosphere is set in place (and also when the first big cities have been established): not only does the idea of returning to the "original" planetary conditions come to seem conservative as well as unrealizable, the thawing of the aquifers and the dramatic unleashing of the great floods foretell the definitive emergence of some irreversibly blue Mars. As for the other axis, which relates the settlers to Earth itself and its power structures, here two changes on both sides modify it ceaselessly. Mars becomes populated and urban, and its younger generations take the premise of Martian independence for granted, so that, after the second – more officially successful – revolution to that effect, political debate turns around the degree to which even a token emigration should be allowed and Earth's many dilemmas publicly acknowledged. But the very nature of Terran power has also evolved and been restructured over this period: an initial United Nations surveillance is undermined by the evolution of multinational corporations into trans- and then finally meta-nationals, with only a few enormous groups left, themselves divided into the traditional capitalist-rapacious ones and a new more experimental type of corporate power more dependent on the World Court (the Praxis group), at the same time that the status of the nation-state begins to oscillate perilously between the nominal flag-renting countries and the few economic giants, later displaced by the immensely populated states, particularly China and India, which support Martian independence at the same time that their overpopulation threatens it. The intricacies of these developments are then intensified by the threefold crisis of famine, the longevity treatment and its social consequences, and finally the break-up of the West Antarctic ice sheet and the disastrous rise in Terran sea level. Yet the *Mars* trilogy does not narrate this grim series of unresolvable crises in any direct or chronicle-like fashion; rather, we learn to read it indirectly off Martian developments themselves and deduce the shifts in the Terran power structure from the modification of political constellations which are the response and the result on Mars itself. It is a system which allows a novel disposition of the utopian and the dystopian, if you like: the latter reserved for the seemingly inevitable degradation of Terran conditions, the former the invention of a range of political positions in that "realm of freedom" which is the Martian public sphere.

It would not be possible to sort the immense proliferation of groups and movements out without distinguishing between the political, the social and the economic levels as such; and indeed on some first general assessment it becomes clear that groups can emerge around concerns centered in any one of these three areas. The political ones are most likely to have come into being in response to the crises of Terran geopolitics outlined above, while the social groups are more likely to organize around what have come in postmodernity to be called "lifestyle" issues. And surely one of the vocations of the Mars trilogy is to have projected a "blank slate" so immense that an unimaginable variety of such social micro-systems can be housed: the descriptive or botanical level of the allegory indeed gives us the clue here:

> The closer he looked, the more he saw; and then, in one high basin, it seemed there were plants tucked everywhere … The diversicolored palette of the lichen array; the dark green of pine needles, bunched spray of Hokkaido pines, foxtail pines, Sierra junipers. Life's colors. It was somewhat like walking from one great roofless room to another, over walls of stone: a small plaza; a kind of winding gallery; a vast ballroom; a number of tiny interlocking chambers; a sitting room. Some rooms have krummholz bonsai against their low walls, the trees no higher than their nooks, gnarled by wind, cut along the top at the snow level. Each brand, each plant, each open room, as shaped as any bonsai – and yet effortless. (*G* 71)

The niches correspond to the varieties of social life, and ask us to fill them and to strain the utopian imagination itself for their tangible specification. One is reminded of Deleuze's celebration of the niches of life forms in Fellini: "The honeycomb-presentation ("alvéoles") the cubicled images of huts, niches, cabins and windows."[16] On the other hand, from any postmodern perspective centered on the "new social movements" or on micropolitics, the social experimentation here scarcely knows the frenzied baroque formations one finds, extensively, in Bruce Sterling's *Schismatrix*, or, intensively, in Delany's *Trouble on Triton* (Olaf Stapledon, the great precursor in this respect, was perhaps reacting against racist ideologies, rather than anticipating this more properly 1960s' spirit). Alongside these utopian objections, then, the *Mars* trilogy also draws on a variety of cultural ones, after the initial Cold War "superstate" division of power of the *Ares*, it is a variety of Terran "cultures" in the national and anthropological sense we are given to observe, from Arabs to Swiss to Japanese and South African (with Sufi interludes and Cretan overtones): indeed, few novels can have projected a global post-coloniality of such range and dimensions, in a spirit so alien to US parochialism and commodity universalism.

As for the economic, to turn our attention to it is at first to recall a certain initial bemusement at Darko Suvin's language (in the generic definition that we have taken as a motto): a "socio-political sub-genre"… but why not a socio-economic one? Or does he mean to imply, on the one hand, that the "economic" is a rather late mode of thinking and interpretation in human social and political thought and thereby in utopian thought as well? Yet utopias from Plato to More have specified an absence of private property as one of their defining characteristics. Or, on the other hand, does Suvin imply that some structural blindness of the utopia to economics as such betrays the

---

16 Gilles Deleuze, *Cinema*, II (Minnesota, 1989 [1985]), p. 89.

fundamental limitation of the form? Or betrays the fundamental limitation of narrative itself?

Yet there is no lack, in the *Mars* trilogy, of socialist and cooperativist alternatives and ideologies, among which anarchism and Bogdanovism hold the pride of place, but also the Mondragon cooperatives in Spain. New economic systems are pioneered, the so-called "eco-economics", an elaborate calculation of value in terms of calories (R 268–270, G 316–317, B 117–118, B 240); or more rudimentary gift or barter economies ('it's a sort of two-track thing, where they can still give all they want, but the necessities are given values and distributed properly" [G 34]). In the old days, the revival of these various schemes and their ideological authorities could often be shown to be an anti-Marxist strategy and a deployment of "utopian socialism" in exactly the spirit of Marx's critique of it. Today, it seems more likely to serve as a kind of collective Left anamnesis and a reflowering of elaborate and varied Left traditions and alternatives that were historically undeveloped, not least owing to the hegemony of Marxism itself.

Leninism does not in fact loom large here, although we are told about the existence of paleo-Marxist communes and splinter groups; but I think that has as much to do with revolutionary strategies as it does with Marxian economics; and indeed the debate about the nature of revolution itself is unsurprisingly one of the central themes of this trilogy, which tells the story of several of them. In that respect, the word does seem to be confined to a very narrow sense indeed when we are told repeatedly by significant characters that revolution as such is outmoded, and is indeed itself a Terran concept ("it never even worked on Earth, not really" [R 315]) and are offered various substitutes, such as the notion of "phase change" from physics (G 497). The Leninist revolutionary party seems, however, to be the main target here, as political movements on Mars are grasped in terms of the dynamics of mass demonstrations, as in the Iranian revolution, where so great a percentage of the population is on the streets (B 598) that the only alternative for the power structure would be, as Brecht famously put it, "to dissolve the people and elect another one". Yet this politics of the mass movement yields splendid Eisensteinian images, such as the immense line of people against the sky, leaving the drowned city and thus also symbolically "walking away" (G 523) from the old system, the old way of life.

What identifies the Mars trilogy as a utopia, nonetheless, rather than a political novel about recurrent revolution as such, is the place of its unexamined premise, which in the traditional utopian text is to be found in the great trench itself, the separation, as has been said above, from everyday Terran reality. The politico-economics of Mars is here and throughout mainly anti-capitalist, although it should be noted that the liberal corporatist ideology of the Praxis metanational is given a more sympathetic hearing than it may deserve. Yet private property has already disappeared from the Martian environment, or, rather, was never implanted there in the first place. This is, then, the sense of the so-called *Werteswandel*: "right here on Mars we have seen both patriarchy and property brought to an end. It's one of the greatest achievements in human history" (B 346). Yet it is an achievement that must constantly be renewed, since one of the latest political problems is the wave of Terran immigrants who cannot be assimilated because they have not absorbed such changes (the issue of some properly cultural revolution). And it is also a structural pre-supposition of this utopia, since we do not ever witness its evolution as a narrative event; perhaps indeed we could not do so. Yet utopia as a form is not the representation of radical alternatives; it is rather simply the impera-tive to imagine them.

Afterword

Of the many other things that could be said about the *Mars* trilogy, I want only to add this one which responds, as one always must, to Robert C. Elliott's test of the imaginative qualities of a given utopian text, namely their capacity to imagine properly utopian art works.[17] I do like the mysterious town of Medusa, in which solid blocks of whitish rock are surrounded by statues: "small white figures stood motionlessly between these buildings, on white plazas ringed by white trees" (G 265). But that is a relatively uncharacteristic note in this mainly "realist" utopia. So I prefer to submit this one:

> Mangalavid was showing the premiere performance of an aeolia built by a group in Noctis Labyrinthus. The aeolia turned out to be a small building, cut with apertures which whistled or hooted or squeaked, depending on the angle and strength of the wind hitting them. For the premiere the daily downslope wind in Noctis was augmented by some fierce katabatic gusts from the storm, and the music fluctuated like a composition, mournful, angry, dissonant or in sudden snatches harmonic: it seemed the work of a mind, an alien mind perhaps, but certainly something more than random chance. The almost aleatory aeolia, as a commentator said. (R 293)

2000

17   Robert C. Elliott, *The Shape of Utopia* (Chicago, 1970).

Acknowledgments

The author and publishers would like to thank the journals and publishers listed below for permission to reprint the essays collected in Part Two. Original publication details as follows:

1: "Ontology and Utopia," *L'Esprit Créateur*, vol. XXXIV, No. 4, 1994, pp. 46–64.

2: "Generic Discontinuities in Science Fiction: Brian Aldiss' *Starship*," *Science Fiction Studies* #2, 1973, pp. 57–68.

3: "World Reduction in Le Guin: The Emergence of Utopian Narrative," *Science Fiction Studies* #2 (iii), 1975, pp. 221–30.

4: "Progress versus Utopia; or, Can We Imagine the Future?" *Science Fiction Studies* #27, 1982, pp. 147–58.

5: "Science-Fiction as a Spatial Genre – Generic Discontinuities and the Problem of Figuration in Vonda McIntyre's *The Exile Waiting*," *Science Fiction Studies* V, 14, 1987, pp. 44–59.

6: "The Space of Science Fiction: Narrative in A. E. Van Vogt," *Polygraph* 2/3, 1989, pp. 52–65.

7: "Longevity as Class Struggle," in *Immortal Engines: Life Extension and Immortality in Science Fiction and Fantasy*, eds. G. Slusser, G. Westfahl and E. Rabkin, University of Georgia Press, 1996, pp. 24–42.

8: "Futuristic Visions that tell us about right now" (on P. K. Dick), *In These Times* VI (23), 17 May 1982, pp. 5–11.

9: "After Armageddon: Character Systems in P. K. Dick's Dr. Bloodmoney," *Science Fiction Studies* #2 (i), 1975, pp. 31–42.

10: "History and Salvation in P.K. Dick", previously unpublished.

11: "Fear and Loathing in Globalization," *New Left Review*, vol. 23, 2003, pp. 105.

12: "'If I Find One Good City I'll Spare the Man': Realism and Utopia in Kim Stanley Robinson's *Mars Trilogy*," in *Learning from Other Worlds: Estrangement, Cognition and the Politics of Science Fiction and Utopia*, ed. Patrick Parrinder, Liverpool University Press, 2000.

A version of Chapter 3 of Part One originally appeared as: "Morus: The Generic Window," *New Literary History*, vol. 34, no. 3, 2003, pp. 431–51.

Index